GRANDMASTER OF CHESS
The Complete Games of
Paul Keres

by Paul Keres

Translated and Edited by
Harry Golombek

AN
ARCO PUBLISHING COMPANY, INC.
BOOK
219 Park Avenue South, New York, N.Y. 10003

An ARC Book
Published 1972 by Arco Publishing Company, Inc.
219 Park Avenue South, New York, N.Y. 10003

Copyright © 1964, 1966, 1969
by Paul Keres and Harry Golombek

Library of Congress Catalog Card Number 72-642
ISBN 0-688-02645-6

Printed in the United States of America

FOREWORD

IT is now nearly thirty years since I first entered the international chess arena, on the occasion when I took part in the Chess Olympiad at Warsaw as a member of the Estonian team. During these years I have taken part in many different tournaments and played against hundreds and hundreds of players. Many good, but also many bad, games have been played and successes and failures have often followed each other. In these years I have often been able to rejoice over good results and equally I have had the less pleasant experiences of suffering from poor results. In the more than 1,000 tournament games that were played by me in these years are best reflected both my chess development and my creative peak and low points.

This collection of games furnishes the best that I have so far been able to achieve over the chess-board. On the basis of these games an expert could trace the various changes that have taken place in my chess characteristics during the respective periods of time covered by the book, whilst the young chess enthusiast may perhaps find useful indications as to how the development of a chess-master is perfected. Nobody is born a master. The way to mastery leads to the desired-for goal only after long years of learning, of struggle, of rejoicing and of disappointment.

It is indeed not all that easy to choose the hundred best from such a great profusion of games. In the first place it depends very much on the individual taste of each chess-player and in the second place the choice from amongst one's own games suffers to a certain degree from various subjective influences. In my selection I have been concerned particularly with two points: that they should embrace all my chess career up to the present and should contain all the games that have found recognition from the wider chess public. That, incidentally, my earlier games bear no artistic comparison with those of later years, should, in my opinion, play a not particularly important role.

One rather substantial problem did indeed appear—what kind of annotations should be given to the game? Should the commentaries on the earlier games be reproduced unaltered, or should they be re-edited in accordance with modern theory? Should the notes be brief summaries or should they elucidate the course of the game in exhaustive fashion, so that the games collection could also serve at the same time as a manual of instruction to some degree at any rate? And finally the question also had to be answered: should only my won games be taken into account or could not perhaps some drawn and lost games be introduced into the work?

After long reflection I decided upon the following principles. As concerns the games of the earlier period I have tried to retain the general character of the annotations, but have also made an exhaustive check-up of the individual variations and opinions passed in the course of these annotations and, when necessary, I have altered them in accordance with present-day ideas. The notes on the various games should be, I decided, as exhaustively done as possible so as to increase the value of the book as a manual of instruction. And finally I decided to take only games won by me, although here too other opinions might be fully justified.

The games are ranged in their chronological order. As regards opponents, I have tried to include the widest possible selection, so that in this collection of games practically all the leading chess-masters of the world are to be found. A list of opponents and a summary of the openings employed will be found by the reader at the end of this book. There too will be found a list of my tournament and match results up to the present time. Before each year, or group of years, a short essay appears, showing in what tournaments I have played during the period in question and what games deserve special attention. The games are illustrated by numerous diagrams so as to facilitate the study of the variations adduced in the notes.

With this I hand my work over to the reader. I hope it will find welcome acceptance not only as reading for tournament players but also as a manual for the less advanced player.

PAUL KERES.

Tallinn, Estonia.

CONTENTS

THE LATER YEARS OF PAUL KERES

THE EARLY GAMES
OF PAUL KERES

TRANSLATOR'S PREFACE

THE collection of games of which the present volume is the first part is designed not only to give a selection of the best games of one of the greatest players of all time but also to show how the mind of a great chess-player works, the deep strategy that lies behind and guides the tactics of each game, and the thoughts that the player had when playing the games. For this purpose Keres has devoted the utmost care and attention to his annotations which, in my opinion, are the best that have ever been lavished on a book of this type. If to study the games of a great master and to strive to understand them is one of the best ways of improving one's own game, as I firmly believe, then this collection should rank high as a manual of the game. As the reader will see, it was partly the author's intention to provide his readers with a manual of instruction.

I have written partly, and the other aim was quite certainly to divert and to please. How, in fact, anyone can fail to be entertained by the remarkable games that Keres has played is hardly to be envisaged. Here the reader will find dazzling combinations blended with a subtle artistry and a refinement of thought almost beyond parallel in modern chess. In his foreword Keres mentions that it is nearly thirty years since he made his début in international chess, at the Warsaw Olympiad of 1935. It so happens that this was my first international tournament too and I well remember with what delight I watched the games played by the young Estonian genius.

In the present volume the reader will find displayed the development of the earlier part of Keres's career, from his beginnings right up to the period when he became recognised as the rightful challenger for the world title, only to have this right taken from him by the outbreak of the Second World

War. It is a privilege and an honour for me to introduce this work to an English-speaking public and I can only hope they derive as much pleasure and instruction from it as I did in translating the book.

H. GOLOMBEK

FIRST STEPS, 1929–1935

I MADE my acquaintance with the game of chess very early, round about the age of 4 to 5 years, when, together with my elder brother, I watched the games my father played with his friends. In this way we learned the moves and the elementary rules of chess, and then naturally there followed the first tries one against the other. How slowly, however, one penetrates into the secrets of the art of chess in this way is shown by the fact that for many a year we were quite unaware that games of chess could be written down. Only after we discovered in the daily papers some mysterious inscriptions together with diagrams did we eventually arrive at the knowledge that these imported written games of chess.

In the small town of Parnu there were naturally great difficulties in the way of widening and perfecting one's chess knowledge. We had no chess literature at our disposal and, in order to fill this want, I wrote down every possible game I could get my hands on. In this way I soon had a collection of almost 1,000 games. My first contact with opening theory occurred through the small Dufresne manual, which I succeeded in borrowing from a chess-friend for some days. It goes without saying that we let no problem or end-game study that had appeared in the newspapers pass unnoticed without embarking on an attempt to solve it. But my chief chess activity still consisted in the practice games with my brother.

My chess work only became more varied when new "rivals" appeared in the shape of school friends and this also led to a gradual increase in my playing strength. I had already achieved very good results against my father and my brother and now wanted to test my strength against other, somewhat

stronger, players. The opportunity for this came quite unexpectedly. In the year 1928 Mikenas, already one of Estonia's
best players, paid a short visit to Parnu, and on this occasion
he gave a simultaneous display in the town's chess club. I
went of course, together with my father, to the club for the
display, and I even managed to take away a whole point from
the master. This success naturally endowed me with fresh
courage and self-confidence and spurred me on to further
steps.

In the next year a lightning championship of the town took
place in Parnu. The winner was the player who amassed the
most points from six successive tournaments. Here I succeeded
in gaining the first prize and because of this success I was
selected to play in the team for the city-match against
Wiljandi. I had to play two games against the young Ilmar
Raud, who had by then already made a name for himself.
The first game ended in a draw and in the second I came
down to an ending with two pawns more. Then suddenly
Raud put a whole Rook en prise! Without thinking for a
single second I took the Rook and . . . in a few moves I was
mated. These first hours of instruction were painful, but also
very useful.

My first tournament was in the year 1929 when I took part
in the Parnu Championship. I played with great ardour and
succeeded in occupying the second place below Wirkus, who
had been city champion many times. This decided me to take
part in the schoolboy championship of Estonia, at that time
a highly popular event. My first visit to Tallinn in 1930 in
this connection brought with it an unexpected success—I won
the first prize with ease. In the following years I won the
Estonian Schoolboy Championship again in Tartu in 1932 and
Parnu in 1933, my participation in the tournament at Wiljandi
in 1931 having been prevented through illness.

On the ground of good results in the Schoolboys' Championships and also in local tournaments I was chosen to be a candidate in the first-class players' tournament. The winner of
this tournament was to have the right to take part in the next
Estonian Championship. The tournament took place in 1933
in Tallinn. I was able to keep the lead right up to the very last

round, but then lost it through a thoughtless handling of the opening (I chose as Black the defence 1 P–Q4, P–K4; 2 PxP, Kt–QB3; 3 Kt–KB3, Q–K2) and thus remained half a point behind the joint winners. This first attempt had failed, but it was with all the more zeal that I stormed through to the cherished first place in the next year at Rakwere. But here too the old story repeated itself. In the last round I had the weakest player in the tournament as my opponent, but played so carelessly against him that I only just managed to emerge with a draw and once again remained half a point behind the winner. But since we had obtained the first two places a great distance away from the rest of the field, both of us were admitted into the next national championship. Thus the way lay open to the highest peak of chess in Estonia!

Life in the small town of Parnu unfortunately did not offer much chance of chess development and so I looked around for other possibilities of practice. This brought me to correspondence chess. My first steps in this field were taken as early as the year 1931. Since I continually increased my activities as correspondence chess-player, after some years I found myself conducting as many as 150 games simultaneously. I utilised correspondence chess chiefly for the purpose of trying out various experiments, especially in the sphere of openings. Many extremely risky opening variations on my part are to be found at this time, such as, for example, the gambit 1 P–K4, P–K4; 2 P–KB4, PxP; 3 Kt–QB3, Q–R5ch; 4 K–K2. Furthermore, I sought complications in practically every game at any price, in order to develop still further my combinational powers. The reader will find in this collection games No. 1 and 2 dating from this period. From the chess point of view they are not on a particularly high level, but they are marked out, nevertheless, by a lively and interesting course and are thoroughly characteristic for my style of that time. There may be observed in these games the compelling desire to combine, though the solving of technical problems is accompanied by very great inaccuracies.

At the turn of the year 1934–35 there came at last the long-awaited moment—the championship of Estonia began. In the meantime my style had grown somewhat more mature, and this enabled me to meet on equal terms even players with well-known names. I began the tournament in promising style with three successive wins. Then there followed once again a risky experiment in the opening, and my meeting with Raud resulted in my having a nought on the tournament table. The ensuing win against Willard was succeeded by a fresh loss against Turn, and this meant that my chances of winning the tournament had sunk to the lowest possible point. But then I managed to win two more games and when the last round commenced it turned out that I was standing at the head of the tournament together with Gunnar Friedemann. In the last round, however, we were due to meet each other.

The struggle was an unequal one—against a youth with no tournament experience there was pitted one of the most noted players of the country. But youthful ardour enabled me to finish up with an honourable draw from this encounter, although for some time matters on the King's wing looked very bad for me. So I shared first prize, a great success for me.

With this, however, the struggle was not at an end, since eventually a match of three games was due to be played off to settle the question of the championship. I had an unhappy start in this match. It is true I obtained rather the better position in the first game, but I underestimated a clever tactical continuation by which Friedemann seized hold of the initiative and forced back my pieces into defensive positions. Soon I was material to the bad and had to resign. However, from the two games I had now played against G. Friedemann I had drawn some useful indications as regards my own weaknesses and the quality of my opponent's play. My self-confidence grew, especially after I managed to win the second game in a style characterised by really continuous pressure. Everything now hung on the third and decisive game. The reader will find this game under No. 4, and I must confess that at the end of this game I was rejoicing in the fact that my chess labours up to this point had achieved such apparently concrete results.

I was now at the highest point that could be attained by a chess-player in Estonia, but I was far from satisfied with the artistic side of my achievements. I often suffered from lack of experience in important games since I had played all too few against good opponents. I therefore decided after the Championship to take part in as many events as possible. I took part in the city championship of Tartu, an event which comprised 25 players, and completed a practice match against Kibberman, one of the leading masters in Tartu. I also participated in the Jubilee Tournament of the German Chess-League in Tallinn, in which some international masters also played. In this tournament I won a highly interesting game against Danielsson (Game No. 4), and after managing to win my last-round game against Samisch with a bit of luck, I gained the second prize below P. Schmidt.

I had played without a break for half a year in various chess events and now I felt I was sufficiently prepared to withstand the proof of my first serious international tournament. In the autumn of that year the next Chess Olympiad was due to take place in Warsaw, and in this for the first time the Estonian team was due to participate. As champion of Estonia I would therefore be playing in this tournament against many of the world's leading grandmasters, amongst others with the then world champion, Dr. Alekhine.

Game 1

QUEEN'S GAMBIT, ALBIN COUNTER-GAMBIT

Played by correspondence, 1931–32

	A. Karu	P. Keres
1	P–Q4	P–Q4
2	P–QB4	P–K4

I played many correspondence games against Karu in his time and often employed Albin's Counter-Gambit against him. One may observe here the desire that characterised most of my games of that period to strive to attain lively piece play and complications at an early stage in the game.

3	Kt–QB3	

In the other games Karu invariably captured the KP. The text-move is an experiment that can hardly be more commendable for White than the usual 3 PxKP.

3	. . .	KPxP
4	QxP	Kt–QB3

Black can also get a really good game here by the simple 4 . . . PxP; but at that time so early a Queen exchange never entered my head. In any case the pawn sacrifice of the text-move provides Black with adequate counter-play.

5	QxQP	B–K3
6	Q–QKt5	

The best reply. After 6 QxQch, RxQ, Black regains his pawn with a good game since, in addition to the threat of 7 . . . BxP, there are the unpleasant Kt moves 7 . . . Kt–Kt5 and 7 . . . Kt–Q5.

6	. . .	P–QR3
7	Q–R4	

Too dangerous, of course, would be the capture of the second pawn by 7 QxKtP, since after 7 ... Kt–Q5; 8 Q–K4, Kt–KB3 Black would obtain a strong attack. After the text-move Black wins his pawn back.

7 ...   B–QKt5
8 B–Q2

Here I cherished the rather slight hope that White would commit the blunder of 8 P–QR3? For then, in fact, would follow 8 ... P–QKt4!; and if then 9 PxP, Kt–Q5!; 10 PxP dis ch, P–B3; and White has no adequate defence against the threat of 11 ... B–Kt6. The continuation selected by Karu likewise fails to disembarrass him of all difficulties.

It was only later on that I learnt that the identical position had already occurred in the game Marshall–Duras, Carlsbad, 1907. White continued in that game with 8 P–K3! and obtained a satisfactory position.

In the ensuing part of the game White keeps back the P–K3 move for too long.

8 ...   BxP
9 P–QR3   P–QKt4!

With this move Black seizes the initiative and forces his opponent to take up a laborious defensive position. White cannot now well play 10 Q–Q1, since then I have the reply 10 ... Kt–Q5! with the threat of 11 ... B–Kt6.

10 Q–B2   Kt–Q5
11 Q–K4ch   B–K2
12 Kt–B3?

This was White's last opportunity of occupying himself with the development of his Kingside by 12 P–K3, since then, after 12 ... Kt–Kt6; 13 R–Q1, BxB White rescues his threatened piece by 14 B–B1!

Black would therefore reply to 12 P–K3, with 12 ... BxB; 13 PxKt, B–B5; 14 Q–B6ch, K–B1; thereby retaining the rather better position.

12 ...   P–QB4!

Now, it is already too late for 13 P–K3, since after 13 ... Kt–KB3; 14 Q–Kt1, BxB; 15 RxB, White's QR would be

placed totally out of play by 15 . . . Kt–Kt6. Hence Karu
develops this Rook immediately, so as not to shut it in by
Q–Kt1, but now becomes hopelessly backward in development. White is already in serious difficulties.

13	R–B1	Kt–KB3
14	Q–Kt1	Q–Q3

Black once again prevents 15 P–K3, since after that move
15 . . . KtxKtch; 16 PxKt, R–Q1; would be decisive. 15 . . .
R–Q1 is, however, now a threat. White therefore decides upon
some exchanges, but is still unable to relieve his position to
any notable extent. Black's advantage in development ensures
him a lasting attack in any case.

15	KtxKt	PxKt
16	Kt–K4	KtxKt
17	QxKt	

Apparently White has now got over the worst of it, since the
QR is attacked and in addition he threatens the very awkward
18 B–Kt4. Castling appears to be impossible on account of
18 B–Kt4, but in this respect White is due for a disagreeable
surprise.

Black (Keres) to play

White (Karu)

17	. . .	O–O!

This move comes all the same. But what happens after
18 B–Kt4? During the game I intended to reply to this move
with the combination 18 . . . QxBch; 19 PxQ, BxPch; 20 K–Q1,

B–Kt6ch; 21 R–B2, QR–B1. However, in this variation White has the better 21 Q–B2, with a difficult but not entirely hopeless defence.

It would therefore be objectively better to reply to 18 B–Kt4, simply with 18 . . . Q–R3!; 19 B–Q2, B–Kt4 when White must lose on account of his undeveloped Kingside.

18	B–B4	Q–Q1
19	R–Q1	B–B3
20	Q–B3	

Here, or on the previous move, P–K3 is no good on account of Q–R4ch, but how else is White to develop his Kingside?

20	. . .	R–K1
21	P–QKt3	

With this White hopes at least to relieve some of the pressure on K2. 21 P–K3 still fails against 21 . . . Q–R4ch, and after 21 P–K4 Black can simply pocket a pawn by 21 . . . Q–Q4. After the text-move Black has the good and strong continuation 21 . . . B–Q4 followed by R–QB1. Instead, however, he decides upon a small combination.

21	. . .	P–Q6!

This piece sacrifice is the quickest way of revealing the helpless nature of White's undeveloped position. The opening of the diagonal KB3–QR8 now speedily decides the issue.

22	P–K4

Acceptance of the piece by 23 PxB is simply answered with 23 . . . PxP! The main line as intended in the game runs as follows: 23 P–K4, B–B6ch; 24 B–Q2, BxBch; 25 RxB, P–B6!; 26 RxP, P–B7; 27 RxQ, QRxR and Black wins. Possibly not the best, but in recompense a most pleasing variation.

22	. . .	B–B6ch
23	B–Q2	Q–Q5

Now there is no longer any defence against the threat of RxPch.

24	BxB	QxBch
25	R–Q2	RxPch!

White resigns.

After 26 QxR, Q–B8ch; 27 R–Q1, there comes the mate with a pawn by 27 . . . P–Q7. The game is characteristic of my style at the time. Not the strongest but the most complicated and striking continuation is the motto!

Game 2

FRENCH DEFENCE

International Correspondence Tournament of the Deutschen Schach-zeitung, 1932–33

	M. Siebold	P. Keres
1	P–K4	P–K3

In the earliest years, when I was taking my first essays in international correspondence chess life, I practically invariably played the French Defence against 1 P–K4. Only later was I to specialize in the open development systems arising out of 1 . . . P–K4.

2	P–Q4	P–Q4
3	Kt–QB3	Kt–KB3
4	B–Kt5	B–Kt5

In the French Defence my favourite system was the Mac-Cutcheon variation and I tried to use it at every opportunity. Here, too, the wish to make the game as violent as possible from the very first moves was dominant.

5	P–K5	P–KR3
6	B–Q2	BxKt
7	BxB	

During the years 1932–36 Siebold and I had the same variation in many correspondence games, in which almost without exception the continuation 7 PxB was employed. The text-move is regarded as inferior by theory, but apparently my opponent wanted to try something different for once.

7	. . .	Kt–K5
8	Q–Kt4	K–B1

In such positions I always preferred the King move at that time to the alternative 8 . . . P–Kt3. White cannot exploit

the position of the King by 9 B–Kt4ch, since after 9 ... P–B4;
10 PxP, Kt–QB3 Black has an excellent game.

	9	B–Q3	KtxB
	10	PxKt	P–QB4
	11	P–KR4	

At the time this game was played I deemed the text-move
not good and recommended as better for White 11 Q–B4,
Q–R4; 12 Q–Q2, Kt–B3; 13 Kt–B3, so as to keep the pawn
position in the centre compact. This would, however, lead to
a quieter level position, whereas after the text-move the game
pursues an interesting and exciting course.

	11	...	Q–R4
	12	K–Q2	Kt–B3

During the game I thought that after 12 ... PxP; 13 QxQP,
Kt–B3; 14 Q–KB4, P–Q5 White could play with advantage
15 Kt–K2, but in reply to this Black could very well play
15 ... PxPch; 16 KtxP, QxKP. Nevertheless, the variation is
good for White, only he must give up the pawn in another
way: 15 Kt–B3!, QxPch; 16 K–K2, etc.

13 Kt–B3.

Here, too, there exists a difference in the appreciation of the
position, then and now. Whilst I then thought that the capture
13 PxP would be bad for White on account of 13 ... P–Q5;
14 Kt–K2, PxPch; 15 KtxP, QxBP; it now seems to me that
White's position is not bad after 16 P–B4. In addition, White
can also continue after 13 ... P–Q5 (but not 13 ... KtxP;
14 Q–Kt4); 14 Kt–B3, QxPch; 15 K–K2, very much as in the
previous note.

	13	...	PxP
	14	KtxP	KtxP
	15	Q–Kt3	KtxB

Here I refrained from protecting the attacked Knight by
15 ... P–B3 because of 16 P–KB4. Still, the closing of the
diagonal QKt8–KR2 would not be unfavourable for Black and
would have vouchsafed him an easier defence after 16 ...
KtxB; 17 PxKt, B–Q2. In fact, however, protection by 15 ...
P–B3 would be extremely dangerous for Black owing to the

reply 16 QR–K1 ! threatening an exchange sacrifice on K5.
Furthermore, Black could not then play 16 . . . KtxB; because of
17 KtxPch, BxKt; 18 Q–Q6ch, etc. After the text-move White
also retains a lasting initiative in return for the pawn sacrifice.

	16 Q–Q6ch!	K–K1

Black wishes to ensure that his Bishop can be developed via
Q2, but in so doing his King remains in a most precarious
position. Hence 16 . . . K–Kt1; 17 PxKt, K–R2 deserved
serious consideration.

17	PxKt	B–Q2
18	KR–K1	R–QB1

White was, of course, threatening 19 Kt–B5. The text-move
gains an important tempo for the defence.

19	QR–B1	Q–B4!

Obviously, Black cannot afford the time to take the QRP,
but also 19 . . . Q–B2 is bad on account of 20 Kt–B5! Now
White cannot make this move as his KBP would be *en prise*.

20	Q–K5	K–B1
21	P–Kt4	

The first storm is over and the situation arising therefrom
can now be ascertained. White has undoubtedly good attacking chances in return for the pawns sacrificed, but the position
has concealed in it a number of interesting and complicated
possibilities, since the White King is also not particularly safe.
In addition to the text-move 21 R–K3 also merits consideration
so as to be able to reply to 21 . . . P–QKt4 with 22 Kt–Kt3,
followed by P–Q4.

It should, however, be observed that at that time in our
correspondence games we paid less regard to a careful defence
than to direct attacks on the King. Once this is taken into
consideration the following moves are easy to understand.

21	. . .	P–QKt4
22	P–KB4	P–Kt5
23	PxP	

Naturally, 23 P–B4 was more prudent and would have led to
an approximate equal ending after 23 . . . PxP; 24 RxP, QxQ;

25 RxRch, BxR; 26 RxQ. But our intentions were obviously far away from the endgame.

> 23   ...   QxPch
>
> 24   K–K3

It is true that after 24 K–K2, Q–Kt7ch; 25 K–B3 Black cannot well play 25 . . . RxR because of KtxPch but 25 . . . K–Kt1 would yield him a good game.

> 24   ...   P–B3!

It is easy to see that White must not capture either on B8 or K6. Now, however, a position has arisen which offers excellent opportunities for various combinations and is thus very much to the taste of both players.

> 25   Q–R5   P–K4

Nowadays I would first have prepared this thrust with 25 . . . R–K1, but at that time I was especially entranced by the forced continuation of the text-move with all its combinational possibilities. And indeed it must be granted that the ensuing portion of the game is not wanting in complications.

> 26   PxP   R–K1
>
> 27   R–B1!

The only counter, but a very strong one, Black must not yet immediately continue 27 . . . K–Kt1, since then 28 RxP! leads to a mating attack. So as to be able to renew the threat of K–Kt1, Black must first protect the point B3 once more.

> 27   ...   Q–Kt3!
>
> 28   R–QKt1   Q–B2
>
> 29   Kt–B3   Q–B4ch

Since White has now adequately protected the K5 square Black goes over to another plan of attack. With the text-move he makes use of the circumstance that White cannot well escape with his King to Q2 on account of 30 . . . K–Kt1 to force the advance of his QP to Q4. With this advance the diagonal QKt1 to KR7 becomes open and Black can forge plans to entrap the enemy Queen.

> 30   P–Q4   Q–B7

Now the win of the Queen is threatened by 31 . . . P–Kt3 and apparently the game is already decided in Black's favour.

But Siebold knows how to present his opponent with new and difficult problems.

31   Kt–Kt5!

Threatening a mate on B7 and thus enforcing Black's reply since the continuation 31 . . . PxKt; 32 QxRch, K–B2; 33 RxPch! would afford White an attack good enough for at least a draw.

31   . . .   P–Kt3
32   RxPch   K–Kt2

Apparently White's counterplay is now over, since after 33 R–B7ch, K–Kt1 he has no more means of giving check and must therefore concede the loss of his Queen. But even in this difficult position the resourceful conductor of the white pieces understands how to set his opponent some serious problems.

33   R–Kt7!

It is interesting to observe that White still has an attacking continuation at his disposal that even now puts the win in doubt. It is true that in the ensuing play White will only have a Knight for the Queen but his Rooks develop a remarkably effective fire-power on the seventh rank.

33   . . .   PxQ

Again forced, since after 33 . . . R–K2; 34 Kt–K6ch would ensure White at least a draw.

Black (Keres)

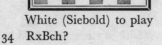

White (Siebold) to play
34   RxBch?

But this is a mistake which makes things much easier for Black. White should continue here with 34 R–B7ch, K–Kt1; 35 R(B7)xB! threatening mate in two. During the game I had prepared the following variation: 35 . . . Q–Kt3 (there seems nothing better since in reply to Queen checks the White King moves up and down the K3 and K2 squares); 36 PxP, Q–B4 (or 36 . . . QxP; 37 R–Kt7ch, K–B1; 38 Kt–R7ch, RxKt; 39 RxR, etc.); 37 R–Kt7ch, K–B1; 38 R(Kt7)–B7ch, QxR; 39 KtxQ, R–R2; 40 Kt–Q6, though all the same a win for Black here is not certain.

It is very natural that, in the case of a young player, his concrete analyses betray much fewer inaccuracies than his positional appraisements. This is a circumstance that we can discover in this case. Whereas in this game I formerly judged quite a number of positions in a manner either open to dispute or even incorrect, the concrete analysis reproduced above is in fact quite good. Only the conclusion is open to doubt, since after 40 . . . RxR; 41 KtxR(Kt7), K–K2 Black retains excellent winning chances.

But the analysis also is itself not wholly accurate. At the time I had not at all noticed that instead of 36 . . . Q–B4 Black could also try 36 . . . Q–KB3. Apparently this move wins without much difficulty since both 37 Kt–R7, RxKt; 38 RxR, Q–B4; as well as 37 R–KB7, RxPch; 38 PxR, QxPch; 39 K–Q3, PxKt; 40 R(B7)–K7, Q–B4ch followed by 41 . . . Q–B1 end in a clearly won position for Black. Nevertheless White disposes of a most surprising defensive resource here, to wit, 37 R–KB7, RxPch; 38 K–Q2! It becomes manifest that Black's own Rook renders the win difficult. If the Rook on K4 is removed then simply QxPch followed by 39 . . . PxKt wins. Now, however, if Black wants to play on for a win, he has nothing better than 38 . . . Q–Q1; when there follows 39 PxR, PxKt. A detailed analysis of this position would lead us too far and in any case does not pertain to the annotations already made here, but it is clear that Black retains some winning prospects. In any event a most interesting variation.

| 34 | . . . | K–Kt1 |
| 35 | R(B6)–B7 | Q–B6ch! |

When the White Rooks stand, as in the game, on Q7 and KB7 this check wins much more quickly than 35 . . . Q–Kt3; 36 PxP, QxR; 37 KtxQ, R–R2. For then White would obtain excellent defensive chances by 38 Kt–Q6, RxPch; 39 PxR, RxR; 40 K–Q4.

36   K–K2   RxPch!

Now it becomes clear why, on move 34, White should have captured with the other Rook on Q7. With the Rooks placed on Kt7 and Q7 this sacrifice would be useless since a mate with the Rook on Q8 would be subsequently threatened.

37   PxR   QxPch
38   K–Q3

After 38 K–B1, PxKt; 39 R–B5, Black wins simply by 39 . . . Q–Kt1.

38   . . .   PxKt

Making the win for Black quite clear since the White Rooks can no longer constitute a mating threat.

39   R–B5

After 39 R(B7)–K7, the following winning variation was planned: 39 . . . Q–Kt6ch; 40 K–K2 (forced, since White must not allow a check on the KB file because of the possibility of Q–KB1. And if 40 R–K3, Black wins by 40 . . . Q–Kt1; 41 R(K3)–K7, Q–KB1; etc.), 40 . . . QxPch; 41 K–K1, QxPch; 42 K–K2, Q–Kt5ch; 43 K–K1, Q–Kt5ch; 44 K–K2, QxRch; 45 RxQ, R–R2. After the text-move the finish is simpler.

39   . . .   Q–K5ch

resigns.

I demonstrated the following variation to my opponent: 40 K–B3, Q–B5ch; 41 K–Q2, Q–Kt5ch; 42 K–K3 (or K–B1), RPxP; 43 RxPch, K–B1; 44 R–Q8ch, K–K2; 45 RxR, Q–B6ch followed by 46 . . . QxR, whereupon White realised the hopeless nature of his position and desisted from further play.

This game is typical for my style of that period—not precisely blameless from the positional point of view, but in compensation for this extremely complicated and full of interesting moments.

Game 3

QUEEN'S GAMBIT DECLINED

Championship of Estonia, 1935. 3rd Match-Game.

	G. Friedemann	P. Keres
1	P–Q4	Kt–KB3
2	P–QB4	P–K3
3	Kt–KB3	P–Q4
4	Kt–B3	P–B3
5	B–Kt5	QKt–Q2

This was the deciding game of the match. The first two had given the result of 1–1, and the winner of this game was to receive the title of champion of Estonia. It is therefore understandable that Black does not want to content himself with relatively passive variations of the Queen's Gambit Declined and tries for the more vigorous Cambridge Springs Defence. At the time when this game was played the counter-attacking system starting with 5 . . . PxP was not yet known.

But Friedemann apparently does not like any great complications in so important a game and therefore proceeds to exchange pawns, thereby assuring himself of a quiet position with some initiative. Naturally, this choice was not particularly welcome to Black.

6	PxP	KPxP
7	P–K3	B–K2
8	B–Q3	O–O
9	Q–B2	R–K1
10	O–O	

White continues with his plan of gradually outplaying his youthful opponent by quiet positional play. Otherwise one might have expected that a temperamental player like Friedemann would have adopted the keen attacking line 10 O–O–O.

10	. . .	Kt–B1
11	P–KR3	

White wants to continue with 12 Kt–K5 and therefore prevents Black's Kt–Kt5 in reply. Nowadays it is common

knowledge that the most enduring attacking method on the
Queenside lies in the manoeuvre P–QKt4–5 and this would be
best prepared here by 11 QR–Kt1.

11 . . .   Kt–K5
12 BxB

Here 12 B–KB4 offered White better prospects of obtaining
an advantage. Black experiences no difficulties after the exchange on K7.

12 . . .   QxB
13 BxKt

White gets nowhere with this exchange but preparations for
P–QKt4 no longer yield so good a result as they would have
done a couple of moves earlier. If now, for instance, 13 QR–
Kt1, then 13 . . . P–QR4; 14 P–R3, Kt–Q3 could follow and
then if 15 P–QKt4, PxP; 16 PxP, P–QKt4! All the same this
variation afforded White better chances than the colourless
exchange on K4.

13 . . .   PxB
14 Kt–Q2   B–B4

Better than 14 . . . P–KB4; since White cannot now play
15 P–B3, on account of 15 . . . Q–Kt4. Further preparation is
necessary for the advance P–B3.

15 QR–K1   Q–K3

At the time the game was played I thought this move was
bad and was convinced that I had a better continuation in
15 . . . Q–R5; 16 P–B3, BxP; 17 Kt(Q2)xP, B–B4. But in this
case, too, White would have got the better of the bargain by
exchanging his RP for a centre pawn. However, Black appears
to have a good line here in 15 . . . P–B4. Then 16 Kt–Q5,
Q–Q3; 17 QxBP, QxQ; 18 PxQ is not good because of
18 . . . QR–Q1; and 16 Kt–Kt3 can be simply met by 16 . . .
P–QKt3. Also possible was 15 . . . B–Kt3; 16 Q–Kt3, Q–K3;
with an approximately equal game.

16 P–B3!   Q–Kt3?

After 16 . . . PxP; 17 P–K4, I reckoned only on the possible
piece sacrifice 17 . . . BxRP; 18 PxB, Q–Kt3ch; 19 K–B2,

Q–Kt7ch; 20 KK3, and came to the conclusion that this was
good for White. But I overlooked the normal move 17 . . .
B–Kt3; which would give Black a really good game after
18 KtxP, QR–Q1.

17   PxP

White could have ensured himself a rather better position
by 17 Kt(Q2)xP, BxP; 18 Q–B2, but an attacking player like
Friedemann cannot resist the temptation to open up the KB
file. The game now becomes most interesting.

17	. . .	BxRP
18	Kt–B3	B–K3
19	Q–B2?	

It is difficult to say whether this was intention or oversight;
in any case, with this move White trifles away his chances for
the initiative. He should, of course, have played 19 Kt–KR4,
Q–R4; 20 Kt–B5, followed by R–B3 with far from poor prospects on the Kingside.

19	. . .	B–B5
20	Kt–KR4	

Perhaps Friedemann had overlooked that 20 Kt–K5 would
not do here because of 20 . . . RxKt. Instead of the text-move
which gives up the exchange the protective move 20 Kt–K2
deserved more attention. Black could not then win any
material immediately since 20 . . . QxP or 20 . . . RxP would
be met by 21 Kt–K5. But if Black first exchanges by 20 . . .
BxKt; 21 RxB, then capture on K4 would allow White to win
back his pawn at once by 22 Kt–Kt5 and 22 Kt–K5 res-
pectively.

Black would, however, have obtained rather the better position after 20 Kt–K2 as well since he could have continued
with 20 . . . P–B3; 21 P–K5, Kt–Q2. Still, White would have
had much better chances then after 22 PxP, QxP; 23 P–QKt3,
than he gets in the game after the exchange sacrifice.

20   . . .   Q–R4

After 20 . . . Q–K3 White could again play 21 Kt–K2, and
get real attacking chances in return for the pawn by 21 . . .
QxP; 22 P–QKt3, B–K3; 23 Q–Kt3. Now White must

surrender the exchange, since 21 Kt–K2, RxP would leave
Black with a marked advantage.

21	Kt–B5	BxR
22	RxB	Q–Kt3

Black is the exchange to the good but must however play
most accurately in order to weaken the attacking threat of
23 P–K5, followed by 24 Kt–K4. For this purpose it would
have been best to have played 22 ... P–B3! During the game
I refrained from this move because of the possibility of 23
Q–Kt3, Q–Kt3; 24 Q–B7, but Black can play better. By
23 ... Kt–K3! and then if 24 P–Q5, Kt–Kt4 Black would have
every prospect of evaluating his material advantage. After
the text-move his task is more complicated.

23	P–K5	P–B3!

Black must not remain passive and allow his opponent to
build up his attack with Kt–K4, Q–R4, etc.

24	Q–R4	Q–Kt4

Naturally, not 24 ... PxP, because of 25 Kt–K7ch; nor
would the continuations 24 ... K–R1; 25 Kt–K4, PxP;
26 Kt(K4)–Q6, or 24 ... Kt–K3; 25 P–Q5, PxQP; 26 KtxQP
be good for Black. With the text-move Black accepts a worsening of his pawn position and also gives up the attack on White's
K5 pawn, but at the same time the White assault on the
King's wing is brought to a standstill. Black's advantage of
the exchange should eventually tell in the endgame.

25	QxQ

White cannot well avoid the exchange of Queens since he
would lose the valuable pawn on K5 after 25 Q–K4, PxP;
26 PxP, P–KKt3.

25	...	PxQ
26	Kt–K4	Kt–Q2!

Black cannot afford the time to protect his KKt pawn
since after 26 ... Kt–K3; 27 Kt(K4)–Q6 would win back the
exchange, and also 26 ... P–KR3; 27 Kt(K4)–Q6, R–K3
(or 27 ... KR–Kt1; 28 P–K4, followed by 29 P–Q5, etc.);
28 KtxQKtP, and 29 Kt–B5 is far from agreeable for Black.

27	Kt(K4)xP

If 27 Kt(K4)–Q6, R–K3; 28 KtxQKtP, when Black should
not play, according to my recommendation at the time,
28 . . . QR–Kt1; 29 Kt(B5)–Q6, KtxP; 30 PxKt, RxP; since
after the further 31 R–B1 he would hardly retain any real
winning chances.

But by 28 . . . R–KB1 he could force an exchange of Rooks
and so preserve very good winning chances.

27   . . .   KtxP!

By means of this Knight sacrifice Black frees himself of all
difficulties and sets his opponent some grave problems in the
ensuing endgame, a correct handling of which demands good
technique.

28   Kt–Q6?

Despite the many drawbacks White should have gone in
for the endgame with 28 PxKt, RxP; 29 P–KKt4. It is true
that after 29 . . . P–KKt3 White would lose another pawn, but
he would retain good prospects of saving the game none the less.
Though White regains the exchange with the text-move he
loses a lot of pawns and the resulting ending does not offer
too difficult a technical problem to Black.

Black (Keres) to play

White (Friedemann)

28   . . .   Kt–Kt5!
29   KtxR   RxKt

Now White can no longer protect his KP.

30	P–K4	P–KR3
31	R–B4	Kt–B3
32	Kt–B3	

After 32 Kt–B7, Black has the pleasant choice between
32 . . . KtxP and 32 . . . KxKt; 33 P–K5, R–K3; 34 PxKt,
RxP.

32	. . .	RxP
33	RxR	

Avoidance of the Rook exchange by 33 R–B5 loses still more
quickly after 33 . . . R–K7.

33	. . .	KtxR

The Knight ending is won for Black without much difficulty,
since in addition to the pawn plus he also has the better position. White puts up a stubborn resistance but cannot, however,
alter the inevitable result.

34	Kt–K5	K–B1
35	K–B1	K–K2
36	K–K2	K–K3
37	K–K3	Kt–Q3
38	P–QKt3	K–Q4

Black prepares the advance P–B4, in order to remove White's
last centre pawn and thus deprive the enemy Knight of its
support. An immediate 38 . . . P–B4 will not do yet because
of 39 Kt–Q3, Kt–B4ch; 40 K–K4.

39	K–Q3

After this, White's pieces are forced into totally passive
positions. Better, therefore, was 39 P–KKt4, P–B4; 40 Kt–B3,
although in that event the continuation I intended during the
game 40 . . . P–B5; 41 Kt–K5, P–B6; 42 K–Q3, P–B7, etc.
would also retain Black's advantage.

39	. . .	Kt–B4
40	Kt–B3	

Forced, since he loses another pawn after 40 Kt–Kt4, P–KR4;
or 40 Kt–B4, P–QKt4.

40	. . .	P–KR4!

Now White is still in zugswang and has to surrender a second pawn. With this the endgame is already decided.

41	P–QKt4	P–QKt4
42	P–R3	P–R3
43	Kt–K5	

After 43 K–B3, the simplest way to win is 43 . . . Kt–K6.

43	. . .	KtxP
44	Kt–Kt6	Kt–K3
45	Kt–K7ch	K–Q3
46	Kt–Kt6	P–B4

Now Black creates a passed pawn on the Queen's wing and this wins quickly.

47	PxPch	KxP
48	K–B3	P–R4
49	P–Kt3	P–Kt5ch
50	PxP	PxPch
51	K–Kt2	K–Kt4
52	K–Kt1	

It is naturally not agreeable to have to give up the chance of a championship title but White could have resigned a long time since.

52	. . .	P–Kt6
53	K–Kt2	K–R5
54	Kt–K5	Kt–B4
55	Kt–B6	P–Kt4
56	Kt–Q4	P–R5
57	PxP	PxP
58	Kt–B3	P–R6
59	Kt–R2	K–Kt5
60	Kt–Kt4	Kt–R5ch
61	K–R1	P–R7

This destroys White's last slender hope: 61 . . . K–R6; 62 Kt–K3, P–R7? 63 Kt–B2ch, PxKt; stalemate.

62	KtxP	K–R6
	resigns.	

Game 4

ALEKHINE'S DEFENCE

International Tournament at Tallinn, 1935

	P. Keres	G. Danielsson
1	P–K4	Kt–KB3
2	P–K5	Kt–Q4
3	P–Q4	P–QB4

This continuation apparently constitutes the sort of opening experiment that many practised players are wont to use against youthful opponents in order to give the game a sharp character from the very start. When this game was played Danielsson was already a recognised international master, whereas I was making my first steps in international chess. In this game, however, Black does not attain the hoped-for result as in the ensuing tactical struggle he turns out to be on the losing side.

4	P–QB4	Kt–B2
5	P–Q5	P–Q3
6	PxP	

White contents himself with the minimal opening advantage that flows from the bad position of the Knight on B2 and some slight advantage in space. An interesting attempt to refute Black's line of play was here the pawn sacrifice 6 P–K6!, PxP; 7 B–Q3, by which White obtains excellent attacking chances.

6	. . .	PxP

Nor is Black's task easier after 6 . . . QxP; 7 Kt–QB3, P–K3; 8 Kt–B3, since White is threatening an eventual Kt–K4 and the further opening up of play can only benefit White in view of his better development. But now Black is handicapped by the bad position of his Knight on QB2.

7	B–Q3	B–K2
8	Kt–K2	Kt–Q2
9	P–B4	B–R5ch

Black aims at further complications and is soon himself punished as a result. Black must play here 9 . . . O–O and

then prepare for the advance P–QKt4 which constitutes the
only chance of counter-play based on the position. With the
text-move Black seeks to force the weakening 10 P–KKt3,
but something quite different occurs.

10   Kt–Kt3   Q–K2ch?

With this move Black must have only taken into account the
Queen exchange by 11 Q–K2, since, otherwise, this check is
hard to understand. As a matter of fact, however, this move
turns out to be a mistake that results in a very bad position
for Black. Given that Black has already played 9 . . . B–R5ch,
then he should here continue logically with 10 . . . BxKtch;
11 PxB, Kt–B3 so at least to obtain control of the KKt5 square.

11   K–Q2!

This King move undoubtedly was a complete surprise for
my opponent. On account of the double threat of 12 R–K1
and 12 Kt–B5, Black must now exchange on Kt3 and afterwards forgo the right to castle, all this leading to a very constricted position for him. It should be observed that White's
King must go to Q2 since if, for instance, 11 K–B2, Black could
avoid the worst by 11 . . . O–O; 12 R–K1, Q–Q1.

11   . . .   BxKt

Forced, as after 11 . . . O–O; 12 Kt–B5, Black would lose
material.

12   PxB   K–Q1
13   R–K1   Q–B1

After 13 . . . Q–B3; 14 Kt–B3, the threat of 15 Kt–K4 would
be very troublesome. But after the text-move it becomes clear
to what fatal consequences the thoughtless check on the tenth
move has led.

White is better developed, possesses more space in addition
to the two Bishops, and finally is in a position to thwart any
counter-play whatsoever on Black's part. It appears that even
with the best play Black can hardly emerge with a satisfactory
position.

14   P–Kt3

so as to reply to 14 . . . Kt–B3 with 15 B–Kt2, and thus to
prevent 15 . . . B–Kt5. The text-move is more exact than

14 P–R4, for this reason. Counter-play by 14 . . . P–QKt4 is not immediately dangerous.

                14 . . .   P–QKt4

It is already difficult to recommend an acceptable plan of play for Black. The text-move forms the only possibility of obtaining some counter-play on the Queen's wing, but on the other hand it makes it easier for White's attack to open up lines.

                15   B–Kt2   PxP
                16   PxP   Kt–Kt3
                17   Q–K2   P–B3

White was, of course, threatening 18 BxKtP. It would have been better to have played immediately 17 . . . B–Q2 to counter this threat, but one can understand that Black does not want to have his Queen tied down for ever to the defence of the Knight pawn.

After the text-move a fresh weakness appears in Black's position, *viz.* his K3 square. White's play is aimed against this point in the ensuing phase; the pieces that protect this point, the Bishop on Q2 and the Knight on B2, must be exchanged off.

                18   Kt–B3   B–Q2
                19   P–Kt4   K–B1
                20   P–R4   P–QR4

Practically forced, since Black cannot allow the further advance of this pawn. But now White has affirmed his control of the squares KB5 and QKt5, from which points he can proceed to exchange off the Black pieces protecting Black's K3.

                21   B–B5   BxB
                22   PxB   Q–Q1
                23   Q–Q3   Q–Q2

If Black plays 23 . . . R–K1 in order to relieve his plight a little then White can make the exchange sacrifice 24 R–K6!, KtxR; 25 BPxKt. Black would then have no counterplay and would scarcely be able to find an adequate defence to the adversary's numerous threats.

Black (Danielsson)

White (Keres) to play

24 Kt–Kt5!	KtxKt

After 24 . . . R–K1 the reply 25 R–K6! would be even more effective.

25 RPxKt	P–R5
26 B–R3	

A useful move that prevents in advance the eventual possibility of P–R6 and also prepares a sacrifice on QB5 if the occasion arises.

26 . . .	P–Kt3

Black's position is hopeless. The attempt initiated by the text-move, to conjure up tactical complications, leads to an unhappy result for Black.

27 R–K6	R–QKt1

White was already threatening, amongst other things, 28 BxP.

28 QR–K1	PxP
29 R–K7	KtxPch

A desperate last throw, but also 29 . . . Q–Q1; 30 QxPch, Kt–Q2; 31 R–B7 is hopeless for Black.

30 QxKt	QxP
31 Q–B2	

It goes without saying that 31 QxQ, RxQ; 32 R–R7 would

win as well, but the continuance of the attack against the King brings about a quicker decision.

| 31 . . . | Q–R4ch |

More stubborn was 31 . . . R–Kt3. The ensuing active counterplay loses at once.

32	K–Q1	R–Kt6
33	QxPch	K–Kt1
34	R–K8ch	RxR
35	RxRch	K–R2
36	Q–Q7ch	R–Kt2
37	QxQP	R–Kt8ch
38	K–B2	R–Kt7ch
39	BxR	resigns

FIRST INTERNATIONAL APPEARANCE 1935–1937

I WENT with very mixed feelings to my first international tournament, the Warsaw Chess Olympiad. After the Estonian Championship I had taken part in a number of events and attained what seemed like good form; but it must be observed that these events bore a local character and it was also known that at that time Estonian chess life was far from being on an international level. Hence it might perhaps be feared that my first contact with the top class of international masters would result in a veritable catastrophe.

The tournament commenced for me with an alternation of successes and failures. After a win in the first round I at once had to meet the world champion, Dr. Alekhine. I managed to keep on level terms for a long time, but in the end the world champion's might prevailed. I made a simple mistake, had to give up two pieces for a Rook and then of course soon resigned. This game was enough to show that I was lacking in the necessary chess maturity, the technique and the experience to fit me to meet the world class type of player. It is therefore no coincidence that at Warsaw I succumbed to Flohr, Tartakower and L. Steiner without being able to put up any noticeable resistance to my experienced opponents.

Amongst these defeats there were also a number of interesting wins full of incident, of which the short sacrificial game against the English master Winter (No. 5) is undoubtedly the most well-known. In the end I succeeded in amassing a good total, 12 points out of 19 games, and thus attained fifth place on first board. But the most important victory for me in the tournament was the conviction that a successful contest with leading international players was indeed possible for me. For this purpose I must, in the first place, acquire more tournament experience and tend to my further chess development, in particular as regards purely technical matters.

In the autumn of the same year I took part in a small tournament in Helsinki and obtained second place after P. Frydman. I lost right in the first round against Frydman, and the shortness of the tournament rendered it impossible for me to make good this loss in the subsequent course of the event. In the last round I achieved a most important win as Black against Stahlberg and that in a complicated game full of combinations where, too, for a long time I had to conduct a difficult defence.

The year 1936 was also characterised by many events in which I took part. At the beginning of the year I played in a training tournament in Tallinn and obtained first place without much difficulty. After that I had to play a match against P. Schmidt, who had challenged me to a match for the championship of Estonia. This match turned out to be most exciting and was very instructive for me in many respects. After a comparatively easy win in the first game I won a piece in the second by a simple combination. In consequence I regarded the issue as already settled and started to play rather superficially. Schmidt, on the other hand, utilised the chances offered to him in exemplary fashion, complicated matters by a surprise Queen sacrifice, and after some further inaccuracies on my part he even achieved a win in the end.

One might have thought that after this defeat I would have played more cautiously in the sequel, but nothing like this occurred. After a quick draw in the third game I chose in the fourth an extremely risky, one might even term it weak, opening variation, and a good positional performance on my opponent's part brought me another nought. In the next and fifth game Schmidt was obviously playing for a draw from the very start, since he chose the exchange variation against the French Defence. An attempt to win at all costs eventually resulted in a loss for me in this game.

My situation was in consequence highly critical, since, with only two more games to play, my opponent was leading by two points. But now apparently Schmidt's nerves gave way under

In the tournament at Ostend that followed on immediately after Margate I had an excellent start in that I achieved a fine win against my chief rival Fine in the first round (No. 12). But the ensuing losses against, first, Tartakower and then Grob, in which latter game I forgot to make my last move before the time-control, and so lost on time, coupled with some tournament luck, brought me eventually to a tie for 1–3 prizes, together with Fine and Grob. One of the most original games in my tournament praxis hitherto was played against Dunkelblum (No. 13).

From Ostend I travelled directly to Prague. There I continued playing in the same light, easy style and achieved a fresh success with it. In fact, I managed to win the first eight games one after the other and after this the gain of the first prize was no longer a difficult task. In this tournament I again had a series of interesting games, amongst which, in addition to that against Foltys (No. 14) and Hromadka (No. 15), the encounter with Eliskases also deserves mention. The march with the King from KKt1 to QKt7 that I undertook in this game is particularly original.

After a small tournament in Vienna, in which the moves 1 P–Q4, Kt–KB3; 2 Kt–KB3, Kt–K5 were prescribed in advance and in which I again proved successful, I went off to the strongest tournament of the year, that at Kemeri. Once again I had the opportunity of crossing swords with the world's leading masters. I began the tournament in very mediocre style but then gradually came into form and was almost able to catch up with my rivals. A draw in the last round against Feigin left me "only" tieing with Alekhine for the 4th and 5th prizes, Alekhine also having been unable to win his last round game against Berg. We were, however, only half a point behind the three first prize-winners. From this tournament the reader will find a pretty brevity against Book (No. 16) which has a final combination of a very pleasing character.

Before the Olympiad in Stockholm there was still time for a small tournament at Parnu, in which, amongst others, Flohr, Stahlberg, Tartakower and Opocensky took part. Here the surprise winner was Schmidt, against whom I lost in the first round and that through a careless handling of the opening.

In this tournament I had to squander much energy on various organisational questions as the event was one of my ideas at the time for enlivening the chess life of Estonia. An almost crazy and in any case complicated game took place between Flohr and myself, the issue of which was a peaceful draw. Also worthy of notice is the original combination in the game with Raud (No. 17).

I again played really well at the Stockholm Chess Olympiad and on first board I eventually obtained second place. Amongst a number of lively games the good attacking achievement against Reshevsky (No. 18) merits especial mention. This was, moreover, my first win against the American grandmaster.

With this event what might be termed my preparation for the Semmering Tournament terminated, since this last tourney was now close at hand. During the last six months I had taken part in seven international tournaments. These undoubtedly introduced more solidity into my play and allowed me to amass the necessary experience for the forthcoming great event.

The question has often been put: how should one behave before a strong tournament? Should one take part in as many chess events as possible, or should one uniquely confine oneself to preparation at home, or finally, should one entirely lay aside chess and simply have a good rest? Naturally, it is difficult to find one completely right answer to this question since it depends on many circumstances, such as, for example, character, age, the health of the player, etc. It seems to me that the best form of preparation for a young player lies in as many other tournaments as possible in which preferably he should encounter players of varying strengths.

In between the tournaments I occupied myself as far as it was possible, in playing tennis, so as to be at the peak physically. When I now look back and consider how easily I played in this very strongly contested tournament, then I am more and more impressed with the conviction that the prime cause was just those seven tournaments which I had worked through before the commencement of this most strenuous event.

Game 5

SICILIAN DEFENCE

Chess Olympiad at Warsaw, 1935

	P. Keres	W. Winter
1	P–K4	P–QB4
2	Kt–KB3	Kt–KB3

With this line, introduced by Nimzowitsch, Winter wants to lead his youthful opponent to paths not so well-mapped out by theory and thus make use of his greater knowledge and experience. He is partially successful in that at the time I had a rather vague idea of the whole variation. The consequences, however, of this tactical plan turn out to be a little different from those Black might have imagined.

3	P–K5	Kt–Q4
4	Kt–B3	P–K3

The variation 4 ... KtxKt; 5 QPxKt is playable for Black, but it gives his opponent a lasting initiative after 5 ... P–Q4; 6 PxP e.p. It was exactly this, in fact, that Black wanted to avoid with his second move.

5	KtxKt	PxKt
6	P–Q4	P–Q3
7	B–Kt5!	

This position was at that time well-known theoretically. White usually continued with 7 B–Kt5ch, or also 7 KPxP, BxP; 8 PxP, with play against the isolated Queen's pawn. The interesting idea bound up with the text-move came into my mind during the game and I decided to try it out. Black is now posed with some most disagreeable problems, so much so that the whole variation has lost its popularity in modern tournament praxis.

7	. . .	Q–R4ch

The main idea of the sortie 7 B–Kt5 lies in that Black cannot well reply 7 ... B–K2 on account of 8 BxB, QxB; 9 PxP, when White wins a pawn. The text-move is Black's logical reply since the pawn sacrifice 7 . . . Q–Kt3; 8 PxBP, PxBP; 9 QxP scarcely affords him sufficient compensation. For example after 9 . . . P–KR3; 10 O–O–O! White obtains a very strong attack and also the continuation 9 . . . B–K3; 10 B–Kt5ch, Kt–B3; 11 Q–Q3, P–KR3; 12 B–Q2 leaves White the better game. With the text-move Black wants to force 8 B–Q2, and then play 8 . . . Q–Kt3.

	8	P–B3	BPxP
	9	B–Q3!	

An original idea that converts this Sicilian to a kind of Danish Gambit. Although White could also play here very well 9 QxP, Kt–B3; 10 Q–K3, the game continuation must be deemed more energetic and it poses Black some difficult defensive problems.

	9	. . .	PxBP

After the game there was considerable discussion in chess literature as to whether Black should accept the pawn sacrifice or not. It seems to me that acceptance of the pawn sacrifice constitutes Black's only logical continuation here, if he wants to have any compensation for his opponent's better development.

Thus, for example, White could simply play after 9 . . . Kt–B3; 10 O–O!, and if then 10 . . . PxKP; 11 KtxKP, KtxKt; 12 R–K1, when White obtains a dangerous attack. In the game Eliskases–Frydman, Lodz, 1938, Black tried 9 . . . PxKP; 10 KtxKP, Q–B2, but here also White had the better position after 11 O–O, B–Q3; 12 PxP.

	10	O–O	PxKtP

But the validity of this capture is very debatable, since now White obtains fine attacking chances which certainly outweigh the sacrificed material. More prudent in any case was 10 . . . Kt–B3; 11 R–K1, B–K3; although also after this White can win back one of the pawns by 12 PxBP and retain a lasting initiative. A possible variation thereafter, 12 . . . PxP; 13 KtxP, KtxKt; 14 RxKt, B–Q3; 15 RxBch, PxR; 16 Q–R5ch gives White excellent attacking chances in return for the exchange sacrifice.

	11	R–Kt1	PxP?

If the validity of the previous pawn capture is unclear, then this capture is certainly incorrect. Black now remains so far behind in development that he can no longer parry the ensuing attack. Here the continuation 11 ... Kt–B3; 12 R–K1, B–K3 was already obligatory.

At the time I conducted a discussion with a German correspondence chess friend about this position. He thought the position was better for Black and challenged me to continue the game from this point by correspondence. The game took the following course: 13 RxP, Q–B2; 14 Q–R4, PxP; 15 KtxP, B–Q3; 16 R(Kt2)–K2, BxKt; 17 RxB, Q–Q2; 18 R(K5)–K3, O–O; 19 BxPch!, KxB; 20 Q–R4ch, K–Kt1; 21 B–B6, B–B4; 22 P–Kt4, and Black resigned.

Obviously this game cannot be adduced as proof that White has an overwhelmingly won game after 11 ... Kt–B3. It shows, however, most clearly with what difficulties Black has to struggle in the defence, especially when one considers the limited time limit in an over-the-board game.

12   KtxP   B–Q3

Black no longer has a satisfactory defence. After 12 ... B–K3 White can again play simply 13 RxP, or else continue with a decisive attack by 13 R–K1, B–QKt5; 14 KtxP!, BxR; 15 KtxR. After the text-move Black's position speedily collapses.

Black (Winter)

White (Keres) to play

13   KtxP!

This Knight sacrifice is immediately decisive since the

deserted King cannot resist the concentrated attack of all the White pieces. Acceptance of the sacrifice is naturally forced.

| 13 | . . . | KxKt |
| 14 | Q–R5ch | P–Kt3 |

After 14 . . . K–K3; 15 B–B5ch wins at once and also the continuation 14 . . . K–Kt1; 15 Q–K8ch, B–B1; 16 B–K7, Kt–Q2; 17 B–KB5 leads to inevitable loss. If, however, Black had played 14 . . . K–B1, then I had prepared the following variation: 15 KR–K1, B–Q2; 16 Q–B3ch (also good is 16 R–K3), 16 . . . K–Kt1; 17 B–K7! and White wins.

| 15 | BxPch! | PxB |
| 16 | QxR | B–KB4 |

Black's position is hopeless. After 16 . . . Kt–Q2 there could follow 17 Q–R7ch, K–B1; 18 B–R6ch, K–K1; 19 QxPch, when the Bishop on Q3 would be lost. Now White wins by a mating attack.

| 17 | KR–K1 | B–K5 |
| 18 | RxB! | |

Removes the last defensive piece from the Black King.

| 18 | . . . | PxR |
| 19 | Q–B6ch | resigns |

Black is soon mated after 19 . . . K–Kt1; 20 QxPch, K–B1; 21 QxBch.

Game 6

QUEEN'S PAWN, KING'S INDIAN DEFENCE

7th game of the match for the Estonian Championship, 1936

	P. Schmidt	P. Keres
1	P–Q4	Kt–KB3
2	Kt–KB3	P–KKt3

This was the last game of the match. Schmidt was leading by 3½–2½, and therefore it was imperative for me to win the game in order to retain the title of champion of Estonia. This explains my choice of opening since I played the King's Indian Defence only very occasionally in tournaments.

3	P–B4	B–Kt2
4	P–KKt3	O–O
5	B–Kt2	P–Q3
6	O–O	QKt–Q2

When this game was played systems such as 6 . . . Kt–B3 followed by P–QR3 were not yet known in the chess-world. However, such a system would have been very useful for bringing about the desired complications.

7	Kt–B3	P–K4
8	PxP	

Schmidt is, of course, content with a draw. He therefore chooses the exchange variation by which the tension in the centre is released and a quiet level game obtained.

8	. . .	PxP
9	P–KR3	Q–K2
10	B–K3	P–B3
11	Q–Kt3	Kt–K1

In the game Spielmann-Bogoljuboff, Bad Kissingen, 1928, Black continued here 11 . . . P–KR3 and 12 . . . K–R2; but was soon in great difficulties. There is naturally no point in Black's voluntary weakening of his King's position and instead he must strive for counter-play as quickly as possible by P–KB4. With the text-move Black clears the way for his KBP to advance, but perhaps 11 . . . Kt–R4 with the same idea was more energetic.

12 Kt–KKt5?

White suddenly conceives the ambitious plan of forcing Black's P–KR3 and thereafter exploiting this weakness. But two lost tempi for this weakness are too high a price and from now on Black seizes the initiative. Much better was the move Schmidt suggested after the game, 12 P–B5 so as to engineer pressure on the Queen's wing. Black cannot then well reply 12 . . . KtxP on account of 13 Q–R3.

But Black also has good chances of active counter-play after
12 P–B5. In the variation recommended by Schmidt 12 . . .
Kt–B2; 13 Q–B4, Kt–K3; 14 P–QKt4, Black can continue
vigorously with 14 . . . P–B4 after which a complicated position
occurs with chances for both sides.

12	. . .	P–KR3
13	Kt–B3	P–KB4
14	QR–Q1	K–R1

Better was 14 . . . K–R2. White intended to reply to this
move with 15 Q–B2, but then 15 . . . P–K5 followed by 16 . . .
Kt–K4 gives Black an excellent game.

15	Kt–KR4	R–B3

To 15 . . . Q–B3 White had prepared the surprising reply
16 Kt–K4, which after 16 . . . PxKt; 17 BxKP, with an eventual P–B4, would have yielded him really good attacking prospects. The text-move enables Black to protect his KKt3 square
once again by Kt–B1 thereby repelling his opponent's attempts
at attack.

16	P–Kt4	Kt–B1!

After this White's attack is at an end and he must occupy
himself with the defence of his own King-side where Black now
has attained a dangerous initiative.

17	P–Kt5	R–B2
18	PxP	B–B3
19	Kt–B3	P–KKt4
20	Kt–QR4	

Black's pawn mass on the King-side is now very threatening
and White must therefore try for some counter-play on the
other wing. Black could simply thwart this attempt by 20 . . .
P–Kt3, but he deems it harmless and quietly continues with
his plans on the King's wing.

20	. . .	R–R2
21	B–B5	Q–KB2
22	Q–B3	Kt–Kt3
23	B–Q6	

Black (Keres) to play

White (Schmidt)

The one point in the Black camp against which White can direct an attack is the pawn on K4. With the text-move White attacks it once again and hopes after the exchange on Q6 to utilise his active Rook for further threats.

Nevertheless, White seems to have here a better chance of stubborn defence, to wit, the advance 23 P–K4! After 23 ... PxP White plays 24 Kt–R2, protecting himself against an attack on his KR pawn by Kt–Kt4 and finally winning the square K4 for his pieces. Should, however, Black proceed 23 ... P–B5 then he deprives his Knight of a good square on KB5 and White can after 24 Kt–R2, form once again a strong defensive position with Kt–Kt4. It seems to me that if White was still in possession of adequate defensive chances at all then these lay in the advance 23 P–K4!

23	...	KtxB
24	RxKt	P–Kt5

Black is over-precipitate with this advance, which after the ensuing exchange allows the opposing pieces to occupy the good post on K4. Black should quietly continue here 24 ... RxP, since he must in any case make this move sooner or later, and thereafter he can adjust his plan of campaign in accordance with whatsoever White plays.

25	PxP	PxP
26	Kt–Q2	Kt–B5
27	R–K1	RxP

Despite the inaccuracy on his 24th move Black has still a very strong attacking position and White is hard put to it to find a good defence. However, in the ensuing phase of the game he does find a good idea for counter-play in the shape of pressure against the K5 square.

28	Kt–K4	B–K3
29	KtxB	

White has no time to play here 29 Kt(R4)–B5, on account of 29 . . . Q–R4; 30 Q–KKt3, B–R5 with a winning attack for Black. By the exchange on KB6 White removes a strong attacking piece of his opponent's, deprives Black's K4 of a reliable defence and at the same time simplifies the position, thereby improving his chances of a successful defence.

29	. . .	QxKt
30	Kt–B5	R–KB1

Threatening 31 . . . Kt–R6ch and so forcing his opponent to protect his KB2. An immediate 30 . . . Q–R5 naturally fails here because of 31 QxPch.

31   Kt–K4

White quite unnecessarily removes his Knight from its strong post where it was attacking the Black Bishop and markedly hindering the enemy attack. True, 31 Q–K3 would not do because of 31 . . . KtxB; 32 KxKt, P–Kt6! (this is even stronger than 32 . . . B–Q4ch), but much better was 31 Q–KKt3. After this 31 . . . Kt–R6ch; 32 BxKt, RxB; 33 Q–Kt2, P–Kt6 leads to nothing because of 34 QxRch! and Black must therefore play 31 . . . Q–B4. In that event, however, the further exchange 32 KtxB, KtxKt would somewhat relieve White's troubles.

31	. . .	Q–B4
32	Q–K3	

After 32 Q–KKt3, Black should not play 32 . . . R–R6; 33 BxR, KtxBch; 34 K–R2, QxKt because of 35 P–B3, by which White would ensure at least a draw. But 32 . . . R–KKt1! would yield him a decisive attack. Then 33 P–K3 fails against

33 ... Kt–R6ch; and after 33 K–B1 the following pretty variation could occur: 33 ... KtxB; 34 QxKt, P–Kt6!; 35 KtxP, RxKt!; 36 QxR, Q–R6ch; 37 Q–Kt2, R–Kt3! and Black wins. Otherwise, however, Black was threatening 33 ... R–R6.

| 32 | ... | Q–R4 |
| 33 | Q–KKt3 | BxP |

This move wins material, since now White can no longer protect his K2 square. But White still manages to find counter-chances.

| 34 | RxRch | QxR |
| 35 | P–K3 | |

In practice, the best chance, since, for example, after 35 Q–K3, B–Q4, White would be condemned to passive play and speedy loss of material would be inevitable.

| 35 | ... | KtxB? |

Both players have already got into time trouble and commit some inaccuracies in the final stages. Black hopes to exploit the pin of the Knight on K4, but this hope proves illusory. Correct here was 35 ... Kt–K7ch; 36 RxKt, BxR; 37 QxPch, K–Kt1; after which the realisation of the advantage of the exchange would only demand careful technical handling.

| 36 | KxKt! | |

After 36 QxKt, B–Q4; White would really be lost on account of the pin.

| 36 | ... | B–Q4 |
| 37 | P–B3? | |

With this mistake White makes good his opponent's error on the 35th move and now soon has a lost game. Schmidt was apparently of the opinion that here 37 QxPch, K–Kt1; 38 R–KR1 was not playable on account of 38 ... Q–Kt2 (if 38 ... Q–B3; 39 QxBch!); but in his time trouble he overlooked the possibility of 39 R–R5!

Black could then still try to exploit the pin on the Knight but should not be successful against correct counter-play. For example: 39 ... QxQ; 40 RxQ, R–B4; 41 R–K8ch, K–B2; 42 K–Kt3! when, with 42 ... KxR; 43 Kt–Q6ch, K–Q2; 44 KtxR, BxP, Black can only obtain rather the better ending.

Therefore Black does better to play at once 41 . . . K–Kt2!;
42 K–Kt3, BxP; after which he would still retain concrete
winning chances.

37	. . .	PxPch
38	K–B2	BxKt
39	QxPch	Q–Kt2!
	resigns	

After 40 QxB there comes, of course, 40 . . . Q–Kt7 mate,
and 40 R–R1ch, B–R2; 41 RxBch, KxR obviously is insufficient
for perpetual check.

Game 7

QUEEN'S PAWN, NIMZOWITSCH DEFENCE

International Tournament at Bad Nauheim, 1936

	G. Stahlberg	P. Keres
1	P–Q4	P–K3
2	P–QB4	B–Kt5ch

This particular sequence of moves was often employed by
me at the time, even against some of the world's best players,
and with quite good results. The idea of the order of moves
chosen consists in this, that after 3 Kt–B3, Black, in addition
to the Nimzowitsch Defence 3 . . . Kt–KB3, can also choose
to transpose into the Dutch Defence by means of 3 . . . P–KB4,
a defence in which the early development of White's Q Knight
is not held to be the best. But the chief reason for my choice of
moves lies in the fact that quite often positions that had been
but little investigated by theory tended to occur and in consequence from the very first moves players would be forced to
think for themselves.

	3 Kt–B3

In many games my opponents would play here 3 B–Q2, to
which I usually replied 3 . . . Q–K2, transposing into positions
similar to the Queen's Indian Defence. The text-move is more
energetic and leads to more interesting positions.

| 3 | . . . | P–QB4 |
| 4 | P–K3 | |

In the same tournament Alekhine played against me 4 PxP,

great complications resulting from 4 . . . BxKtch; 5 PxB, Q–R4; 6 Kt–B3. Black could very well answer the text-move with 4 . . . P–B4 but instead decides to transpose into the Nimzowitsch Defence.

| 4 | . . . | Kt–KB3 |
| 5 | P–QR3 | |

Theory recommends here 5 Kt–K2. The text-move transposes into a Samisch system.

5	. . .	BxKtch
6	PxB	O–O
7	B–Q3	P–Q4

Nowadays this advance is seldom played, since now White can select a system of development against which Black experiences great difficulty in gaining any active counter-play. More usual are 7 . . . Kt–B3 or 7 . . . P–Q3 aiming at P–K4 for Black.

| 8 | BPxP | KPxP |
| 9 | Kt–K2 | |

This method of developing the Knight which inaugurates a system evolved by Botvinnik is held to be best for White. White's further strategic plan is as follows: first to complete his development by O–O and Kt–Kt3, and then to play P–B3 and carry out the advance P–K4 after due preparation. Practical experience shows that it is very difficult for Black to obtain active counter-play against this plan, and therefore this variation is met with but seldom in modern tournament praxis.

At the time that this game was played the Botvinnik system had not yet been worked out and so both players were faced by new problems over the board. It is not therefore to be wondered at that the play that ensues is not carried out in accordance with the last word of modern theory.

| 9 | . . . | P–QKt3 |

The idea that begins with the text-move, to exchange off White's K Bishop, is one of the best existing in this position.

| 10 | O–O | B–R3 |
| 11 | B–B2? | |

Today this move can be given a question mark since it is common knowledge that White can here assure himself a

promising position with the better chances by 11 P–B3, BxB;
12 QxB, R–K1; 13 Kt–Kt3, Kt–B3; 14 B–Kt2, followed by
QR–K1. With the text-move Stahlberg wants to keep his
Bishop to strengthen the square K4, but the Black Bishop on
R3 is too well placed and noticeably impedes White in carrying
out his plans. In addition White loses an important tempo
so that Black obtains an advantage in development.

11	...	Kt–B3
12	R–K1	

This move, also, should be criticised since in the ensuing
phase of play the Rook is badly placed on K1. Better, as
recommended by Stahlberg, was 12 P–B3 followed by R–B2.

12	...	R–K1
13	P–B3	R–QB1
14	PxP?	

But this antipositional exchange results in a speedy disadvantage for White. If the variation 14 Kt–Kt3, PxP; 15 BPxP,
KtxP; 16 BxPch, followed by 17 QxKt, does not appeal to White
here then he should be content with the loss of a couple of tempi
and play back with his Bishop, 14 B–Q3, so as to carry out the
advance P–K4 if possible. Perhaps Stahlberg had not taken into
consideration the possibility of 16 BxPch, and therefore deemed
an exchange on B5 as an indispensable preparation for Kt–Kt3.

14	...	PxP
15	Kt–Kt3	P–Q5!

Black (Keres)

White (Stahlberg) to play

Black could also get here a good position by means of 15 . . . Kt–K4, but this central thrust is much more energetic. Usually, opening up the centre when one's opponent has the two Bishops is a dubious operation, but here this advantage of the opponent's is counter-balanced by superior development, and Black once again holds the initiative in his hands.

16 KPxP

White would also not have fared better with 16 BPxP, PxP; 17 P–K4, avoiding the opening up of the centre. There could then follow 17 . . . P–Q6; 18 B–R4, Kt–Q2; or also immediately 17 . . . Kt–Q2, by which Black would have obtained an overwhelming middle-game through his strong passed pawn.

16 . . . PxP

Black could also first exchange Rooks by 16 . . . RxRch; 17 QxR, and then play 17 . . . PxP; but in that case after 18 PxP, KtxP White would have at his disposal the good square Q1 for his Bishop. After the text-move White must exchange on K8, since 17 PxP would lose material on account of 17 . . . QxPch!

17	RxRch	QxR
18	PxP	KtxP
19	B–R4	

White is forced to place his Bishop on the edge of the board in a passive position since 19 QxKt? is, of course, impossible because of 19 . . . Q–K8ch, and the line 19 B–Q3, BxB; 20 QxB, Q–K8ch; 21 Q–B1, QxQch loses a piece after Kt–Kt6. No better also is 19 B–K4, since White would be in a horrible position after 19 . . . R–Q1.

19	. . .	Q–K4

Threatening 20 . . . KtxPch; and thus practically forcing White's reply.

20	R–Kt1	Kt–Q4!

Black's two centralised Knights have an overwhelming effect. White has nothing better than the game continuation against the threat of 21 . . . Kt–B6 since the attempt at centralisation by 21 Kt–K4 loses material after 21 . . . B–K7 and BxP.

21	B–Kt2	Kt–B6
22	BxKt	RxB
23	K–R1	

Temporarily protecting the QRP since 23 . . . RxRP? would
now be a big blunder because of 24 QxKt! At the same time
the King is removed from the threatened diagonal KKt1–QR7.
In the event of 23 Kt–K4, Black could either have captured on
QR6 or else played 23 . . . R–Q6.

23	. . .	P–R4!

Frustrating all possible mating threats on the back rank
and initiating the disagreeable threat of P–R5–R6. White can
no longer hope to organise a satisfactory defence with his
scattered pieces entirely lacking in co-operation. After 24
Kt–K4, for example, there could follow 24 . . . B–K7 with an
ensuing sacrifice on KB6.

24	B–Q7	R–Q6

Here it appears that Black misses a chance of winning
quickly by 24 . . . P–R5; 25 Kt–K4, B–K7! followed by KtxP,
which would completely demolish White's King's position. The
game was played in the last round and if I won it I could still
overhaul Alekhine. It is, therefore, very natural that I was a
little excited and so did not manage to find the strongest continuation. For the rest, the text-move is also very strong,
although now White can defend himself stubbornly.

25	Q–R4	

After 25 Q–K1, the simplest way to win is 25 . . . QxQch;
26 RxQ, P–Kt3; since White loses the QRP on account of the
threat of 27 . . . Kt–B7. Black can also interpose the move
26 . . . P–R5 which forces White to play 27 Kt–B1, because of
the possibility of Kt–B7. With the text-move White wins a
tempo by attacking the Bishop and would like to utilise the
move to build up a defence.

25	. . .	B–Kt2
26	Kt–K4?	

Allows Black to bring off a pretty finish, but it is very difficult
by now to find an adequate defence. Best practical chances
are afforded by 26 Q–B4. The sacrifice 26 . . . RxBP; 27 PxR,

BxPch; 28 K–Kt1, Q–K6ch; 29 K–B1 would then lead to nothing and the complicated variation 26 ... R–K6; 27 RxB, R–K8ch; 28 Kt–B1, Kt–K7; 29 R–Kt1, RxR; 30 Q–B8ch, K–R2; 31 Q–B2ch!, P–Kt3; 32 QxR, Q–Q5; 33 Kt–Kt3 only results in an approximately equal ending. But also in this line with the simple protection 26 ... Q–K6! Black ensures for himself a decisive attack, since after 27 Kt–B1, or 27 Kt–B5, Black's 27 ... Q–K7 has threats on KB6 and the back rank that cannot be parried.

Also the attempt 26 B–R3 would have afforded White no salvation since after 26 ... P–R5; 27 Kt–B1 (or 27 Kt–K4, BxKt; 28 PxB, RxB!, etc.) 27 ... Q–K7 there comes a decisive sacrifice on KB6.

	26	...	BxKt
	27	PxB	Kt–B6!
		resigns.	

After 28 PxKt, R–Q7 mate on White's R2 is not to be prevented.

Good Ending ∨

Game 8

Q.P. DUTCH DEFENCE

Chess Olympiad at Munich, 1936

	P. Keres	K. Richter
1	Kt–KB3	P–KB4

Master Richter is well-known to us all as a vigorous player with a wealth of combinations, a player who does not hesitate to sacrifice pawns in the opening, in the hope of complicating the position and rendering it unpredictable. So the choice of opening in this game bears witness to Richter's aggressive intentions. Taking these circumstances into consideration, I refrained here from playing the interesting gambit variation 2 P–K4, PxP; 3 Kt–Kt5, and chose a quiet, positional method of play in the hope that this would not suit my opponent.

2	P–Q4	Kt–KB3
3	P–KKt3	P–QKt3

The development of the QB on Kt2 does not fit in well with
the Dutch Defence, the reason being that thereafter White
often has the opportunity of obtaining a positional advantage
by the advance P-Q5. But Richter intentionally embarks on
this line in the hope of remedying the positional inadequacies
of the variation by his tactical skill.

4	B-Kt2	B-Kt2
5	O-O	P-K3
6	P-B4	P-Q4

Black certainly did not make this move willingly, since in
the first place it blocks up the fine diagonal for the Bishop and
in the second it weakens the Black central squares. On the
other hand, Black no longer has to reckon with White's P-Q5
which, for example, would have set him some difficult problems
after 6 . . . B-K2; 7 P-Q5, PxP; 8 Kt-Q4.

7	Kt-K5	B-Q3
8	B-B4	

An idea worth considering here also was 8 B-Kt5, by which
pressure on the central Q5 square is accentuated and the
possible sortie Kt-K5 is prevented. But in any case White
obtains the better position in the ensuing phase of the game
always providing he pays sufficient attention to the possibility
of Black playing P-QB4.

8	. . .	O-O
9	Kt-B3	Kt-K5

It is true that with this sortie Black relieves his situation in
the centre but he will now have difficulties in developing his
Queen-side pieces. 9 . . . QKt-Q2 at once will not do because
of 10 PxP, PxP; 11 Q-Kt3, but 9 . . . P-B3, so as to develop
the QKt by Q-K2 and QKt-Q2, offered Black better chances
of valid counter-play.

10	PxP	PxP
11	Q-Kt3	K-R1

In addition to 12 KtxP, White was also threatening to win a
pawn on K4. With the text-move Black wards off both threats
(12 KtxP?, KBxKt!). White's next move once again renews
the threat on Q5.

12	KR–Q1	P–B3
13	KtxKt	

By quiet and methodical play White has obtained a clear
opening advantage in that he possesses, together with the better
development, objects of attack in the centre and on the Queen's
wing. With the text-move he begins a manoeuvre to open
up the centre and so give his two Bishops full scope, but does
not in the end obtain the desired result.

And this is precisely because Black can utilise the time lost
in the enemy central operation to complete his development.
In consequence White retains only a minimal advantage.

Taking this into consideration a different plan of play must
be recommended for White consisting in the strengthening of
the positional pressure by 13 QR–B1! In that case Black would
still experience great difficulty in developing his Queen-side
pieces, and White could also carry out the manoeuvre undertaken in the game—KtxKt followed by P–B3—later on.

13	. . .	BPxKt
14	P–B3	PxP
15	BxP	

This method of capture also does not stand the test of
criticism, since White does not arrive at the intended P–K4
in the ensuing phase of the game. Stronger seems 15 PxP,
which would open up the important K file for the Rook. The
Bishop could then be brought into play along the diagonal
KR3–QB8. Black too would still have difficulties with his
Queen-side and would not find it easy to obtain active counter-
play.

15	. . .	Q–K2
16	QR–B1	

Pursuing the struggle over the undeveloped QKt. Because
of the attack on his QB3 Black cannot now play 16 . . . Kt–Q2
and therefore the ensuing exchange is practically forced.

Although White now obtains the advantage of two Bishops
and in addition exercises uncomfortable pressure on the Queen-
side, Black does succeed in eventually developing the pieces
on this wing and gains control of the important centre square
K5. The game now enters a new phase.

Unfavourable for White, moreover, is the "logical" continu-
ation 16 P–K4, since after 16 . . . BxKt; 17 PxB (or 17 BxB,
PxP; 18 BxP, Kt–Q2; etc.), 17 . . . P–KKt4!; 18 B–Q2, P–Q5
Black would get a good game.

16	. . .	BxKt
17	BxB	Kt–Q2
18	B–B4	Kt–B3

After the game Richter thought this move inexact and proposed 18 . . . QR–K1, so that the Knight on Q2 can protect
the Queen-side. One cannot, however, see what advantage
in contrast to the game continuation Black could have then
achieved if White had, for instance, replied 19 P–QR4 or 19
R–B3; besides which, the Knight is needed on B3 so as to
control the K5 square.

Now, once the situation in the centre has become clarified,
White utilises his advantage in space to obtain a dangerous
initiative on the Queen's wing.

19	P–QR4!	Kt–K5
20	P–R5	PxP

Practically forced, since after 20 . . . P–QKt4; 21 P–R6!
is decisive.

21 BxKt!

At first glance this exchange seems somewhat surprising,
since now we get the notorious Bishops of opposite colour
which usually give a marked increase to the defender's chances
of a draw. On the other hand, it is also known that Bishops
of opposite colour often afford excellent attacking chances since
the one Bishop is unable to protect points attacked by the other.
This is, in fact, what occurs in the game. In spite of the following
Queen exchange Black eventually gets into unsurmountable
difficulties since he is unable to protect adequately the Black
squares in his position, above all the points QB2 and KKt2.

It might appear that White could now gain the upper hand
immediately, since after 21 . . . PxB; 22 P–Q5 Black cannot
capture on Q4 because of 23 R–B7. But matters are not all
that simple. Black has the resource of a cunning intermediary
move that renders the development initiated by the text-move
much more complicated.

21 . . .   P–R5!

Black places all his hopes on this intervening move. Apparently all is well now as 22 QxRP can be met by 22 . . . QxB, and the diversionary attempt 22 B–Q6 leads after 22 . . . QxB (K5); 23 QxB, Q–K6ch only to perpetual check. But now there comes a nasty surprise.

22   Q–K3!   QxB

After long thought Black decided to exchange Queens and come down to an endgame with Bishops of opposite colour. As a matter of fact it is difficult to suggest anything better for him. After 22 . . . PxB; 23 P–Q5 he must not play 23 . . . PxP because of 24 R–B7, Q–Kt5; 25 B–K5, R–KKt1; 26 Q–R6! when White wins. If, however, Black tries 22 . . . QR–K1, then, in addition to 23 B–K5, PxB; 24 R–B5, White can attain a very favourable ending by 23 B–Q3!, QxQch; 24 BxQ, RxB; 25 R–R1.

23   QxQ   PxQ
24   P–Q5!

In this advance, which also appears in many of the variations given above, lies the idea of the combination begun by White on his 21st move. Black must not now reply 24 . . . PxP since then the planned attack by Bishops of opposite colour comes into full operation: 25 R–B7, B–R3; 26 B–K5, R–KKt1; 27 RxQP, etc. and Black's position completely collapses. The ensuing answer is therefore practically forced, but as a result White obtains a very strong passed pawn in the centre which yields him excellent winning chances.

24   . . .   QR–Q1
25   P–Q6   R–B4
26   R–B4   P–B4

Black cannot undertake any activity, since, for example, 26 . . . P–Kt4; 27 B–K3, R–Q4 would lead to a rapid loss after 28 RxR, PxR; 29 R–B7. With the text-move he does at least avert direct material loss.

27   RxRP   P–QR3
28   R–R5   P–Kt3

Directed against the threat of 29 P–QKt4, which would have

given White two united passed pawns. 28 . . . B–B1 would have been no better. White could then reply 29 B–K3, and now 29 . . . P–B5 fails against 30 B–Kt6, RxR; 31 BxR(Q8)!

Black's play after the Queen exchange can hardly be criticised. He has made the normal defensive moves and obtained the maximum amount of activity for his pieces. If all this, however, is insufficient to save the game, then this only shows all the more clearly the strength of White's attack which, despite the Queen exchange and the Bishops of opposite colour, continues with undiminished force.

Black (Richter)

White (Keres) to play

29   P–QKt4!

This thrust is certainly one of the greatest surprises Black experiences in the game. White now wins practically by force a piece for two pawns by a very pretty, if far from complicated, combination. But the ending that ensues still demands exact calculation before White can evaluate his small material advantage.

29   . . .   PxP

This, and the ensuing moves, are well-nigh forced.

30   RxR   PxR
31   P–Q7   B–B3
32   R–QB1!

The idea of White's combination! Since 32 . . . B–Kt2 would lose at once on account of 33 R–B7, Black must capture on Q2 after which there comes a decisive pin on the Q file.

32	. . .	BxP
33	R–Q1	P–Kt6

There is no longer any defence against the threats of 34 B–Kt5, or 34 B–B7. However, though White now wins the Bishop the Black passed pawns on the Queen-side advance right down the files in the meantime and still make White's task really difficult.

34	B–B7	R–QB1
35	RxB	K–Kt1

The last and most important point of White's combination consists of the fact that 35 . . . P–Kt7 would fail here against 36 B–K5ch. But now this advance even threatens to win for Black.

36	B–K5	R–B4

Black tries at least to get his Rook behind the QKt pawn. The win would be still simpler after other moves, e.g. 36 . . . R–B7; 37 R–Kt7, RxP; 38 RxKtP, etc. or 36 . . . P–QR4; 37 R–Kt7ch, K–B1; 38 R–R7, R–B7; 39 RxQRP, P–Kt7; 40 BxP, RxB; 41 RxPch, K–Kt2; 42 K–B2, and wins, since the KP will also fall.

37	R–Kt7ch!

Probably good enough for a win here was also 37 B–Q4, R–Kt4; 38 B–Kt2, though thereafter Black would still have some troublesome counter-play. With the text-move White forces the exchange of Rooks and reaches an ending in which he has a Bishop for two pawns. This still requires quite exact calculation but it is completely won for White and the sequence of moves is practically forced.

37	. . .	K–B1

Naturally not 37 . . . K–R1; 38 B–B6! and White wins.

38	B–Q6ch	KxR
39	BxR	K–B2

The same theme reoccurs a second time; again Black must not play 39 . . . P–Kt7, because of 40 B–Q4ch.

| 40 | B–R3 | K–K3 |

In this position the game was adjourned and White now had the opportunity of checking his intended winning idea by home analysis. Everything however was in perfect order.

41	K–B2	K–Q4
42	K–K3	K–B5
43	K–Q2	

Here 43 P–Kt4!, PxP; 44 KxP, also would have won as 44 ... K–B6; 45 K–B4 leads into the actual game.

| 43 | ... | P–K6ch |

The best counter-chance. In reply to other moves White would play 44 P–K3, drive back the Black King and then win without any difficulty.

| 44 | KxP | |

Clearly 44 K–B1, K–B6; 45 B–Kt2ch, would also win but the text-move is the most forcing and allows the opponent no possible loophole of escape. One should always choose such variations, in particular when one can, as in this case, check them exactly in home analysis.

| 44 | ... | K–B6 |
| 45 | K–B4 | P–QR4 |

It is of no importance whether Black advances at once with the QRP or whether he inserts the moves 45 ... P–Kt7; 46 BxPch, KxB when 47 P–Kt4! transposes back into the game. An attempt to pursue the Bishop perpetually would also be fruitless; e.g., 45 ... K–B7; 46 P–Kt4!, PxP; 47 P–K4, K–Kt8; 48 P–K5, K–R7; 49 B–B1, K–Kt8; 50 B–K3, K–B7; 51 B–Q4, K–Q6; 52 B–R1, and wins.

| 46 | P–Kt4! | |

The last finesse. After 46 KxP?, P–Kt7; 47 BxPch, KxB; 48 P–K4, P–R5 Black would queen his pawn one move quicker and White would then have to finish off a toilsome Queen ending. White now wins the ending by just one tempo!

46	...	PxP
47	P–K4	P–R5
48	P–K5	P–Kt7

At last Black must eliminate the Bishop.

49	BxPch	KxB
50	P–K6	P–R6
51	P–K7	P–R7
52	P–K8=Q	P–R8=Q
53	Q–R8ch	K–R7
54	QxQch	KxQ
55	KxP	K–Kt7
56	K–Kt5	K–B6
57	K–R6	K–Q5
58	KxP	K–K4
59	K–Kt6!	resigns

The Black King has failed to reach its objective; a very interesting and original fighting game.

Game 9

Q.P. QUEEN'S INDIAN DEFENCE

International Tournament at Margate, 1937

	P. Keres	C. H. O'D. Alexander
1	P–Q4	Kt–KB3
2	P–QB4	P–K3
3	Kt–QB3	B–Kt5
4	Kt–B3	P–QKt3
5	P–KKt3	

This move, usually so good in the Queen's Indian, is here out of place in view of the fact that Black has pinned the QKt. In many variations, after the exchange on QB3, the pawn on QB4 can become an object of attack, since the development of the Bishop robs it of its natural protection. Better was the more usual 5 B–Kt5.

5	...	B–Kt2
6	B–Kt2	Q–B1

Nimzowitsch usually continued in this position with 6 ... BxKtch; 7 PxB, P–Q3; 8 O–O, QKt–Q2, so as to play an eventual P–K4 and then take action against the weaknesses on the opponent's Queen-side. But Alekhine has already shown that White can successfully defeat this intention by playing

9 P–Q5! If, then, 9 . . . PxP, White wins back the pawn with
a good game by 10 Kt–R4. If, however, 9 . . . P–K4, then
Alekhine recommended 10 Kt–R4! followed by P–K4 and
P–B4 with such a strong pressure on the King's wing that
Black would be accorded no time to exploit the weakness of
White's QB4. Moreover, White can also carry out the P–Q5
advance already on his eighth move. With the text-move
Alexander follows another plan. He wants to threaten the
pawn on QB4 indirectly by playing himself P–QB4 and for
this purpose he protects his Bishop so as to render White's
P–Q5 innocuous.

          7   O–O   P–B4?

A mistake that gives Black a lost position practically by
force. It was essential to prepare this move by the exchange
7 . . . BxKt; 8 PxB.

After the game Alexander expressed the opinion that Black
could very well have played here 7 . . . Kt–K5 followed by
P–Q3, Kt–Q2 and P–KB4. But this Knight sally seems premature and needs to be prepared by 7 . . . O–O, since in reply
to an immediate 7 . . . Kt–K5 White can offer a most promising
pawn sacrifice by 8 P–Q5!

          8   Kt–QKt5!

The despised Knight now takes a fearsome revenge. On
account of the threats of 9 Kt–Q6ch and 9 P–QR3 Black's
reply is forced.

          8   . . .   PxP
          9   B–B4   Kt–R3

After 9 . . . O–O; 10 Kt–B7, Black does not obtain sufficient
compensation for the loss of the exchange. But now, however,
he does not even succeed in getting castled.

          10   B–Q6!

The fact that White must surrender a pawn as a consequence
of this move clearly is not worth considering in view of the
circumstances. His first objective is to prevent the opponent's
castling and the text-move is the most effective means of so
doing. Now, too, he threatens, amongst other things, to win a
piece by 11 BxB.

10 ...   QxP

Once again one can see nothing better for Black since after
10 ... Kt–K5; 11 BxB, KtxB; 12 Kt–Q2! wins a piece, as also
does 10 ... Kt–B4; 11 P–QR3.

A very interesting and original position could have arisen
here after 10 ... B–B4. Then White could have gone in for
the practically forced variation 11 P–QKt4, KtxP; 12 Kt–K5,
BxB; 13 KxB (and not 13 Kt–B7ch, QxKt; 14 BxQ, BxR;
with sufficient compensation for the Queen), 13 ... Kt–R3
(after 13 ... Q–Kt2ch; 14 P–B3, Black has no adequate means
of parrying the threat of 15 BxB); 14 Q–Q3! and Black no
longer has any reasonable moves. White, in fact, threatens
to strengthen his position even more by 15 Q–KB3 (16 BxB!).

11   Q–R4

Threatening 12 Kt–K5, Q–B1; 13 BxKB, or simply 12 QR–B1,
or else 12 P–Kt3. If Black tries 11 ... Kt–B4, then, in addition to
12 Kt–B7ch, K–Q1; 13 BxKt, White can get a winning position
by 13 Q–Q1.

11   ...   B–B3
12   Kt(B3)xP   BxB(Kt7)
13   QxKt!

Now he threatens to win the Queen by 14 Kt–B7ch, and,
in addition the Bishop is *en prise* on White's Kt2. It seems that
Black must resign, but Alexander still manages to find a way
of putting up further resistance.

13   ...   BxR

Black (Alexander)

White (Keres) to play

14   RxB!

Black hopes that after 14 Kt–B7ch, he can still put up a
dour resistance by 14 . . . QxKt; 15 BxQ, B–KR6. But the
text-move is much stronger since, now, White retains an enduring attack against the enemy King in the centre.

14   . . .   QxKt(Q5)

Alexander can find nothing better than to surrender his
Queen in order to put up some resistance with Rook, Bishop
and pawn against Queen. Materially speaking, Black's position
would not be so bad, but in addition one must bear in mind
that White's attack continues with unabated force.

It is impossible to see, however, how Black can successfully
defend himself against the numerous threats. After 14 . . .
Q–B1 or 14 . . . QR–B1 he loses the Bishop and has a hopeless
position, as he would also do after 14 . . . K–Q1; 15 P–Kt3.
But if Black plays 14 . . . Kt–Q4, so as to give up the Queen
under more favourable circumstances than in the game by
15 Kt–B7ch, KtxKt; 16 QxQ, BxB, then White has at his
disposal a much stronger continuation in 15 P–K4!

15   KtxQ   BxB
16   Kt–Kt5!

Black does not stand so badly from the point of view of
material but the attack fanned into flame by the text-move
breaks down all resistance in a few moves. At the moment
his Bishop has no move of retreat.

16   . . .   K–K2
17   R–Q1   B–B4

And not 17 . . . Kt–K1, because of 18 KtxB, KtxKt; 19
Q–R3, etc. There is no other square for the Bishop, since after
17 . . . B–K4; 18 P–B4, BxKtP; 19 R–Kt1, wins at once.

18   P–QR3   Kt–K5

The threat was 19 P–QKt4 winning a piece. After 18 . . .
K–B1; 19 P–QKt4, B–K2; 20 Q–Kt7, Black loses both Queen-
side pawns, and after 18 . . . P–Q4; 19 P–QKt4, B–Q3; 20

Q–Kt7ch, Kt–Q2; White has the decisive 21 KtxP, with the threat of 22 Kt–B6ch. The text-move allows of a pretty finish.

| | 19 RxPch! | K–B3 |

Black loses both Rooks after 19 . . . KxR; 20 Q–Kt7ch.

| | 20 Q–Kt7 | resigns. |

If 20 . . . Kt–Kt4; 21 P–KR4, forces the win.

Game 10

RUY LOPEZ

International Tournament at Margate, 1937

	Sir G. A. Thomas	P. Keres
1	P–K4	P–K4
2	Kt–KB3	Kt–QB3
3	B–Kt5	P–QR3
4	B–R4	Kt–B3
5	Kt–B3	

This restrained method of play is a favourite continuation of Sir George Thomas's in the Ruy Lopez, and one with which he has obtained many fine successes. The line is similar to the Four Knights', with the exception of the moves P–QR3 and B–R4, and these basically alter the character of the position. For instance, now, after 5 . . . B–Kt5, which is a normal move in the Four Knights', White can reply very strongly 6 Kt–Q5. The mechanical reply 6 . . . KtxKt would, after 7 PxKt, P–K5; 8 PxKt, PxKt; 9 PxPch, etc., simply lose a pawn.

Black can, however, make use of these extra moves to protect his KP quietly by P–QKt4. This small differentiation from the normal Four Knights' is sufficient to dispel the drawish nature of the opening in certain cases.

| 5 | . . . | P–QKt4 |
| 6 | B–Kt3 | P–Q3!? |

This seemingly highly risky move is psychologically well motivated. Sir George Thomas is known to be a quiet positional

player who usually avoids complications and feels most at home
in peaceful positions where he can exert some light positional
pressure on his opponent. His intended "methodical" continuation in this variation would probably be: 6 . . . B–K2;
7 O–O, P–Q3; 8 P–QR4, P–Kt5; 9 Kt–Q5, as, for instance,
occurred in the game Sir George Thomas–Alekhine, Hastings,
1922. Therefore, Black tries with the text-move to give the
game quite another turn and to this end he is ready to embark
on unforeseeable complications.

The sequence of moves chosen by Black has the advantage
that White can no longer arrive at the usual variation. After
7 P–QR4, P–Kt5; 8 Kt–Q5, Black can, in addition to 8 . . .
KtxP, also very well play 8 . . . Kt–QR4. On the other hand
White can now play 7 Kt–Kt5, and how then is Black to
protect his KB2? It would appear that Sir George Thomas
could find no reply to this query during the game, and he
plunges into complications in which even in subsequent analysis
it is practically impossible to find absolutely the right continuation.

7   Kt–Kt5

There are probably very few players who would not have
embarked on this sally here. Now Black is forced to make the
ensuing pawn sacrifice, but he retains thereafter an enduring
initiative and sets his opponent some difficult problems. The
system initiated by the moves 5 . . . P–QKt4 and 6 . . . P–Q3
does, in any case, merit further notice and is probably a
playable way of avoiding the various unpleasantnesses threatened by 5 Kt–B3.

7 . . .   P–Q4

This pawn sacrifice is already known in positions where White
can only capture by 8 PxP. In the position in the game,
however, White can also capture with the Knight and this
makes matters much more complicated.

8 KtxQP

After 8 PxP, there would equally follow 8 . . . Kt–Q5 and if
then White by 9 P–Q6, KtxB; 10 PxP, QxP; 11 RPxKt went
in for winning a pawn then Black after 11 . . . B–Kt2 obtains
a fine position with excellent attacking prospects.

8 ...   Kt-Q5!

Surprisingly enough, this Knight attack proves to be strong enough in this position to ensure Black adequate counter-play. Despite manifold analyses and researches published in chess literature after the game it is still not clear how White could obtain here concrete chances of an opening advantage. Rather the opposite is the case. White must play most carefully in the ensuing phase of the game so as not to fall victim to a withering attack on the part of his better-developed opponent.

Black (Keres)

White (Sir George Thomas) to play

9 Kt-K3

White fails to obtain a satisfactory result with this retreat, but what should he play? We append some of the many possibilities from which White can choose here.

I. 9 KtxKtch, QxKt; 10 P-Q3 (bad, of course, is 10 KtxBP, KtxB; but also 10 BxPch, K-K2; 11 P-Q3, P-R3 leads to loss of material since 12 P-KR4 can be met by 12 ... PxKt; 13 BxP, QxB!); 10 ... P-R3 (this is stronger than 10 ... KtxB; 11 RPxKt, etc.); 11 Kt-R3 (11 Kt-B3 would naturally be met by 11 ... B-KKt5; and after 11 KtxP, KtxB; 12 KtxR, KtxR; 13 Q-R5ch, K-Q2! White has not enough attack for the piece); 11 ... Q-KKt3! (even stronger than 11 ... BxKt; 12 PxB, Kt-B6ch, which was played in the game Esser–Barton, Cologne, 1911, though this too led to advantage for Black); 12 K-B1, B-KKt5, with a won position for Black.

II. 9 P–Q3, KtxB; 10 RPxKt (and not 10 KtxKtch, PxKt!);
10 ... KtxKt; 11 PxKt, QxP; and Black has regained his pawn
with the better game.

III. 9 Kt–QB3 (perhaps this retreat offers White relatively
the best chances) 9 ... KtxB; 10 RPxKt, P–Kt5; 11 Kt–R4,
P–R3; 12 Kt–KB3, KtxP; 13 Q–K2, B–Kt2; 14 P–Q3, Kt–Kt4;
and in return for the pawn Black has a fine position with good
attacking chances.

| 9 ... | KtxB |
| 10 RPxKt | P–R3 |

With his two Bishops and better development Black naturally
seeks to open up the position and therefore both the centre
pawns are exchanged.

| 11 Kt–B3 | KtxP |
| 12 KtxP | |

Naturally it would be pleasant for White first to force the
Knight to retire by 12 P–Q3, and only then to capture on K5,
but in reply to 12 P–Q3, there can come the very awkward
12 ... B–Kt5ch! If White now does not want to lose the right
to castle or the pawn he has won then he must play 13 P–QB3,
but this would allow Black an excellent position after 13 ...
KtxBP!; 14 PxKt, BxPch; 15 B–Q2, BxR; 16 QxB, QxP.
After the text-move White has great difficulty in completing
his development in a normal fashion.

12 ...	Q–B3
13 Kt–B3	B–Kt2
14 Q–K2	O–O–O
15 O–O	B–Q3

Now we can see the first fruits of Black's pawn sacrifice.
He has developed his pieces ideally and they are aiming at
White's King-side, whereas the White pieces are still lacking
in co-operation. It is clear, beyond all doubt, that Black
possesses here more than adequate compensation for the pawn
and that the White position is scarcely to be defended even
with the best play.

Naturally we cannot maintain that the position arising after
9 Kt–K3 could be attained by force. White could have chosen

other ways of developing his pieces at earlier stages in the game. It must, however, certainly be conceded that Black always retains sufficient opening advantage to justify his small material sacrifice.

16 Kt–Kt4

White still cannot proceed with the development of his Queen's wing, since after 16 P–Q3, there would come the very awkward 16 . . . Kt–Kt4. However, White has just as painful an experience with the text-move.

16 . . .   Q–B4

More exact here was 16 . . . Q–Kt3, so that, after 17 P–Q3, Kt–Kt4; 18 Kt–R4, Black is able to reply with 18 . . . Q–R4. Nevertheless, the text-move is also adequate.

17 P–Q3

White has nothing better, since 17 Kt–R4, or 17 Kt–K3, would be met by 17 . . . Q–R4, with a decisive attack for Black.

17 . . .   Kt–Kt4

Black also would like to avoid simplifying too much and he therefore refrains from 17 . . . QxKt (Kt5); 18 PxKt, KR–K1, though this would regain the pawn with an excellent position. With the text-move he hopes to decide the game in his favour by a direct Kingside attack, but White still has some stubborn defensive chances.

18 Kt–R4   Q–Q4
19 P–QB4?

After this inaccuracy Black's strategy is justified as now White succumbs to an irresistible Kingside attack. A much better defence here was 19 P–KB4! Black would then reply 19 . . . Kt–K3 and still retain some very dangerous threats.

19 . . .   Kt–R6ch!
20 K–R1   Q–R4!

This is immediately decisive, since the Knight on R4 cannot now be protected. The ensuing counter-play can already be classed as desperation.

21 P–B5   KR–K1
22 Q–B2

White avoids the line 22 B–K3, QxKt(R5); 23 PxB, BxPch!; 24 KxB, Kt–B5ch, winning the Queen. In reply to the text-move Black could simply play 22 ... BxBP with a won position; instead he still persists in playing for mate and thereby makes his task more difficult.

22	...	QxKt(R5)
23	PxB	

This is what Black had expected. Also hopeless was 23 P–B6, BxBP; 24 QxB, KtxPch!; 25 K–Kt1, KtxKt; with a piece more for Black, but 23 P–B3! would still have made further resistance possible. Black would stand much better also after this and he would have a number of good lines, amongst which 23 ... BxBP; 24 QxB, R–K7! appears one of the simplest, by which he could utilise his advantage in position. After the text-move White is mated in three moves.

23	...	BxPch!
24	KxB	QxKtch
25	K–R1	Q–B6 mate

An interesting game that possesses some theoretical worth from the opening point of view.

Game 11

RUY LOPEZ

International Tournament at Margate, 1937

		P. Keres	A. Alekhine
1		P–K4	P–K4
2		Kt–KB3	Kt–QB3
3		B–Kt5	P–QR3
4		B–R4	P–Q3
5		P–B4	

Alekhine was fond of using this variation of the Steinitz Defence and employed it in some important tournament games, achieving a number of fine successes with it. So, since my opponent was very well acquainted with the opening, I decided to try this move which was seldom played, but which,

from the positional aspect, scarcely compares with the usual
5 P–B3.

5	. . .	B–Q2
6	Kt–B3	P–KKt3

Although the manoeuvre 6 . . . B–Kt5 followed by KKt–B3–
Q2–B4 is held by many to be better here, the Bishop development on KKt2 also has its advantages. Moreover, Alekhine
had almost without exception always employed this last line.

7	P–Q4	B–Kt2

Many theoreticians regard this as inexact and recommend
here the immediate exchange by 7 . . . PxP. Naturally Black
can also play this way, always providing that after 8 KtxP,
B–Kt2; 9 KtxKt, PxKt (also possible is 9 . . . BxKt); 10 O–O,
he plays with the utmost accuracy. A mistake, for example, is
10 . . . Kt–K2 because of 11 P–B5!, which resulted in great
advantage for White in the game Boleslavsky–Fine, Radio
Match, U.S.S.R.–U.S.A., 1945. Instead Black must continue
10 . . . Kt–B3 with a satisfactory game (Unzicker–Keres,
Hastings, 1954–55).

8	B–K3

After 8 B–KKt5, P–B3; 9 B–K3, which many people hold
to be the refutation of Black's last move, Black gets a satisfactory position by 9 . . . Kt–R3! This Alekhine himself had
often shown, amongst others also in a similar position in his
match against Bogoljuboff, 1929.

8	. . .	Kt–B3

But this is an inaccuracy that enables White to gain a firm
hold of the initiative. Black should continue here with 8 . . .
KKt–K2, or else, before he plays the text-move, exchange
on Q5.

9	PxP	PxP

And here it would be better to play 9 . . . QKtxP so as to
obtain more space for his pieces through some exchanges. White
would then also stand somewhat better, since after 10 KtxKt,
PxKt; 11 O–O, in addition to the freer position he would control the strong outpost on Q5.

10	B–B5!

With this strong move White prevents the enemy castling and poses him some difficult problems. Now Black finds it very difficult to inaugurate counter-play that promises to be successful.

10 . . .   Kt–KR4
11 Kt–Q5

Black plans to obtain counterplay by occupation of the Q5 square, e.g. 11 P–KKt3, P–Kt3! (but not 11 . . . B–Kt5?; 12 BxKtch, PxB; 13 Q–R4!, etc.); 12 B–R3, Kt–Q5, etc. The text-move is aimed against this plan. If now 11 . . . P–Kt3; 12 B–R3, Kt–Q5, then there follows the very strong 13 KtxKt, PxKt; 18 P–KKt4! The text-move also prevents the manoeuvre Kt–KR4–B5–K3.

11 . . .   Kt–B5
12 KtxKt   PxKt

Black (Alekhine)

White (Keres) to play

13 P–K5!?

After long thought I decided upon this promising pawn sacrifice, since I could find nothing better against the threat of 13 . . . Q–B3 followed by O–O–O. Only later was it discovered by L. Steiner that White could assure his opening advantage by the simple move 13 O–O!

The chief idea of this move becomes clear when Black, as intended, continues with 13 . . . Q–B3. Then follows the

surprising 14 B–Q4!, KtxB; 15 BxBch, KxB (White also has
an overwhelming advantage after 15 . . . K–K2; 16 P–K5,
KtxKtch; 17 QxKt); 16 P–K5, Q–Kt3; 17 KtxKt, BxP
(otherwise Black has not even material compensation for his
bad position); 18 Kt–B3 dis ch, B–Q3; and now 19 Kt–K5ch,
results in a clear advantage for White; for example: 19 . . .
K–K2; 20 Q–Q5, or 19 . . . K–B1; 20 P–B5!, BxP (or 20 . . .
QxBP; 21 KtxP, etc.); 21 Q–Q7ch, K–Kt1; 22 Q–Q5, K–B1;
23 QR–B1, and white Wins.

Also when Black abandons the idea of playing 13 . . . Q–B3,
he attains no better result. Thus, for example, 13 . . . BxP; 14
R–Kt1, followed by 15 RxP, leads to a clear advantage for
White, as also does 13 . . . Kt–K4; 14 KtxKt, BxKt; 15 Q–Q5,
B–Kt2; 16 BxBch, and 17 QxP. But if Black tries 13 . . .
Kt–K2, then there comes 14 P–K5, and after 14 . . . BxB;
15 QxBch, Q–Q2; 16 Q–R3, Black has not been successful
in relieving his position to any noticeable extent. Therefore,
relatively best was perhaps 13 . . . P–Kt3, so as to continue with
14 . . . Q–B3 (after White's 14 B–R3), but even in this case
his position does not look very trustworthy.

The pawn sacrifice offered by the text-move has not altogether clear consequences but it ensures White excellent practical chances. And this is particularly important in over-the-
board play where exact analysis of the variations arising out
of the acceptance of the sacrifice is well-nigh impossible owing
to a limited time for thought.

13   . . .   P–KKt4?

Alekhine thought a long time before making this move and
eventually came to the conclusion that acceptance of the pawn
sacrifice would imperil his game too much. After the game a
joint analysis led us to the following variation which we deemed
best for both sides: 13 . . . KtxP; 14 Q–K2 (if immediately
14 KtxKt, BxKt; then Black, after 15 Q–Q5, has the defence
15 . . . B–Q3, and also 15 Q–K2, P–KB3; 16 O–O–O, gives
Black a tenable game after 16 . . . P–B3, or even 16 . . . BxB),
14 . . . P–KB3 (the variation 14 . . . BxB; 15 KtxKt, BxKt;
16 QxBch, K–Q2; 17 O–O, is certainly advantageous for White);
15 O–O–O, P–B3; 16 B–Q6, Q–R4; 17 KtxKt, PxKt; 18 BxKP,

QxB(K4) (after 18 . . . BxB; 19 R–Q5!, PxR; 20 QxBch, White
obtains a most dangerous attack); 19 QxQch, BxQ; 20 KR–K1,
and White wins back his piece with only slightly the better
endgame.

But it seems unlikely that White cannot extract more out
of this position that a minimally better endgame. And a closer
consideration of the position soon brings us to the idea that
White should not hurry to win back the sacrificed pawn. He
can, for example, instead of 16 B–Q6, continue strongly with
16 Q–K4!, threatening to win back the pawn by 17 QxP,
without having to simplify the position thereby. If Black replies 16 . . . Q–R4; then 17 KtxKt, PxKt; 18 RxB, KxR;
19 Q–Q5ch, K–B1; 20 BxP! leads to a decisive attack for
White, so that 16 . . . Q–B2 must be regarded as the normal
continuation. But the reply to this is 17 Q–Q4!, preventing
O–O–O, and threatening to increase White's pressure by 18
KR–K1. It is clear that Black would be in serious difficulties
after this.

But one can also look for better defensive possibilities for
Black. Attention in the first place should be given to the
Queen sacrifice 15 . . . BxB (instead of 15 . . . P–B3;). After
16 RxQch, RxR, Black has a Rook, Bishop and pawn for the
Queen that is almost material equality. Nevertheless, White
should also retain the better chances here, since he can continue
with 17 B–Q4, O–O; 18 BxKt, PxB; 19 Kt–Kt5, followed by
20 P–B3.

To summarize all this: it can be maintained that 13 O–O is
probably White's strongest continuation objectively speaking.
But the gambit line embarked on in the game also offers outstanding attacking chances. Black is faced with very difficult
defensive problems, and in consequence White obtains some
small advantage even against the best counter-play.

14   Q–Q5!

Alekhine intended disquieting his opponent by the threat of
14 . . . P–Kt5, but the text-move is a complete answer.

14 . . .   B–KB1

Black observes the danger threatening him in time and
rightly desists from the intended 14 . . . P–Kt5. For then

would come 15 P–K6!, and White would obtain a won position after 15 . . . BxKP (15 . . . PxP?; 16 Q–R5 mate!); 16 BxKtch, PxB; 17 QxPch, B–Q2; 18 Q–K4ch, B–K3; 19 R–Q1. With the text-move Black succeeds in relieving his position to some extent, but material loss is still not to be averted.

        15   BxB   RxB
        16   O–O–O   Q–K2

Black finds it difficult to obtain a satisfactory defence against the threat of 17 KtxP. In reply to 16 . . . P–Kt5, there again comes 17 P–K6, and after 16 . . . P–R3 White can either force the opening of the KR file by 17 P–R4 (17 . . . P–Kt5; 18 P–K6!), or else continue 17 BxKt, BxB; 18 Q–R5, followed by 19 Kt–Q4 with many strong threats.

With the text-move Alekhine sets a cunning trap and hopes thus to escape from the noose himself.

        17   BxKt!

White has, as the chief idea of his attack, the aim to keep the enemy King fixed in the centre. For this reason he avoids playing 17 KtxP, after which Black would arrive at 17 . . . O–O–O! and suddenly several disagreeable threats would surge up.

        17   . . .   BxB
        18   Q–Q3   B–Q2

It is essential for Black to get his King some sort of protection and so for a second time he offers up a pawn for the purpose. The endgame after 18 . . . BxKt; 19 QxB, P–QB3; 20 R–Q6 is clearly to White's advantage, and after a preparatory 18 . . . P–R3, White can commence an enduring attack by the pawn sacrifice 19 P–K6!, PxP; 20 Kt–K5, R–KKt1; 21 Q–KR3, Q–B3; 22 KR–K1.

        19   KtxP   O–O–O
        20   Kt–B3

The capture 20 KtxRP, could have led to very risky complications on account of 20 . . . B–Kt5; e.g.: 21 Q–K4, BxR; 22 KtxR, B–R5!; and if then 23 Kt–R7, Q–Q2, with a number of threats. With the text-move, which, moreover, threatens

21 QxP, White assures himself of an extra pawn with a good position.

20 . . .   P–KB3!

Thus Black gets rid of his doubled pawns, opens up the position and procures more freedom of action for his pieces. Alekhine does his utmost to get even a little counter-play.

21   PxP   RxP?

Through this mistake Black surrenders his last chance of saving the game. 21 . . . QxP! was essential. White can then force the transition to a good endgame with a solid pawn plus by 22 Q–Q4, QxQ; 23 KtxQ, or else he can choose the vigorous 22 QxP. This last line is, however, very risky and allows Black some most dangerous counter-play by 22 . . . B–B4; 23 Q–R4, RxRch; 24 RxR, Q–B3. One example is the following interesting variation: 25 QxP, Q–R5; 26 Kt–K1, QxRch (the attempt at attack by 26 . . . QxP; 27 Kt–B2, Q–R5; is repulsed by 28 R–Q2); 27 KxQ, B–B7ch; 28 KxB, RxQ; 29 Kt–Q3, RxQBPch; 30 K–Q2, and the strong passed pawns on the King-side assure White some winning chances.

It is interesting to observe that Alekhine was afraid of a possible 22 QxP, as he said after the game. I, on the other hand, would have contented myself with 22 Q–Q4, having regard to the fact that my time on the clock was by now rather restricted.

22   KR–K1   Q–Kt5?

A bad mistake in a difficult position, but also after 22 . . . R–K3; 23 Q–Q4, or 22 . . . Q–Kt2; 23 Q–Q4, White's win would not be in doubt. White always retains a good extra pawn with excellent play for his pieces.

23   QxBch!   resigns

Mate or loss of both Rooks follows.

Game 12

QUEEN'S GAMBIT, SEMI-TARRASCH DEFENCE

International Tournament at Ostend, 1937

	P. Keres	R. Fine
1	Kt–KB3	P–Q4
2	P–Q4	Kt–KB3
3	P–B4	P–K3
4	Kt–B3	P–B4
5	BPxP	KtxP
6	P–K4	

Nowadays this advance that results in a simplification of the position is held to be less lasting than 6 P–K3. But both lines display basic differences. With 6 P–K3, White maintains the tension in the centre and the game takes on the character of a Queen's Gambit Accepted, whereas 6 P–K4, permits Black to simplify the position to some extent by a long and forced variation. In the latter case the position becomes comparatively clear and concrete plans of campaign can be marked out far in advance for both sides.

6	...	KtxKt
7	PxKt	PxP
8	PxP	B–Kt5ch

It is advantageous for Black to exchange off as many pieces as possible, since in the first place, White's chances of a King-side attack are thereby lessened, and in the second Black gets nearer to his eventual objective—the endgame. Praxis shows that the Queen-side pawn majority affords Black here really good chances in the endgame.

9	B–Q2	BxBch

Black could bring about further simplifications here by 9 ... Q–R4; but this would be at the expense of his development. After 10 R–QKt1, BxBch; 11 QxB, QxQch; 12 KxQ, O–O; White would obtain strong positional pressure by the move recommended by Rubinstein 13 B–Kt5!, so that Black would not be able to think of evaluating his Queen-side pawn majority.

10   QxB   O–O
11   B–B4

This position is characteristic of the opening variation that
starts with 6 P–K4. White possesses a strong pawn centre and
excellent piece development, but the Black position has no
weaknesses and contains good chances of counter-play once his
development is complete. With mechanical play in the next
phase of the game Black will, for example, attain exchange of
the major pieces along the QB file and then reach an advantageous ending.

White can direct his ensuing play according to two positionally based plans. The first consists of an attempt to realise
his preponderance in the centre and force through P–Q5 with
the resulting strong passed pawn and the second is a concen-
tration of all his pieces on a King-side attack. It is naturally
hard to say which of the two plans offers the best chances of
success and therefore it is reasonable to keep both possibilities
open for the time being. Since the move 11 B–B4 is of use in
both cases it appears to me to be more logical than the other
possible moves that are played here, 11 B–K2, or 11 B–Q3.

11   . . .   Kt–Q2

Black, too, has to solve here the problem of a plan for further
play. With the text-move he transfers his Knight to the King-
side as protection against an eventual attack. Another possibility here was 11 . . . Kt–B3; so as to use the Knight to promote
an action on the Queen-side. Tournament praxis has shown
that this plan, too, gives Black a reasonable game, for example,
12 O–O, P–QKt3; 13 KR–Q1, B–Kt2; 14 Q–B4, and now
simplest is 14 . . . Q–B3!; 15 Q–K3, KR–Q1; 16 P–K5, Q–R3!
(Reshevsky–Fine, Hastings, 1937–38), when White's attack is
quite held. Were White now to exchange on R3 then the
control of the central square Q5 (18 P–Q5?, Kt–R4!) would
amply compensate for the pawn weakness on the King-side
and even give Black the better endgame prospects.

12   O–O   P–QKt3
13   QR–Q1

As we have already noted, placing a Rook here on the QB
file would serve no purpose and would lead sooner or later

to further exchanges. With the text-move White is carrying out a sound plan. He places his Rooks behind the two centre pawns and is always threatening either P–Q5 or P–K5, so that Black has to pay great care to his defence.

13	. . .	B–Kt2
14	KR–K1	R–B1
15	B–Kt3	Kt–B3

Many commentators have criticised this move and recommended that Black should bring his Knight to KB1 to protect his King-side. Undoubtedly the Knight is better placed on KB1 for defensive purposes, but on the other hand Black would then experience much more difficulty in getting a counter-attack going. But such passive play is not to everyone's taste and therefore Fine's choice is not to be censured, especially since Black does arrive at a tenable position with it.

16	Q–B4	Q–B2
17	Q–R4	

Obviously a Queen exchange does not come into consideration for White here.

17	. . .	KR–Q1

Now both sides have completed their development and concrete plans must be devised for the middle game. By posting his Knight on KB3 Black is adequately ensured against the thrust of P–Q5 and is also ready, in event of P–K5, to occupy at once the important central square, Q4, with his Knight. In reply to 18 Kt–K5, Black has the unpleasant answer 18 . . . Q–B6; when 19 R–K3, will not do because of 19 . . . QxP, White must find an active plan since, otherwise, Black himself would start getting awkward with P–QKt4 followed by P–QR4.

After long thought White decided on the following plan. He would like to make a pawn sacrifice, by P–Q5 and if then PxP to continue the attack by P–K5. But this is not possible immediately, since after 18 P–Q5, PxP; 19 P–K5, Black answers 19 . . . Kt–K5, and if then White tries the intended exchange sacrifice by 20 RxKt, PxR, then his Rook on Q1 is *en prise* and he cannot continue with 21 Kt–Kt5. Therefore, in preparation of this combination, White first removes his Rook from the Q file.

It turns out, however, that the entire plan scarcely affords
success against proper counter-play, since the numerous preparatory moves required for White's combination can be
thwarted by only one prophylactic defensive move on Black's
part, viz. P–KR3. White attains success in the ensuing play
only because Black is too late in observing the danger threatening him and plays over-dogmatically for the realisation of
his Queen-side pawn majority.

18   R–K3?

As already mentioned, the plan commenced by the text-move
offers little chance of success against correct counter-play.
White should, therefore, at once initiate an action against the
enemy King-side—and that by 18 P–K5!. In so doing he would
have ensured for himself a most promising position as the following brief variations show:

I. 18 . . . Kt–Q4; 19 Kt–Kt5, P–KR3; 20 Kt–K4, Kt–B6
(otherwise White threatens 21 Kt–Q6, or 21 R–Q3); 21 Kt–
B6ch!, with a very strong attack.

II. 18 . . . BxKt?; 19 PxKt, BxR; 20 Q–Kt5, K–B1; 21
QxPch, K–K1; 22 RxPch!, and Black will be mated.

III. 18 . . . Kt–Q2; 19 Kt–Kt5, Kt–B1; 20 Kt–K4 (or also
first 20 R–K3), 20 . . . BxKt; 21 QxB, and White obtains a
positional advantage.

18 . . .   P–QKt4!

A very strong move that not only prepares the advance of
the pawns on the Queen-side but also gives the Queen the
important square QKt3.

19   R(Q1)–K1   P–QR4

Black still discerns no danger and thinks he will be able
to continue his advance on the Queen-side unhindered. Here
however he should of necessity have first interpolated the defensive move 19 . . . P–KR3. In that event White would have
experienced great difficulty in forcing through his attack to
a successful end. The logical continuation 20 P–Kt4 fails
against 20 . . . Q–KB5, and 20 P–Q5, PxP; 21 P–K5, Kt–K5
yields White absolutely nothing. Apparently White must then
return to his 20 P–K5, but now this advance no longer has

the same force as before.   After 20 . . . Kt–Q4; 21 R–K4, Q–K2
Black has every prospect of beating back the enemy attack and
retaining his positional advantage.

> 20   P–R4   P–Kt5?

But this is already a mistake after which White can successfully carry out his plan.   Here the possibility still existed of
obtaining the better game by 20 . . . PxP; 21 BxRP, P–KR3.

Black (Fine)

White (Keres) to play

> 21   P–Q5!

At last White succeeds in carrying out the thrust he has so
long and assiduously planned.   With the ensuing pawn sacrifice
White drives away the last piece protecting the enemy King
and so obtains a powerful attack that can hardly be met
successfully in over-the-board play.   The following complications are very interesting and provide the analysts with a
fruitful field for research.

> 21   . . .   PxP

After 21 . . . P–K4; 22 Kt–Kt5, R–Q3; 23 P–B4, or also
22 Q–Kt5, Kt–Q2; 23 Kt–R4, White would obtain a strong
attack without any sacrifice in material.

> 22   P–K5   Kt–Q2

This retreat was characterised by many commentators as the
decisive mistake and instead 22 . . . Kt–K5 was recommended

as the only right move. During the game I thought this move was best and had planned to play in reply 23 P–K6!, PxP; 24 RxKt, PxR; 25 Kt–Kt5, when White's attack would appear to be decisive. However, in this difficult position for Black the strong defensive move 25 . . . Q–B6! was discovered. It is then difficult for White to continue his attack successfully, e.g.: 26 QxPch, K–B1; 27 KtxPch, K–K2; 28 Q–R4ch, Q–B3; or 26 BxPch, K–B1; 27 Q–B4ch (or 27 KtxPch, K–K1; 28 Q–R5ch, K–K2; 29 Q–B7ch, K–Q3; etc.), 27 . . . K–K2; 28 Q–B7ch, K–Q3, and Black's King escapes from the mating net.

However, it seems unlikely that Black, in view of his broken King-side, can put up so successful a defence. And a closer analysis shows that White has in fact a more enduring continuation of the attack. He must play 26 BxPch, K–B1; 27 R–KB1!. With this White threatens Q–B4ch–B7ch–xB, or also the simple 28 BxR, when he would regain the exchange with an enduring attack. It seems to me that in this variation Black could hardly hope for a more successful defence than that in the game.

23 Kt–Kt5	Kt–B1?

But this is a fatal error. By 23 . . . P–R3! Black could have still put up an obstinate resistance. White would then continue 24 P–K6!, PxKt; 25 PxPch, KxP; 26 R–K7ch, after which the following variations could arise.

I. 26 . . . K–Kt3; 27 Q–Q4, Q–B6; 28 B–B2ch, K–R4 (or 28 . . . QxB; 29 RxPch, K–R4; 30 P–Kt4ch, K–R5; 31 Q–K3, etc.); 29 B–Q1ch, K–R3; 30 R(K1)–K3!, winning the Queen.

II. 26 . . . K–Kt1; 27 QxP(Kt5), (after 27 Q–R5, Black has the good defence of 27 . . . Q–KB5!, and 27 Q–Q4, is of course answered by 27 . . . Q–B6) 27 . . . Q–B6; 28 P–R4! (this seems even stronger than 28 BxPch, BxB; 29 QxBch, K–R1; 30 Q–R5ch, which would also afford White some winning chances), 28 . . . Q–KB3 (one can see nothing better since 28 . . . Kt–B4 allows the reply 29 R(K1)–K5, and 28 . . . Kt–B1; 29 R(K1)–K3, Q–R8ch; 30 K–R2 also leaves Black hopelessly placed); 29 BxPch, BxB; 30 QxBch, K–R1; 31 RxKt, and White has some winning chances owing to his opponent's weakened King-side. Perhaps in this variation

28 P–R3 is still stronger so that, in the last line, White's KRP will not be attacked.

The variations given provide convincing proof of the difficulties Black has to contend with even in the best defence. It is therefore understandable that it is difficult to decide, in view of the time-limit, which of the many dangerous variations offers him the best chances of saving the game.

24 KtxRP!

This typical Knight sacrifice is speedily decisive, since the Black King-side, so bereft of its own pieces, cannot resist the ensuing attack. Acceptance of the sacrifice is practically forced, since 24 ... Kt–Kt3; 25 Q–R5, Kt–B5; 26 Q–B5 would leave White a powerful attack with level material.

24	...	KtxKt
25	R–R3	Q–B8

Black puts his hopes in this counter-attack, but they prove illusory. White parries the individual enemy threats without trouble, and that without also weakening his own attack.

26	QxKtch	K–B1
27	R–K3	P–Q5

Apparently Black has now obtained really good counter-play, but the opening up of the diagonal for White's Bishop that results from the text-move is utilised to strengthen the attack decisively.

28	Q–R8ch	K–K2
29	QxP	R–B1

Mate is threatened on B2, and after 29 ... B–Q4, White wins by 30 Q–B6ch, K–Q2; 31 BxB, or 30 ... K–K1; 31 P–K6!, etc.

30	Q–B6ch	K–K1
31	P–K6!	resigns.

After the forced continuation 31 ... PxR; 32 PxPch, RxP (or 32 ... K–Q2; 33 Q–K6ch, K–B2; 34 RxQch, etc.); 33 BxRch, K–Q2; 34 Q–K6ch, Black either loses his Queen or is mated.

Game 13

QUEEN'S PAWN OPENING

International Tournament at Ostend, 1937

	A. Dunkelblum	P. Keres
1	P–Q4	Kt–KB3
2	Kt–KB3	P–B4

This game was played a couple of rounds before the end of the tournament. Through previous losses to Grob and Tartakower I had so much worsened my tournament position that it was imperative that I should win this game. For this reason I chose here an opening variation which was little known at the time and virgin ground to theory, and I hoped thereby to lure my opponent, a player accustomed to play in a most restrained style, into a middle-game rich in combinations. But Dunkelblum does not try for an opening advantage. Instead of the logical advance 3 P–Q5, he selects a quiet method of development and leaves it to his opponent to discover new ways of complicating the game.

3	P–K3	P–KKt3
4	B–K2	B–Kt2
5	O–O	O–O
6	P–B4	

As a matter of fact this advance does not fit in with the quiet system of development chosen by White, since now White can create some tension in the centre. This naturally does not yet lead to any tangible result, but something is all the same attained. Namely, White must abandon his waiting strategy and accept the offer of a hand-to-hand fight.

6	...	P–Q4

The line 6 . . . PxP; 7 PxP, P–Q4; would lead to a position in the Tarrasch Defence with reverse colours and an extra tempo for White.

7	BPxP	KtxP
8	PxP	

Here I comprehended that my opponent was remaining true to his tactics of simplifying the position and if possible of reaching a quiet endgame. As a first step on this way he naturally plans to play P–K4 and Kt–B3 after an eventual Queen exchange. But what then can Black do against this? With his ensuing moves Black entices his opponent to exchange off on QR3, thereby weakening the Black pawn structure and allowing White the opportunity of defending his extra pawn.

| 8 | . . . | Kt–R3! |
| 9 | BxKt? | |

Nowadays everyone knows that such an exchange is not to be recommended since Black then retains the two Bishops, gets open lines for his pieces and finally outruns his opponent in development. Black now not only obtains a positional but also a psychological advantage. He gets what he has striven for from the very first move, viz. a complicated middlegame full of fighting possibilities.

Instead of the faulty text-move White must play 9 P–K4, Kt(Q4)–Kt5; 10 Kt–B3, and this, after 10. . . KtxBP; 11 B–K3, would assure him a thoroughly acceptable position.

| 9 | . . . | PxB |
| 10 | Kt–Q4 | |

Misfortunes are rarely single. White, in trying to defend his extra pawn, gets more and more behind in development. He should at least essay 10 QKt–Q2, so as to develop his Queen-side at long last.

10	. . .	Q–B2
11	Kt–Kt3	R–Q1
12	Q–K2	P–QR4!

Commencing a deeply calculated and highly complicated combination in which White does not feel at home and where he eventually misses the right path. Who could have supposed in this position that in this combination the Black QR pawn which seems for the moment to be so humble will eventually play a decisive role!

13	B–Q2	P–R5

This move is typical of my style at the time. Today, instead of the following hair-raising complications I would probably have chosen the quieter way 13 . . . Kt–Kt5, which equally leads to an advantageous position for Black. But in that case we would have missed the following richly combinative middle-game, which fully justifies the inclusion of this otherwise mediocre game in this collection.

14	B–R5	Q–B3
15	BxR	

Forced, since after 15 Kt–Q4, BxKt; 16 PxB, Black can, in addition to 16 . . . Kt–B5, play as well 16 . . . B–QR3; 17 Q–Q1, BxR; 18 BxR, BxP, thereby obtaining a decisive attack.

15	. . .	B–QR3 !

Black logically follows up the plan commenced by his 13th move. Very attractive here was the exchange sacrifice 15 . . . PxKt; 16 PxP, B–Kt2; and then if 17 B–R5, Kt–B5; 18 Q–B3 (or 18 Q–Kt4, P–KR4;), 18 . . . Kt–K7ch! winning. But White can play in this variation instead of 17 B–R5, the stronger 17 P–K4!, by which he would retain the advantage of the exchange.

16	Kt–R5

White puts up an excellent defence. After 16 Q–Q2, there would come 16 . . . BxR with considerable advantage to Black.

16	. . .	Q–K3 !

Coming down to an ending by 16 . . . BxQ; 17 KtxQ, BxR yields Black nothing since White would liquidate the main danger by 18 Kt–B3! After the text-move the torrent of combinations is at full spate; most of the pieces are either directly attacked or indirectly threatened. In over-the-board play it is naturally very difficult to find the right way in this maze and it is therefore understandable that White does not play the best defence in the ensuing moves and soon gets into a lost position.

Black (Keres)

White (Dunkelblum) to play

17 Q–Q2?

This move is altogether weak and gives Black no difficulty in evaluating his advantage. But the chief question is whether Black has a possibility of strengthening his attack decisively against the best defence 17 Kt–B4!, or whether with this move White can succeed in demonstrating the inadequacy of the enemy action.

It is not so easy to answer this question since the position is so complicated and contains so many hidden possibilities that even in subsequent analysis it is scarcely practicable to find a clear way through the jungle. After 17 Kt–B4, Black can fall back on two chief possibilities which both seem to lead to a promising position for him. Let us now examine them a little more exhaustively.

I. 17 ... Kt–B5 (whilst awaiting my opponent's 17th move, this was the principal possibility that I had taken into consideration); 18 Q–B3, BxKt (here 18 ... RxB also comes into consideration after which, by 19 Kt(Kt1)–R3, White could transpose into the line given in the next paragraph); 19 QxR, B–Q4; 20 Q–Kt8, Kt–K7ch (unfortunately Black has no time for the pretty 20 ... Q–R6; since White gets his mate in first by 21 BxP dis ch); 21 K–R1, BxPch; 22 KxB, Q–Kt5ch; 23 Q–Kt3, KtxQ; 24 RPxKt, BxP; and now we have a very complicated and unclear position which is very difficult to judge. Black will win the exchange and remain with Queen against enemy Rook, Bishop and Knight. The

White pieces are very poorly placed but his strong passed pawn on the QB file gives him adequate defensive possibilities.

II. 17 . . . RxB (this simple recapture is probably best); 18 Kt(Kt1)–R3, Kt–B5; 19 Q–B3 (after 19 Q–B2, KtxP; Black gets a most dangerous attack in return for the exchange), 19 . . . Kt–Q6 and Black wins back his sacrificed material with a good game.

Whatever result further investigation of this position might produce one thing is, in any case, clear—White must try here 17 Kt–B4! which is the only line that guarantees him prospects of a successful defence.

| | 17 . . . | BxR |
| | 18 Kt–B3 | |

This loses at once, but also after 18 KxB, RxB; White's position with its undeveloped Queen-side would be hopeless.

| | 18 . . . | BxP! |

This Bishop sells its life as dearly as possible. Once the White King-side is so broken up Black soon gets a decisive attack.

| 19 | KxB | RxB |
| 20 | K–R1 | P–R6! |

This unobtrusive pawn now provides the finishing stroke.

21	R–Q1	PxP
22	KtxKt	RxKt!
	resigns	

There could follow 23 Q–B2, RxRch; 24 QxR, Q–K5ch, and the Kt pawn queens. It is interesting to observe that, in a position where nearly all the pieces on the board are attacked, in the end the little RP brought about the decision.

Game 14

FRENCH DEFENCE

International Tournament at Prague, 1937

	J. Foltys	P. Keres
1	P–Q4	P–K3
2	P–K4	

After 2 P–QB4, I often used to play at that time 2 . . . B–Kt5ch, and with results that were not bad. Apparently this possibility did not attract Foltys and he therefore decides to transpose the game to the French Defence.

	2 . . .	P–Q4
	3 Kt–QB3	Kt–KB3

The Nimzowitsch move, 3 . . . B–Kt5; was not then so popular as it is nowadays.

	4 B–Kt5	B–K2
	5 BxKt	

This exchange was often employed in his time by the world champion, Anderssen, but has of recent years tended to disappear almost entirely from tournament play. In my opinion there are two main reasons for this. Firstly, White does not obtain particularly good attacking chances with this exchange, and, secondly, he attains good play without much trouble by the normal 5 P–K5.

	5 . . .	BxB
	6 Kt–B3	

White mixes up two different systems and so loses prospects of getting anything out of the opening. Once having plumped for the exchange on B6 White must continue here with 6 P–K5, B–K2; 7 Q–Kt4, which would at least keep him some prospects of attack.

	6 . . .	O–O

It would have probably been better to have postponed castling here for a little and to have first played 6 . . . P–B4, since, now, White can engineer some nasty threats against the enemy King-side.

	7 B–Q3	P–B4
	8 P–K5	B–K2
	9 PxP	

Here Foltys misses the strong continuation 9 P–KR4! which threatens 10 BxPch and sets Black some really difficult problems. If Black then replies 9 . . . PxP, he can get into great trouble after 10 BxPch, KxB; 11 Kt–Kt5ch. In illustration of this we append the following possible variation: 11 . . . K–R3;

12 Q–Q3, P–KKt3; 13 P–R5!, BxKt; 14 PxP dis ch, B–R5; 15 Q–Kt3!, PxP; 16 RxBch, K–Kt2; 17 R–Kt4, and White has a really strong attacking position in return for the piece sacrifice (17 ... Q–K1; 18 Kt–Kt5!, etc.)

Also after 9 ... P–B4; 10 PxP e.p., PxBP, the sacrifice 11 Kt–KKt5! gives White a dangerous attack. Although the appended lines have no claim to be at all exhaustive, they serve to convince us that White could only have justified his previous play by 9 P–KR4.

| 9 ... | Kt–Q2! |
| 10 P–KR4? | |

The move that was good a moment ago is now bad. Since Black can now easily defend himself against the threat of 11 BxPch, the text-move proves to be merely a weakening of White's own King-side. The attempt, too, to protect the BP by P–QKt4 would be unsuccessful because of 10 ... P–QKt3; 11 PxP, BxP; but by 10 O–O, White could have maintained an approximate equality.

| 10 ... | P–B4 |

The simplest way of parrying White's threat. After the practically forced exchange on KB3 both Black Bishops obtain full scope for action in the open centre. In addition White must aim only at castling Queen-side on account of the weakness on his KR4.

| 11 PxP e.p. | BxP(B3) |
| 12 Q–Q2 | |

Now the sacrifice 12 BxPch, KxB; 13 Kt–Kt5ch no longer comes into consideration since Black could completely repulse the attack by 13 ... K–Kt1; 14 Q–R5, BxKtch; 15 PxB, Kt–B3.

| 12 ... | KtxP |
| 13 O–O–O | Q–R4 |

Black's attack on the Queen-side now develops markedly quicker than the White counter-action on the King's wing. He is already threatening to win a pawn by 14 ... KtxBch, followed by BxKt and QxP, and, in addition, White has to reckon with the possibility of P–K4.

| 14 P–R3 |

Such a weakening of the castled position is certainly not pleasant, but what else can White do to protect his QRP? 14 K–Kt1 will not work since Black can then win a pawn by 14 ... BxKt; 15 QxB, QxQ; 16 PxQ, Kt–R5. Now, however, Black threatens to obtain a powerful attack against the King.

        14   . . .   B–Q2
        15   QR–K1

White still cannot play 15 K–Kt1 because of 15 ... BxKt; and 15 Kt–K2 could be met by 15 ... Q–Kt3 followed by P–K4. The text-move is aimed against P–K4, but now White's QB3 turns out to be a fatal weakness.

Black (Keres) to play

White (Foltys)

        15   . . .   QR–B1!

This simple move sets the adversary an insoluble problem. Now Black threatens not only 16 ... KtxBch, followed by 17 ... BxKt, but also 16 ... P–Q5, when White cannot move the Knight on account of Kt–Kt6ch. White, therefore, decides to make an exchange sacrifice in the hope that he will obtain some counter-play on the White squares.

        16   Kt–K5

Undoubtedly the best practical chance. Both of the enemy threats could, indeed, be prevented by 16 B–B1, but then Black would decisively strengthen his attack by 16 ... P–QKt4.

        16   . . .   BxKt

After 16 ... P-Q5, White has the resource 17 KtxB, PxKt; 18 KtxBch, although Black would still obtain much the better ending after 18 ... RxKt. The text-move wins the exchange.

17	RxB	P-Q5!

If now 18 Kt–K4, then 18 ... KtxBch wins a whole Rook. White must therefore capture on QB5.

18	RxKt	QxR

The presence of the Queen increases Black's chances since in the ensuing phase of the game the White King is subjected to all possible kinds of attack. White now tries to consolidate his central position on the White squares, thereby rendering his opponent's task as difficult as possible.

19	Kt–K4	Q–Q4
20	K–Kt1	P–K4
21	P–B3	P–KR3
22	P–QKt3	

This fresh weakening of White King's position is inevitable sooner or later, since Black threatens to penetrate to QR7 after B–K3. Now, however, Black has a clear plan of campaign. He will try to force through his QRP to R5 and if White prevents this by P–R4 then he will be able to break up his pawn position by P–QKt4.

22	...	B–K3

This move is playable because 23 B–B4 can be met by 23 ... RxB!; 24 PxR, QxP; with a winning attack for Black.

23	P–R5	P–R4
24	P–R4	K–R1

Black is in no hurry. Before he starts on the decisive action on the Queen's wing he first removes his King from the dangerous diagonal KKt1–QR7. So as not to go down without a fight White now begins a desperate attack against the Black King, but he only accelerates his loss thereby.

25	R–Kt1	R–QB3

So as to strengthen the attack by bringing his Rook to Kt5.

26	B–Kt5	R–QB2
27	B–Q3	B–Q2

Now all is prepared for the P–QKt4 thrust. White feels bound to accelerate his action on the other wing but in practice 28 K–Kt2 would have afforded better chances, since Black cannot yet play 28 . . . P–QKt4 because of 29 QxP. But this would hardly have altered the result of the game.

28	P–KKt4	KRxP
29	P–Kt5	B–B4!

Liquidating the chief point of support for the opponent on K4, which is equivalent to deciding the fate of the game. The following desperation sacrifice merely permits of a number of checks.

30	PxP	BxKt
31	PxPch	RxP
32	RxR	

Or 32 Q–R6ch, R–R2; and both the mating squares on KB3 and KB1 are protected.

32	. . .	KxR
33	Q–Kt5ch	K–B2
	resigns	

After 34 B–B4, RxPch! wins at once.

Game 15

QUEEN'S PAWN, KING'S INDIAN DEFENCE

International Tournament at Prague, 1937

	P. Keres	K. Hromadka
1	P–Q4	Kt–KB3
2	P–QB4	P–B4
3	P–Q5	P–KKt3

The method of play chosen by Black here is nowadays one of the well-known variations of the King's Indian Defence and has been recognised as valid in international chess for some time. But when this game was played the line was regarded as unfavourable for Black. Despite which, Master Hromadka used it in a number of games and so contributed much towards working out and popularising the whole method of play.

4	Kt–QB3	P–Q3
5	P–KKt3	B–Kt2
6	B–Kt2	O–O
7	P–K4	

Nowadays 7 Kt–B3 is the recommended move. But, as we have already remarked, at that time the development system for both sides had not yet been worked out and it occurred but seldom in tournament play.

7	...	P–QR3

But now the manoeuvre Kt–R3–B2 as preparation for P–QKt4 was in order.

8	P–QR4	R–K1
9	KKt–K2	P–K3

Black adopts the right plan. By the ensuing exchange in the centre he opens up lines for his pieces and at the same time gets rid of White's QBP after which it becomes easier to carry out the advance P–QKt4. Nowadays, however, this strategy is already common knowledge and needs no further explanation.

10	O–O	PxP
11	BPxP	QKt–Q2
12	P–R3	

White could also play 12 P–Kt3, since the combination 12 ... KtxKP; 13 BxKt, RxB; 14 KtxR, BxR leaves White with a clearly overwhelming game after 15 B–Kt5 or 15 KtxQP. But White does not want to play an early P–QKt3 as he wishes to avoid giving his opponent an object of attack on QKt3 after the QKt file has been opened. The text-move is necessary as preparation for P–B4, or for P–KKt4 followed by Kt–Kt3.

12	...	R–Kt1
13	P–R5	Kt–K4

The Knight sally turns out to be merely a loss of tempo. He should play at once 13 ... P–QKt4; 14 PxP e.p., RxKtP; after which Black would have real counter-play on the Q wing in compensation for White's preponderance in the centre.

14 P–B4   Kt(K4)–Q2?

Black, in making this move, marks out his previous one as a mistake, which costs him two valuable tempi. Black's original idea was to play here 14 ... Kt–B5; 15 Q–R4, P–QKt4; but he renounces it at the last moment since he is afraid of losing his Knight after 16 Q–R2. In actual fact, however, Black would then obtain an excellent game by 16 ... Kt–Q2!, since 17 P–Kt3 is not to be feared because of 17 ... P–Kt5; and otherwise there is threatened the disagreeable P–KB4.

Therefore White would play after 14 ... Kt–B5; 15 Q–R4, P–QKt4 simply 16 PxP e.p., KtxP(Kt3); 17 Q–B2, after which the long Knight manoeuvre Kt–Q2–K4–B5–Kt3 would prove to be mere loss of tempi.

15 P–KKt4!   P–QKt4
16 PxP e.p.

Hromadka plays most resourcefully. White was threatening 16 P–Kt5, and at the first glance 16 P–Kt5, Kt–R4; 17 B–B3 still seems very strong. An exchange by 17 ... BxKt; 18 PxB, Kt–Kt2 would then leave White with a clear advantage and in any case there is the threat of 18 BxKt. In fact this line would now lead to most undesirable consequences for White because of the variation 17 ... P–Kt5!; 18 Kt–Kt1, P–B5. Then, if 19 BxKt, PxB, White suddenly finds himself at a loss how to protect his K4 square. White must, if he wants to retain his strong centre, ensure the position of his Kt on QB3 at all costs.

16 ...   QxP?

Black is all too optimistic in his appreciation of the position. After the text-move White forces his opponent to displace his Knight on KR4, and, in order to bring back this Knight into the game again, to exchange off his strong K Bishop. But in so doing Black weakens his King-side to a marked degree and White gets the opportunity of initiating a most promising attack.

The normal continuation of 16 ... KtxKtP, which vacates the Q2 square for the other Knight, was apparently avoided by Black because of the possibility of 17 P–K5, PxP; 18 PxP. Then, in fact, 18 ... RxP would not do because of 19 B–B4

winning the exchange, but 18 . . . KKt–Q2! would have been
playable. Although after the further 19 P–K6, PxP; 20 PxP,
RxP Black's position looks to be in great danger it is difficult to
see how White can achieve any concrete advantage.

Naturally, White need not force matters after 16 . . . KtxKtP
by 17 P–K5. He could, for example, play either 17 Q–Q3 or
17 Kt–Kt3, and retain a marked advantage.

17	P–Kt5	Kt–R4
18	B–B3	B–Q5ch

Black apparently had counted on this move. If now 19 KtxB,
PxKt; 20 Kt–R4, then there follows 20 . . . Q–Kt5 and after
21 BxKt, PxB White has no time to utilise the weaknesses on
the enemy King-side on account of his own weakness on K4.
White, however, has at his disposal a cunning manoeuvre that
convincingly demonstrates the inadequacy of the enemy's plan.

19	K–Kt2!	Kt–Kt2
20	R–R4!	

It is with this move that White makes his positional advantage clear. By his last move Black had to block the only field
of retreat for his Bishop and now, on account of the threat
of 21 KtxB, he must himself exchange the piece against the
enemy Knight. With this White has attained his strategic
objective and his position can be regarded as won from this
point of view.

20	. . .	BxKt
21	KtxB	P–B4

Black must try some sort of counter-play, as otherwise he
soon gets into a clearly lost position after White's P–R4–5.
White could also very well meet the text-move with 22 PxP e.p.,
KtxP; 23 R–K1, with the threat of 24 P–K5, but he prefers to
operate along the K file instead.

22	R–K1	Q–Q1
23	P–Kt3	

In this way White affords his opponent some unnecessary
counter-play. Better was an immediate 23 P–R4 followed by
an eventual P–R5, since it is impossible to see what Black can
do against it.

23 ...   Q–Kt3

Black takes immediate advantage of his opportunity. Although the threat on the pawn on QKt6 is not particularly effective it still does noticeably impede White's attack.

24 PxP   RxR

After 24 ... PxP; 25 RxRch, KtxR; 26 Q–K1, Kt–Kt2 we have the position in the game, and 24 ... QxP; 25 RxRch, KtxR; 26 Q–K1 yields White a decisive attack.

25 QxR   PxP

Here Black was faced with the difficult choice of how he should recapture on KB4. It is true that with the text-move Black deprives White's pieces of the fine square K4, but in so doing he leaves his Knight almost in a stalemate position and relinquishes hope of active counter-play. Therefore the recapture by 25 ... KtxP also came into consideration. After this direct attempts at attack on the Black King would be unsuccessful, e.g.: 26 Q–K8ch, Kt–B1; 27 Kt–K4, B–K3! or 26 Q–K6ch, K–B1! (27 R–K4, Q–Q1) and Black has an adequate defence.

It cannot, however, be maintained that Black's position would have been noticeably relieved by 25 ... KtxP. White would still retain an excellent attacking position thereafter and he could strengthen this in various ways. Thus he could at once protect the threatened point QKt3 by 26 B–Q1, or also after 26 R–K4, Kt–B1; 27 B–Q1. But also possible is the more energetic continuation 26 B–Kt4, Kt–B1; 27 Kt–K4, QxP; 28 Kt–B6ch, followed by 29 R–K4, with numerous threats.

26 R–R2

White retires his Rook to the second rank in order to strengthen his pressure in the centre. The pawn on QKt3 is of no importance as after 26 ... QxP White can even quietly continue 27 P–R4, and the Black pieces cannot get back in time to protect the King-side. Even more forcing, however, would be an immediate 26 P–R4, since the advance of this pawn to R5 would deprive Black of any possibility whatsoever of counter-play on that wing.

26 ...   Kt–B1
27 R–K2

Also here 27 P–R4 merits consideration. The occupation
of the K file turns out to be, by itself, insufficient to break down
enemy resistance.

Black (Hromadka) to play

White (Keres)

27 ...   Q–Q1?

Once Black has, of his own free will, placed his Queen
in a passive defensive position by the text-move the further
strengthening of White's attack meets with no difficulties.
Therefore, here 27 ... B–Q2 must be tried. During the
game I had worked out the following winning variation against
this move: 28 R–K7, R–K1; 29 B–Kt2, Q–Q1; 30 RxKtch,
KxR; 31 Kt–K4 dis ch, K–Kt1; 32 Q–B3, or, in this line, 29 ...
QxP; 30 Kt–Q1, RxR; 31 QxR, Kt–K1; and after 32 K–Kt3
Black has no good move. There is, however, a snag: instead
of 28 ... R–K1, Black can play the stronger 28 ... QxP
(29 Kt–Q1, Q–B7ch) and White cannot easily manoeuvre his
Bishop to the QR1–KR8 diagonal.

White must therefore conduct his attack in a much more
subtle way. The move that will serve very well to start off
matters is 28 Kt–Q1!, since now 28 ... QxP fails against
29 R–Kt2. If Black plays 28 ... R–K1 then follows 29 B–Kt2,
after which 29 ... QxP; 30 R–K7 would transpose into the
line given above. Or if 29 ... Kt–Kt3; 30 Q–B3 wins for White.
Black would also have an unsatisfactory end to the attempt

to use this move after 28 . . . Kt–Kt3; 29 P–R4, Q–Kt5; 30 Q–Kt3, followed by 31 P–R5. It would appear, therefore, that the continuation 28 Kt–Q1! would, in the event, too, of 27 . . . B–Q2, ensure White control of the long diagonal and this, in turn, would mean a decisive attack.

28 P–R4!

Surprisingly enough, Black is quite helpless against the further advance of this pawn. The capture on QKt3 now has a much weaker effect than in the variations considered above, since the Rook cannot fulfil the same function as the Queen from that square.

28	. . .	RxP
29	P–R5	B–Q2
30	P–R6	Kt–K1

Black can indeed save the loss of a piece, but his position is hopelessly passive and must therefore collapse sooner or later.

31	B–R5	Kt–Kt3
32	BxKt	PxB
33	R–K7	P–R4

Black now has hardly a move, and White needs only to get his Bishop on the long diagonal in order to break down the ultimate resistance. Naturally, 33 . . . RxKt? would fail against 34 P–R7ch, and after 33 . . . Kt–B2 the simplest way of deciding the game is by 34 R–Kt7ch and 35 RxP.

34	Kt–Q1	Kt–B2
35	Q–K2	

The simplest win here was by 35 R–Kt7ch, K–R1; 36 Q–K7!, QxQ; 37 RxQ, and Black loses at least a piece. But, in view of the opponent's time trouble White plays for mate.

35	. . .	KtxP

White would have greater difficulties to surmount after 35 . . . Kt–Kt4. Then there could follow 36 R–Kt7ch, K–R1 (or 36 . . . K–B1; 37 Q–K7ch!, QxQ; 38 RxQ, etc.); 37 B–Kt2, Kt–Q5; and now simply 38 BxKt, PxB; 39 RxP, when the pawn on Q6 cannot be defended.

After the text-move it is all over.

36	P–R7ch	resigns

It is interesting to observe that the White Q Bishop has not made a single move throughout the whole game. Now the intention is to play it to Kt2 and this threat is so strong that it compels Black to strike his flag at once.

Game 16

CATALAN SYSTEM

International Tournament at Kemeri, 1937

	P. Keres	E. Book
1	Kt–KB3	P–Q4
2	P–B4	P–K3
3	Kt–B3	

A more accurate sequence of moves would have been 3 P–Q4, Kt–KB3; 4 Kt–B3, since now Black, by 3 . . . P–Q5; 4 Kt–QKt1, P–QB4, could have transposed to a variation of the King's Indian Defence, with colours reversed.

3	. . .	Kt–KB3
4	P–Q4	B–K2

Book is an expert in the Lasker Defence to the Q.G.D. and therefore aims at the line 5 B–Kt5, O–O; 6 P–K3, P–KR3; 7 B–R4, Kt–K5. For this reason, too, he refrains from the continuation recommended by theory 4 . . . P–B4.

5 P–KKt3

Although the transposition to the Catalan in this position is not as effective as when White has not played Kt–QB3, it is psychologically well based. Black is to be confronted with quite other strategical problems than those for which he had hoped with his last few moves.

5	. . .	O–O
6	B–Kt2	P–B3

The choice of this constricted system of defence shows that the opening variation does not quite suit Black's taste. The simplest continuation by which Black obtains really valid counter-play is here 6 . . . PxP; but the energetic thrust 6 . . . P–B4 also ensures Black a more promising game than the text-move. Now the game once again returns to normal theoretical paths.

7	O–O	QKt–Q2
8	P–Kt3	P–QKt3
9	B–Kt2	P–QR4?

With this advance Black loses an important tempo and thus incurs a clear disadvantage. Here essential was 9 . . . B–R3; 10 Kt–Q2, R–B1, which would give Black a satisfactory game. If White then played as in the game 11 P–K4, there would follow 11 . . . PxBP with the ensuing possibilities:

I. 12 P–K5, Kt–K1 (there also comes into consideration 12 . . . Kt–Q4; 13 PxP, KtxKt; 14 BxKt, P–QKt4; though then White can embark on a promising exchange sacrifice: 15 P–B5!, P–Kt5; 16 BxKtP, BxR; 17 QxB, etc.); 13 KtxP (or 13 PxP, P–QB4; and White cannot play 14 P–Q5, because of 14 . . . KtxP), 13 . . . P–QKt4; 14 Kt–K3, P–QB4; and Black has a good game since 15 P–Q5 again fails against 15 . . . KtxP.

II. 12 PxP, P–K4; 13 P–Q5, PxP; 14 KPxP, and now Black cannot, it is true, play 14 . . . BxP because of 15 KtxB, RxKt; 16 P–Q6. But by 14 . . . Kt–B4 or 14 . . . Kt–K1 he would obtain a good position.

III. 12 KtxP, P–QKt4 (also 12 . . . BxKt; 13 PxB, P–K4; deserves consideration); 13 Kt–K3, P–B4; 14 P–Q5 (after 14 P–K5, Kt–K1 we arrive at a position in Variation I), 14 . . . P–Kt5; 15 Kt–K2, Kt–Kt3; and Black has a thoroughly satisfactory position.

Black (Book)

White (Keres) to play

10   Kt–Q2!

Now Black can no longer prevent White's P–K4 because of his own weakness in the centre and he has the worse game.

10 . . .   B–R3

Naturally, here Black could quietly continue 10 . . . B–Kt2; 11 P–K4, PxKP; 12 Kt(Q2)xP, KtxKt; 13 KtxKt, Kt–B3; after which a well-known position is reached with advantage in both space and position for White. It is, however, easy to comprehend that no player would choose such a method of play in which he can hope only for equality after a laborious defence. It is, therefore, quite natural for Black to institute a counter-attack with the text-move on the Queen-side in the hope of obtaining adequate counter-chances with it.

The further course of the game shows, however, that White's advantage ensures him the upper hand whereas Black's counter-play on the Queen's wing does not get into action at all.

11   P–K4   PxBP

The attempt to create complications by 11 . . . P–B4 gives White a clear advantage after 12 KPxP, BPxP; 13 Kt–Kt5!, e.g.: 13 . . . BxKt; 14 PxP, or 13 . . . PxP; 14 KtxP, R–B1; 15 R–K1, etc. With the text-move Black puts his original plan into action.

12   P–K5!

This intervening move thwarts all Black's plans. He would have a satisfactory game after 12 PxP, P–K4; and also 12 KtxP, BxKt; 13 PxB, P–K4 would ensure him the necessary space in the centre for counter-play.

12 . . .   Kt–Q4

Now there is no longer any point in retreating the Knight to K1 since then after 13 PxP, Black must still lose a tempo in preparing for P–QB4 by 13 . . . R–B1.

13   PxP   KtxKt
14   BxKt   R–B1
15   R–K1!

A good prophylactic move by which White prepares, in reply to 15 . . . P–QB4, the thrust 16 P–Q5, and at the same time makes it more difficult for Black to play P–B3. Black

would now soon be hopelessly placed if he were to proceed to
play passively. Therefore his ensuing attempt to obtain counter-play cannot be criticised. Black still manages to create
various tactical threats and so compels his opponent to exert
the greatest care in the further course of play.

| 15 ... | P–QKt4 |
| 16 P–B5 | P–B3 |

Black pursues his plan logically, but only hastens the loss
by opening up the position. White was already threatening
17 Kt–K4, and 18 Kt–Q6.

17 PxP!

The possible win of a pawn by 17 B–R3, or 17 Q–Kt3,
would yield Black after 17 ... PxP good play for his pieces
and some chances of counter-attack.

17 ... BxP

Black cleverly creates counter-chances for himself. White
cannot now continue 18 RxP because of 18 ... KtxP! since the
line 19 PxKt, BxB; 20 R–Q6 (or also 20 Q–Kt3), comes to
nothing after 20 ... BxR. But White need be in no hurry
with the capture on K6, since this pawn is a permanent weakness and must fall sooner or later in any case.

| 18 Kt–K4 | P–Kt5 |
| 19 B–Kt2 | P–K4 |

On account of his many weaknesses and the strong enemy
threat of 20 Kt–Q6, Black is hopelessly placed from the positional point of view. So his last saving chance lies in tactical
complications. With the text-move Black offers an exchange
sacrifice in order to destroy the enemy pawn centre and in the
hope of obtaining one or two pawns for the exchange. There
now ensue some interesting and tense moments.

| 20 Kt–Q6 | PxP |

As is easy to see—forced. After a Rook move 21 PxP wins
easily.

| 21 KtxR | KtxP |

Black's idea of defence lies in this capture. Now White
experiences difficulties in saving his Knight on QB8, whilst,

meanwhile, Black has built up a powerful pawn mass in the
centre which threatens to advance at the first opportunity. All
this, however, constitutes no adequate compensation for the
Rook, in particular having regard to the fact that White can
institute a dangerous King-side attack at once with his well-
developed pieces.

22   Q–R5 !

Here White has undoubtedly more than one way of con-
solidating his advantage. Thus, for example, he could keep his
extra Rook by 22 Kt–R7, although this would allow Black
really dangerous counter-play after 22 . . . Q–Kt3; 23 KtxP,
Kt–Q6. White could also assure himself of a favourable endgame by 22 Kt–K7ch, BxKt; 23 QxP. However, White decides
upon the third, but undoubtedly strongest, possibility, viz.: a
direct King-side attack which brings about a speedy decision.

22   . . .   Kt–R5

A more obstinate defence could have been put up by 22 . . .
Kt–Q6, which would prevent any direct mate. White would
then continue on a par with the game by 23 B–K4, P–Kt3;
24 BxKtP, PxB; 25 QxPch, K–R1; 26 Kt–K7, BxKt; 27 RxB,
QxR; 28 BxPch, Kt–K4; 29 Q–R5ch, K–Kt1; 30 BxKt, when,
in addition to a material advantage he retains a decisive attack.
After the text-move Black is checkmated in an intriguing way.

23   B–K4 !   P–Kt3

Or 23 . . . P–R3; 24 Q–Kt6, threatening mate in two moves.

24   BxKtP   PxB
25   QxPch   K–R1
26   Kt–K7 !

The despised Knight comes into play at last and brings about
the immediate end. 27 Q–R6 mate is threatened.

26   . . .   BxKt
27   RxB !   resigns

After 27 . . . QxR; naturally 28 BxPch is decisive.

Game 17

RUY LOPEZ

International Tournament at Parnu, 1937

	P. Keres	I. Raud
1	P–K4	P–K4
2	Kt–KB3	Kt–QB3
3	B–Kt5	P–QR3
4	B–R4	Kt–B3
5	O–O	B–K2
6	R–K1	P–Q3

Black pays little attention to the accurate sequence of moves in the development of the Kecskemet Variation. As he plays, White could now adopt the unpleasant line 7 BxKtch, PxB; 8 P–Q4, which would lead after 8 ... PxP; 9 KtxP, to a variation of the Steinitz Defence favourable to White. However, if Black tries to protect his centre by 8 ... Kt–Q2, then White, with the manoeuvre Kt(Kt1)–Q2–B4, obtains strong pressure on the Queen-side and in the centre; e.g.: 9 QKt–Q2, O–O; 10 Kt–B4, PxP; 11 KKtxP, Kt–Kt1; 12 Q–B3, B–B3; 13 B–K3, with a clear opening advantage for White (Boleslavsky–Keres, Moscow, 1952). If Black wishes to employ the Kecskemet Variation then he should do it on the previous move by playing 5 ... P–Q3.

In the present game the transposition of moves is not damaging as with his next few moves White gets back into the normal variation.

7	P–B3	O–O
8	P–Q4	B–Q2

Black, too, does not seem to want to make use of the somewhat peculiar sequence of moves. Here in fact 8 ... P–QKt4; 9 B–B2, B–Kt5 comes into consideration, a line in which Black can commence an enduring pressure on the White centre similar to that in some variations of the Tschigorin Defence.

9   P–Q5

In pre-war days the Kecskemet Defence was generally

regarded as thoroughly correct. Only after subsequent research
and practical experience has it been shown that Black, after
the quiet development move 9 QKt–Q2, still has a number of
hurdles to surmount before he obtains full equality. The
action begun with the text-move to obtain some initiative on
the Queen-side offers poor chances of success, since after the
relaxation of the tension in the centre Black finds sufficient
opportunities for counterplay in P–QB3 or P–KB4.

9	. . .	Kt–Kt1
10	B–B2	P–B3

In this position Black must come to a decision as regards his
future plan of play. In several games the pin by 10 . . . B–Kt5
has been tried in similar positions, but this does not appear to
me to be logical. Usually B–KKt5 is played in order to exert
pressure on White's centre and so force him either to exchange
off the KP or to close the centre by P–Q5. Here, where White
has already decided upon P–Q5 of his own free will, the pin
with the Bishop has in consequence little point. And in fact
after 11 P–KR3, Black is faced with the disagreeable choice
between playing his Bishop back to the inactive position on
R4 and exchanging on KB6 which, however, would leave White
the better game.

The text-move, on the other hand, is quite logical. Since
the thrust of P–KB4 would be possible only after some preparatory moves and, in addition, White would obtain the
strong square K4 for his Knight after an exchange on KB4,
Black aims at counter-play on the Queen-side. All the pre-
requisites are at hand for this, since, in the first place, the pawns
on Q5 and QB4 (after White's P–QB4) are good objects of
attack and, in the second, Black is somewhat ahead of his
opponent in development. 10 . . . P–B3! seems to me to be
one of Black's best continuations in this position.

Finally the manoeuvre 10 . . . P–QR4, followed by Kt–R3–
B4, should also be mentioned, as by this means Black assures
for himself the strong Knight post on QB4 on a parallel with
the King's Indian Defence. The world champion, Alekhine,
often employed this method of play.

11	P–B4	Q–B2

With this Black inaugurates a plan of pressure along the QB file that is obviously insufficient by itself for completely worthwhile counter-play. Very strong, on the other hand, seems a continuation of the attack by 11 . . . P–QKt4! which would have inevitably led to further opening up of lines on the Queenside.

| 12 | Kt–B3 | PxP |

Here, too, 12 . . . P–QKt4 came into consideration, although now Black after 13 QPxP would have to recapture with the Bishop instead of the normal 13 . . . KtxP.

| 13 | BPxP | R–B1 |
| 14 | B–K3 | Kt–Kt5? |

Black has emerged from the opening with a satisfactory game and should now continue with 14 . . . P–QKt4 so as to ensure his Knight the strong post of QB4 by an eventual P–Kt5. Instead of this he undertakes with the text-move a totally unsuitable manoeuvre, solely in order to achieve a very dubious win of a pawn. Apart from the fact that White can protect the pawn by 15 B–B1, Black's scheme must also be censured since it leaves him behind in development and hands over the initiative completely to his opponent.

| 15 | B–Q2! | |

This temporary pawn sacrifice is much stronger than 15 B–B1. Given that Black has already played 14 . . . Kt–Kt5, then, logically speaking, he must now continue with 15 . . . Q–Kt3.

15	. . .	Q–Kt3
16	R–K2	QxP
17	R–Kt1	Q–R6
18	RxP?	

White intends to play an enticing variation involving the sacrifice of two pieces for the Rook, but the consequences are far from clear. On the other hand the normal move 18 R–Kt3! would ensure White a clear advantage. In reply 18 . . . Q–B4 would not do because of 19 P–KR3, Kt–KB3; 20 B–K3! winning the Queen, and Black must content himself with 18 . . . Q–R4. Only then can White proceed with 19 RxP (19 . . . RxKt?; 20 R–Kt3!) with a clear advantage.

After the text-move a very complicated position arises with possibilities for both sides, and in such positions it is difficult to find the right line given the limited amount of time for thought.

18   . . .   RxKt

Obviously, Black must accept the sacrifice, since after 18 . . . Q–B4, White would obtain extremely strong pressure by 19 B–R4!, and that without making a sacrifice of material.

19   BxR   QxB
20   Q–Kt1 !

It was this position at which White was aiming with his 18th move, and then it seemed to him that 20 . . . Q–B1 was Black's best reply. To this I intended to reply 21 B–Q3, with the threat of 22 R(K2)–Kt2, after which Black has hardly anything better than 21 . . . B–KB1. Then would follow 22 R–B2, Q–Q1; 23 R(B2)–Kt2, B–Kt4; 24 BxB, PxB; 25 R(Kt2)xP, Kt–Q2; 26 P–KR3, KKt–KB3; 27 Kt–Q2, and White is probably a little better on account of his passed pawn and his actively placed pieces.

This was, in fact, Black's best defence and he should have played it. Instead of this Black hopes by the ensuing piece sacrifice to turn matters in his favour, but he has, however, overlooked the hidden possibility for his opponent on the 23rd move.

20   . . .   B–QKt4?

It was also here exceedingly difficult to foresee that a move so seemingly strong should turn out to be the decisive mistake. Black must, as already mentioned, play 20 . . . Q–B1.

21   RxB(K7)   K–B1
22   R–Kt7   BxR

This was the position that Black had envisaged on his 20th move. Now he had only reckoned with 23 RxKtch, RxR; 24 QxRch, K–K2; when the triple threat of 25 . . . QxB, 25 . . . BxKt, and 25 . . . Q–B4, would leave him with a clear advantage. White has, however, a cruel surprise in store that not only saves the situation but also soon ensures a won position.

23   Q–Kt6!

Black had completely overlooked this surprising continuation. However he plays now Black cannot avoid a decisive disadvantage.

23   . . .   Kt–QB3

Black could find nothing better after deep consideration, but there is no longer any adequate defence against the various threats. Here are some sample lines:

I. 23 . . . P–Kt3; 24 Q–Q8ch, K–Kt2; 25 RxPch!, KxR; 26 Kt–Kt5ch, K–Kt2; 27 Kt–K6ch and mates next move.

II. 23 . . . Q–B1; 24 R–B7, Q–K1; 25 Kt–Kt5 (very strong also is 25 Q–Kt7), 25 . . . Kt–R3; 26 QxPch, K–Kt1; 27 QxKP, and White wins since 27 . . . Q–KB1 can, as Belavienetz has observed, be met by 28 Kt–K6!.

III. 23 . . . Kt–Q2; 24 QxPch, K–Kt1; 25 QxKt, etc. with mating threats.

Black (Raud)

White (Keres) to play

24   Q–B7!

Naturally 24 QxKt would also have won, but the text-move is stronger and much prettier.

24   . . .   Kt–R3
25   QxQPch   K–Kt1

Also hopeless was 25 . . . Kt–K2; 26 QxKtch, K–Kt1; 27 Q–B7, etc.

26 PxKt!   K–R1

On account of the mating threat on QKt8 Black has no time to capture the Bishop. After the text-move White, who now has a pawn more, has naturally many ways of realising his advantage. The ensuing way is one of the clearest and simplest.

27 R–Kt8ch   RxR
28 QxRch   Kt–Kt1
29 P–B7!   B–Kt4

After 29 . . . QxB, Black would indeed threaten mate, but then would follow 30 P–KR4! and Black would no longer be able to contain the pawn, e.g.: 30 . . . Q–B8ch; 31 K–R2, Q–B5ch; 32 P–Kt3! and now 32 . . . QxKt is not possible because of 33 QxKtch!.

With the text-move Black threatens mate on QR8 and could, for instance, hold back the pawn by 30 . . . B–Q2. White, however, finds a way of forcing through the pawn.

30 Q–Q8!   QxB
31 K–R1

Also 31 P–KR4, Q–B8ch; 32 K–R2, Q–B5ch; 33 P–Kt3, QxKt; 34 QxKtch won easily, but White wants to bring about an amusing analogy—he protects himself against the threat of mate in the same extraordinary way in which his opponent had done on move 26.

Since Black no longer has any adequate defence against the threat of 32 P–B8=Q, he could now quietly resign.

31 . . .   P–B3
32 P–B8=Q   Q–Kt8ch
33 Kt–Kt1   QxRP
34 Q–KB8   resigns

The game is interesting on account of the richly combinative middle-game and the surprising lines of attack.

Game 18

RUY LOPEZ

Chess Olympiad in Stockholm, 1937

	P. Keres	S. Reshevsky
1	P–K4	P–K4
2	Kt–KB3	Kt–QB3
3	B–Kt5	P–QR3
4	B–R4	Kt–B3
5	O–O	B–K2
6	R–K1	P–QKt4
7	B–Kt3	P–Q3
8	P–B3	Kt–QR4

A more accurate sequence of moves here would be 8 ... O–O; and then Kt–QR4 after White has played 9 P–KR3. Black, by playing Kt–QR4 at once, leaves open too many possibilities to his opponent, one of which being that White can manage without playing the move P–KR3.

9	B–B2	P–B4
10	P–Q4	Q–B2
11	P–QR4!	

In this position, where Black has not yet castled, this thrust is awkward to meet and forces a marked weakness on the Queen-side. Black cannot now in fact continue 11 ... B–Q2, since this would cost a piece after 12 PxP, PxP?; 13 P–QKt4.

11	...	P–Kt5
12	PxKtP	PxKtP
13	P–R3	

This move was not necessary as Black was not immediately threatening B–Kt5. Better, therefore, was 13 QKt–Q2 at once.

13	...	O–O
14	QKt–Q2	B–K3

This development of the Bishop is more to the point than 14 ... B–Q2; 15 Kt–B1, KR–B1; 16 Kt–K3, which resulted in a clear advantage to White in the game Keres–Tylor,

Margate, 1937, after 16 . . . PxP; 17 KtxP, Kt–B3; 18 Kt(K3)–
B5!. On K3 the Bishop protects the important Q4 square and
allows thereby the ensuing counter-play with Kt–KR4.

15	Kt–B1	KR–B1
16	Kt–K3	P–Kt3

The passive defence 16 . . . Kt–K1; 17 P–QKt3, P–B3;
18 B–Kt2, B–B1; 19 B–Q3, led, in the game Keres–Berg,
Kemeri, 1937, to advantage for White. With the text-move
Black protects the point on KB4 where White might try to
break through and prepares to play Kt–R4. From there Black
can eventually penetrate with his Knight to KB5 and in addition the good square KB3 is made free for the Bishop and from
this point it can exert pressure on the White centre. The
struggle is coming to its climax.

17	P–QKt3	Kt–R4
18	B–Kt2	B–B3

This defence of the K4 point is much more aggressive than
the method chosen by Berg through P–B3.

19	R–QB1	PxP

The crisis of the middle-game is approaching, and therefore
both players must make a concrete plan of play. It is true that
this pawn exchange was criticised by a number of commentators, but what should Black have played? In any case 19 . . .
Kt–KB5 is inadequate since then White could present his opponent with serious difficulties by carrying out his main threat
20 Kt–Q5!.

In my opinion the exchange in the centre is in no way bad,
since, in the first place, Black thwarts further pressure against
his K4 by its means, in the second, he sets his opponent a
cunning trap and, in the third, he procures for himself chances
of active play for his pieces. Now the position becomes highly
interesting.

20	KtxP	

Had White here played 20 BxP; so as to weaken his opponent's King-side by an exchange of Bishops, then he would
have fallen into the cunning trap already mentioned. For
then would come 20 . . . KtxP!; for example: 21 BxKt, QxR;

22 QxQ, RxQ; 23 RxR, BxB(Kt6); when the attempt to win
a piece by 24 P–Kt4, fails against 24 . . . Kt–B5!

| | 20 . . . | Q–Q2 |

Black could, by 20 . . . Q–R2, renew the threat of 21 . . .
KtxP, but would then only succeed in putting his Queen in a
poor position. White would reply 21 B–R1, and would then
himself be threatening 22 KtxB, or 22 Kt–Kt4.

| 21 | R–Kt1 | R–B4 |
| 22 | Kt(Q4)–B5! | |

A pretty tactical stroke by which White hopes to eliminate
the chief defence of the enemy King-side, the KB. In addition,
Black must take steps to defend his Q3. Both players have
very little time left on the clock for the working out of the
ensuing complicated possibilities.

| | 22 . . . | BxKt? |

After the exchange of both Bishops Black remains in a most
dubious position, since both his Knights are badly placed on
the edge of the board and also have no point of support in the
centre. Much better chances are offered here by the quiet
protection of Q3 by 22 . . . B–K4!, after which White would
not find it easy to increase his initiative.

Black could, however, hardly have attained full equality
with this continuation as well. White could then play, for
instance, 23 B–Q4! and so force the exchange 23 . . . BxB, since
retiring the Rook would, as can readily be seen, lose the exchange. After 24 QxB, BxKt; 25 PxB, Kt–QB3, Black would
indeed win a tempo in comparison with the game continuation,
but White's advantage in position would be quite clear.

For the rest, Black cannot well accept the piece sacrifice,
since after 22 . . . PxKt; 23 PxP! (but not 23 QxKt, PxP; etc.)
23 . . . BxBP; 24 BxQB, RxB; 25 Q–Kt4ch, Kt–Kt2; 26 BxB,
would win. But if Black plays first 22 . . . BxB; 23 RxB, and only
then 23 . . . PxKt; there could follow 24 PxP, BxBP; 25 KtxB,
RxKt; 26 Q–Q3, Kt–Kt2; 27 P–Kt4 and wins.

| 23 | PxB | BxB |
| 24 | RxB | R–K1 |

Black has now beaten back the first wave of attack, but his

positional weaknesses still remain. The Knights are badly placed, the pawns on the Queen-side and in the centre are weak, and Black has no prospects of active counter-play. White, on the other hand, still possesses good attacking possibilities on both wings.

Meantime the finger on the clock had so far advanced that for the next 26 moves White had 20 minutes and Black only 10 left. It is, therefore, understandable that it is not so simple to find the correct method of play in such a complicated position with practically no time left for reflection.

25   B–Q3

The first inaccuracy, which allows Black the opportunity of activating his pieces. Much stronger here was 25 Q–Kt4, which threatened 26 PxP, as well as 26 QxP. After 25 . . . Q–Kt2 there could follow 26 Q–Q4! and Black would experience difficulties in protecting his QP.

25   . . .   Q–B3
26   Q–Kt4   Q–Kt3?

Black (Reshevsky)

White (Keres) to play

This passive defence by which Black removes his Queen far from the King-side is hopeless. Hence Black must utilise the opportunity for counter-attack with 26 . . . R–B6!, which would have set the opponent a number of tactical traps. Let us examine some of the possibilities:

I. 27 QxP, RxB; 28 QxKt, Kt–B5! and Black has excellent counter-play for the pawn with all his pieces taking up active positions.

II. 27 R–Q1, RxKt!; 28 PxR, RxB; 29 RxR, Q–B8ch; 30 K–R2, QxR; and Black, with two Knights against a Rook, has a good game.

III. 27 R–B2, RxR; 28 BxR, R–Kt; 29 RxR, QxB; 30 Q–Q4!, with a very strong attacking position for White. Black can, however, play better here 27 . . . Q–B4! threatening 28 . . . KtxP.

White could, nevertheless, retain the better position after 26 . . . R–B6 if he replied 27 B–B1!. Then Black cannot capture the pawn by 27 . . . RxP because of 28 RxR, KtxR; 29 PxP, RPxP; 30 B–B4! etc. He could, it is true, force the White Queen to retreat by 27 . . . R–K5; 28 Q–Q1, but even then his position would be worse on account of the numerous pawn weaknesses. After the text-move White's advantage takes on a particularly threatening character.

27   R(Kt2)–K2   R(B4)–K4

Perhaps Black hoped he had secured his position adequately with this move, but White demonstrates that the opposite is the case with the ensuing sacrifice.

28   PxP   RPxP
29   BxKtP!

This sacrifice is undoubtedly correct since by its means the remaining pawns protecting the Black King are destroyed and White obtains an overwhelming attack.

In addition White also gets sufficient compensation in material. When one also takes into consideration the time-trouble factor then it seems most improbable that Black can still successfully defend himself.

29   . . .   PxB
30   QxPch   K–R1?

A mistake that leads to immediate loss. 30 . . . Kt–Kt2 also would not do because of 31 Kt–B5!, Q–B2; 32 KtxKt, QxKt; 33 QxRch!, etc., but by 30 . . . K–B1! Black could still have put up a stubborn resistance. There could then

follow: 31 Kt–Q5!, Q–Q1 (an approximately similar endgame
also results from 31 ... Q–B4; 32 RxR, PxR; 33 Q–B5ch,
followed by 34 ... QxKt, or also 32 ... RxR; 33 RxR, PxR;
34 Q–B5ch, K–Kt1; 35 QxP, etc.); 32 RxR (after 32 QxKt,
RxQ; 33 RxRch, QxR; 34 RxQch, KxR; 35 Kt–B6ch, K–Q1;
36 KtxR, KtxP; the Black pawns on the Queen-side could
still prove dangerous), 32 ... RxR (or 32 ... PxR; 33 Q–B5ch,
followed by 34 QxKt); 33 RxR, PxR; 34 Q–B5ch, K–Kt1;
35 QxP!, and White should win the ending without much
trouble.

| | 31 | Kt–B5! | R(K1)–K3 |

Black no longer has anything better, since 32 QxKtch,
followed by mate was threatened. Now, however, White
finishes off the game.

32	QxKtch	K–Kt1
33	Q–Kt5ch	K–B1
34	Q–Kt7ch	K–K1
35	KtxPch	resigns

Black loses a whole Rook.

★ 3 ★

ON THE WAY TO THE GRANDMASTER TITLE
1937–1938

I WENT to the Semmering Grandmaster Tournament without
any special hopes of a great success, since with my comparatively small tournament experience I had no reason to
believe that I could successfully compete with such names as
Capablanca, Reshevsky, Fine, Flohr and others. I took as my
objective simply to play good chess and thus to occupy a satisfactory place in the final table. But already in the first round
I emerged badly from a position in which Flohr had exerted
positional pressure against me and soon had to surrender two
pieces for a Rook. Fortunately for me the counter-play I
obtained proved sufficient for a draw. In the second round,
too, I lost a pawn against Ragosin and managed only with
difficulty to get a draw. The third game against Fine produced
a quiet draw, whilst in the fourth I succeeded in outplaying
Petrov in a nerve-racking game and thus forcing a win.

So far my play was far from satisfactory and I became convinced that my chances would be very slim if I continued to
play in the same style. My opponents were superior to me in
quiet positional play, and therefore I decided to strive for much
more complications.

In the very next game, against Eliskases, I chose the notorious
gambit against the Sicilian–P–QKt4. Black, it is true, did
obtain a satisfactory middle-game in this encounter, but in
the succeeding whirlpool of combinations I was able to achieve
a decisive King-side attack (No. 19). The following game,
against Reshevsky, was a quiet positional struggle, and in this
I obtained one of the best of my endgame wins of my pre-war
tournament praxis (No. 20). This game showed that I had

also made clear progress in strictly positional play and also that I was already playing the endgame better, although I still felt very uncertain in this field. This particularly came to light in my next game against the ex-world champion, Capablanca. I succeeded in gaining the advantage in a complicated middle-game and then winning a pawn, but in the ensuing elementary endgame I played so uncertainly that the great endgame powers of Capablanca enabled him in the end to escape with a draw.

The first half of the tournament was over. To my own not inconsiderable astonishment I suddenly found myself in first place, a half a point ahead of Fine, whilst the other players were even further behind. This gave me fresh courage and energy, and in the next four rounds I played a series of my best games from the pre-war period. In the game against Flohr (No. 21) I gained the advantage by the most original and surprising attacking move of my tournament praxis (Kt–R7!); then I was able to refute the over-optimistic pawn sacrifice made by Ragosin (No. 22), and when, in the next round, Petrov was unable to find any adequate counter to White's pressure I had already the first prize in my pocket practically speaking. Three rounds before the end of the tournament, after I had drawn yet another extremely complicated game against Fine, my margin of advance above the next competitors had already grown to two points.

But even in this tournament a certain careless attitude towards the decisive games on my part could not quite be avoided. Nowadays I would have played the three remaining games, if not quietly, at least not for a win at all hazards. But what did I do then? In the next game Eliskases was obviously playing for the draw, but instead of falling in with this, I played in risky fashion for the win and soon I had to suffer my first loss in the tournament. After losing yet again in the next round, this time to Reshevsky, I had to draw with Capablanca in the last round in order not to let the first prize escape my grasp.

The Semmering tournament noticeably strengthened my position in the chess world and placed me amongst the leading grandmasters. At last I had attained the dream of all chess-masters—I was now accepted as one of the numerous family of international grandmasters. This position now had to be defended. It was necessary to show that I had not strayed by chance into this select company.

After the tournament I stayed for a long time in Holland, where I remained to watch the match between Alekhine and Euwe. When Euwe won the title in the year 1935 he wanted to hand over to F.I.D.E., the International Chess Organisation, the conduct of any further world championship matches and the choice of the suitable candidates for such matches. The result of these deliberations was the far-famed AVRO tournament. All the leading grandmasters of the world agreed to participate in this tournament, amongst them Alekhine, who had in the meantime regained the title. In addition to the world champion, invitations went to the grandmasters Botvinnik, Capablanca, Euwe, Fine, Flohr, Reshevsky and myself. The winner would have the right to a match with Alekhine.

Participation in such a tournament could be regarded as the dream of every chess-player and, moreover, in the event of a successful appearance in such a contest one could even attain a match for the world championship. So, once again it was necessary to decide on what lines a plan of further events should be drawn to form the best preparation for this great tournament.

This time I decided upon a different method from that which I had employed before the Semmering tournament. Since I had taken part in many tournaments in the year 1937 and, in consequence, found myself in satisfactory form from the sporting, competitive point of view, I decided not to play very much before the AVRO tournament. My first appearance as a newly-minted grandmaster was not bad, viz.: the sharing of second and third place with Alexander at Hastings. First prize was won by Reshevsky, but Fine, Flohr and others were below us. Then I played a training match with Grandmaster Stahlberg, which, after an interesting and lively course, ended in a friendly draw 4–4. In the fourth game of this match I succeeded in utilising a minimal endgame advantage for winning purposes. This showed that I had once again made some progress in the technical aspect of the game. The last serious test before the great tournament was the international tournament at Noordwijk. Here I gained second place below Eliskases, who rescued a difficult Rook ending in our game by an endgame study continuation. In this tournament I won my first tournament game against Euwe (No. 23), and the combinational struggle with Spielmann (No. 24) caused a considerable stir at the time in the chess world.

At last came the long-awaited moment when the eight best grandmasters of the world assembled in Holland in order to pick out the candidate for the match for the world championship against Alekhine. This tournament naturally aroused great interest throughout the chess world, in Estonia amongst other countries. For the first time in the chess history of Estonia a special reporter was sent to the tournament to keep our bigger daily papers informed as to the progress of the struggle.

The tournament began with a great surprise. Fine commenced in so dashing a style that it seemed quite hopeless for anyone to overtake him. After the sixth round he had obtained five points, one point ahead of his nearest rivals, and this with only eight games remaining to be played. I began this tournament, as I had at Semmering, in mediocre style. After I had saved a half-point in the first round in a difficult position against Euwe by an interesting tactical manoeuvre, I made in the next two rounds quick draws with Botvinnik and Flohr. After this came a victory over Reshevsky who fell into a trap in the very opening and lost a piece, and then a difficult defensive game against Alekhine. This game was adjourned in a position where Alekhine could have won by force, providing he had sealed the right move. Despite long consideration, however, Alekhine did not find the winning line, sealed another move and had, in the end, to content himself with a draw. I played one of my best games in this tournament against Capablanca (No. 25), although I committed some inaccuracies in the realisation of the positional advantage. And then there came in the seventh round my meeting with the leader of the tournament, Grandmaster Fine (No. 26).

This game turned out to be one of the most interesting of the tournament and played a far from unimportant role in determining the eventual placings of the contest. I defended a

Ruy Lopez and Fine chose a rarely used variation. I was able to employ an interesting method of defence that, however, as was later discovered, had already been played before. It was apparently a surprise for Fine since he missed the right path and allowed me to reach a won ending by an exchange sacrifice. Time trouble on both sides and a great nervous tension resulted in a number of inaccuracies in this ending, but when the game was at last adjourned the win no longer provided any difficulties for Black.

With this important victory I came up to within half a point of Fine and now I decided to play more cautiously in the second half of the tournament. I made four draws in succession and as, meanwhile, Fine had lost to Reshevsky and Euwe I found myself, surprisingly enough, at the head of the table. Botvinnik had greatly bettered his tournament position since he had won against Capablanca and thus overhauled Fine. But there remained only three rounds to be played.

The next, and twelfth round, proved to be the decisive one. In the first place, Botvinnik committed a gross blunder against Euwe, lost the game and thus, for all practical purposes, disappeared from the struggle for first prize. Flohr and Fine produced a quick draw, whilst I had to fight out a difficult positional struggle with Alekhine. In this game I chose to play in seemingly risky fashion for a win in the middle-game, and in fact I did succeed in winning two pawns and adjourning the game in a won position. Apparently with this the struggle was over, since in the event of a victory over Alekhine I would have held a lead of one full point over Fine and we had to play each other in one of the two remaining games. In the other game Fine had Alekhine and I had Capablanca as an opponent.

But now once again, as so often before, I took the task confronting me in unforgivably light fashion. I was so convinced of an easy win that I did not even bother to look at my adjourned position against Alekhine. In consequence, with Alekhine devoting all his great defensive powers to the ending, once I had lost the right way, then there happened what often occurs in such cases—the position gradually evened out and the game ended in a draw. But this was not the end of my

ill-fortune. I drew my next game against Capablanca, but
Fine destroyed Alekhine's position in unexpectedly easy style
and thus, by the time the last round came we were once again
equal in points. In the event of a tie for first prize the Sonneborn-Berger system was due to be used and this was in my
favour owing to my wins against my chief rivals. Therefore
in the last round against Fine I made a quick draw.

So I shared first and second prizes with Fine, but obtained
the right to challenge the world-champion, Alekhine, to a
match for the title. I had made a giant step forward on the
road of my chess career and was now very near indeed to the
highest point that a chess-master can reach. All this had cost
me colossal energy and a great nervous and physical strain.
But there was no question of rest. The chess enthusiasts of
my native land were understandably stirred by the result, and
one reception followed on another. This, in turn, meant
appearances in various cities. And so sped by the couple of
weeks before the next event, the Training tournament at Leningrad-Moscow, without my being allowed the necessary repose,
not to mention any fresh preparation for play.

Game 19

SICILIAN DEFENCE

International Tournament at Semmering, 1937

	P. Keres	E. Eliskases
1	P–K4	P–QB4
2	Kt–KB3	P–Q3
3	P–QKt4	

Eliskases is well-known as a good positional player who
prefers quiet positions in which strategy dominates over tactics.
Therefore in this game I played from the very beginning for
great tactical complications. Of course I would not claim that
the pawn sacrifice offered by the text-move is wholly correct,
but in this does not lie, in my opinion, the heart of the matter.
One can only find a definitive conclusion about the correctness
of such a sacrifice by exhaustive private analysis, whereas over

the chess-board Black has to defend himself in a complicated position which does not really suit his taste.

3 . . .   PxP

This game subsequently aroused considerable discussion amongst many commentators. The champions of the combinational style of play were delighted that so vigorous and risky a type of play could also occur in games between grandmasters. Others, on the contrary, maintained that White's play was chiefly based on bluff and that Black could have obtained a clear advantage for practically the whole game. In my opinion the truth lies somewhere in a compromise solution. It is naturally difficult to demonstrate the correctness of the White pawn sacrifice in clear-cut variations, but on the other hand it is likewise not so easy to conduct the Black defence as the further course of this game shows to perfection.

Afterwards, Black's method of play throughout almost all the game came under criticism which began already with the text-move in that it was held that 3 . . . Kt–KB3 was simpler. I take, however, the liberty of claiming that the gambit continuation P–QKt4 would appear much more often in tournaments if in reply 3 . . . Kt–KB3 were the best answer.

4   P–Q4   Kt–KB3
5   B–Q3   P–Q4

In later games when I tried this gambit line again, Black usually defended himself with 5 . . . P–KKt3 followed by 6 . . . B–Kt2. Perhaps this system is more logical, since the opening up of the centre which is bound up with the text-move can only be of use to the better-developed side—White—but on the other hand by its means Black demolishes the opponent's powerful pawn centre.

6   QKt–Q2   PxP
7   KtxP   QKt–Q2

This normal development move was criticised by many people and instead 7 . . . KtxKt; 8 BxKt, Kt–Q2 was recommended. It goes without saying that Black can also play this way, but whether he would have fared better is not so certain. White could, for example, have replied 9 P–B4!, and would

have retained considerable initiative after 9 . . . PxP e.p.; 10
Q–Kt3, or after 9 . . . Kt–B3; 10 B–B2.

8   Kt(K4)–Kt5

White continues play in the way that prepares the most
unpleasantness for his opponent. After 8 O–O, KtxKt; 9 BxKt,
Kt–B3; 10 B–Q3, P–K3; 11 Kt–K5, White would, too, have
a certain compensation for the pawn, but the position would
lead to a quiet type of positional play that would specially suit
Eliskases.

In addition to the text-move 8 P–B4, PxP e.p.; 9 Q–Kt3
also came into consideration and this likewise would have led
to a lively and interesting position.

8 . . .   Q–B2

The question as to whether, after 8 . . . P–KR3, the possible
piece sacrifice 9 KtxP, KxKt; 10 Kt–K5ch, KtxKt; 11 PxKt
is correct or not, did not particularly concern me during the
course of the game. I intended, after 8 . . . P–KR3, to reply
simply 9 Kt–K6, Q–Kt3; 10 KtxB, followed by 11 O–O.

9   P–B4

Thus White obtains a strong pawn centre, since he has
utilised the tactical possibility of 9 . . . PxP e.p.; 10 Q–Kt3,
P–K3; 11 KtxP! Black can now make use of the unfavourable
position of the Knight on Kt5 to complete the development
of his King's wing with gain of tempo.

9 . . .   P–KR3
10   Kt–R3   P–KKt4

For this move, too, Eliskases was criticised by a number of
commentators, whereas others held this advance to be quite
correct. Naturally in considering this move each person's taste
plays a great role. It seems to me that 10 . . . P–KKt4 is no
bad move, at any rate not weaker than, for instance, 10 . . .
P–K3. Black now threatens 11 . . . P–Kt5; forces his opponent
in this way to lose more time, and can himself in the meantime
complete his development. That White wins the square KB5
for his pieces in the ensuing play is the lesser evil, since, in
order to occupy it, White must lose yet more valuable time.

11   Kt(R3)–Kt1!

Out of the eleven moves, White has made no less than five with this Knight, and the result of all this is that the piece has moved from one original Knight position to another! But nevertheless White has a more or less satisfactory position, since Black, too, has been unable to undertake anything in the meantime to strengthen his position to any marked degree.

	11 . . .	B–Kt2
	12 Kt–K2	P–K4

Black must undertake this advance so as to break up the enemy centre, since otherwise his previous play would be without any logical basis. But now, however, White obtains counter-play through Black's weakness on KB4.

13 Kt–Kt3

White's Queen's Knight displays quite astonishing activity in this game. It now has to its account seven moves out of the thirteen made.

	13 . . .	O–O
	14 O–O	P–K5!

Very well played. In the first place Black liquidates the opposing pawn centre with this thrust; in the second he diverts the Knight from the KB5 square, and in the third he assures his pieces the strong supporting square on Q4. Weaker would have been 14 . . . PxP; when, in addition to 15 Kt–B5, Kt–K4; 16 KtxB, etc. White could also very well play 15 P–KR4!, P–Kt5; 16 KtxP.

	15 KtxKP	KtxKt
	16 BxKt	QxP
	17 B–Q3	

White is still a pawn down, but in compensation he possesses, in addition to the better development, an advantage in the centre and on the King's wing. With the text-move he begins a bold plan to increase his attacking chances by sacrificing the centre pawn on Q4. This idea is absolutely valid, since, for example, after 17 B–K3, Kt–B3, Black would arrive at full control of the important central square Q4, and this White must prevent at all costs.

17 ...   Q–Q4
18 R–K1   P–Kt5

Yet another position in which Eliskases had to incur criticism
from many quarters. With the text-move Black's King's position is further weakened and the White Knight reaches the
important KB5 square. However, with the thrust 18 ... P–Kt5
not only is the Queen's pawn attacked but also the White
Knight is turned away from K5. For example, after 18 ...
Kt–B3; 19 Kt–K5, or 18 ... Kt–Kt3; 19 P–KR4!, P–Kt5;
20 Kt–K5, etc. Black's King would be in considerable trouble.
As can be seen, Black still does not find it easy to solve the
problem of the development of his Queen's wing.

                    19   Kt–R4!

Naturally not 19 Kt–K5, KtxKt; 20 PxKt, B–K3 when
Black is excellently placed. The pawn sacrifice offered by the
text-move calls up new and great complications.

Black (Eliskases) to play

White (Keres)

19 ...   Kt–Kt3

After long reflection Eliskases declines to accept the pawn
sacrifice by 19 ... QxQP. White would not then play to win
the exchange, since after 20 R–Kt1, Kt–B4; 21 B–K3, QxKB;
22 BxKt, QxQ (but not 22 ... R–Q1?; 23 R–K8ch!); 23
QRxQ, Black would obtain an excellent position by 23 ...
B–K3! During the game I had in mind the keen attacking
line 20 Kt–B5!, QxR; 21 QxP.

This position became a repeated and controversial subject for analytical discussion amongst a number of commentators. First of all, Euwe claimed that White obtained a decisive attack after 21 ... Kt–B4; 22 KtxPch, K–R1; 23 Q–R5. It was also pointed out that 21 ... Q–B3; 22 BxP, Kt–K4; 23 Kt–K7ch! or 21 ... R–Q1; 22 KtxPch, K–B1; 23 QxPch would not rescue Black from a loss.

Then Riumin discovered that Black had a better defence in 21 ... K–R1!, and that in this way he could obtain an advantage. As demonstration of his idea Riumin adduced the following complicated main variation: 22 KtxB, Q–B6! (or 22 ... QxKt; 23 Q–R4!) 23 Kt–B5, QxRch; 24 B–B1, R–KKt1 (after 24 ... Q–K4; follows 25 BxP, R–KKt1; 26 Q–R5! etc.); 25 B–Kt2ch, K–R2 (weaker would be 25 ... Kt–K4; 26 Q–KB4, or 25 ... P–B3; 26 Q–R5! etc.); 26 Q–R5, R–Kt3 (26 ... Q–K3 allows the reply 27 KtxP!); 27 KtxP, Kt–B3; 28 BxKt, RxB; 29 Kt–B5 dis ch, K–Kt1; 30 Q–Kt5ch, K–B1; 31 Q–Kt7ch, K–K1; 32 Q–R8ch, K–Q2; 33 QxR, Q–K3 and Black retains some winning chances in the endgame.

Accepting that this analysis is without flaw, then it provides us with a characteristic picture of the dangerous nature of White's attack. Therefore it is quite logical and easy to understand that Black desists from this unfathomable and unclear turn of events in favour of a quieter method of play, and one by which he obtains a thoroughly satisfactory position.

However, turning once again to Riumin's analysis, we find in it some debatable points. Thus, for example, the very first move provokes well grounded doubts, since instead of 22 KtxB, serious consideration should be given to 22 KtxP! Black cannot well take this Knight since after 22 ... BxKt; 23 Q–R4, K–Kt1 (or 23 ... Q–B3; 24 B–Kt2!); 24 QxB, Q–Kt2; 25 Q–R4! yields White an overwhelming attack. For example, there could follow 25 ... Kt–B4; 26 B–Kt2!, P–B3; 27 B–B4ch, B–K3; 28 RxB, KtxR; 29 BxKtch, R–B2; 30 BxP, and White wins.

Also lines such as 22 ... Q–B3; 23 Q–R5, or 22 ... Kt–B3; 23 Q–R4, or 22 ... Q–Q5; 23 Q–R3, give White a decisive attack. So Black is left only with the defence 22 ... Q–B6, but then White has at least a draw. He can continue with 23

KtxPch (23 . . . RxKt; 24 Q–R4ch), or with 23 Kt–B5!,
QxRch; 24 B–B1 (24 . . . Q–K4; 25 B–Kt2!), and is sure of
at least perpetual check in both cases.

20	R–Kt1	B–Q2
21	R–K4?	

It is not clear to me, to this very day, why I refrained here
from the capture 21 RxP, by which White would have restored
the balance of material and would certainly not have the worse
position. The attempt begun by the text-move to bring about
further complications is very risky and has little positional
basis.

                21 . . .   KR–K1

At first glance the incursion of the Knight by 21 . . . Kt–R5
appears to be very strong since after 22 B–Q2, Kt–B6; 23
BxKt, PxB Black clearly stands better. But in this case White
has a combinational resource in 22 RxKKtP! If then 22 . . .
BxR, White, after 23 QxB, has a fine attacking position as
compensation for the exchange. But if Black plays 23 . . .
Kt–B6, there comes the surprise 23 BxP!, and after 23 . . .
KtxQ; 24 RxBch, White has made sure of perpetual check,

22	R–B4	Q–Q3

Both sides are by now a little fatigued by the tense middle-
game and for this reason a crop of inaccuracies spring up in
the ensuing play. With the text-move Black has the intention
of getting his Knight into play with gain of tempo via Q4,
and this, by itself, is a very good plan. But he could also set
his opponent some very awkward problems by 22 . . . Kt–R5!,
threatening 23 Kt–B6. If now 23 RxQKtP, then 23 . . . Kt–B6;
24 Q–B1 (after 24 Q–Q2, the reply 24 . . . QR–B1!, threatening
25 . . . Kt–K7ch or 25 . . . KtxP, is very strong), 24 . . . KtxP,
and Black obtains a most dangerous attack after 25 B–B4,
KtxR; 26 BxQ, KtxB; 27 R–B5, B–Kt4! Or if White plays
in this variation 27 P–R3, then Black's advantage in material
after 27 . . . KtxR; 28 BxKt should be enough for a win despite
his somewhat weakened King's position.

But White could also initiate really dangerous counter-play
after 22 . . . Kt–R5 by continuing 23 B–Q2! After 23 . . . Kt–
B6; 24 BxKt, PxB, White plays 25 B–B2!, thereby obtaining

the threats of 26 B–Kt3, and 26 Q–Q3. Although Black now has a pawn more, he can hardly hope to make use of this advantage since the weakened Black King's position affords the opportunities for the creation of dangerous threats.

23 B–Q2   Kt–Q4
24 RxKKtP!

Of course White makes use of the first opportunity to attack the enemy King. The exchange sacrifice is naturally absolutely correct, since after its acceptance White gains the square KB5 for his pieces and obtains a wonderful attacking position.

24 . . .   BxR?

Now it is Black's turn to make a mistake, and this time one with the most serious consequences. Black should on no account give up his best defensive piece, not even for a Rook. He should by all means carry out the second half of his plan and play 24 . . . Kt–B6! 25 BxKt, PxB (but not 25 . . . BxR; 26 QxB, PxB; 27 QxBch!).

In this position White can continue 26 Kt–B5, BxKt; 27 BxB, or also 26 B–B5, QR–B1; 27 Q–B2, and try to gain control of the square KB5. Then White's tactical chances, which are mainly based on the weakened enemy King's position, should enable him to neutralize the power of the enemy passed pawn on QB6.

25 QxB   Q–KB3

White was threatening, in addition to 26 Kt–B5, also 26 QxBch!

26 Kt–B5   K–B1

No better would be 26 . . . K–R1; 27 Q–R5, Q–KKt3; 28 Q–R3, etc.

27 KtxB!

Once White has eliminated the strong defensive Bishop of his opponent, he soon obtains a decisive attack.

27 . . .   QxKt
28 Q–R5   Kt–B3
29 Q–R4   P–KR4

29 . . . Kt–Kt1 was no better. White could reply 30 BxPch, Kt–K2; 31 B–Kt5, winning the exchange back at once.

30	RxP	QR–B1
31	P–KR3!	

White need not be in a hurry, since his opponent cannot
do anything anyway. With the text-move he protects himself
against possible counter-attacks such as R–B8ch or Q–Kt5 and
himself threatens simply 32 RxP.

31	. . .	R–B2
32	R–Kt5	R–K3

Parrying the threat of 33 B–Kt4ch, followed by 34 R–Kt5,
but nevertheless allowing quite another decisive line.

33	RxRP!	resigns

After 33 . . . KtxR; 34 Q–Q8ch, R–K1; 35 B–Kt4ch, mate
follows in a few moves.

Game 20

Q.P. QUEEN'S INDIAN DEFENCE

International Tournament at Semmering, 1937

	S. Reshevsky	P. Keres
1	Kt–KB3	Kt–KB3
2	P–Q4	P–K3
3	P–B4	P–QKt3
4	P–KKt3	B–Kt2
5	B–Kt2	B–Kt5ch

Usually 5 . . . B–K2 is played here, since with the text-move
Black makes his opponent a present of a valuable tempo in
development. On the other hand, through the exchange of
Bishops, Black's situation, in which he has allowed his opponent
some advantage in space, becomes somewhat less difficult.
Providing that Black is not pursuing too high an aim and is
only striving for equality, then the text-variation offers him
very good prospects of achieving this last goal.

6	B–Q2	BxBch

Nimzowitsch often played 6 . . . Q–K2 here, but this move
has no individual importance. White replies 7 O–O, upon

which Black must exchange on Q2 just the same, since after
7 ... O–O; 8 B–B4, his Bishop would be in a dangerous
plight on QKt5.

| | 7 | QxB | O–O |

Here the interesting possibility of 7 ... P–Q3; 8 Kt–B3,
Kt–K5? should be mentioned. Normally this sally with the
Knight is the best method of meeting White's Kt–QB3, but
here it proves to be a mistake and yields White a clear opening
advantage after 9 Q–B4! (9 ... KtxKt?; 10 Kt–Kt5!).

| | 8 | O–O | |

A more accurate sequence of moves, so as to force through
P–K4, is 8 Kt–B3, with the further intention of 9 Q–B2. If
Black seeks to thwart this plan by playing 8 ... Kt–K5, then
he is forced to concede White the exchange after 9 Q–B2,
KtxKt; 10 Kt–Kt5!: then comes 10 ... Kt–K5; 11 BxKt,
BxB; 12 QxB, QxKt; 13 QxR, Kt–B3; 14 Q–Kt7, KtxP. This
line occurred in the tenth game of the Euwe-Capablanca
match, 1931. Subsequent analysis showed that by the pawn
sacrifice 15 O–O!, KtxPch; 16 K–Kt2, White retains the better
chances here, since Black experiences difficulties in protecting
his Queen-side.

| | 8 | ... | P–Q3 |
| | 9 | Q–B2 | |

Had White played 9 Kt–B3 here then Black could have
quietly replied 9 ... Kt–K5, since a continuation analogous
to that in the preceding note 10 Q–B2, KtxKt; 11 Kt–Kt5
fails because of 11 ... KtxPch!

| | 9 | ... | QKt–Q2 |

Black fails to take advantage of his opponent's inaccurate
8th move. By 9 ... B–K5; 10 Q–Kt3, Kt–B3! he could have
successfully dealt with the threatened advance of P–K4 and
reached an approximately equal position. After the text-move
White can force through his P–K4 and then, by reason of his
greater control of space, obtains rather the better position.

| | 10 | Kt–B3 | Q–K2 |
| | 11 | P–K4 | QR–B1! |

Black has fallen into a constricted position without prospects of active counter-play. He must, therefore, assume a kind of waiting pose so as to wait for any further enemy plans. The Rook move is a good prophylactic measure. Black has in mind to carry out the central advance P–K4, and then, should White reply P–Q5, or also Kt–Q5, KtxKt; BPxKt, the posting of the Rook on QB1 facilitates immediate counter-play by P–QB3.

	12	KR–K1	P–K4
	13	QR–Q1	

The idea behind Black's 11th move can best be seen in the variation 13 Kt–Q5, KtxKt; 14 BPxKt, P–QB3! with which Black attains good counter-play on the QB file. Hence, White does not want to make a definitive plan of campaign as yet and first completes his development, retaining the rather better position owing to his advantage in space. This plan is naturally very good and suits the nature of the position since, in the meantime, Black cannot in any case undertake anything active.

	13	. . .	P–B3
	14	Q–R4	

White naturally has the better position and he must at long last construct a concrete plan so as to realise his advantage in some way. The manoeuvre on the Queen-side commenced by the text-move, however, proves to be unfitting for the purpose and at best imports a loss in time for White. In fact, he has at least three good plans which would have posed Black some difficult problems.

Firstly 14 P–QKt4 came into consideration here. White could then continue with 15 Q–Kt3, and a pawn attack on the Queen-side, and against this Black, with his passively placed pieces, would experience difficulty in finding an adequate defence.

Secondly here 14 Kt–KR4, P–Kt3; 15 Q–Q2! would be very strong, threatening as it does to transfer the Queen to the King-side followed by an eventual P–B4. And thirdly, simply doubling the Rooks on the Q file, eventually followed by B–R3, deserved earnest consideration.

Naturally White could also return later to one of these plans, since Black can hardly make use of the time he has gained in the interim to better his position to any marked extent.

14	...	R–B2
15	Q–R3	R–K1
16	P–Kt3	P–Kt3
17	PxP?	

White can find no suitable way to increase his positional advantage and therefore decides to come down to an ending in which he hopes to make use of his control of the only open file. This plan, however, turns out to be mistaken. Firstly because every exchange only helps the constricted Black position, and secondly because the control of the Q file constitutes only a theoretical advantage as Black can adequately protect all the squares along which the White forces might try to penetrate.

The disadvantage of this exchange lies, however, not solely in the circumstance that in so playing White surrenders bit by bit his positional advantage. Much more important is the circumstance that Black in the ensuing phase of the game is able to make his pieces fully active and that afterwards he obtains excellent counter-play on account of White's weakness on Q4. The fact that White underestimates this possibility for his opponent in the ensuing moves and also continues to "play for a win" eventually proves fatal for him in the ending that approaches.

It is clear that White, instead of this exchange, should choose one of the plans that we have mentioned in the note to move 14. In that case he would have had every prospect of increasing his small positional advantage bit by bit.

17	...	PxP
18	QxQ	RxQ
19	B–R3	B–B1
20	P–QKt4	

With this move White shows that he still reckons his position to be better, whereas in actual fact Black's chances are by now not worse than White's. The attack planned on the Queen-side does not hold out any prospect of success for White and merely creates fresh weaknesses there and these in turn become most awkward for White later on. A better plan, therefore, was the quiet continuation 20 R–K2, with the idea of Kt–K1, P–B3, Kt–B2 and R(K2)–Q2 after which the position would soon equalise out.

White, by continuing to play obstinately for a win, merely seriously disturbs his own position.

20	. . .	Kt–B1
21	BxB	RxB
22	R–Q6	

White wants to double his Rooks on the Q file but with the text-move he makes his opponent a present of an important tempo for the regrouping of his forces. Better was 22 R–K2, and, as soon as possible, Kt–K1–B2.

22	. . .	Kt–K1
23	R–Q3	P–B3
24	R(K1)–Q1	K–B2
25	P–QR4	

Here we can already see clearly what White has attained by his descent into the endgame on his 17th move. He does, indeed, control the Q file, but his Rooks cannot penetrate anywhere from that line. An attacking plan holding out prospects of success is also difficult to find on the Q wing. In contrast, Black's plan of campaign is straightforward and logical and, in addition, most effective. First of all he wants to exchange off a Rook, so as to weaken the pressure on the Q file to some extent, at any rate. Next, attention is turned to the outpost on Q5, for which purpose the Knight is to be brought to K3. We can already incline towards the idea that Black's chances are to be rated rather higher than White's.

It should not be thought, however, that White is already in real difficulties. The position is still level, and if White, instead of the "attacking" move 25 P–QR4, had continued here, for example, with 25 Kt–K1–B2 followed by P–B3 and K–B2–K3, then a draw would have been the probable result. The reason for White's subsequent difficulties lies in this; that he still believes he stands better and must strive for attacking chances on the Q wing, whereas in reality he ought to pay more attention to the defence of his own position.

25 . . .   K–K3

Now White can no longer prevent the exchange of one pair
of Rooks. The ensuing manoeuvre merely puts off this operation for a couple of moves.

26 R–Q8   R(K2)–QB2
27 K–B1   K–K2
28 R(Q8)-Q3   R–Q2

With this Black has obtained his first objective—one pair of
Rooks are exchanged. In the distance, however, we can already
perceive the further perspectives of Black's game, above all,
the positioning of the Knights on K3 and Q3. One of these
pieces aims at occupying the important outpost on Q5, whilst
the other will attack the pawns on K5 and QB5 and it should
be observed that it is very difficult for White to defend his
QBP satisfactorily. From this it becomes apparent that the
preceding pawn advances on White's Q wing have only
weakened him on that side. Already White must contend
with difficulties from which he is never free right to the end of
the game.

29 RxRch   KtxR
30 K–K2

In order to achieve positional equality White must carry
out the pawn advance to QKt5, and so seize hold of the outpost on Q5 for his own pieces as compensation for the one on
Black's Q5. This advance, however, cannot be carried out so
quickly in practice, since after 30 P–Kt5 Black can, in the first
place, gain control of the important QB file by the pawn
exchange 30 . . . PxP, and in the second he can leave the
situation as it stands and allow White to exchange on QB6
himself, when the pawn on QB4 will become hopelessly weak.
Since, too, 30 P–R5 would lead to a clear advantage for Black
after 30 . . . PxP; 31 PxP, R–Kt1 followed by Kt–B4, White
is condemned to play a waiting game. This, however, shows
that the initiative has already passed into Black's hands and
the latter systematically strengthens his position with the ensuing moves.

30 . . .   Kt–Q3
31 Kt–Q2   Kt–B1!

This Knight is aimed at K3 where it will assume a dominating position. White's attempt to arrive at counter-play in the next phase of the game does not lead to the wished-for success.

32   R–QR1   Kt–K3
33   P–R5   P–QKt4!

Of course Black does not allow the opening up of the QR file, which would have afforded White good counter-play. After the text-move White appears to attain his long-awaited goal—the occupation of Q5 by his Knight.

34   PxP   Kt–Q5ch!

This intervening check destroys White's hopes which were bound up with the variation 34 . . . PxP; 35 Kt–Q5ch, K–B2; 36 K–Q3, etc.

35   K–Q3   PxP
36   R–QB1

Now it suddenly becomes apparent that it will not be so easy for White to gain possession of the outpost on Q5, since after 36 Kt–Q5ch, K–K3 his Knight is insecurely placed owing to the threats of R–B7 and RxKtch and also of P–KB4. With the text-move White threatens to simplify the position still more, but this Black does not permit. In fact he takes advantage of the pin on the QB file to increase his positional advantage.

However, White was already in a very uncomfortable position, and one cannot see how he could put up a noticeably better defence. After 36 P–B4, hoping for the variation 36 . . . K–K3; 37 PxP, PxP; 38 R–KB1, etc., Black has two possible ways of increasing his advantage. Firstly 36 . . . K–K3; 37 PxP, KxP!, or, secondly, 36 . . . Kt–B3; 37 Kt–Q5ch, K–K3; etc.

36   . . .   K–K3
37   Kt–K2   Kt–B3!

With this move Black forces the enemy Rook to occupy a passive position on the QKt file and gains still greater activity for his own pieces. It is interesting to observe that the position offers excellent Knight outposts for both sides (for White his QB5 and Q5 and for Black his QB5 and Q5). But the White

Knights are never able to reach these squares throughout the whole endgame, whereas their Black counterparts take up practically ideal positions. A similar picture prevails with regard to the Rooks. White's must content itself with the protection of the QKt pawn whilst Black's is in full control of both the open lines. Hence it is no wonder that Black's positional pressure soon begins to manifest itself in really concrete results.

38   R–QKt1   R–Q1 !

Driving the White King from the centre, since 39 K–K3, Kt–B5ch; 40 KtxKt, PxKt would lead to an easily won ending for Black.

39   K–B3   P–B4 !

With this the support point on K4 is liquidated and Black now obtains the superiority in the centre as well. An attempt to protect this point by 40 P–B3 would not succeed since after 40 . . . PxP; 41 PxP (or 41 KtxP, KtxKtch; 42 PxKt, R–KB1, etc.), 41 . . . R–KB1 the Black Rook has a decisive effect on the KB file (42 R–KB1, KtxPch!). Therefore the ensuing exchange is practically forced.

40   PxPch   PxP
41   P–B3   R–QB1

The manoeuvres with the Black Rook are very interesting and instructive. Now White's King must abandon the protection of the QKtP and leave this task to the Rook.

42   K–Q3   Kt–K1 !

This Knight now gets to Q4 via B3, thereby attacking the QKtP once again. White's position is already critical.

43   Kt–B3

An attempt to obtain new outposts in the centre by 43 P–Kt4 leads to loss in material after 43 . . . R–Q1ch!; 44 K–B3 or B2, PxP; 45 PxP, Kt–B3 threatening either KtxP or Kt–Q4.

43   . . .   Kt–B3 !

A surprising reply but one which is, however, based on good logical grounds. After 44 KtxP, there would follow 44 . . . Kt–Q4 with the threat of 45 . . . Kt(B3)xPch; 46 K–K2, P–

QR3; and 47 . . . Kt–B6ch, winning the Rook. White has no good defence against this threat, e.g.: 45 R–Kt3, P–QR3; 46 Kt–R3, Kt(B3)xPch; 47 K–K2, R–B8 and Black's Rook penetrates into the White position with decisive effect.

White therefore refrains from playing this variation and intends to wait until Black has played his P–QR3. He has prepared a pawn sacrifice for this eventuality that affords him good saving chances.

| 44 | R–Kt2 | P–QR3 |
| 45 | P–Kt4 | |

White's situation is grave. He is completely bereft of active counter-play and must therefore wait to see how Black intends to strengthen his position. But, in the position that has now arisen, this is no longer difficult. Against a passive resistance Black can, for example, continue with P–R4–R5 and after that penetrate the K side with his Rook, or, at the indicated moment, he can execute the advantageous exchange of Kt–Q4, KtxKt; KxKt. It is clear that passive tactics no longer suffice to hold the position.

So as not to surrender without a struggle White makes a pawn sacrifice with the text-move. After its acceptance by 45 . . . PxP; 46 PxP, KtxP White hopes to obtain counter-play by 47 Kt(Q2)–K4!, threatening 48 Kt–B5ch. It should be observed that in this variation, too, Black would retain sufficient advantage for winning purposes, for example, after 47 . . .

Black (Keres) to play

White (Reshevsky)

R–Q1ch followed by 48 . . . K–B4 and an eventual 49 . . . R–Q3. But, in any case, this would allow White active counter-play and this is exactly what Black wants to prevent.

| 45 . . . | P–K5ch! |

This continuation is, in my opinion, more convincing than the win of a pawn as given in the variation above. Black now obtains the pawn majority on the King's wing by force, com-pletely blockades the enemy pawn on K4 and keeps the enemy pieces in passive positions just as much as before. The ensuing ending is won without much difficulty.

| 46   PxP |

Forced, since 46 K–B2, Kt–Q5ch loses a Knight and the variation 46 K–K2, Kt–Q5ch; 47 K–K3, RxKtch; 48 KxKt, R–Q6ch; 49 K–B5, R–Q3; 50 PxPch, K–K2 leads to mate. After 46 K–K3, Black assures himself of a marked advantage in every variation by 46 . . . Kt–K2.

| 46 . . . | Kt–K4ch |
| 47   K–B2 | PxKtP |

Now we can see what exactly Black has achieved by the combination begun on his 45th move. White's pieces are posted ineffectively on the Q wing, whereas on the other wing Black threatens to procure a speedily decisive passed pawn by P–R4–5. In addition his Knights and King are very actively stationed in the centre, whilst White's pieces have no chance of showing any activity in the near future.

| 48   K–Kt3 | Kt–B5! |

Vacating the strong post of K4 for Black's King and so winning, in practice, the pawn on the K file. For this reason the line chosen is simpler than 48 . . . P–R4; 49 Kt–K2.

| 49 KtxKt. |

Once again, a forced move, since after 49 R–B2, KtxKtch; 50 RxKt, Black wins at once by 50 . . . RxKtch!; 51 KxR, KtxPch followed by KtxR.

| 49 . . . | RxKt |
| 50   R–K2 |

White is unable to penetrate the enemy camp at all quickly with his Rook, since 50 R–Q2 or 50 R–KB2 fail against 50 . . . RxKtch. The ending is hopeless by now.

	50 . . .	K–K4
	51 R–K1	P–R4!

Black need not hurry to capture the KP as it will not run away. With the text-move he prepares to obtain a passed pawn on the K wing, and this will rapidly decide the game.

	52 R–Q1	P–R5
	53 R–Q8	P–Kt6!

Naturally here there were many ways of winning but the method chosen is one of the prettiest. There follow some more combinational touches.

	54 PxP	PxP
	55 R–Q3	

After 55 Kt–K2, Black can win by either 55 . . . P–Kt7 or 55 . . . RxP, and 55 R–Q1 is naturally hopeless because of 55 . . . KtxP.

	55 . . .	P–Kt7!

The idea of this move becomes apparent in the variation 56 R–Kt3, RxKtch!; 57 KxR, KtxPch. After 56 R–Q1, Black would win by 56 . . . KtxP.

	56 Kt–K2	RxP
	57 Kt–Kt1	R–K8!
	White resigns	

After 58 Kt–B3ch, K–K5; 59 KtxR, there comes, of course, 59 . . . P–Kt8 = Q. In this game I played one of my best endings from the pre-war period.

Game 21

Q.P. GRUNFELD DEFENCE

International Tournament at Semmering, 1937

	P. Keres	S. Flohr
	1 P–Q4	Kt–KB3
	2 P–QB4	P–KKt3
	3 Kt–KB3	B–Kt2
	4 P–KKt3	P–B3

If Black is seeking for speedy equality then the text-move is admirably designed for the purpose and usually leads to symmetrical positions. But if, however, Black has aggressive intentions and intends in the event of an exchange on Q4 to recapture with the Knight, then the text-move is superfluous and an immediate 4 ... P–Q4 should be played.

5   B–Kt2   P–Q4
6   PxP

With this exchange White goes in for a symmetrical position in which his extra tempo will be difficult to utilise, but this will still yield him some slight initiative.

6 ...   KtxP

Playing the Grunfeld Defence with a tempo less is a risky experiment that can scarcely be excused by the desire to bring about greater complications than such as occur after the normal 6 ... PxP. Now White obtains a lasting initiative.

7   O–O   O–O
8. Kt–B3   KtxKt

White could, of course, have also very well played 8 P–K4 here, and this would have led, after 8 ... Kt–Kt3, to a well-known line of the Grunfeld Defence. However, with the Knight move White wanted to entice his opponent to make the exchange on QB3—a procedure Flohr very readily employs in such positions. But, carrying out the idea of the main variation of the Grunfeld Defence with a tempo less is a dangerous undertaking, since with the further opening up of the position, White's advantage in development becomes more and more important.

9   PxKt   P–QB4
10 B–QR3   PxP
11 KtxP!

An interesting and rather surprising idea that, as far as I know, was used for the first time in this game. After the "normal" continuation 11 PxP, Black would reply 11 ... Kt–B3 and then develop his Queen-side without any trouble. But pressure on the enemy Queen's wing is precisely one of the main aims of the text-move. The White Knight has now taken up a dominating position in the centre, both Bishops have beautiful diagonals at their disposal, and the weakness on QB3 plays little role in the game in view of White's excellent development. In the ensuing phase of the game Black has to contend with great difficulties.

	11 ...	Q–B2
	12 Q–Kt3	B–B3

Black wants to carry out the Knight manoeuvre Kt–Q2–Kt3–B5, or Kt–Q2–B4, but must first protect the pawn on K2. But this imports fresh loss of time. The other possible continuation here, 12 ... Kt–B3, is, however, equally unpleasant for Black. After 13 KtxKt, PxKt we would once again have a practically symmetrical position in which White, by 14 Q–R4!, could initiate lasting pressure on the QBP.

	13 KR–Q1	Kt–Q2
	14 P–QB4!	

By means of this good move White foils the enemy plan since now 14 ... Kt–Kt3 would meet with the very strong reply of 15 P–B5. The same aim could be obtained by 14 QR–B1, when 14 ... Kt–Kt3 can be met by 15 P–QB4, and 14 ... Kt–B4 would allow White to reach an advantageous ending by 15 Q–B4, Kt–K3; 16 QxQ, KtxQ; 17 QR–Kt1.

	14 ...	Kt–B4
	15 Q–Kt4	Kt–K3?

This "consequent" move must, however, be regarded as a mistake since now Black is unable to achieve normal development of his Queen's wing. Although the move 15 ... Kt–R3 looked very ugly and did not fit in well with Black's plan of play it was, nevertheless, the only chance of obtaining a more or less acceptable position. To this White could reply 16 Q–Kt5, R–Kt1 (16 ... R–Q1; 17 P–K3, would not alter the position to any marked degree); 17 P–B5!, R–Q1; 18 P–K3, B–Q2; 19 P–B6, and after the further 19 ... BxKt (or 19 ... B–K1; 20 QR–B1); 20 RxB, BxP; 21 RxRch, RxR; 22 BxB, QxB; 23 QxQ, PxQ; 24 BxP, would retain the better endgame.

	16 Kt–Kt5	Q–K4
	17 QR–B1!	

In view of his excellent development White need not fear the capture of his KP. With the text-move White protects himself against the threat of 17 ... P–QR3 and threatens to play 18 Kt–B3–Q5, once again threatening Black's K2.

17 ...   R–Q1

In reply to 17 ... QxP White intended to play 18 Kt–B3. If then 18 ... BxKt, then there threatens, after 19 QxB, both 20 B–B3 and 20 BxKP, or 20 B–Kt2. But if Black replies 19 ... Q–K4 there follows 20 Kt–Q5 and White at least wins the pawn back while retaining an enduring attack.

18 R–Q5

Very strong also here was 18 RxRch, KtxR; 19 Q–B5! when Black would experience great difficulties with his Queen-side. However, the continuation of the attack intended by the text-move is more energetic.

18 ...   RxR

It is difficult to find any better line for Black. After the capture 18 ... QxKP White has a number of ways to attack, of which the simplest is 19 Kt–B3, BxKt (or 19 ... Q–Kt5; 20 P–R3); 20 QxB, with various threats. But if Black tries 18 ... Q–Kt1 then the reply 19 QR–Q1 is most unpleasant for him.

19 PxR   P–QR3

Black (Flohr)

White (Keres) to play

Black had relied upon this move. He had hoped to put up a stubborn resistance with his strong central Knight after 20 Kt–B3, Kt–Q5, but suffers a cruel awakening in the next move.

20   Kt–R7!

One of the most original moves of attack that has occurred in my tournament career. Surprisingly enough, Black now loses a whole piece.

20   . . .   Kt–Q5

After 20 . . . RxKt; 21 RxBch, Kt–B1, White wins a whole Rook by 22 Q–Kt6, Q–Q5; 23 B–B5, and 20 . . . B–Q2; 21 PxKt, or 21 QxP, is equally hopeless for Black. With the text-move Black still hopes to conjure up some slight threats.

21   RxBch   RxR
22   KtxR   QxKP

No different is 22 . . . KtxPch; 23 K–B1.

23   P–R4   Kt–B4
24   Q–K4   resigns

Game 22

CATALAN SYSTEM

International Tournament at Semmering, 1937

P. Keres   V. Ragosin
1   P–Q4   Kt–KB3
2   P–QB4   P–K3
3   Kt–QB3   P–Q4

It is well known that Grandmaster Ragosin is no lover of the Nimzowitsch Defence and that he favours positions in which the pawns in the centre come into direct contact. With the text-move Black tries to transpose the game into the variation 4 Kt–B3, B–Kt5, a line exhaustively analysed by Grandmaster Ragosin and which is called after him.

4   P–KKt3

If White wants to thwart his opponent's intentions then 4

B–Kt5 would be a better method for the purpose. Transposition into the Catalan System after the Knight has been developed on QB3 is not particularly to be recommended.

4	...	PxP
5	Q–R4ch	

After 5 B–Kt2, Black can embark on the attempt to retain his extra pawn by 5 ... P–B3.

5	...	Kt–B3!

With this move Black initiates an interesting plan of development by which the disadvantages of an early development of the Knight to QB3 are laid bare. An attempt to bring about simplifications by 5 ... Q–Q2; 6 QxBP, Q–B3 here would be inferior on account of the reply 7 P–K4. But a transposition into more normal channels by 5 ... QKt–Q2 was of course equally playable.

Grandmaster Ragosin is, however, fond of extraordinary methods of play and the system begun by the text-move is very much to his taste.

6	B–Kt2	B–Q2
7	QxBP	Kt–QKt5

A logical demonstration of the drawback of having the Knight posted on QB3. In order to protect his QB2 White must now lose a move and Black can make use of this to carry out the advance P–B4, by which he easily equalises. In addition the other advance in the centre 7 ... P–K4 was also possible here, and this, too, would have led to satisfactory play for Black after 8 P–Q5, Kt–QKt5; 9 Q–Kt3, P–B3.

8	Q–Kt3	P–B4!

Once this advance has been made Black can be thoroughly satisfied with the result of the opening struggle. He can finish his development normally; he exerts a marked pressure on the enemy centre and in addition his pieces are rather more actively posted than his opponent's. White must now play very carefully in order to avoid the disadvantage.

9	Kt–B3

In order to avoid all possible complications White could here continue with 9 PxP, BxP; 10 Kt–B3, O–O; 11 O–O, but this would allow his opponent a good position without putting up a fight. With the text-move he sets his opponent a little positional trap that, in the event of its success, will assure White a lasting initiative.

Bad was naturally the capture 9 BxP? since after 9 . . . R–QKt1 White cannot retreat the Bishop because of 10 . . . Kt–Q6ch.

| 9 . . . | B–B3? |

White's trap works! With the text-move Black further strengthens his pressure on the centre and hopes thereby to force the line mentioned in the previous note 10 PxP, BxP; 11 O–O, O–O, etc. White has, however, a stronger continuation at his disposal by which he destroys the enemy plans. Naturally, Black should here exchange pawns by 9 . . . PxP; 10 KtxP, and now not 10 . . . B–B4 because of the simple reply 11 O–O, but 10 . . . P–K4! White would then have nothing better than the retreat 11 Kt–B3 (after 11 Kt–B2, Black can, if he so pleases, force a repetition of moves by 11 . . . B–K3; 12 Q–R4ch, B–Q2). 11 . . . B–K3; 12 Q–R4ch, and now both 12 . . . B–Q2 and 12 . . . Q–Q2 would give Black about a level game.

10 O–O!

A surprise, setting Black some seemingly awkward problems. White now threatens simply to continue 11 R–Q1, fully protecting his centre and obtaining a positional pressure characteristic of the Catalan. Black, therefore, has little choice.

| 10 . . . | PxP |
| 11 R–Q1 | Q–R4 |

Ragosin decides to give back the pawn, since an attempt to retain it by 11 . . . BxKt; 12 BxB, Q–Kt3 would, in any case, prove fruitless on account of 13 Kt–QR4. Also pointless would be 11 . . . B–B4 since White could continue with 12 KtxP, in any case.

| 12 KtxP | BxB |
| 13 KxB | B–K2 |

As a consequence of his inaccurate 9th move Black now experiences some difficulties since, in the ensuing phase of the

game, he will have difficulties with the defence of the Queen's
wing. Moreover, White is somewhat ahead in development,
and therefore Black must hurry up and castle. Since, however,
White, too, has not completed his development, it will prove
difficult for him to build up still further his hardly noticeable
advantage.

14   P–QR3

White could also try here 14 B–Q2, although then one
cannot see how, after 14 ... O–O, he can exploit the insecure
position of the Knight on QKt5. If, for example, 15 Kt(B3)–
Kt5, then Black has a good counter by 15 ... P–QR3; 16
P–QR3, PxKt; 17 BxKt, BxB; 18 QxB, QxQ; 19 PxQ, R–R5!
etc.

14   ...   O–O
15   B–Q2

After 15 B–K3, 15 B–B4, or 15 R–QKt1 Black gets rid of
all difficulties by 15 ... QKt–Q4. The text-move is aimed at
preventing this counter. Now 15 ... QKt–Q4 would be
simply met by 16 QxKtP, and if then 16 ... QR–Kt1, White
would ensure himself of a solid extra pawn by 17 KtxKt!

15   ...   Kt–B3?

Black had to calculate complicated possible variations the
whole time. Now he relaxes his attention for one moment and
at once falls into great difficulties. Here Ragosin could have
played the strong 15 ... Q–Kt3! so as to meet 16 PxKt, with
16 ... QxKt. In reply White would have nothing better than
16 B–Kt5, by which, however, he could have reached an ending
with the barest possible advantage. For example: 16 ...
Kt–B3; 17 QxQ, PxQ; 18 Kt(Q4)–Kt5, or 16 ... Kt(Kt5)–
Q4; 17 KtxKt, KtxKt; 18 QxQ, PxQ; 19 BxB, KtxB; 20
Kt–Kt5, etc.

16   KtxKt

Perhaps Ragosin had only reckoned on 16 QxKtP, KtxKt;
17 QxB, which would have allowed him strong counter-play
after 17 ... Kt–Kt6; 18 QR–Kt1, Kt–Q4! The text-move,
however, is much simpler and markedly stronger.

16   ...   PxKt
17   Q–B4

But now it is White's turn to be guilty of an inaccuracy. He wants to fix the pawn on QB3 and then exert strong positional pressure on the QB file, but in so doing he overlooks the much stronger tactical sally of 17 Q–Kt7! In reply Black could not play 17 ... Q–QB4 on account of 18 B–K3, and he is therefore compelled to surrender the QBP. Moreover, one cannot see how he can attain even comparative compensation for his pawn. Thus, for example, after 17 ... Kt–Q4; there would follow simply 18 QxBP, when Black cannot play 18 ... QR–B1, because of 19 KtxKt!

After the text-move White has only a minimal positional advantage.

| 17 | ... | Q–Kt3 |
| 18 | P–QKt4 | P–QR4? |

Black (Ragosin)

White (Keres) to play

White threatens to obtain definite possession of the QB5 square by 19 B–K3, or 19 QR–B1, and this Black seeks to prevent by a counter-attack on the QKtP. But the text-move imports a pawn sacrifice. Apparently Ragosin regards the acceptance of such a sacrifice as not particularly dangerous for him since now White gets a doubled Pawn on the QR file, and Black thinks he will soon regain his pawn. But the further progress of the game shows that the winning back of the pawn is not so simple and in fact eventually Black remains a pawn down.

Black must naturally take the opportunity here of carrying out the advance 18 . . . P–B4. In reply White is practically forced to play 19 P–Kt5 (19 Kt–QR4?, Q–B3ch). But then follows 19 . . . P–QR3; 20 P–QR4, PxP; and though White stands a little better after both 21 KtxP, and 21 PxP, Black still retains every opportunity of a successful defence.

Now there ensues a very interesting endgame.

	19	Kt–R4!	Q–Kt4

After other Queen moves there follows simply 20 PxP.

	20	QxQ	PxQ
	21	Kt–Kt6	R–R3
	22	PxP!	

This is the turning point; although his Q-side pawns are doubled White has a clearly better endgame, this being because of the excellent position of his pieces. The White Bishop has a fine post on QKt4, the Knight deprives the opponent of the important squares Q4 and Q2, and finally Black's weakness on QKt4 furnishes White with a good object of attack. All this brings one to the conviction that Black no longer possesses any adequate defence in this ending.

	22	. . .	B–Q1
	23	B–Kt4	

Instead of this move White could also win a pawn by 23 KR–QKt1, BxKt; 24 PxB, RxKtP; 25 P–QR4, since after 25 . . . KR–Kt1; 26 RxP, Black cannot capture twice on QKt4 because of the mating threat on the back rank. The text-move, by which White retains his outpost on QKt6, is perhaps even more convincing.

	23	. . .	R–K1
	24	R–Q6	B–B2

Naturally not 24 . . . BxKt; 25 PxB, when the passed QKtP wins, but there still came into consideration 24 . . . B–K2; 25 R–B6, BxB; 26 PxB, Kt–Q4. Then White could consolidate his advantage in two ways. First, simply by 27 R–QKt1, and if 27 . . . KtxKt, then 28 R–Q1 followed by 29 R(Q1)–Q6, with an easy win. Secondly, however, White can also play 27 P–K4,

KtxP; 28 R–B5, and after the QKtP has fallen White is a strong pawn up on the QR file.

| 25 | R–B6 | Kt–Q4 |

Now after 25 . . . BxKt; 26 PxB, Kt–Q2, there would follow 27 R–Q6, and Black cannot capture on QKt3 by 27 . . . KtxP, since then 28 R–QB1, followed by 29 R–B6, would soon win material.

| 26 | P–K4! |

This forces the exchange on QKt4, since after 26 . . . KtxKt White can win by either 27 PxKt, BxQKtP; 28 B–B5, R–Kt1; 29 R–QKt1, or 27 RxB, Kt–B5; 28 P–QR4!, etc. But once his Queen-side pawns are once again united the ensuing endgame offers no difficulties to White.

| 26 | . . . | KtxB |
| 27 | PxKt | B–K4 |

Now after 27 . . . BxKt the reply 28 RxB wins at once, since then the pawn simply goes right through to Queen by 28 . . . RxR; 29 PxR, followed by 30 P–Kt7. After the text-move, however, the QKtP is soon lost and this means the end.

28	R–Q1	P–Kt3
29	R–B5	B–B3
30	Kt–Q7	

Thwarting the last theoretical chance of resistance: 30 RxP, R–Kt1 followed by an eventual B–Q1. Black could already have quietly struck his flag.

30	. . .	B–K2
31	RxP	R(R3)–R1
32	R–Kt7	R–R3
33	Kt–Kt8	R–R1
34	Kt–B6	B–B1
35	P–Kt5	KR–B1
36	P–R6	B–B4
37	R(Q1)–Q7	R–B1
38	P–R7	P–R4
39	R–Kt8	K–Kt2
40	P–Kt6	resigns

Game 23

RETI SYSTEM

International Tournament at Noordwijk, 1938

P. Keres	M. Euwe
1 Kt–KB3	P–Q4
2 P–B4	P–Q5

After the return match, Alekhine–Euwe, 1937, this line of play became one of the topical problems of international tournaments. Naturally, I knew that Euwe was one of the leading experts in this variation. Nevertheless, I decided to employ it in this game, though this was a very important one for me, with the idea of trying out a new line.

3 P–K3	Kt–QB3
4 PxP	

I had had only bad results with the move 4 P–QKt4, having got into difficulties equally after 4 . . . KtxP; 5 PxP, P–K4!; 6 P–QR3, P–K5; 7 PxKt, PxKt (Keres–Flohr, Parnu, 1937); and after 4 . . . PxP; 5 KPxP, KtxP; 6 P–Q4, P–K4! (Keres–Stahlberg, 7th match-game, 1938).

After the exchange on Q4 an interesting position arises in which White, it is true, obtains a slight advantage in development, but Black is able to exert a certain positional pressure on the backward QP. The question as to which of these advantages weighs the heavier constitutes the chief opening problem of this game.

4 . . .	KtxP
5 KtxKt	QxKt
6 Kt–B3	B–Kt5

White's further plan of play is clear. He would like to force through P–Q4 by means of 7 P–Q3 and 8 B–K3 and thus obtain a marked preponderance in the centre. So, for example, Black played passively in the 22nd match-game, Alekhine–Euwe, 1937: 6 . . . Kt–B3; 7 P–Q3, P–B3; and allowed White a small but clear opening advantage after 8 B–K3, Q–Q2;

9 P-Q4, P-KKt3; 10 B-K2, B-Kt2; 11 P-KR3, O-O; 12 O-O, etc.

Attempts have been made in later games played with this variation to better Black's game in various ways and eventually the text-move has been chosen, which seems the simplest method of equalising the position. In the game Fine–Flohr, Hastings, 1937–38, Black did in fact have no more difficulties to contend with after 7 B-K2, BxB; 8 QxB. But it was precisely against the sally 6 . . . B-Kt5 that I wanted to try a new continuation and in this game, at any rate, it proves to be very successful.

Objectively considered Black does not stand worse at this point of course, and the simplest way to equalise seems to be the advance recommended by Alekhine 6 . . . P-K4. After 7 P-Q3, Black can either play 7 . . . B-QB4; 8 B-K3, Q-Q3; 9 Kt-Kt5, Q-K2; 10 BxB, QxB, with easy equality (Alekhine) or he may carry out the scheme of 7 . . . P-QB3; 8 B-K3, Q-Q3; followed by Kt-R3-B4 (Flohr).

7 Q-R4ch!

This check constitutes the innovation planned by White. Black must now meet with much greater difficulties than would arise after 6 . . . P-K4.

7 . . .   P-B3

White stands a little better after 7 . . . Q-Q2; 8 QxQch, followed by 9 P-Q4, and also 7 . . . B-Q2; 8 Q-Kt3, gives White the better prospects. If Black then protects his pawn by 8 . . . O-O-O, he will have to undergo a dangerous attack against his King by 9 P-Q3 and 10 B-K3; whilst if he plays 8 . . . B-B3, then, after 9 P-Q3, he must always reckon with the possibility of B-K3 followed by P-Q4-5. On the basis of this game the move 6 . . . B-Kt5 must be regarded as having marked drawbacks.

8	P-Q3	Kt-B3
9	B-K3	Q-Q2
10	P-Q4	

With this advance White has attained his objective and now clearly stands better. In addition to being behindhand with his development, Black will soon have troubles with his QB.

	10 ...	P–K3
	11 P–B3	B–KB4
	12 O–O–O	

A little more accurate here was 12 P–KKt4, B–Kt3; 13 P–R4, since now Black could have prevented this advance by 12 . . . P–KR4. Naturally, Black would also not be particularly well placed thereafter, since the move 12 . . . P–KR4 noticeably weakens the K wing and would deprive Black of the opportunity of O–O. Since also O–O–O cannot be carried out except after long preparation, Black would soon be at his wits end as to what he should do with his King, trapped as it is in the centre.

	12 ...	B–Q3?

Regardless of the weaknesses involved, Black must still try 12 . . . P–KR4 here. After the text-move White obtains by force a marked advantage.

	13 P–KKt4!	B–Kt3
	14 P–R4	P–KR4

Black has to choose between two evils, and it is difficult to say which of the two is the greater. It is true that after 14 . . . P–KR3 the ensuing combination in the game would not be possible, but on the other hand Black would then be in a hopelessly passive position. White could, for instance, continue with 15 B–R3 and threaten eventually P–R5 and P–Kt5 or also P–Q5, and Black would once again be faced by the insoluble problem as to where to hide the King.

With the text-move Black does indeed ensure himself of the possibility of Castling King-side, but he also allows his opponent to make a tactical break-through in the centre which results in a decisive positional advantage for White.

	15 P–Kt5	Kt–R2
	16 P–B5!	B–K2
	17 P–Q5!	

This thrust in the centre which has its tactical justification in the variation 17 . . . KPxP; 18 KtxP!, PxKt; 19 B–Kt5, assures White an important advantage. Black's reply is

practically forced, since 18 PxBP is threatened and 17 . . .
Q–B1 leads to loss of a piece after 18 P–Q6.

<table>
<tr><td>17 . . .</td><td>O–O</td></tr>
<tr><td>18 PxBP!</td><td></td></tr>
</table>

It may appear at first glance too modest for White to abandon
any attempt to destroy the opponent's position in the middle-
game and to aim instead for the ending with the text-move.
But as a matter of fact this way is the simplest method of
realising his positional advantage. After the Queen exchange
Black's pieces are very awkwardly placed and White soon wins
at least a pawn.

Moreover, attempts to take the enemy position by direct
storm yield no tangible result. Thus, for example, after 18
P–Q6, B–Q1 Black is indeed very constricted, but it would also
be not so easy to suggest a plan of attack promising success
for White, since the position is really closed. Nor would 18
B–R3 furnish a better result, since this only leads, after 18 . . .
B–B4, to an exchange of the Bishops on White coloured
squares.

<table>
<tr><td>18 . . .</td><td>QxP</td></tr>
<tr><td>19 QxQ</td><td>PxQ</td></tr>
<tr><td>20 R–Q7</td><td>KR–K1</td></tr>
<tr><td>21 B–R6!</td><td></td></tr>
</table>

Black (Euwe) to play

White (Keres)

Now we can see what White has attained with his Queen exchange. He has penetrated into the opponent's position, whereas Black must still lose much time in bringing into play the pieces that have accumulated unused on the King-side. In consequence of all this White now wins the QBP by force, and a pawn plus together with the better position signifies in practice the decision in White's favour. Euwe still defends himself very resourcefully in the remainder of the game, but can, however, find no really promising defensive possibility.

21 . . .   P–K4

Depriving the White Bishop of the important square KB4 and giving his Knight an outlet on K3. Better, however, was first 21 . . . Kt–B1; 22 R–B7, and only then 22 . . . P–K4, when White would have less choice in the ensuing phase of the game.

22   R–B7

The text-move is, of course, good enough, but 22 B–Kt7 seems even more energetic. Since then 22 . . . Kt–B1; 23 BxR, KtxR; 24 BxP, or 22 . . . QR–Q1; 23 BxP, RxR; 24 BxR, would be both hopeless for Black, the only continuation left him would be 22 . . . QR–Kt1; 23 BxP. In the resulting position Black would indeed have a wealth of tactical possibilities, but none of these leads to the wished for result. Consider, for example: 23 . . . QR–B1; 24 RxB!, RxR; 25 Kt–Q5, etc., or 23 . . . BxBP; 24 BxB, QR–B1; 25 R–Q6, R–K3; and then White wins easily by 26 KR–Q1, or 26 B–Q5.

22 . . .   Kt–B1
23   B–Kt7

In realising his advantage White commits a certain number of inaccuracies and allows his opponent to bring about some tactical complications. Simpler from the technical point of view was undoubtedly 23 RxP, Kt–K3; 24 Kt–Q5, etc.

23 . . .   QR–Kt1
24   BxP   Kt–K3!

Euwe conducts a difficult defence with great skill. After 24 . . . KR–QB1 White would have won quickly by 25 RxR, RxR; 26 Kt–Q5!, B–Q1; 27 B–Kt7, followed by 28 P–B6.

25   BxR

White rightly refrains from capturing the pawn by 25 RxP,
as this would have opened up fresh tactical possibilities for his
opponent. Firstly, he must then reckon with the possible
counter-attack 25 . . . KtxBP; 26 BxR, Kt–Q6ch; or also
25 . . . BxBP; 26 BxB, KR–QB1; though this would eventually
result in White's advantage: 27 B–Q6!, R–Kt3; 28 B–Q7,
RxKtch; 29 PxR, R–Kt8ch; 30 K–Q2, RxR; 31 BxKt,
followed by 32 BxP, etc.

Secondly, however, Black can continue more quietly with
25 . . . KR–QB1! After 26 RxB (26 B–Q7, BxBP!), 26 . . .
RxB he would attain quite good counter-play, since White
would have to give back one of the pawns he has won. It can
be seen with what skill Euwe knows how to manoeuvre even
in hopeless positions so as to procure counter-chances.

Another possibility for White here was 25 RxB, RxR; 26
Kt–Q5, though this could scarcely have been stronger than
the game continuation.

25	. . .	KtxR
26	B–Q7	P–R4
27	P–B6	R–Kt5

Black still provides his opponent with the greatest possible
difficulties. But White's preponderance on the Queen-side is
too great for his opponent to hope for any successful attempt
in combating the first player.

28	P–Kt3	P–B3
29	K–Kt2	PxP
30	PxP	B–B2

White was threatening 31 P–R3, followed by 32 B–R7, and
33 B–Kt6.

31	R–Q1	R–KR5
32	R–Q2	R–R8

There was no longer any adequate defence against the
threat of 33 B–Kt6. With the text-move Black intends to meet
33 B–Kt6 by 33 . . . BxP, but White does not bestow on him
even this last chance.

33   P–B4!

This wins yet another pawn as Black may not capture on

KB5 on account of 34 BxP. The rest of the game no longer gives us anything interesting.

33	. . .	B–Kt5
34	PxP	B–Kt3
35	P–R3	BxKtch
36	KxB	P–KR5
37	P–K6	R–K8

After 37 . . . P–R6 there would, of course, have followed 38 B–B4.

38	K–Q4	K–B1
39	B–B2	KtxPch
40	K–Q5	Kt–B2ch
41	K–B5	resigns

This game possesses a certain theoretical value.

Game 24

FRENCH DEFENCE

International Tournament at Noordwijk, 1938

| | R. Spielmann | P. Keres |
| 1 | P–K4 | P–K3 |

At the time this game was played I usually replied to 1 P–K4 with 1 . . . P–K4. In this game, however, I chose the French Defence on psychological considerations. Spielmann had, in fact, published shortly beforehand a commentary on the variation 1 P–K4, P–K3; 2 P–Q4, P–Q4; 3 Kt–QB3, Kt–KB3; 4 P–K5; KKt–Q2; 5 QKt–K2, in which he estimated this method of play good for White. Moreover, Spielmann had made good his claim in a number of tournament games and achieved beautiful victories with this variation against Miss Menchik (Hastings, 1937/38) and some rounds earlier in Noordwijk against Schmidt. I therefore assumed that Spielmann would also employ this method of play against me, especially taking into consideration that his place in the tournament was not amongst the leaders.

However, in the meantime adequate methods of dealing

with the line recommended by Spielmann had been found, above all, the Pirc variation 5 . . . P–QB4; 6 P–QB3, P–B3; 7 P–KB4, KBPxP; 8 BPxP, PxP; 9 PxP, B–Kt5ch! after which White gets into difficulties because of the threat of 10 . . . Q–R5ch. It is true that later on it was discovered that the Pirc variation is not all that terrible for White, if, for example, he plays 8 QPxP, instead of 8 BPxP, or perhaps even better, instead of 7 P–KB4 plays 7 Kt–B4. But at the time this game was played the variation was thought very strong and there was even talk of it as a refutation of the 5 QKt–K2 line.

It is, therefore, understandable that I wanted to combat this variation in a serious tournament game and therefore adopted the French Defence, which very rarely happened in my tournament praxis of that time.

2	P–Q4	P–Q4
3	Kt–QB3	Kt–KB3
4	P–K5	KKt–Q2
5	P–B4	

But Spielmann, too, had in the interim already heard of the wicked designs of Pirc against his pet variation and therefore chose another continuation here. So the game now definitely departs from all prepared variations and pursues a normal course.

5	. . .	P–QB4
6	PxP	

A logical reply. Whereas White, in the 5 QKt–K2 variation, aims at supporting his pawn centre by P–QB3 and P–KB4, here he wants to occupy the central square of Q4 with his pieces. But for this the QP must be exchanged for Black's QBP and this is best done at once. Grandmaster Boleslavsky has tried here in a number of games 6 Kt–B3, Kt–QB3; 7 B–K3, but then can follow 7 . . . PxP; 8 KKtxP, B–B4; 9 B–Kt5, O–O! with a good game for Black (Boleslavsky–Guimard, 1954).

6	. . .	Kt–QB3

Of course, Black could also here recapture at once by 6 . . . BxP, but there is no need to be in a hurry to do so. Besides, in some cases, for example, after 7 B–Q3, Black can very well play 7 . . . KtxBP.

7	P–QR3	BxP
8	Q–Kt4	P–KKt3

This continuation is new and this game shows it to be really good. Usually there is played here 8 . . . O–O; 9 Kt–B3, Kt–Q5; 10 B–Q3, P–B4; 11 Q–R3, P–QR3; followed by 12 . . . P–QKt4, which also holds out prospects of a good game for Black, but allows White some opportunities for a King-side attack. By the text-move Black avoids this possibility and prevents in practice the possible thrust of P–B5. The weakening of the black squares does not matter at the moment as White is unable to exploit it in any way.

9	Kt–B3	P–QR3

The commencement of a good counter-attack on the Queen-side by P–QKt4–5 and the consequent hindering of White's Queen-side castling. Since White cannot at once castle King-side he must leave his King in the centre and this, in view of the eventual possibility of an attack on the King, can prove to be really awkward.

10	B–Q3	P–QKt4
11	P–Kt4	

Although fresh weaknesses appear in White's position (in particular on QB4), this advance is practically forced. White cannot allow Black's P–QKt5.

11	. . .	B–R2
12	P–KR4	P–KR4
13	Q–Kt3	Q–K2?

But this move is imprecise and enables Spielmann to commence a very dangerous attack. Since 14 BxKKtP, does not constitute a threat on account of 14 . . . R–KKt1, Black should take the opportunity of playing 13 . . . Kt–Q5, which would have given him an excellent position. 13 . . . Q–B2 would also have been good, depriving White of any possibility of P–B5, through the threat on his K5.

14	P–B5!

A brilliant tactical stroke, as one might, of course, have expected from such a master of the attack as Spielmann. White now obtains a powerful attack and it is indeed by no means sure that Black should succeed in escaping with a whole skin with correct further play.

This advance did not come as a surprise to Black. By means of his counter-move he hoped to beat off the attempt at attack by the enemy easily enough. But in so hoping he under-estimated the many possibilities that the position afforded to a resourceful attacking player.

14 ...   B–Kt1!

It is on this counter-attack that Black has placed his hopes. White cannot now adequately defend the K5 square and Black believes that with the fall of this important pawn White's attack, too, will be quenched. In actual fact matters are not so simple as the following analysis shows.

The point of White's attack lies in the fact that 14 . . . KtPxP can be met by 15 BxBP! since 15 . . . PxB; 16 KtxQP, would yield White a decisive attack. It is true that 15 . . . B–Kt1 is then possible and we will examine the possibilities that arise after the Bishop move in our next note. Finally, 14 . . . Kt(B3)xKP; 15 KtxKt, B–Q5 merits consideration (after 15 . . . B–Kt1; 16 B–KB4, a position arises which will be examined in the next note). But then White attains a strong attack by 16 Kt–B6!, BxKtch; 17 K–Q1: for example: 17 . . . Q–B3; 18 B–Kt5, Q–Kt2; 19 Q–Q6, or 17 . . . Q–B1; 18 Q–B7, etc.

The text-move is undoubtedly Black's best practical chance.

15 PxKtP?

The text-move is the best proof that Spielmann was not in his best form at Noordwijk. Here he abandons all possible chances of developing a highly dangerous attack in the position and instead chooses a tame continuation that at best holds out promise of a bare equality. White would also have obtained nothing by 15 PxKP, Kt(Q2)xP; or by 15 P–B6, QxBP!, and also 15 B–Kt5, could have been answered by 15 . . . Kt(Q2)xP!, in every case with an advantageous position for Black. But with 15 B–KB4!, White could have successfully continued his attack, and then it would not have been easy for Black to find an adequate defence.

During the game I was of the opinion that 15 B–KB4 could have been met by 15 . . . KtPxP with advantage to Black. After 16 BxBP, PxB; 17 KtxQP, the QB2 square is protected and Black can continue with 17 . . . Q–K3. But this is not the end of the matter. If we consider the position more deeply then we soon observe that the further 18 O–O–O yields White an overwhelming attack. Consider, for instance, 18 . . . Kt–K2 (after 18 . . . Q–Kt3 White can play, in addition to 19 Q–K1, 19 P–K6, winning back the piece sacrificed); 19 KtxKt (also 19 Kt–Kt5, QxKt; 20 RxQ, KtxR; 21 R–K1, is very strong), 19 . . . QxKt; 20 Kt–Q4!, KtxP; 21 KR–K1, P–B3; 22 Kt–B6!, with a decisive attack.

We are driven to the conclusion, then, that the acceptance of the piece sacrifice in the given circumstances can scarcely be Black's best continuation. But how, then, should Black proceed after 15 B–KB4?

In the first instance 15 . . . KtPxP; 16 BxBP, Kt(Q2)xP; 17 KtxKt, KtxKt; leaps to mind, so as to meet 18 BxKt, with 18 . . . PxB. White has, however, the stronger continuation 18 O–O–O!, obtaining a very strong attack, whether Black accepts the piece sacrifice or not.

Secondly, an immediate 15 . . . Kt(Q2)xP deserves consideration, without having exchanged first of all on KB4. After 16 KtxKt, KtxKt Black would be threatening to exchange on Q6, and then 17 BxKt, KPxB would free him of all his troubles. But here, too, White would attain a strong attack by continuing 17 PxKtP (very strong, too, is 17 O–O–O, KtxBch; 18 RxKt, BxBch; 19 QxB, KtPxP; 20 R–K1), 17 . . . KtxBch; 18 QxKt! Then, after 18 . . . BxB; 19 P–Kt7, R–KKt1; 20 Q–R7, Black, in order to avoid worse, must give up the exchange.

The variations assembled here naturally lay no claim to being exhaustive, but, if the possibility of 15 . . . KPxP; 16 BxBP, P–Q5; 17 B–K4! is added to them, then they give a characteristic picture of what kind of dangerous attacking chances White possesses in this position. It is a great pity that Spielmann misses the strong attacking continuation 15 B–KB4!

which could have resulted in making this game one of the best in the whole tournament.

15   . . .   Kt(Q2)xP!

After this reply, with the deadly threat of 16 . . . KtxBch, White's attack is in practice at an end and it is only a question as to whether White is in a position, in the remaining phase of the game, to beat back the enemy attack or not.

16   PxPch   QxP
17   Kt–Kt5

17 Q–B2 fails against 17 . . . Q–Kt2.

17   . . .   Q–B3

Black (Keres)

White (Spielmann) to play

18   R–B1?

It is well known that it is especially difficult for every chess-player to accustom himself to the defence after an attack that has failed. Praxis shows that the defender in such cases rarely finds the best resource and often collapses quickly. Such a psychological collapse does indeed take place here. Spielmann is concerned over the failure of his attack and his normal resourcefulness is now wanting in the defence.

The text-move is a grave error that leads in surprising fashion to the loss of a piece, after which the struggle is at an end to all intents and purposes. Despite the seemingly irre-sistible threats on his position Spielmann could have still put up a stubborn resistance here by 18 B–Q2! Although at first glance it appears that Black could then realise his advantage in various ways, matters are not in reality so simple. Let us now adduce some characteristic sample lines.

I. 18 . . . KtxBch; 19 QxKt, Kt–K4; 20 Q–B1! and apparently Black must content himself with only a better ending.

II. 18 ... Kt–Q5; 19 O–O–O!, Kt–B5. (After 19 ... Kt–Kt5; 20 Q–K1, Kt–B7 there comes naturally 21 R–B1, and both 19 . . . Kt(K4)–B6 and 19 . . . Kt(Q5)–B6 are dealt with by 20 Q–B2.) 20 Q–K1 and if 20 . . . KtxB then 21 KtxQP! and already Black must struggle for equality.

III. 18 . . . Kt–Kt5; 19 Q–B3, Q–K4ch; 20 K–Q1!, R–B1; 21 B–Kt6ch, K–K2; 22 Kt–B7! and in this complicated position it is not clear who will finally gain the upper hand. For example: 22 . . . Q–Kt2; 23 KtxPch! or 22 . . . Q–Q5; 23 K–B1, etc.

IV. 18 . . . Kt–B5; 19 Q–B3, Q–K4ch; 20 K–Q1, KtxB; 21 Q–B7ch, K–Q1; 22 KxKt, and White has a really good position.

The variations given show adequately that after 18 B–Q2! Black would hardly be in a position to obtain concrete advantage by direct attack. He would rather have to return to quiet play and to build up his positional advantage still more. A good continuation, for example, would be 18 . . . Kt–B5; 19 Q–B3, B–K4!; 20 QxQ, BxQ. White would then still have to contend with great difficulties, but would, however, obtain some chances of saving the game.

	18 . . .	Kt–Kt5!

By this surprising move, which is easily enough overlooked, Black wins at least a piece.

| 19 | Q–B3 | QxKtch |
| 20 | K–Q1 | Q–Kt2 |

Naturally 20 . . . QxR could also have been played since White's attack would be obviously insufficient after 21 Q–B7ch, K–Q1; 22 KtxPch, BxKt; 23 QxB, Kt–K2. But Black also has enough with his extra piece for the win.

21	Q–K2	R–B1
22	RxRch	KxR
23	KtxPch	BxKt
24	QxB	Kt–B7ch
25	K–K1	KtxBch
26	PxKt,	

White resigned without waiting for his opponent's reply.

A very interesting struggle of which, unfortunately, the general impression is damaged by some marked inaccuracies on both sides.

Game 25

FRENCH DEFENCE

AVRO World-championship tournament in Holland, 1938

	P. Keres	J. R. Capablanca
1	P–K4	P–K3
2	P–Q4	P–Q4
3	Kt–Q2	P–QB4

Capablanca had little luck with the French Defence in the AVRO tournament. Already, in the first round, he got into great difficulties with this defence against Fine; he was also unable to solve the opening problem satisfactorily in the present game, and, finally, he lost with it to Alekhine, on the very anniversary of his fiftieth birthday.

| 4 | KPxP | KPxP |
| 5 | KKt–B3 | Kt–QB3 |

This Knight development, allowing the ensuing pin, must already be deemed an error. Better is an immediate 5 . . . Kt–KB3, so as to be able to meet 6 B–Kt5ch, with 6 . . . B–Q2.

| 6 | B–Kt5 | Q–K2ch |

This check is the equivalent of a tacit offer of a draw: 7 Q–K2, QxQch; etc. But White is aggressively inclined in this round. Better therefore would be 6 . . . B–Q3; 7 O–O, Kt–K2, when White at best could obtain an insignificant initiative.

| 7 | B–K2! | PxP |

White did not lose a tempo by the manoeuvre B–Kt5–K2, since the Black Queen, too, is not at all well placed on K2 and must soon leave this square. The exchange on White's Q4 only aids the opponent's development and it would have been better to have substituted 7 . . . Q–B2; 8 O–O, Kt–B3.

| 8 | O–O | Q–B2 |
| 9 | Kt–Kt3 | B–Q3 |

Capablanca wants to post his pieces as actively as possible, but the text-move costs him another tempo, since after capturing on Q4 White threatens Kt–QKt5 and thus forces P–QR3. A quicker development of his forces by 9 . . . Kt–B3; 10 Kt(Kt3)xP, B–K2 followed by O–O would therefore have been preferable.

| 10 | Kt(Kt3)xP | P–QR3 |
| 11 | P–QKt3 | |

A plan worthy of consideration here was 11 P–B4! so as to give more weight to his advantage in development by opening up the position with 11 . . . PxP; 12 BxP. The text-move, bringing the Bishop on the long diagonal, is, however, very very good.

| 11 | . . . | KKt–K2 |
| 12 | B–Kt2 | |

Simpler was an immediate 12 KtxKt, PxKt; 13 B–Kt2 so as to eliminate the possibility of 12 . . . Kt–K4. However, Black would hardly have procured for himself any particular advantage by this since White could have continued with 13 Q–Q2, O–O; 14 KtxKt, BxKt; 15 B–Q3, still retaining the better game.

| 12 | . . . | O–O |
| 13 | KtxKt! | |

Apparently illogical, since now Black is relieved of his isolated pawn, but in reality very disagreeable for Black. Black now gets new weaknesses on QR3 and QB3, and the defence of these entails just as much trouble as would that of the isolated pawn.

| 13 | . . . | PxKt |
| 14 | P–B4 | B–K3 |

Black must protect the square Q4 once again since he is threatened with the very awkward 15 PxP, PxP; 16 Q–Q4.

15 Q–B2   PxP

Although Black is now left with weak pawns on QR3 and QB3, this exchange is practically forced. Black must reckon with, in addition to 16 Q–B3 and 16 Kt–Kt5, the positional threat of 16 P–B5, B–B5; 17 P–Kt3, B–R3; 18 B–K5, followed by 19 Kt–Q4, which would ensure White of a completely overwhelming position.

16 BxBP   BxB
17 QxB   KR–Kt1

An interesting idea. Capablanca wants to bring this Rook into play via QKt4, from where it can also protect the King-side. The other Rook must remain for the present at its post so as to protect QR3

18 P–KR3

White has acquired a marked positional advantage out of the opening and thinks that now the time has come to relieve the uncomfortable pressure against his KR2. But there was no necessity for this just yet, and the resulting loss of time gives Black the opportunity of suitably regrouping his pieces.

White has here several very strong continuations at his disposal. Firstly, he could here, by 18 Q–B3, enforce the weakness 18 . . . P–B3, since 18 . . . Kt–B4 loses material because of 19 P–KKt4!, B–Kt5; 20 Q–K5, QxQ; 21 BxQ, Kt–Q3; 22 P–QR3, B–B4; 23 P–Kt4. Secondly, here 18 KR–Q1 would be most effective, since it would result in various tactical possibilities. And finally, if White indeed wanted to free his KR2 from attack then he could have done this better by 18 P–Kt3, which would also have deprived the opposing pieces of the important KB5 square.

18 . . .   R–Kt4
19 QR–B1   R–QB1
20 KR–Q1   Kt–Kt3

Black's position is very difficult. He must try something against the threat of 21 Q–KKt4 (21 . . . Kt–Kt3; 22 RxB!), and in addition he must also bear in mind the possibilities of

Q–B3 or Q–Q4. An intervening 20 ... B–B5; 21 R–B2, would have altered matters very little, since then, too, White could have replied to 21 ... Kt–Kt3; with 22 Kt–Q4 (22 ... R–Q4; 23 R–K1, etc.). Moreover, the simple reply of 22 Q–Q4 would be also very disagreeable for Black.

With the text-move Black opens up for his Bishop a retreat to KB1, whence it can conveniently protect the KKt2 square. In addition he sets his opponent a positional trap.

In fact, after 21 Kt–Q4, Black intends to offer his opponent a promising pawn sacrifice by 21 ... R–Q4, the acceptance of which with 22 QxRP, B–K4! would allow Black excellent counter-play. Unfortunately, however, there is a hole in the trap.

21 Kt–Q4!   R–Kt3

Only now could Capablanca have noticed that the intended 21 ... R–Q4 would not work. White would then continue 22 KtxP!, RxRch; 23 RxR, QxKt; 24 RxB! and retain a good pawn more with the better position. The text-move is the only way in which Black can avoid material loss, but now White initiates a dangerous attack against the enemy King.

22 Kt–K6!

A pretty and exceedingly strong attacking continuation. Naturally the Knight cannot be immediately captured because of 23 QxPch, followed by RxB, but also after the intervening check 22 ... B–R7ch; 23 K–R1, 23 ... PxKt fails against 24 QxPch, K–R1; 25 R–Q7. But if Black tries 23 ... Kt–K4 then White gains a marked advantage by 24 BxKt, QxB; 25 Kt–B5, or 25 R–K1. In addition the simplifying line 24 KtxQ, KtxQ; 25 KxB, KtxB; 26 R–Q2 with the threat of 27 Kt–Q5! is also very strong.

22 ...   Q–Kt1!

Capablanca made this good defensive move almost without thinking and it would appear that he had already prepared for it. The main idea of Black's defence lies in the variation 23 KtxP, B–K4! after which White has some difficulties in connection with his Knight on Kt7. An attempt at attack 24 R–Q7, R–B1; 25 Kt–B5, BxB; 26 Kt–R6ch, K–Kt2; 27 KtxP, would lead to no tangible success on account of the reply

27 ... R–Kt2, and therefore White is practically forced to play 24 BxB. The endgame resulting after 24 ... KtxB! (24 ... QxB; 25 Q–KKt4!); 25 Q–B3, KxKt; 26 P–B4, would, however, afford Black really substantial chances of saving the game by 26 ... R–Kt4.

White therefore rightly decides to proceed with the attack, which seems to promise better results.

| 23 | Kt–Kt5 | R–Kt2 |
| 24 | Q–KKt4 | B–B5 |

Once again we see how much more advantageous it would have been for White to have played P–KKt3 instead of P–KR3.

| 25 | R–B4 | R–Kt4? |

Capablanca, having repulsed the first wave of the enemy attack, becomes over-optimistic and in consequence must now endure a fresh and powerful onslaught. Although Black's position after 25 ... BxKt; 26 QxB would not have been enviable, he should have gone in for it, willy-nilly. Capablanca must, indeed, have said to himself that his position, after the exchange on KKt4, would be lost, slowly but surely, and he therefore decided on further complications in the hope that, in the ensuing combinational play, his young opponent could be led away from the right path.

Black (Capablanca)

White (Keres) to play

26 KtxBP

With both sides short of time White "believes in" his great opponent and does not calculate out the combination 26 RxB! to its end. In reply 26 . . . KtxR; 27 KtxBP, is of course hopeless for Black and 26 . . . P–KR4 fails against 27 Q–Q7, so that Black is reduced to 26 . . . RxKt. But then there follows 27 QxR, QxR (or 27 . . . P–R3; 28 Q–KB5, KtxR; 29 B–K5, etc.); 28 R–Q8ch, RxR; 29 QxRch, Kt–B1; 30 B–R3, P–QB4. Thus far White had calculated and seen that now 31 BxP would not do because of 31 . . . Q–B8ch, and consequently rejected the whole variation. Had he only devoted a couple of minutes more to it, then it could scarcely have escaped him that Black, after 31 Q–B8!, possesses no defence against the threat of 32 BxP, since an attempt at perpetual check would also be fruitless.

However, with the text-move White also obtains an excellent position, and this was one of the reasons why I did not bestow any more exhaustive consideration on the possibilities arising out of 26 RxB!

26   . . .   R–K1 !

Capablanca's cool and resourceful defence in this game certainly deserved a better fate. Capturing by 26 . . . KxKt was, of course, unavailing on account of 27 R–Q7ch, and after 26 . . . R–B1 White can simply continue with 27 Kt–Q6.

27   P–Kt3

Simpler here was 27 Kt–Q8!, RxKt; 28 RxRch, QxR; 29 RxB, etc. With the text-move White gives his King an escape square from the back rank, thereby thwarting all possible threats on that line.

27   . . .   Q–B1 ?

Bearing the time-trouble in mind, Capablanca should have seized his last chance and played 27 . . . BxP. There would then have been several possible ways for White to go wrong. That, however, with correct play the issue of the game would not have been changed by this, is best shown by the following variations:

I. 28 QxB, QxQch; 29 PxQ, KxKt; 30 RxP, and White has a good pawn more with the better position in the endgame.

II. 28 PxB, Q–R2ch (or 28 . . . KxKt; 29 R–Q7ch, etc.);
29 R(B4)–Q4, QxKt; (29 . . . KxKt; 30 K–Kt2, is hardly
better); 30 R–Q7, and there is no satisfactory defence here
against White's attack.

> 28   RxB

White was so absorbed in calculating the consequences of
27 . . . BxP that Black's reply took him completely by surprise
and he quite forgot his original plan of 28 R–Q7! However,
the transition to an endgame with two pawns more that is
forced by the text-move is equally satisfactory. The rest is
no longer of any interest.

28	. . .	QxQ
29	RxQ	KxKt
30	R–Q7ch	R–K2
31	RxRch	KxR

To save such a position not even the endgame skill of a
Capablanca is sufficient.

32	BxP	R–QR4
33	P–QR4	R–QB4
34	R–Kt4	K–K3
35	K–Kt2	P–KR4
36	R–QB4	RxR
37	PxR	K–Q3
38	P–B4	resigns

Game 26

RUY LOPEZ

AVRO World Championship Tournament in Holland 1938

R. Fine   P. Keres

> 1   P–K4

Usually Fine liked to start off with the move 1 P–Q4. But
he had expressly taken up 1 P–K4 for the AVRO tournament
and thoroughly prepared himself for the open type of game.
With White Fine started no less than six out of the seven games
played with 1 P–K4, and achieved splendid success with them.

The present game was played in the last round of the first tour and had a most important bearing on the further course of the tournament. Fine had started brilliantly and with $5\frac{1}{2}$ points out of 6 games he had assured for himself a notable margin above his nearest rivals. In the event of his winning the present game nobody could hardly have threatened to overhaul him, having regard to the short duration of the tournament.

1	...	P–K4
2	Kt–KB3	Kt–QB3
3	B–Kt5	P–QR3
4	B–R4	Kt–B3
5	O–O	B–K2
6	Q–K2	

This Queen move was quite a surprise for Black, as at that time the usual continuation was 6 R–K1. Seemingly Fine had also worked out some innovation here, since otherwise he would scarcely have chosen a continuation which was then still hardly investigated at all.

6	...	P–QKt4
7	B–Kt3	P–Q3

Perhaps Fine had expected here the wild gambit continuation 7 ... O–O; 8 P–B3, P–Q4, taking into account that Black had to play for a win at all costs. Black, however, was not aiming at achieving anything by experiments in the opening, but placed all his hopes in the middle-game, and had as his goal the attaining of a position rich in fighting possibilities. In this respect his opponent comes to meet him halfway in the ensuing phase of the game.

8   P–QR4

This advance was probably the continuation on which Fine had set his hopes. At that time 8 ... R–QKt1 was considered the best reply, since the pawn sacrifice that occurs in this game was held to be good for White. Despite all this I decided to go in for this complicated continuation, since the position that arises after 8 ... R–QKt1; 9 PxP, PxP; 10 P–B3, O–O; 11 P–Q4 in no way attracted me.

        8 . . .   B–Kt5
        9 P–B3

Of course not 9 PxP, Kt–Q5, with advantage to Black.

        9 . . .   O–O!

If Black does not want to go in for this pawn sacrifice then
his only alternative is 9 . . . R–Kt1. But in reply to this White
would seize the initiative by 10 PxP, PxP; 11 P–R3.

        10 PxP

Nowadays everyone knows that White gets nothing with this
exchange, and instead theory recommends 10 P–R3. If then
10 . . . B–R4; 11 P–Q3, whilst if 10 . . . B–Q2; 11 P–Q4.

        10 . . .   ·PxP
        11 RxR   QxR
        12 QxP

At that time this position was regarded as favourable for
White, since at first glance one cannot see how Black can get
his pawn back. An immediate 12 . . . KtxP? naturally fails
because of 13 B–Q5, and after 12 . . . R–Kt1, 13 Q–R4 protects
everything. Moreover, the attempt at refutation 12 . . .
Kt–QR4; 13 B–B2, KtxP in the game Book–Alexander,
Margate 1938, yielded White an advantage after 14 KtxP!,
e.g. 14 . . . R–Kt1 (or 14 . . . PxKt; 15 QxP, and White wins
his piece back); 15 BxKt, RxQ; 16 BxQ, when White retains
his extra pawn.

When I went in for this variation I was convinced that
Black's advantage in development would, nevertheless, ensure
him sufficient counter-chances. After some thought, too, I
succeeded in finding a continuation that deprived the method
of play chosen by White of all its poison.

        12 . . .   Kt–R2!

In this simple move lies the key to the whole method of play.
Black now wins his pawn back and eventually even retains
some slight advantage in development, so that White must
already be thinking of how he can equalise matters. It seems
to me that in the future hardly anyone will display an inclination to go in for capturing the Kt pawn in this variation.

During the game I was convinced that I had introduced an

innovation with my 12 . . . Kt–R2, but soon the contrary appeared to be the truth. The whole variation had already been played in the year 1935 in a game Rogmann–Rellstab, with the continuation 13 Q–R5, QxP; 14 QxKt, BxKt; 15 PxB, Q–Kt3ch; 16 K–R1, QxKt; 17 QxP, Q–Q6; 18 K–Kt1, Kt–R4; 19 Q–B4, QxKBP; 20 B–Q1, Q–B5; 21 QxQ, KtxQ and an eventual draw. But in this line Black, instead of 18 . . . Kt–R4, could have tried the better 18 . . . B–Q1; 19 Q–B4, QxKBP, which would have left him still with some prospects of attack and also with equality in material.

13   Q–K2

After Fine had become convinced that the continuation 13 Q–R5 held out nothing of any promise for him, he wanted to lead back the game with the text-move into quiet paths. But Black's advantage in development ensures him a lasting initiative.

13   . . .   QxP

After 13 . . . KtxP White can either continue 14 P–Q4, or also 14 Q–K3. There is no reason for Black to avoid the ensuing exchange of Queens.

14   QxQ   KtxQ
15   P–Q4

White must allow the weakening of his pawn position on the King's wing and complete his development as soon as possible. For example, after 15 B–Q1, Kt–B4 could be very troublesome.

15   . . .   BxKt
16   PxB   Kt–KKt4
17   K–Kt2

White must choose between two unpleasant alternatives. With the text-move he presents his opponent with yet another valuable tempo for the attack, but he retains his two Bishops and good chances of a successful defence. On the other hand, Black's position after 17 BxKt, BxB, despite the Bishops of opposite colour, would be decisively advantageous. In the first place he would be threatening an attack on the QKt file, and in the second it is possible that White would later on experience difficulties by reason of his weakened King's wing. Which

method of play one recommends depends upon the taste of
the individual master, since in both cases Black's advantage
is unquestionable.

17	. . .	R–Kt1
18	B–QB4	PxP
19	PxP	Kt–K3
20	P–Q5	

Fine certainly did not make this move gladly, since now the
Black Knights take up dominating positions on the Queen's
wing. But White has no choice. After 20 BxKt, PxB the ending
is clearly better for Black, and also the try 20 R–K1, B–B3;
21 BxKt, PxB; 22 RxP, BxP carries in its train only difficulties
for White.

20	. . .	Kt–B4
21	Kt–B3	Kt–B1

One can readily comprehend that Black would like to bring
those of his pieces that are placed on the edge of the board into
play as quickly as possible. Here, however, it would have been
more logical to challenge the enemy Bishop immediately by
21 . . . R–Kt5. After the probable continuation 22 R–K1,
K–B1; 23 B–B1 (or 23 B–R2, Kt–Q6 etc.), 23 . . . P–B4,
followed by 24 . . . B–B3, Black would have an excellent
position and would allow his opponent fewer opportunities
than in the game.

22	R–K1	K–B1
23	R–K2	

With this White closes the diagonal QR6–KB1 for his
Bishop and thus increases his difficulties, but a satisfactory
continuation is hard to find. After the game 23 Kt–K4, was
recommended here, but then there would follow 23 . . . R–Kt5!
and Black would be clearly in the advantage both after 24
KtxKt, RxKt, as after 24 B–B1, Kt–R5.

Comparatively best was probably still 23 Kt–Kt5, but then
Black can, as in the game, capture a pawn by 23 . . . Kt–Kt3;
24 P–Kt3, KtxQP!

23	. . .	P–B4?

Up to here Black has played well and obtained a clear advantage in position, but with the faulty text-move he gives up the greater part of his advantage. White cannot now it is true get his Knight to K4, but the unprotected pawn on KB4 enables him to gain an important tempo, in consequence of which White is in a position almost to even out the game.

So as to increase his advantage Black must naturally continue with 23 . . . R–Kt5! The limited scope of activity for the Bishop would have then set White some difficult problems, e.g. 24 B–QKt5 (or 24 B–R2, Kt–Q6 winning a pawn), 24 . . . Kt–R2; 25 B–B6, KtxB; 26 PxKt, R–QB5 and Black would win the pawn on QB3 with the better position.

After the imprecise text-move some highly interesting complications arise.

24	Kt–Kt5	Kt–Kt3
25	P–Kt3	KtxQP!

As a result of his thoughtless 23rd move Black's advantage has practically disappeared, and he must look around for ways and means to retain the initiative at any rate. With the text-move he commences a deeply calculated combination that, in its main variation, leads to a winning position for Black in the end. Of course White, in what follows, could defend his position on a number of occasions quite differently, but one can also understand how he rejects many of these possibilities, which would leave him with the worse position, in favour of the game continuation in which he seemingly obtains most dangerous counter-play.

Black has no other possibility, in place of the text-move, of bringing about complications that favour him. White threatens, in addition to 26 KtxBP, also 26 B–K3, and the try 25 . . . P–B3?; 26 PxP, P–Q4; would, after 27 P–QKt4!, KtxB; 28 P–B7, followed by PxKt, even work to White's advantage.

26   Kt–Q4

This was White's first opportunity to diverge from the main variation, which was by 26 KtxQP. After the further moves 26 . . . BxKt; 27 BxKt, KtxP; 28 R–Kt2, B–R6; 29 RxKt, RxR; 30 BxR, BxB, an ending would result in which it would

be not at all sure that the Bishops of opposite colour would
yield White a draw. A possible winning plan would be as
follows: Black blockades the enemy BP by P–B5, gets his
Bishop then to QKt3, his King to Q5, and then advances his
QBP. Once this manoeuvre has been carried out then White
must soon give up his pawn on KB2, after which he would
retain merely end-game study type of drawing chances.

It is naturally possible that a penetrating analysis of this
ending would show that White could make a draw, but one
does not go in for such a position of one's own free will.
In addition, in practice the text-move seems much more
plausible, since it threatens 27 BxKt, 27 KtxP, and also 27
Kt–B6.

26 . . .   Kt–Kt5

After other Knight moves, for instance after 26 . . . Kt–Kt3,
there would naturally follow 27 RxB!

27   B–Q2?

It is only this move, with its enticing threat of 28 BxKt, that
is the decisive mistake which allows the opponent to execute
his intended combination. Here White should play simply
27 KtxP, B–B3; 28 B–B4, with good prospects of equality,
although his adversary would still retain the initiative after
28 . . . Kt(B4)–Q6. Apparently White was convinced that
after the text-move Black would have nothing better than to
transpose into this variation by 27 . . . B–B3; 28 KtxP, but
now comes a cruel surprise.

27 . . .   P–Q4!

Black had placed all his hopes on this thrust. The ensuing
complications are more or less forced and lead eventually to a
position where the Black passed pawns on the Queen's wing,
without paying attention to the lost exchange, ensure him an
advantage sufficient for a win.

28   BxKt

White has no choice, since 28 B–QKt5 fails on account of
28 . . . KtxP!

28   . . .   RxB
29   Kt–B6

The endgame after 29 RxB, KxR; 30 Kt–B6ch, K–Q3; 31 KtxR, PxB; 32 PxP, Kt–Q2, is won for Black without much trouble. With the text-move White was perhaps hoping for 29 . . . R–Kt3, whereupon 30 BxP, or 30 KtxB, would have ensured him equality. But Black has quite other plans.

29   . . .   PxB!
30   KtxR   PxP

This concludes the first part of Black's combination. The two passed pawns on the Queen's wing now give him excellent winning chances. But he still has quite a number of technical problems to solve, which, in the ensuing phase of the game, seem far from simple. Firstly Black must take good care that his passed pawns are not blocked. Secondly he must advance his QBP as soon as possible and unite the passed pawns, since the QKtP cannot bring about a decision by itself. In what follows Black manages to solve these problems in combinational fashion.

31   Kt–Q5

Both players had already got into some time trouble, and hence White here makes the most plausible move, but one which is not perhaps the best. Black has greater practical difficulties to surmount after 31 R–Kt2, when White can meet 31 . . . B–B3; 32 R–Kt1, P–Kt7 with 33 Kt–Q5!

But in this case also Black's passed pawns should eventually prove the decisive factor. There could follow: 31 . . . K–B2; 32 K–B1 (after 32 Kt–B6, B–B3 followed by 33 . . . K–K3, or 32 Kt–Q5, B–Q3, Black's task is an easier one); 32 . . . K–K3 (after 32 . . . B–B3; 33 R–Kt1, B–B6; so as to meet 34 Kt–Q5 with 34 . . . B–K4; 35 P–B4, K–K3! White has the defence 34 Kt–Q3!, KtxKt; 35 RxP, etc.) 33 K–K2 (33 R–K2ch, K–Q2 provides White with no relief), 33 . . . B–B3; 34 R–Kt1, P–Kt7 and Black's victory should be only a question of time.

With the text-move White hopes to force his opponent to play 31 . . . B–Q3, which would enable him to make a stubborn resistance after 32 R–Q2. But Black has a surprising and much stronger continuation at his disposal.

Black (Keres) to play

White (Fine)

31   . . .   Kt–Q6!

Now White cannot capture on K7, since both 32 RxB,
P–Kt7, and 32 KtxB, Kt–B5ch lead to immediate loss. But
32 . . . P–Kt7 is threatened, so White has no great choice.

32   R–Q2   P–Kt7
33   R–Q1

After 33 Kt–B3, Black wins both by 33 . . . B–Kt5; 34 RxKt,
BxKt; and by 33 . . . Kt–B5ch; 34 K–Kt3, Kt–R4ch, followed
by B–Kt5, etc.

33   . . .   P–B4

Black, in time trouble, does not find the best continuation.
Technically much simpler here was 33 . . . Kt–B8; 34 Kt–B3,
B–Kt5; 35 Kt–Kt1, K–K2; etc. White's pieces would now be
well-nigh stalemated, whereas Black would be threatening to
advance his QBP. After the text-move White can organise a
further resistance.

34   R–QKt1!   P–QB5
35   K–B1   B–B4!

Black discerns that he cannot force his passed pawns through
willy-nilly, and therefore looks around for more pawns to
capture. White cannot now protect the KBP, since after 36
Kt–K3, BxKt; 37 PxB, P–B6 is immediately decisive. But he
finds another way to procure counter-play.

36 K–K2   BxP!

Apparently very risky, since the ending after 37 Kt–K3, BxKt; 38 KxB, affords White good chances of recovery because of the threat of 39 K–Q4. But Black has once again prepared a surprise.

37 Kt–K3   P–B6!

White must not now play 38 KxKt, BxKt; 39 KxP, since then 39 . . . B–B8 would cut off his Rook completely and the ending would be hopeless for him. But his defensive resources are still not exhausted.

38 Kt–B2   Kt–K8!

Everything fits together beautifully! After 39 KtxKt, BxKt White cannot of course capture on K1 because of 40 . . . P–B7, and after 40 K–Q3, B–Q7 Black wins the ending easily.

39 Kt–R3   B–B4?

After all this complicated and exciting play Black now makes, in his time trouble, an imprecise move, that almost deprives him of the fruit of his method of conducting the game so far. Naturally, he should here have continued with 39 . . . B–R5! when 40 RxKt, BxR; 41 KxB, will not do because of 41 . . . P–B7. Now White suddenly gets a new lease of life.

40 KxKt?

Fine, too, in great time trouble, cannot calculate out all the possibilities. With the text-move he noticeably relieves his opponent's technical task. He must naturally play here 40 RxKt!, BxKt; 41 K–Q3, B–Kt5; 42 K–B2, which would still pose Black some most complicated problems. Consider the following variations:

(1) 42 . . . K–B2; 43 R–K5, K–B3; 44 R–Kt5, B–Q3; 45 R–Kt6, followed by 46 KxP, and Black can scarcely have any winning chances.

(2) 42 . . . P–Kt3; 43 R–K6!, B–B4; 44 R–B6, B–Q5; 45 R–B7, K–Kt1; 46 R–Kt7, and, with his King cut off, it is very difficult for Black to advance his King-side pawns.

From these variations we see that White possesses the disturbing threat of playing his Rook on the QKt file behind the pawns, whereupon in many cases the pawn on QB6 falls and

White obtains good drawing chances. Despite this there exists
here a way by which Black can ensure his advantage in
practically forced fashion. He plays 42 . . . K–B2; 43 R–K5,
B–Q3; 44 RxPch, K–Kt3! Now the RP falls and Black
obtains a passed pawn as well on the other wing, which also
signifies the end. After the further 45 R–Kt5, BxP; 46 KxP,
B–K4ch; 47 K–Q3, K–B4; 48 K–K3, P–Kt4! Black wins by
the advance of his KRP.

We see what complicated problems White could still have
set his adversary by 40 RxKt. After the text-move, on the
other hand, Black's task is no longer difficult.

40	. . .	BxKt
41	K–Q1	B–Q3
42	K–B2	

White has no time to get his RP into safety by 42 P–R3, since
there was threatened 42 . . . B–B5–B8, etc.

42	. . .	BxP
43	R–KR1	B–K4

With this move Black summons up unnecessary difficulties.
He could have won very easily here by 43 . . . B–B5; 44 RxP,
K–B2; followed by 45 . . . B–Q7, after which the advance of
the King-side pawns would be decisive. After the text-move
the ending is still interesting.

44	RxP	K–B2
45	R–R1	P–Kt4
46	R–K1	K–B3
47	R–KKt1	K–Kt3
48	R–K1	B–B3
49	R–KKt1	P–Kt5!

Fine has given his opponent the greatest possible difficulties
by preventing his making a passed pawn on the King's wing
as long as possible. However, with this temporary pawn
sacrifice Black's problem is solved satisfactorily.

50	PxP	P–B5
51	P–Kt5	

Otherwise 51 . . . K–Kt4, followed by P–B6, is quickly
decisive.

| | 51 · · · | B–Q5 |
| | 52 R–Q1 | B–K6! |

The QBP no longer plays any role in the game as it is the KBP which is going to bring about a decision.

| | 53 KxP | B–B8 |
| | 54 R–Q6ch | |

After 54 K–B2, KxP Black wins with his KBP very much as in the game. White no longer has a defence.

	54 · · ·	KxP
	55 R–Kt6	P–B6
	56 K–Q3	K–B5
	57 R–Kt8	K–Kt6
	resigns	

There could still follow: 58 R–Kt8ch, K–B7; 59 K–B2, K–K7; 60 R–K8ch, K–B8; 61 R–KB8, P–B7; 62 R–B7, K–K7; 63 R–K7ch, K–B6; 64 R–B7ch, B–B5 and the BP goes on to Queen.

LIST OF EVENTS

Below we list every event in which Keres took part in the earlier part of his career. The reader will find the year, the place, the result, the number of games played, how many were won, how many lost and how many drawn and the number of points obtained (in that order along the page).

1. *Tournaments*

1929	Parnu	II	18	13	4	1	13½
1930	Tallinn	I	9	7	0	2	8
1932	Tartu	I	9	9	0	0	9
1933	Parnu	I	12	11	0	1	11½
1933	Tallinn	III–IV	7	5	2	0	5
1934	Rakvere	II	9	6	1	2	7
1935	Tallinn	I–II	9	6	2	1	6½
1935	Tartu	I	24	22	0	2	23
1935	Tallinn	II	8	5	2	1	5½
1935	Warsaw	V	19	11	5	3	12½
1935	Helsinki	II	8	6	1	1	6½
1936	Tallinn	I	10	8	0	2	9
1936	Nauheim	I–II	9	4	0	5	6½
1936	Dresden	VIII–IX	9	2	4	3	3½
1936	Zandvoort	III–IV	11	5	3	3	6½
1936	Munich	I	20	12	1	7	15½
1937	Tallinn	I	9	6	0	3	7½
1937	Margate	I–II	9	6	0	3	7½
1937	Ostend	I–III	9	5	2	2	6
1937	Prague	I	11	9	0	2	10
1937	Vienna	I	6	4	1	1	4½
1937	Kemeri	IV–V	17	8	2	7	11½
1937	Parnu	II–IV	7	3	1	3	4½
1937	Stockholm	II	15	9	2	4	11
1937	Semmering-Baden	I	14	6	2	6	9
1938	Hastings	II–III	9	4	0	5	6½
1938	Noordwijk	II	9	4	0	5	6½
1938	Avro	I–II	14	3	0	11	8½
			320	199	35	86	

2. *Matches*

1935	G. Friedemann	3	2	1	0	2
1935	F. Kibbermann	4	3	1	0	3
1936	P. Schmidt	7	3	3	1	3½
1938	G. Stahlberg	8	2	2	4	4
		22	10	7	5	

3. *Other Events.*

1929 Parnu–Wiljandi (Raud)	2	0	1	1	$\frac{1}{2}$
1930 Parnu–Wiljandi (Leoke)	2	0	0	2	1
1932 Parnu–Moisakula (Peet)	2	2	0	0	2
1936 Parnu Team Matches	3	1	1	1	$1\frac{1}{2}$
1937 Esthonia–Lithuania (Mikenas)	2	1	0	1	$1\frac{1}{2}$
1938 Tallinn Team Matches	6	4	0	2	5
1938 Esthonia–Latvia (Petrov)	2	0	1	1	$\frac{1}{2}$
1938 Tartu Student-Matches	3	2	1	0	2
1938 Esthonia–Finland (Salo)	2	2	0	0	2
	24	12	4	8	
Total	366	221	46	99	

OPENINGS INDEX

(The numbers are those of the games)

LIST OF OPPONENTS
(The numbers are those of the games)

THE MIDDLE YEARS
OF PAUL KERES

TRANSLATOR'S PREFACE

THE present volume traces the career and gives a selection
of the games of the middle years of Paul Keres. In the
preceding volume, devoted to the early years, we saw
the fresh brilliance of the young genius inflicting crushing
defeats on the world's best players. Here, in the years 1939 to
1952, we have a more mature Keres, a grandmaster of world
class, who, without losing one whit of his pristine brilliance,
has developed and deepened his style of play. Whilst an
examination of the games contained in this book shows that the
capacity for producing a startling move or an original idea is
just as great as ever, we now observe a rather sterner, more
responsible attitude towards the game. Violence is used when
necessary; but, instead of a careless rapture we get a careful
rapture.

Two most important attributes that go to make up the skill
and genius of the really great chess-player are to be discerned
in Keres's games here. Firstly we begin to see a wonderful
mastery of end-game technique and an understanding the
subtleties of that branch of the game that puts him amongst
the very greatest of end-game experts in the history of chess.
Next, signs develop, more particularly towards the end of this
volume, of a mastery of a fresh field in chess strategy. An
acknowledged grandmaster of the attack, he now shows a
corresponding interest and even delight in the art of defence.

From the material point of view this period is significant in
that it contains a number of great tournament successes and
one bitter disappointment. To take this last first: it will
perhaps be remembered that, just before the Second World
War broke out, Keres had become recognised as a natural
(and indeed official) challenger of Alekhine's for the World
Championship title. The coming of war deprived him of the
opportunity of such a match and, when he did have a chance
of gaining the title a few years after the end of the war in the

match-tournament at the Hague and Moscow, 1948, it was Botvinnik who was in form and who emerged victor. Thus Keres joined the ranks of that very small number of great players of whom it can be said that though they played like a world champion they never held the title. As some compensation in this period Keres won a U.S.S.R. Championship three times, which feat must be round about as arduous as winning the world championship itself. Also, at the beginning of this phase in his career he defeated Dr. Euwe in a match, in very similar fashion to the way both Alekhine and Capablanca won matches against Dr. Euwe, with the one difference that, unlike them, he did not win the world championship either before or after.

Here, as in the previous volume, the reader will find the wealth of Keres's chess mind reproduced in annotations of similar calibre. I have numbered the games in succession to those in the first volume which will explain why the first game here starts off with number 27.

H. GOLOMBEK

★ I ★

THE LAST PRE-WAR YEARS
(from the Russian point of view—translator's note)

IT was often said in the earliest part of my career that I conducted single, decisive games with an insufficient sense of responsibility and earnestness. But my participation in the training tournament at Leningrad and Moscow showed that such was also the case with me in whole events. It was naturally my desire to make acquaintance with the chess-masters of the Soviet Union and measure my strength with them over the board and, finally, to get to know their method of play and their various researches into the game of chess. But I should not in any way have undertaken this in the sort of form I found myself after the AVRO Tournament. I should have copied the example of Botvinnik who quite rightly refrained from taking part in this training tournament.

Naturally, the consequences of this thoughtless behaviour on my part were not long in coming, especially when one takes into consideration the good playing calibre of the tournament participants. I lost two games in the very first rounds and had to make a vastly concentrated effort in order not to collapse completely. I succeeded in winning three good games in the middle part of the tournament, these being a highly complicated struggle against Tolush (No. 27), one with an interesting exchange sacrifice against Levenfish (No. 28) and a well carried out King-side attack against Smyslov (No. 29). But in a whole series of games I conducted play in a style beneath criticism, as for example in easily won endings against Reshevsky and Rabinowitsch, or in the encounter in the last round with Alatorzev. I stood well for quite a long time, but in the end my physical reserves were exhausted. I lost both the last two games and finished up in the lower half of the table.

The result of this tournament was indeed bitter for me, but also extremely instructive. Shortly after the Leningrad-Moscow Tournament I was invited to take part in a fine international tournament at Kemeri, but this time I did not repeat my mistake. I refrained from participating and only took part in national matches against Latvia and Lithuania. The next tournament in which I took part was some months later, the Easter Tournament at Margate. This time I was fresh once again, played very good chess and won the first prize, one point ahead of Capablanca and Flohr. My best achievement in this tournament was against Najdorf (No. 30) where I succeeded in refuting a little combination of my opponent's in interesting style.

Then there ensued participation in the Chess Olympiad which this time was organised in Buenos Aires. Practically all the European teams made the long journey on the same ship, which enabled one not only to have a fine rest but also to get good chess training. Hence I played in the Olympiad easily, without any particular over-exertion, and obtained the second-best result on top board. I achieved a very good game in the preliminary group against Stahlberg in which I exploited the more active position of my pieces in an ending with all the major pieces on the board, and with material equality. This Chess Olympiad was a triumph for the Esthonian team which obtained a most creditable third place against strong opposition. Even a first place was very possible, had not Schmidt been quite out of form on third board and obtained only 33% of the total possible points.

After the Olympiad I stayed for some time in the Argentine and took part in a tournament held by one of the clubs there. I succeeded in sharing first prize with Najdorf, and was able to obtain a revenge this time in our individual game for the defeat I had suffered at Margate.

Before I left for Buenos Aires, I had agreed in principle with Dr. Euwe to play him a friendly match. Although it was a question officially of a friendly match, the general opinion in the chess-world was that the winner would have the moral right of challenging the world champion, Alekhine. My prospects of bringing about such a match through the results of the AVRO tournament, had not proved realisable. In reply to the challenge that went out to the world champion when this tournament was at an end Alekhine answered with conditions that were inacceptable to the AVRO and so further negotiations were broken off. I had to look around for other ways to arrive at this longed-for match. Now, whilst I was in Buenos Aires, I received a telegram from Dr. Euwe saying that all preparations for our friendly match had been made and that play was due to begin at the end of the year. I therefore hurried to return home and by the last days of December we were sitting opposite each other at the chess-board in Amsterdam.

The match began quietly. Both players were testing each other out, and the first two games ended in a draw. The third game was won by Dr. Euwe in good style, and the Dutch grandmaster was also successful in the fourth game, after I had declined a draw and then played for a win in a highly risky way. So the match stood at 3–1 in favour of Euwe, and there remained only ten more games to be played. Therefore I was faced by a difficult choice in the fifth game. I had obtained a slight advantage by a tactical thrust in the opening, and, at one moment, I had to decide whether I would allow exchange of Queens and come down to the rather better ending, or else retain the Queens and surrender my minimal advantage. Finally I decided in favour of the endgame and after Euwe had missed the best defence, I obtained a valuable victory in an ending with Bishops of opposite colour (No. 32).

The sixth game was very important for the further course of the match. I was able to emerge from the opening with a small advantage in space and soon the game had reached an ending with the major pieces. Euwe had a passive position and he had to play a waiting game to see whether his opponent would find a way of achieving a break-through on the King's wing. The critical moment came when the game was due to be adjourned. If Euwe had sealed the right move then he would have been justified in having hopes of saving the game. But the ex-world champion failed to seal the best move and, after a stubborn resistance, he had to acknowledge himself beaten (No. 33). The match was once more equal in score and the struggle could start all over again.

In the seventh game I had a depressing piece of bad luck. A complicated and unclear middle-game arose out of an interesting opening variation, in which Euwe it is true won a pawn, but in return had to allow me quite good chances of attack. But suddenly I put a piece en prise and once again Euwe was in the lead with 4–3. The fate, however, of the match was sealed in the next three games. In the eighth game I succeeded in making a distinct improvement in a variation which had been used in the match between Alekhine and Euwe. I obtained an overwhelming position and won, after Euwe had missed a good opportunity of saving the game. The course of the ninth game was the most interesting of all. Euwe played the opening imprecisely and lost a pawn, with only problematical counter-chances on the King's wing. So as to thwart even these chances I played a positional Queen sacrifice, after which the Black Rooks and Bishop developed formidable fire-power. By my win in this game (No. 34) I was able to take the lead for the first time. Apparently Euwe played the tenth game whilst still under the impression of the preceding loss. He made a terrible blunder in the middle-game, lost two pawns and also, after a long resistance, the ensuing endgame.

In the following game Euwe convincingly refuted my opening experiment and won in good style. This advantage, however, he lost back in the twelfth game which, moreover, was the weakest of the match on his part. With a draw in the 13th game I ensured for myself the win of the match. In the last game Euwe won by excellent play and thus he contrived to lose the match by the smallest possible margin. I had then won the match by 6½–5½ and thus gained a worthwhile victory on the road to the world championship. But in the meantime the possibilities of a title match had sunk to a minimum in consequence of the war that had broken out in Europe.

Game 27

QUEEN'S PAWN, NIMZOWITSCH DEFENCE

Training Tournament in Leningrad and Moscow 1939

	A. Tolush	P. Keres
1	P–Q4	Kt–KB3
2	P–QB4	P–K3
3	Kt–QB3	B–Kt5
4	Q–Kt3	

At the time this game was played, next to the text-move, the most popular continuation was 4 Q–B2, whereas the move that is so popular nowadays, 4 P–K3, was only very seldom seen.

4	. . .	Kt–B3
5	Kt–B3	O–O
6	P–K3	

White has better chances of the initiative here with 6 P–QR3, BxKtch; 7 QxB, P–Q3; 8 P–QKt4, or 8 B–Kt5. After the text-move Black has little difficulty in surmounting all the opening hurdles.

6	. . .	P–Q4
7	B–Q2	

This developing move is more useful for White than 7 P–QR3, after which Black would also continue with 7 . . . PxP; 8 BxP, B–Q3 etc. The manoeuvre can only be averted by 7 PxP, PxP, but in so doing White can scarcely hope for an opening advantage.

7	. . .	PxP!

The capture on QB5 appears to be illogical since it only develops the White pieces, but it is in fact bound up with a deep idea. This becomes clear on the next move.

8	BxP	B–Q3

Now we can see what Black was aiming at with his last move. He wants to force through 9 . . . P–K4, and White cannot well prevent it. In addition to this positional threat Black, however, possesses another, viz. to exchange off the strong enemy Bishop by 9 . . . Kt–QR4. White cannot prevent both.

9   Kt–QKt5

It seems at first glance that White can defeat the enemy plans by 9 B–Kt5, but in actual fact this is not the case. Black can then offer a promising pawn sacrifice by 9 . . . P–K4! In the game Capablanca–Ragosin, Moscow 1936, when, for the rest, the method of play used by Black here was introduced, Black obtained excellent attacking chances after 10 BxKt, PxP; 11 KtxP, PxB; 12 KtxP, Q–Q2; 13 Kt–Q4, Q–Kt5 (in this game, though, Capablanca had continued with 7 P–QR3, instead of 7 B–Q2).

White gets nowhere with the text-move, since Black need not play 9 . . . P–K4 at once. Perhaps therefore it would have been better to have played 9 B–K2, P–K4; 10 PxP, KtxP; 11 Kt–QKt5, or 11 R–Q1, by which, at any rate, White would avoid greater simplification.

9	. . .	Kt–K5
10	KtxB	PxKt
11	O–O	Kt–K2

Black is not too keen on simplifying the position, since 11 . . . KtxB; 12 KtxKt, Kt–R4 would probably lead to a speedy draw. It is true that with the text-move he leaves White with the two Bishops, but in return he prepares counter-play along the long diagonal by P–QKt3 and B–Kt2. A very interesting middle-game now occurs.

12	B–K1	P–QKt3
13	Kt–Q2	KtxKt
14	BxKt	B–Kt2

The position has all the same simplified out to some extent, and White still has his two Bishops. These are however counter-balanced by the powerful position of the Bishop on QKt2, so that the chances of both sides must be appraised as approximately equal.

15   KR–Q1

After 15 P–QR4, Black can continue 15 . . . B–Q4; 16 BxB, KtxB; with a good game, and this is of course possible after the text-move as well. Instead of which Black plunges boldly into complications the outcome of which cannot possibly be reckoned out beforehand.

15 ...   Kt–B4
16 P–Q5

Black had the disagreeable threats of 16 ... Q–Kt4 and 16 ... Kt–R5. With the text-move White does indeed close the long diagonal, but he also limits thereby the scope of his own Bishop and allows his opponent supporting posts in the centre. Now the struggle takes on a sharper character.

16 ...   P–K4
17 Q–Q3   Kt–R5
18 P–B4!

A good move by which White permanently cuts out the possibility of Black's Q–Kt4 and also protects himself against the threat of P–KB4. The hardly noticeable weakening of his own King's position that is bound up with the move has no importance for the moment, since Black has insufficient forces in play to initiate a successful attack on the King.

18 ...   R–B1

Preventing 19 PxP, after which 19 ... Q–Kt4! would follow when White could not well protect the KKt2 square. White's best way of replying to the text-move is by 19 QR–B1, so as to continue with B–R6 as the occasion arises and ensure himself control of the QB6 square.

19 B–Kt3   R–K1
20 B–B3   P–B3

Black wants to maintain his post on K4 at all costs, but these tactics are very dangerous and permit White to develop a threatening initiative. A better method here was 20 ... Q–Q2, so as to meet 21 PxP, by Q–Kt5 and eventually continue himself with 21 ... PxP; 22 PxP, Q–B4. On account of his poor place in the tournament Black must, however, play for a win at all costs and was therefore ready to plunge into great complications.

21 B–R4   R–K2
22 P–B5

Black's situation seems highly precarious, since suddenly his Knight is cut off and White already threatens to win it by

23 Q–K4. An attempt to help matters by 22 . . . P–K5 fails
against 23 Q–B1, threatening 24 Q–KB4, or 24 B–K1. White
had in fact played 21 B–R4, so that Black, in the last mentioned
variation, could not continue with 23 . . . Q–Q2. Apparently
Black is now forced to accept the fact that he must lose material.
But precisely in this difficult position he possesses a surprising
continuation which completely thwarts the opposing plan.

When this circumstance is taken into consideration then
perhaps one must acknowledge Euwe to be right when he
recommends here 22 PxP, BPxP; 23 Q–K4, so as to open up
more lines for the Bishops. It is hardly likely however that,
after this, for instance after 23 . . . R–KB2, White can hope for
an advantage, since Black's pieces are actively placed and can
easily create various tactical threats.

Black (Keres) to play

White (Tolush)

22 . . .   P–QKt4!

A successful tactical stroke right on the other wing! At first
glance one cannot see what Black is aiming at with this pawn
sacrifice. After 23 QxP, Black can of course continue 23 . . .
KtxBP, but White can also capture with 23 BxKtP, and what
has Black then achieved?

A detailed analysis of the position shows that in this case too
Black obtains excellent counter-play, inasmuch as he can make
a combined attack on QKt4 and KB4. He can for example
play 23 . . . Q–Kt3, with the threat of 24 . . . KtxBP. After
the only way of protecting the pawn 24 R–KB1, there comes
24 . . . R–B4; 25 B–B4, P–K5; (25 . . . B–B1 was also good)

26 Q–K2, (or 26 Q–Q4, B–B1;) 26 . . . BxP and Black has regained his pawn with a good game.

Black can however continue differently after 23 BxP, namely 23 . . . P–K5; 24 Q–B1, R–B4. Now there is threatened 25 . . . KtxBP, and after 25 B–Kt4, or 25 B–Q4, there follows 25 . . . R–B7. Or if White tries 25 B–B4, then Black wins his pawn back by 25 . . . Q–QB1, and also after 25 B–R4, Q–QB1 White must give back the pawn on KB5, if he does not want to go in for the highly risky continuation 26 P–KKt4, Kt–B6ch.

23   B–Kt3

Taking the foregoing possibilities into account, Tolush decides upon this simple retreat, but with this Black has attained his aim. Now the Bishop no longer attacks the Q7 square and Black can free his Knight by a correctly timed attack on KB4.

23   . . .   P–K5
24   Q–B1   Q–Q2

Black has solved the problem of his Knight satisfactorily, since White can no longer protect his KB5. Apparently Black is now getting the advantage, but Tolush has prepared a clever defence by which he retains equality.

25   Q–KB4   KtxBP
26   R–KB1

Setting Black a disagreeable choice, since his Knight has once again got into difficulties. After 26 . . . P–Kt3; 27 BxP, R–KB2; 28 B–B3, the White Bishop has too strong a position on the long diagonal QR1–KR8, and there remains therefore only 26 . . . Kt–R3. Then there follows, however, 27 BxP, R–KB2; 28 Q–Kt5, and after 28 . . . R(B1)–B1; 29 B–Q4, RxRch; 30 RxR, RxRch; 31 KxR, P–R4 the endgame should be drawn.

Since it was impossible for Black to accept such a result he decided on the following exchange sacrifice, so as to complicate the situation even more.

26   . . .   RxB!

This exchange sacrifice has good positional grounds. In the first place Black wins a pawn for the exchange, in the second he ensures for his pieces the central point on K4, and thirdly

weaknesses are created in the opposing camp on QB3, Q5 and
K3. Despite this Black should not have been able to break
through even with this sacrifice against a correct defence. It
would appear that the problems of defence that now ensue are
complicated and offer many possibilities for going astray.

27   PxR   R–K4
28   P–QR4

White has conceived the right idea, which is to obtain
counter-play on the Queen's wing, since otherwise he would
soon get into difficulties owing to his pawn weaknesses. Here,
however, he should seize the opportunity of eliminating his
weakness on QB3 by 28 P–B4. Black would then best continue
28 . . . P–Kt5; 29 P–QR3, PxP; 30 RxP, Q–QB2 and thus
assure for himself the control of the black squares on the
Queen's wing.

28   . . .   Q–QB2!
29   PxP

White must carry out the plan conceived in logical fashion.
An attempt to protect the QBP would result in a clear advantage for Black, both after 29 QR–B1, PxP; 30 BxP, BxP, and
29 KR–B1, Q–B4 etc. After the text-move the complications
become even more unclear.

29   . . .   QxP
30   RxP   KtxP!

Black cannot afford to lose time defending his Bishop since,
for example, after 30 . . . Q–B2; 31 R–R4, the advantage would
go over to White. Now White has to return the exchange,
since 31 R–Kt1, Q–Q5! would soon lead to a catastrophe.

31   RxB   KtxR

31 . . . R–B4 would lead to no better result, since after 32
R–Kt8ch, K–B2; 33 R–Kt7ch, a draw is inevitable. This
could be reached immediately by 33 . . . K–Kt1; or more
complicatedly by 33 . . . K–Kt3; 34 QxKP, KtxR; (the pretty
34 . . . Q–Q5 would fail against the simple reply 35 B–B2!)
35 P–Kt4, when 35 . . . Q–B4ch; 36 K–R1, Kt–Kt6ch; 37
PxKt, Q–B8ch; leads to perpetual check.

32   QxKt?

The decisive mistake, which is in fact difficult to explain. White could here get an easy draw by 32 Q–Kt4! since after 32 ... P–Kt3; 33 R–Kt8ch, the Black King cannot escape the checks as can readily be seen. White must only avoid trying to play for a win by 33 Q–Q7, since after 33 ... Q–K6ch; 34 K–R1, Kt–Kt6ch; 35 PxKt, R–R4ch; this would end sadly for him.

Black (Keres)

White (Tolush) to play

Good enough for a draw was also the immediate 32 R–Kt8ch, K–B2; 33 R–Kt7ch. Neither 33 ... K–Kt3; 34 Q–Kt4ch, R–Kt4; 35 QxKPch, nor 33 ... R–K2; 34 RxRch, KxR; 35 QxKPch, would then yield Black winning chances. After 33 ... K–K1; 34 R–Kt8ch, K–K2; however, there can follow 35 Q–Kt4! whereupon it is Black who has to bethink himself how he can get a draw.

Perhaps Tolush cherished here the illusory hope of being able to utilise the position of his Rook on the seventh rank for a mating attack. This plan is however baseless and it soon becomes apparent that the position of the White King is in much more danger. Now Black gets an attack and conducts it, with the help of his strong passed pawn, to a speedy victory.

32	...	QxB
33	Q–B1	P–R4
34	P–R4	P–K6!

Black has here naturally a number of good continuations to put a halt to the enemy attack, but the text-move is the most effective. After an immediate 35 Q–B7, Black now wins easily by 35 ... Q–Q8ch; 36 K–R2, Q–Kt5 etc.

	35	K–R2	P–K7
	36	Q–B7	

White's last hope. Black can now no longer protect his Kt2 directly, but the problem allows of a combinational solution.

	36	. . .	Q–Kt6ch!
	37	KxQ	P–K8 = Qch
		resigns	

Game 28

RUY LOPEZ

Training Tournament in Leningrad and Moscow 1939

	G. Levenfish	P. Keres
1	P–K4	P–K4
2	Kt–KB3	Kt–QB3
3	B–Kt5	P–QR3
4	B–R4	Kt–B3
5	O–O	B–K2
6	R–K1	P–QKt4
7	B–Kt3	P–Q3
8	P–B3	O–O
9	P–QR4	

This move had been played by Ragosin against me a few rounds earlier. He obtained the better position in the middle-game, and eventually won the game. Apparently Levenfish was influenced by this game when he used this continuation here again and he hoped it would once more succeed. In actual fact, the thrust 9 P–QR4 is not particularly dangerous for Black, at any rate not in the form in which it was used in both these games.

The usual continuation here is 9 P–KR3, and praxis shows that White obtains better prospects of the initiative with it than with the rather nervous text-move.

	9 . . .	P–Kt5

This advance is held to be one of the best ways of meeting the line for Black.

	10	P–Q4	KPxP

It is well known that after 9 P–Q4, the best reply is 9 . . .
B–Kt5, pinning the Knight. The interpolation of the moves
9 P–QR4, P–Kt5 has however somewhat altered the situation,
and now 10 . . . B–Kt5 would be a pawn sacrifice of doubtful
validity. White would then continue with 10 P–Q5, followed
by 11 PxKtP, and it is doubtful if Black could then obtain
sufficient compensation for the pawn.

Instead of the text-move 10 . . . KtPxP also merits consideration, so as to reply to 11 KtPxP, with 11 . . . PxP; 12 PxP,
P–Q4; 13 P–K5, Kt–K5, or also simply 11 . . . B–Kt5. Therefore, after 10 . . . KtPxP, White would do better to play 11 QPxP!,
for example: 11 . . . QKtxP; 12 KtxKt, PxKt; 13 KtxP, and
White's position must be regarded as somewhat more promising
(Keres–Smyslov, XXII U.S.S.R. Championship, 1955).

11   PxQP

After 11 KtxP, Black has a thoroughly satisfactory reply in
11 . . . B–Q2, since 12 KtxKt, BxKt; 13 PxP, would be simply
met by 13 . . . BxKP.

11   . . .   B–Kt5
12   B–K3

This move was also employed by Ragosin in the game already
mentioned. In that game Black continued 12 . . . P–Q4; 13
P–K5, Kt–K5; 14 P–R5, Kt–R2; 15 QKt–Q2, K–R1; and
after 16 B–KB4, he tried the pawn sacrifice 16 . . . P–KB4;
17 PxP e.p., BxP; but later got the worse of it. This however
was not because of the opening variation but was due to the
later planless play on the part of Black. With 14 . . . P–B4;
15 PxP e.p., RxP, or also with 14 . . . K–R1, Black could have
obtained a thoroughly satisfactory game. In this game Black
finds an even more convincing reply, which should stamp the
idea begun by White with 12 B–K3 as scarcely acceptable.

If, however, White wanted to arrive at the position in the
game Ragosin–Keres so much, then he could have attained it
had he first played 12 P–R5. Since thereupon 12 . . . BxKt;
13 PxB, would be hardly the best for Black, then it seems he
must continue 12 . . . P–Q4; 13 P–K5, Kt–K5, and then 14
B–K3 yields the desired position. White gets nowhere with
12 Q–Q3. Black can then continue with 12 . . . P–Q4; 13

P–K5, (13 PxP, Kt–QR4) 13 . . . Kt–K5, or also with 12 . . .
Kt–QR4; 13 B–B2, P–B4; 14 QKt–Q2, Kt–Q2, in both cases
with a good game.

12   . . .   Kt–QR4!

This move, universally known in the position without the
moves 9 P–QR4, P–Kt5, is also very strong here and ensures
Black an excellent game. Naturally, 12 . . . KtxKP? fails
against 13 B–Q5.

13   B–B2   P–B4

The attack against the central point Q4 is most uncomfortable for White and disturbs the normal development of his
pieces. Moreover, White must always reckon with the possibility of P–QB5, by which Black obtains a threatening
preponderance on the Queen's wing. On these grounds
White's ensuing move is readily understood. But through it
the QR1–KR8 diagonal is weakened and naturally Black
takes the first opportunity of occupying this line with his
Bishop.

14   P–QKt3   Kt–Q2
15   QKt–Q2   B–B3
16   Q–Kt1

Although so far White has made a series of normal
developing moves, his position is already a little uncomfortable,
this being chiefly due to the pinned nature of his Knight and
to the enemy pressure on the central square Q4. With the
text-move White strengthens his Q4 and threatens an eventual
P–K5 followed by BxPch, but naturally the Queen is not
particularly well placed on QKt1. It is clear that Black has
emerged from the opening with the initiative in his own hands.

16   . . .   P–R3
17   R–R2   Kt–B3

Forces a clarification of the centre since White can no longer
protect his Q4.

18   B–B4?

It goes without saying that the advance 18 P–Q5, is not to
White's taste. Black would thereby command the beautiful
long diagonal with his Bishop and would gain the K4 square

for his pieces. For example, after 18 . . . Kt–R4; 19 B–Q3, R–K1, followed eventually by B–B6 Black would have a lasting hold on the initiative. Nevertheless, this was the only continuation which would allow White a hope of achieving equality.

With the text-move White seeks to solve the problem of the position by combinational means, but in so doing overlooks a tactical finesse and then soon declines into a lost position.

18 . . .   BxKt!

The right sequence of moves! After an immediate 18 . . . KtxP, White can prevent the worst by 19 BxQP.

19 KtxB   KtxP
20 BxQP

Only now does White observe that the intended 21 KtxKt, BxKt; 21 BxQP, would lead to the loss of a pawn by 21 . . . BxPch! He must therefore allow his King-side to be broken up. But with this Black gains the opportunity of initiating a powerful King-side attack in combinational fashion, and against this attack there is no satisfactory defence.

20 . . .   KtxKtch
21 PxKt   B–K4!

Black (Keres)

White (Levenfish) to play

Levenfish probably thought his position strong enough at any rate to ward off direct threats. Thus, for example, the White Bishop would ensure him sufficient counter-play after

21 ... R–K1; 22 P–B4, and also 21 ... Kt–K4, which seems
such a strong continuation, is not entirely convincing. In the
first place White can then, by 22 BxR, KtxPch; 23 K–Kt2,
KtxRch; 24 QxKt, bring about a position in which the opposite
coloured Bishops leave open for him chances for equality, and
in the second place the pawn sacrifice by 22 R–Q1, KtxPch;
23 K–Kt2, Kt–R5ch; 24 K–R1, deserves notice since by these
means the White pieces suddenly become most active.

With the surprising text-move, however, Black makes his
opponent's calculations quite false. White is faced by a disagreeable choice. Either he accepts the exchange sacrifice and
then tries to find a defence against his opponent's powerful
attack, or he exchanges the Bishops and then, in view of his
weaknesses on the black squares stands positionally hopeless.

22   BxR

White prefers the first possibility, since now he has at least a
material equivalent for his bad position. If instead 22 BxB,
KtxB; 23 Q–Q1, (or 23 B–Q1, Kt–Q6, followed by 24 ...
Kt–B5, etc.), 23 ... Q–B3, followed by QR–Q1, when Black
would control the whole board and would soon attain a decisive
attack as well.

22   ...   Q–R5!

Black need not be in a hurry to recapture the Bishop, since
there is time enough for this. For example, after 23 B–K7, in
addition to 23 ... QxB, there is also the very strong 23 ...
Q–R6!, which would have posed the adversary insoluble
problems. After 24 P–B4, BxP; 25 P–B3, Black wins quickly
by 25 ... QxPch; 26 K–B1, Q–R6ch, and also after 24 B–Q3,
BxPch; 25 K–R1, B–B5 dis ch; 26 K–Kt1, Kt–K4; followed
by 27 ... R–K1, Black's win is assured. Worse than useless
too for White would be the possible win of a pawn by 23
BxKtP, since then, after 23 ... KxB, Black could utilise the
open KKt file for attack.

In consideration of all this White tries in his next few moves
to eliminate the threat of 23 ... Q–R6 at least, but his weaknesses on the Black squares render all defence hopeless in the
ensuing phase of the game.

23   B–Q3   QxRPch
24   K–B1   KtxB

This Knight now comes decisively into play via K3 or Kt3. White's position is hopeless.

25	K–K2	Kt–K3
26	B–B4	Kt–B5ch
27	K–Q1	R–Q1ch
28	B–Q5	

White has nothing better, since 28 R–Q2, RxRch; 29 KxR, B–B6ch; or 28 K–B1, Kt–Kt7!; 29 K–B2 (or 29 R(K1)–K2, B–B6 etc.), 29 . . . B–B6!; 30 R–K2, Kt–K6ch!; 31 PxKt, R–Q7ch, etc. lead to an immediate loss. But the text-move is also no great help.

28	...	Q–Kt7

Once Black has attained a clearly won position he relaxes here a bit and allows his opponent to put up a stubborn resistance. An immediate win was to be got here by 28 . . . B–B6; 29 R–B1, Q–Kt7; 30 K–B2, KtxB; 31 PxKt, Q–Kt3ch, or also by 28 . . . KtxB; 29 PxKt, RxPch; 30 K–K2, B–B6 etc.

29	R–Q2	QxPch
30	K–B2	KtxB
31	PxKt	

After 31 RxKt, RxR; 32 PxR, QxBPch, White would also lose the QP.

31	...	B–B6
32	R–K3	

Otherwise White has to give back the exchange.

32	...	Q–B4ch
33	R(Q2)–Q3	QxPch
34	K–Q1	P–B4
35	Q–B1	P–B5
36	R–K7	

After 36 R–B3, there could follow 36 . . . Q–K8ch; 37 K–B2, Q–K7ch; 38 K–Kt1, RxP etc. Now Black once again obtains a mating attack.

36	...	R–Q3
37	R–K6	

There was no longer any defence against the threat of
37 . . . R–KKt3.

37	. . .	RxR
38	PxR	Q–B8ch
39	K–B2	Q–K7ch
	resigns	

Game 29

QUEEN'S GAMBIT DECLINED

Training Tournament at Leningrad and Moscow 1939

	P. Keres	V. Smyslov
1	P–Q4	Kt–KB3
2	P–QB4	P–K3
3	Kt–QB3	P–Q4

The Orthodox Queen's Gambit is a rare bird in modern
tournament praxis with all its Indian systems. The then still
young Master Smyslov wanted to use the classical set-up
against his more experienced opponent, so as to cut out, at
any rate, all possible complications from the opening.

4	B–Kt5	B–K2
5	P–K3	O–O
6	Kt–B3	P–QKt3

Black chooses a quite old defence, which places him in a
comparatively passive position and allows the adversary a
simple initiative. Nowadays the continuation P–QKt3 is used
in conjunction with the defence 6 . . . P–KR3; 7 B–R4,
P–QKt3; so as to continue after 8 PxP, with 8 . . . KtxP, and
thereby forcing a freeing exchange. This method of play,
elaborated by the grandmasters Tartakower and Bondarevsky,
is quite good and has proved itself in a number of tournament
games.

7	PxP	PxP

Without the move P–KR3 7 . . . KtxP is less favourable,
since in many cases White gains a valuable tempo in development by an eventual attack on KR7.

8 B–Q3   B–Kt2

The most natural, but not the best, continuation, since the
Bishop is too passively placed on Kt2. Better is Tartakower's
recommendation 8 . . . B–K3, so as to carry out P–QB4 when
the occasion arises. Then, after 9 Kt–K5, Black gets a satisfactory game by 9 . . . KKt–Q2!

9 Q–B2

Pillsbury, one of the greatest experts in this old variation,
was accustomed to play here 9 Kt–K5, and then to protect his
Knight by P–B4. Later on he castled K and commenced an
attack on the King's wing. In so doing he was wont to allow
counter-play on the other wing by P–QB4 and P–B5. With
this plan Pillsbury won many beautiful games, and even today
9 Kt–K5 is still deemed one of the best methods of meeting
the system chosen by Black.

With the text-move White immediately threatens the pawn
on KR7 and in the second place he leaves himself the option
of castling either side, so as to make his decision only after
seeing his opponent's further plan of campaign.

9 . . .   QKt–Q2
10 O–O

A sharper line here was 10 O–O–O, with a King-side attack
to follow. With this system Grandmaster Rubinstein won
many a beautiful game in his time, amongst others, against
Znosko-Borovsky at the St. Petersburg Tournament of 1909.
But the text-move is equally good and ensures White excellent
play.

10 . . .   P–KR3

Black wants to carry out the sally, Kt–K5, but this would
not be particularly good at once on account of 11 B–KB4. If
then 10 . . . P–KB4; 11 Kt–QKt5! would be disagreeable for
Black, since 11 . . . P–B3; could be met by 12 Kt–B7, threatening
13 KtxR, and 13 Kt–K6. Hence Black would like to drive
back the White Bishop to KR4 with the text-move, and only
then to proceed with 11 . . . Kt–K5.

11 B–KB4

The question is, whether the intended 11 . . . Kt–K5 was in
any case good and whether White could not have set a cunning

trap here by 11 B–R4? However, the position arising from
11 . . . Kt–K5; 12 BxB, QxB; 13 KtxKt!?, PxKt; 14 QxP, is
very complicated and hard to see through. At first glance,
though, one cannot see how Black can obtain adequate compensation for his pawn. Thus, for example, 14 . . . B–Q4, or
14 . . . QR–Kt1 would be met by 15 Kt–K5, and 14 . . . B–B1
allows White the defence 15 Q–B6!

11 . . .	P–R3

Black loses too much time with all these preparatory moves
and thereby gets into a very constricted position. Better is the
immediate 11 . . . P–B4, since Black certainly need not fear the
sally with the Kt to QKt5.

12 KR–Q1	Kt–K1

But now 12 . . . P–QB4 would be met by 13 PxP, PxP; 14
B–B5, after which White would exert powerful pressure in the
centre. With the text-move Black seeks to relieve his position
by a Bishop exchange on Q3, but this is obviously insufficient
to neutralise White's positional advantage.

13 QR–B1	B–Q3
14 Kt–K2	Q–K2
15 BxB	QxB

Black could also recapture here with 15 . . . KtxB, since then
16 QxP? would be of course impossible on account of the loss
of the Queen through 16 . . . QR–B1. After 16 Kt–B4, though,
Black's situation would not be easier than in the game.

16 Kt–Kt3	P–Kt3

This signifies a fresh weakening of Black's King-side, but
otherwise the Knight's penetration to KB5 would be burdensome. Thus, for example, after 16 . . . P–QB4; 17 PxP, PxP;
18 P–K4, P–Q5; the advance 19 Kt–B5, would cause Black
much anxiety. Now, however, White initiates a direct attack
against the enemy King.

17 P–KR4!	P–KR4
18 Kt–Kt5	

Here White has yet another good plan by which he could
have assured himself of an excellent position, to wit 18 P–K4,

PxP; 19 BxKP, BxB; 20 KtxB, followed by 21 Q–B6, etc. One can however understand that White would like to exploit the weakness of the enemy King-side and therefore plays for a direct attack. It should be said, too, that this continuation is no less enduring than 18 P–K4.

18 . . .   P–QB4

At last Black decides upon this thrust, which is the only line holding out any counter-play for him, but now he loses material. It is, however, not easy to find a satisfactory continuation for him. If, for example, 18 . . . P–KB4, then White can already make a most promising Bishop sacrifice by 19 BxBP!, PxB; 20 KtxBP, since after 20 . . . Q–KB3; 21 Kt–Q6! would win back the piece with a won position.

19 B–B5

With this move White commences a fine combination, which however eventually reveals fresh defensive possibilities for Black and therefore does not turn out to be the strongest continuation of the attack. The simplest way to ensure an advantage here for White was the sacrifice 19 KtxRP! After 19 . . . PxKt, he would win his piece back by 20 BxP, and 19 . . . P–B5 would be simply met by 20 B–K2. Also 19 . . . PxP; 20 PxP, R–B1; 21 Q–Kt1, in no way alters the situation.

The ensuing method of attack is however so original and interesting that it seemed a pity to me to reject it in favour of a simple win of a pawn.

19 . . .   PxP

Black must not accept the sacrifice, since after 19 . . . PxB; 20 KtxP(B5), he could scarcely ward off the attack any more, for example: 20 . . . Q–B2 (20 . . . Q–KB3; 21 Kt–K7ch, leads to mate); 21 Kt–K7ch, K–Kt2; 22 Q–R7ch, K–B3; 23 Kt–Kt8ch, RxKt; 24 QxP mate. The text-move is forced, since White was also threatening 20 BxKt, and 21 PxP, winning a pawn.

20 B–K6!

The point of White's plan of attack! Black must not of course capture the Bishop, and otherwise one cannot see any good defence against the threat of 21 QxPch. After 20 . . . Kt–K4 White wins easily by 21 PxP, PxB; 22 PxKt. In this difficult

situation Smyslov finds an excellent defence that occasions his
opponent the greatest difficulties.

20   . . .   P–Q6!

Black gains an important tempo for the defence with this
move as after 21 QxP, there comes the reply 21 . . . Kt–K4,
attacking the White Queen. Another interesting possibility
here lay in 20 . . . K–Kt2; 21 KtxPch, K–R3. If then 22
Kt–B4, P–Q6, and if 22 BxBP, there, without any qualms,
22 . . . KxKt. White can however utilise the exposed position
of the enemy King all the same by simply continuing 22 PxP!,
with the threat of 23 Q–Q2. In the main variation that can
then arise 22 . . . PxB (22 . . . KxKt; 23 Q–Q2! threatening
24 P–Kt4ch, or 24 KtxP); 23 Q–Q2, KxKt; 24 Kt–B7! Black
is checkmated, and the Queen sacrifice by 23 . . . PxKt; 24
Kt–B7ch, followed by 25 KtxQ, and 26 R–B7, in no way alters
the end result.

21   QxP

After 21 RxP, PxB; 22 RxP?, PxR; White is protecting his
KKt3!

21   . . .   Kt–K4
22   Q–Kt1   PxB

Black has no alternative, since in addition to 23 P–B4, he is
threatened with 23 BxP, and 24 P–K4. After 22 . . . Kt–B2
White can force a decision in the following combinational
way: 23 Kt–B5!, Q–Q1 (after 23 . . . PxKt; 24 QxP, K–Kt2;
White wins easily by 25 BxBP!); 24 Kt–R6ch, K–Kt2; 25
Kt(R6)xP!, KtxKt; 26 BxKt, RxB; 27 RxKt! and wins.

23   P–B4!

Black must now return the piece and at the same time
protect his KKtP where, after the capture on K4, an immediate
catastrophe is threatened.

23   . . .   K–Kt2
24   PxKt   QxP

By his resourceful defence Black has beaten back the first
wave of the attack and now looks hopefully to the future,
especially having in mind the possibility of 25 KtxPch, K–R3!
when the White Knight has no square of retreat. But White
still possesses a chance of instilling new life into his attack.

25 R–B1 !

This game is particularly characterised by the great number of different sacrificial lines. With the text-move White seeks to eliminate the strong defensive piece on KB1, so as then to be able to attack the isolated King with success. It is clear, moreover, that Black must not accept the offer of the piece, since after 25 ... QxKt (Kt6); 26 KtxPch, or 25 ... RxRch; 26 RxR, QxKt(Kt6); 27 R–B7ch, all is over.

25 ...   RxRch

Again the best defence. The seemingly good continuation 25 ... Kt–B3, would lose at once on account of 26 R–B7ch, K–R3; 27 RxKt, since mate is threatened on KR7. Weak also is 25 ... QxPch; 26 K–R2, RxR; 27 RxR, when Black no longer has a defence, for example: 27 ... Kt–B3 (after 27 ... Kt–Q3; 28 R–K1, followed by RxP is decisive); 28 RxKt, KxR; 29 Q–B1ch, K–K4 (29 ... K–K2; 30 Q–B7ch, followed by QxB is hopeless for Black); 30 Q–B7, B–B1; 31 Q–B7ch, K–Q5; 32 Kt–B3ch, and White wins.

26 RxR   Kt–Q3?

After a careful and successful defence Black makes a blunder at the decisive moment and now loses quickly. It was absolutely essential for him to play here 26 ... Kt–B3! The seemingly very dangerous sacrificial continuation 27 RxKt!, KxR (after 27 ... QxR White wins by 28 KtxRPch!, PxKt; 29 Q–R7ch, K–B1; 30 QxB, with the double threat of 31 Kt–R7ch, and 31 QxRch); 28 Q–B1ch, K–K2; 29 Q–B7ch, K–Q3; 30 QxB, is still in no way decisive. White is unlucky in that Black, in his otherwise hopeless position, has the resource of 30 ... QxKt(Kt6)!, and after the further 31 QxR, QxKPch; 32 K–B1, Q–B8ch; can bring about perpetual check. White can indeed undertake further winning attempts by 31 QxKtPch, K–Q2; 32 QxPch, K–B2; 33 Q–B7ch, but it is not at all certain that this would lead to success after a careful defence on Black's part.

Instead of 30 QxB, White could also try and win by 30 Kt(Kt3)–K4ch, and only after 30 ... PxKt; play 31 QxB. Then 31 ... Q–Q4; 32 Kt–B7ch, K–B4; 33 Q–B7ch, K–Kt5! would lead to an unclear position in which White would not be without winning chances. But here too Black can play better by not capturing the Knight at all and by continuing with 30 ... K–B3! After 31 KtxP, P–QKt4!, the Black King can escape via QKt3, and one cannot see how White can continue the attack successfully.

We see from these variations what dangers the Black King must surmount and how narrow is its escape from destruction. It is therefore not to be wondered at that Smyslov, after a long and tiring defence and with a limited amount of time at his disposal, could not accurately reckon through all these complicated variations, and decided upon another method of defence. With this Black does indeed protect himself against all immediate threats, but in the long run he cannot succeed in warding off the enemy attack.

Black (Smyslov)

White (Keres) to play

27	KtxRPch!	K–R3
28	Kt–B6	QxPch

Once again the only defence, since 29 Kt–Kt4ch was threatened, and after 28 ... K–Kt2; 29 Kt–Kt4, Q–KKt6; 30 R–B6!, Kt–K5; 31 R–B7ch, leads to mate.

29	K–R1	Q–Q5

Here too the Black King would fall into a mating net after 29 ... K–Kt2; 30 Kt–Kt4, Q–K7; 31 R–B6!, etc.

30	KtxKP	QxPch
31	K–Kt1	P–Q5

Black no longer has any satisfactory defence against the many threats. If, for example, 31 ... R–QB1, in order to prevent the check on QB1, then White wins at once by 32

R–B4, Q–Kt6; 33 R–B3. Now, however, an equally speedy finish comes about.

32	Q–B1ch	P–Kt4
33	Q–B7!	resigns

A very interesting and combinational game in which the mistake committed by Black on his 26th move should not particularly affect the logical nature of play.

Game 30

QUEEN'S GAMBIT DECLINED

International Tournament at Margate, 1939

	P. Keres	M. Najdorf
1	P–Q4	Kt–KB3
2	P–QB4	P–K3
3	Kt–QB3	P–Q4

Usually Najdorf favours sharper systems of development, such as occur in the King's Indian or the Nimzowitsch Defences. The Orthodox Defence to the Queen's Gambit is in any case rarely found in his opening repertoire.

4	B–Kt5	B–K2
5	P–K3	o–o
6	Kt–B3	QKt–Q2
7	PxP	

Black apparently desired, if his choice of opening be any guide, to play a quiet positional game, and White declares with this that he accepts the offer. I had a very good position in the tournament table and therefore the exchange variation suited me very well, since in this line White, with a secure position, retains the initiative for a long time.

7	. . .	PxP
8	B–Q3	P–B3
9	Q–B2	R–K1
10	P–KR3	

This move, which comes in useful for White in many cases, was not exactly necessary at the moment, since Black was not yet threatening anything on Kt5. Hence better was an immediate 10 0–0, Kt–B1; 11 QR–Kt1, followed by P–QKt4, by which a worthwhile tempo could have been saved.

10   ...   Kt–B1

11   0–0

This quiet continuation appears to me to be better based positionally than sharp play for attack by 11 0–0–0. Black's King's position contains no weaknesses and it is well supported by its own pieces, so that a direct attack affords little prospects of success. At the same time, too, Black can undertake a disagreeable manoeuvre designed to break open the Queen-side by B–K3, R–B1 and P–B4.

11   ...   Kt–R4

Sooner or later Black must clear up the situation on the King's wing, even though this costs him a couple of tempi. With the text-move he puts his Knight into an unfavourable position on the edge of the board, but the other possibility 11 ... Kt–K5 also has its dark sides. White would then reply 12 B–KB4, whereupon Black must, if he does not want to resign himself to 12 ... P–KB4, and yet still wishes to exchange off the black coloured Bishops, decide upon the exchange 12 ... KtxKt; 13 QxKt, and only then play 13 ... B–Q3. In reply to this, however, 14 BxB, QxB; 15 P–QKt4, would lead to a position where Black, in comparison to the game continuation, would have made no great progress.

12   BxB   QxB

13   QR–Kt1

With this move White prepares the advance on the Queen's wing by P–QKt4–5 that is characteristic of the whole variation. After this manoeuvre Black would be faced by a disagreeable choice. Either he permits the exchange on his QB3 and takes on the weakness on QB3, or he himself exchanges on QKt4, whereupon the pawns on QKt2 and Q4 become objects of attack. Praxis shows us that Black finds it difficult to make a good defence against this plan, since a counter-attack on the other wing is not easy to carry out and, furthermore, offers little prospect of success. In this present game too Najdorf does not succeed in solving the opening problem satisfactorily.

13   ...   Kt–B3

Many experts would certainly criticise Najdorf for not trying anything against his opponent's plans, and would here advocate 13 ... P–QR4. In fact, however, with this move Black would achieve only what he actually obtains later with his P–QR3, this being the exchange of a couple of pawns, by which, too, the QR file is opened up. The question whether this circumstance relieves Black's defence, is however arguable, and is indeed a question of taste for each player. After 13 ... P–QR4 White could continue with an immediate 14 P–R3, or else first 14 Kt–QR4, and would then pursue his attack as in the game.

	14	P–QKt4	B–K3
	15	Kt–QR4	

Naturally, not immediately 15 P–Kt5, when Black, by 15 ... P–B4 would obtain a comparatively satisfactory position. After the text-move Black, by a skilful tactical manoeuvre, gets his Knight to the strong square, Q3. White could however hardly prevent this, since after 15 KR–B1, there could follow 15 ... KR–B1, and Kt(B3)–K1–Q3 can no longer be prevented.

	15 ...		Kt–K5!

Black makes use of the circumstance that, after 16 BxKt, PxB; 17 QxKP, White's QRP would be unprotected. Black could then play at once 17 ... BxQRP, with the continuation 18 QxQ, RxQ; 19 R–R1, B–B5; 20 KR–B1, B–R3; 21 Kt–B5, B–Kt4, etc. but stronger still would be 17 ... Q–B3! with a very good position for Black. White naturally refuses to go in for this and quietly continues with his own plans.

	16	Kt–B5	Kt–Q3

Here the Knight is beautifully placed, since it assumes control of a whole row of important central squares. White must now also always reckon with the possibility of P–QKt4 followed by Kt–B5, by which pressure on the QB file would be neutralised.

	17	P–QR4	P–B3
	18	KR–B1	B–B2
	19	Kt–Q2	P–KKt3

Black already has to decide here what plan of play he intends to select in the event of White executing his threatened

P–QKt5. If he wants to allow his opponent to exchange pawns on QB3, then 19 . . . B–Kt3 comes into consideration here, so as to get rid of the passive Bishop. But should he want himself to capture on QKt4, then the Bishop must remain where it is as a protection of Q4. Najdorf has plumped for the latter plan and with his last move he has muffled the threat on his KR2 so as to be able to move his other Knight.

20   P–Kt5   PxP

With this direct exchange, however, Black meets his opponent's plans more than half-way. Better, at any rate, would have been 20 . . . KR–B1, so as to meet 21 PxP, with 21 . . . RxP. Thereby Black would have gained time and not assisted a White pawn to establish itself on QKt5, as happens in the game. Now indeed Black gets into serious difficulties.

21   PxP!

Stronger than 21 BxQKtP, KR–B1 which would have permitted Black prospects of counter-play on the QB file. White now threatens, as the occasion arises, to advance with his pawn to Kt6 which, in the event of P–QR3, would leave him with a strong point of support on QB7, or, after an exchange on QKt6, would create a good object of attack on QKt7.

21   . . .   KR–B1
22   Q–Kt3   Kt–Q2

22 . . . Kt–K5 would be worse than useless, as after 23 Kt(Q2)xKt, PxKt; 24 B–B4, BxB; 25 QxBch, followed by 26 Q–Q5, Black would experience great difficulty in protecting his pawns. With the text-move Black parries the threat of 23 P–Kt6, and intends himself to play 23 . . . Kt–Kt3, so as to gain control of the QB5 square.

23   Q–Kt4!   Kt–K5?

White has prevented 23 . . . Kt–Kt3 by means of the threat of 24 KtxP. Bad also would be 23 . . . K–B1; on account of the answer 24 P–K4, and after 23 . . . R–K1 there could follow simply 24 KtxKt, QxKt; 25 P–Kt6, etc. Hence Black should have tried here 23 . . . Kt–K1, although then White would have a clear superiority after 24 R–B2.

With the text-move Black embarks on an attempt to solve the problem of the position in combinational fashion. He is counting upon the fact that after the double capture on K5 the reply P–Kt3 would attack a number of enemy pieces. There is, however, a hole in this combination which enables White to attain a won position immediately.

Black (Najdorf)

White (Keres) to play

24	Kt(Q2)xKt	PxKt
25	BxP!	P–Kt3

It was on this move that Black had based his hopes. After 26 KtxKt, there would now come 26 . . . RxRch; 27 K–R2, QxQ; followed by QR–QB1, and other Knight moves would naturally be answered by 26 . . . QxB. After 26 BxR, PxKt; White apparently also loses his Bishop but now Black is faced by a cruel surprise.

26	BxR	PxKt
27	RxP!	

With this the enemy combination is utterly refuted, since now White obtains an easily won endgame with two plus pawns. Also here White has the possible line 27 PxP, RxB; 28 P–Kt6!, with good winning chances. But in this case Black could still put up a tough resistance with 28 . . . Kt–K4!, for instance: 29 P–Kt7, R–Kt1; 30 P–B6, Q–B2, or also 29 Q–K4, R–Q1; 30 P–Kt7, Q–B2, etc. The game continuation is more forcing and certainly prettier.

27 . . .	KtxR

After 27 . . . RxB; White wins the Queen by 28 R–B8ch!

28	B–B6!

Now the Knight on QB4 is pinned and must be lost, after which White has an easily won endgame.

    28   ...   P–QR3

The last hope: 29 QxKt?, QxQ; 30 PxQ, PxP; and White loses his QBP.

    29   PxKt   PxP
    30   QxP   resigns

Perhaps a little prematurely, but the endgame after 30 ... Q–B2; 31 B–Q7, followed by 32 P–B6, would certainly afford Black no satisfaction.

Game 31

CARO KANN DEFENCE

International Tournament at Buenos Aires 1939

	P. Keres	M. Czerniak
1	P–K4	P–QB3
2	P–Q4	P–Q4
3	PxP	

This game was played in the last round, when Najdorf was half a point above me. I therefore had to play for a win at all costs. The exchange on Q5 seemed to me to be much in favour of this aim, since usually one gets a full middle-game therefrom, without having to fear any immediate and considerable exchanges.

3	...	PxP
4	P–QB4	Kt–KB3
5	Kt–QB3	Kt–B3

Nowadays 5 ... P–K3 is usually played here, after which the game takes on similar characteristics to those of the Queen's Gambit. Czerniak had, however, prepared an innovation for the present game, with which he wished to surprise his opponent.

6	B–Kt5	Q–R4

This is the innovation already mentioned. It is naturally very unpleasant to meet with a prepared innovation over the

board, especially when one is so placed that one must strive
for an advantage at all costs.

7   Q–Q2

Undoubtedly one of the best ways of meeting the system
chosen by Black. The other continuation that deserved consideration here, 7 BxKt, KPxB; 8 PxP, did not exactly appeal
to me because of 8 . . . B–QKt5, when, after 9 PxKt, BxKtch;
10 PxB, QxPch; 11 K–K2, Black, by 11 . . . o–o!, obtains an
overwhelming attack in return for the piece. White could play
better here of course, the right line being 9 Q–Q2, BxKt; 10
PxB, QxQP; 11 Kt–B3, with perhaps a minimal superiority,
though the reverse of the medal being the simplified position.

7   . . .   PxP

Now, however, Black should have undertaken something for
the defence of Q4. Apart from the text-move the sharp thrust
7 . . . P–K4 advocated by Pachman deserves consideration,
since it leads to very complicated positions that have been but
little studied in practice. It is however doubtful if Black would
have had more success with it than with the text-move. For
example, in the main variation given by Pachman 8 BxKt,
KtPxB; 9 KtxP, QxQch; 10 KxQ, B–R3ch; 11 K–B3, PxPch;
12 K–Kt3, o–o White need not indeed capture on B6, but can
try 13 B–Q3, in order to make clear White's advantage on the
white squares.

The move recommended by Czerniak, 7 . . . B–B4, which
leads to equally complicated variations, is also not convincing.
Without going in for a thorough analysis, I should like to
question the validity of the following variation given by
Czerniak: 8 PxP, KKtxP; 9 B–QB4, KtxKt; 10 PxKt, B–K5;
11 Kt–B3, BxKt; 12 PxB, P–K4. After this Black would have
to struggle against great difficulties if White played 13 o–o!

8   BxP   P–K4

The execution of this advance was one of the advantages of
the move 6 . . . Q–R4. Black can now completely free his
position, but this in turn will open it up, when White's better
development will ensure him the initiative.

9   P–Q5   Kt–Q5
10   P–B4!

By an energetic attack against the Q 5 and K 5 squares White forces the enemy pieces to adopt defensive positions. Black has now little choice, since counter-attack by 10 . . . B–KB4 would permit White to make a most promising exchange sacrifice: 11 PxP!, Kt–B7ch; 12 K–B1, KtxR; 13 PxKt, etc.

	10 . . .	B–Q3
	11 KKt–K2	Kt–B4

The other possible method of play here, 11 . . . KtxKt; 12 QxKt, o–o (12 . . . B–KKt5; 13 B–Kt5ch!); also yields White the better game. He should not then play for the trap 13 PxP, BxP?; 14 QxB, R–K1; 15 BxKt, RxQch; 16 BxR, with advantage to White, since this would be thwarted by the intervening move of 13 . . . B–KKt5! and then 14 . . . BxP.

The simple continuation 13 BxKt, PxB; 14 o–o! would also ensure him here of a clear positional advantage.

The text-move leads to no better result, and in addition Black now loses the right to castle.

	12 B–Kt5ch	B–Q2
	13 BxKt	PxB

The continuation 13 . . . BxB; 14 BxKP, would lose a pawn without adequate compensation. Now White obtains a clear preponderance on the white squares.

	14 BxBch	KxB
	15 o–o	

An inexactitude, after which Black is able to bring his Knight into play with the win of a tempo and can then set up some worrying threats. Better was 15 Q–Q3, or also immediately 15 PxP, BxP, and only then 16 o–o

	15 . . .	Kt–K6!
	16 R–B3	

Also worthy of consideration was the exchange sacrifice by 16 PxP, KtxR (or 16 . . . B–B4; 17 K–R1, KtxR; 18 RxKt, etc.); 17 P–K6ch! and then RxKt with a very strong attack.

	16 . . .	Kt–Kt5
	17 Q–Q3!	

The threats of 17 . . . Q–Kt3ch, or 17 . . . B–B4ch could also have been parried by 17 QR–KB1, but the text-move is

stronger. Black must not now accept the exchange sacrifice,
since after 17 . . . Q–Kt3ch; 18 K–R1, Kt–B7ch; 19 RxKt,
QxR; 20 Q–Kt5ch, K–B2; White wins by 21 Kt–K4! After
17 . . . B–B4ch; 18 K–R1, Kt–B7ch; 19 RxKt, BxR; however,
20 PxP, threatening 21 Q–B5ch, is decisive.

17	. . .	QR–KKt1
18	K–R1	Q–Kt3
19	QR–KB1	K–B1

At long last Black gets his King into safety. Black would now
have a very good position if it were not for the fact that White
has retained his absolute preponderance on the white squares.
This circumstance prevents the co-operation that is essential
for the Black pieces in the ensuing phase of the game.

20	P–KR3	P–KR4

Black does not want to put this piece entirely out of play by
20 . . . Kt–R3, but the text-move signifies merely a temporary
protection of the piece.

21	Kt–K4	K–Kt1
22	Q–Kt3!	

With this strong move White forces the enemy Queen to
abandon the QR2–KKt8 diagonal, since he threatens now 23
QxQ, followed by 24 KtxB, and the Queen exchange 22 . . .
QxQ; 23 RxQ, would, surprisingly enough, cost Black a piece.

22	. . .	Q–R3
23	Kt(K2)–Kt3	PxP

White was threatening a decisive strengthening of his position
by 24 Kt–KB5. It is instructive to observe how Czerniak, in
a situation that is so difficult for him, always finds fresh defensive
resources and thereby forces his opponent right to the end to
play the most exact and accurate moves.

24	Kt–KB5

At first glance Black's position now appears quite hopeless.
His Bishop is attacked, and if 24 . . . B–B1; then 25 P–Q6, or
also 25 RxP, with a won game for White. After 24 . . . B–K4,
however, White even wins the Queen by 25 Kt–B5.

24	. . .	Kt–K6!

A clever defence! A superficial consideration would at once reject this move, since after 25 Kt(B5)xB, KtxR; 26 Kt–QB5, the Black Queen is trapped. But it is precisely in this variation that there lies the cunning trap devised by Czerniak. Black would, after 26 Kt–QB5, play the unexpected 26 . . . Kt–Kt6ch! If then 27 RxKt, Black wins by 27 . . . Q–B8ch, and after 27 K–Kt1, Q–Kt3! the White Knight would be pinned. Hence White must continue with 27 K–R2, whereupon there would come 27 . . . Kt–B8ch. Now White would have to be content with a draw, since the attempts to win by 28 RxKt, RxPch!; 29 KxR, Q–K7ch; or by 28 K–Kt1, RxPch!; 29 KxR, Q–K7ch, would in both cases lead to mate. A very pretty variation!

It is a pity that this resourceful defence by Black is of little use, since White is not indeed forced to play for the win of the Queen. Instead of this he can reach a favourable major piece ending with a good pawn more.

Black (Czerniak)

White (Keres) to play

25	KtxKt!	PxKt
26	QxP	B–K4
27	KtxP	

In view of the fact that White is threatened by time trouble, his decision to get down to an ending is most judicious.

27	. . .	BxKt
28	RxB	QxP
29	Q–K5ch	K–R1
30	RxP	

The plus pawn, together with the active position of his pieces and the strong passed pawn, now ensure White the victory, although exact technical work is still demanded for this. The immediate threat is 31 QxR!

30 ...   Q–B5

Black protects himself against the threat in combinational fashion (31 QxR, QxRch;) and at the same time gets his Queen into play.

31 P–QKt3   Q–B7

Naturally not 31 ... QxKtP? because of 32 QxR!

32 R(B1)–B2   Q–QB4

After this White can bring about a Queen exchange under favourable circumstances, but other moves too would not be much better. After Czerniak's recommended 32 ... Q–B8ch; 33 K–R2, P–R3, White can either continue 34 P–Q6, or 34 Q–K7, so as to answer 34 ... R–Kt1 with 35 R–R2.

33 Q–K7

Undoubtedly the simplest continuation in view of White's time trouble. Otherwise here 33 P–QKt4! would have been very strong since in fact 33 ... QxKtP fails against 34 R–Kt2.

33 ...   QxQ

Practically forced, since 33 ... Q–B1; 34 R–B2, or 33 ... QxP?; 34 R–B8ch, give an even more painful end for Black. The Rook ending, however, is won for White without much trouble.

34 RxQ   R–Q1
35 R(B2)–B5   P–R5
36 K–Kt1   R–QB1

With this Black gets his Rook behind the passed pawn but only hastens his loss in so doing since his King has no escape square. A more stubborn resistance here could have been put up by 36 ... P–R3.

37 P–Q6   R–B8ch
38 K–R2   R–Q8
39 P–Q7   R–Q1

Black thinks he has built up a solid defensive position with this move and that now his King can get to QB2 so as to win the QP. But the fact that Black has no loophole for his King allows White to finish off the game by a pretty mating combination. The same line would also have come after 39 . . . R–QKt1.

40	R–K8 !	RxP
41	R(B5)–B8 !	resigns

Black loses at least a whole Rook.

Game 32

QUEEN'S PAWN, NIMZOWITSCH DEFENCE

Fifth game of the match in Holland 1939/40.

	M. Euwe	P. Keres
1	P–Q4	

The earlier games of this match all commenced with the Ruy Lopez and yielded Euwe a lead of 2:0 with two draws. It is therefore rather surprising that Euwe here himself refrains from the move 1 P–K4 of his own accord, in view of his having obtained such good results with it hitherto.

1	. . .	Kt–KB3
2	P–QB4	P–K3
3	Kt–QB3	B–Kt5
4	Q–B2	o–o

One of the most elastic continuations for Black in this variation by which he leaves his further plan of play quite open.

5	B–Kt5

Apparently Black's last move enabled his opponent to carry out the advance 5 P–K4 unhindered, which indeed was the main purpose of 4 Q–B2. Praxis shows, however, that Black would then have a very satisfactory position, if he were then either to play the sharp 5 . . . P–Q4, or the positional 5 . . . P–Q3 followed by 6 . . . P–K4.

5	. . .	P–KR3
6	B–R4	Kt–B3

After White has developed his Bishop on KKt5 this move is inexact and allows White to seize the initiative, as the sixth

game of the match (No. 33) shows. Much better here was
6 ... P–B4 which, after 7 PxP, Kt–R3, would lead to a position
arising out of the variation 4 ... P–B4 that would be good for
Black.

7   P–K3

Stronger here is 7 Kt–B3, which would have led to a position
in the sixth game of the match. After the text-move Black can
more easily force the important advance of P–K4.

7 ...   R–K1

An interesting idea. Black wants to carry out the thrust
P–K4 without a preparatory 7 ... P–Q3, with the idea of

Black (Keres)

White (Euwe) to play

utilising with the text-move his opponent's King's position on
K1 for various tactical finesses.

8   B–Q3?

White wants to achieve the development plan of B–Q3
followed by Kt–K2 and o–o, but in so doing he fails to reckon
with his opponent's possibilities. The text-move is in any case
inexact and allows Black to seize the initiative. The right
continuation here was 8 Kt–B3, although here too after 8 ...
P–K4 the gain in time allowed by the omission of P–Q3 would
display its advantage (9 P–Q5, Kt–Q5!).

Not particularly strong here on the other hand was 8
P–QR3, BxKtch; 9 QxB, since then Black can utilise his
advance in development with the energetic thrust 9 ... P–K4!
After 10 P–Q5, there follows once again 10 ... Kt–Q5!

together with an eventual Kt–B4, and after 10 PxP, KtxP,
Black plays later on Kt–Kt3. Very interesting complications
may arise in the event of White trying to defend the centre by
10 Kt–B3. Black can then in fact bring about complications
that are favourable to him by 10 . . . PxP; 11 KtxP, P–KKt4.
If then 12 KtxKt, QPxKt; 13 B–Kt3, Kt–K5 etc., and after
12 B–Kt3, Kt–K5 White cannot play 13 Q–Q3, because of
13 . . . Kt–B4; 14 Q–Q1, KtxKt; 15 QxKt, Kt–Kt6; when
Black wins the exchange.

8 . . .   P–K4

Once again Black can execute this important thrust without
a preliminary P–Q3. From now on White is confronted by
some really serious problems.

9 P–Q5?

Subsequent analysis showed that White could still have
obtained a tenable position here by continuing with 9 PxP,
KtxP; 10 Kt–K2, (in reply to 10 B–K2, there comes 10 . . .
Kt–Kt3). It is easily understood, however, that no one would
willingly go in for such a continuation. Hence Euwe selects
another way and pursues the contest in a game of fighting
character.

In actual fact this advance turns out to be a mistake which
already ensures Black a real superiority. The ensuing complications are highly interesting.

9 . . .   P–K5!

White had seemingly underestimated the force of this
intervening move, since now he gets into great difficulties. It
is interesting to observe that another sharp continuation was
possible here, namely 9 . . . Kt–Q5, which would also have
afforded Black a most promising position after 10 Q–R4,
P–K5! White could, however, play better with 10 PxKt, PxP
dis ch; 11 Kt–K2, PxKt; 12 PxP, followed by 13 0–0, with a
reasonable game.

10 PxKt

Capture on K5 would give Black, after 10 . . . RxB!, a
marked advantage, e.g. 11 BxKt, QxB; 12 QxR, BxKtch; 13
K–B1 (White loses a piece after 13 PxB, QxQBPch; 14 K–K2,
Q–Kt7ch), 13 . . . BxP; 14 PxKt, P–Q4! (even stronger than

14 . . . QPxP); 15 Q–K8ch (after 15 QxP, B–K3 White loses
his QR), 15 . . . K–R2; 16 R–Q1, KtPxP with a won game for
Black.

After 10 B–B1, Kt–K4 White experiences difficulties in
developing his King's wing. The text-move is perhaps the best
way out of his dangerous situation.

        10   . . .   PxB
        11   QxP   QPxP!

Black could also get a good game here by 11 . . . KtPxP
followed eventually by B–R3, but the text-move is more
forcing and leads in the end to a very good endgame for
Black. Despite the ensuing exchange of Queens, Black still
retains a most dangerous initiative.

        12   QxQ

White has no choice. The attempt to get castled by 12
Q–B2, and then Kt–K2, gives Black a clear advantage after
12 . . . Q–Q5!; 13 BxKt, QxB.

        12   . . .   BxKtch!

It is true that Black would have the two Bishops after 12 . . .
RxQ; 13 BxKt, PxB; 14 R–B1, but White's better pawn
position would yield him prospects of successful defence. After
the text-move White must not, however, continue with 13
PxB, RxQ; 14 BxKt, PxB, since the ending would be won for
Black, for example: 15 Kt–B3, B–K3; 16 Kt–Q2, R–Q6; 17
R–QB1, QR–Q1; etc.

        13   Q–Q2   BxQch
        14   KxB   Kt–K5ch

Despite considerable simplification the resulting endgame is
clearly better for Black. In the first place his pieces are better
developed and have more active posts; in the second place
White's King can find no safe haven of refuge, and thirdly,
with his Rook Black controls the only open file. The Bishops
of opposite colour do not constitute any danger of drawing
here and merely increase the possibilities of attack for Black.

It is naturally difficult to say if all these advantages suffice
to yield Black a decisive superiority. But one thing is clear:
Black has a superiority and in the ensuing phase of the game

White has to conduct a difficult defensive struggle without prospects of counter-attack.

15   K–K2

The White King disposes of no square from which it does not interfere in some way with the development of its own pieces. After 15 K–K1, or 15 K–B1, Black has the disagreeable 15 . . . Kt–B4, threatening 16 . . . Kt–Q6ch.

15   . . .   B–K3
16   R–QB1

After 16 P–QKt3, there can follow 16 . . . P–KKt4; 17 B–Kt3, QR–Q1; 18 Kt–B3, B–Kt5, when White must not play 19 KR–Q1, because of 19 . . . Kt–B6ch.

16   . . .   P–KKt4
17   B–Kt3   QR–Q1
18   Kt–B3   P–QB4!

The enticing possibility of 18 . . . P–Kt5; 19 Kt–Q4, RxKt; 20 PxR, BxPch, so as to meet 21 RxB, with 21 . . . KtxB db. ch, followed by 22 . . . KtxR, does not lead to the desired goal. White can still defend himself by 21 K–Q1!, BxP; 22 K–B2, etc. With the text-move, on the other hand, Black deprives the enemy Knight of the Q4 square and threatens to win offhand by 19 . . . P–Kt5. The question now is whether White could capture the pawn offered him on QB7.

19   KR–Q1

After long thought Euwe rejects the proposed gift. In the event of 19 BxP, Black would have had two continuations that ensure him the superior game, namely:
(1) 19 . . . P–Kt5; 20 BxR, RxB; 21 KR–Q1 (after 21 Kt–K5, R–Q7ch, followed by 22 . . . RxBP, Black's advantage is naturally beyond all doubt), 21 . . . PxKtch; 22 PxP (or 22 KxP?, RxR; 23 RxR, B–Kt5ch! and wins), 22 . . . RxR; 23 KxR, and now not 23 . . . KtxPch; 24 K–K2, Kt–R6; 25 P–B4! when the Black Knight cannot get out, but simply 23 . . . Kt–Q3; 24 P–Kt3, K–Kt2 when the ending should be rather better for Black.
(2) 19 . . . R–Q2; 20 B–R5, P–Kt3; 21 B–K1, KR–Q1, and Black is now threatening a very strong exchange sacrifice by

22 ... P–Kt5 and 23 ... R–Q7ch. During the game I had the
intention of choosing this variation.

It is understandable that Euwe did not like to choose this
highly dangerous possibility, especially when one takes into
consideration the fact that with the text-move he at last arrives
at the development of his King's wing.

19 ...		RxR
20 KxR		P–Kt5!

At last Black can force the penetration of his Rook to Q7.
White's Knight now has five squares at its disposal, but which
is the right one?

Black (Keres)

White (Euwe) to play

21   Kt–Kt1?

To this question White could find no satisfactory answer
during the game and with the text-move he commits a decisive
mistake. Let us now consider in detail what consequences
would result from each Knight move.

(1) 21 Kt–K1?, R–Q1ch; followed by 22 ... R–Q7ch with a
won position.

(2) 21 Kt–K5, KtxB; 22 RPxKt, B–B4!; 23 P–B4, and now
Black can get down to an endgame in which he has a material
superiority by either 23 ... PxP e.p.; 24 KtxP, RxP; or 23 ...
P–KB3; 24 P–K4, PxKt; 25 PxB, PxP; (26 PxP, R–K5).

(3) 21 Kt–Q2, R–Q1; 22 R–B2, B–B4!; 23 B–R4, R–Q2; and
all White's pieces are badly placed, whilst Black has the very
strong threat of 24 ... P–Kt6. For example: 24 K–B1, P–Kt6!;
25 BPxP, Kt–B7 (26 P–K4, BxP!) and Black has at his disposal

in this ending such effective threats that White can scarcely hope to defend them successfully.

Since the move played in the game, 21 Kt–Kt1, also proves insufficient, there remains for White only the reply 21 Kt–R4!, and it was this continuation that he should have chosen. After 21 . . . R–Q1ch; 22 K–K1, Black cannot unfortunately play 22 . . . R–Q7, because of 23 P–B3, winning a piece. But despite this he retains the better endgame owing to the unhappy position of the White pieces. If, for example, he should then continue 22 . . . KtxB; 23 RPxKt, P–QR4, Black would have good winning chances since in the ensuing phase of the game White would have much trouble in extricating his Knight from R4. Moreover, Black need be in no hurry to exchange on Kt6, but could for instance continue with 22 . . . P–QB3, preparing for P–QKt4 as the occasion arises.

It is naturally still questionable whether White could have saved the game or not by 21 Kt–R4, but in any case he should have played it. Now Black obtains a decisive material and positional advantage.

| | 21 | . . . | R–Q1ch |
| | 22 | K–K1 | R–Q7! |

Now this move is possible since the Knight is badly placed on Kt1.

| | 23 | P–B3 | RxKKtP |
| | 24 | PxKt | |

Euwe had overlooked in his previous calculations that, in reply to the intended 24 K–B1, Black possessed the simple 24 . . . PxP, which wins at once. With the text-move he hopes for Bishops of opposite colour, but Black's advantage is already so great that the Bishops of opposite colour cannot help White any longer.

| | 24 | . . . | RxKtch |
| | 25 | K–Q2 | RxR! |

25 . . . R–Kt7ch; also won apparently, but the Rook exchange is simpler and leads to a clearly won ending.

| | 26 | KxR | BxP |
| | 27 | P–Kt3 | B–Q6 |

Two plus pawns are not always sufficient to win in an endgame with Bishops of opposite colour, but here in addition

Black possesses a considerable positional advantage. Namely, he possesses the pawn majority on both flanks and is in a position to create passed pawns there when necessary. Such an advantage is usually decisive, even when one has not got a material superiority.

28	BxP	P–KR4!

Black need be in no hurry to capture the KP. He prefers to advance his KRP as quickly as possible, and thereby forces the enemy Bishop to keep on watch against the further onmarch of this pawn. For these reasons Black need not worry about his Queen-side pawns, e.g.: 29 B–Kt8, P–KR5; 30 BxP?, P–Kt6; 31 PxP, P–R6 and the pawn Queens.

29	K–Q2	B–Kt8
30	K–B3	P–R5!

Now Black has attained his goal and the win is practically reached. White could have put up a little further resistance if he had played his Bishop over to KR4, but this also would not have sufficed to save the game.

31	P–R4	BxP
32	K–B4	P–Kt3

Black can quietly place his pawns on the black squares since the opposing Bishop cannot attack them because of the advancing KRP.

33	P–R5	PxP
34	KxP	B–B7
35	K–Kt5	BxP
36	KxP	K–Kt2

The QRP is not essential for the win and is therefore not defended.

37	K–R6	K–Kt3
38	P–K4	P–Kt6!
39	PxP	P–R6
40	P–Kt4	K–Kt4
	resigns	

The Black passed pawn will cost White his Bishop in a few moves.

Game 33

QUEEN'S PAWN, NIMZOWITSCH DEFENCE

Sixth Game of the match in Holland, 1939/40

	P. Keres	M. Euwe
1	P–Q4	Kt–KB3
2	P–QB4	P–K3
3	Kt–QB3	B–Kt5
4	Q–B2	Kt–B3

At the time this game was played this so-called Zurich variation was very fashionable and was used most of all in the Nimzowitsch Defence. In this match, too, the system was often tried and we came to accept that 5 P–K3 offered White best chances of obtaining an active game. In the present game White chooses, however, another possibility.

	5 Kt–B3	0–0

This inexactitude constitutes the reason for the ensuing difficulties that afflict Black, since now the development of White's Bishop to Kt5 is very effective. The exact sequence of moves lay here in 5 ... P–Q3, whereupon White must continue with either 6 P–QR3 or 6 P–K3. But if he plays, as in the game, 6 B–Kt5, then 6 ... P–KR3! provides him with a disagreeable choice. The exchange 7 BxKt, QxB; is naturally unacceptable, and the retreat 7 B–R4, implies a pawn sacrifice: 7 ... P–KKt4; 8 B–Kt3, P–Kt5; followed by 9 ... KtxP; etc.

	6 B–Kt5	P–KR3
	7 B–R4	P–Q3

Once Black has castled the continuation 7 ... P–KKt4; 8 B–Kt3, P–Kt5 was naturally already too risky. Apart from this, it does not lead to the win of a pawn, since White can indeed proceed with 9 Kt–R4, KtxP; 10 Q–Q2, with simultaneous attack against the Knight and the pawn on KR6. After the text-move White has a lasting initiative, since his Bishop on R4 exerts a very uncomfortable pressure on the opponent's King's position.

	8 P–K3

Euwe's recommendation here of 8 0–0–0 is very interesting. In so doing White would unpin his Knight, prevent the advance P–K4 and at the same time prepare an advance on the King's-side. But White regarded his position as also very good after the text-move, and with good right. It goes without saying that there was no point here in wasting time over the move 8 P–QR3, since sooner or later Black will exchange himself on QB6 in any case.

> 8 . . .   Q–K2
> 9 B–K2   P–K4
> 10 P–Q5

There can naturally be diverse opinions as to the worth of this advance, as, for the rest, is nearly always the case when it is a question of closing the centre. At first glance more natural seems 10 0–0, which threatens 11 Kt–Q5, and thereby forces BxKt. If now 11 QxB, then there follows of course 11 . . . P–KKt4; 12 B–Kt3, Kt–K5; with 13 . . . P–B4 and an excellent position for Black. After 11 PxB, however, Black still plays 11 . . . P–KKt4; 12 B–Kt3, Kt–KR4, exchanges off the Bishop and has an approximately equal position.

For this reason White would like to refrain from castling for the moment, so as to be able to initiate an attack on the King's wing in the event of P–KKt4.

> 10 . . .   Kt–Kt1
> 11 Kt–Q2!

Now 11 0–0, would be in fact bad because of 11 . . . P–KKt4; 12 B–Kt3, BxKt; which would lead to a good game for Black after both 13 PxB, QKt–Q2, and 13 QxB, Kt–K5; 14 Q–B2, P–KB4.

> 11 . . .   QKt–Q2

White's plan lies in 12 0–0, followed by QR–K1 and P–B4, with the idea of preparing a King-side attack. If Black plays 11 . . . R–K1 to prevent this, in the intention of attaining an approximately equal game after 12 0–0, BxKt; 13 QxB, Kt–K5, there comes a surprise with 12 BxKt! Now 12 . . . QxB fails against 13 Q–R4, and after 12 . . . PxB; 13 B–Q3, White's advantage is indubitable.

12	O–O	P–QR4
13	QR–K1	R–K1
14	P–B4!	

White has now realised his plan and threatens to build up a very strong attacking position by 15 P–B5, followed by 16 Kt(Q2)–K4. With his last few moves, however, Black has already taken precautions against this threat and now inaugurates a long exchanging combination by which practically all the minor pieces disappear from the board.

          14 . . .   BxKt

Another possibility here was to play to win a pawn by 14 . . B–B4. This, however, had its dangers as White could simply continue with 15 K–R1, BxP; 16 PxP! After this Black would be faced by a difficult choice. Naturally 16 . . . QKtxP fails against 17 Kt(Q2)–K4, and also 16 . . . QxP; 17 Kt–Kt5 is anything but pleasant for Black. There remains only 16 . . . PxP, but even then White obtains, for example, a strong attack for his pawn by 17 Kt–Kt5, B–Kt3; 18 Kt–K4.

The text-move is, at all events, more prudent and more in accordance with the needs of the position.

          15   QxB

In this position 15 PxB, really came into consideration, despite the weakness on QB5. White would have avoided further simplification with this move, but whether he would have obtained a better result than in the game after 15 . . . PxP; 16 PxP, Q–B1 is very dubious.

          15 . . .   Kt–K5!

Naturally Black must seize the first opportunity to ease his constricted position by exchanges.

16	KtxKt	QxB
17	P–KKt3	Q–K2
18	B–Kt4	

Now there is threatened 19 BxKt, followed by P–KB5 with a marked positional advantage. The text-move, however, permits the exchange of the remaining minor pieces and therefore it was better to continue immediately with 18 P–B5. After 18 . . . Kt–B3; 19 B–Q3, KtxKt; 20 BxKt, White would retain the two Bishops, and Black would find it more difficult to obtain any counter-play on the Queen's side.

18 . . .   Kt–B3

After 18 . . . Kt–B4; there could follow 19 KtxKt, PxKt; 20 BxB, QRxB; 21 Q–RP and one cannot see what Black has obtained in return for the pawn.

19	KtxKtch	QxKt
20	BxB	QRxB

If 20 . . . KRxB, then White could obtain a rather better Rook ending by 21 PxP, QxP; 22 QxQ, etc. After the text-move 21 QxRP, gives White nothing as Black simply replies 21 . . . PxP, followed by 22 . . . QxKtP.

Now an ending with equal material has arisen and here perhaps many players would have contented themselves with a draw. But in actual fact White stands better. Firstly, he enjoys greater command of space, and secondly he can inaugurate an action on the King's wing by P–B5, followed by P–K4 and P–KKt4–5. It is naturally not proven that this small advantage can be translated into a win, but in any case Black is faced by the prospect of a long and patient defence in which the slightest inexactitude may have the most serious consequences.

21   R–B2

With this move White unnecessarily departs from his clear plan of play and, in the ensuing phase of the game, allows his opponent to make a choice amongst various methods of defence. Although the text-move threatened to win a pawn by 22 QxRP, an immediate 21 P–KB5, with the idea of 22 P–K4, was better. If Black tries to prevent this by 21 . . . P–K5, then he gets into a very unfavourable Rook ending by 22 QxQ, PxQ; 23 R–Q1. White plays, later on, R–B4, brings his King to Q4, and then proceeds with R–R4, followed by R(Q1)–KB1–B4, and thus succeeds in winning the KP. Black can hardly undertake anything against this plan since his position contains too many weaknesses.

21 . . .   P–QKt3?

It would appear that this move, by which Black destroys all possibilities of eventual counter-play on the Queen's wing, is

the one that definitely ruins his position. It is clear that after
the closing of the centre the threat of P–KKt4–5 must be met
by a counter-action on the Queen's wing, and the only chance
of this is afforded by the thrust P–QB3. But in order to make
this thrust effective Black must have the possibility of recapturing with a pawn after the exchange on his QB3. Hence the
pawn should have been left on QKt2 and the Rook move
21 ... R–R1, should have been played in order to protect the
QRP.

As Euwe himself remarked after the game, he was already
quite dispirited here by the fact that he was faced by a long
and wearisomely passive defence. In such a situation the
mistakes come of their own volition and this game too is no
exception in this respect.

22   R(K1)–KB1

Here too 22 P–KB5, or also 22 P–K4 and then 23 P–KB5,
was the right move. After the text-move Black could transpose
to a Rook ending in which it would be not at all certain that
White's advantage would be sufficient for the win.

22 ...   Q–Kt3?

Black fails to utilize the excellent opportunity here of getting
into a Rook ending which would have offered very good drawing prospects by 22 ... PxP; 23 QxQ, PxQ; 24 RxP, RxP.
White would not then play at once 25 RxP, because of 25 ...
R–K7! with strong counter-play on the seventh rank, but
first of all 25 R(B1)–B2! so as to guard the second rank. Only
then would 26 RxP ensue, and on account of the weaknesses
on KB7 and KR6 White would have rather the better ending.
It is more than doubtful however whether this advantage
could be turned into a winning one.

With the text-move Black does, it is true, defend the threat
of 23 PxP, since the possible win of the Queen by 23 ... RxP;
24 RxP, QxR; 25 RxQ, KxR, would be scarcely advisable for
White, but the execution of the main plan of P–KB5 and P–K4
is even invited with gain of tempo. Black now gets into a
difficult and thoroughly passive position.

23	P–B5!	Q–B3
24	P–K4	P–B3

Now the drawbacks of Black's 21st move are apparent. If the pawn still stood on QKt2 then this thrust would have given Black valid counter-play; but in the present position it only leads to fresh weaknesses on QKt3 and Q3. Black must however try to do something, since if he remains passive then White, in addition to his main plan of P–KKt4–5, can also think of the possibility of P–QR3, followed by P–QKt4 and P–B5.

25	PxP	RxP
26	P–QR4!	

White now completely blockades the Queen's wing, thereby depriving his opponent of all chances of counter-play, and then prepares to carry out the pawn advance P–KKt4–5. Black utilises the time at his disposal to remove his King from the danger-zone.

26	. . .	K–B1
27	R–Q1	R(K1)–B1
28	P–Kt3	K–K2

If Black tried to thwart the enemy plans by 28 . . . Q–Kt4, then the reply 29 P–B6 would be most uncomfortable for him.

29	Q–B3	K–Q2
30	P–R4	K–B2
31	K–B1	K–Kt2
32	K–K2	

White, too, seeks for a more secure place for his King, in anticipation of the coming opening up of lines on the King's wing.

32	. . .	R(B1)–B2

The attempt to prevent the advance P–KKt4 by 32 . . . R–KR1; 33 R–R2, P–R4, does not lead to the hoped-for result. White would then continue with 34 R–KKt1, would open up the KKt file and obtain pressure against the point KKt7 of just as much force as in the game. The chief tragedy of the position from the Black point of view is that, although he can choose amongst a number of defensive methods, he cannot, however, obtain a completely satisfactory result with any of them.

33	R–R2	Q–Q1
34	P–KKt4	P–B3

This move is necessary sooner or later, since otherwise White, by playing P–Kt5, would obtain a decisive positional advantage. Black could have set a small trap for his opponent here by 34 . . . R–Q2. If then White were to make the careless reply 35 R–KKt1, there would follow the surprising 35 . . . P–Q4!; 36 KPxP, RxQP etc. White would, however, play simply 35 R–R3, and then continue with R–KKt1 and P–Kt5, so that Black would not have achieved any alteration of the situation.

35   R–Kt2

Simpler was the immediate 35 R–KKt1, followed by P–Kt5 before Black could get his Rook round to the KR file. It was, however, White's first aim to get past the time control on the 40th move with success, before he started on his decisive breakthrough on the King's wing.

35	. . .	R–B1
36	R–Kt3	Q–Q2
37	Q–Q3	Q–KB2
38	R–KR1	R–KR1
39	R(R1)–R3	

This placing of the Rooks does not seem so effective as 39 R(Kt3)–R3, but in the latter case Black would not be forced to exchange on Kt4 after P–Kt5.

39	. . .	R(B3)–B1
40	P–Kt5!	

At long last White carries out this advance that has been so long in preparation, and thereby forces the opening up of a line on the King's wing. Naturally, there would have been no point in capturing by 40 QxP, since after 40 . . . R(R1)–Q1 Black would have obtained good counter-play on the Q file.

40	. . .	RPxP
41	PxP	Q–B2
42	Q–Q5ch	K–R2
43	R–Q3	

Here the game was adjourned and Black sealed his move. Black's position is naturally difficult, but White's task is still not so easy, especially when one takes into account the comparatively open nature of his King's position. If Black were to succeed in penetrating into the White camp with any one of his pieces then the problem of winning could become highly complicated.

Whilst I was studying the position during the adjournment I noticed that Black had very good chances of counter-play with 43 . . . PxP! Then, if 44 RxR, RxR; 45 QxQP, QxQ; 46 RxQ, Black obtains excellent drawing prospects by 46 . . . R–R5! Let us look a little more closely at some of the variations.

It is clear that White must not give up his KP, and hence the moves 47 K–B3, R–B5ch; 48 K–K3, are readily comprehensible. Then, however, Black plays 48 . . . P–Kt5! and

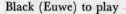

Black (Euwe) to play

White (Keres)

threatens R–B6ch, R–B5 etc. The attempt to capture the Black KP by 49 R–Q5, leads to nothing after 49 . . . P–KKt4! since then 50 RxKP?, P–Kt6! would even lead to a loss for White. Nor does more than a draw arise from the continuation 50 PxP e.p., P–Kt6; 51 R–Q2, R–Kt5; 52 R–KKt2, RxP; 53 K–B3, R–B3ch; 54 KxP, R–B5; etc. It seems as though White possesses only very problematical winning possibilities in the Rook ending, if they indeed exist at all.

One cannot, however, maintain that Black would have attained a draw by 43 . . . PxP, since in the end White is not indeed forced to capture on Q6. He could, for example, continue with 44 K–B2, so as to get his King to KKt2 and only then to capture on Q6, or else to continue with R–KKt3. But it is in any case obvious that the continuation 43 . . . PxP! would have assured Black of good drawing prospects and hence should most certainly have been adopted.

43 . . .   RxR?

One can imagine my relief when the envelope was opened
and it became apparent that my opponent had not sealed the
best move 43 . . . PxP! The remaining play is comparatively
simple and did not cause me any headaches, even though I
had not at all considered this line in my analysis at home.

44   RxR   PxP

This is now indeed too late as the White Rook penetrates to
the seventh rank with some decisive threats.

45   R–R7   Q–K2

46 P–B6 was threatened. Now, before he proceeds to the
decisive attack on the Queen's wing, White places his King in
a position that may increase its activity.

46   K–B3   R–B1
47   K–Kt4   R–B2

Now that White has posted his King in an active position
he is already threatening 48 Q–K6, since the Rook ending
would be easily won for him. With the text-move Black defends
this threat since now 48 Q–K6, QxQ; 49 PxQ, R–K2, would
still leave open for Black many very good defensive possibilities.
White therefore turns his attention to the other wing, where
the Black King is placed quite alone.

48   P–Kt4!

The strategy employed by White here is already universally
known. When the opposing pieces are occupied with the
defence of one wing, then, suddenly, an action is commenced
on the other wing, and by this the enemy pieces usually are
unable to come to the aid of the defence in time. With the
text-move White opens up new lines against the enemy King
and soon obtains a decisive attack.

48   . . .   PxP
49   P–R5   Q–Kt2

The only defence as after 49 . . . PxP; 50 QxPch, K–Kt2;
51 QxPch, K–B1; 52 Q–R5, K–Kt1; 53 R–R3, White wins
with a mating attack. But now too White proceeds with his
attack with undiminished strength.

50	PxPch	KxP
51	QxPch	K–R2
52	QxKP	P–Kt6

A last desperate attempt to obtain counter-play on the QKt file with the passed pawn, and one which, owing to the open position of the Black King, is doomed to failure. Black has, however, nothing better, since if he tries to build a protective wall for his King by 52 ... R–B2, then he is demolished by 53 P–B6!

53 R–R3!

Threatening 54 Q–R5ch, and thus winning the passed pawn, as after 53 ... P–Kt7; 54 R–R3ch, is decisive.

53 ... R–B3

Rather more stubborn was 53 ... Q–Kt3, after which White can force the win by 54 Q–R1ch, K–Kt2; 55 Q–Q1!, P–Kt7; 56 Q–Q5ch. The text-move loses more quickly.

54 Q–Q4ch R–Kt3

Or 54 ... Q–Kt3; 55 Q–Q7ch, Q–Kt2; 56 QxQch, followed by RxPch, with an easy win. In addition White can also continue his attack by 55 P–B5.

55 RxP resigns

Game 34

QUEEN'S PAWN, QUEEN'S INDIAN DEFENCE

Ninth game of the match in Holland, 1939–40

	M. Euwe	P. Keres
1	P–Q4	Kt–KB3
2	P–QB4	P–K3
3	Kt–KB3	

After the eighth game the match was level at 4 to 4. Euwe had had poor results with the Nimzoindian in the fifth game (No. 32) and therefore seemingly wanted to choose a quieter opening in the present game. The crisis of the struggle was designed to be put off till the middle-game.

3	. . .	P–QKt3
4	P–KKt3	B–Kt2
5	B–Kt2	B–K2
6	o–o	o–o
7	Kt–B3	Kt–K5

I too, with the black pieces, had no particular inclination to play for complications and therefore there now comes a simplifying continuation with quiet play.

| 8 | Q–B2 | KtxKt |
| 9 | QxKt | P–Q3 |

This careless move gives White an opportunity of seizing the initiative. Simple and usual continuations such as 9 . . . B–K5 or 9 . . . P–KB4 are, according to practical experience, sufficient to permit Black an easy equality.

| 10 | Q–B2 | P–KB4 |

If Black wants to prevent the advance 11 P–K4, then this thrust, which somewhat weakens Black's central position, is practically forced. After 10 . . . Kt–B3; 11 P–Q5! would be an awkward reply to meet. Thus, for example, after 11 . . . PxP; 12 PxP, Kt–Kt5; 13 Q–Kt3, KtxQP; White would win back his pawn by 11 Kt–Q4, and would have the better position.

| 11 | Kt–K1 |

By an exchange of the Bishops on the white-coloured squares White seeks to lay clear the enemy weaknesses in the centre, but he obtains but little with this. Therefore the advance of 11 P–Q5 merited consideration here. After 11 . . . P–K4; 12 P–K4, PxP; 13 QxP, Kt–Q2; 14 Q–B2, White would have obtained rather the better position.

| 11 | . . . | Q–B1 |

In my game against Alekhine at the Buenos Aires Olympiad of 1939 I continued here with 11 . . . BxB; 12 KtxB, P–B3, but this led to the somewhat better position for White after 13 P–K4. Instead of 12 . . . P–B3, however, 12 . . . P–K4 would have been more energetic and would have yielded Black satisfactory counter-play in the centre. After the text-move Black has to contend with greater difficulties.

| 12 | P–K4 |

After 12 P–Q5, Black would also continue with 12 . . . Kt–Q2, and if then 13 PxP, Kt–B4; etc.

| 12 | . . . | Kt–Q2 |
| 13 | P–Q5? | |

With this advance White surrenders his chances of gaining an advantage, which could have been maintained here by 13 PxP. For example, after 13 . . . PxP; 14 P–Q5, or 13 . . . BxB; 14 KtxB, PxP; 15 P–Q5, Black has to contend with difficulties on account of the weakness on his K3. Probably he would then have to continue 13 . . . PxP; 14 P–Q5, P–B3!, with good prospects of counter-play in the centre which would in turn afford him equality.

13 . . .   BPxP!

With this capture his opponent is faced with an unpleasant choice. If White now recaptures with 14 BxP, then he is, after 14 . . . Kt–B3, practically forced to give up his KB for the Knight, whilst after 14 PxP, Kt–B4, assures Black of an excellent position.

| 14 | QxP | Kt–B4 |
| 15 | Q–K2 | |

After 15 Q–B2, PxP, gives Black a fine position, e.g.: 16 PxP, B–R3, or 16 BxPch, BxB; 17 PxB, Q–B4; etc., whilst if 16 P–QKt4, Black wins a pawn by 16 . . . Kt–R3. With the text-move White pins the KP and hopes to get an advantage by directing his attack against it in the ensuing phase of the game.

| 15 | . . . | B–BK3 |
| 16 | B–R3 | |

The logical continuation of White's plan, but this pin fails to lead to the desired result. Hence it would have been best for White here to have abandoned all attempts at gaining an advantage and simply to have continued 16 PxP, BxB; 17 KtxB, KtxP; 18 B–K3, with about equal chances. Black's fine development does not permit White to play for an advantage.

16 . . .   R–K1!

With the tactical threat of 17 . . . PxP! which, for instance, could follow after 17 Kt–Q3.

17 B–K3

Now he threatens 18 BxKt, followed by 19 BxPch, but Black can free himself from the troublesome pin by combinational means.

| 17 | . . . | Q–Q1 |
| 18 | BxKt | PxP! |

With this intervening move Black entirely frees his position, thereby demonstrating the purposeless nature of his opponent's play.

19 B–K6ch?

But this leads in the end only to the loss of a pawn. By now White should be thinking of equality and should, with this in mind, continue 19 B–K3, P–Q5; 20 B–Kt2, which, after 20 . . . BxB; 21 KtxB, PxB; 22 KtxP, B–Q5; 23 QR–K1, BxKt; 24 PxB, R–K4, would have led to a rather better ending for Black. Now the balance definitely swings in Black's favour.

| 19 | . . . | K–R1 |
| 20 | R–Q1 | |

A similar result is achieved by 20 PxP, BxQP, or by 20 B–QR3, Q–K2; 21 PxP, BxQP; etc.

20 . . .   QPxB

Simpler still would have been 20 . . . KtPxB; so as to meet 21 PxP, with 21 . . . BxQP; 22 RxB, Q–K2. After 21 Kt–Kt2, Black can quietly play 21 . . . PxP. But the text-move is also sufficient to make clear Black's advantage.

21 Kt–Kt2

After 21 PxP, Black could have continued with 21 . . . BxQP; 22 Q–K2, or also with 21 . . . B–Q5. With the text-move White tries to strengthen the position of his Bishop.

21 . . .   P–Q5

This thrust limits the effectiveness of his own Bishop and markedly interferes with the evaluation of the advantage he has already gained. The right move here was 21 . . . B–Q5, so as then to take off on QB5 and allow his two Bishops their maximum scope for action. After the text-move White gains fresh possibilities of making a stubborn resistance.

22 P–B4?

Black (Keres)

White (Euwe) to play

White has conceived the right idea but carries it out in-exactly. He wants to protect his Bishop by P–B5 and then initiate a King-side attack by Kt–B4 and Q–R5, but for this purpose he should first have played 22 KR–K1! Perhaps White was not content with the possible simplification that might have then occurred by 22 ... B–B1; 23 Q–Kt4, BxB; 24 RxB, RxR; 25 QxR, Q–K1, but he certainly need not have feared it. After 26 ... QxQch, RxQ; 27 K–B1, the win would be indeed very difficult to force for Black since he exerts no control over the white squares.

22 ...   P–Q6!

Black at once utilises his opportunity of making good his mistake and opens up the diagonal for his KB.

23 RxP   QxR!

He could also have justified his pawn sacrifice by 23 B–Q5ch; 24 K–R1, Q–B3. The Queen sacrifice is, however, more elegant and destroys his opponent's one well-placed piece. The following moves are practically forced.

24 QxQ   B–Q5ch
25 R–B2

After 25 K–R1, RxB, the Black Bishops and Rooks would command the whole board, so that White would have been unable to achieve anything against the threat of 26 ... QR–K1, followed by 27 R–K7. With the text-move White offers an exchange sacrifice so as to get rid of the strong Bishop on Q5, but, as the game continuation shows, this aim is not so easily attained.

| 25 . . . | RxB |
| 26   K–B1 | QR–K1 ! |

This strengthening of the positional pressure is much more
lasting than the win of the exchange by 26 . . . BxR; 27 KxB,
QR–K1; when White could still put up a stubborn resistance
by 28 Kt–R4. With the text-move Black is in fact threatening
27 . . . BxR, since 28 KxB, R–K7ch, would eventually leave
Black a piece up.

| 27   P–B5 | R–K4 |
| 28   P–B6 | |

If White plays an immediate 28 R–Q2, then Black wins a
piece by 28 . . . B–K5; 29 Q–Kt3, RxPch; 30 Kt–B4, P–KKt4.
White now makes use of the fact that 28 . . . BxR; 29 KxB,
R–K7ch?; 30 QxR, RxQch; 31 KxR, BxKt, fail against 32
P–B7, to lure the Black KtP to B3. After that, in the variation
mentioned above, Black would no longer have at his disposal
the move P–KKt4.

In any case, White has nothing better, since after 28 R–B4,
R–K7 wins at once.

| 28   . . . | PxP |
| 29   R–Q2 | |

Now this move is possible, and after 29 . . . B–K5; 30
Q–Kt3, R–B4ch; 31 Kt–B4, White would have avoided the
worst dangers. But a new trouble has appeared, to wit, the
strong diagonal on QB1–KR6 for the Queen's Bishop, which
lends Black's attack decisive power.

It should also be pointed out that 29 RxP, fails here because
of 29 . . . BxKtch; 30 KxB, R–K7ch, followed by 31 . . . BxR.

| 29   . . . | B–B1 ! |
| 30   Kt–B4 | R–K6 |

Here Black has many ways of evaluating his advantage.
For example, he could have played 30 . . . R–K8ch; 31 K–Kt2,
R(K1)–K6; 32 Q–B2, B–Kt5; etc. However, the combination
beginning with the text-move is the most effective.

| 31   Q–Kt1 | R–B6ch |
| 32   K–Kt2 | RxKt ! |

This exchange sacrifice shows in the clearest possible form
the immense power of two Bishops in an open position.

33	PxR	R–Kt1ch
34	K–B3	B–Kt5ch
	resigns	

After 35 K–K4, R–K1ch, there follows mate in two moves, and 35 K–Kt3, B–B4 dis ch, would lose the Queen.

Game 35

QUEEN'S PAWN, NIMZOWITSCH DEFENCE

Team Match at Tallinn, 1940

	G. Friedemann	P. Keres
1	P–Q4	Kt–KB3
2	P–QB4	P–K3
3	Kt–QB3	B–Kt5
4	Q–B2	Kt–B3
5	Kt–B3	

This game was played shortly after the Euwe–Keres match in which this opening system was tried out in a number of games and which I therefore knew very well indeed. On the basis of these match games I came to the conclusion that the Knight development is premature here and that White would do better to play 5 P–K3. It must however be observed that the preference for one or another move at such an early stage in the game is more or less a matter of taste.

5 . . .   P–Q3

This is more exact than 5 . . . O–O, when White could continue with 6 B–Kt5, to great effect. Now, however, 6 B–Kt5, P–KR3; 7 B–R4 would entail a pawn sacrifice, since it is well known that after 7 . . . P–KKt4; 8 B–Kt3, P–Kt5, Black can quietly capture on Q5 with 9 . . . KtxP.

6 B–Q2

If White wants any opening advantage then he must try here the sharper continuation 6 P–QR3, BxKt ch; 7 QxB, etc. After the text-move Black obtains easy equality.

6 . . .   P–K4
7 P–QR3

Usually pawns are exchanged first here by 7 PxP, PxP, but the text-move too is quite playable and eventually transposes to the same position.

	7 . . .	BxKt
	8 BxB	Q–K2

After 8 . . . P–K5 the reply 9 P–Q5 would be troublesome. The text-move provides White with the opportunity of giving the opening an original cast by continuing 9 P–K3. Instead of this White decides to transpose to customary variations, and he exchanges off on K5 after which, however, Black has no more problems to solve.

	9 PxP	PxP
	10 P–K3	P–QR4

Black must prevent White's pawn advance 11 P–QKt4, since otherwise he might experience difficulty in protecting his K4. In the game Flohr–Keres, Leningrad, 1947, Black carelessly continued 10 . . . O–O; and after 11 P–QKt4, B–Kt5; 12 B–K2, P–K5; 13 P–Kt5!, PxKt; 14 PxP, he was in distinct difficulties.

	11 B–K2	O–O
	12 O–O	P–R5

A double-edged move. With it Black does indeed gain control of QKt6, but on the other hand the important QKt4 square is yielded to the enemy pieces. Also the pawn on R5 could become weak later on, especially in the event of both Rooks being exchanged on the only open file. A natural and better continuation here was 12 . . . B–Kt5.

| | 13 P–R3! | |

A good move which deprives the enemy Bishop of a fine square of development on Kt5. Black in fact has troubles in developing his Bishop and is forced to grasp at artificial measures.

| | 13 . . . | Kt–Q2 |

It is true that the Knight is well posted on QB4, but such manoeuvres can become most dangerous in undeveloped positions. However, Black has no alternative if he wants to develop his Bishop.

| | 14 QR–Q1 | |

Mechanically played—and the result is that Black can once again set his position right and that he ends up by standing very well indeed. Here White could have utilised the circumstance that the enemy Knight has quitted KB3 to play the active 14 B–Q3! and after 14 . . . P–KKt3 or 14 . . . P–R3 he could have continued 15 B–K4. The Bishop would be beautifully posted there and could eventually occupy the strong square Q5, and could also help in an attack on the point K5. It seems that 14 B–Q3! would have best demonstrated the drawbacks of Black's rather superficial 12th move.

| 14 . . . | Kt–B4 |
| 15 B–Kt4! | P–B3 |

Black must in the first instance protect the K4 point since, for example, after 15 . . . KtxB; 16 PxKt, Kt–R3; 17 QxP, he would simply lose a pawn. Bad too would be 15 . . . B–K3 because of the possibility of 16 BxKt, QxB; 17 Kt–Kt5! etc.

16 R–Q5

With this manoeuvre White eventually obtains only an approximately equal endgame. Hence stronger was 16 BxKt, QxB; 17 R–Q5, Q–K2; 18 Kt–Q2, so as to meet 18 . . . B–K3 simply by 19 R–Kt5 and eventually to continue with P–B5. By playing this way White could still have attained some slight positional advantage.

| 16 . . . | KtxB |
| 17 PxKt | Kt–R3 |

After the game the criticism was voiced in various quarters that White should have continued 14 KR–Q1 instead of 14 QR–Q1, since in the ensuing phase White really needs the Rook on QR1. However, this recommendation is accompanied by a number of "buts". In the first place Black would be in no way forced to choose this continuation, and secondly he could very well play 17 . . . Kt–Kt6 in the position now reached, thereby attacking the Rook on R1 and in consequence winning the pawn on QKt4.

18 QxP   QxP

Here Black could try to harass the enemy Rook before making this capture, but this would have led to unnecessary complications. 18 . . . B–K3 would naturally be unsatisfactory

because of 19 R–R5!, but also after 18 . . . P–B3; 19 R–R5,
could lead to great complications. An example is the variation
19 . . . P–QKt3; 20 QxP, B–Q2; 21 QxKtP, KR–Kt1; 22
RxKt, RxQ; 23 RxRch, K–B2; 24 P–Kt5, when White would
possess more than enough compensation for his Queen.
Furthermore, the line 20 . . . B–Kt2 (instead of 20 . . . B–Q2)
21 QxKtP, KR–Kt1 would not be at all clear. White could
for example continue 22 Q–Kt5, BxKt; 23 BxB, RxQ; 24
PxR, P–K5; 25 RxKt! and again he would obtain sufficient
material for his Queen, since the try 25 . . . RxR; 26 PxR,
PxB would have seemingly sad consequences for Black after
27 R–R1, Q–R2; 28 P–Kt5.

19   R–R1?

A move characteristic of Friedemann's style. The young
master always strives for complications at every opportunity.
The pawn sacrifice offered by the text-move is, however, all
the more welcome to Black in that after, for example, 19, QxQ
KtxQ; 20 R–Kt5, Kt–B3; 21 P–B5, he would be left with
rather the worse ending. At any rate, in the great complications that now ensue White is unable to demonstrate the
correctness of his pawn sacrifice.

19   . . .   QxKtP
20   P–B5!

White takes advantage of the fact that Black cannot play
20 . . . QxB on account of 21 R–Q2, winning at least the
exchange, to open up the strong diagonal QR2–KKt8 for his
Bishop. In any case White has no choice since there is threatened
simply 20 . . . Q–Kt3, and 20 R–Kt5 can now be answered by
20 . . . QxB. Now there is threatened, amongst other things,
21 R–Q2.

20   . . .   Kt–Kt5!

Much stronger than 20 . . . B–K3; 21 R–Q2, Q–Kt5; which,
after 22 QxQ, KtxQ; 23 R–Kt1, would have led only to an
approximately equal position since the pawn on Kt7 falls.

21   B–B4

It is upon this very pretty move, teeming with possibilities,
that it appears White has set his hopes. It is easy to see that
Black cannot capture either the Queen by 21 . . . RxQ;

22 R–Q8 dis ch, or the Rook by 21 ... KtxR; 22 BxKtch,
followed by 23 QxR. Finally, White would also have some
prospects of equalizing matters after 21 ... QxRch; 22 R–Q1
dis ch, K–R1; 23 RxQ, RxQ; 24 RxR on account of the
active position of his pieces.

As, however, his opponent's reply shows, this pretty continuation is not the strongest. Better chances would have been

Black (Keres)

White (Friedemann) to play

afforded here by the prosaic line 21 QxR, KtxR; 22 B–B4,
B–K3; 23 Q–R5, when his well placed pieces would compensate to some extent for the lost pawn.

    21   ...   B–K3!

This simple move thwarts all White's attempts at attack and
in addition forces the exchange of Bishops, after which Black
is left a solid pawn to the good. The ensuing moves are forced.

    22   QxR   BxR

Naturally, not 22 ... RxQ?; 23 RxRch, K–B2; 24 R–Q7ch,
followed by 25 BxB etc. Weaker, too, is 22 ... KtxR; 23
Q–R5, as has already been mentioned earlier.

    23   BxBch   KtxB
    24   Q–R7

The attack on QKt7 in no way hinders Black's ensuing
manoeuvres. More to the point therefore was 24 Q–R5, with
which White would have brought his Queen into more active
play.

| 24 | . . . | Kt–B6 |
| 25 | R–K1 | Q–Kt5! |

Now Black controls the whole board and threatens, after due preparation, to launch a decisive attack on the weakness on QB5. In this difficult situation Friedemann embarks on a last attempt to free his position but succeeds only in hastening the inevitable loss.

| 26 | P–B6 | PxP |
| 27 | QxP | P–K5! |

Winning a piece, since after 28 Kt–Q2, or any other Knight move, there follows the decisive 28 . . . Kt–Q4. After the loss of the piece further resistance is naturally hopeless.

28	QxP	PxKt
29	QxP(B3)	P–B4
30	R–R1	Q–K5
31	Q–R5	P–B5
32	PxP	

This allows a pleasant little finishing touch.

32	. . .	Kt–K7ch
33	K–R1	QxPch
34	KxQ	KtxPch
35	K–Kt3	KtxQch

The following moves, as far as the time control, occurred merely because White could find no time to resign.

36	K–Kt4	P–Kt3
37	R–R7	RxP
38	K–R4	P–R3
39	R–R8ch	R–B1
40	R–R4	R–B5ch
41	RxR	KtxR
	White resigns.	

Game 36

VIENNA GAME

XII U.S.S.R. Championship, Moscow, 1940

A. Konstantinopolsky   P. Keres

1	P–K4	P–K4	
2	Kt–QB3		

The Vienna is a rare bird in modern tournament praxis. Round about half a century ago it was extremely popular, but now it has lost most of its bite. In my opinion, one of the main reasons for this lies in the fact that Black, by a timely P–KB3 or P–KB4, attains easy equality in the principal variations and in addition he simplifies the position to a marked degree. Hence the Vienna Game has been employed but rarely in recent times and then only with the main aim of posing the opponent some unexpected problems. It is with this last aim that White probably plays it in the present game.

2	. . .	Kt–KB3	
3	P–B4	P–Q4	
4	PxKP	KtxP	
5	Kt–B3	B–K2	

This quiet development, which prepares O–O followed by P–KB3, is held nowadays to be Black's simplest reply.

6	P–Q4	O–O	

Here the paradoxical move 6 . . . B–QKt5 so as to meet 7 Q–Q3, with 7 . . . P–QB4, leads to interesting complications. Hence White should play simply 7 B–Q2, and if then 7 . . . P–QB4; 8 P–QR3 with a good game.

7	B–Q3	P–KB4	

With this Black has carried out his opening idea and now he has a thoroughly satisfactory position. White is practically forced to exchange pawns on KB6 since otherwise the Black Knight would be too strong on K5. But after the capture on KB6 the position simplifies out and soon takes on a drawish appearance.

8	PxP e.p.	BxP	

Were Black here forced to recapture with the Knight then
White would indeed stand rather better after 9 O–O, owing
to his superior development. But the capture by 8 . . . BxP!
is distinctly better and is facilitated by the fact that White
cannot capture twice on K4 owing to the ensuing pin.

9	O–O	Kt–B3
10	KtxKt	

After this capture the position becomes even more simplified
and the draw is almost tangibly imminent. But White has no
reason for avoiding complete equality, since, for example, after
10 Kt–K2, Black can attain an excellent position by 10 . . .
Kt–Kt5; 11 B–QKt5, B–Q2; 12 BxB, QxB.

10	. . .	PxKt
11	BxP	KtxP
12	Kt–Kt5	B–B4!

With this strong move, which was first used in the game
Spielmann–Reti, Vienna 1922, Black thwarts all enemy attempts
at attack and forces complete equality. In the game mentioned
above White was soon convinced that he no longer had any
prospects of obtaining an advantage and hence he forced an
equal endgame by 13 P–B3, BxKt; 14 BxKB, QxB; 15 QxKt,
BxB; 16 QxB, etc. Konstantinopolsky is apparently of the
opinion that the position still allows of some attempts to procure
an advantage, but in the end he has, however, to pay dear for
his experiments.

13	BxB	KtxB
14	Kt–K6?	

Curiously enough this incursion with the Knight turns out
to be a decisive mistake after which it is indeed difficult to find
a satisfactory continuation for White. Too great strictures should
not, however, be passed on White since in such a quiet position
Black's surprising 15th move was most difficult to foresee.

White could still have ensured himself an equal game by the
Queen exchange, 14 QxQ to which Black would reply 14 . . .
QRxQ; 15 Kt–K6, B–Q5ch; 16 KtxB, KtxKt; 17 B–Kt5,
RxRch; 18 RxR, R–Q4; leading to an approximately equal
endgame.

14	. . .	QxQ
15	RxQ	KR–K1

At first glance this move seems quite paradoxical, or even senseless, since now White not only loses his pawn on QB2 but even allows his two Rooks to be forked. When, however, one looks more deeply into the position then the secret of Black's plan is revealed. After 16 KtxBP, QR–Q1 Black in the first place saves the exchange and in the second obtains, by means of his fine development, a very strong positional initiative that leads at the very least to the recovery of the pawn sacrificed. Furthermore, the White pawns on the Queen's wing are weakened, since after the loss of the QKtP the others are isolated and constitute a valid object of attack for Black. In the sequel White is forced to busy himself with the completion of his Queen-side development and thus does not attain in time the requisite counter-play. Hence he must allow himself to be led into a difficult endgame.

Naturally, the simple 15 . . . R–B2 was also possible. But in reply to this White could complete his development by 16 B–B4, and it is just this that Black seeks to prevent.

Black (Keres)

White (Konstantinopolsky) to play

| 16 | KtxBP | QR–Q1 |
| 17 | B–B4 | |

Neither 17 KtxR, RxRch; 18 K–B2, B–Kt4; nor 17 Kt–Q5, B–Q5ch will do, whilst 17 RxR, RxR; 18 B–B4, BxP would not bring about any substantial alteration in the position.

| 17 . . . | R–K7 |

17 . . . RxRch; 18 RxR, R–K7 would also lead to the position in the game.

18   RxRch   BxR
19   R–Q1

After 19 Kt–Q5 Black does not play at once 19 . . . RxP on
account of 20 R–QB1 !, but he first plays 19 . . . P–KKt4 !. Another
good continuation too was 19 . . . Kt–R5 with which Black would
regain his pawn and have the more active piece position.

19   . . .   B–B3

Naturally not 19 . . . BxKt; 20 BxB, RxP; 21 B–K5, when
White certainly has not the worse game.

20   R–Q2   R–K5

Now the way back to QB1 for the White Bishop is cut off
and White loses his QKtP, and with this Black attains his
objective. The realisation of the positional advantage thus
acquired affords Black surprisingly few technical problems in
the ensuing phase of the game.

21   Kt–Q5   BxP
22   R–Q3

Not only preparing for counter-play by 23 R–QKt3, but
also protecting himself against the threat of 22 . . . B–B8. But
Black gains further ground by attacking the QRP.

22   . . .   R–R5 !
23   P–Kt4

Black's Knight is too strong on KB4 and must be driven
away, but this is done at the cost of new weaknesses on the
King's wing. Inadequate, however, was the counter-attack
by 23 R–QKt3, RxP; 24 RxP, since after 24 . . . B–Q5ch;
25 K–B1, RxP Black, in addition to a solid pawn more, retains
an enduring attack.

23   . . .   Kt–Q5
24   R–K3   Kt–B3 !

The 7th rank must be made safe against possible attack by
the enemy Rook. Thus, for example, after 24 . . . RxP;
25 R–K8ch, K–B2; 26 R–K7ch, White obtains enough counter-
play to save the game. Now the numerous threats, such as,
for example, 25 . . . B–Q5, 25 . . . RxP or 25 . . . P–KKt4
(26 BxP, B–B8) leave White little choice.

25   R–QKt3   B–Q5ch
26   K–Kt2

A little better here was 26 B–K3, so as to get his pieces into active positions after 26 . . . RxP; 27 RxP, RxP; 28 R–QB7!. With this White would have had good prospects of holding the position. Black would therefore simply reply to 26 B–K3, with 26 . . . P–QKt3. After 27 BxB, RxB; (27 . . . KtxB; 28 R–Kt4!) 28 Kt–K3, R–R5! would leave Black with the markedly better endgame. Also 26 . . . Kt–R4; 27 R–Q3, B–K4 would have been a good continuation and would have ensured Black the upper hand.

After the text-move Black's task is lighter since now White loses a pawn at once.

	26 . . .	P–QKt3
	27 P–QR3	B–B4!

Now White must surrender either the QRP or else the KKtP, and with this the game is practically over.

	28 B–B1	RxPch
	29 R–Kt3	RxRch

With both players pressed for time Black chooses the simplest continuation. The rest is easily understood.

	30 PxR	Kt–Q5
	31 P–B4	

Losing yet another pawn, but the continuation 31 P–B3, Kt–Kt6; 32 B–Kt2, K–B2 followed by the advance of the Black King was equally hopeless for White.

	31 . . .	Kt–Kt6
	32 B–B4	Kt–R4
	33 P–R4	KtxP
	34 B–Kt8	P–QR4
	35 B–B7	K–B2
	36 K–B3	K–K3
	37 Kt–B3	B–Q3
	38 B–Q8	K–Q2
	39 B–Kt5	K–B3
	40 B–B1	B–K4
	41 Kt–Kt5	K–B4
	42 P–Kt4	

And White resigned without waiting for the reply 42 . . . K–Kt5.

★ 2 ★

TOURNAMENTS OF THE WAR YEARS, 1942–44

IN spite of the limitations enforced by the War international chess life went on in this period too. Although, of course, markedly fewer events than usual took place, still some international tournaments were held in various countries. My chess activity in this period commenced with a participation in the Estonian Championship at Tallinn in 1942 where I succeeded in winning all 15 games. Then there followed the international tournament at Salzburg in which, too, the World Champion, Alekhine, took part. I lost both the games we played against each other and in the second of these used an interesting innovation in the King's Gambit, without, however, having thoroughly prepared it beforehand. In the tournament I obtained second place after Alekhine.

In the autumn of this year I played in the tournament at Munich where I once again ended up second to Alekhine and also again lost my individual game with him. It was obvious that the difficult war years had a bad effect on my play. The games I played lacked both ideas and freshness whilst several gross inaccuracies cropped up on the technical side.

Nor did the beginning of the year 1943 hold out promise of anything better. In the Championship of Estonia I managed to occupy first place only after great efforts. I lost one game and made four draws and, in addition, in some others I got into positions with genuine losing chances. The ensuing tournament in Prague also had a far from satisfactory course. It is true that I played much better than in the previous tournaments, but I was still unable to produce any signs of really satisfactory play. Alekhine proved to be in great form since he finished up in the tournament with 17 points out of 19 games and passed me by no less than $2\frac{1}{2}$ points. I did indeed win the small event at Poznan following on the Prague tournament with a 100 per cent score, but there was no real opposition there.

Only by the middle of 1943 had I more or less regained my sureness of play and performed in two tournaments really good achievements. It was in Salzburg that I played some of my best games from this period. As examples I have given two games in this book, against Bogoljuboff (No. 37) and Foltys (No. 38), where I succeeded in breaking down enemy resistance as early as shortly after the opening stages. This time there were two draws against Alekhine, both after a hard struggle. In the end I shared first and second places with him, with a margin of a full three points over the third placed player. With only ten games played this represented a really solid advantage!

I played really good chess, too, at the end of the year in the international tournament at Madrid where I won first prize with 12 wins and only 2 draws. In addition, I twice visited Finland, in the years 1943 and 1944, played a number of individual games and gave a series of simultaneous displays. After the Finnish trip in 1944 I travelled to Stockholm at the invitation of the present F.I.D.E. President, Folke Rogard. I played hors concours in the Swedish Championship at Lidköping, but, however, lost as many as 2 games out of the 7 played, and in the end had to content myself with second place. In the ensuing match against Ekstrom, however, I once again played distinctly better and, after the first two draws, I won the next four games and thus won the event by the score of 5–1.

My achievements in the war years cannot be regarded as satisfactory either from the sporting or from the artistic point of view. These tournaments, however, served the purpose of keeping my form, to some extent at any rate, up to a good level and prevented me from quite forgetting how to play chess.

Game 37

SICILIAN DEFENCE

International Tournament at Salzburg, 1943

P. Keres	E. D. Bogoljuboff
1 P–K4	P–QB4
2 Kt–K2	

I have employed this peculiar move in several tournament games with very good success. This development of the Knight is not intended to inaugurate a new system of development, but sets itself much more modest aims. White intends, after 2 . . . P–Q3, to play the close system 3 P–KKt3, which would hardly be in place at once because of 2 . . . P–Q4. After 2 . . . P–Q3 Black can, however, carry out this advance only after the loss of tempo involved in P–Q3–Q4. But if Black chooses the usual development 2 . . . P–Q3; 3 P–KKt3, Kt–KB3 then White need not play the move Kt–QB3 and instead plays 4 B–Kt2, so as to continue, in certain circumstances, with P–B3 and P–Q4. Incidentally, this idea was also employed by Capablanca in some of his games.

All the same, the text-move has little intrinsic importance, since usually the game soon transposes into normal paths.

| 2 . . . | P–K3 |

Simpler here is 2 . . . Kt–KB3 or 2 . . . Kt–QB3, to which White replies 3 QKt–B3, and later transposes to the usual variation by P–Q4. With the text-move Bogoljuboff is aiming at a Scheveningen variation.

| 3 | P–Q4 | PxP |
| 4 | KtxP | Kt–KB3 |

The present-day fashionable 4 . . . P–QR3 was not then, of course, practised.

| 5 | Kt–QB3 | P–Q3 |
| 6 | P–KKt4! | |

This interesting idea came into my mind during the course of the game. In this position the continuation 6 P–KKt3, followed by B–Kt2 was often employed and an attack on the King's wing was begun only later by P–KB4 and P–KKt4. The thought came into my head, however, why not save a tempo and begin immediately with P–KKt4?

In order to appraise the worth of 6 P–KKt4 we must first of all consider the possible replies 6 . . . P–K4, 6 . . . P–Q4, and 6 . . . P–KR4. Since 6 . . . P–KR4 is useless because of 7 P–Kt5, and also 6 . . . P–Q4; 7 PxP, KtxQP; 8 B–Kt5ch, B–Q2; 9 KtxKt, PxKt; 10 Q–K2ch, would leave White with a most agreeable position, then only 6 . . . P–K4 comes into serious consideration.

I came to the conclusion that this advance seemed highly dubious for Black without a most exact preparatory analysis, since after 7 B–Kt5ch, B–Q2 White gains the strong square KB5 for his Knight. In fact the position is critical for Black after 8 BxBch, QxB; 9 Kt–B5. After 9 . . . P–KR4 White need not continue with 10 P–Kt5, KtxP; 11 KtxKtPch, BxKt; 12 KtxKt, P–Q4 with a double-edged game (O'Kelly–Christoffel, Groningen, 1946) but he has at his disposal a much more enduring continuation in 10 B–Kt5!. After 10 . . . KtxKtP; 11 P–KR3, White then wins at least his pawn back with an excellent position.

Black (Bogoljuboff) to play

White (Keres)

6 ...   Kt–B3

Bogoljuboff wants to avoid all these unclear possibilities and decides upon a quiet developing continuation. Such tactics are, however, not without certain dangers, as the game continuation shows. More prudent, at all events, was 6 . . . P–KR3 which does at least safeguard the position of the Knight on KB3.

7 P–Kt5   KtxKt?

This exchange which merely facilitates enemy development cannot of course be satisfactory and it soon gets Black into difficulties. Here 7 . . . Kt–Q2 should have been played, although then 8 Kt (Q4)–Kt5 could pose Black several disagreeable problems. After 8 . . . Kt(Q2)–K4; 9 P–B4, or 8 . . . Kt–B4; 9 B–KB4, Kt–K4; 10 P–Kt4, or finally 8 . . . Kt–Kt3; 9 B–KB4, Kt–K4; (9 . . . P–K4; 10 B–K3) 10 P–QR4, P–QR3;

11 Kt–R3, positions arise that are hardly acceptable for Black without much further consideration. But unfortunately practical data is lacking in each case.

8	QxKt	Kt–Q2
9	B–K3	

This move is directed against 9 . . . Q–Kt3 after which there would now follow simply 10 QxQ (10 . . . KtxQ; 11 Kt–Kt5). At the same time O–O–O is prepared and the threat of 10 Kt–Kt5, Kt–K4; 11 O–O–O is set up.

9	. . .	P–QR3
10	B–K2	

Usually the Bishop is developed on Kt2 in this variation but here White has other plans. Since Black cannot arrive at the development of his King's wing all that quickly on account of the dominating position of the Queen on Q4, White must devote his attention to the Queen-side and that more particularly to the advance P–QKt4. In order to be able to meet this as powerfully as possible with P–QR4 White leaves his Bishop on the diagonal KB1–QR6 and for the same reason he refrains from an early O–O–O.

10	. . .	Q–B2
11	P–B4	P–QKt3

As already mentioned, 11 . . . P–QKt4 does not seem really good on account of 12 P–QR4, and another method of developing his pieces is not so easily discernible for Black. With the text-move Black plans to play 12 . . . B–Kt2 followed by an eventual O–O–O, but with his next move White opposes this plan too.

12	P–B5 !	Kt–K4

White was threatening 13 PxP, PxP; 14 B–R5ch, when Black must abandon the right to castle. Black has now, it is true, an ideal post for his Knight on the centre, but at the same time White has assured himself a number of distinct advantages. He is better developed, exerts a lasting pressure on the weak points QKt6, Q6 and K6, and soon is in control as well of the open KB file. In particular, the defence of QKt6 will cause Black much trouble.

13 PxP   PxP

After 13 . . . BxP; amongst other lines, 14 Q–R4ch, B–Q2;
15 Kt–Q5! would be very awkward for Black. Now, however,
Black will have further troubles with his QKt pawn.

14 P–QR4

Fixing the weakness on QKt6 and now actually threatening
15 QxKtP, which, played at once, would lead to nothing after
14 . . . QxQ; 15 BxQ, R–QKt1 followed by 16 . . . RxP.

14 . . .   B–K2
15 P–R4   Q–B4

16 QxKtP was once again threatened and 15 . . . B–Q1 fails
against 16 O–O–O. But if Black plays 15 . . . R–QKt1, then
there comes 16 R–KB1 and the Black King would be forced
to remain in the centre, castling on either side being prevented.
The text-move, however, provides only a temporary relief for
Black.

16 Q–Q2   Q–B2

Here 16 . . . Q–Kt5 only appeared to be more active. White
must not indeed reply 17 R–QR3, because of 17 . . . Kt–B5!
(18 Q–Q4?, KtxR!), but after 17 O–O!, Black's situation
becomes critical. Then 17 . . . Kt–B5 fails because of 18 Q–Q4,
and after 17 . . . B–Kt2; 18 R–QR3! is very strong.

17 R–KB1

Before White proceeds with the decisive attack he prevents
O–O, thereby keeping the enemy King fast in the centre.

17 . . .   B–Kt2
18 B–Q4!   R–KB1

After 18 . . . O–O–O White wins a pawn by 19 Q–K3. Black
seeks to lighten his heavy task but in so doing his King's wing
is further weakened.

19 O–O–O   RxR

A little better was an immediate 19 . . . B–Q1 since now a
catastrophe befalls him on the KB file.

20 RxR   B–Q1

20 . . . O–O–O still will not do because of 21 Q–K3, and after
20 . . . Kt–B5; 21 Q–B4, O–O–O; 22 Q–Kt4 wins easily

enough. With the text-move Black prepares to defend his
King-side by 21 . . . Q–K2.

	21	Q–B4	Kt–Kt3

After 21 . . . Q–K2 White need not content himself with the
mere win of a pawn by 22 BxKt, PxB; 23 QxP, but he can
continue his attack energetically by 22 Kt–Kt5!, PxKt; 23
BxKt. The text-move, however, loses a valuable pawn.

	22	Q–Kt4!

Weaker was 22 B–R5 because of 22 . . . Q–K2. Now Black
no longer has any defence against the double threat of 23
QxPch, and 23 Q–R5.

	22	. . .	Q–K2

A prettier finish to the game would be 22 . . . K–Q2; 23
Kt–Q5, Q–B3; 24 QxPch!, KxQ; 25 B–Kt4 mate!

	23	Q–R5!

Now the KRP falls and with this the game is decided. With
the ensuing despairing defence Black can naturally no longer
hope for any success.

	23 . . .		P–K4
	24	B–K3	B–B2
	25	QxP	Kt–B5

Also 25 . . . Kt–B1; 26 B–R5ch etc. is no better. Black's
plight is hopeless.

	26	BxKt	PxB
	27	B–R5ch	K–Q2
	28	B–Kt4ch	K–B3

If the King returns to the back rank then White wins simply
by 29 RxP.

	29	Q–B5	P–Kt4
	30	Q–Q5ch	K–Kt3
	31	Q–Q4ch	K–B3
	32	Kt–Q5	resigns

Game 38

SICILIAN DEFENCE

International Tournament at Salzburg, 1943

	P. Keres	J. Foltys
1	P–K4	P–QB4
2	Kt–K2	

As already mentioned in the notes to the previous game, this move usually possesses no individual importance, but leads to known variations. In the present game, however, Foltys chooses a plan which concentrates on the carrying out of P–Q4 and with this the whole system acquires quite another look.

2	...	Kt–KB3
3	QKt–B3	Kt–B3

Several games have demonstrated that an immediate advance of 3 . . . P–Q4 is not wholly without objections here. White continues simply with 4 PxP, KtxP; 5 KtxKt, QxKt; 6 P–Q4, and if 6 . . . PxP; then 7 QxP!, ensuring White a small but lasting advantage. As regards the energetic thrust 6 . . . P–K4 it must be observed that too little practical data exists to enable one to offer an opinion one way or the other.

4	P–KKt3

The close system is bound up here with a certain risk since in the sequel Black can launch a really formidable attack against the KB3 square. Simpler, at all events, was 4 P–Q4, transposing to the normal variation.

4	...	P–Q4

This energetic thrust is stronger than the usual 4 . . . P–KKt3.

5	PxP	KtxP

A much bigger headache would have been inflicted on White by the pawn sacrifice 5 . . . Kt–Q5, and after its acceptance by 6 KtxKt, PxKt; 7 Kt–Kt5, a very obscure and complicated position would arise. Black should, however, obtain a really dangerous initiative by 7 . . . P–K4. On the other hand, if

White plays 6 B–Kt2, then 6 . . . B–Kt5; 7 O–O, KtxP gives Black a good game.

After the text-move White gets an excellent game with the better development.

6   B–Kt2   KtxKt

Black wished to play P–K3 a little later on but it would have been better to have done it at once. The exchange on QB3 enlarges the scope of the Bishop on Kt2 and opens up the QKt file for the Rook.

7   KtPxKt!

This way of recapturing is certainly stronger than 7 KtxKt, which would give the important square Q4 to the adversary. The pressure on QKt7 is now very disagreeable for Black.

7   . . .   P–K3

Since White will soon develop his Bishop on the diagonal QR1–KR8, 7 . . . P–KKt3 followed by B–Kt2 came into consideration here and this would have been more in keeping with the nature of the position.

8   O–O   B–K2
9   R–Kt1   O–O
10   P–QB4!

This advance is positionally more logical than 10 P–Q4, which would weaken the QB4 square and leave Black with a good game after 10 . . . Kt–R4. At the same time a fine diagonal is opened up for the Queen's Bishop by the text-move. On the other hand, however, the square on Q4 is left free for Black's occupation and this may enable him to obtain counter-play in the centre.

10 . . .   Q–Q2

Black wishes to continue with 11 . . . P–QKt3 and then 12 . . . B–Kt2 but for this purpose the Queen is unfortunately placed on Q2. Better, therefore, was 10 . . . Q–B2 followed by 11 . . . P–QKt3 and 12 . . . B–Kt2 with a satisfactory position.

11   B–Kt2   P–QKt3?

This natural looking move is, surprisingly enough, a mistake that gets Black into great difficulties. An essential preparation for this move was 11 . . . R–Q1 to which White intended replying 12 Kt–B4!. If then 12 . . . QxP; 13 Kt–Q5! gives White the advantage, e.g.: 13 . . . QxQ; 14 KtxBch, KtxKt; 15 KRxQ, R–K1; 16 B–QR3, when White wins back his pawn with the clearly better position. So then Black must play 12 . . . Kt–Q5, but after 13 R–K1, he would still be confronted with the problem of developing his Queen's wing.

Possible also of course was an immediate 11 . . . Kt–Q5, which, however, after 12 Kt–B4, leads to a similar position to that mentioned above.

Black (Foltys)

White (Keres) to play

12   P–Q4

The tactical justification for this thrust lies in the fact that after 12 . . . PxP; 13 KtxP, B–Kt2; 14 KtxKt, BxKt; 15 QxQ, Black would lose the exchange. Black is now set some very difficult problems.

12   . . .   B–Kt2

Black hopes to emerge into safety at the cost of a pawn: 13 PxP, R–Q1! (but not 13 . . . QxQ; 14 KRxQ, BxP; 15 R–Q7, etc.) 14 PxP, PxP and the weakness on White's Queen's wing gives his opponent good counter-play. But White has a much more enduring continuation at his disposal.

13   P–Q5!   Kt–R4

Black must keep his Bishop on Kt2 protected on account of the possibility of P–Q6, whilst after the exchange 13 . . . PxP; 14 PxP, White would obviously stand better. With the text-

move Black hopes to obtain equal chances through the counter-
attack on QB5.

14   Kt–B4   KtxP

It was on this capture that Black had placed all his hopes.
But by this time he had nothing better, since 14 . . . PxP;
15 PxP, would be clearly advantageous for White and otherwise 15 Q–Kt4 was threatened. Comparatively best was
probably 14 . . . P–K4; 15 BxP, KtxP etc.

15   BxP!

By means of this temporary piece sacrifice White destroys
the enemy King's position and obtains a decisive attack. Black
has now little choice.

15   . . .   KxB
16   Q–Kt4ch   K–R1

Equally unavailing was 16 . . . K–R3; 17 PxP, Q–B2 (or
17 . . . PxP; 18 BxB, QxB; 19 QxPch, followed by 20 QxKt,
etc.), 18 Q–R3ch!, K–Kt2; 19 Kt–R5ch, K–R1; (or 19 . . .
K–R3; 20 Kt–B6 dis ch, K–Kt2; 21 QxPch, KxKt; 22 Q–R6ch,
etc.) 20 BxB, QxB; 21 Q–Kt4, followed by 22 QxKt, and
White wins.

17   PxP!

But not immediately 17 Kt–R5, R–KKt1; 18 QxKt, which
would allow Black good play after 18 . . . PxP.

17   . . .   R–KKt1?

In a difficult situation Black makes a mistake that leads at
once to a loss. He no longer has, however, any adequate
defence. The main variation as planned by White runs as
follows: 17 . . . PxP; 18 KtxP, R–KKt1; 19 QxKt, B–B3;
20 QR–Q1, with a healthy pawn more and a marked positional
advantage for White. 17 . . . P–B4 fails against 18 . . . Kt–Kt6ch
and also the continuation 17 . . . Q–B2; 18 BxB, QxB (or
18 . . . Kt–K4; 19 Q–R5, etc.); 19 Kt–R5, R–KKt1; 20 QxKt,
does not alter the position to any extent.

18   QxRch   resigns

After 18 . . . KxQ; 19 PxQ, BxB White wins by either
20 KR–K1, or else by 20 KxB, Kt–Q7; 21 QR–K1, KtxR;
22 RxB, K–B1; 23 R–K2, etc.

★ 3 ★

BEFORE THE WORLD CHAMPIONSHIP
TOURNAMENT, 1945–1947

AT the turn of the year 1944–45 the Latvian chess-players
decided to organize a Baltic Tournament in Riga. In
this, however, only chess-players from Latvia and
Estonia took part. I again played pretty well in this tournament, winning all my games with the exception of one draw.
In addition to this tournament I also played in some club
matches in Riga and in the match between the cities of Tallinn
and Riga. My most important tournament in the year,
however, was at Tallinn in the autumn, this being the championship of Estonia in which some players from abroad were
participating hors concours. The tournament had a most
exciting course and was a particularly hard test for me since
I had been absent from serious tournament chess for quite a
time. I had, however, in this tournament an advantage that
should not be underestimated, in that I knew the home players
better and so acquired more points against them than my chief
rivals. But in any case all went well for me and I attained first
place, conceding only four draws. Round about this time I
was very busily engaged with chess matters, less in serious
tournament games and more with literary and pedagogic
work, a circumstance that had a positive influence on my own
play.

In the following spring I went on a tour in the far south
together with Master Mikenas and there we took part, hors
concours, in the Georgian Championship. I won this tournament with a fine total of 17 wins and 2 draws, but the task of
achieving this was not so easy as it might seem. Thus, for
example, I had to defend for a long time a really difficult ending
in my game against Ebralidze and it was only after some

inaccuracies on my opponent's part that I managed to obtain the draw through some variations resembling an endgame study. The other draw I made against a youngster of 16 years of age whose name was—Petrosian! Curiously enough, the decisive game of this tournament was already played by Round 3 when I obtained a win against Mikenas. After this, however, Mikenas won 14 games in succession! From these two tournaments I give my game against Tolush in the Tallinn event (No. 39).

In the year 1946 I made my first reappearance on the international scene since the end of the war. In the summer a match by radio took place between teams representing the U.S.S.R. and Great Britain and I had to play two games against Master Klein. The first game ended in a draw after an interesting course and in the second I succeeded in obtaining a positional advantage and then in winning the ending. After this a team came to Moscow from the U.S.A. to play a match v. the U.S.S.R. In this after a long interval I met my old opponent, Grandmaster Fine. Of our games the first one was the more interesting. After I had obtained a slight positional advantage I was able to win material by a small but very pleasing combination and then converted this advantage to a win (No. 40). The other game resulted in an early draw.

The year 1947 brought with it fresh chess activity for me and the old question of the world championship was once again raised. The world champion, Alekhine, had died the previous year and taken his title with him to the grave. The chess world was confronted with the problem as to how the question of the new world championship was to be settled. After lengthy discussion and much controversy it was eventually agreed that the new world champion should emerge from a tournament with many rounds in which Botvinnik, Euwe, Fine, Reshevsky, Smyslov and I should take part. Each player was to play 5 games against each other and the tournament was to be held in two cities, in the Hague and in Moscow. It was to begin early in the year 1948. I was faced with the prospect of some hard exhausting work so as to prepare for an important tournament of far-reaching consequences.

Bearing in mind that I had not taken part much in big tournaments in the years preceding this event I came to the conclusion that the best way of preparing for my participation in it lay in playing in as many strongly contested tournaments as possible. I began with the XV U.S.S.R. Championship which took place at Leningrad. This tournament was very strongly constituted and contained, with the exception of Botvinnik, all the chess elite of the Soviet Union. From the very first round there began for me a stiff struggle with Smyslov who made an excellent start and was in the lead at the end of the ninth round with 7 points. I also commenced the tournament in very good style and won my first three games. Then, however, I lost to Klaman and, despite great efforts, I was unable to overhaul Smyslov. Up to our decisive encounter in the tenth round I was still half a point behind him. In this deciding game Smyslov committed a hardly perceptible mistake in the opening. He lost a valuable tempo and I was able to utilize this factor to gain a decisive attack in the centre. This valuable victory (No. 41) put me in first place alone. The tournament continued with its ups and downs, but I succeeded in avoiding any further losses and held my leading position till the very end. And so I won, for the first time, the title of champion of the Soviet Union. I played really good chess once again in this tournament and won several well-played games.

After the U.S.S.R. Championship I played in a match against Latvia and then I busied myself with the organisation of a masters' tournament at Parnu in which the best players of the U.S.S.R. were due to compete. It exacted a great deal of work, but in the end the tournament actually did take place and, in order to give them practice, two of the home masters, Randviir and Renter, were allowed to take part. Despite the exhausting nature of the play, this tournament constituted an agreeable relaxation for the participants, thanks to the prevailing splendid summer weather. I played well in this tournament too and produced some interesting games, although life in a spa did not exactly provide the right atmosphere for tournament play. The rivalry for first place went on till the very last round. Only then, when Kotov failed to realise a marked advantage against Lilienthal, did I succeed in passing him by half a point. Thus in the period of some six months I had attained a second fine result and this allowed me to entertain hopes of a good result in the tournament for the World Championship which was due to start shortly.

After the tournament at Parnu I went to London as a member of a team representing the U.S.S.R. to play a match against Great Britain. I played against Alexander, with whom I had already played a number of games before the War. We always had lively and interesting encounters and these two also were no exception. After a complicated struggle rife in combinations I was able to obtain victory in the one game, whilst the other ended in a draw.

Towards the end of the year an international tournament in memory of M. I. Tschigorin was held in Moscow. I started off the tournament in excellent style and did in fact obtain, if one considers the mere points, a really fine success, but somehow or other my play was not quite convincing. It is quite certain that the organisation of the tournament bore some responsibility for this, since it was not, unfortunately, of the usual high quality this time. With two rounds to go I seemed to be very near ultimate victory, but at this point the tournament, to all intents and purposes, finished for me. My play in the last two games was totally lacking in energy; I suffered defeats in both and in the end achieved only a sharing of sixth and seventh places.

This was obviously a really bitter blow, only a few months before the World Championship tournament. It was not the sixth and seventh places that caused me anxiety but the indifferent chess that I played in this tournament. My games against Bondarevsky, Boleslavsky and Plater were "achievements" that I had no wish to repeat in the next tournament. Some small consolation was the good ending against Sokolsky. In this theoretically drawn endgame with Rook and two pawns against Rook I succeeded in discovering an original winning idea and also in forcing the win after some inaccuracies on the part of my opponent.

I assumed that my failure in this tournament was to be ascribed rather to circumstances beyond my control and then plunged hopefully into my next task—preparation for the decisive struggle for the World Championship.

Game 39

QUEEN'S PAWN, NIMZOWITSCH DEFENCE

Played in the Estonian Championship, 1945

	A. Tolush	P. Keres
1	P–Q4	Kt–KB3
2	P–QB4	P–K3
3	Kt–QB3	B–Kt5
4	P–K3	

In the years following the war this quiet move has become the most frequently used continuation in the Nimzo-indian and it has put every other line on one side, amongst them too the once almost inevitable 4 Q–B2. The main reason for the great popularity of the text-move resides in the fact that it retains the tension in the position for a long time and does not allow Black to obtain the more or less clear positions that occur after most other continuations.

4	. . .	P–Q4
5	Kt–B3	O–O
6	B–Q3	P–B4
7	O–O	Kt–B3
8	P–QR3	

After many years' practical experience and theoretical research it has eventually become established that it is with this thrust, which forces the enemy Bishop to declare its intentions at once, that White retains best prospects of keeping the initiative.

8	. . .	BxKt
9	PxB	P–QKt3

In recent years 9 . . . QPxP; 10 BxP, Q–B2 has become the most fashionable variation. The problems arising therefrom have not been definitely solved, despite innumerable practical essays. The text-move is generally regarded as unfavourable for Black.

10 BPxP

Practically forced, since Black was threatening to exchange off the powerful Bishop on Q3 by 10 . . . B–R3.

10 . . .	KPxP
11 P–QR4	

A good move which threatens 12 PxP, followed by 13 B–R3
and which induces the opponent to release the pressure on
White's centre by 11 . . . P–B5.

11 . . .	P–B5
12 B–B2	B–Kt5

After 12 . . . Kt–K5 White has the very strong continuation
13 BxKt, PxB; 14 Kt–Q2, eventually gaining the initiative after
14...P–B4; 15 B–R3, R–B3; 16 P–B3. The text-move is stronger.

13 Q–K1

Another good move with which White takes his first step
along the path of the execution of his main plan, the carrying
out of the central thrust P–K4. White now threatens to seize
the initiative in the centre by 14 Kt–R4, or 14 Kt–Q2, followed
by P–B3 and P–K4. Since now the exchange 13 . . . BxKt;
14 PxB, followed by 15 K–R1, would scarcely be very satisfactory for Black the second player has his fill of difficult
strategical problems to solve in the ensuing phase of the game.

13 . . .   R–K1?

This natural reply does nothing to refute the enemy plan and
hence Black now gets into real difficulties. 13 . . . B–R4 was
also not altogether satisfactory, since the intended 14 . . .
B–Kt3 would be thwarted by 14 Kt–R4! But by 13 . . . Kt–K5,
preventing 14 Kt–R4, Black could have obtained adequate
counterplay.

14 Kt–Q2

Stronger still here was the Knight leap 14 Kt–R4! which
ensured White a clear positional advantage in a match-game
Taimanov–Botvinnik, 1953 after 14 . . . B–R4; 15 P–B3, B–Kt3;
16 KtxB, RPxKt; 17 P–K4. After the text-move Black's task is a
little easier.

14 . . .   Kt–K2

Black's original intention here was 14 . . . B–R4 so as to
meet 15 P–B3, with 15 . . . B–Kt3 etc. Only now did I notice
that then, instead of 15 P–B3, there could follow the very
unpleasant 15 P–B4!, after which Black could get into difficulties with his Bishop.

15 P–B3

Here White fails to utilise the strong possibility 15 B–R3! which prevents 15 ... B–B4 and once again threatens 16 P–B3. If then 15 ... Q–Q2; 16 P–B3, B–B4 and White can in the first place choose the game continuation 17 P–K4, B–Kt3, with Black having made the passive move Q–Q2. But stronger still seems 17 BxB, KtxB; 18 P–K4! with which White would have been able to carry out his thrust as planned with the better game.

15 ...   B–B4
16 P–K4

Now 16 BxB, KtxB; 17 P–K4, would fail against 17 ... PxP; 18 PxP, KtxQP!.

16 ...   B–Kt3
17 B–R3

Now, once the Black Bishop has become ensconced on Kt3, this move loses its point. In order to thwart Black's ensuing tactical counter-chances it would have been better to have protected once again the central points of QB3 and Q4 by 17 B–Kt2.

17 ...   PxP
18 PxP   Kt(K2)–Q4!

Black utilises the circumstances that the KP is doubly pinned so as to gain control of the important central square Q4 and at the same time to threaten the pawn on B6. The position that has now arisen is full of tension and rich in tactical possibilities so that even the slightest inaccuracy can give the opponent the opportunity of forcing a decisive advantage for himself. Hence both sides must now proceed with the utmost care.

The positional problem is not intrinsically complicated. Black will attain a completely satisfactory position once he succeeds either in establishing himself on Q4 or exchanging off one of the centre pawns. But should White manage to frustrate the tactical threats of his opponent and force his pieces to retreat, then, with his strong pawn centre and his two Bishops, he has every likelihood of getting a decisive advantage. It is clear that a sharp and exciting struggle is about to take place.

19   R–B3

No better defence of the QBP can be seen, since 19 B–Kt2 makes possible a fresh attack on the KP by 19 . . . Q–K2. After the text-move 19 . . . KtxBP; 20 RxKt(B3), QxPch fails against 21 Q–K3.

19   . . .   R–QB1

Protecting the BP and threatening to strengthen the pressure against K5 by R–B3–K3 should White fail to undertake anything in the meantime so as to unpin his pawn.

20 K–R1

White's best chance to free himself from the burdensome pin is undoubtedly Q–Kt1. This, however, was not possible at once because of 20 . . . KtxBP; 21 RxKt, QxPch, etc. Hence White moves his King away so as to make this line a valid one.

One cannot see how White could procure for himself a positional advantage in any other way since he has to take into account a whole host of tactical counter-thrusts. If, for example, 20 Q–R4, then Black can make the capture 20 . . . KtxKP and 20 B–Kt2 would be met by 20 . . . Q–K2. Also 20 Q–B2, so as to regain with advantage the pawn on KB7 after the double exchange on K4, will not do on account of 20 . . . KtxBP!; 21 RxKt(B3), Kt–Kt5, etc.

20   . . .   R–B3

Now Black is indeed threatening 21 . . . KtxKP, so as to regain his sacrificed piece afterwards by R(B3)–K3. White is

Black (Keres)

White (Tolush) to play

therefore forced to free himself from the pin somehow or other. The game is nearing its critical moment.

21 Q–QKt1?

At last, so White believes, the time has come to carry out this move that has been intended so long, but it becomes apparent that this Queen move is still not sufficiently prepared. Now in fact 21 Q–R4 came into consideration, since once one of the Rooks has left the back rank Black can no longer reply 21 . . . KtxKP. He has, however, another continuation and that is the sacrifice 21 . . . KtxBP! 22 RxKt(B3), QxP. Then White has nothing better than 23 Kt–Kt1, but then follows 23 . . . BxP, with a decisive attack.

In this variation White, instead of 22 RxKt(B3), can play stronger 22 P–Q5, but then could follow 22 . . . Kt(B6)xQP; 23 PxKt, QxP; 24 BxB, RPxB; and with three pawns for the piece together with a more active position Black's prospects must be deemed superior.

The best continuation for White was, however, 21 Q–KB1! Since then 21 . . . KtxBP; 22 RxKt(B3), QxP; will not do on account of 23 RxP, Black, in view of the threat of 22 PxKt has nothing better than 21 . . . KtxKP. After 22 KtxKt, he can, however, choose between two continuations. Firstly the pawn sacrifice 22 . . . BxKt; 23 BxB, RxB; 24 RxP, R–B3; 25 RxR, KtxR; 26 QxPch, Q–Q4; when he should have sufficient recompense for the pawn in the active position of his pieces and in his control of the white squares. But still more interesting is the second possibility, that of the exchange sacrifice by 22 . . . RxKt; 23 BxR, BxB. After 24 R–Kt3, P–B4 Black has certainly adequate compensation for the exchange, and therefore 24 RxP must be investigated. Then, however, follows 24 . . . BxPch; and after 25 QxB (or 25 KxB, Kt–K6ch, etc.) 25 . . . KxR Black keeps his extra pawn with a good position.

Although the couple of exemplary lines given above cannot of course bring out all the hidden possibilities of the position, they give an approximate picture of what problems both sides must solve in this position. Here too, however, one gains the impression that Black's middle game strategy is well based and that there exists no clear way open to White by which he can repulse the enemy pieces.

21   . . .   KtxBP!

This threat, which was always in the offing, now decides the
fate of the game. White can no longer avoid loss of material.

22   RxKt(B3)   QxP

With his 21st move White has taken away the QKt1 square
from his Knight, so that now protection by 23 Kt–Kt1 has
become impossible. Now Black wins his piece back and has
two extra pawns into the bargain.

23   B–Kt4

No better too was 23 RxP, RxR; 24 KtxR, QxKt when
White will also lose his pawn on K4.

23   . . .   QxKt
24   P–R5

Tolush, when making his 21st move, had thought in his
calculations that he could now capture first the pawn and then
the Rook by 24 RxP. But in making these calculations he overlooked the simple protection by 24 . . . Q–Q2. The text-move
is a desperate attempt to gain something yet by the threat of
25 B–R4, but this can no longer lead to any possible success.

24   . . .   BxP

White resigns.

After 25 BxB, KtxB; 26 RxP Black can play 26 . . . Q–K6
and if then 27 RxR, simply 27 . . . Kt–B7ch; 28 K–Kt1,
Kt–Q8 dis ch followed by mate in two moves.

Game 40

ENGLISH OPENING

Played in the match between the U.S.S.R. and U.S.A. in Moscow, 1946

	P. Keres	R. Fine
1	P–QB4	P–QB4
2	Kt–KB3	Kt–KB3
3	Kt–B3	P–Q4
4	PxP	KtxP
5	P–K3	

This seemingly restrained method of play constitutes in fact one of the best continuations for White in this position. In the ensuing phase of the game Black will have some little troubles in connection with a comparative weakness on the diagonal K1–QR5. Thus for example 5 . . . Kt–QB3; 6 B–Kt5 would lead to a Nimzoindian with colours reversed and with an extra tempo for White.

Praxis has shown that after 5 P–K4, both 5 . . . KtxKt; 6 KtPxKt, P–KKt3; transposing to the Grunfeld Defence and 5 . . . Kt–Kt5; 6 B–B4, B–K3!, which would exploit White's weakness on Q3, are thoroughly satisfactory for Black. Also the continuation 5 P–KKt3, Kt–QB3; 6 B–Kt2, Kt–B2 has in practice produced very good results for Black.

5 . . .   KtxKt

Black would like to lead the game along the paths of the Grunfeld Defence, but he cannot, however, play 5 . . . P–KKt3 at once because of 6 Q–R4ch, Kt–B3; (or 6 . . . B–Q2; 7 Q–B4, etc.) 7 B–Kt5, with an enduring pin. But the exchange on B3 strengthens White's centre and gives him an easy game. Hence here 5 . . . P–K3 seems best for Black, after which, by 6 P–Q4, a position in the Queen's Gambit could be reached.

6 KtPxKt   P–KKt3
7 Q–R4ch

With this move White had in mind a combination that, however, after a further check, turned out to be incorrect. There came therefore into consideration the idea of taking advantage of the absence of a Knight on Black's King-side to embark on an attack by 7 P–KR4. If then 7 . . . P–KR4; White obtains lasting pressure on Black's King's position by 8 B–B4, B–Kt2; 9 Kt–Kt5, O–O; 10 Q–B2.

After the text-move Black attains a satisfactory position.

7 . . .   Kt–Q2
8 B–R3

White originally had in mind the following combination after 7 . . . Kt–Q2; 8 B–B4, B–Kt2; 9 BxPch, KxB; 10 Kt–Kt5ch, but now notices just in time that there is a hole in it. After 10 . . . K–K1; 11 Kt–K6, Q–Kt3; 12 KtxBch, K–B2 the Knight has no square to retreat and is lost.

Nevertheless it would have been logical for White, either

here, or in the course of the next few moves, to have interposed
the moves 8 P–KR4, P–KR4; so as to have called into being a
certain weakness in Black's King's position.

8	. . .	Q–B2
9	B–K2	B–Kt2
10	O–O	O–O
11	P–Q4	P–QR3

This merely signifies a weakening of the Queen's wing since
an advance by P–QKt4 proves to be impracticable here.
Simpler therefore was 11 . . . P–QKt3 followed by 12 . . .
B–Kt2 and then P–K4.

12	P–B4	P–K4

A good reply that makes use of the fact that White cannot
play 13 P–Q5, because of 13 . . . P–K5. An immediate 12 . . .
P–Kt3 yields White an excellent game after 13 QR–Q1,
threatening the very awkward 14 P–Q5.

13	QR–Q1	KPxP
14	PxP	P–Kt3

The possibility of winning the Queen by 14 . . . P–QKt4;
15 BPxP, RPxP; 16 QxR, B–Kt2; 17 Q–R7, R–R1; does not
appeal to Black since after 18 QxRch, BxQ; 19 PxP, Black
clearly stands better. Now White gets his P–Q5 in and obtains
some small preponderance in the centre.

15	P–Q5	B–Kt2
16	Q–Kt3	

16 . . . P–QKt4 was of course threatened and Black tries to
execute this thrust in the next few moves at all costs.

16	. . .	QR–Kt1
17	B–B1	

White plays the middlegame anyhow and without a well-
thought out plan, thereby eventually allowing his opponent
to free his Queen-side. Very strong here would have been
17 B–Kt2, exchanging off the powerful enemy Bishop. After
17 . . . BxB; 18 QxB, P–QKt4; 19 PxP, PxP; 20 BxP, B–R3;
21 P–QR4, BxB; 22 PxB, Q–Kt2 Black does, it is true, win back
the pawn, but he remains, on account of the strong enemy
passed pawns and his weakened King's position, in a seemingly
difficult plight.

17 . . .   P–QKt4!

After the carrying out of this essential thrust, which, more-over, must be done at once on account of the threat of 18 P–QR4, Black is rid of his greatest trouble, the weakened Queen's wing. Now the position becomes simplified and White's positional advantage is really dubious.

18 PxP   PxP
19 BxP

Interpolating 19 P–Q6, Q–Kt3 would merely result in White's no longer being able to play 20 BxP, on account of 20 . . . BxKt.

19 . . .   B–QR3
20 P–QR4   BxB
21 PxB   Q–Kt2

Black could here have made use of the circumstance that White's Bishop makes it impossible to protect the KtP by R–Kt1 and played the stronger 21 . . . Q–R4. If White then continues as in the game with 22 Kt–Kt5, then there comes 22 . . . RxP; 23 Q–KR3, Kt–B3 when White lacks the possi-bility of the important tempo win by 24 B–B4.

22 Kt–Kt5!

With this White utilises the fact that Black King's position is comparatively insecure to initiate a direct attack that will give his opponent many a headache in the ensuing phase of the game.

22 . . .   QxKtP
23 Q–KR3   Kt–B3

The other possibility that came into consideration here, 23 . . . P–R3, would set Black some difficult problems after 24 Kt–K4. The threat is 25 BxP, and even after 24 . . . K–R2 there could follow 25 BxP!, BxB; 26 QxKt, etc. The defence 24 . . . P–B4; 25 Kt–Kt3, would, however, seriously weaken Black's King's position and allow White to strengthen his position noticeably by KR–K1 or Kt–K2–B4. Finally, the continutaion 24 . . . Q–R5; 25 QR–K1! is also disagreeable for Black since 26 BxP is still threatened and after 25 . . . KR–K1; 26 Kt–B3! Black must give up his strong Bishop.

24 B–B4   QR–B1?

Black has not seen the ensuing little combination and in consequence loses a pawn without any compensation whatsoever. Necessary was 24 ... R–Kt2, so as to be able to meet 25 B–K5, with 25 ... Q–Q2. But even in this case White would stand better after 26 Q–QB3!, e.g. 26 ... Q–B4; 27 P–B4, or 26 ... KtxP; 27 RxKt!, QxR; 28 BxB, QxKt; 29 BxR, KxB; 30 Q–R8ch, K–K2; and it is doubtful whether the Black King can emerge safe and sound.

Not particularly good for Black too was the defence 24 ... QR–Q1 to which White can reply 25 B–B7, R–B1; 26 B–K5, Q–Q2; 27 Q–QB3, Q–B4; 28 P–B4, when a similar position to that in the previous variation would arise. Here Black cannot play 27 ... KtxP because of 28 BxB! (but not 28 RxKt, QxR; 29 BxB, QxKt; etc.) 28 ... KtxQ; 29 RxQ, KxB; 30 Kt–K6ch, etc.

Perhaps Black, after 24 ... R–Kt2, could have eventually equalised the position by a careful defence, but in any case he would have had to play with the utmost circumspection for quite a while.

Black (Fine)

White (Keres) to play

25 KtxBP!

It is clear that Black cannot capture the Knight in either way and must accept the loss of a pawn. In addition, the ensuing Queen exchange is practically forced, after which, however, the ending is also lost for Black.

25	...	Q–Q2
26	QxQ	KtxQ
27	Kt–Q6	QR–Q1
28	B–K3!	

By attacking the QBP White deprives his opponent of a good opportunity for counter-play by 28 . . . Kt–Kt3, which, for example, would have given Black good drawing prospects after 28 B–Kt3.

28 . . .   Kt–Kt3

Black nevertheless decides upon this counter-attack, although it now costs him a second pawn. He is convinced that passive defence would be hopeless, e.g. 28 . . . Kt–B3; 29 BxP, R–Q2; 30 KR–K1, KR–Q1; 31 R–K6 etc. No better also was 28 . . . B–Q5; 29 BxB, PxB; 30 Kt–K4! when Black again loses a second pawn.

29   BxP   Kt–R5
30   B–R3!

But not 30 Kt–Kt7, KtxB; 31 KtxKt, R–B4! when the QP is lost.

30 . . .   Kt–B6
31   Kt–Kt7!

Breaking down all further possible resistance.

31 . . .   KtxR
32   KtxR   resigns

Game 41

ENGLISH OPENING

From the XV U.S.S.R. Championship at Leningrad, 1947.

P. Keres	V. Smyslov
1 P–QB4	Kt–KB3
2 Kt–QB3	P–B4
3 Kt–B3	P–K3

Black may have wanted to play P–Q4 later and then to recapture with the Kt on Q4 after the pawn exchange, but all the same he should have played the QP advance at once. After P–K3 Black loses a valuable tempo in many variations involving the advance of the QP and thus brings upon himself unnecessary difficulties.

	4	P–KKt3	P–Q4
	5	PxP	KtxP

After 5 . . . PxP; 6 P–Q4, we get the normal position arising out of a Tarrasch Defence, which is not, however, to everyone's taste. With the text-move Black transposes to the normal variation of the English Opening, but with the not particularly useful move P–K3.

	6	B–Kt2	Kt–QB3
	7	O–O	Kt–B2

With this move Black chooses an ambitious idea designed to gain control of the important Q5 square by carrying out the advance P–K4. This idea is, however, very risky, as it is bound up with the loss of tempi by P–K3–K4. Better therefore was the quiet 7 . . . B–K2, after which White would bring about a variation of the Catalan by 8 P–Q4.

	8	P–Kt3	B–K2
	9	B–Kt2	P–K4

Smyslov pursues his idea logically. The thrust P–K4 must be made immediately since, for example, after 9 . . . O–O; 10 R–B1, Black is already too late with the move as now 10 . . . P–K4 would cost a pawn on account of 11 Kt–QR4. Seeing that in the ensuing phase of the game Black must lose much time in protection of K4 and QB4, he remains dangerously behindhand in his development.

	10	R–B1	P–B3
	11	Kt–QR4	P–QKt3?

But this move is already a direct mistake which gets Black into great difficulties. The weakening of the diagonal QR1–KR8 allows White to open up the centre in the ensuing phase of the game, after which through his better development White attains some dangerous threats. For good or ill, Black must continue here 11 . . . Kt–K3 when White retains the better chances by 12 Kt–R4 followed by P–B4.

	12	Kt–R4	B–Q2

With 12 . . . B–Kt2 Black would in the first place weaken the important KB4 square and in the second allow of the strong advance 13 P–QKt4! After the text-move this thrust would no longer possess the force White would wish as Black could give

up the exchange with good counter-play by 13 . . . KtxP!;
14 BxR, QxB.

Black (Smyslov)

White (Keres) to play

13   P–K3!

Curiously enough, this seemingly so quiet move sets Black
practically insoluble problems. The point of course does not
reside in the threat to win the exchange by 14 Q–R5ch, as
this can be parried easily enough. Much more serious, however, is the positional threat of 14 P–Q4! With this thrust, that
comprises a variety of threats, White would force the opening
up of the centre and this, in view of Black's retarded development, could lead easily to a catastrophe.

Inasmuch as Black possesses no satisfactory defence against
the last-mentioned threat, his opening strategy can be classed
as a failure. White now has a clear advantage.

13   . . .   O–O
14   P–Q4   KPxP

P–Q5–6, winning a piece, was threatened, and in addition
the simple win of a pawn by 15 PxBP. With the text-move
Black does at least ward off the first threat since he frees the
square Q5 for his Knight.

15   PxP   R–B1

Black now intends to meet 16 P–Q5 simply with the reply
16 . . . Kt–Q5 and then after 17 BxKt, PxB; 18 QxP, to build
up an apparently adequate defensive position by 18 . . .
Kt–Kt4 followed by 19 . . . Kt–Q3. White therefore chooses

another continuation which opens up the position still more
and enables him to win a pawn under more favourable
circumstances.

16	PxP	P–QKt4
17	Kt–QB3	P–B4

Bad of course was 17 . . . BxP because of 18 KtxP.

18   R–B2 !

This Rook move, which threatens 19 R–Q2, a move that
cannot be prevented, is much stronger than simply going back
with the Knight by 18 Kt–B3, B–B3 etc. Now Black's position
falls to pieces quickly.

18	. . .	BxKt
19	R–Q2	R–B2

Black has nothing better, since after 19 . . . Kt–Kt1; 20
P–B6 is decisive, whilst if 19 . . . Kt–K4; 20 PxB.

20   PxB !

This simple recapture is much stronger than winning the
Queen by 20 BxKt, BxB; 21 RxQch, RxR, which would still
leave Black with comparatively reasonable defensive chances.
Now Black cannot do anything against the threat of 21 BxKt.

20	. . .	Kt–K3
21	KtxP	KtxP

Otherwise, with two pawns less in a hopeless position Black
could already have resigned with a good conscience.

22	Kt–Q6	R–K2
23	KtxR	QxKt
24	B–QR3	Kt–K5
25	BxKt	PxB
26	BxR	KtxB
27	RxB	resigns

* 4 *

THE WORLD CHAMPIONSHIP AND OTHER
TOURNAMENTS, 1948–1950

In the Spring of 1948 I went to Holland in order to contest, at long last, the highest chess title in the world. For various reasons Fine declined to participate and so this left five of us to embark on this momentous conflict. From the very first rounds a fierce struggle developed and this continued right to the very last games. I began the tournament with two wins, against Euwe and Smyslov, but then lost in the ensuing rounds against Reshevsky and Botvinnik and at the end of the first tour I stood equal with Smyslov in third and fourth places. Thus far my play was unsatisfactory since, apart from the two lost games I also committed unforgiveable inaccuracies in the two won ones. There was wanting in my play the ease with which I had disposed of several tournaments in the year 1947 and this naturally had a negative influence on my results. Botvinnik began with great eclat, produced a very certain and assured style of play and at the end of the first tour was securely in the lead with $3\frac{1}{2}$ points.

I cherished the hope that my play would improve as the tournament progressed, but this alas was not the case. It is true that in the next tour I won my game against Smyslov (No. 42), but then I lost a most weakly played game against Botvinnik and the draws too with Euwe and Reshevsky were full of small mistakes. It was clear that I found myself in far from my best sporting form and when in addition one takes into consideration that by the end of the second tour Botvinnik had already obtained a two point lead over me, then my prospects for first place had already practically disappeared.

It was in the third tour that I undertook my last attempt to struggle to the top and I initiated this by a theoretically interesting lightning victory over Euwe (No. 43). After a fighting draw with Smyslov I then played my most up and down game of the whole tourney against Reshevsky. I got into difficulties in the opening and lost a pawn, but then I was able to obtain marked counter-play before the adjournment and the game was in fact adjourned in a position where I had good drawing chances. However, on resumption of play there came a great surprise. Reshevsky fell into a cunning trap, lost the exchange and, after a long and vicissitudinous ending, eventually the game as well. With this win I came to within $1\frac{1}{2}$ points of Botvinnik and now everything hung on our individual encounter. In event of a win I would come to within half a point of the leader and the issue of the tournament would be once again wide open.

This deciding encounter had a most complicated and exciting course and constituted a stiff test for the nerves of both players. Out of a complicated middle-game I succeeded in evolving a position of the most promising kind. Then, however, I failed to utilise my opportunities to the best advantage and the scales tipped over in Botvinnik's favour. Then there ensued a whole series of inaccuracies committed by both sides and when the game was eventually adjourned a double Rook endgame with an extra pawn for Botvinnik had arisen.

When play was resumed Botvinnik did not find the best line and a Rook ending resulted that should have been easily drawn. But the vicissitudes of this game were by no means ended. Both sides conducted the ending imprecisely and it was I who made the last mistake. By the time the second adjournment came Botvinnik had an easily won position and I suffered a bitter defeat. With this win Botvinnik had in practice ensured for himself victory in the tournament since with only eight more games remaining to be played he already had a lead of $2\frac{1}{2}$ points.

In spite of this loss I still stood very well in the tournament, especially after winning the game in the next round against Euwe. By this time I enjoyed a lead of $1\frac{1}{2}$ points over both Smyslov and Reshevsky and seemed to have second place firmly in my grasp. Then, however, I committed a great tactical blunder. Instead of resigning myself to the hopeless nature of the struggle for the World Championship title and contenting myself with the assurance of second place, I concentrated my efforts on trying to overhaul Botvinnik in a desperately forced style of play. The consequences of such thoughtless tactics soon manifested themselves. I lost in succession to Smyslov, Reshevsky and Botvinnik and, when the fourth tour was at an end, I was in mere fourth place, a whole point behind Reshevsky and Smyslov. Thus, through thoughtless play in a few rounds I spoilt the whole tournament.

In the fifth tour there was nothing left for me but to try and somehow or other improve my position in the tournament and this I more or less succeeded in achieving after the utmost expenditure of effort. I won a game full of complications and blunders against Euwe, then made draws against Reshevsky and Smyslov, and in the final round I succeeded in administering a defeat to the newly fledged World Champion in an interesting game that was rich in combinations (No. 44). Through this good result in the last tour I overhauled Reshevsky and eventually attained the sharing of third and fourth places, a half a point below Smyslov. The new World Champion, Botvinnik, undoubtedly played the best chess of all, and I am of the opinion that this tournament is qualitatively the best result in his chess career. A disagreeable surprise was Euwe's bad form in consequence of which the tournament practically became a four man contest. Nor was I at all satisfied with my own play. In the first place many uncalled for inaccuracies occurred in my games and in the second the tactical scheme I employed in the whole tournament was not right.

Every player has in the course of his career periods in which he at times plays very well and at other times plays in quite mediocre fashion, and this is indeed only natural. It seems to me that in my case a depression in my form had already begun with the Tschigorin tournament and that this continued in ensuing tournaments. Thus for example in the XVI U.S.S.R. Championship nothing seemed to go right for me. The ill luck began already in the first round when, against Cholmov in a very promising Queen ending I overlooked a resourceful stalemate combination by my opponent. I drew my first five games, then came a loss to Furman, a draw in an endgame with a plus pawn against Taimanov, and then another loss, against

Kotov. My wretched position was then somewhat bettered by winning a game full of ups and downs against Levenfish, a game that was characterised by a most interesting Rook ending. Then, however, there came yet another loss against Konstantinopolsky, and I was just as badly placed as before. Only by exerting the utmost efforts towards the end of the tournament did I manage to improve my tournament position a little and in the process I did play a few really good games. The most interesting of these was undoubtedly my meeting with Bronstein (No. 45), the joint winner of the tournament, in a game of original cast and a pendulum-like struggle that eventually yielded me a valuable point in the ending. This end spurt of mine got me as far as to a sharing of 6th to 9th places.

I played rather better in the next XVII Championship where I gained a valuable victory over Geller (No. 46) after a complicated and involved game. Despite committing some inaccuracies in the draws with Cholmov and Aronin, I resumed my winning vein in the ensuing rounds. The victories over Mikenas and Petrosian (No. 47) were good achievements from the artistic point of view. Having obtained $5\frac{1}{2}$ points out of the first seven rounds and played really good chess in so doing, I had reason to hope that I had overcome the crisis in my creative period. The further course of the tournament showed, however, that this was not quite yet the case. Once again my play was exceedingly variable, wins alternating with losses. In a highly complicated and indeed obscure position against Bronstein I made a terrible blunder in great time trouble and was checkmated. Against Taimanov I lost a reasonably good position practically with one move, whilst against Lublinsky, wishing to win at all costs in an even position, I once again had to add yet another nought to my tournament table. Thus, though I did also win some really good games, as for example against Levenfish, a number of losses cut me off from competing for first place. Eventually, despite an excellent start, I had to content myself with the 8th place only.

My next great tournament was the Candidates' Tournament at Budapest in the Spring of 1950. Now once again I had thoroughly prepared for the event and I felt I was in good form. The tournament too started off most auspiciously for me. I won in the first round against Stahlberg and also obtained a clear advantage in my next game against Boleslavsky, though this game did only end in a draw. In the further course of the first tour I succeeded in winning an interesting sacrificial game against Kotov (No. 48), and, since I drew the other games, I stood in second place at the end of the tour with the good result of 5½ points out of 9 games. Only Boleslavsky had a half a point more.

With the commencement of the second tour the exciting struggle continued. Although Boleslavsky scored a victory over Flohr, I once again reduced the difference between us to half a point by winning against Szabo. Then, however, I suffered a loss in an extremely complicated game against Kotov and after I had failed to make proper use of my winning chances in an interesting sacrificial game against Flohr it became apparent that I could no longer overhaul Boleslavsky. Hence I played in the final rounds without any real dash, and, after losing the last game against Bronstein I finished up eventually in fourth place.

However, in this tournament I was already playing in markedly better form than in the preceding tournaments of this period and it was to be hoped that I should soon regain my good form. The first five players in this tournament obtained the right to participate in the next Candidates' Tournament. Thus my fourth place assured my participation in a tournament of the same nature after an interval of three years.

Game 42

CATALAN SYSTEM

From the World Championship Tournament at the Hague and Moscow,
    1948

	V. Smyslov	P. Keres
1	P–Q4	Kt–KB3
2	P–QB4	P–K3
3	P–KKt3	P–Q4

One of the best and most used replies for Black in this opening. Of recent years the system 3 . . . P–B4; 4 P–Q5, PxP; 5 PxP, P–Q3 has also been often employed, when the development of the Bishop on KKt2 is reckoned as not particularly advantageous for White.

| | 4   B–Kt2 | PxP |

In my view this exchange gives Black an easier game than the system of development by 4 . . . B–K2; 5 Kt–KB3, O–O; 6 O–O, QKt–Q2; followed by P–B3 and P–QKt3. Now White must lose time in regaining his pawn and Black can utilise this circumstance to develop his pieces.

| | 5   Q–R4ch |

After 5 Kt–KB3, Black could try to retain the pawn by 5 . . . P–QR3; 6 Q–B2, P–QKt4; 7 Kt–K5, R–R2; or 7 . . . Kt–Q4 etc. Unfortunately this continuation has not as yet been tried out in practice.

| | 5   . . . | B–Q2 |

The usual continuation here is 5 . . . QKt–Q2. The text-move leads to a type of middle-game postulating a difficult positional struggle.

| | 6   QxBP | B–B3 |
| | 7   Kt–KB3 |

Naturally, White does not want to exchange off Bishops and after 7 P–B3, Black would get a good game by 7 . . . QKt–Q2. Now, however, Black obtains counter-play on the white centre squares.

| | 7   . . . | QKt–Q2 |

7 . . . B–Q4 came into consideration here in order to gain speedy equality. After 8 Q–B2, Kt–B3 or 8 . . . B–K5 would be troublesome, and 8 Q–R4ch, B–B3; 9 Q–Q1, P–K4! also gives Black a good game too. The text-move is, however, equally good and avoids any quick simplification.

| | 8   Kt–B3 | Kt–Kt3 |

Black must take good care in this variation to see that his opponent does not arrive at the advance P–K4. The main struggle in the present game is precisely concerned with this advance which forms the chief target for White's aims in the course of the next twenty moves. It is for this reason that one cannot recommend for Black a quiet piece development by 8 . . . B–K2; O–O, O–O; 10 Q–Q3, Kt–Q4 (Kotov–Romanov-

sky, Moscow, 1944). White could then get a clear advantage
by the pawn sacrifice 11 P–K4!, KtxKt; 12 PxKt, Kt–B4;
13 Q–K3, KtxP; 14 Kt–K5!

	9 Q–Q3	B–Kt5

Continuing the struggle for the white central squares.

	10 O–O	O–O
	11 R–Q1	

By 11 B–Kt5, P–KR3; 12 BxKt, QxB; 13 P–K4, White
could enforce the KP advance, but it would be at too high a
price. After 13 . . . KR–Q1; Black would possess sufficient
compensation in his two Bishops for the opponent's advantage
in space.

	11 . . .	P–KR3

Black did not like the possible pin after 11 . . . Q–K2; 12
B–Kt5, but this was not to be feared. After 12 . . . P–KR3;
13 BxKt, QxB; 14 P–K4, KR–Q1; the tempo plus of White's
KR–Q1 would have no real significance.

	12 B–Q2	

Simpler was an immediate 12 P–QR3, KBxKt; 13 QxB,
since as the game goes White does not recapture with the
Bishop on B3 in any case.

	12 . . .	Q–K2
	13 P–QR3	KBxKt
	14 QxB	

After 14 BxB, B–K5; followed by 15 . . . KR–Q1 or 15 . . .
Kt–Q4 would give Black an excellent game. But now, however, the central white squares are firmly in Black's hand,
temporarily at any rate.

	14 . . .	KR–Q1

Here 14 . . . Kt–K5 was also possible since after 15 Q–Kt4,
Q–K1; the threat of 16 . . . P–QR4 is very troublesome. If,
however, White should continue with 15 Q–B2, then there
follows 15 . . . KtxB; 16 RxKt, P–B4 with complete control
of K5.

	15 B–K1	QR–B1

Black has emerged from the opening with a good game and
is for the moment to be reckoned as victor in the struggle for

the white squares in the centre. In the ensuing middle-game, however, he does not at first find the right plan of play and so soon gets into pronounced difficulties. The advance of P–QB4 planned eventually by the text-move is easily parried and hence here 15 ... P–QR4 was to be recommended. With this Black would thwart all active play on his opponent's part on the Queen's wing and would himself threaten to fix the weaknesses on the white squares by an eventual P–R5.

16 B–B1!

An excellent idea. White now plans to force P–K4 after P–B3, thereby retaining his two Bishops. Since Black in the meantime enjoys no opportunity of active play he is forced to occupy himself with defending this threat. But this means that White, as a result of Black's inaccurate 15th move has by now obtained the initiative.

	16 ...	B–Q4
	17 P–QKt4	

Naturally, White is not going to allow the advance 17 ... P–B4. Already he is threatening 18 Kt–K5, followed by 19 P–B3 and 20 P–K4.

	17 ...	Kt(Kt3)–Q2

Depriving the enemy Knight of its K5 square and planning to meet 18 Kt–Q2, with 18 ... P–K4. Therefore White plays his Knight to R4 so as in the event of 18 ... P–K4, to have at his disposal the strong reply of 19 Kt–B5.

	18 Kt–R4	Kt–K5
	19 Q–B2	Kt–Q3
	20 P–B3	P–KKt4

An immediate 20 ... P–KB4 would be met by 21 Kt–Kt6, followed by 22 Kt–B4, when White would quickly attain the strong square of Q3 for his Knight. Through the text-move Black does indeed prevent this, but he has, however, to weaken his King-side, a circumstance that later on becomes unpleasantly apparent.

	21 Kt–Kt2	P–KB4

Black has been able to prevent the advance of P–K4 only by the greatest efforts, and has had to create in consequence some marked weaknesses in his position. Moreover, White is in a position to concentrate the fire of his Knight, Bishop and Rook on the K4 square and thus can eventually force through his P–K4. For these reasons Black must seek counter-play as quickly as possible and best prospects of this are afforded by the Queen-side since fewer White pieces are present there. So, in the ensuing phase of the game, White must devote his attention to the possibility of Black playing P–Kt3 and P–B4 and it is with this in mind that he plays his next move. At the same time he opens up the way to the strong post on Q3 for his Knight, and will then proceed with B–Kt2 and R–K1 as a preparation for the P–K4 advance.

It is naturally hard to say whether the plan devised by White is the best, but in any case it is in keeping with the demands of the position and is characterised by a strictly logical approach, Alternatives such as 22 B–B3, P–Kt3, with the eventual threat of P–B4, or 22 Kt–K3, Q–Kt2, permitting Black in some variations to play P–KB5, are anyway not stronger than the text-move.

22	B–B2	Kt–B3
23	Kt–K1	P–QR4

Black (Keres)

White (Smyslov) to play

Here Black could permanently dispose of the danger of an advance by P–K4 if he were to continue 23 ... P–Kt5. But with this he would create hopeless weaknesses on the black squares of his position and would give his opponent a much superior game after 24 B–Kt2, followed by 25 Kt–Q3. The

diversion begun by the text-move on the Queen's wing is
unpleasant enough for White and at least forces him to abandon
his main plan, the P–K4 advance, for the time being.

24   Kt–Q3

Instead of this move it would have been simpler to have
played 24 PxP, so as to manoeuvre his Bishop to the strong post
of QKt4 after 24 . . . R–R1 ; 25 Kt–Q3, RxP; 26 B–K1. After
the text-move Black should immediately open up the QR file
by 24 . . . PxP; 25 PxP, R–R1 so as to worry his adversary on
the Queen's wing. But for some time now both players have
been in time trouble and this circumstance strongly affects the
ensuing part of the game.

24	. . .	R–R1
25	B–Kt2	R–R2

Black does not want at all to eliminate the possibility of PxP but
would like to double his Rooks before the exchange on QKt4.

26   R–K1   Q–R2!

A good move by which Black increases his control of White's
K4 and, in the event of White continuing with Kt–B5 followed
by P–K4, will have a troublesome pin on that square after a
pawn exchange. Now there has arisen a critical situation in
which White has to show how well based was his previous
strategy of executing the P–K4 advance.

27   P–Kt5?

By means of this pawn sacrifice White at last carries out his
idea and arrives at P–K4, but he has, however, to pay too
highly for it all. In the first place Black will now have a pawn
more and in the second this advance no longer possesses the
force it was once supposed to have. Hence it seems to me that it
would be best for White here to renounce the direct carrying
out of his plan but that he should also try to seize the initiative
on the Queen's wing by continuing 27 PxP, RxP; 28 KR–QB1,
followed by B–K1–Kt4. I believe that White could have
obtained real prospects of a positional advantage with this plan,
whereas now Black easily frees himself from all difficulties.

27	. . .	KtxP
28	Q–B5	P–B3
29	P–QR4	Kt–Q2!

Perhaps Smyslov, in his time trouble, had overlooked this simple defence, one by which Black makes certain of a solid pawn more.

30   Q–B2   Kt–Q3
31   Kt–K5?

This move proves to be merely a loss of time. By 31 Kt–B5 White could here force the long prepared thrust of P–K4 since Black cannot well play 31 . . . P–B5 because of 32 QxQch, KxQ; 33 PxP, and if then 33 . . . PxP; 34 B–R4, winning the exchange. So, after 31 Kt–B5, Black would have to play 31 . . . Kt–B3 when there would follow 32 P–K4, PxP; 33 PxP, P–Kt3 with a tense position that would, however, rather favour Black. An instance would be the following possible variation: 34 QR–B1, PxKt; 35 PxB, QxQ; 36 RxQ, KPxP; 37 RxP, R–QB1; 38 R–K6, Kt(B3)–K5; 39 BxKt, KtxB; 40 KRxBP, RxR; 41 RxR, R–QKt2 and Black stands a little better in the endgame owing to his strong Knight.

31   . . .   Kt–B3!

And so Black gains sufficient control of the K5 square. White must now, if he wants to force through P–K4, retreat with his Knight soon and with this the purposeless nature of his 31st move is demonstrated.

32   QR–B1   QR–R1
33   Kt–Q3   QR–Kt1

Perhaps it would have been better here not to allow the Knight to get to B5 and to play 33 . . . P–Kt3. But Black regards the ensuing complication as not dangerous, for him at any rate.

34   Kt–B5   P–Kt3
35   P–K4!

Smyslov makes excellent use of the opportunity afforded him and obtains attacking chances with the text-move. After 35 Kt–Kt3, with the intention of 36 Kt–Q2 followed by P–K4 Black's 35 . . . P–B5 can be troublesome and with 35 Kt–Q3 White would finally abandon his plan of forcing through P–K4. After the text-move great complications suddenly arise.

35   . . .   PxP
36   KtxP(K4)

In view of the time trouble this capture is far more dangerous for Black than going over to the endgame by 36 PxP, PxKt; 37 PxB, QxQ; 38 RxQ, KPxP; 39 RxP, which would offer Black the better prospects after 39 ... Kt(Q3)–K5; 40 RxBP, R(Q1)–QB1. In the sharp position that has now arisen it is not easy, even in later analysis, to find the best moves for both sides. And certainly not during the game when under time pressure.

36	...	Q–Kt3
37	Q–K2	R–Kt2
38	Kt–B3	B–B5
39	Q–Kt2	P–Kt4

It is not easy for Black to make use of his extra pawn. His pieces possess no firm outposts in the centre and the open position enables White to set up dangerous tactical threats. With the text-move Black seeks to exploit his Queen-side pawn preponderance, but in so doing he has to allow his opponent dangerous counter-chances. Perhaps, therefore, it would have been better to prepare this advance by playing 39 ... R–KB1, so as to meet 40 Kt–K4, with 40 ... Kt(B3)xKt; 41 PxKt, R–KB2 etc.

40	PxP	PxP
41	Kt–K4!	

This strong move was White's sealed move. Now he threatens to win a piece by 42 KtxKt, followed by 43 RxB, which would also follow for example after 41 ... R–KB2. In addition White threatens in many variations 42 Kt–B5, 42 Q–R3, and even 42 P–Q5, and hence the following exchange is practically forced.

It should be observed that 41 P–B4, was much weaker as then Black would reply 41 ... R–KB2 and obtain control over the important squares K5 and KKt5.

41	...	Kt(Q3)xKt
42	PxKt	Kt–Kt5!

After a detailed analysis during the adjournment I came to the conclusion that the surprising sacrificial combination begun by Black with the text-move offers the best winning chances in practice. The point is that White now not only threatens 43 RxB, but also the very strong 43 P–Q5!, when, at the cost of a second pawn, all kinds of lines of action would be opened up for his Bishop and Rooks.

Such an event would, however, be very dangerous for Black in view of the open position of his King. Thus for example after 42 ... R–KB2 White would continue 43 P–Q5!, PxP; 44 PxP, so as to attain after 44 ... KtxP; 45 QR–Q1, a position in which Black's extra pawns are practically worthless.

After the game many people thought that 42 ... R(Kt2)–Q2 might have been stronger, but I had discarded this move on account of 43 P–Q5! Then, after 43 ... PxP; 44 B–Kt6, the White pieces suddenly become extremely active and I am not at all convinced that Black's extra pawns would ensure him an advantage.

43   RxB   Q–R4!

It is in this move that the point of Black's piece sacrifice lies. Apparently Black gave up his Bishop here so as to recover the piece now by 43 ... KtxB since both 44 QxKt, PxR and 44 KxKt, R–B2ch followed by 45 ... PxR would lead to loss of the exchange. But after 43 ... KtxB White would continue 44 R–B3, Kt–Kt5; 45 P–R3 and would suddenly arrive at an excellent position.

It would appear that White was far from expecting the text-move since he now used up the greater part of his time on the clock without succeeding in finding the right continuation.

Black (Keres)

White (Smyslov) to play

44   R–B2?

Retaining the piece allows his opponent a decisive attack and speedily brings White to a lost position. Bad too was 44 P–R3

because of 44 . . . KtxB with the threat of 45 . . . Kt–Q6 or
else of 45 . . . KtxPch. But 44 P–R4! was essential and offered
White adequate defensive chances. Black would then have to
reply 44 . . . KtxB and we would like to investigate a little more
exhaustively some of the possible continuations here.

1. 45 Q–Kt3 (After a Rook move there would come a fork
with the Knight, e.g. 45 R–B3, Kt–Q8, or 45 R–B6 Kt–Q6
etc.) 45 . . . PxR! (better than 45 . . . Kt–Q6; 46 R–KB1, which
would transpose into the variation given below) 46 QxR, PxP
with good prospects for Black since an acceptance of the piece
sacrifice by 47 KxKt, would give Black a winning attack after
47 . . . R–B1ch.

2. 45 R–KB1! (Undoubtedly the best defence) 45 . . .
Kt–Q8; (after 45 . . . Kt–Q6; 46 Q–Kt3, R–KB2; White even
gets the advantage by 47 R–B6!) 46 Q–Kt3, PxR!; (46 . . .
Kt–K6 allows White the saving clause of 47 R–B8! etc.)
47 QxR, Kt–K6 and, though Black has retained his extra pawn,
the open nature of Black's King affords him good prospects of
equalising the position.

With Smyslov having left these variations unnoticed in his
adjournment analysis, one can hardly blame him for not
discovering the only way of saving the game on coming so
unexpectedly to these complications over the board.

44	. . .	QxPch
45	K–B1	R–KB2
46	R(K1)–K2	

Forced, since Black was threatening to capture twice on
KB7 with R–KB1 to follow.

46	. . .	QxP
47	Q–B3	

This loses quickly, but there was no longer any saving move.
After 47 R–B3 for example, Black wins by 47 . . . Q–Q3 with
the threat of 48 . . . R(Q1)–KB1, or 48 . . . QxP, and 47 P–K5
would not avail White either. Black can simply play 47 . . .
P–R5, with the threat of 48 . . . P–R6 and would win very
much as in the game.

47	. . .	QxQ

Black could also win with 47 . . . KtxB; 48 QxQ, KtxP dis

ch; 49 Q–B3, RxQch; 50 BxR, Kt–Kt6ch followed by 51 . . .
KtxR and 52 . . . RxP. But the text-move is simpler.

	48	RxQ	R(Q1)–KB1
	49	R(B3)–B2	KtxB

But not at once 49 . . . P–R5 because of the intervening
50 B–R3. The ensuing general exchange leads the quickest to
the desired end.

	50	RxKt	RxRch
	51	RxR	RxRch
	52	KxR	P–R5!

White can no longer stem the advance of this pawn. The
rest needs no commentary.

	53	B–R3	K–B2
	54	P–Q5	PxP

Simpler still was 54 . . . P–R6; 55 BxPch, K–B3 and the
QRP will Queen. But the text-move is also convincing enough.

	55	B–Q7	K–B3
	56	B–B6	PxP
	57	BxKtP	P–R6
		White Resigns	

Game 43

RUY LOPEZ, STEINITZ DEFENCE DEFERRED

From the World Championship Tournament at the Hague and Moscow,
    1948

	M. Euwe	P. Keres
1	P–K4	P–K4
2	Kt–KB3	Kt–QB3
3	B–Kt5	P–QR3
4	B–R4	P–Q3
5	P–B3	P–B4

This interesting variation was introduced into tournament
praxis by Capablanca in the Budapest Tournament, 1929. In
the ensuing years it was subjected to numerous analyses and
investigations and the general conclusion reached was that

White, with correct play, should get the advantage. But the lines recommended are not altogether convincing and allow a resourceful master full opportunity of adducing improvements to the main variations.

Owing to my position in the tournament I was compelled to play for a win in this game at all costs, so as to retain any chance whatsoever of the first place. For this reason the opening variation suited my purposes admirably.

6	PxP	BxP
7	P–Q4	

·Of recent years the variation 7 O–O, B–Q6; 8 R–K1, P–K5; 9 R–K3, followed by 10 Kt–K1 has become highly fashionable. With it White either forces the Bishop to retreat or else wins a pawn. Though it is generally assumed that it is with this variation that White gains the advantage in simplest style, yet this view must be regarded with certain reservations. The possibilities that are at Black's disposal here have been by no means exhausted in the investigations made up to now.

At the time this game was played, however, 7 P–Q4, was held to be best for White and in what follows Euwe continues with the plan held to be best by theory.

7	. . .	P–K5
8	Kt–Kt5	

Very interesting here was the piece sacrifice 8 O–O, PxKt; 9 QxP. With it White would retain a lasting initiative with good attacking prospects, but it goes without saying that such a method of playing is not to everyone's taste.

8	. . .	P–Q4

Undoubtedly one of the best replies for Black. After 8 . . . P–R3 or 8 . . . Kt–B3; 9 Q–Kt3 is very troublesome, but after the text-move 9 . . . P–R3 becomes a real threat.

9	P–B3	P–K6!

This pawn sacrifice is not new but in this game Black essays the attempt to rehabilitate its dubious reputation. And since he succeeds in this it is incumbent on White to give proof in other games that he could play stronger somewhere or other. In practice 9 . . . P–K6 is undoubtedly Black's best chance since

both 9 . . . PxP; 10 O–O! and 9 . . . P–R3; 10 PxP, PxKt;
11 PxB, give White the better game.

10 P–KB4

Black gets an excellent position after 10 BxP, P–R3;
11 Kt–R3, BxKt; 12 PxB, B–Q3. With the text-move White
makes certain of winning a pawn, since the far advanced KP
is of course beyond protection. In compensation, however,
Black gets very fine play for his pieces and an advance in
development that render highly problematic any realisation of
White's small material advantage.

10 . . . B–Q3

Black (Keres)

White (Euwe) to play

11 Q–B3

With this move, which deprives the White Knight of the
important square of KB3 (on its way to K5), White cannot, at
all events, expect to obtain an advantage. Nor is it altogether
clear whether the other possible continuations here are calculated so to do. Better, however, than the text-move was 11
Q–R5ch, so as to continue as in the game after 11 . . . P–Kt3;
12 Q–B3, Q–B3; 13 QxPch, Kt–K2; 14 O–O, etc., since this
would block off the important square KKt3 from the Black
pieces. And after 11 . . . B–Kt3; 12 Q–B3, Q–B3; 13 QxPch,
Kt–K2; White would have the possibility of the disagreeable
14 Q–K6. But these variations too are not completely convincing since Black always obtains a dangerous initiative in
return for his pawn.

That 11 O–O, BxP; 12 RxB, QxKt; 13 BxP, Kt–K2; is not particularly hopeful for White on account of his opponent's excellent development is obvious enough. Hence the capture 11 BxP, must be regarded as the other main variation, but after this too the situation is far from clear. We append a possible continuation: 11 . . . Q–K2; 12 Q–K2, Kt–B3; (the combination 12 . . . B–Q6; 13 QxB, BxP; gives White a clear advantage after the surprising reply 14 Kt–B7! as also does 12 . . . B–KKt5; 13 QxB, QxBch; 14 Q–K2, etc.) 13 Kt–B3, B–KKt5; 14 P–KR3, Kt–R4; 15 K–B2, (15 PxB, fails against 15 . . . Kt–Kt6) and now Black has the following choice: if he does not want to carry on play with Queen against three minor pieces by 15 . . . BxBP; 16 PxB, Kt–Kt6; 17 R–K1, KtxQ; 18 RxKt, etc., then he can play simply 15 . . . KtxP; 16 BxKt, QxQch; 17 KxQ, BxKtch; 18 KxB, O–O; 19 P–KKt3, P–KKt4; with an approximately level game.

Naturally, the variations given here cannot take into account all the hidden possibilities of the position. But they nevertheless furnish a characteristic picture of the sort of dangerous initiative that Black can attain in return for the pawn sacrifice. Therefore one must treat with certain reservations the opinion cast by theory on the pawn sacrifice 9 . . . P–K6 and at the very least wait until it has been tried in more games over the board.

| 11 | . . . | Q–B3 |
| 12 | QxPch | |

Too dangerous was naturally 12 QxP, because of 12 . . . BxP, and after 12 BxP, White is in difficulties on account of 12 . . . P–R3. But the position is not noticeably changed by 12 O–O, Kt–K2, since on account of the threat of 13 . . . P–R3 White must then continue 13 QxKP in any case.

| 12 | . . . | Kt–K2 |

In this position Black, with his excellent development and taking into account the many weaknesses in his opponent's position, has attained full compensation for his pawn. White must now play very carefully if he does not wish to get the disadvantage.

13   BxKtch?

This exchange is undoubtedly a mistake since in the first place White strengthens the enemy centre with it, in the second

he weakens the white squares in his own camp and in the third
he gives his adversary the advantage of two Bishops. In my
opinion in this position there exists only one satisfactory plan
of play for White—to wit, the transfer of the Knight to K5.
In preparation of this plan 13 O–O must be played. It should
be observed that an immediate 13 Kt–B3, O–O does not alter
the situation since then 14 Kt–K5 would not be good because
of 14 . . . BxKt; 15 QPxB, Q–Kt3, whilst after 14 QKt–Q2,
B–Kt3 can be very troublesome.

After 13 O–O, O–O White cannot well play 14 Kt–Q2,
because of 14 . . . Kt–Kt3!; 15 P–KKt3, P–R3; 16 Kt(Kt5)–
B3, B–KR6 with a decisive attack; but he can continue 14
Kt–B3! Now at long last the Knight does threaten to attain
the K5 square. In reply Black might try 14 . . . B–K5; so that
if 15 Kt–K5?, he can win material by 15 . . . BxKt; 16 QPxB,
Q–Kt3. But White has the stronger continuation 15 Kt–Kt5,
whereupon Black has nothing better than to return to the old
position by means of 15 . . . B–KB4; 16 Kt–B3, etc.

Nevertheless, Black can still try and play for an advantage
after 13 O–O, O–O; 14 Kt–B3, by continuing 14 . . . BxKt;
15 RxB, Q–Kt3; 16 B–Q2, RxP. Then Black will have regained his pawn, caught up with his opponent's development
and attained a position in which White must be thinking of
trying for equality.

13 . . .   PxB
14 O–O

14 Kt–B3, O–O would lead to the position in the game since
now 15 Kt–K5 would not be good because of 15 . . . BxKt(Kt8);
16 RxB, BxKt; followed by 17 . . . Q–Kt3 etc.

14 . . .   O–O
15 Kt–Q2?

The decisive mistake after which Black obtains an irresistible
attack against his opponent's undeveloped position. Here
White must try, willy-nilly, 15 Kt–B3, although this move
would not now be so effective as it was before the exchange on
QB6. Black can then reply, for example, 15 . . . BxKt (after
15 . . . B–K5; White returns with his Knight by 16 Kt–Kt5)
16 RxB, Q–Kt3; 17 B–Q2, RxP and would then stand rather
better on account of his control of the white squares.

15	. . .	Kt–Kt3
16	P–KKt3	QR–K1!

This continuation is now stronger than 16 . . . P–R3; 17
KKt–B3, B–KR6, since White cannot play 17 Q–B3, because
of 17 . . . P–R3, winning a piece. It is clear that White's
undeveloped position must sooner or later collapse.

17	Q–B2	B–Q6

Good enough too for winning purposes was the piece sacrifice
17 . . . P–R3; 18 KKt–B3, BxP! etc. but the text-move is
simpler.

18	R–K1	RxRch
19	QxR	BxP!

With this sacrifice Black destroys the enemy King's position
and now obtains an attack that is speedily decisive. Here,
however, Black must avoid the other enticing sacrificial
opportunity 19 . . . KtxP; 20 PxKt, QxP, since then White
could force an exchange of Queens by 21 Q–K6ch, K–R1;
22 QKt–B3.

20	PxB	

White cannot offer to exchange Queens by 20 Q–K6ch,
since then, after 20 . . . QxQ; 21 KtxQ, Black wins at once by
21 . . . B–K6ch; 22 K–R1, R–B8ch!; 23 K–Kt2, R–B7ch, etc.

20	. . .	KtxP
21	QKt–B3	

After 21 KKt–B3, Q–Kt3ch is decisive, whilst if 21 Q–R4,
Kt–K7ch; 22 K–Kt2, B–K5ch, etc. Nor does the interposition
of 21 P–KR4, P–R3 help White's plight.

21	. . .	Kt–K7ch
22	K–Kt2	P–R3!

Winning back the piece and retaining an irresistible attack.

23	Q–Q2	Q–B4
24	Q–K3	PxKt
25	B–Q2	B–K5

White resigns.

An interesting game not without theoretical value.

Game 44

FRENCH DEFENCE

From the World Championship Tournament at the Hague and Moscow,
1948

	P. Keres	M. Botvinnik
1	P–K4	P–K3
2	P–Q4	P–Q4
3	Kt–QB3	

This game was played in the last round when Botvinnik was already assured of the World Championship title. In contra-distinction White had to go all out for the win if he wished to retain chances for third place. This is why he chooses a very sharp opening variation so as to bring about complications from the very first moves onwards.

3	. . .	B–Kt5
4	B–Q2	

This move obtained wider recognition after the game Alekhine–Flohr, Nottingham, 1936, which ended in a brilliant win for White. In any case, White's pawns sacrifices are highly promising and their acceptance ensures him a lasting initiative.

4	. . .	PxP
5	Q–Kt4	

In the game mentioned above, Alekhine–Flohr, White captured the pawn at once with 5 KtxP, and after 5 . . . QxP was forced to offer up another pawn by 6 B–Q3, BxBch; 7 QxB. Flohr refrained from taking the second pawn but later analyses have shown that in this case White would scarcely have sufficient attacking possibilities to compensate for the loss in material. The text-move, given by Alekhine himself as better after the game, is certainly much stronger.

5	. . .	Kt–KB3

Botvinnik refuses the second pawn. After 5 . . . QxP; 6 O–O–O, P–KB4; 7 Q–Kt3, B–Q3; 8 B–KB4, White, together with his excellent development, would obtain an enduring attack in return for his pawns, as was shown in the game

Keres–Levenfish, Moscow, 1948. With the text-move Black
even gives the pawn back in the hope of gaining a harmonious
cooperation for his pieces.

6	QxKtP	R–Kt1
7	Q–R6	Kt–B3

Another possibility here was 7 ... QxP, which, however, after
8 O–O–O, could lead to incalculable complications. These are
best shown by the possible variation 8 . . . R–Kt3; 9 Q–R4,
R–Kt5; 10 Q–R3, QxP; 11 B–K2!, R–R5; 12 QxR!, QxQ;
13 P–KKt3, when Black loses back the Queen and remains
the exchange down. It is easy to understand why Botvinnik,
having regard to his tournament position, wishes to avoid
complications of this nature and selects a continuation that will
guarantee him an acceptable position.

8	O–O–O!	R–Kt3

Now a capture on Q5 by 8 . . . KtxP, would be really
hazardous since then White could simply recover his pawn by
9 KtxP, or else play for further complications by 9 Kt–Kt5.

9	Q–R4	BxKt
10	BxB	Q–Q4

A good manoeuvre by which Black once more protects his
KP and at the same time gains a tempo in development.

11	P–QKt3	Kt–K2
12	P–B3!	

White has fallen a little behind with his development in the
opening and, too, the enemy Knights dispose of excellent
outposts in the centre. But in compensation White possesses
two powerful Bishops. In order to procure wider scope for
these the position must be opened up still further and the first
immediate task is the subjugation of the strong pawn on Black's
K5 which hinders a normal development of White's King's
wing. The game now assumes a very sharp character and
exacts resourceful play from both sides in its further course.

The other possible continuation here, 12 Kt–K2, would be
less to the purpose. Black could then continue, for example,
with 12 . . . Kt–B4; 13 Q–B4, B–Q2; preparing for 14 . . .
O–O–O. If then 14 QxBP, R–B1; 15 Q–K5, QxQ; 16 PxKt,

Kt–Kt5, when Black wins back his pawn with an excellent game.

12   ...   B–Q2

Now 12 . . . Kt–B4 would be useless since White's Queen has a good retreat on K1. In this position Botvinnik offered me a draw. Such a result could not, of course, satisfy me, especially in so sharp and complicated a position.

13   B–Kt2

An unnecessary loss of time as a result of which Black is given the opportunity of strengthening his central position. Here an immediate 13 PxP, should have been played. After either 13 . . . KtxP; 14 B–Kt2, followed by 15 Kt–B3, or 13 . . . QxKP; 14 Kt–B3, White would have retained a fine game, despite the possible Queen exchange in the second variation.

13   ...   B–B3
14   P–QB4

Now an exchange of pawns by 14 PxP, was no longer good since after 14 . . . QxKP, Black controls all the centre squares and exerts troublesome pressure on KKt7. Thus, for example, after 15 QxQ, BxQ, as well as after 16 Kt–B3, Kt–Kt5, or also 16 R–Q2, Kt–B4, Black would have some unpleasant threats, and after 15 Kt–B3, Kt–B4; 16 QxQ, KtxQ, would be very strong for Black. White is therefore forced to open up his King's position with the text-move and strive after even greater complications.

14   ...   Q–KB4!

Botvinnik finds the best reply. A number of annotators recommended here the piece sacrifice by 14 . . . Q–QR4; 15 P–Q5, PxQP; 16 BxKt, Kt–B4, which would, apparently have opened up the way for a fierce attack by Black, for example: 17 QxP, RxB; 18 Q–R8ch, K–K2; 19 QxR, Kt–K6, or 17 Q–B4, RxB; 18 Q–K5ch, R–K3; 19 QxKt, QxP etc. Although in this last variation White would still have some resources after 20 PxQP.

In actual fact, however, this continuation is considerably weaker for Black, since there exists the possibility for White of simplifying the position by 17 Q–K1!: 17 . . . QxQ; 18 RxQ,

RxB; 19 PxQP, BxP; 20 PxP, R–K3; 21 Kt–B3! After the
further 21 . . . RxP; (but not 21 . . . BxKP; 22 Kt–Kt5)
22 B–Q3, RxR; 23 RxRch, Kt–K2; 24 BxP, we get an ending
in which White stands better in view of his passed pawn on the
Rook file.

Black (Botvinnik)

White (Keres) to play

15   P–Q5!

A positional pawn sacrifice in order to obtain the initiative.
In compensation for the sacrificed pawn White now opens up
lines for his Bishops and for the Rook, whilst at the same time
keeping the enemy King fixed in the centre. Thereby he
obtains the opportunity of initiating a dangerous attack.

| 15 . . . | PxQP |
| 16 PxKP | PxKP |

Here it is not easy for Black to decide how best he should
recapture. Since there are no positive threats the choice must
be made on the grounds of general positional considerations.
16 . . . QxP being very bad because of 17 BxKt, Q–K6ch;
18 K–Kt1, Kt–B4; 19 R–K1!, only 16 . . . KtxP really comes
into consideration as an alternative. White intended then to
proceed with 17 Kt–B3, and this after 17 . . . R–Kt5; 18 Q–K1,
O–O–O; would lead to a position quite different from that in
the game. There would arise a sharp battle with the minor
pieces, together with a speedy opening up of the centre, and
in this, after, for instance, 19 Kt–Q4, White's chances should
not be underestimated.

It is difficult to say, even after subsequent analyses, which of these two variations would provide Black with the better prospects, since in both cases there is no forced continuation. At any rate, the line chosen by Black in the game also has its advantages and the strong pawn on K5 noticeably hinders the normal development of White's King's wing in the ensuing phase of the game.

17 Kt–R3   Kt–Kt5

Black must make haste with his counter-action on the King's wing, since otherwise White threatens to start a decisive attack by 18 B–K2, followed by 19 KR–B1. Already it is apparent that the game is nearing its decisive crisis.

18 Q–Kt3

Thus White wins back his pawn, since protection of the BP by 18 . . . R–B1 would allow White a fierce attack after 19 B–K2. However, Black does manage to attain some simplifications and so averts the worst dangers. Here, therefore, the sharp attacking continuation 18 B–K2, Kt–K6; 19 P–KKt4, came into consideration. I noticed the possibility during the game but eventually rejected it because of the reply 19 . . . Q–QR4!

In fact, a satisfactory continuation for White is not then to be seen. In reply to 20 R–Q2, there comes 20 . . . QxP, with the very troublesome threat of 21 . . . QxP (21 Kt–B4, R–Q3) White could try an exchange sacrifice by 20 P–R3, but in this case too Black stands very satisfactorily after, for example, 20 . . . KtxR; 21 P–Kt4, Q–R5; 22 BxKt, Q–R3; 23 P–Kt5, BxP; 24 PxB, QxKtP; or also in this line 21 . . . Q–R3; 22 RxKt, (22 P–Kt5, Q–Kt3;) 22 . . . P–Kt4, etc.

Taking these circumstances into consideration, the text-move, by which, moreover, White ensures himself against any danger of losing, must be regarded as very good. In addition, by this time both adversaries were plagued by acute time-trouble, and this rendered the calculation of the various complicated lines still more difficult.

18 . . .   Q–B4!

Threatening 19 . . . Q–K6ch, and thus practically forcing White to go in for the ensuing simplification.

19	QxP	R–B1

Weaker here was 19 ... Kt–K6; 20 R–Q2, KtxB; 21 RxKt, P–K6; 22 R–K2, R–B1; 23 Q–B4, when Black cannot capture on Kt7 because of the threat of 24 QxPch, etc.

20	Q–B4	Q–K6ch
21	R–Q2	QxQ?

It is difficult to understand why Black did not choose to give check here by 21 ... Q–K8. He could at least have tried to see whether White was satisfied with a draw by 22 R–Q1, Q–K6ch; 23 R–Q2, Q–K8ch etc. An attempt to win by 22 K–B2? would in any case fail, since Black could then win the Queen by 22 ... Kt–K6ch; 23 K–B3, Kt(K2)–Q4ch. Good too for Black would be the continuation 23 QxQ, KtxQ, followed by 24 ... KtxB when White loses his KKtP.

If White still wanted to play for a win in reply to this line then he would have to try 23 K–Kt1. Then, however, there could follow 23 ... QxQ; 24 KtxQ, Kt–B7; 25 KtxR, KtxKt; 26 B–K2, KtxR(R8); 27 RxKt, P–B4, with a very good end-game for Black in which the White Bishops could scarcely come into real action.

22	KtxQ	P–K6
23	R–QB2!	

It would seem that Botvinnik, when exchanging Queens, had underestimated this good move and, in all probability, had anticipated only 23 R–K2, R–Q3, with counter-play on the Queen file. With the text-move White leaves the square K2 free for his Bishop and thereby arrives at a speedy development of his king's wing.

23	...	R–Kt4

Later on this proves to be a poor post for the Rook, but Black's position is already difficult. If, for example, 23 ... R–Q3, then there follows 24 B–K2, Kt–B7; 25 R–B1, threatening 26 R–B3. A possible counter-attack by 25 ... B–K5; 26 R–B3, R–Q7, would, however, yield White a clear advantage after 27 B–B3!.

Not noticeably better, too, was 23 ... R–R3, whereupon White again continues with 24 B–K2. After 24 ... RxP; 25 RxR, KtxR; 26 R–B3, Black loses his important pawn on

K6 and White gets a clear advantage by the continuation
24 ... KtxP; 25 R–K1, in conjunction with the threats of
26 B–Kt7, or 26 R–B3. Finally, 24 ... Kt–B7; 25 R–K1, RxP;
26 R–B3, is the reverse of pleasant for Black.

24	B–K2	Kt–B7
25	R–K1	R–Q1

Naturally Black must not here capture the pawn with
25 ... BxP, because of 26 R–Kt1, and also an attempt to defend
the KP by 25 ... B–K5; 26 R–B3, Kt–B4, would not be good
because of 27 P–KKt4!, KtxP; 28 R–Kt1, etc. With the text-
move Black still furnishes his opponent with the most technical
difficulties.

26   P–Kt3?

With time trouble on both sides White fails to utilise his
advantage in the best possible way and allows his opponent still
to put up a stubborn defence. Here he should certainly have
played 26 B–B1!, preventing both 26 ... B–K5, and 26 ...
Kt–B4, because of the reply 27 RxKt. White would then
himself be threatening 27 B–B6, followed by 28 BxKt, and
29 RxPch, with a quick win.

26   ...   R–KB4?

With this Black makes good his adversary's previous inaccuracy and the game resumes its normal course. Much better
defensive possibilities were afforded here by 26 ... B–K5;
27 R–B3, Kt–B4, by which Black protects his vital KP at least
temporarily. After that White would still have to overcome

Black (Botvinnik)

White (Keres) to play

some technical difficulties, but, with correct play, should in the end attain a decisive advantage. He could, for example, continue with 28 B–B1, and if then 28 . . . R–Q7; 29 Kt–Q5!, BxKt; 30 R(B3)xPch, KtxR; 31 RxKtch, etc. with obvious advantage. Probably too the sharp continuation 28 P–KKt4, could be played, since after 28 . . . KtxP; 29 R–Kt1, Kt–Q5; 30 BxKt, P–B4, there would come 31 RxP, and also the try 29 . . . R–Q7, would seem to be insufficient because of 30 P–KR3!(30 BxKt, R–B7!).

After the text-move White's task is considerably simpler, since now the important KP falls and the White King escapes from all danger.

| 27 | B–B1 | RxKt |

Desperation, but it in no way alters the situation. White was threatening 28 B–QR3 and 27 . . . B–K5 fails on account of 28 RxKt.

28	PxR	Kt–Q6ch
29	BxKt	RxB
30	R–B3!	

With this the chief prop of Black's position, the pawn on K6, falls and this in turn signifies the end of the game.

30	. . .	RxRch
31	BxR	Kt–B4
32	B–Q2!	K–Q2
33	BxP	P–Kt3
34	B–B2	P–B3
35	K–Q2	P–KR4
36	K–Q3	Kt–R3
37	B–R4	P–B4
38	R–K7ch	K–Q3
39	P–KR3	resigns.

This sharp game, rich in vicissitudes, was my first win over Botvinnik.

Game 45

RUY LOPEZ, STEINITZ DEFENCE DEFERRED

XVI U.S.S.R. Championship at Moscow, 1948

	D. Bronstein	P. Keres
1	P–K4	P–K4
2	Kt–KB3	Kt–QB3
3	B–Kt5	P–QR3
4	B–R4	P–Q3

The Steinitz Defence, with or without the move 3 . . . P–QR3, gives Black a firm, if somewhat constricted, position. In the present game I wanted to introduce a little improvement on the game Euwe–Keres, Hague–Moscow, 1948.

5	P–B3	B–Q2
6	P–Q4	KKt–K2
7	B–Kt3!	P–R3
8	QKt–Q2	Kt–Kt3
9	Kt–B4	B–K2
10	Kt–K3	

Euwe continued here with 10 O–O, to which Black could reply with the move recommended by Bondarevsky 10 . . . B–Kt4. This move is also possible, however, after the text-move, since the continuation 11 KtxB, PxKt; 12 Q–B3, is not dangerous on account of 12 . . . Kt–B5. Black has, however, other intentions.

10	. . .	O–O
11	O–O	R–K1!

This is the improvement that Black wished to try out. In two games of the World Championship at the Hague–Moscow, 1948, Black played here 11 . . . B–B3 (Euwe–Keres and Smyslov–Reshevsky), but after 12 Kt–Q5, he had scarcely anything better than to surrender the centre with 12 . . . PxP, which also in fact occurred in the game earlier mentioned.

With the text-move Black intends to retire his Bishop to KB1 and thus to exert noticeable pressure on the K5 square, but here too his position remains rather cramped. White, at

all events, retains a free game with good prospects in the centre
and on the King's wing.

                    12   R–K1

Better here was an immediate 12 B–B2, leaving the Rook on
KB1 to support the eventual thrust of P–KB4.

                    12   . . .   B–KB1
                    13   B–B2   Kt–R5

In order to free his position a little, Black exchanges off his
Knight for the Knight that is blockading the KBP and thereby
makes it easier for White to execute the advance of P–KB4.
Hence, further passive defence by 13 . . . QKt–K2 came into
consideration so as to obtain counterplay by P–QB4, or else to
continue with his development by P–QB3, Q–B2 and QR–Q1.

                    14   KtxKt   QxKt
                    15   Kt–Q5

The drawbacks of Black's 13th move are best revealed by
the line 15 P–KKt3, Q–Q1; 16 P–KB4, with which White
would exert strong pressure on Black's centre. To this Black
could not very well reply 15 . . . Q–R6, because of 16 B–Q3.
With the text-move White complicates his task unnecessarily.

                    15   . . .   QR–B1

In reply to the retreat 15 . . . Q–Q1, White could at once
play 16 P–KB4, and retain a fine position with good attacking
possibilities after 16 . . . PxBP; 17 BxP, Kt–K2; 18 Kt–K3.
After the text-move it is more difficult for White to force through
the P–KB4 advance, since an immediate 16 P–KB4, PxQP;
17 PxP, fails against 17 . . . B–Kt5, followed by 18 . . . KtxP,
and also the continuation 17 P–KKt3, Q–Kt5; 18 PxP, QxQ;
19 RxQ, B–Kt5; 20 R–Q2, B–B6; 21 Kt–B3, P–Q4!, is very
satisfactory for Black.

Since also a preparation of P–KB4 by 16 P–KKt3, Q–Kt5;
17 P–B3, Q–R4, does not look very good, Bronstein decides to
take back his 12th move and return his Rook to KB1.

                    16   R–B1   Kt–K2
                    17   Kt–K3

White could assure himself of some slight positional advantage here by 17 KtxKtch, followed by 18 P–KB4, but it

would seem that Bronstein does not want to simplify the position and hopes for more in the sequel. However, once Black has manoeuvred his Knight to its good square on KKt3 he possesses adequate defensive resources to repulse enemy aggression.

	17 . . .	Kt–Kt3
	18 P–KKt3	

Now White has no other way of forcing through the thrust P–KB4. The game develops into some very interesting and entangled complications.

	18 . . .	Q–R6
19	P–KB4	PxBP
20	PxP	P–KB4!

This temporary pawn sacrifice is forced if Black is not to succumb to a fierce King-side attack. White must now not only give up his plans of attack but must also break up his fine pawn centre, after which his extra pawn possesses no particular value. Quietly one must accept the fact that with this thrust Black has satisfactorily solved the problem of the position.

	21 R–B3

It is clear that he must not immediately capture the pawn Black offers him since both 21 PxP?, RxKt, and 21 KtxP, BxKt; 22 PxB, Kt–R5 would assure Black a marked advantage. Apart from the text-move only the pawn advance 21 P–K5 came into consideration, but this would be most hazardous for White. Black would continue with 21 . . . PxP; 22 BPxP, Kt–R5, threatening eventually to commence a fierce King-side attack, once he has brought his Bishop on to the diagonal QR1–KR8.

	21 . . .	Q–R4

But not 21 . . . Q–R5; 22 PxP, KtxP? because of 23 Q–B1! with advantage to White. Now exchanges are forced.

22	PxP	Kt–R5
23	R–B1	QxQ
24	RxQ	P–B4

Both adversaries have used up so much time in the exciting opening variations that they are already perturbed by signs of imminent time-trouble. Instead of the text-move

24 . . . P–B3 was much more to the purpose as it simply threatens to regain the pawn by 25 . . . B–K2, followed by 26 . . . R–B1. With this Black would have obtained a thoroughly satisfactory game, whereas after the imprecise text-move the positional advantage clearly swings over to White's side.

25   K–B2   B–K2!

Suddenly Black has become assailed by various difficulties. After 25 . . . PxP; 26 RxP, he could, it is true, attack the pawn on B4 for the third time by 26 . . . R–B4, but he still does not threaten to capture it. White can simply play 27 B–Q2, and if then 27 . . . KtxP; 28 BxKt, BxB; 29 P–Kt4, when Black loses at least the exchange. On the other hand, Black cannot simply stand by doing nothing since 26 P–B6 is already threatened and if then 26 . . . PxBP; 27 K–Kt3, winning the exchange.

In this difficult situation Black comes to a decision of considerable gravity. He allows White to get rid of his doubled pawns on the KB file and to create a strong passed pawn on K6 in order to obtain counter-play by means of his superior development and by reason of the many weaknesses in his opponent's position. It is clear that such tactics are bound up with great dangers, but Black has by now no alternative.

26   B–Kt3ch   K–R1

It would have been better to have put the King on R2, from whence it could be brought more speedily into play.

27   B–K6   BxB
28   PxB   PxP
29   PxP

One can readily comprehend why White recaptures here with the pawn in the hope of being able soon to protect his passed pawn by P–Q5. In fact, probably most players as White would have chosen this move. Surprisingly enough, however, the natural moves proves not to be the best. In the first place, of course, Black does not allow the P–Q5 move, and in the second, the open QB file now becomes a basis from which the Black Rooks threaten to penetrate the White position with decisive effect. Another example of the fact that "natural" moves are not always the best.

If White had had more time in which to look into the position, then he would have hardly missed the stronger continuation 29 RxP.

Although after that White would not have disposed of such a fine defence as P–Q5, on the other hand Black too would have found it not so easy to get a counter-attack going. If Black tries 29 . . . B–Q1, then White would play, not 30 RxP, B–B2 etc. but the stronger 30 R–K4!, fully protecting his KP.

After 29 RxP, Black appears to have one and one only more or less reasonable continuation, and that is the pawn sacrifice 29 . . . P–Q4!. Otherwise White threatens to play 30 P–B4, assuring himself mastery of the white squares and depriving his opponent of all chances of counter-play. After 29 . . . P–Q4; 30 RxP, R–B3; 31 P–B5, P–KKt3!, however, Black has good prospects of valid counter-play since he is making use of his superior development and the somewhat uncertain position of the enemy King. All the same, White should have chosen this continuation, since after the text-move Black emerges from all his difficulties in the most surprising fashion.

Black (Keres) to play

White (Bronstein)

29 . . .   P–Q4!

A pawn sacrifice that is vitally necessary as otherwise White would continue with 30 P–Q5, with much the better of it. Apart from this, however, the sacrifice is very strong, since now the Black pieces attain active positions and White must play with great care if, having regard to his own undeveloped position, he does not wish to get into difficulties himself.

Although now White is temporarily two pawns to the good, Black's counter-play becomes so effective that it is impossible to see how, in the ensuing phase of the game, White could have extracted any concrete advantage out of the position.

30	KtxP	B–Q3
31	B–Q2	

An attempt to protect the KP by 31 R–K1, cannot meet with success, since after 31 . . . R–B7ch, White is practically forced to play 32 R–K2. After 32 . . . RxRch; 33 KxR, RxPch; 34 K–B2, Kt–B4, Black wins back, however, the second pawn as well.

31	. . .	RxP
32	QR–B1	R–B1

It now becomes clear that White must soon give back his other extra pawn. Perhaps it would have been prudent for him to have chosen the simplifying method of play mentioned in the previous note. But who would go in for an equalizing variation in a position with two extra pawns!

33	R–K1	R–Kt3
34	R–KKt1	R–B4!

With this the KBP falls and thus material equality is once again restored. White, apparently somewhat upset at having so speedily lost back his advantage in material, plays the ensuing part of the game uncertainly. So he even gets into difficulties eventually.

35	RxR	KtxR
36	Kt–B3?	

If White really wished to bring back his Kt to B3 then it was essential for him first to get his Rook back into play by 36 R–B8ch. But probably still better was 36 Kt–K3!, RxPch; 37 K–K2. If Black then captures the pawn by 37 . . . RxP, a position arises after 38 Kt–B5, followed by exchanges on Q6, in which White should obtain a draw despite his pawn less, owing to the active nature of his pieces. Also after 37 . . . R–R5; 38 R–B8ch, K–R2; 39 Kt–B5, RxPch; 40 K–Q3, the White pieces are so well placed that Black will have hardly any real prospects of utilising his extra pawn.

After the text-move, on the other hand, White's position is
critical.

36   ...   KtxP
37   K–K3

The ending after 37 BxKt, BxB; 38 R–Q1, BxP dis ch;
39 K–K3, K–Kt1, is extremely difficult for White. The
Bishop is much superior to the Knight and in addition Black
still possesses two united passed pawns on the King's wing.
Better than the text-move, however, was the calm advance
37 K–B3! since Black has no effective discovered check.

After the text-move Black wins a pawn and comes down to
an ending in which he retains good winning prospects.

37   ...   Kt–Kt7ch
38   K–Q3

Better was 38 K–K4, R–B7; 39 R–Q1, BxP; 40 P–Q5,
forcing the actual continuation in the game.

38   ...   BxP
39   P–Q5   R–B6ch

In time-trouble Black unnecessarily makes his opponent a
present of a valuable tempo. Correct was at once 39 ...
K–Kt1; or also 39 ... P–KR4, so as to advance at once with
his passed pawns on the King's wing.

40   K–K4   R–B7
41   R–Q1

Here the game was adjourned and Black sealed his 41st
move. Despite Black's pawn more and the two united passed
pawns on the King's wing, it is not easy to force the win, since
White's pieces are very actively placed. The passed pawn on
the Queen file will prove very troublesome for Black and the
White King, too, is very well placed. Black's pieces, in particular the Knight, are far removed from the central field of
action, and Black must expend valuable time in order to bring
them back into play. All these factors taken together give
White the chance of putting up a stern and far from hopeless
resistance.

41   ...   K–Kt1

Better was an immediate 41 ... Kt–R5 so as to bring the

unemployed Knight once again into play. The text-move allows his opponent dangerous counter-play.

42   Kt–R4

During the game the move 42 B–K3, struck me as very strong, since in reply Black must not capture the pawn by 42 ... RxP because of 43 P–Q6. But a simple exchange by 42 ... KtxB; 43 KxKt, R–B2 would yield Black a highly promising endgame. The good Bishop and the two united passed pawns should provide him with all the possibilities of crowning the ending with a victory.

With the text-move White aims at getting his Knight to the strong QB5 square, thereby supporting an advance of his own passed pawn.

42   ...   Kt–R5
43   B–K3

If immediately 43 Kt–B5, then the check 43 ... R–K7 is very troublesome. After 44 K–Q3, R–K4 the passed pawn falls and 44 B–K3 would be met by 44 ... Kt–Kt7; 45 K–B3, KtxB, etc.

43   ...   R–Kt7

By means of the attack on the enemy pawns on the Queen's wing Black seeks to make the Kt–B5 move more difficult for White to execute, and at the same time he threatens 44 ... R–Kt5ch. Despite all these advantages it would have been more prudent to have played 43 ... R–B2, blockading the passed pawn. How playable the move is still, is shown by the fact that White cannot well reply 44 P–Q6, because of the simple retort 44 ... BxP; 45 RxB, R–K2ch; 46 K–Q3, RxBch etc. Thus, however, Black gains time for the manoeuvre 44 ... R–K2ch followed by 45 ... Kt–B4. Thereafter it could be said that the win for Black would be merely a matter of technique.

After the text-move, on the other hand, Bronstein is able to conjure up fresh complications and solving the problems set by these is not so simple over the board.

44   Kt–B5!

Very well played. By giving up a second pawn White gets his pieces into very active positions and converts his passed pawn into a most powerful force.

44   ...   RxP

Some notion of the great technical difficulties confronting Black is given by the following variations. Apparently Black can win here without any trouble by continuing with 44 ... P–QKt3; 45 KtxP, R–Kt5ch; 46 K–Q3, R–R5. The White Knight has no retreating square and counter-attack by 47 R–KR1, B–Kt6; 48 R–R3, Kt–B4 seems likewise without success. But it is precisely in this last variation that we see best why Black must, above everything else, render the enemy passed pawn innocuous. For White continues with 49 RxB!, KtxR; 50 P–Q6, and now Black has no good reply. If 50 ... RxKt; then 51 P–Q7, R–R1; 52 BxKtP, whilst after 50 ... K–B2; 51 P–Q7, K–K2; White has the resource of 52 BxKtP!, KxP; 53 Kt–B5ch, etc. Black could still try 50 ... R–R4, but then too after 51 Kt–Kt4, R–R2; 52 B–B4, White would have excellent drawing chances, chiefly because of the great activity of his pieces.

With the text-move Black does indeed win a second pawn, but here too the winning process is still bound up with great difficulties. The White King is beautifully placed and, in conjunction with the passed pawn, it causes the opponent many a headache.

45   R–Q2!

Bronstein defends himself in exemplary style in his difficult situation. Black cannot well now exchange Rooks since this would mean he would have to give back one of his pawns and, taking into account the active position of the White pieces, he could then hardly be said to have any winning chances. Incidentally, a mistake here would have been 45 P–Q6?, because of 45 ... R–Kt5ch; 46 K–Q5, BxP, when Black wins.

45	. . .	R–Kt5ch
46	R–Q4	R–Kt3
47	Kt–K6	B–Q3?

A loss of time that gives White real drawing chances. He should undoubtedly have played at once 47 ... K–B2, or else 47 ... Kt–Kt3, avoiding an exchange of Bishops.

48   B–B4!

Once again, much the best move. It is clear that the piece that holds up the progress of the passed pawn must be removed, and in addition a Bishop exchange opens up fresh squares for the White King. A win for Black already appears dubious.

On the other hand, an attempt by 48 R–B4, R–Kt8; 49 R–B8ch, K–B2; 50 R–Q8, to uproot the blockader yields White nothing since Black can simply reply 50 . . . R–K8! etc.

48 . . .   Kt–Kt3

It was high time that this Knight was at last brought back into play.

49 BxB   RxB
50 K–B5?

After a long and outstandingly good defence Bronstein, no doubt very tired by the hard struggle, suddenly makes a weak move after which Black can realise his advantage without any special trouble. Black's task would have been much more complicated after the correct continuation 50 R–B4!, threatening 51 R–B7. If then 50 . . . Kt–K2; 51 R–B7, KtxP (or 51 . . . K–B2; 52 KtxP, etc.) 52 RxPch, K–R1; 53 R–Kt6, when White should have a sure draw. Hence Black is practically forced to play 50 . . . R–Q2, after which there follows 51 Kt–B5.

Now again Black has hardly anything better than 51 . . . R–K2ch; 52 K–Q4, (weaker is 52 Kt–K6, K–B2; followed by 53 . . . R–Q2) and now 52 . . . Kt–B1. After 53 P–Q6, Black can play 53 . . . R–KB2, or, still more actively, 53 . . . R–K7. Naturally, with his two extra pawns Black should eventually win, but at all events his task would have been much more

Black (Keres) to play

White (Bronstein)

complicated and a number of opportunities for making a mistake would have been left open. After the faulty text-move, on the other hand, the struggle is practically over.

50	...	K–B2
51	Kt–B5	R–B3ch
52	K–K4	P–Kt3!
53	KtxP	K–K2

By returning one of his extra pawns Black has gained a number of advantages. Firstly, the dangerous QP is definitively blockaded; secondly, Black's pieces are more actively placed than his adversary's, and thirdly, now at long last Black threatens to advance one of his passed pawns on the King's wing. In fact, the issue of the game is already decided.

54	Kt–B7	Kt–B1

Naturally, there is no point for Black in exchanging Rooks. This would increase the activity of White's King and once again the QP could become dangerous.

55	Kt–Kt5	P–Kt4
56	P–Q6ch	K–Q2
57	K–K3	Kt–K3
58	R–QKt4	

After 58 R–QR4, there comes, of course, 58 ... K–B3.

58	...	Kt–Kt2!

At last the QP, which had caused Black so much trouble, falls.

59	Kt–Q4	RxP
60	R–R4	K–K2
61	R–R6	

Or 61 R–R7ch, K–B3; 62 RxKt, RxKt; etc.

61	...	K–B3
62	P–R4	Kt–B4ch
63	KtxKt	KxKt
	resigns.	

After 64 P–R5, there naturally follows 64 ... R–K3ch. A very exciting struggle, the general picture of which should not be marred by some inaccurate moves.

Game 46

RUY LOPEZ, MORPHY DEFENCE

XVII U.S.S.R. Championship in Moscow, 1949

	E. Geller	P. Keres
1	P–K4	P–K4
2	Kt–KB3	Kt–QB3
3	B–Kt5	P–QR3
4	B–R4	Kt–B3
5	O–O	P–QKt4
6	B–Kt3	P–Q3

An opening system worked out by Master Rabinovitch about 20 years ago, but one which usually leads back to normal lines. Individual importance pertains only to the line commencing with the premature 7 Kt–Kt5 which, in accordance with the experience of the games already tried out on these lines, leaves Black with a satisfactory position.

7	P–B3	B–K2

Black hardly has anything better than to aim at a transposition into normal lines. Should he continue here with 7 . . . Kt–QR4; 8 B–B2, P–B4; 9 P–Q4, Q–B2, so as to meet 10 QKt–Q2, with 10 . . . P–Kt3, then White obtains a strong initiative with the line recommended by Master Suetin 11 P–QKt4!, PxKtP; 12 PxKtP, Kt–B3; 13 B–Kt2!

Not particularly good too is the pin 7 . . . B–KKt5, since White has not yet played P–Q4 and so can stamp the sally as loss of time by 8 P–Q3, and QKt–Q2.

8	P–Q4

After 8 R–K1, or 8 Q–K2, known positions in the main lines would arise, but White need not as yet bother about the protection of his K4. Instead of the text-move 8 P–KR3 also deserved consideration. With this White would prevent the ensuing pin and he could then carry out P–Q4 without the preparatory move R–K1, which, as contrasted with the main variation, represents the win of a tempo.

| 8 | . . . | B–Kt5 |
| 9 | P–KR3! | B–R4 |

As was shown in the game Tal-Teschner, Vienna 1957, Black obtains a fierce attack after the acceptance of the pawn sacrifice by 9 . . . BxKt; 10 QxB, PxP; with 11 Q–Kt3! The text-move is Black's only acceptable continuation, even though his Bishop is not particularly well-placed on R4.

10   P–Q5

An advance that is usually held to be not really advantageous and with good reason, but in the present circumstances White has, nevertheless, some prospects of obtaining an advantage owing to the unfavourable position of the Bishop on R4. Instead of the text-move 10 B–K3 also came into consideration, protecting the pawn on Q4 and maintaining the tension in the centre.

10	. . .	Kt–R4
11	B–B2	P–B3
12	PxP	Q–B2
13	P–QR4?	

An attempt at attack which leads to no positive results and only makes unnecessary weaknesses on the Queen's wing, which the opponent can exploit later on so as to give him counterplay. Calm continuation of his development by 13 QKt–Q2, O–O; 14 R–K1, followed by Kt–B1 and Kt–K3 or Kt–Kt3 yielded, on the other hand, a very promising attacking position for White as was later shown in a game from the same tournament between Boleslavsky and Keres. In this latter case Black experienced difficulties with the protection of his Q4 and KB4 owing to the bad position of his Bishop on R4.

13   . . .   P–Kt5!

With his thrust Black thwarts his opponent's plans. After 14 PxP, there would now follow 14 . . . KtxBP; 15 B–Q2, BxKt; 16 PxB, P–Q4! when Black has a fine position in return for the pawn. Probably White should have fallen back on this variation, only, instead of 15 B–Q2, he should play 15 Kt–B3, KtxKtP; 16 B–Kt3, O–O; 17 B–K3, with an approximately even game.

14   Q–Q3

White wants to rid himself of the troublesome pin, and hence makes a careless move which, however, as a result of Black not undertaking adequately active counter-measures, turns out to be really successful. Better was, as already remarked, simply 14 PxP.

14   . . .   O–O

Here Black misses an excellent opportunity of siezing the initiative by 14 . . . P–Q4!. White cannot then well play 15 PxQP, since after 15 . . . P–K5; 16 Q–Q4, R–Q1 the advantage swings over to Black. In addition Black can also simply play 16 . . . PxKt; 17 PxP, KtxBP, etc. Whilst if White protects his K4 by 15 QKt–Q2, then there could follow 15 . . . O–O with a fine position for Black.

After the "natural" text-move, however, White obtains the initiative and sets his adversary some disagreeable problems.

15   Kt–R4!   KR–B1

The attempt to retain the two Bishops is here not really justified and allows White to get his pieces into active positions with a gain of tempo, whilst at the same time Black has to retreat with his own pieces. Furthermore, White also eventually gains control of the important central square Q5.

Correct therefore was 15 . . . KtxBP, so as to meet 16 Kt–B5 with 16 . . . B–Kt3, threatening an eventual BxKt followed by P–Q4. In that event Black, with a normal development, would have obtained about an even position, whereas White now clearly gains the advantage.

16   Kt–B5   B–B1

16 . . . B–Kt3 was still the better continuation.

17   B–Kt5   Kt–K1
18   Kt–K3

After White has obtained a clear superiority in position, he here commits a small inaccuracy and allows his opponent to obtain troublesome counter-play on the Queen's wing. Much stronger was first 18 P–Kt4, B–Kt3; and only then 19 Kt–K3. Thus White would control the important square Q5 and assure himself of an advantage after, for instance, 19 . . . KtxP; 20 Kt–Q5, Q–Kt2; 21 P–R5. Black would therefore have to try for counter-chances in this line by 19 . . . P–Kt6; 20 B–Q1, QxP, but after 21 Kt–Q2, White would stand better.

After the text-move Black succeeds in exchanging off the white-squared Bishops and thus considerably lightens his task

18	. . .	P–Kt6!
19	B–Q1	BxB
20	RxB	QxP

Now we can see that Black, by blockading the Queen-side, has procured for himself a good target for attack in the pawn on White's QR4, and it is therefore not an easy task for White to exploit the dominating position of his Knight on Q5 so as to obtain a concrete advantage. Then too, White must concern himself in the ensuing part of the game with seeing that his pawn on QKt2 does not fall victim to the enemy Knight.

| 21 | Kt—Q2 | Kt–B2 |
| 22 | B–R4 | |

Obviously, Geller does not relish the idea of allowing his strong point in the centre to become blockaded by 22 Kt–Q5, KtxKt, but all the same this continuation deserved consideration. After 23 PxKt, White would undoubtedly stand somewhat better, although Black, too, would not be without counter-chances.

With the text-move Geller chooses a double-edged plan. He aims at winning by a direct attack on the King and leaves his Queen-side to take care of itself. However, should the attack fail, then such tactics would signify a sure loss. It seems to me that White, in view of his good position, is in no way bound to go in for such a risky method of play and that therefor 22 Kt–Q5 was to be preferred. After 22 ... Kt–K3, White would continue 23 B–K3.

| 22 | . . . | Kt–K3 |
| 23 | Kt–Q5 | Kt–B4 |

Black proceeds with his attack on the Queen's wing in logical fashion, but the taking of such a strong defensive piece away from the King's wing is bound up with considerable risks. More prudent and better, therefore, was first 23 ... R–R2, helping in the defence of the King-side and also preparing for 24 ... Kt–B5.

24 Q–B3!

It is clear that White can no longer directly protect the pawn

on QR4. It is all the more interesting to observe how skilfully,
in the ensuing phase of the game, Geller combines an indirect
protection of this pawn with attack on the King's wing. If
now, for instance, Black were to capture it carelessly by 24 . . .
KtxRP?, then White would obtain a decisive attack after 25
Kt–B6ch!, K–R1 (or 25 . . . PxKt; 26 Q–Kt4ch, etc.) 26 Q–R5,
PxKt; 27 BxPch, B–Kt2; 28 QxP, followed by Kt–B3.

Black therefore keeps in reserve the defensive possibility of
Kt–K3 and brings yet another piece to protect his King's wing.

      24   . . .   R–R2
      25   Kt–B1   Kt–B5

Now the capture 25 . . . KtxRP? would be at once disastrous,
since White would reply 26 RxKt!, QxR; 27 Kt–B6ch, K–R1;
28 Q–B5, with simultaneous attack on R7 and B8. With the
text-move Black reminds his opponent for the first time that he
has a pawn on QKt2.

Black (Keres)

White (Geller) to play

26 Kt(B1)–K3?

Once White, with his 22nd move, has already chosen a
risky attacking continuation and burnt his bridges behind him,
then he must continue to play in the same style and move here
26 Kt–Kt3! Black could scarcely then risk 26 . . . KtxKtP,
in reply to which there could follow either 27 Kt–B5, or 27
Kt–B6ch, K–R1; 28 Q–R5, P–R3; 29 B–Kt5, with the chief
threat of 30 BxP, PxB; 31 Q–B5, etc.

It is hard to believe that Black could have saved his King from
the massed attack of all the White pieces.

Hence, after 26 Kt–Kt3!, Black would have been forced to give up the idea of winning a pawn and would have to provide a satisfactory defence for his King's wing, for instance, by 26 . . . P–B3. But after this too, Black would have to reckon with a strong attack and it is not at all clear as to which side the pendulum would have eventually swung.

With the text-move White plans a similar continuation, but now of course Black no longer captures on QKt7, and instead takes the opportunity of exchanging off one of his opponent's strong attacking pieces. After this Black's King's position is rendered practically safe against any attack and he can then try to slowly exploit his advantage on the Queen's wing.

26	. . .	KtxKt!
27	QxKt	P–QR4
28	P–KB4?	

It is with this thrust, which is obviously still bound up with his dream of a King-side attack, that Geller finally compromises his position. He will now have to defend a weakness on K4 in addition to that on QR4, and, through the opening up of lines in the centre, the Black pieces will acquire greater activity.

He should have tried here 28 Q–K2, so as to be able to protect, if necessary, the pawn on QR4 by Q–B4. Black cannot then play 28 . . . KtxRP? because of the continuation 29 RxKt!, QxR; 30 Kt–B6ch, K–R1; 31 Q–R5, PxKt; (or 31 . . . P–R3; 32 Q–B5 etc.). 32 Q–Kt4! when White wins his Rook back and has a decisive attack. In this way White would have satisfactorily protected his Queen's wing and obtained every prospect of evening out the struggle.

28	. . .	PxP
29	QxP	R–K1!

At once attacking the fresh weakness. White must now protect his pawn since an attempt at attack by 30 Kt–B6ch, PxKt; 31 Q–Kt3ch, B–Kt2; 32 BxP, Kt–K3 would cost him a piece without sufficient compensation.

30	R–K1	R–K3

Completely protecting his King's wing and threatening both 31 . . . KtxRP and 31 . . . KtxKP. Bad of course was 30 . . . Kt–Q6, because of 31 Kt–B6ch! etc.

31   B–B2

This loses rapidly, but by now it is difficult to recommend a satisfactory continuation for White. After 31 R–K3, there would follow 31 . . . KtxKP and if then 32 R–Q1, R–K4! Nevertheless, White should have gone in for this line of play, since he would have obtained some counter-play in return for the pawn, whereas now Black clearly gains the advantage.

31   . . .   Kt–Q6
32   Q–Q2

After 32 Q–Kt3, KtxR; 33 BxR, Black wins by 33 . . . KtxP! etc.

32   . . .   KtxR
33   BxR   Kt–B7

Now the KP falls and with it the White position, too, collapses.

34   R–KB1   RxP
35   R–B3   R–K4

Once the dominating White Knight is driven away, the realisation of Black's advantage causes no difficulties. Hence Geller essays a desperation-sacrifice which, however, can no longer lead to anything for him.

36   Kt–B6ch   PxKt
37   R–Kt3ch   K–R1

Naturally not 37 . . . R–Kt4 because of 38 RxRch, PxR; 9 QxPch, with a draw by perpetual check. Another way of winning was 37 . . . B–Kt2; 38 Q–R6, R–KKt4, etc.

38   Q–B4   P–Q4

In this hopeless position White exceeded the time-limit.

Game 47

QUEEN'S PAWN, KING'S INDIAN DEFENCE

XVII U.S.S.R. Championship in Moscow, 1949

	P. Keres	T. Petrosian
1	P–Q4	Kt–KB3
2	Kt–KB3	P–KKt3
3	P–B4	B–Kt2
4	Kt–B3	P–Q3
5	B–B4	

The usual moves here are either 5 P–K4, or 5 P–KKt3. With the text-move White aims at a quiet game but Black allows him no opportunity for this and with his next few moves creates some tactical complications.

5	. . .	Kt–R4

This Knight sortie does, it is true, lead at once away from the theoretical path, but it looks a little premature. In any case, a better result would have been achieved by Black with the quiet move 5 . . . O–O, either continuing with P–QB4 followed by Kt–B3 or else preparing for the advance P–K4.

6	B–Kt5	P–KR3
7	B–K3	

White is not willing to allow his good Bishop to be exchanged, as would occur after 7 B–R4, P–KKt4 etc. Provoking Black to play 6 . . . P–KR3 was a useful manoeuvre since if now the second player were to continue carelessly with 7 . . . O–O, then he could easily fall victim to a strong attack after 8 Q–Q2, K–R2; 9 P–KR3.

7	. . .	P–QB3
8	P–KKt3	

Instead of this quiet development there also came into consideration at once 8 P–KR3 followed by P–KKt4, winning a valuable tempo in comparison with the game continuation. 8 Q–Q2, which, for the moment, prevents enemy castling, also has its good points.

8 ...	Kt–Q2
9 B–Kt2	KKt–B3

Showing Black has comprehended the fact that his plan commencing with the 5th move has proved a vain one. In the meantime White has made normal developing moves and attained an excellent position. The text-move serves as preparation for P–K4, which would not be good at once because of 10 Kt–K4.

10 P–KR3	O–O
11 O–O	K–R2

This King move was not as yet necessary, and therefore an immediate 11 ... P–K4 was preferable.

| 12 P–KKt4 | |

A good move, limiting the action of the enemy pieces and setting up an eventual threat of P–Kt5.

12 ...	P–K4
13 Q–Kt3	

The Queen is badly placed on QKt3, since it deprives the Pawn on QB4 of its natural protection by P–Kt3 and is itself a point of attack for a Black Knight. Better, therefore, was 13 Q–B2, planning to exert further pressure along the Queen file.

| 13 ... | PxP! |

Petrosian makes excellent use of his adversary's inexact moves, ensuring with the text-move a good square for the Knight on K4 and at the same time pinning down the enemy Queen to the protection of the pawn on QB4. Perhaps, therefore, it would have been better for White to recapture with 14 BxQP, thereby gaining the time to play Q–B2.

| 14 KtxP | Kt–K4 |

Now Black has the positional threat of 15 ... KKt–Q2 followed by Kt–B4 or Kt–Kt3, and it is not all that easy to find a good defence against it. At all events, 15 P–B4 will not serve the purpose, as then the sacrifice 15 ... Kt(K4)xKtP!; 16 PxKt, KtxP would allow Black a fierce attack.

| 15 QR–Q1 | Q–K2 |

An immediate 15 ... KKt–Q2 allows of the reply 16 ...

Kt–K4, but now Black really has taken all preparatory steps for this move.

16   B–B4

16 P–Kt5 came into consideration in order to thwart the enemy plan, although in so doing White would have weakened his King's position.

16 . . .   P–KR4?

Petrosian wants to force the White pawn to advance to Kt5 before he executes his plan, in the hope that thereby the White King's position will be weakened. It turns out later, however, that this manoeuvre is in fact fatal for Black, since it is precisely because of the pawn on Kt5 that White is eventually able to bring off a combination that ensures him a clear advantage. Correct was an immediate 16 . . . KKt–Q2, with the strong threats of 17 . . . Kt–Kt3 and 17 . . . Kt–B4. Should White wish to avoid great complications then he could reply 17 Kt–R4, with an approximately even position.

17   P–Kt5   KKt–Q2
18   Kt–K4   Kt–Kt3?

But now, surprisingly enough, this move proves to be a decisive mistake, allowing the opponent a deeply calculated winning combination. Here 18 . . . Kt–B4; 19 Q–B2, B–Q2 should have been played, with only an insignificant positional advantage for White.

19   Q–Kt3!

Now this long Queen move is extremely powerful. White threatens not only 20 P–Kt3, with a clear positional advantage but also 20 P–B5!, PxP; 21 Kt–B6ch, BxKt; 22 PxB etc. Black is therefore practically forced to capture on QB5.

19 . . .   Kt(K4)xP

19 . . . Kt(Kt3)xP; 20 P–Kt3, Kt–Kt3 would have also led to the game position.

20   P–Kt3

Probably here Petrosian had only reckoned with the capture 20 KtxQP, which would have given him a good game after 20 . . . KtxP.

20 . . .   Kt–K4
KtxQP!

This is the point of the combination foreshadowed by White's
19th move. However Black now defends himself, White at
least wins back his sacrificed piece together with the better
position. In what follows Black in no way succeeds in taking
advantage of the White Knight's position, cut off from its own
pieces on KKt7, whilst in fact it displays an astonishingly
energetic activity on that square.

21 . . .   QxKt

Practically forced, since, for example, after 21 . . . Kt–Q4;
22 KtxB, QRxKt; 23 B–B1, White, with his two Bishops and
prospects of attack both in the centre and on the Queen's wing,
is obviously in a far superior position.

22 Kt–B5   Q–R6

Black (Petrosian)

White (Keres) to play

Black has here a whole assortment of different defensive
possibilities, but none of these would lead to a satisfactory
result. Let us look at them a little more closely:

1. 22 . . .QxR; 23 RxQ, BxKt; 24 BxKt, and Black has
insufficient compensation for his Queen.

2. 22 . . . Q–B2; 23 KtxB, Kt(Kt3)–Q2; 24 RxKt, QxR;
25 BxKt, and White is a piece up.

3. 22 . . . Q–B4 (comparatively the best reply and one by
which Black at least avoids material loss) 23 KtxB, Kt(Kt3)–
Q2; (after 23 . . . P–R5; 24 QxPch, KxKt; White wins by
25 R–Q5!, KtxR; 26 Q–R6ch, K–Kt1; 27 QBxKt etc.)
24 B–K3 (naturally he can also play 24Rx Kt, KtxR; 25 B–Q6,

Q–R4; 26 BxR, KtxB; 27 Kt–K8 etc.), 24 ... Q–K2; 25 P–B4, KxKt; 26 PxKt, with great advantage to White since 26 ... Kt–B4 would be met by the strong reply 27 P–K6!.

With the text-move Black not only returns the piece he has captured but also eventually loses the exchange.

	23	KtxB	Kt(K4)–Q2

There is no way for Black to protect his Knight on K4.

	24	B–Q6	Q–R4

Black cannot capture the QRP by 24 ... QxRP, since then after 25 BxR, KtxB; 26 Kt–K8, he has no defence against the threefold threat of 27 Q–K5, 27 Q–QB3, and 27 Kt–B7. A little better, however, was 24 ... Q–Kt7 since now, before capturing on KB8, White could interpose the move 25 P–Kt4, and thus ensure the Queen either the square QB3 or K5.

	25	BxR	KtxB
	26	Kt–K8!	

Freeing the Knight and deciding the issue since, in addition to being the exchange to the good, White still possesses a powerful attack. Not altogether convincing on the other hand was the pawn sacrifice 26 P–Kt4, QxKtP; 27 Kt–K8, since after 27 ... B–K3!; 28 Kt–B6ch, K–R1; 29 Q–K5, Black still has at his disposal the defence 29 ... Kt–B5!

	26	...	B–K3
	27	Kt–B6ch	K–R1
	28	Q–B4	Kt–R2
	29	Q–Q4	KtxKt
	30	QxKtch	K–R2
	31	P–K4	

Another easy way of winning here was by 31 R–Q6, and if then 31 ... Kt–Q4; 32 BxKt, BxB; 33 P–K4, or if in this line 32 ... PxB; 33 RxB, PxR; 34 Q–B7ch, K–R1; 35 R–B1, etc. With the text-move, however, White aims at ending the game by a mating attack and for this purpose he sacrifices all the Queen's wing pawns.

	31	...	QxRP
	32	P–B4	BxKtP
	33	R–Q6	R–KKt1

There was no longer any defence against the threat of 34 P–B5.

	34 P–B5	R–Kt2

35 R–Q8 was threatened and if then 35 ... RxR; 36 PxPch, PxP; 37 Q–K7ch, etc. Another strong threat was simply 35 P–K5–6.

35	R–Q8	Q–R4
36	Q–Q6	P–B3
37	Q–B8	KtPxP

Or, 37 ... B–Kt1; 38 PxBP, etc.

38	Q–R8ch	K–Kt3
39	Q–R6ch	resigns

Game 48

SICILIAN DEFENCE

F.I.D.E. Candidates' Tournament at Budapest, 1950

	P. Keres	A. Kotov
1	P–K4	P–QB4
2	Kt–KB3	P–Q3
3	P–Q4	PxP
4	KtxP	Kt–KB3
5	Kt–QB3	P–QR3
6	B–K2	

The usual continuation here is 6 B–Kt5, and this, according to the most recent results, holds out better prospects of the initiative than the quiet text-move. I had definite reasons, however, for choosing the move in this game. Kotov always employed in this variation a development system akin to the Scheveningen with the moves Q–B2, P–K3 and B–K2, and I had prepared a new type of attacking continuation precisely against this. For the next few moments everything went according to my preconceived plan.

6	...	Q–B2
7	B–KKt5	QKt–Q2
8	O–O	P–K3
9	B–R5!	

The chief idea of White's system of play centres round this original Bishop move which is designed to prevent Black's

method of development by B–K2 followed by O–O. On
account of the threat of 10 KtxP, Black must now choose other
paths far removed from the Scheveningen line.

After the game there arose a hot discussion amongst various
commentators about the whole variation, a discussion with
which I do not intend to concern myself here. With the text-
move White has achieved a psychological victory in that he has
diverted his opponent from the prepared opening variation.
And in such cases it is not easy to find the right move at once
over the board.

$$9 \ldots \qquad\qquad \text{Q–B5?}$$

It is interesting to note that in my own preparatory study of
the line I had not at all taken into account this natural move.
I chiefly examined the possibilities arising out of 9 ... Kt–K4;
10 BxKt, PxB; 11 K–R1, with an eventual P–KB4 to follow,
and also those coming from 9 ... KtxB; 10 QxKt, P–KKt3;
11 Q–R4, B–Kt2; 12 QR–Q1, both of which yield White the
more promising game. On the other hand, to an almost unpredictable future leads 9 ... P–KKt3; 10 B–K2, B–Kt2, by
which, it is true, Black has won a couple of tempi, but only at
the cost of creating a cruel weakness on Q3.

Black (Kotov)

White (Keres) to play

10 KtxP!

My first impression was that White, on account of the threat
of 10 ... KtxB, followed by 11 ... QxKt, had nothing better
than the retreat 10 B–K2, which, however, after 10 ... Q–B2,
would have led to a repetition of moves. After an exhaustive

examination of the position, however, the interesting idea occurred to me of initiating a sharp attack with this Knight sacrifice aimed at the enemy King which has been left too long in the centre.

The sacrifice in question is not based on exactly calculated variations but more on general considerations. I thought that after accepting the sacrifice Black would have great difficulties with the defence, since White is considerably ahead in development and will soon be in a position to set up some harassing threats. The game shows that in the end the supposition is a correct one.

    10   ...   QxKt(K3)

Acceptance of the sacrifice is forced since the capture 10 ... KtxB would lead to White's winning the exchange with a better position after 11 Q–Q5!, Kt–Kt3; (11 ... QxQ?; 12 Kt–B7 mate!) 12 QxQ, KtxQ; 13 Kt–B7ch.

    11   Kt–Q5!

In this Knight move lies the point of the Knight sacrifice. Black can now only parry the threat of 12 Kt–B7ch by an exchange on Q5 or by a King's move to Q1. Both moves have, however, grave positional drawbacks.

    11   ...   K–Q1

Kotov decides upon a laboriously passive defence. It is, however, clear that the Black King is most insecurely placed on Q1 and that his undeveloped pieces cannot assure him adequate protection. Moreover, White can also continually set fresh threats to his opponent.

Hence 11 ... KtxKt; 12 PxKt, Q–B4 deserved consideration here. Closer analysis shows us, however, that White would also have a very strong attack in this line. The variation which is more or less forced is 13 Q–K1ch, Kt–K4; (or 13 ... Q–K4; 14 P–KB4 etc.) 14 P–KB4, P–KR3; (after 14 ... B–K2 White wins by 15 PxKt, QxB; 16 PxP, and also 14 ... P–KKt3; 15 PxKt, QxB; 16 PxP dis ch leads to no better result) 15 PxKt, QxB; 16 PxP dis ch and White has a mating attack.

    12   B–Kt4   Q–K4

After 12 ... Q–K1 White's strongest continuation is 13 Q–Q2! with the main threats of 14 BxKt, and 14 Q–B3.

	13 P–KB4	QxKP

No better for Black is the capture by 13 . . . QxKtP; 14 R–Kt1, when, after 14 . . . Q–R6, White can win by 15 BxKt, BxB; 16 KtxKt, or, in this line, 15 . . . KxB; 16 BxKt, PxB; 17 Kt–Kt6ch.

	14 BxKt	BxB

After 14 . . . KxB; 15 BxKt, Black achieves nothing by 15 . . . K–B3 since, in addition to 16 R–B3, White can gain a decisive advantage by 16 P–B4, PxB; 17 Q–R4ch.

	15 KtxKt	PxKt

Naturally 15 . . . Q–Kt3; 16 Q–Q4, or 15 . . . Q–B3; 16 Kt–Q5 dis ch, P–B3; 17 KtxP etc. were no longer adequate defences, but this last variation would still have given Black some possibilities of playing on further. After the text-move, however, we get a speedy end to the game.

	16 BxPch	K–B2
	17 BxR	B–B3

At last Black has succeeded in beating off the attack—but at too great a cost in material. With the exchange and a pawn to the good White has a clearly won game.

	18 Q–Q2	B–R3
	19 QR–K1	Q–Kt3
	20 R–K7ch	K–Q1
	21 KR–K1	P–R4
	22 B–Q4	R–R3
	23 Q–B2	B–B1

Attempts at attack, such as 23 . . . BxBP, now come too late, since White can then reply 24 B–Kt6ch, K–B1; 25 R–B7ch, K–Kt1; 26 RxB, PxR; 27 R–K8ch, K–Kt2; 28 R–K7ch, and wins: e.g. 28 . . . K–Kt1; 29 B–B7ch, followed by 30 . . . QxB, or 28 . . . K–B1; 29 QxB, RxB; 30 Q–Q4, K–Q1; 31 R–R7, or finally 28 . . . K–R1; 29 B–Q4! when the threats of 30 . . . QxB, or 30 . . . Q–K2, are decisive.

	24 B–Kt6ch	K–B1
	25 R–K8ch	BxR
	26 RxBch	K–Q2
	27 RxB	resigns.

★ 5 ★

EVENTS AND TOURNAMENTS OF THE
YEARS 1950–52

AFTER the Budapest Tournament I was given little time to rest since shortly afterwards there commenced at Bad Salzbrunn (Sczawno-Zdroj) a great international tournament dedicated to the memory of the well-known Polish master Przepiorka. I went to this tournament with mixed feelings, since the second half of the Budapest tournament had shown that I had not yet surmounted a crisis in a period of my creative evolution. The first games in the tournament showed, however, that things had developed very much for the better in this respect. Once again, after a long interval of time, I was playing in an easy, care-free style, and for this reason my results were correspondingly better. I maintained my position in the leading group the whole of the time and of this group the most dangerous rival was the Hungarian master, Barcza. And until our individual meeting (No. 49) it was not clear which would succeed in breaking away from the other in the race for first place. I succeeded in winning this vital game in good positional style and thereafter the way to first place lay wide open.

Thus it was that I went to the XVIII U.S.S.R. Championship which was held at Moscow towards the end of the year in a much more confident frame of mind. But the begining of the tournament was far from promising. After three uncertainly played draws I managed to obtain a victory over Geller, after the latter had missed the best continuation in a complicated position and lost material through a bad blunder. Then I lost a very weakly played game against Alatortzev, salvaged a draw out of a lost position against Suetin and reached the same result out of a position with a good pawn more against Tolush. From the first eight rounds I had obtained only four points, was two points behind the leaders and now had only nine more rounds to play.

My position was not exactly rosy, but now commenced a series of successes. There was repeated, more or less, the experience I had in the Semmering tournament where every plan I devised was crowned with success. By the fourteenth round I had overhauled the leaders and after the fifteenth round I was in the sole lead, a half a point ahead of my nearest rivals. From the last seven games I had acquired no less than six and a half points. It is difficult for me now to explain the reason for such a long series of successes (or failures for that matter). But they do seem to occur quite frequently in tournaments, even in those in which the opposition is very strong.

With this series of successes, however, the tournament was far from being decided, even though only two games remained to be played. In the next round I obtained a clear advantage with White against Petrosian, but then allowed myself to be drawn into great complications quite unnecessarily, lost my way in these and eventually had to admit defeat. Now there arose a strange position in which three players were equal when the last round commenced and in which therefore the decision hung on one single last game.

I had to play with Black against Averbach and my disappointment can be imagined when my opponent commenced with the Four Knights Game (No. 50). However, Averbach's choice of opening was not prompted by a desire for a boring drawish variation and hence there soon arose an interesting middle-game. Eventually I succeeded in obtaining a small positional advantage and the game was adjourned in an ending that was rather in my favour. Of my other rivals, Tolush had already drawn with Boleslavsky, whilst Aronin also possessed somewhat better chances against Borisenko. When play was resumed I managed to break through Averbach's position and win an endgame that was full of combinations, although the nervous tension was not without influence on the play of both sides. Aronin tried for a long time to break down Borisenko's stubborn defence, but without success. After a three-year pause I had once again captured the title of champion of the U.S.S.R.

No less exciting was the course of the next, the XIXth Championship, which was also held in Moscow. In this tournament I played more consistently than in the previous year, but here too the question of the winner was only decided in the last round. I began well with three wins and a loss, amongst these games an interesting sacrificial victory over Geller (No. 51). Thereafter the struggle evened out, and, after I had let escape an excellent winning chance against Botvinnik, the following intriguing tournament position was reached at the end of the thirteenth round. Botvinnik, Geller, Smyslov and I led with 8½ points and only half a point behind us came Averbach and Petrosian. It was clear that in such a position every single game was of outstanding importance.

In the following round there came my decisive meeting with Smyslov (No. 52). I was able to seize the initiative in an exciting middle-game and, once my opponent had missed a favourable opportunity of transposing to an equal endgame, I obtained a strong attack despite the few remaining pieces. The game then transposed to a Bishop ending that was to my advantage and in this I was able to score the point that was so vital for me. In the same round, too, Geller beat Botvinnik, Petrosian, Simagin and Taimanov Averbach, so that the question of the lead was still open. We had only three more rounds to play. The next round, too, brought no final solution as both Geller and myself won, whilst Petrosian and Smyslov also obtained a full point.

The games of the next round had a vital bearing on the first place. As in the previous Championship, I was playing against Petrosian in the penultimate round. Perhaps owing to my evil memory of the game of the previous year, or perhaps the tension of the tournament was to blame, but my position worsened from move to move. Soon I had lost two pawns and in addition to this was afflicted by acute time-trouble. But then apparently Petrosian did not make the best of his chances. I managed to extract a Rook ending from the game in which I was only a pawn down and on the next day I did in fact obtain a draw. Things did not go so well with my chief rival Geller, who was beaten by Bronstein. Since Smyslov also won his game I had, by the time the last round was reached, a lead of only half a point above my three rivals, Geller, Petrosian and Smyslov. Botvinnik, after his loss to Geller, was practically cut off from any competition for the first prize.

So, for the second time in succession, I had to play a game in the last round that was to be decisive as regards the first prize. This time I had grandmaster Taimanov as my opponent, and against him I played one of the most hair-raising games of the tournament (No. 53). I obtained an overwhelming attack against the enemy King position, and, although I did not execute it quite precisely, this attack still was enough to win the game. The audience was so carried away by this vital game that play in its last few minutes had to be transferred to another, quieter, room. This valuable victory assured for me the championship of the U.S.S.R. for the third time, but at the same time also demonstrated that I had made good progress in the matter of conducting single, deciding games to their successful conclusion. This capacity is indeed of the utmost importance for every tournament player.

Game 49

RUY LOPEZ

International Tournament at Sczawno-Zdroj, 1950

	P. Keres	G. Barcza
1	P–K4	P–K4
2	Kt–KB3	Kt–QB3
3	B–Kt5	P–QR3
4	B–R4	KKt–K2

It is well-known that Grandmaster Barcza does not feel particularly at home in positions that contain many tactical possibilities and require exact and concrete calculation. He prefers methods of play of a positional character in which his excellent powers of strategic manoeuvring can be brought into full force. Hence Barcza is not especially happy when defending against 1 P–K4. The text-move is characteristic of his style. He tries to get the game off theoretical paths in the hope that thereby he may confuse his adversary.

5 B–Kt3

Theory recommends here either 5 P–Q4 or 5 Kt–B3, for both of which moves, however, Black must have been fully prepared. At the time the game was played the text-move seemed very good to me and at least in this present game the experiment turns out to be very well grounded.

5 . . .   P–B3

One does not make a move like this very readily, but White had the unpleasant threat of 6 . . . Kt–Kt5. Should Black play 5 . . . P–R3 then 6 P–Q4 would certainly be more effective than it might have been a move earlier, whilst after 5 . . . Kt–Kt3 White's attack by 6 P–KR4 could become most troublesome. With the text-move Black hopes eventually to be in a position to drive off the White Bishop from the diagonal QR2–KKt8, but this is not so easily accomplished.

6 P–Q4   P–Q3
7 P–B3   Kt–QR4

In order to complete his development Black is reduced to snatching at artificial aids. But the Bishop was indeed much too strong along the QR2–KKt8 diagonal. Bad, for example, would be 7 . . . B–Kt5, when 8 KtxP!, KtxKt; 9 P–B3, could occur, with advantage to White.

8 B–B2   P–KKt3

There is no time for Black to occupy the critical diagonal by 8 . . . B–K3, since then, after 9 P–QKt4, Kt–B5; 10 B–Kt3, he would be held in the grip of an uncomfortable pin. It turns out that Black has procured a temporary alleviation only of his troubles by 7 . . . Kt–QR4.

9 QKt–Q2   B–Kt2

Once Black has managed to castle then his position will be most satisfactory. With the ensuing exchange White works against this plan and the measures he now takes are designed to prevent enemy castling. In fact, the struggle over Black's castling has now become the strategic core of the game.

10 PxP   QPxP

Bad is naturally 10 . . . BPxP, since after 11 P–QKt4, QKt–B3; 12 B–Kt3, Black must reckon with the threats of 13 Kt–Kt5 and 13 P–KR4.

11 P–QKt4   QKt–B3
12 B–Kt3   B–Q2

Black's idea is to challenge the diagonal by 13 ... Q–B1 and 14 ... B–K3 and thus at last get himself castled. For this purpose 12 ... Q–Q3 also came into question but then 13 P–QR4, B–K3; 14 P–Kt5, followed by 15 B–R3, could be very awkward for Black. White could also of course simply play 13 Q–B2, B–K3; 14 Kt–B4, Q–Q2; 15 O–O, with the better game.

13   Kt–B1

Here White could have obtained a fine game by the normal continuation 13 O–O, Q–B1; 14 Kt–B4, B–K3; 15 Kt–K3, or also in this line 15 Kt–K1, followed by 16 Kt–Q3, but in so playing he would allow Black to castle. In order to prevent this White, already with his 10th move, had conceived a firm plan and now he pursues its logical course. If Black now continues with his original plan by 13 ... Q–B1; 14 Kt–K3, B–K3, then there comes 15 Kt–Q5! when Black still cannot castle because of 16 KtxBP etc.

Hence in the next phase of the game Black tries to carry out his plan in a somewhat different form. Naturally, White is not prepared to allow this.

13	. . .	B–Kt5
14	Q–B2	Q–Q2
15	Kt–K3	B–K3

Of course not 15 ... BxKt; 16 PxB, when the strong Bishop on Kt3 cripples Black's entire position. With the manoeuvre 13 ... B–Kt5 followed by 14 ... Q–Q2 Black has at any rate managed to prevent White from playing an immediate 16 Kt–Q5.

16   O–O   Kt–Q1

At last Black has got so far as to be in a position to castle, but suddenly he desists of his own free will. And with good reason, since after 16 ... O–O; 17 R–Q1, Q–B1; 18 Kt–Q5, White would have the advantage in every respect and his opponent would be without counter-play. With the text-move Black tries to regroup his pieces and in particular to manoeuvre the Knight to a better square from its poor position on QB3.

17   R–Q1   BxB

The continuation 17 ... Q–B3; 18 Kt–Q5, would naturally have been worse for Black.

18	QxB	Q–B3
19	Kt–Q5	Kt–B2
20	P–B4	Kt–Q3 ?

Up to here Black has defended his difficult position extremely well. Now, however, he fails to take into consideration the strong threat that follows and falls into a game that positionally is hopelessly lost. Here it was essential for him to get rid of the strong central Knight by 20 . . . KtxKt; 21 KPxKt, Q–Q2; although even then White would clearly have much the better game after 22 P–B5.

Black (Barcza)

White (Keres) to play

21   P–Kt5!

With this thrust he breaks up his opponent's defence, whilst keeping the enemy King fixed in the centre.

21	...	PxP
22	PxP	Q–Q2

It almost goes without saying that if 22 . . . KtxKtP; White wins by 23 QxKt.

23   B–R3

Very strong here too was 23 P–Kt6, forcing the reply 23 . . . KtxKt. White would, however, scarcely have achieved a quicker win with this since both 24 RxKt, P–B3; 25 R–Q3, and 24 QxKt, would allow Black to put up a stubborn resistance by Q–B2! With the text-move White threatens in the first place 24 KtxQBPch and thus forces an exchange on Q5.

23	...	KtxKt
24	RxKt	P–Kt3

Again practically forced since if he tries 24 ... B–B1 White would have a decisive attack after 25 P–Kt6, P–B3; 26 KtxP! (26 R–Q3, Q–B2!) 26 ... PxKt; 27 RxPch, K–Q1; 28 R–Q1 etc. Now, by leaving his opponent with a bad Bishop and gaining absolute control of the white squares, White attains a positionally won game.

25	BxKt	PxB
26	Kt–Q2	

In bringing his Knight to QB4, from which point it attacks the weaknesses on Q6 and QKt6, White once again underlines the superiority of this piece over his opponent's Bishop. Another good continuation was 26 R–QB1 followed by 27 R–B6.

26	...	Q–QB2
27	Kt–B4	B–B1
28	R(R1)–Q1	R–Q1
29	R(Q5)–Q2	

Once White has attained a winning position he proceeds to play imprecisely, under the influence of approaching time trouble, and so allows Black to get some counter-play. The simplest way to win was undoubtedly 29 P–QR4, B–K2; 30 P–R5! and this, after 30 ... PxP; 31 P–Kt6 would have soon convinced Black of the uselessness of further resistance.

29	...	P–Q4!

White was intending, after 30 Kt–K3, to manoeuvre his Knight to a dominating position on Q5 and then to occupy the QB file with his Rooks. The pawn sacrifice comprised by the text-move is therefore practically forced. Black now arrives at a good development for his Bishop and is in a position, in the ensuing phase of the game, to put up quite a stubborn resistance.

30	RxP	RxR
31	PxR	

Here too 31 RxR, B–B4; 32 P–QR4, with the threat of 33 P–R5, was simpler. But White pursues another plan.

31	...	B–B4
32	P–Q6	Q–Q2
33	P–QR4	

A logical continuation of White's plan, but one which, on closer examination, proves to be faulty. Much stronger here was immediately 33 Q–KB3, which would have prevented the enemy King from escaping to the comparatively safe square of KKt2.

33 ... K–B1
34 Q–KB3

White notices only just in time that his intended continuation 34 P–R5, PxP; 35 Q–KB3, K–Kt2; 36 Q–B6, will not work on account of 36 ... Q–Kt5! Black now at last manages to get his Rook into play, but White's plus pawn, in conjunction with the active position of his pieces, still assures him a winning position.

34 ... K–Kt2
35 P–R3 R–QB1
36 Q–Q5 B–Q5

Taken together with the threat of 37 ... R–B4, this represents Black's only chance of active counter-play. Now, however, White has the opportunity of finishing off the game by a pretty combination, easy enough to find it should be said.

37 RxB! R–B4

Equally hopeless is the endgame after 37 ... PxR; 38 KtxKtP, R–B8ch; 39 K–R2, followed by 40 P–Q7 etc.

38 KtxKtP RxQ
39 RxR Q–B4

After 39 ... Q–Q1; 40 P–Q7, the advance of the QRP wins quickly.

40 P–Q7 resigns.

Game 50

FOUR KNIGHTS' GAME

XVIII U.S.S.R. Championship at Moscow, 1950

	J. Averbach	P. Keres
1	P–K4	P–K4
2	Kt–KB3	Kt–QB3
3	Kt–B3	

This game was played in the last round and its result had a decisive bearing on the question of the first place, since before the last round three players were in the lead—Aronin, Tolush and I. So, who would win the tournament depended upon the results of these three players in the last round.

In view of the circumstances White's choice of opening was most unwelcome to Black. It is known that the Four Knights' Game is one of the best proved systems of avoiding all complications in the opening, and it is therefore regarded by masters as a drawish opening. However, there are certain lines in which Black can aim at a fighting middle-game. In the first place, however, he refrains here from making dubious opening experiments whilst endeavouring to. discover his opponent's actual intentions.

3	. . .	Kt–B3
4	B–Kt5	B–Kt5
5	O–O	O–O
6	P–Q3	P–Q3
7	Kt–K2	

After 7 B–Kt5, Black would have been faced by a difficult choice as the main variation 7 . . . BxKt; 8 PxB, Q–K2 would allow White if he so wished to bring about a dead drawn position by 9 KBxKt. Probably in that case I would have chosen a continuation not particularly recommended by theory, but in compensation a complicated one, such as for example 7 . . . Kt–K2.

With the text-move, however, Averbach shows that his choice of the Four Knights' Game is not connected with designs on a draw. The game now moves towards an interesting middle-game.

7	. . .	Kt–K2
8	P–B3	B–R4
9	Kt–Kt3	P–B3
10	B–R4	Kt–Kt3
11	P–Q4	B–K3

A symmetrical position has arisen in which, as a rule, the first player's possession of an extra tempo ensures him a lasting initiative. Hence here White has been able to carry out the thrust P–Q4 first, thereby driving his opponent on the defensive. Black could indeed have continued in symmetrical style 11 . . . P–Q4, but thereafter, too, White would have obtained the initiative by 12 B–KKt5.

In order to reach a feasible middle-game full of fighting possibilities Black must seek other methods of developing his pieces. In the game Alekhine–Euwe, Amsterdam, 1936, Black tried here 11 . . . R–K1; 12 B–Kt3, PxP with the idea of exerting pressure on K5. But after 13 PxP, it turned out that Black could not well play 13 . . . KtxP on account of 14 KtxKt, RxKt; 15 Kt–Kt5, or 15 BxPch, and therefore he had to continue with 13 . . . B–K3. After 14 Kt–Kt5, BxB; 15 QxB, Q–Q2; 16 P–B3, White, however, obtained rather the better position.

With the text-move Black embarks on an attempt to improve Euwe's method of play. He wants, after 12 B–Kt3, to play 12 . . . R–K1 without exchanging on White's Q4. After that, at all events, 13 Kt–Kt5 would be purposeless and White would have to seek out other ways of assuring himself an initiative.

12   B–B2

White should have, as mentioned earlier, continued with 12 B–Kt3. After the text-move Black gets a good game without any trouble.

12   . . .   R–K1
13   R–K1

Through this careless move, which puts the Rook on the same diagonal as the enemy KB, Black gets the opportunity of gaining the initiative in quite a surprising manner. After 13 B–K3, on the other hand, White would have stood rather better, chiefly because of his advantage in space.

13   . . .   B–KKt5!

An unexpected counter, which poses White some awkward defensive problems and gives Black the initiative. Now the chief threats are 14 . . . PxP and 14 . . . Kt–R5 with a worsening of White's pawn position from which he would not be saved by 14 PxP, KtxP(K4). Since also 14 R–K3, P–Q4! or 14 B–K3, PxP; 15 BxP, Kt–R5 are unsatisfactory lines for White, Black's position must already be regarded as preferable.

14   Kt–B5?

White, apparently realising that he does indeed stand worse, here chooses a continuation that ensures Black a small but clear advantage. Instead of this, however, he could have brought about complications by the interesting pawn sacrifice 14 P–KR3!, BxKt; 15 QxB, PxP; 16 P–Kt4, B–Kt3; 17 B–Kt5, and such complications are not so easily dealt with in practice. Thus for example the natural continuation 17 . . . Kt–K4; 18 Q–B5, Kt(K4)–Q2; would allow White a really dangerous attack after 19 P–K5!, PxP(K4); 20 Kt–R5, and after 17 . . . R–K4 White need not immediately exchange on KB6, but can further increase his pressure by 18 Kt–B5.

Naturally, Black need not allow his opponent's attack in this variation and can for instance simplify the position by 17 . . . Kt–K4; 18 Q–B5, P–KR3; 19 BxKt, QxB; 20 QxQ, PxQ, whilst at the same time retaining his extra pawn. All the same, White should have launched out on this sharp variation as here it would have been much more difficult for Black to find the correct defence than in the game.

Black (Keres) to play

White (Averbach)

| 14 . . . | P–Q4! |

Opening up the centre and thereby giving Black's advantage a concrete form. The ensuing moves are practically forced.

| 15 | P–KR3 | BxKt(B6) |
| 16 | QxB | KtxP |

After 16 . . . KPxP White could gain an enduring initiative by 17 B–Kt5, and the bold recapture by 17 KtxQP would also come into consideration. The text-move is much simpler.

17	BxKt	PxP
18	KtxQP	B–Kt3!

With this move Black reveals his trump cards. He will in fact simplify the position by the ensuing exchange; but he saddles his opponent with an isolated pawn on Q4 whilst he still has a Bishop on black coloured squares on the board. Meanwhile Black himself retains the good Knight. White can do nothing against all this since after a Knight move there would follow a double exchange on K4 and then a check on White's Q1.

Attempts to extract more than a favourable endgame out of the position are doomed to failure. After 18 . . . Q–K2 White has the defensive resource of 19 Kt–B5 followed by 20 Kt–Kt3, and 18 . . . Q–R5 could even have a tragic outcome for Black after 19 Q–B5! e.g., 19 . . . RxB; 20 B–Kt5, RxRch; 21 RxR, Q–R4; 22 P–KKt4 and White wins! After 18 . . . P–QB4, however, White can either play 19 Kt–Kt3, or else choose the combinative continuation 19 B–Kt5, QxB; 20 BxP, etc.

19	B–Q2	PxB
20	RxP	RxR
21	QxR	BxKt
22	PxB	

This was the position at which Black was aiming. White has a weak isolated pawn on Q4, and Black's Q4 square in front of it forms an ideal point of support for Black's pieces. White's Bishop has no prospects since its own pawns are on the same coloured squares. Black's next task lies in the accomplishment of the exchange of Queens, thereby depriving his opponent of the chance of an eventual King-side attack.

22	. . .	Q–K2
23	Q–Kt4	Q–Q3
24	R–K1	

After this mechanical move Black takes a big step forward in the execution of his plan and forces the exchange of Queens. The ending arising after the Queen exchange is very favourable for Black, probably even won for him, since it is not easy to find a defensive plan holding out any prospects of success to White in the ensuing part of the game.

White should undoubtedly have seized the opportunity here of harassing his opponent on the King's wing by 24 P–KR4! After this Black's task would have been much more difficult. The possible win of a pawn by 24 . . . P–KR4; 25 QxP, QxP; 26 B–B3!, QxP; 27 QxQ, KtxQ offers Black no real winning chances after 28 R–Q1. He would, therefore, have had to continue with 24 . . . Kt–B1; 25 P–R5, Kt–K3; thereby once again asserting his positional advantage.

| 24 | . . . | Q–Q4! |

Now he threatens not only 25 . . . QxRP but also 25 . . . P–KR4, after which White would have to exchange Queens. White cannot parry both threats simultaneously.

| 25 | P–QKt3 | P–KR4 |
| 26 | Q–K4 | |

Otherwise he loses the QP without any compensation.

| 26 | . . . | QxQ |
| 27 | RxQ | P–B3 |

Now Black's plan is to bring his King nearer to the centre and eventually to threaten to get it as far as Q4 where it will constitute a real threat to the pawn on Q5. White cannot undertake anything active in the ensuing phase of the game and must simply wait to see how his opponent proposes to strengthen his position.

28	K–B1	K–B2
29	B–R5	P–Kt3
30	B–B3	R–Q1
31	B–Kt2	R–Q3
32	P–KKt4	

A useful advance for White as it deprives his opponent of the possibility of drawing away the Rook from its protection of the QP by P–KB4. And any exchange of pawns only helps White.

| 32 | . . . | PxP |
| 33 | PxP | R–K3 |

This attempt to free a way for his King to Q4 by a Rook exchange is not the happiest of plans. In the first place he cannot sweep the way clear for his King to reach the desirable post on Q4 and in the second place any further exchange merely alleviates White's position. Despite the fact that the ending, for example, after 34 RxR, KxR; 35 K–K2, K–Q4; 36 K–Q3, is very favourable for Black, White, in view of the reduction in material, still has very good chances of putting up a resistance.

Hence, and more particularly when one takes into account that the game was shortly due to be adjourned, it would have been better here to have continued at once 33 . . . Kt–B1 followed by 34 . . . Kt–K3 and 35 . . . R–Q4, and with this in fact we would have attained a position reached at a later stage in the game.

                34   P–B3

Averbach also is seemingly convinced that the ending would be lost for him after a Rook exchange, and avoids this possibility both now and later.

34	. . .	Kt–K2
35	B–B1	Kt–Q4
36	B–Q2	R–Q3

Black, perceiving that the advance of his King cannot be forced, proceeds to regroup his forces. At the same time he avoids a transition into an ending with Knight against Bishop as after this Black no longer offers an exchange of Rooks.

37	K–K2	R–Q1
38	K–B2	Kt–B2
39	P–R4	

A weakening of the Queen's wing that is practically forced since 39 . . . Kt–Kt4 was threatened. After the Knight move, protection of the QP by 40 B–K3, Kt–B6 or 40 K–K3, Kt–Q3 would lead to the loss of the exchange.

39	. . .	Kt–K3
40	B–K3	R–Q4

In this position the game was adjourned and White sealed his move. Black's positional superiority is beyond doubt, and the only question is, can this be converted into a material advantage. A reply to this demands a narrower examination of the state of affairs.

White's pieces are tethered to the protection of the QP and hence White is in a passive waiting position, since in practice he can only move his King. So Black has time enough in which to prepare for a decisive break-through, and this lies in the advance P–QKt4. Immediately played, this move, for example after 41 K–K2, would be premature since after 41 ... P–QKt4; 42 P–R5, P–Kt5 (a little better is 42 ... P–R3); 43 P–R6, White gains some counter-play, both after 43 ... Kt–B2; 44 K–Q3, KtxP; 45 K–B4, and also after 43 ... R–QR4; 44 P–Q5, PxP; 45 RxP, etc.

Therefore Black conceives the plan of further strengthening his position, providing that White puts up an entirely passive defence, by bringing his King to Q2 and playing P–Kt3, with an eventual P–QR3. Only at the right moment will P–QKt4 be played. It seems unlikely that White could have successfully defended himself against this plan, even if he had remained entirely on the passive defence.

| 41 | K–Kt3 | K–K2 |

After an immediate 41 ... P–QKt4 Black did not quite like the look of the possible pawn sacrifice by 42 K–B2, PxP; 43 PxP, R–QR4; 44 P–Q5, PxP; 45 R–Kt4. With this line White would have activated his pieces and obtained some counter-play. Hence Black intends first of all to bring his King to Q2.

| 42 | P–Kt5? | |

White, no longer able to endure this passive waiting, decides to force some counter-play on the King's wing by his pawn sacrifice. But this action merely lightens Black's task and accelerates the collapse of White's position. After 42 K–B2, Black's task would undoubtedly have been more complicated, although in this case, too, the plan outlined in the previous annotation would have eventually secured him a decisive advantage.

| 42 | ... | P–KB4! |

Naturally Black does not take the pawn, since after 42 ... PxP; 43 K–Kt4, White's pieces would become active.

43	R–K5	K–Q3
44	RxRch	KxR
45	P–Kt6!	

It seems that it was on this clever advance that White, in playing 42 P–Kt5, had set his hopes. Apparently Black can now capture the pawn by 45 ... KtxP without any risk since 46 K–B4 is not to be feared because of 46 ... P–B4. But matters are not so simple.

Black (Keres) to play

White (Averbach)

45 · · ·   P–QR4!

White's cunning trap reveals itself in the ending that arises
after 45 . . . KtxP; 46 BxKt, KxB; 47 K–B4, which at first
glance seems hopeless for White. Black's best continuation
47 . . . P–Kt4!; 48 PxP, PxP; creates a difficult position for
White, but all the same there is a way out. By 49 P–Kt4!,
K–B5; 50 KxP, KxP White can bring about a position in which
he has some surprising resources. There are apparently even
two ways White can save the position. The ending is very
interesting and instructive and it therefore merits closer
consideration.

In the first place 51 K–K6 comes into question with the idea
of ensuring the draw after a King move by K–B7, xP, –B6,
followed by the advance of the Kt pawn. Black, however, has
the stronger 51 . . . P–R4! after which White's situation becomes
critical. For example, he cannot play 52 P–B4, P–R5; 53 P–B5
P–R6; 54 P–B6, PxP; 55 P–Kt7, P–R7; 56 P–Kt8=Q,
P–R8=Q; 57 Q–B8ch, K–Kt6, when Black wins easily. And
also the continuation 52 K–B7, P–R5; 53 KxP, P–R6, bodes
nothing good for White, since after a King move Black forces
the exchange of Queens: 54 K–B7, P–R7; 55 P–Kt7, P–R8=Q;
56 P–Kt8=Q, Q–R7ch etc.

Would it not be high time to resign in this position after
57 K–B8, QxQch; 58 KxQ, K–B5? And yet, in precisely this
apparently hopelessly lost position, there turns out to be a saving
clause for White. Viz. he plays 59 P–B4, K–Q4; 60 K–B7!.
If then 60 . . . K–K5; 61 K–K6!, KxP; 62 K–Q5, with a

drawn position, and after 60 . . . P–Kt5 White likewise reaches a theoretically drawn position by 61 P–B5, P–Kt6; 62 P–B6, P–Kt7; 63 K–Kt7, P–Kt8=Q; 64 P–B7. An astonishing resource!

Perhaps Black might still retain some winning chances in the variation given above if he refrains from exchanging Queens and instead continues 57 . . . Q–R1ch; 58 K–Kt7, QxP. The ending that then arises, however, is one of the most difficult known to chess theory and up to this very day it has not been possible to determine with any certainty whether it is won or not.

And so White's other defensive possibilities, viz. 51 P–B4! must be regarded as the stronger. Now neither 51 . . . K–B4; 52 K–K6!, P–Kt5; 53 P–B5, P–Kt6; 54 P–B6, when the pawn threatens to Queen with check, nor 51 . . . K–B6; 52 K–Kt5!, P–Kt5; 53 P–B5, P–Kt6; 54 P–B6, PxPch; 55 KxP, P–Kt7; 56 P–Kt7, P–Kt8=Q; 57 P–Kt8=Q, gives White any difficulties since the last-mentioned ending yields practically no winning chances. But after 51 . . . P–R4! the situation seems critical for White as then 52 K–K6, P–R5; 53 P–B5, P–R6; 54 P–B6, PxP etc. leads to a position that is, as we have already seen, won for Black. Nevertheless, White still has a saving resource, to wit 52 K–K4!, P–R5; 53 K–Q3, and suddenly the White King comes in time to stop the pawn. In fact, now Black could have trouble in getting the draw.

Naturally, Black was unable to calculate out all these finesses during the game. Nevertheless, he correctly appraised the position after 45 . . . KtxP and refrained from taking the pawn. After the text-move Black is in fact threatening 46 . . . KtxP as his extra tempo with P–R4 would make the pawn ending easily won for Black.

46 K–R4   KtxP

Although this capture was now possible it was not in actual fact logical since it removed a pawn that hemmed in the activity of the White Bishop. Simpler here was 46 . . . P–Kt4 so as to get his pawn to Kt5 before capturing on Q5. Now White gets some counter-play.

47 B–R6!   Kt–K3

It goes almost without saying that Black cannot capture the Bishop because of 48 P–Kt7, whilst after 47 . . . KtxPch;

48 K–R5, Kt–K4; 49 BxP, KtxP; 50 KxKt, P–B. White retains adequate defensive chances by 51 B–B6.

48   B–K3   P–B4

Also possible was 48 . . . P–Kt4; 49 B–Kt6, P–Kt5; 50 BxP, P–B4; etc., but the text-move is just as good.

49   K–R5

After 49 B–B1, Black wins by the manoeuvre 49 . . . P–QB5; 50 PxPch, KxP; 51 B–Kt2, P–Kt4; 52 PxP, KxP; 53 BxP, (White's sole counter-chance) 53 . . . KtxB; 54 K–Kt5, P–R5; 55 K–B6, P–R6; etc. In reply to the text-move Black could also play 49 . . . P–QB5; 50 PxPch, KxP; 51 BxP, K–Kt5 followed by 52 . . . KxP, when the passed QRP should quickly decide the game.

49 . . .   K–K4

Instead of the simple and clear winning method outlined in the previous note Black commences to manoeuvre about whilst his opponent is in time trouble in the hope of attaining a still easier win. Such tactics are not, however, in place here and merely lead eventually to Black's overlooking a hidden defensive resource of his adversary's, thereby imperilling his won position.

50   B–B1   Kt–Q5

Once he has lost the clear winning path Black commences to complicate the position unnecessarily. It is true that 50 . . . K–Q5; 51 B–Kt2ch, K–K6? would be a blunder since after 52 BxP, KtxBch; 53 K–Kt5, no win can be discerned any longer for Black, e.g. 53 . . . KxP; 54 K–B6, Kt–R4ch; 55 KxP, K–K6; 56 K–K5, K–Q6; 57 K–B5! and White threatens a perpetual attack on the Knight. Nor would the attempt 53 . . . Kt–K1; 54 KxP, KxP; 55 K–K6, K–K5; 56 K–Q7, suffice for a win.

With 50 . . . P–KB5 Black could indeed try to win a second pawn, but this continuation too would yield White really good counter-play after 51 K–Kt4, K–B3; 52 B–Kt2ch, KxP; 53 B–K5! in conjunction with the possibility of B–Kt8–R7. With the text-move Black also gets nowhere since in order to win in the simplest way the Knight must go back to K3.

Black's clearest winning method lay in the setting up of a

passed pawn on the Queen's wing, and for this purpose
50 . . . K–Q4 should again have been played. If then 51
B–Kt2, Black wins as follows: 51 . . . P–QB5; 52 PxPch,
KxP; 53 BxP, (otherwise there comes 53 . . . P–Kt4) 53 . . .
KtxBch; 54 K–Kt5, Kt–K1; 55 KxP, K–Q4 and White no
longer has any defence against the threat of 56 . . . P–Kt4.
From this variation we can see that the win for Black has become
much more complicated than it was on move 49.

51 B–R6

Bad of course was 51 B–Kt2, because of the reply 51 . . .
K–B5. After the text-move 51 . . . Kt–K3 was simplest, transposing to a position we have already seen in our notes. Black
is, however, pursuing quite another plan.

51 . . .   K–B3

52 B–Kt5ch   K–K3

53 B–R6?

A terrible blunder in time trouble. White fails to utilise an
excellent saving resource in 53 B–Q8! During the game Black
thought this was bad because of 53 . . . KtxKtP; 54. BxP,
P–QB5, after which White will even lose his Bishop. However,
instead of 54 BxP, White has the much stronger continuation
54 K–Kt5! setting up the troublesome threat of 55 B–B6!
Black would have nothing better then than 54 . . . Kt–Q5;
55 BxP, KtxPch; 56 K–B4, or 56 K–R5, with excellent drawing
prospects for White. 54 . . . P–KB5 leads to no better result
because of the simple reply 55 KxP etc.

All the same, Black can still force a win after 53 B–Q8,
always providing that he plays 53 . . . K–Q2! instead of 53 . . .
KtxP?. If then 54 BxP the Bishop is in fact lost by 54 . . .
KtxKtP; 55 K–Kt5, P–QB5; whilst if White tries 54 B–B6,
Kt–K3; 55 B–K5, then Black wins by the following manoeuvre:
55 . . . K–B3; 56 BxP, (forced on account of the threats of
56 . . . P–Kt4 and 56 . . . K–Q4) 56 . . . KtxBch; 57 K–Kt5,
Kt–K1!; 58 KxP, K–Q3 and Black's Knight proves stronger
than White's passed pawns. If now, for example, 59 P–B4,
then 59 . . . K–Q4; 60 K–Kt5, K–K3; 61 P–B5ch, K–K4 etc.
and after 59 K–B4, K–K3; 60 K–K4, Black wins by 60 . . .
Kt–Q3ch; 61 K–B4, K–B3; 62 P–Kt7, KxP; 63 K–K5, P–B5.
It is clear that after 53 B–Q8, the game could still have been

most interesting, whereas the faulty text-move leads to a speedy end.

53	. . .	PxB
54	KxP	Kt–B3!

Averbach had apparently overlooked this simple move. Now the White pawn is stopped and Black wins easily.

55	P–Kt7	Kt–K2
56	K–R7	K–B2
57	K–R6	K–Kt1
58.	P–B4	K–B2
	White resigns	

Game 51

RUY LOPEZ, MORPHY DEFENCE

XIX U.S.S.R. Championship, Moscow, 1951

	E. Geller	P. Keres
1	P–K4	P–K4
2	Kt–KB3	Kt–QB3
3	B–Kt5	P–QR3
4	B–R4	Kt–B3
5	O–O	B–K2

This close method of development with its ensuing moves, a system introduced by Tschigorin into tournament praxis, is nowadays one of the most popular continuations in the Ruy Lopez. One of the reasons for this is undoubtedly the fact that the Tschigorin development system usually leads to very lively and eventful positions in which the imagination of both players is allowed full scope. A characteristic picture of the complicated nature of the system is furnished by the fact that, despite numerous analyses and practical experience in the course of more than half a century no positive decision has been made to this very day as to which plan of play can give White best chances of retaining an initiative.

6	R–K1	P–QKt4
7	B–Kt3	P–Q3
8	P–B3	O–O
9	P–KR3	Kt–QR4

Here, one of the most interesting of the less usual continuations is the original pawn thrust 9 . . . P–QR4 with which I have obtained very satisfactory results in a number of games.

10	B–B2	P–B4
11	P–Q4	Q–B2
12	QKt–Q2	BPxP

Amongst the various possible continuations tried in thousands of games at this point, as for example 12 . . . B–Q2, 12 . . . B–Kt2, 12 . . . Kt–B3, 12 . . . R–K1 etc., this exchange, with P–Q4 to follow, was very fashionable at the time. Geller had prepared an innovation against the plan and uses it in this game.

| 13 | PxP | B–Kt2 |
| 14 | Kt–B1 | |

Of recent years it has been held that the closing of the centre by 14 P–Q5 is the most likely continuation to yield an advantage against Black's method of development. After 14 . . . B–B1 Bronstein discovered the interesting move 15 R–Kt1, chiefly directed against the manoeuvre Kt–Kt2–B4. After 15 . . . Kt–Kt2 there would in fact follow 16 P–QKt4!, since then 16 . . . P–QR4 could be very well met by 17 P–R3. The Knight on Kt2 would, however, remain badly placed for a long time.

But on the other hand, with the 14 P–Q5 advance White surrenders all his chances in the centre and bases his hopes on the Queen's wing, where, however, success is not to be achieved easily. Therefore, in my opinion, the question as to which method of play affords White best prospects still remains quite open and the choice depends upon each player's own taste.

| 14 | . . . | QR–B1 |
| 15 | B–Kt1 | |

This is Geller's prepared variation. The usual continuations here are 15 B–Q3, or 15 R–K2, whereupon Black makes his pawn sacrifice as planned by 15 . . . P–Q4; 16 KPxP, P–K5, and when it is accepted he usually acquires a lasting initiative. A mistake, on the other hand, is 15 Kt–K3, which, in the game Boleslavsky–Keres, Budapest 1950, led to an overwhelming game for Black after 15 . . . KtxP!; 16 Kt–B5, QxB; 17 KtxBch, K–R1.

| 15 | . . . | P–Q4 |
| 16 | KPxP | PxP!? |

The idea of Geller's innovation appears in the other possible variation, viz. 16 . . . P–K5. White then intended to continue with 17 Kt–Kt5, thereby making use of the circumstance that his Bishop is no longer vulnerable to attack on Q3. Subsequent analysis has shown that Black in that event would also obtain strong counter-play in return for his pawn sacrifice by 17 . . . KR–Q1!; 18 KtxKP, KtxP; but it will be self-evident that I did not want to go in for a variation that had been thoroughly prepared by my opponent.

The idea bound up with the text-move—liquidation of the whole pawn centre—is very risky, as later analyses have demonstrated. The highly involved possibilities explored in subsequent analyses were not, however, so easy to foresee and work out over the board. The position in the game now becomes extremely complicated.

17 B–Kt5!   P–R3?

Though this move pertains to the method of development chosen by Black, it is tactically incorrect, since now White could have initiated an irresistible King-side attack by an interesting Bishop sacrifice. An immediate 17 . . . KtxP would not do because of 18 BxPch, which would have enabled White to gain a decisive attack after 18 . . . KxB; 19 BxB, KtxB; 20 Kt–Kt5ch, K–Kt3; 21 Kt–Kt3! However, in preparation for this capture 17 . . . KR–K1 was necessary, and with this move Black could have obtained a very satisfactory position.

18 B–R4?

Black (Keres) to play

White (Geller)

After this retreat the game returns to its normal course, one in which Black obtains a good, perhaps even somewhat better game. Later analysis has shown that White could have obtained an overwhelming attack here by the surprising Bishop sacrifice 18 BxP, PxB; 19 Q–Q2. As evidence of this consider the following variations:

1. 19 . . . BxP; 20 QxRP, BxKt; 21 Kt–Kt3! and the threat of 22 Kt–B5! ensures White a decisive advantage.

2. 19 . . . KR–Q1; 20 QxRP, RxP; 21 R–K4! (after 21 Kt–Kt3, B–B1!; 22 QxKt, B–Kt2; 23 Q–R4, P–Q6; Black has a good game) 21 . . . R–R4; 22 R–Kt4ch, KtxR; 23 QxR, Kt–KB3; 24 Q–Kt5ch, K–B1; 25 Q–R6ch, K–K1; 26 B–B5, with a winning attack.

3. 19 . . . K–Kt2; 20 Kt–Kt3, Kt–Kt1; 21 Kt–B5ch, K–R1; 22 RxB! and White wins.

From this it may be seen that after 18 BxP, Black can scarcely capture the Bishop and must seek a defence in 18 . . . KR–Q1. But this would hardly suffice for full equality. White could then play, for example, 19 B–Kt5, RxP; 20 Q–Q3, P–Kt3; 21 P–KR4! retaining excellent attacking prospects.

> 18 . . .   KtxP
> 19 Q–Q3

After some inaccuracies in the opening, an interesting middle-game has now been reached. White still thinks he stands better and continues his efforts to attack on the King-side. With the text-move he does, it is true, force the weakening move 19 . . . P–Kt3, but he can make no use of this weakness owing to his opponent's excellent development. It would have been better, therefore, to have given up all idea of gaining an advantage out of the opening and to have aimed at equality by 19 BxB, KtxB; 20 KtxP, KR–Q1; 21 Q–Kt4, etc.

> 19 . . .   P–Kt3
> 20 B–Kt3

White in fact experiences some difficulties in getting back his pawn. After 20 BxB, KtxB; Black has rather the better game after both 21 QxQP, BxKt; and 21 KtxP, KR–Q1; 22 Q–K3, Kt–QB5; 23 QxKt, RxKt.

| 20 | . . . | B—Q3 |
| 21 | BxB | |

An attempt at attack by 21 Kt–K5, is repulsed by 21 . . .
Kt–QB5!, since after 22 KtxKtP, PxKt, Black possesses adequate defensive resources: e.g. 23 QxPch, Q–Kt2; 24 Q–K6ch,
K–R1; 25 BxB, Kt–B5! or 23 R–K6, R–B3; 24 RxR, KtxR;
25 QxPch, Q–Kt2 etc.

| 21 | . . . | QxB |
| 22 | Q–Q2? | |

With the text-move Geller hopes to capture the KRP and
thereby still to obtain some attacking chances, but such tactics
are very risky in an undeveloped position. Here he should have
undoubtedly restored material equality by 22 QxQP, after
which Black's slightly better development would scarcely have
been sufficient to establish a real advantage.

| 22 | . . . | Kt–KB5! |

With this unexpected piece sacrifice Black seizes the initiative
and he obtains a decisive King-side attack after acceptance of
the sacrifice. White's pieces are poorly placed on the Queen's
wing, the Queen is quite out of play on QR5 and the Rook and
Knights are unable by themselves to provide an adequate
shield for the King. Furthermore, Black also gets two pawns
for the piece.

| 23 | QxKt(R5) |

Geller loves sharp and complicated positions and hence he
accepts his opponent's piece sacrifice without further ado.
Objectively better, however, was 23 B–K4! by which White
could at last bring into play his stalemated pieces on the
Queen's wing. Black can then maintain his extra pawn by
23 . . . Kt–B3, but must concede his adversary some counter-
play by 24 Kt–K5, KtxKt; 25 QxKt, P–Kt4, in view of his
somewhat weakened King-side.

However, after 23 B–K4, Black could also return his extra
pawn, for example by 23 . . . Kt–B5; 24 QxP, BxB; 25 RxB,
Kt–K3; or also by 23 . . . KR–K1; 24 BxB, KtxB; 25 KtxP,
RxR; 26 RxR, Kt–B4; in both cases with some slight positional

advantage. At any rate, it is quite clear that with 23 B–K4! instead of acceptance of the sacrifice White could have retained much better prospects in practice of a successful defence.

23	...	BxKt
24	PxB	KtxPch

After 24 ... Q–Q2; 25 Q–Q2, P–Kt4 White has an adequate defence in 26 R–K4.

Black (Keres)

White (Geller) to play

25 K–Kt2

Weaker here was 25 K–R1, since after 25 ... Q–B5! White has no satisfactory defence, e.g.:

1. 26 K–Kt2, Q–R5; 27 Q–Q2, (after 27 Kt–R2, Kt–B5ch; 28 K–R1, QxP wins, as also does 27 R–K4, QxPch followed by 28 ... QxKtch etc.) 27 ... Kt–B5ch; 28 K–Kt1, Q–Kt4ch; 29 Kt–Kt3, Kt–R6ch, winning the Queen.

2. 26 B–K4, KtxPch; 27 K–Kt1, (or 27 K–Kt2, KtxB; followed by 28 ... R–B7ch) 27 ... KtxB; 28 RxKt, QxP; with a won position for Black.

3. 26 Kt–R2, KtxPch; 27 K–Kt2, R–B4! with a winning attack. In addition, an immediate 26 ... R–B4 would be very strong.

25	...	Kt–B5ch
26	K–Kt1	Kt–R6ch
27	K–Kt2	Kt–B5ch

Black repeats a couple of moves in view of the approaching time trouble.

28	K–Kt1	Q–Q4
29	Kt–Kt3	

Simplest after 29 B–K4, is 29 . . . Q–R4! when White no longer has any defence against the threat of 30 . . . Q–R6 (30 Q–Q2, Q–Kt4ch!). Nor can he try 29 R–K4, on account of 29 . . . Q–Kt4ch; 30 Kt–Kt3, R–B8ch.

29 . . .   P–Q6!

White was hoping to put up further resistance after 29 . . . QxBP; 30 B–K4, but the text-move is much stronger. Now all White's Queen's wing is cut off from the centre of combat and two pieces alone are clearly insufficient to defend the King-side. The immediate threat is 30 . . . QxBP followed by mate.

30 Kt–K4   Q–KB4
31 Q–Kt4

A tougher resistance could have been put up here by 31 Q–Q2. Black would then have replied 31 . . . R–B5 with the threat of 32 . . . RxKt, whereupon the following possibilities could have occurred:

1. 32 BxP, R–Q1! (Not, however, 32 . . . RxKt; 33 RxR, Q–Kt4ch; 34 K–B1, Q–Kt7ch; 35 K–K1, when White has the resource of 36 B–B1!) 33 R–K3, RxKt; 34 PxR, Q–Kt4ch; 35 R–Kt3, Kt–R6ch winning the Queen.

2. 32 Q–K3, RxKt!; 33 PxR, Q–Kt5ch; 34 Q–Kt3, P–Q7!; 35 B–B2, PxR=Qch; 36 RxQ, Kt–K7ch; 37 RxKt, QxR, winning the exchange and with an easily won game.

3. 32 R–K3, Q–R6; followed by mate in a few moves.

31 . . .   KR–K1!

White resigns. The threat is 32 . . . RxKt against which there is no defence. If 32 BxP, there could follow 32 . . . RxKt! 33 RxR, Q–Kt4ch; 34 K–B1, Q–Kt7ch; with 35 . . . KtxBch; whilst after 32 Kt–Kt3, Q–R6 leads to mate.

Game 52

RETI OPENING

XIX U.S.S.R. Championship in Moscow, 1951

	V. Smyslov	P. Keres
1	P–QB4	Kt–KB3
2	P–KKt3	P–B3

The system of development with the fianchetto of both Bishops introduced by grandmaster Reti was very popular about 30 years ago. With this system White often obtained, almost without its being noticed, strong pressure on the enemy centre and this resulted in a positional advantage. Hence a number of masters applied themselves to the task of finding a thoroughly satisfactory set-up against the system. This was achieved first by Dr. Lasker in his celebrated game against Reti at the 1924 New York Tournament. In the present game Black employs the same system and demonstrates that it is still a good weapon, even today, against the once so dreaded Reti Opening.

3	Kt–KB3	P–Q4
4	P–Kt3	B–B4
5	B–QKt2	P–K3
6	B–Kt2	QKt–Q2
7	O–O	P–KR3
8	P–Q3	B–B4

In this position Black has at his disposal a whole series of different plans of development and it is not easy to say which of these is the best. In the game against Reti already mentioned Dr. Lasker refrained from P–KR3, developed his Bishop on Q3 and aimed at carrying out the central thrust P–K4. Others, again, hold that the development of the Bishop on K2 is better, so as to be able to attack the KP by Kt–B4 in the event of White's playing P–K4. And finally the text-move, at first glance somewhat strange looking, is also employed, after a P–K4 by White, so as to use the Bishop along the diagonal QR2–KKt8. In so playing Black does not fear the possible gain of a tempo by White with P–Q4 since this would yield his pieces the important square K5. White therefore rightly refrains from this possibility and prepares for P–K4.

9	Kt–B3	O–O
10	Q–B2	B–R2!

A useful retreat in anticipation of White's eventual P–K4. However, it was already essential to proceed with the utmost care so as to prevent his opponent from obtaining a lasting initiative. Thus, for example, after the natural move 10 . . . Q–K2 there could follow 11 P–K4, PxKP; 12 PxP, B–R2;

13 Q–K2! and White would gain an advantage by reason of the possibility of P–K5 followed by Kt–K4.

| 11 | P–K4 | PxKP |
| 12 | KtxP | |

Now 12 PxP would be met by the disagreeable 12 . . . P–QKt4! with troublesome pressure on White's KP. After the text-move Black is practically forced to exchange on K5, since after 12 . . . B–K2; 13 Q–K2, White threatens to gain an advantage in space in the centre by 14 KtxKtch, followed by 15 P–Q4.

12	. . .	KtxKt
13	PxKt	Kt–B3
14	Kt–K5	Q–Kt3

Black has emerged from the opening with a satisfactory game and now threatens to bring about further simplifications by 15 . . . B–Q5. Nor would 15 QR–Q1, QR–Q1 change the situation in any way. Therefore Smyslov decides upon a temporary pawn sacrifice so as to liven up the position a little.

15   Kt–Q3

At first glance White seems to obtain a clear advantage by this interesting pawn sacrifice, since now Black is practically forced to exchange off one of his two Bishops. But Black's pieces now take up very active positions so that the advantage of two Bishops is more than outweighed. All the same, no blame attaches to White for his plan of campaign, since in the first place it seems most enticing and in the second White can still maintain equality by careful play in the ensuing phase of the game.

15   . . .   KtxP!

Despite its apparently hazardous nature, this is the right reply. After 15 . . . B–Q5; 16 P–B5, Q–Q1; 17 KR–K1, followed by 18 QR–Q1, the White Knight will sooner or later attain the square Q6, which would signify an advantage that should not be underestimated.

16	KtxB	KtxKt
17	Q–B3	P–B3
18	Q–K3!	

Now the idea behind the pawn sacrifice becomes apparent. The two threats of 19 B–Q4 and 19 B–QR3 can no longer be both thwarted and hence Black must give back the pawn. If however, White was expecting to obtain an advantage then a bitter disappointment now awaits him.

18 ...   Kt–Q6!

Naturally not 18 ... Kt–K5?; 19 BxKt, QxQ; because of the intervening 20 BxBch. With the text-move an immediate capture on Black's K3 is forced, since 19 B–Q4 is met by 19 ... P–QB4.

19	QxPch	K–R1
20	B–QB3	KR–K1
21	Q–Kt4	QR–Q1

Now we can sum up the results obtained by the combination that started with Black's 15th move. We see that Black's pieces are excellently developed and that they control a large part of the board, whilst White's two Bishops possess a purely academic value. The even balance of the position is, however, not yet significantly disturbed. But it is White who, in the ensuing part of the game, must play most accurately in order not to get the worse of it.

22   Q–R5

Instead of this 22 QR–Q1 was simpler so as to meet 22 ... Kt–K4 with 23 Q–B4. The threat of 23 B–R5 is easily parried.

22	...	Kt–K4
23	QR–Q1	B–Kt3
24	Q–R4	RxR

Before he brings his Knight back to Q6 Black tries to weaken White's hold on the back rank and combines this aim with a simultaneous attack on KB7. If at once 24 ... Kt–Q6 then White has an adequate defence in 25 R–Q2.

25   RxR   Kt–Q6!

The Knight returns with gain of tempo to its dominating square on Q6 and at the same time it ensures control of the King file for the Black Rook. White's situation is now precarious indeed.

26   B–Q4?

This move, with which White hoped to gain time for further defensive measures through the threat of 27 BxKBP, must in fact be regarded as a decisive error. Had Smyslov realised in

time the perils that were threatening then he would certainly
have aimed at further simplification by 26 Q–Q4. Then Black
would have avoided the Queen exchange himself and the ending should in all probability be drawn.

26 . . .   Q–R4!

Probably here White had hoped for 26 . . . P–QB4; 27 B–K3,
which would have meant a valuable gain of time because of
the threat of 28 BxRP. The reply that Black selects is, however,
much stronger since in the first place 27 . . . R–K8ch is now
threatened and in the second Black can now in many variations simply capture on QR7, for example, after 27 B–K3.
White can no longer fend off this threat.

In making this move Black has only to work out exactly the
consequences of the sacrifice 27 BxKBP. They are, in fact,
innocuous for Black. After 27 . . . R–K8ch; 28 B–B1, K–R2!;
29 RxR, KtxR; White would lose a piece because of the threat
of 30 . . . Kt–B6ch. The couple of pawns he gets in return
should scarcely save him from defeat in the ending.

27 P–KR3

White, convinced that he can no longer avoid loss of material,
employs the text-move in order to give his King a necessary
flight square. He hopes after 27 . . . QxP to obtain some
counter-play by 28 Q–Kt4, and after 28 . . . QxP he can even
make the exchange sacrifice 29 QxB. Black therefore decides
to strengthen his position still further, being assured that his
opponent can undertake nothing active in the meanwhile.

27 . . .   K–R2
28 B–KB3   Kt–K8!

Here too the capture 28 . . . QxP was not advisable as White
would get dangerous counter-play by 29 B–R5! With the text-
move Black makes use of the fact that his Queen is attacking
the KR4 square in order to force the enemy Bishop into a
corner. The continuation 29 Q–B4, KtxBch; 30 QxKt, R–K8
ch; 31 K–R2, B–K5; 32 Q–Kt4, P–R4 would lead to an
immediate loss for White.

29 B–KR1   Kt–B7

Naturally Black does not waste his time working out the
possible complications after 29 . . . QxP; 30 BxKBP. With the

text-move 30 BxKBP is again prevented because of 30 . . . R–K8ch.

30   B–KB3?

Both players were already in time trouble and they now commit some inaccuracies. White should have tried here 30 Q–B4, in order to bring his Queen into play. Black would then reply neither 30 . . . R–Q1; 31 B–K4, nor 30 . . . P–QB4; 31 B–QKt2, QxP; 32 BxKBP! when White has good defensive chances, but he should content himself with the assurance of a solid plus pawn by 30 . . . KtxB; 31 QxKt, QxP. After the text-move White's position should rapidly collapse.

Black (Keres) to play

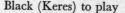

White (Smyslov)

30   . . .   R–K8ch

Here he could have won by 30 . . . P–QB4! with the following possible lines:

1. 31 BxBP, R–K8ch; 32 K–R2, (or 32 K–Kt2, Kt–K6ch!) 32 . . . RxR; 33 BxR (after 33 BxKKtP, Black wins by 33 . . . Q–Q7!) 33 . . . Q–Q7 and wins.

2. 31 B–QKt2, R–K8ch; 32 RxR, (or 32 K–Kt2, RxR; 33 BxR, Kt–K6ch; 34 PxKt, Q–Q7ch) 32 . . . QxRch; 33 K–Kt2, and now the simplest method of winning is by 33 . . . B–Q6; 34 P–KKt4, Kt–K6ch; 35 K–R2, P–KKt4.

3. 31 B–K3, KtxB; 32 PxKt, RxP with a won position for Black.

But the text-move is also not bad and should win easily enough.

31   RxR

After either 31 K–Kt2, or 31 K–R2, Black can transpose into the winning line given in the previous note by 31 ... P–QB4.

31	...	QxRch
32	K–R2	

White loses a piece after 32 K–Kt2, Q–Q7! owing to the double threat of 33 ... Kt–K8ch and 33 ... KtxB.

32	...	P–Kt3?

Black, in time trouble, considers only coming down to a Bishop ending favourable for him and overlooks the immediate win by 32 ... P–QB4!; 33 BxBP, P–Kt3; 34 B–Q4, Q–Q7, when White must give up at least a piece. With the text-move he follows the same idea (33 BxQBP?, Q–Q7!) but in a much weaker form.

33	Q–B4!	

Naturally White takes advantage of the chance of bringing his Queen into play. Now Black has nothing better than the transition to the ensuing Bishop ending. This, however, contains a number of instructive moments.

33	...	P–QB4
34	B–K3	KtxB
35	QxKt	QxQ
36	PxQ	

Black, despite his time trouble, had aimed at this position and adjudged the ending to be very favourable for him—and with good reason. Black possesses here a number of advantages which, taken together, render the ending hopeless for White. In the first place, White's pawns on the Queen's wing are on the same colour squares as his Bishop and in consequence of this White must either soon surrender one of the pawns or else place his Bishop in a totally passive defensive position. In the second place, Black has the strong central square of K4 for his King, from which point, after having played P–B4–B5, it threatens to penetrate into White's camp through either Q5 or KB5. And, finally, Black's King gets to the centre more quickly than White's, thereby enabling him to carry out his plans undisturbed. The ensuing part of the game gives a quite instructive example of how such endings should be conducted.

36	...	B–Kt8
37	P–R3	P–QR4!

Preventing the possibility of P–QKt4 and hence fixing the weaknesses on QKt6 and QB5 which require continual protection by the Bishop. Now the chief threat is 37 . . . B–B7.

38	B–Q1	K–Kt3
39	K–Kt2	K–B4
40	K–B3	K–K4

In this position the game was adjourned and White sealed his move. Adjournment analysis showed very clearly the hopelessness of his position. Moreover, Black's winning idea is quite simple and is based chiefly on zugzwang. Obviously White cannot move his Bishop because of the loss of a pawn after B–B7 and hence he can make only King moves. However, against totally passive play Black proceeds with P–KKt4 followed by P–B4 and P–B5. And then White is forced either to give up a pawn or else to allow the enemy King to penetrate his position via Q5 or KB4 which in turn would lead to inevitable loss of material.

Once we are aware of the winning plan the rest of the game presents no difficulties.

41   P–QR4

Preventing B–Q6 followed by P–R5, but this has no particular affect on the course of the game.

| 41 | . . . | P–KKt4 |
| 42 | K–K2 | B–B4 |

Black could also of course have continued with 42 . . . P–B4 in accordance with his original plan, but he takes advantage of the opportunity of forcing the enemy pawns on the King's wing onto the colour of the Bishop. The endgame after 43 P–R4, B–Kt5ch would naturally be hopeless.

43	P–KKt4	B–Kt8
44	K–B3	P–B4
45	PxP	

Omitting to make this exchange would result in an even speedier loss; e.g. 45 K–K2, P–B5; 46 K–B3, PxP; 47 KxP, B–K5 and White is in complete zugzwang.

| 45 | . . . | KxP |
| 46 | K–B2 | B–K5 |

46 . . . K–K5 leads to nothing because of the reply 47 B–R5.

With the text-move Black deprives his opponent's King of the
KB3 square and prepares to play 47 . . . K–Kt3 and 48 . . .
P–R4.

47	K–Kt3	K–Kt3
48	K–B2	

After 49 P–R4, P–R4!; 50 K–R3, B–Q6; 51 K–Kt3, B–B4!
White would again be in zugzwang and would have to exchange
on KKt5, after which, however, the passed pawn on the KR
file ensures Black an easy win. But now that a fresh weakness
is fixed on White's KR3 the win becomes very easy.

48	. . .	P–R4
49	K–Kt3	P–R5ch
50	K–B2	B–B4
51	K–Kt2	K–B3

Now, sooner or later, the break-through by the King in the
centre will be decisive since White's King is tethered to the
protection of KR3.

52	K–R2	K–K3!

The last finesse. After the forced line 53 K–Kt2, K–K4;
54 K–R2, there would follow 54 . . . B–Kt8!; 55 K–Kt2,
K–K5; 56 K–B2; K–Q6, winning off-hand.

So White resigns.

Game 53

QUEEN'S PAWN OPENING

XIX U.S.S.R. Championship, Moscow, 1951

	P. Keres	M. Taimanov
1	P–QB4	Kt–KB3
2	Kt–KB3	P–K3
3	Kt–B3	P–Q4
4	P–K3	

This game was played in the last round. In order to win
first prize I had to go all out for a victory as my nearest rivals
were only half a point behind me. The somewhat peculiar
choice of opening is due to the fact that I wanted to avoid the
Nimzoindian and Queen's Indian Defences which Taimanov
likes to play and in the systems of which he is a known expert.

4	...	B–K2
5	P–QKt3	O–O
6	B–Kt2	P–QKt3

After an immediate 6 ... P–B4 White could also continue with 7 P–Q4, since Black can in no way utilise White's delay in development on the King's wing for a counter-attack on that side of the board.

7	P–Q4	B–Kt2
8	B–Q3	PxP

In making this exchange Black aims at giving his opponent hanging pawns on Q4 and QB4 so as to make use of them as objects of attack. Praxis has, however, shown that such pawns can very often become really strong, especially in conjunction with the threat of P–Q5. So it has already become apparent that in all probability a tense middle-game will arise, and this in fact is very much what I desired in such a vital game.

9	PxP	P–B4
10	O–O	PxP

Black must make this exchange at once, since, for example, after 10 ... Kt–B3, White can gain the advantage by 11 P–Q5, Kt–QKt5; 12 P–K4.

11	PxP	Kt–B3
12	Q–K2	

With this move white sets his opponent an interesting trap. If now 12 ... KtxP? then 13 KtxKt, QxKt; 14 Kt–Q5! and White wins a piece, e.g. 14 ... Q–B4; 15 BxKt, PxB; (or 15 ... BxB; 16 Q–K4) 16 Q–Kt4ch, K–R1; 17 Q–R4 etc.

All the same, the move 12 Q–K2, cannot here be regarded as best since it allows Black a most troublesome attack on White's centre. Better in any case was 12 R–B1, so as to anticipate the threat of Kt–QKt5.

12	...	R–K1

Black makes this preventive move so as to render an eventual P–Q5 innocuous. But in so doing he gives his opponent time to get his Rooks into play, after which the middle-game is clearly better for White. Hence Black should at once embark on an action against the enemy centre and for this purpose 12 ... Kt–QKt5 was in order.

I naturally took this possibility into consideration during the game and intended replying 13 B–Kt1. My further calculation of this variation ran as follows: 13 . . . BxKt; 14 QxB, QxP; 15 P–QR3, Kt–R3; 16 Q–Kt7, and Black loses a piece. Apparently everything is in apple-pie order but unfortunately there is a hole in the analysis. It turns out that Black can quietly give up a piece by 16 . . . B–Q3, since after 17 QxKt, BxPch he obtains an attack at least good enough for a draw.

White must therefore find another reply to 12 . . . Kt–QKt5. One possibility is 13 B–Kt1, BxKt; 14 PxB, QxP; 15 Kt–K4, with very good attacking chances in return for the pawn he has lost. And secondly White can simply continue with 13 KR–Q1, KtxB; 14 RxKt, when it is true White has given up his strong Bishop, but in return for this he is ahead in development and is threatening such attacking moves as P–Q5 or Kt–K5.

13	KR–Q1	R–QB1
14	QR–B1	Q–Q3

Now that White has completed his development Black experiences difficulties in finding active counter-play. With the text-move he aims at getting his Queen to KB5 so as to threaten later on Kt–KKt5 and Kt–QKt5, but this plan is never realised. Not particularly better is the idea of 14 . . . B–Q3, since White could then reply 15 Kt–K4, KtxKt; 16 BxKt, when, apart from anything else, Black must reckon with White's eventual King-side attack.

Very interesting complications arise from 14 . . . Kt–QKt5; 15 B–Kt1, BxKt. Naturally, White can simply recapture with 16 PxKt, but very interesting also is the pawn sacrifice 16 QxB, RxP; 17 P–Q5!. After 17 . . . KPxP; 18 P–QR3, Kt–B3; 19 B–R2, followed by 20 KtxP, White gets an excellent attacking position.

We see then that Black has not been able to obtain full equality out of the opening. This means that White's hanging pawns are not a weakness, but, on the contrary, constitute a potential attacking force which Black must always keep in mind.

15	B–Kt1	Q–B5

With this Black has carried out his plan but White too has

been allowed time in which to initiate a decisive action. The position now becomes very complicated.

16   P–Q5!

A break-through typical of such positions which is carried out here despite the hidden threat on the White Queen by the Black Rook. It is on this break-through that the whole problem of the position usually turns and when White succeeds in executing it he usually obtains the upper hand.

16 . . .   PxP

Black (Taimanov)

White (Keres) to play

17   PxP

White used up a considerable amount of time on the clock here in working out the possible consequences of 17 KtxP. Since 17 . . . Q–R3; 18 R–K1, would ensure White the better position even without any sacrifice then the reply 17 . . . KtxKt; 18 PxKt, B–B3 is practically forced.

During the game I came to the conclusion that an attempt at attack by 19 Q–B2, BxB; 20 PxKt, would be unsatisfactory. Black can then calmly reply 20 . . . BxR!; 21 QxPch, K–B1, after which there is no good continuation, e.g.: 22 PxB, QR–Q1; or 22 R–Q7, Q–R3; or, finally, 22 Q–R8ch, K–K2; 23 R–Q7ch, (also 23 QxP, RxP; or 23 R–K1ch, K–Q3 lead to nothing) 23 . . . K–B3; 24 Q–R5, P–Kt3 and in every case Black beats back the enemy attack.

I also considered for a long time the Queen sacrifice 19 PxKt!, RxQ; 20 PxB. But I could not work out to the end the extremely complicated variations possible and so I eventually plumped for the simple text-move. And that all the more because White now obtains much the better game. Nevertheless, it is still interesting to investigate the eventual results of the Queen sacrifice. We would like therefore to analyse the position a little more closely and look at the various possible lines for Black one by one:

1. 20 ... RxR; 21 RxR, B–Q1; (or 21 ... R–K1; 22 R–B8, Q–QR5; 23 P–Kt3, Q–Q2; 25 B–B5 and White wins) 22 R–B8, Q–Q3; 23 P–Kt3, RxB; 24 B–K4, and White wins.

2. 20 ... R(B1)–K1; 21 BxB, (but not 21 ... R–B8?, BxB; 22 R(Q1)–Q8, when Black has the saving resource of 22 ... Q–B8ch; 23 RxQ, RxR; 24 R–B8, R(K7)–K1) 21 ... PxB; (after 21 ... QxB White wins by 22 R–B8, Q–K3; 23 R(Q1)–QB1, and 21 ... Q–Kt1 allows the strong reply 22 Kt–Q4!) 22 R–B8, K–Kt2; 23 P–Kt8=Q, (but not 23 R(Q1)–KB1, because of the reply 23 ... Q–Q5!) 23 ... QxQ; 24 RxQ, RxR; 25 P–Kt3, and the endgame is won for White.

3. 20 ... R–QKt1; 21 B–K5!, RxB; 22 KtxR, P–Kt3; (nor would 22 ... QxKt be of any use because of 23 R–B8ch, Q–K1; 24 R(Q1)–QB1, when 24 ... B–K4; 25 RxQch, RxR; 26 R–K1, leads to a lost endgame for Black) 23 Kt–Q7, (Black would have dangerous counter-play after 23 R–B8ch, K–Kt2; 24 RxR, BxKt); 23 ... RxP; 24 P–Kt3!, and Black must give up his Bishop (24 ... Q–B6; 25 B–K4!).

4. 20 ... R–B1; 21 B–R3, (naturally not 21 R–B8?, because of 21 ... RxB! and also after 21 BxB, QxB; 22 R–B8, R(K7)–K1; 23 P–Kt8=Q, RxR; 24 QxRP, Q–Kt7, or 23 R(Q1)–QB1, Q–K3, Black would still have very good chances of saving the game) 21 ... B–K2; 22 BxB, (after 22 R–B8, BxB; 23 R(Q1)–Q8, there would again come 23 ... Q–B8ch!) 23 ... RxB; 24 R–B8, P–Kt3; (or 24 ... RxP; 25 R(Q1)–Q8) 24 P–Kt8=Q, QxQ; 25 RxQ, RxR, when White's advantage in the endgame is not necessarily sufficient for the win.

Summing all this up then we can claim that after 17 KtxP, too, White could assure himself a considerable advantage, though not a direct win. Taking also into account that in the working out of these complicated variations over the board mistakes may be very easily made, then one must regard the capture 17 PxP, as being the most logical in practice.

17 ...   Kt–Kt1

After 17 ... Kt–QR4; 18 R–Q4, Q–Q3; 19 Q–Q3, the Knight would be badly placed on QR4.

18 R–Q4   Q–Q3
19 R(B1)–Q1   B–B1?

In a difficult position Black makes a mistake that allows his opponent a decisive King-side attack. Here he should have brought his QKt into play as quickly as possible by 19 ... QKt–Q2, although even then White would have retained some most dangerous threats as, for example, after 20 Kt–KKt5.

20 Kt–K4!

Taimanov had apparently underestimated the force of this Knight move. After the exchange of the KKt the Black King has no pieces to protect it and falls victim to a concentrated attack by enemy forces against which no adequate defence can be found.

20 ...   KtxKt

20 ... Q–Q1; 21 KtxKtch, QxKt; 22 R–K4, also leads to a position resembling that in the game.

21 RxKt   RxR
22 QxR   Q–R3

Rather better defensive chances were afforded here by 22 ... P–Kt3. After 23 Q–Q4, P–B3; 24 Kt–Kt5?, Black would have the saving tactical resource of 23 ... QxP! But by 24 P–KR4, Kt–Q2; 25 P–R5, White would obtain here too a strong attack.

Another strong attacking line for White after 22 ... P–Kt3 is 23 Kt–Kt5, B–Kt2; 24 Q–KR4. Now 24 ... P–KR3 fails against 25 BxB, KxB; 26 QxPch!, and after 24 ... P–KR4; 25 Kt–K4, Q–Q1; 26 Kt–B6ch, K–R1, the attack would become really powerful with 27 B–B5!, R–B4; 28 Q–Kt5, threatening 29 BxP.

23 Kt–Kt5!   B–Q3

Naturally not 23 ... P–Kt3 because of 24 KtxBP. With the text-move Black offers up his KRP so as to break the force of the enemy attack, but of course White is not satisfied with so little and much prefers to proceed with his attack.

24	P–KR4!	Kt–Q2
25	Q–B5	Kt–B3
26	BxKt	

Both players are now rather tired by the tension of this vital encounter and also by the difficult middle-game, so that now that they are getting into time trouble they play a little imprecisely. Instead of giving up his strong Bishop and yielding his opponent counter-chances on the eighth rank, White could have won more quickly and surely by 26 KtxBP!, KxKt; 27 Q–K6ch, K–B1; 28 QxBch, K–Kt1; 29 Q–K6ch, K–R1; 30 P–Q6, etc.

26 ...   PxB

After 26 ... QxB; 27 QxPch, K–B1; I intended continuing the attack as follows: 28 R–K1! (after 28 Kt–K4, Black can still defend himself by 28 ... Q–Q5!) 28 ... P–Kt3; (also 28 ... B–K4; 29 Kt–B3, or 28 ... Q–R3; 29 Q–B5, would lose immediately) 29 KtxP!, (or 29 BxP, BxP; 30 KtxP!, and wins) when White's attack is a winning one.

For example, after 29 ... QxKt White wins by 30 Q–R8ch, Q–Kt1; 31 Q–B6ch, Q–B2; 32 QxBch, whilst 29 ... R–B2 allows, in addition to 30 BxP, the combinational solution of 30 R–K8ch!, KxR; 31 KtxBch, QxKt; (31 ... K–Q1; 32 QxRch!) 32 BxPch, when, in order to avoid mate, Black must surrender his Queen.

27 KtxBP   Q–B8

But now Black fails to see the much better defensive chance of 27 ... KxKt!, which, especially in view of the time pressure, would have posed his opponent some really awkward problems. White could still then force the win as follows: 28 Q–Q7ch, K–Kt1; (or 28 ... B–K2; 29 P–Q6, R–B8; 30 QxBch, K–Kt1; 31 QxPch!) 29 QxKB, R–B8; 30 Q–Kt8ch, B–B1; 31 RxR, QxRch; 32 K–R2, QxB; 33 QxBch, K–B2; 34 P–Q6, and Black cannot stop the further progress of the pawn.

28 QxPch

I was deeply engaged in analysing the variations arising out of 27 ... KxKt when Taimanov suddenly made the move 27 ... Q–B8. Time pressure did not allow me to spend much time considering the fresh position since otherwise I could scarcely have failed to see the simple win by 28 KtxB!, QxRch; 29 K–R2. Black would then lose quickly, both after 29 . . . QxP; 30 QxQ, BxQ; 31 KtxR, and after 29 . . . R–B2; 30 Q–K6ch, etc.

The ensuing moves were made by both sides at lightning speed.

28	. . .	K–B1
29	KtxB	

After 29 Q–R5, Black could try 29 . . . B–B5, threatning simplification by 30 . . . QxRch. And then he could still have put up a stubborn resistance.

29	. . .	QxRch
30	K–R2	QxP
31	KtxB	

Simpler than 31 Q–R8ch, K–K2; 32 KtxRch, K–Q2; when Black wins the Knight. After the text-move Black's threats are insufficient to provide him with adequate counter-play.

31	. . .	Q–K4ch
32	P–Kt3	R–B2

The counter-attack 32 . . . Q–K8, would be best met by 33 Q–B5, R–B8; 34 B–K4, but also 33 Q–R8ch, K–K2; 34 QxR, is naturally enough to win.

33	Q–R8ch	K–B2
34	P–R5	RxKt

Black no longer has any defence against the threat of 35 B–Kt6ch.

35	Q–R7ch	K–K3
36	QxR	QxRPch
37	K–Kt2	resigns.

LIST OF EVENTS

Below we list every event in which Keres took part in the middle years of his career. The reader will find the year, the place, the result, the number of games played, how many were won, how many lost and how many drawn and the number of points obtained (in that order across the page).

Tournaments

Year	Place	Result				
1939	Leningrad–Moscow	XII–XIII	17	3	4	10	8
1939	Margate	I	9	6	0	3	7½
1939	Buenos Aires	II	19	12	2	5	14½
1939	Buenos Aires	I–II	11	7	1	3	8½
1940	Moscow	IV	11	9	4	6	12
1941	Leningrad–Moscow	II	20	6	4	10	11
1942	Tallinn	I	15	15	0	0	15
1942	Salzburg	II	10	4	2	4	6
1942	Munich	II	11	6	2	3	7½
1943	Tallinn	I	11	6	1	4	8
1943	Prague	II	19	11	1	7	14½
1943	Poznan	I	5	5	0	0	5
1943	Salzburg	I–II	10	5	0	5	7½
1943	Madrid	I	14	12	0	2	13
1944	Lidköping	II	7	4	2	1	4½
1945	Riga	I	11	10	0	1	10½
1945	Tallinn	I	15	11	0	4	13
1946	Tiflis	I	19	17	0	2	18
1947	Leningrad	I	19	10	1	8	14
1947	Pärnu	I	13	7	1	5	9½
1947	Moscow	VI–VII	15	6	3	6	9
1948	Hague–Moscow	III–IV	20	8	7	5	10½
1948	Moscow	VI–IX	18	5	4	9	9½
1949	Moscow	VIII	19	7	4	8	11
1950	Budapest	IV	18	3	2	13	9½
1950	Sczawno Zdroj	I	19	11	1	7	14½
1950	Moscow	I	17	8	2	7	11½
1951	Moscow	I	17	9	2	6	12
			409	223	50	144	

Matches

Year	Place					
1940	M. Euwe	14	6	5	3	7½
1944	F. Ekström	6	4	0	2	5
		20	10	5	5	

Other Events

1939	Estonia–Latvia (Petrov)	2	2	0	0	2
1939	Estonia–Lithuania (Mikenas)	2	0	0	2	1
1940	Estonia–Lithuania (Mikenas)	2	0	0	2	1
1940	Tallin Team Matches	4	4	0	0	4
1940	Tartu Student Matches	5	5	0	0	5
1940	Tallinn–Provinces (Friedemann)	1	0	0	1	½
1944	Tallinn–Nõmme (Arulaid)	1	1	0	0	1
1945	Club match (Solmanis)	2	2	0	0	2
1945	Tallinn–Riga (Koblencs)	2	2	0	0	2
1945	Club match (Beilin)	2	1	0	1	1½
1946	U.S.S.R.–Great Britain (Klein)	2	1	0	1	1½
1946	U.S.S.R.–U.S.A. (Fine)	2	1	0	1	1½
1947	Estonia–Latvia (Koblencs)	2	2	0	0	2
1947	Club Match against Riga	2	2	0	0	2
1947	U.S.S.R.–Great Britain (Alexander)	2	1	0	1	2
1951	Kiev Team Matches	3	1	0	2	2
		38	25	0	11	

OPENINGS INDEX

(The numbers are those of the games)

LIST OF OPPONENTS

(The numbers are those of the games)

THE LATER YEARS
OF PAUL KERES

TRANSLATOR'S PREFACE

IN THIS, the last volume of Keres's games, we get the final maturity of his style. Here we have the grandmaster in the complete and absolute form. The depth of strategy evident in his middle years is even more profound and the end-games are of the finest subtlety. But, and this is what is so striking about the later games of Keres, the brilliance of the early years is not lost; it is still there and is merely refined to the purest gold.

His tournament career continues to be successful, though not perhaps quite so consistently as in his middle years, with the important exception of the Candidates' Tournament in which, time and again, he seems on the point of qualifying to become the challenger for the world championship, only to have the cup dashed from his lips at the last moment. Possibly at this stage in his career he does not possess quite sufficient stamina for the task or else it may be that the full ambition is not wholly there.

Again, as in the previous volumes, his remarkably deep and exhaustive analyses gives one an insight into the way a real grandmaster's mind works. Nothing is more revealing of the gap that exists between the genuine grandmaster and those who have acquired the title by the application of fortuitous and arbitrary rules than the games and the comments to them that appear in this volume. These games are on the same level as those of the best of the great players of the past, as those of Lasker, Alekhine, Capablanca, Rubinstein and Nimzowitsch.

The games in this volume are numbered in succession to those of volume two and hence start with number 54.

H. GOLOMBEK

BUDAPEST 1952—
A GREAT TOURNAMENT

IN the Spring of 1952 I took part in the Maroczy Memorial Tournament, an event which comprised a remarkably strong entry. In addition to the World Champion, Botvinnik, there were also playing, Geller, Petrosian, Smyslov, Stahlberg, Szabo, and Pilnik, amongst others. This tournament turned out to be a successful one for me, and that not only in the purely sporting aspect. I was also able to produce there a series of excellent artistic achievements, as for example the games against Smyslov (No. 1), Geller (No. 2), Barcza (No. 3) and Pilnik. Geller, too, was in fine form. He began with a run of fine victories and after the thirteenth round he was in the lead with 10 points. Close after him there followed the Swedish grandmaster, Stahlberg, who was also in excellent form, with $9\frac{1}{2}$ points. I came next with 9 and Botvinnik had $8\frac{1}{2}$ points. The decision was to be worked out in the last four rounds.

No clear picture of the winner was produced by the next three rounds. Geller made three quiet draws; Botvinnik did likewise and Stahlberg too obtained only $1\frac{1}{2}$ points, losing, incidentally, to Szabo. My final spurt was happier. I won against O'Kelly and Troianescu and drew with Botvinnik, and so I succeeded in overhauling Geller. Half a point behind was Stahlberg and a whole point below him, Botvinnik and Smyslov.

Once again I had to play the deciding game in the last round, and here there came to my mind the good lessons that I had learnt in this respect in the last two U.S.S.R. Championships. I played my game against Barcza in quiet style and, managing to seize the initiative during the opening phase, I was able to convert this into a win by logical play. Geller could only draw with O'Kelly, whilst Stahlberg even suffered a defeat at Benko's hands. Thus I came first alone, crowning

the fine achievement of winning first prize in four great and
strong international tournaments in a couple of years.

Game 54

QUEEN'S GAMBIT ACCEPTED

Maroczy Memorial Tournament in Budapest, 1952

	P. Keres	V. Smyslov
1	P–Q4	P–Q4
2	P–QB4	PxP

Usually Smyslov favours various branches of the Slav and
Grunfeld Defences and one very seldom sees him play the
Q.G.A. In the present game he apparently wishes to repeat the
sharp variation that he employed in his game against Petrosian
in the XVIIIth U.S.S.R. Championship and in which he
probably had found some important improvements. Hence
White, with his very next move, tries to steer the game along
new lines.

3	P–K3	Kt–KB3

According to theory, the simplest reply here is 3. . . P–K4.
But, as already mentioned, Smyslov is aiming at one particular
variation and therefore avoids all by-ways.

4	BxP	P–K3
5	Kt–KB3	P–B4
6	O–O	P–QR3
7	Q–K2	P–QKt4
8	B–Q3	

At the time this game was played the variation in fashion
was 8 B–Kt3, B–Kt2; 9 P–QR4, QKt–Q2, followed by the
risky pawn sacrifice 10 P–K4. In the game previously mentioned
between Petrosian and Smyslov there now followed 10 . . .
BPxP; 11 P–K5 (after 11 PxP, Kt–B4; 12 B–QB4, P–Q6;
13 Q–K3, which occurred in the game Kotov–Flohr, Budapest
1950, Black could have obtained an excellent game with 13
. . . P–QR4!) 11 . . . Kt–Kt5; 12 PxP, B–B4?; 13 PxP, and
White had the advantage. However, subsequent analysis

convinced Smyslov that Black's play could be bettered. Thus, for instance, 11 ... Kt–Q4; 12 PxP, P–Q6!; 13 QxP, Kt–B4, when Black stands very well and possibly even rather better than White.

White, taking this factor into consideration, selects with his text-move another method of play in order to divert his opponent from prepared variations. As the sequel shows, White soon achieves some success with these tactics.

8 ... Kt–B3

This move does not fit in well with the system of development chosen by Black and it sows the seeds of his later difficulties. Better here was 8 ... PxP; 9 PxP, B–Kt2, so as to develop the QKt eventually on Q2 as occurred in the game Barcza–Keres (No. 3) in the final round of the same tournament.

9 P–QR4

Another good continuation here was 9 PxP, BxP; 10 P–QR3, which would have led to a symmetrical position, but with White having an extra tempo. However, the text-move also poses the opponent an awkward problem.

9 ... P–Kt5

Praxis has shown that the Queen-side advance by 9 ... P–B5; yields White the better position after 10 B–B2, B–Kt2; 11 Kt–B3. In addition to the threats on the Queen-side Black must in this case also reckon with the thrust, sooner or later, of P–K4. Not altogether satisfactory, too, is the capture 9 ... Kt P, after which, in addition to 10 Kt–B3, White has the unpleasant reply of 10 B–B2. But after the text-move the QB5 square is markedly weak, of which circumstance White can later make use for an attack on the Queen's wing.

10 PxP

In this position White has to decide at once which further plan of play he is going to choose. With the continuation of the game he is trying for P–K4 and hence he leaves his KR where it is so as to protect the squares KB1 and KB2. Another attractive possibility here was 10 R–Q1, omitting the capture on QB5 and bearing in mind the manoeuvre Kt (Kt 1)–Q2–B4. Finally, there also came into consideration the pawn sacrifice 10 QKt–Q2, acceptance of which by 10 . . . PxP; 11 PxP, KtxP; 12 KtxKt, QxKt would leave White with a most dangerous initiative after 13 R–Q1, or 13 Kt–B4. Clearly White has emerged from the opening with the better game.

10	. . .	BxP
11	P–K4	P–K4

Obviously, Black dare not allow the thrust 12 P–K5. Once the pawn position in the centre is fixed, White focuses the struggle on the Queen's wing and tries to exploit the weaknesses there. First of all, the black squared Bishops must be exchanged in order to obtain control of the QB5 square.

12	B–K3!	BxB

Occupation of Q 5 by 12 . . . Kt–Q 5; 13 KtxKt, BxKt, does not yield the desired result. White simply continues with 14 Kt–Q2! and after 14 . . . BxP; 15 QR–Kt1, B–B6; 16 Kt–B4, he gets a dangerous attack in return for his pawn sacrifice.

13	QxB	O–O
14	QKt–Q2	Kt–KR4

The attempt at counter-play on the King's wing brings Black no noticeable relief and leads only to further exchanges at the cost of some loss of tempi. But it is difficult to find any suitable plan for Black. After 14 . . . Q–K2; 15 QR–B1, B–Kt2; 16 Kt–Kt3, White would also retain the better game through his pressure on the Queen's wing. It is not easy for Black to rid himself of the consequences of his inferior opening variation.

15	Kt–B4

Naturally also possible was an immediate 15 KR–Q1, so as to retain the Bishop after 15 . . . Kt–B5; 16 B–B1. But White does not in fact wish to prevent the ensuing exchange, since this merely increases the scope for action of his pieces.

15	. . .	Kt–B5
16	KR–Q1!	

Of course not 16 Kt (B4)xP?, KtxKt; 17 KtxKt, Q–Kt4, when Black wins a piece. After the text-move Black is practically forced to exchange off on Q6, since after 16 . . . Q–B3; 17

B–B1, Black's "attack" would be at an end and he would have to fend off the troublesome threat of 18 R–Q6.

16 . . .   KtxB

After 16 . . . B–Kt5, White could already pocket the pawn by 17 Kt (B4)xP!, KtxKt; 18 QxKt, BxKt; 19 B–K2! etc.

17   RxKt   Q–K2
18   Kt–Kt6   R–Kt1
19   R–QB1   Q–Kt2

Naturally not 19 . . . B–Kt2 because of 20 Kt–Q7, but with the text-move too Black cannot assure a harmonious development for his pieces.

20   Kt–Q5   B–Q2

White was threatening 21 RxKt.

21   Kt–Q2!

With this White transfers his last remaining piece from the edge of the board to the chief centre of combat and already he threatens to play Kt–B6 ch.

21 . . .   K–R1

After 21 . . . P–B3 the continuation 22 Kt–B4 is very strong.

22   Kt–Kt3

Here too 22 Kt–B4 would have been very troublesome for Black and, setting up the threat of 23 Kt–B5, it is perhaps even stronger than the text-move. If for example 22 . . . B–K3, then 23 Kt–Q6, Q–Q2; 24 Kt–Kt6!, Q–B2; 25 P–R5 and wins since Black has no adequate defence against the threat of 26 Q–B5. However, the text-move also suffices to ensure White a clear advantage.

22 . . .   KR–B1!
23   Kt–Kt6!

With his last move Black had set a little trap for his opponent. If White had now carelessly continued 23 Kt–B5, then Black would have obtained a thoroughly satisfactory position by the sortie 24 . . . Kt–Q5! With the text-move White forces further simplifications and transposes to an endgame in which Black possesses purely minimal chances of saving the game.

23 . . .   QxKt

After the alternative 23 . . . R–Q1 White can choose from amongst a number of favourable continuations. Firstly he can continue 24 RxB, RxR; 25 Kt–B5, R–Q8 ch! (after 25 . . . QxKt; 26 KtxR, QxQ; 27 PxQ, Black loses material) 26 RxR, QxKt; 27 R–Q6, with considerable pressure, and secondly the simple continuation 24 RxB, RxR; 25 Kt–B5, RxR; 26 QxR, wins at least another pawn. Finally 24 R–R5 is also very strong, since Black has no good defence against the threat of 25 Kt–B5.

24	QxQ	RxQ
25	RxB	R(Kt 3)–Kt1!

In his difficult situation Black defends himself very well indeed. White must not now play 26 RxP, on account of 26 . . . Kt–Q5! whereupon, on account of the mating threat on the first rank Black even gains the upper hand.

26   P–Kt3

A slight inaccuracy which renders more difficult realisation of the advantage already achieved. Better was 26 K–B1, so as to bring the King via K1 to the protection of the QB file. If Black replies 26 . . . Kt–Q5, then 27 RxRch, RxR; 28 KtxKt, PxKt; 29 RxQP, P–QR4; 30 K–K2, results in an easily won Rook ending for White.

Black (Smyslov) to play

White (Keres)

26   . . .   P–R3?

After the surrender of the BP the ending soon becomes hopeless for Black, since White can eventually obtain two united passed pawns in the centre. Hence 26 . . . P–B3 was absolutely essential here, after which White would still have some technical difficulties to overcome. If, for example, directly 27 R–Q6, then there follows 27 . . . Kt–Q5!; 28 RxRch, RxR; 29 KtxKt, PxKt; and the Rook ending is not so easy to win. As examples we adduce the possible lines 30 RxRP, P–R3; 31 R–Q6, R–B7; 32 RxQP, RxKtP; or 30 RxQP, P–QR4; 31 K–B1, K–Kt1; 32 K–K2, P–Kt6; 33 K–K3, R–B7; 34 R–Q2, R–B5; 35 R–Q3, RxP and in both cases Black still has very good defensive possibilities.

However, 26 . . . P–B3 would still have been insufficient to hold the position. White need not hurry with the forcing continuation 27 R–Q6, but can, as in the previous note, continue with 27 K–B1, with the intention of 28 K–K1. In this case one can hardly believe that Black, with his passively placed pieces, could have prevented further loss in material.

27	RxP	Kt–Q5

The only possibility of obtaining any counter-play.

28	RxRch	RxR
29	KtxKt	PxKt
30	R–Q7!	

Now White needs only to liquidate the enemy QP and exchange off a couple of pawns on the Queen's wing so as to transpose into a very easily won Rook ending. Black cannot undertake anything against this plan.

30	. . .	R–B7
31	RxQP	RxKtP
32	K–Kt2	

A step from the right path here would have been 32 R–Q6. Black could then reply 32 . . . R–K7! and if then 33 P–B3?, P–Kt6 etc. White does not want the enemy QRP since in any case it plays no role in the final phase of the game.

32	. . .	P–Kt6
33	R–Kt4	K–R2
34	K–B3	

Again it would have been useless to have tried 34 R–Kt6, R–Kt8; 35 RxP, R–K8! etc. But now White is threatening to capture the QRP with 35 R–Kt6 and hence the following manoeuvre is as good as forced.

34	. . .	R–Kt8
35	R–Kt6	P–QR4
36	R–Kt5	P–Kt7

The only way of defending the pawns. The ending after 36 . . . R–QR8; 37 RxKtP, RxP; 38 P–R4, would have been equally hopeless for Black.

37	K–B4	K–Kt3
38	P–R4	K–B3
39	P–R5	K–K3
40	R–Kt6ch	K–K2
41	K–B5	R–QR8

It would have been equally hopeless to have remained passive since then White could either have advanced his KP or else launched an attack on the KKtP.

42	R–Kt7ch	resigns.

After 42 . . . K–B1; 43 RxQKtP, RxPch; 44 K–K6, or 42 . . . K–Q 3; 43 P–K5 ch, K–Q4; 44 RxQKtP, RxPch; 45 K–Kt6, R–Kt4ch; 46 K–B7, etc. further resistance would have been useless.

Game 55

RUY LOPEZ, MORPHY DEFENCE

Maroczy Memorial Tournament in Budapest, 1952

	P. Keres	E. Geller
1	P–K4	P–K4
2	Kt–KB3	Kt–QB3
3	B–Kt5	P–QR3
4	B–R4	Kt–B3
5	O–O	B–K2
6	Q–K2	

I have employed this Queen move a number of times in important games of recent years, and not without success. It is of course hard to say whether here the text-move or the usual

continuation 6 R–K1 offers the better chances, and in the end
the choice must be made according to the taste of each individual player. One of the chief reasons why I have often preferred
6 Q–K2 lies in the fact that it is much more seldom played and
hence not so well-known as 6 R–K1.

6	. . .	P–QKt4
7	B–Kt3	O–O
8	P–B3	P–Q4

The pawn sacrifice is much more promising in this variation
than after 6 R–K1, since after 9 PxP, KtxP; 10 KtxP, Kt–B5;
11 Q–K4, KtxKt; 12 P–Q4, B–Kt2 etc. Black would obtain
adequate counter-play in return for the pawn. And alternatively
Black can, after 9 PxP, also continue energetically with 9 . . .
B–KKt5, which would yield him excellent attacking possibilities
in return for the pawn sacrifice after 10 PxKt, P–K5; 11
P–Q4, PxKt; 12 PxP, B–R4.

| 9 | P–Q3 | |

In my opinion this restrained defensive move constitutes
White's best chance of maintaining the tension in the game.
Black must now take care that in the ensuing phase of the game
his central pawns do not become objects of attack.

| 9 | . . . | R–K1 |

An innovation. Usually Black continues here with 9 . . . B–
KKt5; 10 P–KR3, B–R4, allowing White to exert really
strong pressure on Q5; or else he may play 9 . . . P–Q5. After
this last move praxis shows that by 10 PxP, KtxQP; 11 KtxKt,
QxKt, a position arises in which Black has not had bad results.
Still, it seems to me that White has a promising middle-game
here providing he exerts pressure on the enemy weaknesses on
the QB line by 12 B–K3, Q–Q3; 13 R–B1. Hence, Geller's
attempt to improve Black's defence here merits especial
attention.

| 10 | R–K1 | |

Here, too, winning the pawn by 10 PxP, was not particularly
enticing for White. Black could then reply either 10 . . . KtxP;
11 KtxP, KtxKt; 12 QxKt, B–Kt2, or else 10 . . . Kt–QR4, in
both cases with a strong initiative in return for the pawn. But

if White plays 10 B–Kt5, then Black can defend himself by
10 . . . B–K3. In addition to the text-move 10 R–Q1 deserves
consideration in order to carry out the thrust P–Q4 as the occasion arises.

10   . . .   B–Kt2

With his ninth move, R–K1, Black weakened himself on the
diagonal KKt 1–QR7, especially on the KB2 square, and hence
10 . . . B–K3 came into consideration here. Apparently Geller
did not like the possible reply 11 Kt–Kt5. Black must then
either give up the two Bishops or shut off his Bishop from the
centre of the combat by 11 . . . B–KKt5; 12 P–B3, B–R4.

11   QKt–Q2   Q–Q2
12   Kt–B1   QR–Q1
13   B–Kt5

Very good here too was 13 Kt–Kt3, controlling the important
KB5 square. But the text-move also has its advantages since
now Black must at once clarify matters in the centre.

13   . . .   Kt–QR4

Instead of this many masters have recommended 13 . . . P–
Q5 for Black, in order to exert troublesome pressure on the QP
after 14 PxP, KtxP; 15 KtxKt, QxKt. However, it is doubtful
if Black could have obtained a satisfactory position with it,
since instead of the exchange, White has the better continuation
44 QR–Q1. Black would then not find it easy to formulate a
suitable plan of play, whereas White could strengthen his
position further by Kt–Kt3, opening up the game at the right
moment by exchanging off on Q4.

With the text-move Black forces the enemy Bishop to quit the
strong diagonal QR2–KKt8, since after 14 KtxP, Q–K3; 15
PxP, KtxP White's pieces would be uncomfortably pinned.

14   B–B2   PxP
15   PxP   Kt–B5

Geller again chooses a combinational method of protecting
his KP. If now 16 P–QKt3, Kt–R6; 17 KtxP, Q–K3; and
Black wins back his pawn with a good game. But also very well
playable was the simple 15 . . . Q–K3.

16   Kt–K3   KtxKtP?

Black should not take this pawn since now at last White is given the opportunity of capturing the KP under favourable circumstances. Here, quite certainly, he ought to have played 16 . . . KtxKt which would have led to further simplification after 17 QxKt, Kt–Kt5, and afforded Black well-justified hopes of establishing complete equality. There could, for example, have followed: 18 Q–K2, BxB; 19 KtxB, P–R3; 20 QR–Q1, Q–B1; 21 Kt–B3, Kt–B3; etc.

17   KtxP   Q–K3

Forced, since 17 . . . Q–Q7; 18 B–Kt3, or 17 . . . Q–Q3; 18 B–B4 would lead to marked advantage for White.

18   KtxP!

By this temporary piece sacrifice full use is made of Black's weakness on the diagonal KKt1–QR7. The result of the ensuing combinational complications is that White eventually arrives at an end-game with a pawn more, after which the win only requires good technique.

18   . . .   QxKt

Acceptance of the sacrifice in conjunction with the defensive moves that follow are forced if Black wishes to avoid even bigger material loss.

19	B–Kt3	Kt–B5
20	KtxKt	PxKt
21	BxP	Kt–Q4
22	BxB	QxB

After 22 . . . RxB White can play either 23 Q–Q2, or 23 Q–Kt2, whereupon he eventually remains a pawn to the good as well. However Black tries to defend himself he cannot do better than emerge into an ending with a pawn less.

23	PxKt	QxQ
24	RxQ	RxR
25	BxR	BxP
26	P–QR4!	

Now we can enumerate the results of the combination begun by White on his 18th move. A Rook and Bishop ending has arisen in which White possesses a solid pawn more on the King's wing. The positional advantage too is on White's side,

Black (Geller)

White (Keres) to play

since in the first place his opponent's QRP is an object of attack and in the second Black must protect himself against troublesome pins both on the Q file and along the QR7–KKt1 diagonal.

But before White goes over to the decisive attack the preparatory text-move must be made. If at once 26 BxP, then Black would still retain good chances of saving the game in the Rook ending after 26 . . . R–R1; 27 P–B4, BxKtP; 28 KxB, RxB or also after 27 . . . RxB; 28 PxB, R–R4; 29 P–QR4, K–B1. The immediate pin, too, by 26 R–Q1, would be useless because of 26 . . . R–K1!

Now, however, Black must seriously reckon with these two possibilities.

26 . . .   R–Q3

Black cannot play here 26 . . . P–QR4, since after 27 R–Q1, R–K1; 28 RxB, RxB; 29 P–Kt3, R–B7; 30 R–QB5 he would lose yet another pawn.

27 R–Q1   K–B2

Black defends himself most resourcefully against the threat of 28 RxB. If White now embarks on the pawn ending with 28 RxB, RxR; 29 B–B4, then there follows 29 . . . K–K3; 30 K–B1, K–Q3; 31 BxR, KxB; 32 K–K2, K–B5; 33 K–Q2, Kt–K6 and Black gets adequate counterplay with his active King. On the other hand the end game after 27 . . . B–Kt2; 28 RxR,

PxR; 29 P–R5 would be equally hopeless for Black because of the weakness that has been fixed on his QR3.

28 P–R5!

Thus the weakness on QR3 is definitely fixed and with it all possible Bishop end-games are practically hopeless for Black. In addition there now threatens 29 BxP, winning a second pawn.

28 . . .   R–K3

Some time or other Black must free himself from the pin on the Q file. After 28 . . . K–K3, for example, White can continue with 29 . . . P–B5 and thus deprive his opponent of the chance of a counter-attack because of 30 B–Kt4ch.

29 B–B1

Again 29 BxP was not good because of the reply 29 . . . B–Kt6 and the Rook ending after 29 RxB, RxB; 30 K–B1, R–R7; 31 R–B5, K–B1 still offers Black defensive possibilities. After the text-move Black must surrender yet another pawn, but all the same he knows how to present his opponent with the maximum difficulties.

29	. . .	B–Kt6
30	R–Q7ch	K–B1
31	RxBP	R–K4

Obviously in vain is 31 . . . R–K8; 32 P–B3, R–R8; 33 R–B5. Now Black does at least win the dangerous QRP.

32	R–B6	RxP
33	R–QKt6!	

The last finesse. After 33 RxP, R–QB4 White could lose his QBP, when a win would indeed be very dubious. In the ensuing ending with two pawns less Black naturally no longer has any chance and he merely makes the ensuing moves in order to reach the time control.

33	. . .	B–B7
34	RxP	R–QB4
35	R–R3	R–Q4
36	P–B3	R–Q8
37	K–B2	R–B8

38	P–R4	B–Kt3
39	B–B4	K–K2
40	P–Kt4	P–R3
41	B–Q5	resigns.

Game 56

QUEEN'S GAMBIT ACCEPTED

Maroczy Memorial Tournament in Budapest, 1952

	G. Barcza	P. Keres
1	Kt–KB3	P–Q4
2	P–Q4	

Usually Barcza plays here 2 P–KKt3 and then later on transposes into the system of development stemming from White's P–QB4. As this game was played in the last round and had a vital bearing on the destination of the first prize, Black welcomed the opportunity of transposing the opening into a Queen's Gambit Accepted, thereby obtaining a position full of fighting possibilities.

2	...	Kt–KB3
3	P–B4	PxP
4	P–K3	P–K3
5	BxP	P–B4
6	O–O	P–QR3
7	Q–K2	P–QKt4
8	B–Q3	

As in an earlier game played in this tournament between Keres and Smyslov (No. 54), Barcza also chooses the rarely seen Bishop retreat to Q3 instead of the usual 8 B–Kt3. However, in the present game Black adopts a much better system of defence than Smyslov did in the game mentioned.

8	...	PxP
9	PxP	B–Kt2
10	P–QR4	

It is because of this thrust that theory holds the whole variation to be favourable for White, the basis being the game Landau–Reshevsky, Kemeri, 1937. In that game Reshevsky

continued with 10 . . . P–Kt5; whereupon White, after 11
QKt–Q2, B–K2; 12 Kt–B4, P–QR4; 13 B–B4, O–O; 14 KR–
Q1, obtained the better position on account of the strong post
for his Kt on QB4. The present game shows, however, that
Black's play can be noticeably improved in this variation and
causes one to doubt whether, with 8 B–Q3, White really
obtains better prospects than with the customary 8 B–Kt3.

10   . . .   PxP!

This simple capture is much stronger than 10 . . . B–Kt5 as
was the usual move up to this game. In the first place White
must now lose time in order to win back the pawn, and in the
second the comparative weakness of the QR pawn is outweighed
by counter-play on the QKt file where there is in addition a
strong square for the Kt on QB5. Experience acquired in
actual praxis shows that it is very difficult for White to extract
an advantage out of the opening.

11   RxP

With this immediate recapture White presents his opponent
with no opening problems. Innocuous too is 11 Kt–B3, whereupon there can follow 11 . . . Kt-B3, gaining an important
tempo through the attack on Q5. But the most unpleasant move
for Black seems to be 11 B–B2, threatening to obtain lasting
pressure on the diagonal QR4–K8, e.g. after 11 . . . B–K2;
12 BxPch, QKt–Q2; 13 Kt–K5 etc. However, in this case too,
Black can solve the opening problem in a satisfactory manner
by playing, instead of 12 . . . QKt–Q2, 12 . . . KKt-Q2!
followed by 13 . . . O–O.

Finally, we should also mention the game, Furman–Keres,
XXIVth U.S.S.R. Championship in Moscow, 1957. In this
White tried 11 B–Kt5, but after 11 . . . B–K2; 12 Kt–B3,
O–O; 13 KtxP, Kt–B3; 14 KR–Q1, Kt–QKt5 he also could
obtain no advantage. Practical experience so far thoroughly
justifies the capture 10 . . . PxP.

11   . . .   B–K2
12   QKt–Q2

With this Barcza begins a disadvantageous Knight manoeuvre, not only losing thereby all prospects of an opening
advantage but even getting into a defensive position. The

normal continuation here is 12 Kt–B3, O–O; 13 B–KKt5, whereupon Black can reply 13 . . . P–QR4 or even with an immediate 13 . . . Kt–B3.

<pre>
          12   . . .   O–O
          13   Kt–Kt3
</pre>

Here the Knight is badly placed and constitutes the reason for White's further difficulties. Better was 13 Kt–B4, although Black could utilise the breaking off of the attack on his QR3 to develop his Knight by 13 . . . Kt–B3, with an eventual Kt–QKt5 to follow. It can be seen that Black has emerged from the opening with a good game.

<pre>
          13   . . .   B–B3
          14   R–R1   Q–Kt3!
</pre>

Eliminating, once and for all, the threat on his QRP, since now White has nothing better than 15 Kt–R5. Furthermore, Black will now manoeuvre his QB to an active position on QKt4 from whence it also contributes to the hindering of any eventual King-side attack.

<pre>
          15   Kt–R5   B–Kt4
          16   Kt–B4
</pre>

It is well-known that in the Queen's Gambit Accepted White must aim at active play on the King's wing, otherwise Black, especially after some simplifying exchanges, gets the better position on account of the weakness of White's Q4. Hence one can readily understand why Barcza refrains from the possible simplification here of 16 BxB, QxB; 17 QxQ, PxQ; 18 B–Kt5. For then all he would have would be prospects of a hard-won equality.

<pre>
          16   . . .   Q–Kt2
          17   KKt–K5
</pre>

With this move White merely helps on his opponent's development, since he will be forced in the sequel to exchange off Knights. Better therefore was an immediate 17 B–K3, although in this case too after 17 . . . Kt–B3; 18 QR–B1, Kt–QKt5; 19 B–Kt1, P–QR4 one must prefer Black's position.

<pre>
          17   . . .   Kt–B3
          18   B–K3?
</pre>

An incautious move in consequence of which White's pieces are driven back to unfavourable positions and his chances of active play on the King's wing disappear. Necessary was first the exchange 18 KtxKt, QxKt and only then 19 B–K3, by which at least the co-operation between White's pieces could be maintained.

18	. . .	Kt–QKt5!
19	B–Kt1	QR–B1
20	R–B1	KR–Q1

Black's superiority is now patent. His pieces are excellently placed, the pins on the QR3–KB8 diagonal and on the QB file are very awkward for White, and in addition Black, in face of his opponent's weakness on Q4, possesses absolute control of his own important Q4 square. Although Black does not yet threaten anything directly, he has every chance of further strengthening his positional pressure, whereas White must passively await future events. Experience shows, however, that in such positions the defending side sooner or later allows himself to commit some inaccuracies, and this fact too will be once again demonstrated in the present game.

Black (Keres)

White (Barcza) to play

21	P–QKt3	P–Kt3

Black would like to continue with 22 . . . KKt–Q4. For this, however, he must first make secure the position of his King, since an immediate 21 . . . KKt–Q4 would be an outright mistake because of 22 BxPch.

22   P–B3

This fresh weakness renders White's position still more difficult. Better was 22 Kt–Q3, so as to relieve his position somewhat by further exchanges.

22   . . .   KKt–Q4
23   B–K4?

A mistake that costs at least a pawn. Black was threatening 23 . . . KtxB; 24 QxKt, RxP, and if White parries this with 23 B–KB2 then the reply 23 . . . B–Kt4 would be very troublesome. In view of his difficult position White must try and build up a tough defence, for instance by 23 K–R1. Even though in that event, too, Black would undoubtedly stand better, still, an exploitation of his advantage would be far from easy and would require careful and consistent play.

23   . . .   P–B4!

With this the issue of the game is decided. After the retreat 24 B–Kt1, Black could implement his threat with 24 . . . KtxB; 25 QxKt, RxP, winning a pawn with an overwhelming position. Hence in the next phase of the game White tries to rescue himself by combinational complications, but merely succeeds in hastening the loss.

24   BxKt   PxB
25   Kt–R5   RxRch!

This exchange is made just at the right moment since now White cannot play 26 RxR, because of 26 . . . Q–Kt3 winning a piece. Now White must soon surrender material on account of the unhappy position of his pieces, in particular of the Kt on R5.

26   BxR   Q–Kt3
27   Q–Q1   R–QB1

It was of course also possible to win a pawn here by 27 . . . Kt–B7. But Black is in no hurry and intends first of all to activate his pieces to their maximum extent. With the text-move he threatens amongst other things 28 . . . RxB, winning two pieces for the Rook.

28	K–R1	Kt–B7
29	Kt (R5)–B6	

A desperate attempt that does not, however, alter the
situation. After 29 R–R2, Black wins simply by 29 . . . QxP; 30
QxQ, KtxQ and 29 Kt (R5)–B4, would allow, in addition to
29 . . . QxP, the decisive 29 . . . PxKt; 30 QxKt, QxP; 31
B–Kt2, P–B6 etc.

29	. . .	RxKt
30	KtxR	QxKt

With two pieces for the Rook and the better position Black
has of course no difficulty in forcing the win.

31	R–R2

In the hope, after 31 . . . KtxP, of making his pieces a little
more active by 32 B–K3, so arriving at some counter-play. But
Black refuses to allow his opponent any such chances.

31	. . .	Kt–Kt5!
32	R–KB2	Q–B6
33	B–Kt2	Kt–Q6

Breaking down the last line of resistance. White could
already have quietly struck his flag.

34	R–B2	KtxB
35	Q–QB1	QxKtP
36	RxKt	Q–B5
37	R–QB2	Q–B8 ch

White resigns.

TOURNAMENTS AND EVENTS OF THE
YEARS 1952–1955

INASMUCH as the excellent results I had obtained in the last couple of years showed I was in good form I went in high hopes to the Helsinki Olympiad in 1952. On first board there I was due to contend with heavy opposition. Alas, it must be confessed that I was in my worst form here of recent years. Nothing would go right and in the final group I managed to obtain 50% with the greatest difficulty. This low ebb of my form also lasted right to the end of the year when the XXth Championship of the U.S.S.R. was held. For almost the whole tournament my score was about 50% and it was only shortly before the end that I was able to better my position somewhat. And then, four rounds before the end of the tournament, I lost two games in succession and only by my victory over Korchnoi (No. 57) did I once again reach the 50% level. I finally ended up equal 10th and 11th with Master Suetin. This was my worst result, not only in U.S.S.R. Championships but also in tournaments of the last decade. Furthermore, the quality of my games in this tournament was the lowest that I had displayed during recent years.

Clearly I was once again undergoing a period of depression as far as my creative work was concerned. It was essential, however, to emerge from it as speedily as possible since in the autumn of the following year a tournament of the utmost importance was due to take place—in fact, the Candidates' Tournament for the World Championship in Zurich. And in this tournament it was imperative for me to play well once again. So as to tighten up my form I felt I must play in some tournaments in the interim and hence I decided to take part once again in the Estonian Championship, the first time after a long interval. This tournament took place in the Spring of 1953 at Tartu. Naturally, I could not test my real form in this tournament since the general level of the participants was not of the necessary height, but the tournament certainly performed its function as regards good training. A training tournament with the participation of the members of the national team of the U.S.S.R. that was held at Gagry in summer showed me that I was still far from being in my best form, but by then I was in fact playing reasonably well. I therefore was reduced to hoping that the length of the Zurich Tournament, 28 games in all (for each competitor), would be sufficient to enable me to attain my best form once again.

The commencement of the tournament in Zurich demonstrated something that I had in fact both feared and expected. I had clearly not yet surmounted the crisis in my form and my results in the first half of the tournament, seven points out of 14 games, were far from satisfactory. I shared the 8th and 9th places and was in no way satisfied with the quality of my play. Playing through my three wins in the first half of the tournament reveals that in them Szabo made me the present of a pawn in the first few moves, Boleslavsky was unlucky enough to go in for an incorrect sacrificial line and Stahlberg allowed himself to be outplayed in a clearly drawn position. As regards the lost games, I chose an opening variation against Smyslov that had been refuted, against Bronstein I played the opening weakly and against Averbach I put an important centre pawn en prise. In addition I was unable to secure the victory in a clearly won position against Reshevsky; equally against Petrosian I failed to make use of an extra pawn to win and against Najdorf I escaped a loss only through an inaccuracy by my opponent on the last move before adjournment. This result then was simply bad and I had to put all my hopes in the second half of the tournament.

In fact the first few games of the second half of the tournament did show that my play was on the way to improvement. After much manoeuvring I won by a direct King-side attack against Petrosian, then drew with Averbach, Szabo and Euwe, and, succeeding in winning against Stahlberg, I was standing in fourth place, only two points behind the leader, Smyslov. When, in the next round, I managed to defeat Boleslavsky by means of an interesting theoretical innovation, whilst at the same time Smyslov suffered a defeat at Kotov's hands, I was indeed standing very well. I was only a point behind Smyslov, and only half a point behind Bronstein. But there were still no less than eight more games to play and hence every possibility was still open.

In the next round I won the exchange against Kotov by an interesting combination, but then played weakly and eventually had to content myself with a draw. However, then I obtained an important point against Geller. By now I had overhauled Bronstein and was only half a point behind Reshevsky and Smyslov, with the latter having played one game less. I still had, however, to play the decisive game against Smyslov. Should I succeed in winning this then I would be at the head of the tournament with every chance of emerging with final victory. But a draw too would not have extinguished my hopes, and therefore I should not have played in too risky a style in this game. However, I once again repeated a mistake I had made so often before and put everything on one card. I offered my opponent an extremely complicated piece sacrifice, acceptance of which would have submitted Smyslov's King to a fierce attack. But, after long reflection, Smyslov discovered an excellent defence and once I had given up the chance of securing equality thereafter in favour of an ill-considered plan, the consequences were soon apparent. I suffered an ignominious defeat and in so doing I had not only thrown away all chances of first place but was once again back in fourth place. The stiff struggle for an upwards climb had to be started all over again.

Curiously enough, I was best helped in this endeavour by the events of the next round—when I had the bye! The point was that my nearest rivals suffered defeat, Reshevsky against Smyslov and Bronstein against Geller. So I stood below them, a half a point in one case and a full point in the other, but I still had one more game to play than they had. On the other hand new dangers had sprung up from below since both Kotov and Najdorf had progressed to within half a point of me.

During the next two rounds the situation remained the same, since after draws with Reshevsky and Bronstein I was still lying in fourth place. However, then I achieved a win over

Gligoric and thus, with two rounds to go, I was in third place. I had only half a point less than Bronstein, but with one more game to play, and was half a point above Reshevsky who had lost in this round against Bronstein. In the penultimate round, however, matters were evened up, since Reshevsky won against Gligoric, and so all three of us reached the last round with the same score. In the last round we all drew our games and the final result was that I shared second to fourth prizes with Bronstein and Reshevsky. Although I had played really well in the second half of the tournament and with 9 points out of 14 had obtained the best result, this was insufficient to make good the lapses in the first half. The total result was, however, thoroughly satisfactory and gave me the right to take part in the next Interzonal without having to qualify for it.

The ensuing year, 1954, was characterised by exceptional chess activity on my part; and this not so much in great tournaments as rather in many national matches and in long journeys. At the beginning of the year I met Tal for the first time in the match between Estonia and Latvia. In one game I succeeded in forcing the win, after an interesting middle-game (Game No. 59), whilst the other one resulted in a draw. Then I made the long voyage to the Argentine as a member of the U.S.S.R. team and crossed swords with Julio Bolbochan in four games, winning one, losing one and drawing two games. On the way back we played a match against a team representing France. I encountered the veteran Dr. Tartakower and succeeded in winning both games. Hardly was this journey over than yet another was in being, this time to the U.S.A. In the fight against this team I played four games, against Pavey and Kevitz, and obtained three points therefrom. On the way back I won both my games against Wade in a match versus England and then had the same result in both my games with Stoltz in Stockholm.

It would seem that these national matches exercised a favourable influence on my play, since at the beginning of the Chess Olympiad in Amsterdam I once again found myself in good form. In this event I played without any sort of tension and without getting into time trouble, in a style that was at once simple and clear. Everything worked together wonderfully, one win came after another and the end result was that, with $13\frac{1}{2}$ points out of 14, I achieved the absolutely best total of the Olympiad. I also played really well in the tournament that took place soon after in Hastings and, despite a loss to Fuderer, I contrived eventually to share first prize with Smyslov. In these tournaments I played a number of good games from which I have selected for this book my wins against Sajtar (No. 60) at Amsterdam and against Alexander (No. 61) and Szabo (No. 62) at Hastings.

My next tournament, the XXIInd U.S.S.R. Championship, proved once again a disappointment for me. The reason for this was not that I played badly in this tournament. Not at all, in fact, rather the contrary was the case. I played in this event a number of good games of which perhaps the best was the one against Taimanov (No. 63). What, however, prevented me this time from occupying a higher place was, if one may be allowed to say so, simply bad luck. The ill fortune began already in the first round when I gained a healthy passed pawn against Spassky, only, however, to allow my opponent to escape with a draw. After a draw with Averbach and a win against Simagin there came my encounter with Smyslov. I got into some difficulties but was nevertheless able to extricate myself by a tactical finesse and then, once the position was equal again, I put a piece en prise! But pieces of bad luck seldom come singly. In the next round in the deepest time trouble I lost to Furman, then drew with Flohr, and against Ilivitzky obtained a Rook ending with some winning chances. It was then that there occurred my second piece of really bad luck. I literally put en prise a whole Rook and thus, after the seventh round I found myself in one of the lowest places in the tournament table with $2\frac{1}{2}$ points.

I won my next two games and so managed to improve my position somewhat, but then, in an easily won position against Korchnoi I proved unable to utilise the fact that I was the exchange up to force the win. Then, however, two wins in succession brought a further advance so that, with 7 points out of 12 games, I was only $1\frac{1}{2}$ points behind the leader. At this point, however, came my loss against Mikenas and all hopes for first prize were at an end. The remaining part of the tourna-

ment I played rather listlessly and so I had to content myself
with sharing 7th and 8th places, only half a point below the
players who tied for 3rd to 6th places. In the last round I
succeeded in winning a brief game against Botvinnik who fell
victim to an incorrect opening variation.

In the Spring I took part in the match U.S.S.R.-Hungary
at Budapest and then the U.S.A. team paid its return visit to
Moscow. In this match I played four games against Robert
Byrne out of which I managed to extract $3\frac{1}{2}$ points. In the first
game I was able to save myself in a lost position by getting into
an original kind of ending, and in our third encounter we had
an interesting and up and down struggle that resulted from a
most venerable variation of the King's Gambit Accepted
rarely seen nowadays (No. 64). In addition I played in a
tournament at Parnu that was designed to serve as training for
the Interzonal Tournament which was due to begin shortly at
Gothenburg. A number of the leading grandmasters of the
U.S.S.R. took part and I won this tournament with an excellent
score. I was now ready for the next important event, the
Interzonal tournament at Gothenburg.

Game 57

QUEEN'S PAWN, DUTCH DEFENCE

The XXth U.S.S.R. Championship in Moscow, 1952

	P. Keres	V. Korchnoi
1	P-QB4	P-KB4

Grandmaster Korchnoi is no great believer in long theoretical
opening variations, but instead favours original systems of
development that have been little analysed. The Dutch Defence
is well designed for such purposes and thus the game soon takes
on a quite original character.

2	Kt-KB3	Kt-KB3
3	P-KKt3	P-KKt3

An old continuation in the Dutch Defence that has been
brought into action once again by the Leningrad school of
masters. This school has exhaustively analysed it and worked it

up into a new system of defence. Grandmaster Korchnoi is one of the co-authors of this system and hence he is thoroughly au fait with all the finesses of this method of play.

4	B–Kt2	B–Kt2
5	Kt–B3	P–Q3
6	P–Q4	O–O
7	O–O	Kt–B3

The Knight development is characteristic of the Leningrad System. With it Black prepares for P–K4 and so practically forces his opponent to make the ensuing pawn advance. The position is very similar to a type of play in the King's Indian Defence, but with the one difference that Black has played P–KB4. Whether this circumstance is of any great use for Black is doubtful since in many variations the weakness of the K3 square becomes unpleasantly noticeable.

8   P–Q5   Kt–QR4

An innovation which, it seems, Korchnoi had prepared for this game. The usual continuation here is 8 . . . Kt–K4 and if 9 KtxKt, PxKt; 10 P–K4, then 10 . . . P–K3. Pachman claims that White gets an advantage by the simple exchanges 11 QPxP, BxP; 12 PxP, but this needs to be proved in practice.

The text-move is played in similar positions in the King's Indian Defence but it is doubtful here, precisely because of the weakening of Black's pawn position due to his P–KB4.

9   Q–R4   P–B4
10   PxP e. p.!

In this position an exchange on QB6 is very promising for White in contradistinction to kindred positions in the King's Indian Defence. Black is now left with various positional weaknesses in the centre and he will soon have some real difficulties to overcome.

10   . . .   KtxP (B3)

Black cannot play 10 . . . PxP, since this would lead simply to the loss of a pawn after 11 Kt–Q4, e.g. 11 . . . B–Q2; 12 KtxBP, or 11 . . . Kt–K5; 12 KtxQBP, QKtxKt; 13 KtxKt! etc. However, it becomes apparent in the position arising from the text-move that the P–KB4 advance does not fit in with the development system chosen by Black. One can claim, with quiet confidence, that White has emerged from the opening with the better game.

11 R–Q1   Kt–QR4?

The playing to and fro of this Kt is altogether too original and soon gets Black into great difficulties. In a certain sense therefore this may be regarded as the decisive mistake. Although Black's position would not have been particularly agreeable still he should have tried here ... B–Q2, followed eventually by R–QB1, so as to get some counterplay on the Queen-side.

12 P–B5!

It seems that Korchnoi had underestimated the strength of this pawn thrust by which White initiates a decisive attack against the enemy position in the centre.

12 ...   B–Q2

Naturally Black does not want to make a move like 12 ... P–Q4, which, after 13 B–B4, would leave him positionally lost owing to the weakness of the Black central squares. Hence he tries to solve the positional problem in a tactical way—to no avail.

13 Q–R3!

Now Black cannot capture the pawn by 13 ... PxP since then, after 14 Kt–K5, loss of material would be inevitable. However, the protection of his Q3 provides him with unsurmountable difficulties.

Black (Korchnoi) to play

White (Keres)
13 ... Kt–K1?

Black, having got himself into a difficult situation, should have tried to find the relatively best way out, and this undoubtedly lay in the surrender of the weak point on Q 3. If for example he were to continue with 13 . . . Q–B2; 14 PxP, PxP; 15 QxP, QxQ; 16 RxQ, B–B3; then, by reason of his well-developed pieces he could have caused his opponent noticeable difficulties, despite the extra pawn.

14 B–Kt5!

This move virtually decides the fate of the game since Black no longer has an adequate defence against 15 PxP.

14 . . . B–K3

A little better here was 14 . . . B–KB3 (but not 14 . . . P–KR3; 15 PxP! etc.), but in this case too Black's position, for example after 15 BxB, RxB; 16 Kt–Q5, R–KB1; 17 Kt–B4! etc. would hardly be agreeable. If then 17 . . . P–K4; there could follow 18 KtxKP, PxKt; 19 Kt–K6, and White wins.

After the text-move Black loses two pieces for the Rook, after which further resistance is hopeless.

15 PxP KtxP

Also hopeless is of course 15 . . . Kt–B5; 16 PxP, QxRch; 17 RxQ, KtxQ; 18 PxR–Qch, KxQ; 19 Kt–Q4, BxKt; 20 RxB, etc. since Black loses at least another pawn.

16 RxKt! QxR
17 QxKt P–Kt3

Now White has two Knights for the Rook, together with a good position, and this is of course sufficient for the win.

18 Q–R4 B–Q2
19 Q–R4 BxKt

White was threatening, not only 20 BxP, but also 20 R–Q1, and hence Black cannot protect his K2 by 19 . . . QR–K1. Instead of the text-move Black could just as well have resigned here.

20 BxP Q–K3
21 PxB KR–K1
22 Kt–Q4! resigns.

Game 58

RUY LOPEZ, MORPHY DEFENCE

F.I.D.E. Candidates' Tournament in Zurich, 1953

	I. Boleslavsky	P. Keres
1	P–K4	P–K4
2	Kt–KB3	Kt–QB3
3	B–Kt5	P–QR3
4	B–R4	Kt–B3
5	O–O	B–K2
6	R–K1	P–QKt4
7	B–Kt3	O–O
8	P–B3	P–Q3
9	P–KR3	Kt–QR4
10	B–B2	P–B4
11	P–Q4	Q–B2
12	QKt–Q2	

Thus far the game has followed the well-known paths of the Tschigorin Defence to the Ruy Lopez, and the position now obtained has appeared thousands of times in master games. Despite this immense total of practical play and researches into this variation that have on some occasions gone very deep indeed, it has not yet been decided to this very day what is Black's best continuation. Here moves like 12 . . . Kt–B3, 12 . . . BPxP, 12 . . . B–Q2, 12 . . . B–Kt2, 12 . . . R–K1, and others, have been tried, but nevertheless all the problems in the position have not yet been solved.

I had the same position a few rounds earlier against Averbach. Then I continued with 12 . . . B–Kt2; and then, after 13 Kt–B1, went in for the gambit variation 13 . . . BPxP; 14 PxP, QR–B1, followed by P–Q4 etc. During the game a new idea came into my head. If one intends to carry out the thrust P–Q4, why should one necessarily prepare it by 12 . . . B–Kt2; rather than, for instance, 12 . . . R–Q1? Naturally during the game I was unable to study this idea exhaustively, and had to lay it on one side as being too time-consuming. But after some brief preparations at home the idea was ready for the present game as far as the general guiding lines were concerned and this was a good opportunity to try it out in practice.

12   . . .   R–Q1!

The exclamation mark to this move does not of course mean that it is stronger than the other continuations that have been used here hitherto. In certain concrete cases, however, this move is the most effective, that is to say, the most troublesome for the opponent. It is manifest to White that the idea of the text-move lies in the carrying out of the pawn advance P–Q4 and to meet this a number of ways lie open to him. But to find the right one amongst these during the game with only a limited amount of time at one's disposal is no easy task, especially when one takes into account that this is the first time White has been faced with the problem, whereas his opponent has already been able to study the idea in home analysis.

13   Kt–B1

White has nothing better than to allow the game to go along the paths prepared by his adversary, since after 13 PxKP, PxP, or 13 P–Q5, B–Q2 Black, in contrast with usual variations, has at least gained a valuable tempo.

13   . . .   P–Q4

This thrust is the point of Black's innovation. The Rook on Q1 effectively supports the attack against the enemy centre and exerts an uncomfortable pressure on the opposing Queen. Later, more exact, analysis of this variation has shown that Black would do better to interpolate here the pawn exchange 13 . . . BPxP; 14 PxP. But this was only realised after the whole variation had been used in many games.

14   KPxP

It is not easy for White to determine which is the best of the many possible continuations here. The first move that of course comes into consideration after the text-move is 14 KtxP, but then, after 14 . . . QPxP, one cannot see how White can gain an advantage. Winning a pawn by 15 BxP, KtxB; 16 RxKt, B–Kt2; 17 R–K1, PxP; 18 PxP, Kt–B3, undoubtedly yields Black sufficient counterplay, and also after 15 Kt–Kt3, PxP; 16 PxP, B–Q3, as was played in the game Nilsson-Keres, Amsterdam 1954, Black obtains easy equality. As the present game shows, the continuation in the text also gives Black adequate play.

Only about a year after this game was played did Master Vasiukov succeed in discovering a method by which White could dissolve the tension in the centre to his advantage. He recommended the exchange 14 QPxKP, PxP; (After 14 . . . KtxP; 15 Kt–K3, B–K3; 16 Q–K2, White has the awkward threat of 17 KtxP) and now not the Queen sacrifice 15 PxKt, RxQ; 16 PxB on account of the reply 16 . . . B–K3! but the surprising 15 Kt(B1)–Q2! After the ensuing forced moves 15 . . . PxKt; 16 PxKt, BxBP; 17 QxP, B–K3; 18 Kt–K4 White's position is indeed overwhelming.

From this last variation one can also understand why Black must interpose the pawn exchange 13 . . . BPxP; 14 PxP, before playing P–Q4. For then the QB file would be open and White could not play Kt–K4 as in the last variation since his Bishop on QB2 would be unprotected. But for this possibility, however, Black's game would be satisfactory.

All these circumstances, however, only came to light later on, after the whole variation had been exhaustively analysed and tried many times in practice. Hence one can hardly blame Boleslavsky for not at once finding the strongest continuation in the present game when he was confronted with this innovation for the first time.

14	. . .	KPxP
15	PxP	KtxP
16	Q–K2	

Once he can solve the problem of the defence of his King-side satisfactorily then Black has every reason to be pleased with the result of the opening. Therefore it is clear that White must look for his chances in a King-side attack. However, 16 B–Kt5 does not in any way contribute to this aim since Black can then reply 16 . . . BxB; 17 KtxB, P–Kt3, as well as 16 . . . B–K3; 17 BxB, QxB; etc. But 16 Kt–Kt5! sets Black much more difficult problems.

Naturally Black cannot well reply with either 16 . . . Kt–KB3; 17 Q–B3, threatening 18 QxR and 18 BxPch, or 16 . . .

P–R3; 17 Q–R5, and White also stands better after 16 . . .
BxKt; 17 BxB. But Black can beat back the direct attack by the
quiet move 16 . . . P–Kt3! If then 17 KtxRP, PxP with the
threat of 18 . . . P–Q6 could follow, and also after 17 Q–B3,
B–B1 one cannot see how White can continue his attack
effectively.

All the same, this was precisely the continuation that White
should have chosen, since the loss in time involved by the
text-move allows Black to ensure his position definitively. And
once Black has achieved this then he has nothing more to fear
and White must say goodbye to his chances of an advantage for
good.

16   . . .   B–Kt2

Thus Black thwarts the threat of 17 B–Kt5, since he fully
protects his back rank. For there would then follow simply
17 . . . BxB; 18 KtxB, P–R3. Equally innocuous is also now the
attempt at attack by 17 Kt–Kt5, P–Kt3 since after 18 KtxRP
Black has the strong defensive resource of 18 . . . Q–B3!
Hence White would have best done here to have abandoned
further attempts at attack and played 17 PxP, which would
have led to an approximately equal game.

17   Kt–Kt3   PxP

Better here was an immediate 17 . . . P–Kt3 depriving his
adversary of the opportunity of complicating the position by the
Knight leap to KB5. After the text-move interesting complications could have arisen.

Black (Keres)

White (Boleslavsky) to play

18   KtxP

Undoubtedly better here was 18 Kt–B5, by which White could have brought about almost incalculable complications. Should Black reply to this with 18 . . . B–KB3, then White may surprise his opponent with 19 Kt–R6ch!, since 19 . . . PxKt cannot be played on account of 20 Q–K4 etc. And after 19 . . . K–R1; 20 Kt–Kt5!, BxKt; 21 Q–Q3, would give White a dangerous attack, for example: 21 . . . P–B4, 22 BxB, and if now 22 . . . Kt–Kt5; then 23 BxR, RxB; 24 QxQP! etc. In addition Najdorf's continuation 19 Kt–Kt5 is also quite playable, although then Black could very well defend himself by 19 . . . BxKt; 20 BxB, P–B3.

Not altogether clear are the consequences of Bronstein's move 18 . . . B–Kt5. White can then simply answer 19 R–Q1, but Najdorf's continuation, 19 Q–Q3, is also really dangerous for Black. Whether Black now continues with 19 . . . BxR; 20 Kt–R6 ch, followed by 21 QxRP, or if he plays 19 . . . P–Kt3; 20 Kt–R6ch, K–Kt2; 21 R–K4, in both cases White obtains excellent attacking chances in return for the material sacrificed.

After 18 Kt–B5, Black's best defence appears to be 18 . . . B–KB1, so as to be able to defend himself against 19 Q–Q3, or Kt–Kt5, by 19 . . . P–Kt3. White could then, for example, continue with 19 Kt(B3)xP, whereupon his pieces are at any rate more actively placed than in the game.

18   . . .   P–Kt3!

With this strong defensive move Black deprives the enemy pieces of the important KB5 square and thus thwarts all attempts at attack whilst ensuring for himself the better chances owing to the more active position of his pieces.

19   B–R6

Perhaps Bronstein is right when he recommends here the desperate piece sacrifice 19 Kt(Q4)–B5 as White's best chance. But after 19 . . . PxKt; (also possible of course is the simple 19 . . . B–KB1) 20 KtxP, B–KB1 White's prospects of carrying out an attack are undoubtedly smaller than those of Black for a successful defence. All the same, this would still result in a complicated position with some practical chances for White, whereas after the text-move the advantage slowly but surely swings over to Black.

          19   . . .   B–KB3
          20   Kt–Kt3

After 20 QR–Q1, Black would get nowhere by 20 . . . Kt–Kt5, because of 21 B–Kt1!, but with 20 . . . Kt–KB5! he could obtain the advantage of two Bishops and so get the clearly better position. With the text-move White does indeed defend his pawn on QKt2 for the moment, since 20 . . . BxP? would be met by 21 KtxKt, QxKt; 22 BxP! etc., but this defence is a purely temporary one.

          20   . . .   Kt–QB5

Now the pawn can no longer be defended and hence Black has attained a strategically won position. The practical realisation of this advantage is, however, attended still by considerable difficulties since White obtains marked counter-play on the black squares.

          21   Kt–K4   BxP
          22   Kt(Kt3)–B5

White is convinced that, for instance after 22 QR–Q1, B–Kt2; 23 BxB, KxB, Black's extra pawn will sooner or later prove decisive and so goes in for an exchange sacrifice in order to complicate matters a little. He wants, after the capture on QR1, to utilise the weaknesses on the black squares, in parti-cular on the long diagonal, for a King-side attack; but such hopes prove illusory. By reason of his well developed position Black is able to repulse all enemy attempts at attack in the sequel and after that it is an easy matter to realise his material superiority for winning purposes.

          22   . . .   BxR
          23   RxB   P–B4!

Weakening pawn advances of this nature on the King-side are not usually made voluntarily; but in this particular position it is the best procedure, since it brings about further exchanges and this in turn makes it easier to realise the material advantage.

          24   KtxB

Unfortunately for White, this exchange is forced, since both 24 Kt–K6, Q–K4; and 24 Kt–Kt5, Kt–B5, lead to further loss in material.

24	. . .	QxKt
25	Kt–B5	Q–B3
26	Kt–Q3	Kt–B6
27	Q–K1	Q–B3

Now the Black Knights are so effectively posted that White's attacking chances are practically liquidated. And this means that the issue of the game is decided.

| 28 | P–B4 | Kt–K5 |

Naturally not 28 . . . RxKt; 29 BxR, Q–Q5ch; 30 K–R2, when Black cannot play 30 . . . QxB? because of 31 Q–K6ch. But now he does threaten 29 . . . RxKt.

| 29 | K–R2 | Q–B6 |
| 30 | Q–QKt1 | |

The endgame after 30 QxQ, KtxQ would naturally be hopeless for White. The text-move allows a pretty finish.

30	. . .	Kt(B5)–Q7
31	Q–QB1	RxKt!
32	BxR	QxB
33	Q–B7	Kt–B6ch!
	resigns.	

After 34 PxKt, Q–K7ch White is mated in three moves.

Game 59

Q.P. KING'S INDIAN DEFENCE

Match Estonia-Latvia in Tallinn, 1954

	M. Tal	P. Keres
1	P–Q4	Kt–KB3
2	P–QB4	P–KKt3
3	Kt–QB3	B–Kt2

The King's Indian is an opening that is rarely seen in my repertoire. I knew that Tal is a master with a very sharp style and that he is eager for complications and so I wanted with my choice of opening to afford him every possibility of so doing. And indeed it cannot be said that this game was wanting in interesting complications as it proceeded.

4   P–K4   P–Q3
5   Kt–B3

Of recent years Samisch's continuation, 5 P–B3, has become very fashionable and the possibilities arising from it have been explored deep into the middle-game, both theoretically and practically. Whether White does in fact obtain better results with it or whether the move is merely a question of fashion only the future can give a reply.

5   . . .   O–O
6   B–K2   P–K4
7   B–K3

A little used continuation that does not give Black much difficulty. After 7 O–O the variation that was at that time highly fashionable was 7 . . . Kt–B3; 8 P–Q 5, Kt–K2; 9 Kt–K1, Kt–Q2; 10 Kt–Q 3, P–KB4; 11 P–B 3, P–B5 etc. one in which Black's attack on the King-side is met by White's on the Queen's wing. But despite a considerable mass of practical experience of this line it is not at all clear which attack holds out more chances of success here.

With the text-move Tal intends to try a new plan in that he abstains from castling immediately. After this Black's attack on the King's wing is without its customary force and more chances of success are afforded for the White advance on the other wing.

7   . . .   Kt–B3

Black reacts against the adversary's plan of campaign. But he could also have plumped for simplification here by 7 . . . PxP; 8 KtxP, R–K1; 9 P–B3, P–B3, since White can no longer well prevent the freeing thrust of P–Q4 (Lissitzin-Taimanov, XXIst U.S.S.R. Championship, 1954).

8   P–Q 5

It has been long well-known that after 8 O–O, Black obtains a good position by 8 . . . R–K1 (9 P–Q 5, Kt–Q 5!). But as we have already observed, an early castling is not at all part of Tal's plans.

| 8 | ... | Kt–K2 |
| 9 | P–KR3 | |

The point of this move is to be found in the safeguarding of the position of the Bishop on K3. But if it is White's intention, as in fact does actually occur in the game, to carry out the manoeuvre Kt–Q2 followed by P–B3, then it would be preferable to do it straightaway. As White plays the move P–KR3 merely creates a weakness in his position.

| 9 | ... | Kt–Q2 |
| 10 | Kt–Q2 | |

Once White has already played 9 P–KR3, then 10 P–KKt4 would be more logical here. If Black replies to this with 10 ... P–KB4 then there can follow 11 KPxP, PxP; 12 Q–B2 and 13 O–O–O with a sharp game that is not unfavourable for White. After the text-move Black obtains an excellent position.

| 10 | ... | P–KB4 |
| 11 | P–B3 | PxP! |

This seems at first glance somewhat surprising, but it is, however, based on sound considerations. For White must not now play 12 PxP, because of 12 . . . KtxP! by which move Black utilises the weakness created in the King's position by 9 P–KR3 for the tactical threat of mate by 23 . . . Q–R5ch. After the capture with the Knight, however, Black's Knight gets to the strong square of Q4 via KB4, and this evens out the chances for both sides.

| 12 | Kt(Q2)xP | Kt–KB4 |
| 13 | B–Kt5 | Kt–B3 |

Naturally not 13 . . . Q–K1 because of 14 Kt–Kt5 etc.

| 14 | B–Q3 | Q–K1 |

Instead of this an immediate 14 . . . P–B4 came into consideration, ensuring the Knight the important Q5 square. If in reply White exchanges pawns by 15 PxP e.p., PxP; then Black gets the better position owing to his mobile pawn centre.

| 15 | Kt–K2 | KtxKt |
| 16 | BxKt | B–B3 |

Black has attained a very good position but now he unnecessarily exchanges off his strong Bishop. He hopes thereafter to exploit the weaknesses of the black squares in the enemy position, but in fact obtains nothing tangible. Much more promising here was the thrust 16 . . . P–B4, further strengthening his hold on the Q 5 square.

Again, after 17 PxP e.p., PxP; Black would have an excellent position because of his mobile pawn centre (18 BxKt?, RxB!).

17	BxB	RxB
18	Q–Q2	P–B4

Here too the advance of the pawn is still adequate and forces his adversary to exchange off pawns, since otherwise Black would definitely secure his Knight position on Q 5 and furthermore would obtain good chances on the Queen's wing by P–QKt4.

19	PxP e.p.	PxP
20	P–KKt4?	

With this thrust Tal apparently hopes to make use of the somewhat insecure position of the Black Rook on KB3, but, as the sequel shows, without success. On the contrary, White noticeably weakens his King's wing with 20 P–KKt4, and this later proves fatal. Correct here was simply 20 O–O with an approximately equal position.

20	. . .	Kt–K2
21	O–O	

Black (Keres) to play

White (Tal)

After 21 P–Kt5, R–K3 Black's Rook would not be by any means so badly placed as one might think at first glance and the pawn move would weaken White's King-side still further. The combination 22 B–Q5, PxB; 23 PxP, would result in Black having a clear advantage after 23 . . . KtxP; 24 QxKt, R–Kt1. But there also came into consideration 21 O–O–O, after which the position would become very complicated.

With the text-move White hopes to arrive at 22 P–B4, but Black is able to thwart this plan by action in the centre.

| 21 | . . . | B–R3 |
| 22 | P–Kt3 | P–Q4! |

With this energetic thrust Black grasps the initiative firmly in his hand and drives his opponent completely on the defensive.

| 23 | Q–Kt5 | |

Tal tries to obtain counterplay by attacking the unprotected pawn on K4 and so gives his opponent the most difficulties. Bad of course was 23 PxP, BxKt; 24 QxB, PxP; 25 B–Q3, Kt–B3 with a marked advantage for Black, and the immediate retreat 23 B–Q3, results, after 23 . . . Q–B2, in about the same position as in the game.

| 23 | . . . | Q–B2 |
| 24 | B–Q3 | PxP! |

Though with this Black renounces his beautiful pawn centre the exchange, nevertheless, constitutes the most effective continuation of the attack. White must now allow the exchange of his good defensive piece—the Bishop on Q3—since after 25 PxP, R–Q1 he would incur really troublesome threats on the KB1–QR6 diagonal.

| 25 | BxBP | BxB |
| 26 | PxB | R–KB1 |

Now White is punished for his ill-considered 20th move. The attack on the KBP can no longer be warded off and with the fall of this pawn White's King is subjected to a fierce attack. In addition he is threatened simply with 27 . . . QxP. White's reply is therefore forced.

27	QxP	R–K3
28	Q–R2	

28 Q–Kt2 would also be met by 28 ... R–K6.

28	...	R–K6
29	Kt–Kt3	

Despite his difficult position Tal defends himself most resourcefully. He plans now after 29 ... RxP; 30 RxR, QxR, to consolidate his position by 31 R–K1. But Black first captures on QB5 and leaves the pawn on B3 to remain a burden for White.

29	...	QxQBP
30	Kt–K4!	

Once again Tal finds a clever defence for the KBP. If now 30 ... R(K6)xP; then 31 RxR, RxR; 32 Q–K5, or also 31 ... Q–Q 5ch; 32 K–Kt2, RxP; 33 KxR, QxR; 34 Q–Q6, in both cases with good counterplay in return for the pawn.

30	...	Q–Q 5!

Black definitely assures his advantage with this strong move. White cannot now continue with either 31 K–Kt2, R–K7ch, or 31 K–R1, R(K6)xP; however, Tal still finds a way of avoiding greater loss of material.

31	QR–Q1!	R–Q6dis ch
32	Kt–B2	R(B1)xP

And so Black has won a pawn with the better position, whereupon one may deem the fate of the game to be basically decided. In the remaining part of the game Tal does indeed put up the toughest possible resistance but he is no longer able to change the result of the struggle.

33	RxR	RxR
34	Q–Kt8ch	K–Kt2
35	Q–B7	Q–K6
36	Q–Kt7	

Necessary, since White must avoid the transition into an easily won ending for Black by 36 ... Q–Kt6ch, etc.

36	...	K–R3
37	Q–Kt8	R–Q7
38	Q–QKt3	Kt–Q4

In time trouble, Black wishes to avoid possible complications after 38 . . . Q–B5; 39 P–Kt5ch (39 . . . QxPch?; 40 Kt–Kt4 ch!) and invites his opponent to come down to an ending. In actual fact, however, 38 . . . Q–B5 would have won more quickly, since 39 P–Kt5ch can be simply met by 39 . . . K–R4!

39 P–Kt5ch?

Here of course White should have taken the opportunity of coming down to an ending by 39 QxQ, KtxQ; following this up by 40 R–K1, even though the position would still be won for Black thereafter. In the end-game, however, White could still have put up a stubborn resistance, whereas now Black wins quickly.

39 . . . K–R4!

Naturally not 39 . . . KxP? 40 QxQch, followed by 41 Kt–K4ch, and also after 39 . . . QxPch; 40 Kt–Kt4ch, White would still have some troublesome threats. But the text-move brings about an immediate decision, since now the ending after 40 QxQ, KtxQ would also be hopeless on account of the weakness on KKt5.

40 Q–Kt7 Q–Kt3ch
41 K–R1 RxKt

Simplest. Now the Black King easily escapes the checks.

42 QxPch KxP
43 P–R4ch

Unfortunately 43 R–KKt1, fails against 43 . . . R–R7 mate.

43 . . . K–B3
resigns.

After 44 Q–R8ch, K–B2; 45 Q–R7ch, K–K3; 46 R–K1ch, K–Q3, or 46 Q–Kt8ch, K–Q2; 47 Q–Kt7ch, K–Q3, the checks are ended and White has a piece less in the ending.

Game 60

SICILIAN DEFENCE

The Final of the XI Chess Olympiad in Amsterdam, 1954

P. Keres J. Sajtar
1 P–K4 P–QB4

2	Kt–KB3	P–Q3
3	P–Q4	PxP
4	KtxP	Kt–KB3
5	Kt–QB3	P–QR3

This system of defence, which shows a number of similarities to the Boleslavsky defence 5 . . . Kt–B3; 6 B–K2, P–K4, has gained great popularity in recent years. After 6 B–K2, P–K4 Black, in contrast with the Boleslavsky Defence, has the advantage of being able to develop his QKt either to QB3 or Q2 according to circumstances.

6	B–Kt5	QKt–Q2

Usually 6 . . . P–K3 is played here. But the defensive system inaugurated by the text-move is also not bad for Black and in addition he still retains the possibility of eventually developing his KB on KKt2 in this line.

7	B–QB4	P–K3

With this move Black mixes up two defensive systems, both good by themselves, and hence soon gets into difficulties. If Black did not want to go in for 7 . . . P–KKt3 and 8 . . . B–Kt2 here, then he must play at once 7 . . . Q–R4 and only after 8 Q–Q2 should he adopt the 8 . . . P–K3 move. The numerous games that have commenced in this fashion in recent tournaments show that with it Black gets an acceptable game.

8	O–O	Q–B2?

This continuation allows White to make a most promising piece sacrifice, but by now it is difficult to recommend a satisfactory move for Black. The sacrifice 9 BxKP is also very strong after 8 . . . B–K2 or 8 . . . P–QKt4, and to 8 . . . Q–R4 White can simply reply 9 P–B4. The attempt to win a piece then by 9 . . . Q–QB4; 10 B–Kt3, P–K4 is not to be feared as 11 PxP, PxP; 12 B–K3!, PxKt; 13 BxQP, followed by 14 P–K5 gives White a decisive attack. Comparatively best was perhaps still 8 . . . P–R3; 9 B–R4, Kt–K4; 10 B–QKt3, Kt–Kt3 but this too is not wholly satisfactory.

9	BxKP!

A characteristic piece sacrifice in such positions. In return for the piece White now obtains two pawns together with a excellent development; he also prevents his opponent from castling and gets an exemplary attacking position.

| 9 | ... | PxB |
| 10 | KtxP | Q-B5 |

The best reply, although with it Black gives up yet a third pawn. After 10 ... Q-Kt1 the Black Queen would be quite out of play and White would attain a decisive attack by 11 Kt-Q5.

11 Kt-Q5

White wants to decide the game by a direct attack, but this is not so simple to achieve, since Black has sufficient pieces in play for defence. Although White does retain a very strong attack in the next phase of the game one cannot categorically demonstrate that this would be enough to ensure him the win. Therefore there also came into consideration here the simple win of a pawn by 11 KtxB and 12 QxP. White would then obtain yet a third pawn for his piece and by reason of the threat of P-K5 would obtain equally good attacking possibilities.

11 ... K-B2!

Black finds much the best defence. Markedly weaker would have been 11 ... KtxKt; 12 PxKt, by which White definitively assures the position of his Kt on K6 and retains an overwhelming attack after both 12 ... K-B2; 13 R-K1, and 13 P-QKt3, followed by 14 R-K1. After the text-move, however, White's task is much more difficult.

12 BxKt

Black (Sajtar) to play

White (Keres)

12 ... KxKt?

It is this inaccuracy that gives Black a lost position. Here he should have played the cold-blooded 12 . . . KtxB, despite the weakening of the QKt3 square. If now 13 Kt–Kt5ch, K–Kt1; 14 Kt–Kt6, then, by 14 . . . Q–B4; 15 KtxR, QxKt, Black wins two pieces for a Rook and two pawns and has a very satisfactory position.

During the game I intended to reply to 12 . . . KtxB, with 13 P–QKt3, since after the only retreat-move of the Queen, 13 . . . Q–Kt4, White wins a whole Rook by 14 Kt(K6)–B7. Black has, however, a better defence in that he can give up his Queen by 13 . . . QxRch! 14 QxQ, BxKt. The position arising is difficult to appraise, it being one in which, materially speaking, Black has nothing to complain about, but on account of the insecure position of his King he will have to reckon with a great activity on the part of the enemy Queen. For instance, after 15 Kt–B7, R–B1; 16 KtxB, KxKt; 17 P–KB4, the Black King is most insecurely placed in the centre, and, too, Black must still devote a great deal of time to developing his pieces. And White can utilise this circumstance to increase his command of the initiative.

It seems to me that in this case, too, White's chances would have been preferable. But the result would have been in no way clear and Black would undoubtedly have had better prospects of a successful defence than he now has in the game.

13　B–B3!

The chief aim of this move lies in cutting off the retreat of the Black King via KB2. For if now 13 . . . K–B2; 14 Q–R5ch, P–Kt3; (or 14 . . . K–Kt1; 15 Q–K8 etc.) 15 Q–B3ch, K–Kt1; 16 Kt–B6ch and White wins. Now Black no longer has any good defence against the threat of 14 Q–Kt4ch and so he has to abandon protection of the QKt3 square, after which, however, White forces a decisive gain in material.

13	. . .	Kt–B3
14	BxKt	PxB
15	Kt–Kt6	

With this the game is ended to all intents and purposes. Black has insufficient compensation for the loss of the exchange and attempts at entrapping the Kt on R8 are in vain.

15	. . .	Q–B3
16	KtxR	

An immediate 16 Q–Q5ch, could of course have been played, but White need be in no hurry to make this move.

16	. . .	B–K2
17	P–QR4	P–Kt3

This could not have been played on the previous move on account of 16 . . . P–Kt3; 17 KtxP, QxKt; 18 Q–Kt4ch, etc. but now too White finds a way of saving his Kt.

18	Q–Q5ch	K–Q2
19	R–R3	B–Q1
20	KtxPch!	resigns.

Both 20 . . . BxKt; 21 Q–B7ch, K–Q1; 22 QxPch, and 20 . . . QxKt; 21 Q–B5ch, win for White without any trouble.

Game 61

PETROFF DEFENCE

International Tournament at Hastings, 1954–55

	P. Keres	C. H. O'D. Alexander
1	P–K4	P–K4
2	Kt–KB3	Kt–KB3

Alexander is recognised as one of the leading experts of the Petroff Defence and he has obtained good results with it against the world's best players. Praxis has shown that it is very difficult for White to obtain any noticeable advantage against this defence. More particularly when Black handles the opening accurately. In this game too White attains nothing worth mentioning out of the opening.

3   KtxP

In recent times the method of play 3 P–Q4 , PxP; 4 P–K5, Kt–K5; 5 QxP, P–Q4; 6 PxP e.p., KtxP (Q 3); 7 Kt–B3 has been played often, but in this line too no system has been discovered by which White can obtain an advantage. It would

seem that the Petroff Defence is a good one to choose when one
is not aiming at more than equality out of the opening.

3	. . .	P–Q3
4	Kt–KB3	KtxP
5	P–Q4	P–Q4
6	B–Q3	B–K2

Alexander had already demonstrated himself in 1938 that
the pawn sacrifice 6 . . . B–Q3; 7 O–O, O–O; 8 P–B4, B–KKt5;
9 PxP, P–KB4 is not quite sound. The text-move is regarded
as being best here.

7	O–O	Kt–QB3
8	R–K1	B–KKt5
9	P–B3	

As has been known for quite a time, the simplifying variation
9 BxKt, PxB; 10 RxP, BxKt; 11 QxB, KtxP leads to nothing.
White does retain some prospects of a slender advantage by
9 P–B4, here, since after 9 . . . BxKt (an immediate 9 . . . KtxP?
loses a piece after 10 BxKt) 10 QxB, KtxP; 11 Q–K3, White
has some troublesome threats. According to present theory,
Black, after the text-move, arrives at equality.

9	. . .	Kt–B3?

Once Black has gone in for this opening variation then he
should not avoid the possibility of great complications arising
from 9 . . . P–B4. After 10 P–B4, B–R5! or 10 Q–Kt3, O–O!
positions arise that have been deemed to be satisfactory for
Black by theory, but they are very complicated and so may
conceal many a surprise.

The Kt move is in any case illogical since with it Black
voluntarily leaves the initiative to his opponent and abandons
without a struggle the chief pride of his position, the outpost
on K5.

10	B–KKt5	Q–Q2?

The plan Alexander chooses here is indeed ambitious but it
is scarcely sound positionally speaking. He aims at castling
Queen-side so as to embark on a King-side attack thereafter. But
in the first place White's King's wing has no weaknesses and
hence affords no object of attack and in the second place White

gets in much more quickly with his counter-attack on the Queen's wing. It is for these reasons too that White refrains from exchanging off on KB6 in the ensuing phase of the game since this would open up the KKt file and deprive White's pieces of the important square K5.

The right plan naturally lay in 10 ... O–O, to which White would have replied 11 QKt–Q2, with only a slight positional advantage.

11   QKt–Q2   O–O–O

Black strides straight towards disaster. Despite the loss in time by 10 ... Q–Q2, 11 ... O–O was still in order.

12   Q–R4

Here there also came into consideration 12 B–Kt5, with the troublesome threat of 13 BxQKt, but White wanted to unpin his Knight as quickly as possible. Now indeed Black must reckon with the threatened 13 B–Kt5.

12   ...   P–KR3

In order to prevent the enemy threat Black chooses a method of diverting the Knight from K5. This is, however, bound up with a weakening of his own position and enables White to obtain a decisive advantage in combinational fashion. But by now it is hard to find a reasonable plan for Black since he has placed his King in a most dangerous situation with his Queen-side castling. If, for example, 12 ... B–Q3, then, in addition to 13 B–Kt5, White can continue with (even more strongly) 13 P–Kt4, K–Kt1; 14 P–Kt5, Kt–K2; 15 Kt–K5, BxKt; 16 PxB, and so gain a clear advantage. The same possibility is also very strong after the weakening move 12 ... P–QR3.

13   B–R4   P–KKt4
14   B–Kt3   BxKt
15   KtxB   P–Kt5

Now the idea of Black's defensive manoeuvre becomes apparent. He intends, after 16 Kt–R4, to sacrifice a pawn by 16 ... Kt–K5!; 17 BxKt, PxB. If then 18 RxP, P–B4, with attacking chances on the King's wing (19 R–K2, P–B5!). But there is a hole in the entire plan, as is demonstrated convincingly in the game continuation.

Black (Alexander)

White (Keres) to play

16   Kt–K5!

At first glance surprising, but in reality not so difficult to find. Black is now faced with most awkward defensive problems. White's attack assumes most threatening proportions and exacts the utmost careful defence from the adversary.

It is interesting to observe that there was possible here another solution of the problem—and an equally effective one. White could quietly ignore the attack on his Knight and continue with 16 B–Kt5! and this, after 16 . . . PxKt; 17 BxKt, QxB; (Black would be eventually mated after 17 . . . PxB; 18 QxRP) 18 RxB!, QxQ; 19 RxPch, K–Kt1; 20 R–B4disch, K–R1; 21 RxQ, would leave White in a fine position with a sound pawn to the good. The continuation in the game, however, sets Black harder problems and leaves open more opportunities for him to go wrong.

16   . . .   KtxKt
17   B–B5!

This second piece sacrifice constitutes the main idea of White's conduct of the attack. In order to avoid the worst Black must now return the material he has gained, losing at least a pawn in the process.

In any case, the other piece sacrifice 17 QxP, Kt–B3; 18 Q–R8ch, Kt–Kt1, was far from clear since in reply to 19 R–K5, Black calmly plays 19 . . . Q–Q3, and retains his extra piece, temporarily, at any rate.

17	...	QxB
18	RxKt	Q–Q6?

Black, in a difficult position, commits a mistake that results in immediate loss. However, an attempt at retaining his piece by 18 ... Q–Q2 equally gives White an overwhelming position after, for example, 19 QxP, Q–K1; 20 QR–K1, Kt–K5; 21 Q–R8ch, K–Q2; 22 QxP, or 19 ... Q–Q3; 20 R–K3, when Black must give back the Bishop.

19	RxB	R–Q2
20	R–K3!	

In this important win of a tempo lies the kernel of the matter. Black cannot now afford to surrender his QRP since this would mean that his whole King's position would crumble away. Therefore, his answer is practically forced.

20	...	Q–R3
21	QxQ	PxQ
22	B–K5!	resigns.

After the forced loss of the exchange by 22 ... R–Q3; 23 BxR, PxB; 24 R–K7, further resistance is naturally pointless.

Game 62

QUEEN'S PAWN, KING'S INDIAN DEFENCE

International Tournament at Hastings, 1954–55

	P. Keres	L. Szabo
1	P–QB4	Kt–KB3
2	Kt–KB3	P–KKt3
3	P–QKt3	

It goes without saying that with this move White is not seeking to gain an advantage out of the opening. Instead he wants to build up a solid position and quietly develop his pieces, whilst diverting his opponent from the usual theoretical paths.

3	...	B–Kt2
4	B–Kt2	O–O

5	P–Kt3	P–Q3
6	P–Q4	

Since White, with this pawn thrust, fails to prevent either P–K4 or P–B4, it would have been more logical to have completed his development by an immediate B–Kt2 followed by O–O. After the text-move Black can engineer complications that are in no way unfavourable to him.

6	. . .	P–B4

6 . . . P–K4 could also of course have been played, so as to reply to 7 PxP, with 7 . . . Kt–Kt5. This would have transposed to the normal lines of the King's Indian, whereas the text-move soon results in great complications.

7	B–Kt2

The thrust 7 P–Q5 would have allowed an immediate 7 . . . P–QKt4, but 7 . . . P–K3, too, would have not been bad against the pawn move. The maintenance of tension in the centre undoubtedly results in a more interesting type of game.

7	. . .	Kt–K5!

Black must work out with exactitude the consequences of this Knight sally since, should White succeed in neutralising the pressure on the point Q4 by simple developing moves in the next phase of the game then the text-move would prove to be merely a waste of time. However, Black's calculations are correct, since White now experiences much trouble in the defence of his Q4 square and Black attains a good game without difficulty.

8	O–O

White cannot attack the enemy Knight at once, since 8 QKt–Q2 could be met by 8 . . . Q–R4; whilst after 8 KKt–Q2, Black plays 8 . . . Kt–Kt4 with the plan of strengthening his pressure on White's Q4 by an eventual Kt–K3.

8	. . .	Kt–QB3
9	QKt–Q2	KtxKt?

With this exchange Black nullifies all the advantage he has obtained by his 7th move and so converts the Knight sally into an unnecessary loss of time. But one can only cast a judgment over the development system chosen by Black when one considers the consequences of the best continuation 9 . . . B–B4 from every point of view. With this move Black completes his development, once again ensures control of the central point K5 and strengthens the pressure on White's Q4. It seems then that Black's position would be completely satisfactory after the Bishop move.

During the game I intended replying to 9 . . . B–B4 with 10 Kt–R4, KtxKt; 11 QxKt, but this does not yield anything more than equality. Black can either continue with 11 . . . PxP; 12 KtxB, PxKt; 13 BxKt, PxB; 14 BxP, or also with 11 . . . KtxP; 12 KtxB, followed by 13 BxKtP, in both cases with an approximately even position. This shows, however, that the system of development chosen by Black was very good and that his mistake in the game is to be sought elsewhere.

| 10 | QxKt | B–Kt5 |

This method of attack on White's Q4 is ineffective since White, by simplifying the position, can now obtain an advantage in space.

11	P–Q5	BxB
12	QxB	BxKt
13	BxB	Kt–R4?

It would seem that Black overestimates his position. His aim is to initiate a counter-attack on the Queen's wing by P–QKt4, and for this purpose the Knight is of course well placed on QR4. But it appears that Black quite forgets that after the exchange of the Bishops on the black squares his King's position remains completely bereft of the necessary protection. Black, by removing his last minor piece far from the King's wing, allows his opponent to attain a most dangerous initiative there. Better therefore was 13 . . . Kt–K4, even though then White would retain the better position with 14 B–Kt2, chiefly because of the possibilities of activity both in the centre and on the King-side. All these difficulties are the consequences of Black's ill-considered 9th move.

| 14 | P–KR4 | P–QKt4 |

Owing to the threat of 15 P–R5, Black no longer has the time to prepare for this thrust with 14 . . . P–QR3. Too risky,

however, would have been 14 ... P–R4, since after 15 P–KKt4
White threatens to open up two lines of attack on the King's
wing.

15   PxP   Q–Kt3

Naturally Black would rather have continued here with
15 ... R–Kt1, but this would have allowed the sharp continuation 16 P–R4, P–QR3; 17 P–QKt4! etc. With the text-move
Black does indeed win back his pawn, but in so doing has to
take away yet another piece from the protection of his King's
wing.

16   P–R4   P–QR3
17   P–R5   RPxP

Black could not well play here 17 ... P–Kt4 so as to keep the
position on the King-side closed, since then White would have
the troublesome reply of 18 P–QKt4! at his disposal. And then
Black could not play 18 . . . Kt–B5 because of 19 Q–B1!
threatening both QxKt and QxPch, whilst after 18 ... BPxP;
19 QxP, White would simply retain his extra pawn with the
better position.

However, once the KR file is opened up Black must reckon
with a direct mating attack and therefore has no time in which
to initiate any effective counter-play on the Queen's wing.

18   KRPxP   RPxP
19   K–Kt2   P–B3
20   R–R1   K–Kt2

Black (Szabo)

White (Keres) to play

The threats on the King's wing leave Black no time to capture the pawn on QR5. To 20 ... PxP White could simply reply 21 RxP, but still stronger seems 21 Q–B2, K–Kt2; 23 Q–K4! For then Black would experience great difficulty in protecting his KP since after 22 ... QR–K1 or 22 ... R–R2 there comes 23 Q–K3, and after 22 ... Q–B2; 23 RxP, is enough to retain the positional advantage.

With the text-move Black tries to better his position by offering an exchange with 21 ... R–R1. But White affords him no opportunity for this, since he is able to combine his attack on the King's wing with threats on the Kt.

21   PxP   QxP

Black must give up the projected exchange of 21 ... R–R1, since after 22 RxR, RxR; 23 Q–B3, Kt–Kt2; 24 Q–K3! White not only has a pawn more but also possesses a marked positional advantage. But the text-move also leads to a rapid catastrophe.

22   Q–Q2!

Once again preventing R–R1 since after 23 RxR, RxR the Kt would be hanging. Now, in order to parry the threat of 23 Q–R6ch, Black must weaken his King-side still further.

22   ...   P–Kt4
23   Q–K3   Q–Q2
24   B–Kt4!

Black's plight is of course hopeless by now and there are many ways for White to increase his advantage. Of all these the text-move is the most pleasing. White could also have won by 24 Q–Q3, since after 24 ... R–R1; 25 RxR, RxR, White can quietly capture on QR5 without taking much notice of the check 26 ... Q–R6.

24   ...   Q–B2

Naturally not 24 ... QxB; 25 QxKPch, R–B2; 26 R–R7ch, etc.

25   B–B5   K–B2

Black no longer has a defence against the threatened check on KR2. For example, after 25 ... R–R1; 26 RxR, RxR; White can play 27 RxKt!, QxR; 28 QxKPch, with mate to follow. The text-move merely lengthens resistance by a few moves.

26	R–R7ch	K–K1
27	QR–R1	Q–Kt2
28	R–R8	resigns.

The unhappy position of the Kt on R4 is very apparent. Not only cannot it come to the aid of the Black King but it also interferes with the organising of a successful defence.

Game 63

QUEEN'S PAWN, NIMZOWITSCH DEFENCE

XXII U.S.S.R. Championship in Moscow, 1955

	P. Keres	M. Taimanov
1	P–Q4	Kt–KB3
2	P–QB4	P–K3
3	Kt–QB3	B–Kt5
4	Kt–B3	

This move in the Nimzoindian is held to be innocuous for Black and probably rightly so. In the present game, however, White pursues certain definite objectives. In his game against Gligoric in Zurich 1953 Taimanov made use of a dubious line in this variation against which I had prepared an improvement. I only had to wait and see if, in the meantime, Taimanov had perhaps also discovered the drawbacks of the variation.

4	. . .	P–QKt3
5	B–Kt5	B–Kt2
6	P–K3	P–KR3
7	B–R4	

Naturally White does not want to choose the simplifying continuation 7 BxKt, which, in the 27th match game Euwe–Alekhine, 1937, yielded Black a thoroughly satisfactory position after 7 . . . BxKtch; 8 PxB, QxB.

7	. . .	P–KKt4

Apparently it was just this advance that Euwe feared when he exchanged off pieces in the above-mentioned game. But, as the present game shows, the ensuing advance on the King's wing is a double-edged undertaking since in so doing Black markedly weakens his central and King-side position. In later games in this tournament when this opening variation was again tried out, Black continued more prudently with 7 . . . Q–K2 and this move undoubtedly fits in better with the nature of the position.

8	B–Kt3	Kt–K5
9	Q–B2	BxKtch
10	PxB	P–Q3
11	B–Q3	P–KB4

Seemingly Taimanov scents no danger and exactly repeats his above-mentioned game against Gligoric, in which, after 12 O–O, Kt–Q2; 13 Kt–Q2, QKt–B3, he obtained a good position. But for me too the position that has now arisen was not new. It had already occurred in the game Keres–Rozdestvenski, Estonian Championship, 1953, and I was able to use a new strong continuation that appears to destroy the whole variation chosen by Black.

12 P–Q5!

A logical continuation. With it the proud enemy centre is torn up and the one piece of the adversary that is well placed, the Kt on K5, is removed. That all this happens at the cost of a pawn sacrifice, plays no particularly important role since, in the sequel, owing to the numerous weaknesses in the enemy position, White obtains good attacking chances and adequate counter-play. It is interesting to observe that, in his notes to the game Gligoric–Taimanov, Grandmaster Bronstein also recommended the same pawn sacrifice and after its acceptance esteemed White's chances the better.

12 . . .   PxP

It is clear that only this move can challenge White's previous move, even though Black has a sad experience with it here. However, given that Black already regards his position as bad and is seeking a way out of his dubious plight, then 12 . . . Kt–Q2 would come into consideration. White then has two promising continuations. Firstly 13 PxP, QKt–B4; 14 Kt–Q4, Q–B3; 15 P–B3, KtxBch; 16 QxKt, Kt–B4; 17 QxP, QxQ;

18 KtxQ, KtxP; 19 P–K4, with a solid plus pawn, and secondly
13 Kt–Q4, Kt (Q2)–B4; 14 B–K2, with the threat of P–B3.

13   PxP

In his notes Grandmaster Bronstein recommends here an
immediate 13 Kt–Q4, which, however, after 13 . . . Q–B3,
should lead to approximately the same position as arises later
in the game. It would seem that both continuations are
sufficient to maintain White's advantage.

13   . . .   BxP
14   Kt–Q4!   Kt–Q2

Obviously Black must sooner or later give back the pawn he
has won since KB4 cannot be adequately defended. In the
previously mentioned game Keres–Rozdestvenski Black continued here with 14 . . . Q–B3 which, after 15 P–B3, KtxB; 16
PxKt, Kt–Q2; 17 BxP, O–O–O; led to the position in the
present game. With the text-move Black offers back the pawn
at once so as to meet 15 KtxP with 15 . . . Kt(Q2)–B4. However,
White does not want to stray from the path of attack he has
already marked out.

15   P–B3   KtxB
16   PxKt   Q–B3

Now 16 . . . Kt–B4 would naturally have served no purpose
because of 17 BxP. With the text-move Black attempts to get
his King into safety, but, as the sequel of the game shows, with
Queen-side castling the problems besetting the Black King are
in no way solved.

17   BxP   O–O–O
18   Q–R4!

A very troublesome move for Black, attacking as it does the
vulnerable QRP. The ensuing weakening of his King's position
is practically forced since 18 . . . P–B4 fails against 19 Kt–Kt5.
In the above mentioned game Rozdestvenski tried 18 . . . Q–K4;
19 K–B2, P–QR4; 20 P–Kt4, KR–K1, but only succeeded in
losing his KRP within a few moves. Taimanov finds a more
skilful defence.

18   . . .   P–QR4

By now it is already clear that the opening has gone in favour of White and that Black is in a critical position. White's pieces are much more actively placed, he is threatening a strong attack against Black King's position, and finally no possibility of successful counter-attack can be perceived for Black. Nevertheless, Black does possess a counter-chance. The position of White's King is also somewhat precarious and this could have been exploited by 18 ... Q–K4; 19 K–B2, P–KR4, with the threat of P–R5.

From this one deduces that White's first task must be to eliminate this counter-chance, and, once this is done, Black must sit quietly watching the development of the White attack on the Queen's wing without doing anything himself. A suitable means for such a purpose was 19 P–Kt4!, fixing the weakness on KR6 and thwarting the counter-threat of P–KR4–5. Instead of this White plays a little carelessly during the next few moves and allows his opponent quite considerable counter-play.

19   K–B2   P–R4!

It goes without saying that Black at once utilises the chance of carrying out this advance, before White plays P–Kt4.

20   QR–QKt1

This move too shows that White has strayed from the correct handling of the attack. Very strong here was 20 P–K4, B–Kt2; 21 Kt–K6!, threatening both 22 KtxR, and 22 Q–QB4.

20   . . .   P–R5
21   P–K4

Black's counter on the King's wing has become somewhat troublesome by now. Thus, for example, the natural looking move 21 P–Kt4 could be met by 21 ... Q–K4, threatening the unpleasant Q–Kt6ch. White must therefore accelerate his action on the Queen's wing, if he does not wish to lose the initiative. But the text-move leads to great complications and allows the opponent counter-chances that should not be underestimated.

Better therefore seems 21 PxP, PxP; 22 R–Kt5, B–Kt2; 23 Q–B4!, threatening in the first place 24 RxKtP. Should Black

then try 23 ... P–Q4 the sacrifice of the exchange by 24 RxB!
would give White a decisive attack and after 23 ... K–Kt1; 24
Kt–B6ch, BxKt; 25 QxB, would suffice to demonstrate the
hopelessness of Black's position.

21 ...   B–Kt2

The pawn exchange 21 ... PxPch; 22 KxP, would surrender
the pressure on KKt6 and so merely lighten White's task.

22   PxP   PxP
23   Kt–K6

At last White plumps for the correct plan of attack, as has
already been outlined in the note to White's 20th move. In the
meantime, however, Black has been able to procure some
counter-play on the other wing and therefore he can now put up
a much tougher defence than would have been possible some
moves ago.

Black (Taimanov) to play

White (Keres)

23 ...   Kt–K4?

Black, apparently already convinced of the hopelessness of
his position, throws up the sponge too soon. Instead of the
text-move, which is equivalent to resignation, Black could have
made the opponent's task markedly harder by the capture
23 ... QxP! At first glance this move looks idiotic because of
24 KR–QB1, Q–Q7ch; 25 K–Kt1, but it is precisely at this
point that Black can produce a problem-like resource. He plays

25 ... P–R6!; 26 RxPch, K–Kt1; 27 RxBch, and now not 27 ... KxR; because of 28 KtxRch, but 27 ... K–R1! White no longer has an effective check and after 28 BxP, Q–K6ch; 29 K–R2, RxBch; Black has at least a draw by perpetual check.

But what then should White play after 23 . . . QxP? Naturally, 24 KR–Q1 comes into consideration, but this move too does not have particularly convincing consequences. Black then plays 24 ... B–B3; 25 Q–Q4, QxQ; 26 RxQ and, now not 26 ... QR–Kt1; 27 R–B4, K–Kt2; 28 RxB!, KxR; 29 Kt–Q4ch, K–B4; 30 K–K3, when the Black King has fallen into a mating net, but simply 26 . . . K–Kt2!; 27 KtxRch, RxKt, and Black can still put up a stubborn resistance in the ending.

Although this last variation is quite acceptable for White yet one cannot get rid of the feeling that the position must contain somewhere or other in it a better possibility. A more exhaustive consideration of the position reveals to us that the surprising retreat 24 Q–Q1! poses Black most difficult problems, since in addition to 25 KtxR, White also threatens 25 R–QB1. It is, however, clear in any case that the move 23 . . . QxP!, though scarcely saving the game, still sets White many difficult problems and so would at least have provided Black with some practical chances. After the text-move White's task is easy.

24 Q–Q4!

Naturally White can also take the exchange, but the text-move is still stronger. White's Knight is worth more in this position than the passive Black Rook.

24 . . . QR–Kt1

The only possibility of saving the exchange since after 24 ... R–Q2; 25 P–B4 is at once decisive. Now there comes a combinational finish.

25	KtxPdisch	K–Kt1
26	QxKtP	Kt–Q6ch
27	K–B1	Kt–Kt5

Hoping still to fish in troubled waters after 28 PxKt, Q–B6.

| 28 | RxKt! | PxR |
| 29 | Kt–Kt5 | resigns. |

Game 64

KING'S GAMBIT ACCEPTED

Match U.S.S.R. against U.S.A. in Moscow, 1955

	R. Byrne	P. Keres
1	P–K4	P–K4
2	P–KB4	

The King's Gambit is a rare visitor to modern tournaments and its presence there is greeted with pitying laughter and comparisons are drawn with the sacrificial games of the previous century. But it seems to me that such an attitude towards the King's Gambit is not justified and it must have arisen chiefly because this opening has, for the moment, gone completely out of fashion. It would not be surprising if the King's Gambit were not to assume its proper place in the tournament praxis of the next twenty-odd years, as indeed it had rather more than half a century ago.

2	. . .	PxP
3	Kt–KB3	P–KKt4

As my opponent informed me after the game, he had already made up his mind to play the King's Gambit against me during his preparations for the match. In so doing he had checked over numerous variations anew and furbished up his recollections of them. When, however, the move 3 . . . P–KKt4 came into question then this possibility was accompanied by the observation that a player would not choose such a method of play under any circumstances. I decided upon this classical defence principally because one very rarely has the opportunity of defending against a King's Gambit; it especially interested me to discover whether my opponent had found or not some improvement in his analysis of this old defence.

4	P–KR4	P–Kt5
5	Kt–Kt5	

In view of the present-day refined technique of defence such sacrifices as those in the Allgaier Gambit 5 Kt–Kt5, P–KR3; 6 KtxBP no longer yield any satisfactory prospect of success.

| | 5 . . . | Kt–KB3 |
| 6 | B–B4 | |

Master Byrne chooses one of the oldest lines of play in this variation. At the time 6 P–Q4 was regarded as the stronger continuation, but after that too Black gets a most satisfactory game by 6 . . . P–Q 3; 7 Kt–Q 3, KtxP; or 7 . . . P–B6.

| | 6 . . . | P–Q4 |
| 7 | PxP | B–Kt2 |

This continuation is regarded as more precise than 7 . . . B–Q3, though with the latter move Black likewise gets a good game.

| | 8 P–Q4 | Kt–R4 |
| 9 | O–O | |

The other continuation considered by theory, 9 Kt–QB3, yields Black the better game after 9 . . . O–O; 10 Kt–K2, P–QB4! After the text-move a very complicated position arises, even though it is somewhat simplified by the ensuing Queen exchange.

	9 . . .	QxRP
10	Q–K1!	QxQ
11	RxQ	O–O
12	Kt–QB3	

Undoubtedly better than the restrained protective move 12 P–B3, which is recommended by many theoretical books, since then the pin 12 . . . R–K1 ensures Black a clear advantage. After the text-move Black, in view of the threats of 13 Kt–K2 and 13 Kt–Kt5, must proceed with the utmost energy.

| | 12 . . . | Kt–Q2 |

More precise here was an immediate 12 . . . P–QB4, so as to play Kt–Q2 only after 13 Kt–Kt5 or 13 PxP. The pawn exchange 13 PxPe.p., KtxP would undoubtedly be favourable to Black. The text-move is playable, but allows more possibilities open for White.

| 13 | Kt–Kt5 | P–QB3 |
| 14 | Kt–B7? | |

White pursues the plan of winning the exchange, but in so doing gives the initiative completely into Black's hands. In

addition Black also obtains sufficient material in compensation
for the exchange so that from now on the advantage sways over
to his side.

Obviously White must utilise his opponent's transposition
of move and continue with 14 PxP! Since White would win the
pawn back with a good game after 14 . . . PxP; 15 KtxQBP
Black must reply 14 . . . KtxKt. Now there are two possibilities
open to White. He can play 15 PxP, BxP; 16 PxKt, when Black
can bring about great complications by 16 . . . QR–B1; 17
Kt–Q6, R–B4. The other possibility 15 PxKt, PxP; 16 Kt–B7,
R–Kt1; 17 P–K6 equally leads to very unclear complications
after 17 . . . R–Kt5! After both continuations positions would
arise in which the end-result would depend on the resourcefulness of the two adversaries, whereas now Black gets a clear
advantage in position.

14   . . .   PxP!

Also possible was 14 . . . R–Kt1, after which, in addition to
15 PxP, Black would also have to reckon with the advance
15 P–Q6. But the exchange sacrifice bound up with the text-
move is much more energetic and ensures Black a lasting initiative.

15   KtxR

Declining the sacrifice by 15 BxP, R–Kt1 or 15 KtxQP,
KtxKt; 16 PxKt, B–K3 etc. would give Black a good position
together with an extra pawn.

15   . . .   PxB
16   B–Q2

Black now has two pawns for the exchange, together with
active play for his pieces. Whilst White must lose more time
so as to get the Kt on R8 once again into play. An immediate
16 Kt–B7, however, would after 16 . . . KtxKt; 17 PxKt, R–Q1
have occasioned White a lot of trouble in connection with the
development of his Queen's wing.

The capture, too, by 16 KtxKtP does not seem good, since
after 16 . . . BxPch; 17 Kt–B2, (or 17 K–R2, P–B4 etc.) 17 . . .
Kt–K4! leaves White inadequate protection against the threat
of 18 . . . Kt–Kt5. With the text-move White surrenders yet a
third pawn.

16	. . .	KtxKt
17	PxKt	B–B4
18	Kt–B7	BxBP?

Black is in too much of a hurry to make this capture. Much more lasting pressure would have come from an immediate 18 . . . R–Q1, taking away from the enemy Knight the strong square on Q5, and only after 19 B–B3, BxP. With this Black would have obtained a clear advantage, whereas now White gets considerable counter-play.

| 19 | QR–B1 | B–Q6 |
| 20 | Kt–Q5 | P–Kt4 |

As a result of his imprecise 18th move Black now experiences marked difficulties in defending his KBP. With the text-move, however, he makes his opponent's task all too easy. It would have been much better to have surrendered the pawn by 20 . . . R–Q1; 21 KtxP, KtxKt; 22 BxKt, R–Q4. After this Black could either have carried out the King manoeuvre K–B1–K2–K3 or else have attacked the enemy pawns on the Queen's wing at a favourable opportunity.

| 21 | BxP | |

It would seem that White does not like the end game that would ensue after 21 KtxP, KtxKt; 22 BxKt, and with good reason. The text-move leads to interesting complications, though here too Black has the better chances in the long run.

| 21 | . . . | R–Q1 |

After 21 . . . KtxB; 22 KtxKt, B–B4; 23 Kt–R5, White has some troublesome counter-play. The text-move is stronger.

22	Kt–K7ch	K–B1
23	B–Kt5	R–K1
24	Kt–B6	Kt–Kt6

The position is very complicated and both players are by now harassed by coming time trouble. In an endeavour to force matters Black surrenders too many pawns on the Queen-side in the ensuing phase of the game and in consequence loses practically all his advantage. The text-move is not bad in itself but it would have been more logical first of all to have

deprived the enemy Knight of the QKt5 square by 24 . . .
P–QR4. After 25 KtxP, RxP the pawn on QKt4 would no
longer be under attack and Black would retain his advantage.

	25	QR–Q1	R–K3

Here too 25 . . . P–QR4 could still have been played. On the
other hand, nothing would have come of 25 . . . Kt–K7ch;
26 K–B2, R–K3 on account of the resource 27 RxKt!

	26	KtxP	

Now White omits to take advantage of the opportunity of
playing 26 Kt–Kt4! Apparently, in time-trouble, he did not
like the possible reply 26 . . . Kt–K7ch. If then 27 K–R1,
RxP; 28 KtxB, PxKt; or else 27 K–B2, BxP; 28 KtxB, B–Kt6
etc. in both cases with advantage to Black. But after 26 . . .
Kt–K7ch White has the surprising reply 27 K–B1! at his
disposal, after which it is not easy for Black to find a promising
continuation of the attack. 27 . . . Kt–B6disch fails against 28
RxB, and after 27 . . . Kt–Kt6dbch there follows 28 K–Kt1.

Black would, therefore, after 26 Kt–Kt4, Kt–K7ch; 27 K–B1,
have continued either with 27 . . . Kt–Kt6dbch; 28 K–Kt1,
B–Kt3; 29 Kt–B6, Kt–B4, or with 27 . . . Kt–B5disch; 28
K–Kt1, P–QR4!; 29 BxKt, PxKt; 30 B–Q2, BxP; 31 BxPch, K–
Kt1; 32 B–B3, BxB; 33 PxB, R–QR3; retaining winning chances
in both cases.

	26	. . .	BxP

Before making this capture 26 . . . P–Kt5 came into consideration, since the KP will not run away.

	27	KtxP	Kt–K7ch
	28	RxKt!	

Forced, as is quite apparent. White, by giving back the
exchange, breaks the spearhead of the enemy attack and brings
about an endgame in which Black is met by marked technical
difficulties in making his extra pawn felt.

	28	. . .	BxR.
	29	R–Q8ch	R–K1

Unfortunately Black is compelled to exchange Rooks, since
after 29 . . . K–Kt2: 30 Kt–Q4 he has to take on an ending

with Bishops of opposite colour (30 . . . R–KKt3? 31 Rt–B5 mate). After the exchange of Rooks, however, Black experiences great difficulties in realising the advantage of his small material plus, this being chiefly because, in the ensuing phase of the game, White succeeds in blockading the enemy pawns on the King's wing. After the exciting middle-game an ending has been reached in which the solution of the technical problems still demands very careful work on the part of Black.

30	RxRch	KxR
31	K–B2	B–Q6
32	Kt–B3	K–Q2

Another inaccuracy under time pressure. Black should play here 32 . . . P–R4, so as to meet 33 K–K3 with 33 . . . P–B4. In that event White could not have played 34 B–B4, because of 34 . . . BxBch; 35 KxB, P–R5 with an easily won position for Black. Now White succeeds in completely blockading the Black pawns on the King's wing, thereby markedly increasing the difficulty of Black's task.

33	K–K3	B–R7
34	B–B4	B–Kt8ch
35	K–Q2	P–R4
36	P–KKt3	B–KB7

Threatening 37 . . . P–R5 which would not work at once on account of 37 PxP, B–KB7; 38 P–R5, P–Kt6; 39 B–K3.

37	Kt–Q1	B–Q5
38	Kt–B3	K–B3?

Instead of this he should have played 38 . . . B–B3, so as to force through the essential advance of P–R5. The King's move to B3 presents White later on with a valuable tempo, aiding him to advance his own pawns.

39	P–Kt4!	B–B3
40	P–Kt5ch?	

With his last move before the time control White makes up for his opponent's mistake on move 38. For with the text-move he weakens his pawn formation on the Queen's wing and Black, by blockading it along the diagonal Q1–QR4, renders it practically valueless. If instead White had played 40 P–R4!

Black (Keres)

(Position after
39 ... B–B3)

White (Byrne) to play

then Black would have been set much more difficult problems. One can see nothing better for Black in reply than 40 ... P–R5; 41 PxP, BxP, but then follows 42 P–R5, P–Kt6; 43 P–Kt5ch and the White pawns on the Queen's wing have become very strong. It is doubtful if in fact Black would have a win any longer.

Now time trouble is over and with it the inaccuracies too depart. The game continues along normal lines and the ending that has now arisen still affords us many an interesting moment.

| 40 | ... | K–Kt2 |
| 41 | P–R4 | B–Q1! |

Here the difference in the order in which White's advance of his pawns is made makes itself felt. The Black Bishop now not only blockades the enemy pawns from QR4 but can also pin White's Knight, thereby rendering both it and the White King immobile.

| 42 | Kt–Q5 | |

White cannot well prevent his Knight being pinned, since he dare not allow the QBP freedom to advance and his Bishop cannot guard the two squares KKt3 and QB3 at the same time.

| 42 | ... | B–K5 |
| 43 | Kt–B3 | B–B6 |

An immediate 43 ... B–R4 could be met by 44 K–K3. In addition, in order to render the pin an effective one, Black must first of all limit the freedom of action for the enemy Bishop by P–B3.

44	K–K3	B–Kt3ch
45	K–Q2	P–B3!

At once 45 ... B–R4 achieves nothing after 46 B–K5. Now, however, all the preparations for this pin have been made and White can only wait to see how Black intends to strengthen his position.

46	B–Q6	B–R4
47	B–B4	B–K5!

With this Black's plan of campaign is clear. He intends to bring his Bishop back to Q6 and, when White places his Bishop on B4, then follows B–Kt5 and White will be in zugzwang. One cannot see what White can undertake against such a plan. His Bishop is bound down to the protection of KKt3 and if he tries to transfer his King to the Queen-side then the threat of B–B2 followed by P–R5 is decisive.

48	B–Q6

After 48 K–K3 the simplest way of deciding the game is 48 ... BxKt; 49 KxB, B–K4! since in the pawn ending Black procures yet another passed pawn by P–R5. Now, however, Black carries out his original plan.

48	...	B–Q6
49	B–B4	B–Kt5!

And now Black's problem is solved. White can no longer retain his Bishop on the KR2–QKt8 diagonal, and this means that Black will obtain a passed pawn on the King's wing as well as on the Queen's. The ensuing part of the endgame is merely a matter of technique.

50	B–K3	P–R5!

Now the passed pawn on the KKt file brings a speedy decision.

51	PxP	P–Kt6
52	P–KR5	P–Kt7
53	P–R6	P–B4

This is playable because of the variation 54 P–R7, P–B5!

54	B–B2	P–B5
55	B–Kt1	B–R4
56	B–R2	B–QKt3

A simpler way of winning here was by 56 . . . P–B6; 57 K–K3 (or 57 B–Kt1, B–QKt3 etc.) 57 . . . BxKt; 58 KxP, B–Q7; 59 KxP, P–B6; etc., but of course the text-move is just as adequate.

57	P–R7	

White still finds a way of making some resistance.

57	. . .	BxP
58	K–K2	P–Kt8–Q
59	BxQ	BxB
60	Kt–Q5	B–Q5
61	KtxP	B–B6
62	Kt–Q3	BxKtch!

The quickest way of finishing off the stubborn enemy resistance. By now the end is very simple.

63	KxB	K–Q3
64	K–B2	K–R4
65	K–Kt3	B–K4
66	K–B2	KxP
	resigns.	

An interesting struggle in the good old style of the previous century.

3

FRESH ATTEMPTS
AT THE WORLD CHAMPIONSHIP, 1955–1956

My sharing of 2nd to 4th place at Zurich 1953 gave me no right to participate in the next Candidates' Tournament. For this I still had to take part in the Interzonal Tournament at Gothenbourg. Since the ensuing Candidates' Tournament was to comprise ten participants and of these ten only one, the loser of the match between Botvinnik and Smyslov, was fixed, this meant that the nine top players from the Gothenbourg tournament would qualify for the Candidates. With normal play, then, one had good prospects of advancing further on to the road that led to the World Championship.

In Gothenbourg I was again playing good chess. According to a decision of the F.I.D.E. Congress all the players from the same country had to be paired together at the beginning of the tournament, so that my results in the early rounds were not exactly outstanding. I won against Spassky by an interesting combination involving a Queen sacrifice (Game No. 65), but then lost to Bronstein in a beautiful game full of sacrifices, obtaining only 50% in the first six rounds. Grandmaster Bronstein, on the other hand, was in terrific form, since he obtained 6½ points out of his first seven games. When, at the end of Round 11 all the Soviet grandmasters had played against each other, I was a full two points below Bronstein who had acquired eight points out of his first ten games. Very well placed, too, was Panno with 8 points out of 11 games, whereas I had obtained 6 out of 10. I was then faced by the prospect of some very hard work in the second half of the tournament if I wanted to ensure myself a good place amongst the leaders.

I played distinctly better in the second half of the tournament and up to the 18th round I kept in step with Grandmaster Bronstein, who was still in brilliant form, so that I was only 1½ points behind him. In the interim I defeated Panno in good positional style (Game No. 66), managed to outplay Najdorf in a combinational whirlpool of a game (Game No. 67), won after terrific complications against Guimard and succeeded in outplaying Fuderer in an interesting theoretical variation of the opening (Game No. 68). By means of this series of wins I had secured the second place amongst the leading group, true, only half a point ahead of Panno, but the latter had played one game more. In the next round, however, I lost to Stahlberg, with which not only were all my hopes for the first place buried but also my prospects of gaining the second prize were endangered. I had to beat Unzicker in a wild game and then win too against Sliwa in order to keep up with Panno. But then a draw in the last round against Szabo ensured me the second place since Panno had the bye in the last round.

The next event was in fact the Candidates' Tournament which was held in Amsterdam in the Spring of 1956. This time ten grandmasters were taking part in a double-round tournament as at Budapest in 1950. I employed new tactics in this tournament, the chief idea being to save as much energy as possible. For this purpose I was ready to incur a series of short draws whenever the position offered very little chances of obtaining advantage from the objective point of view. In between whiles I aimed at inserting here and there a whole point. One may indeed entertain varying opinions about such tactics, but in Amsterdam they served very well. In the first tour I drew 7 games, won against Pilnik and Panno and, with $5\frac{1}{2}$ points, was equal 2nd and 3rd with Bronstein, only half a point below Geller.

It was in the opening round of the second tour that I had my decisive meeting with Bronstein who obtained good pressure out of the opening and adjourned the game in a most favourable position for him. But on resumption of play Bronstein failed to find the best continuation, got into great time trouble and during this lost not only all his advantage but also eventually even the game. Since round about this time Geller lost to Petrosian I was now in the sole lead. It was, however, in the next three rounds that the real decision took place. I was not able to convert the strategically won positions against Spassky and Pilnik into wins, and thus Geller and Smyslov gradually overhauled me. By the penultimate round Smyslov was even half a point ahead of me, whilst Geller was in third place with half a point less than me. But then came the unlucky game with Filip. After a middle-game full of vicissitudes I obtained a clearly won position, but then committed a great blunder, whereupon the balance swung in favour of my opponent. Despite a lengthy resistance I could not save the ending and with this my last chances of getting first prize disappeared. In the last round I played most indifferently against Petrosian and only with the help of my adversary did I escape with a draw. But this was enough to secure the second place for me, thus gaining the right to play in the next Candidates' Tournament without having to qualify in previous tournaments.

Shortly after the Candidates' Tournament I went to Hamburg to play a friendly match with Grandmaster Unzicker. The match was of eight games. After a quiet draw in the first game I gained the advantage in the second against an old-fashioned defence by my opponent and decided the game by a direct King-side attack (Game No. 69). The third game was also drawn, though only after an exciting struggle and in the fourth I was able to gain my second win by an interesting combination. The decisive point came in the fifth game. Unzicker conducted it in good attacking style and obtained a marked advantage; but in time trouble he played weakly and eventually even lost. This broke my adversary's resistance. After a draw in the sixth game Unzicker played a listless seventh game and suffered another loss. The last game was a quick draw, so that I won the match by the fine score 6–2. An interesting point about the match is that all the games commenced with the Ruy Lopez.

After the match with Unzicker I went to Yugoslavia as a member of the U.S.S.R. team in a match between the two countries. There I had a win against Karaklaic that was of interest to theory. In the autumn came the next Chess Olympiad, which was held in Moscow. I played really well and finished up with 7 wins and 5 draws, without losing a game. However, I had a much less favourable result in the Alekhine Memorial Tournament which was held in Moscow after the Olympiad. I lost two games in this tournament, the one after an excellently conducted attack by my opponent, Unzicker, and the other through an oversight in a drawn ending against Szabo, but the chief reason for my indifferent result did not reside in these losses. My failure lay in the fact that I was unable to gain any wins against the comparatively weaker opponents, whereas my rivals succeeded in exactly this. I did, it is true, succeed in winning a theoretically interesting game against Golombek (Game No. 70) and also in the last round in an important game as regards the destination of the first prize against Botvinnik I managed to inflict a defeat on the World Champion (Game No. 71), but all this sufficed only for a share of 7th and 8th places in the end.

Game 65

QUEEN'S PAWN, QUEEN'S INDIAN DEFENCE

F.I.D.E. Interzonal Tournament at Gothenbourg, 1955

	P. Keres	B. Spassky
1	P–Q4	Kt–KB3
2	P–QB4	P–K3
3	Kt–KB3	

Usually the Queen's Indian is regarded as a type of opening in which Black experiences no difficulties. In this game, however, play is soon steered along a track where one cannot complain of a lack of complicated problems.

3	. . .	P–QKt3
4	P–K3	B–Kt2
5	B–Q3	B–K2
6	O–O	O–O

Here Black can choose between two different systems of development which are distinguished by the moves P–Q4 and P–QB4. Since Black has castled he has made it clear that he has plumped for the P–Q4 advance. For example, after 7 Kt–B3, P–B4 would no longer be good on account of the possibility of 8 P–Q5. Taking this circumstance into account, White refrains from an immediate Kt–B3, since in some variations this Knight can be usefully developed on Q2.

7	P–QKt3	P–Q4
8	B–Kt2	QKt–Q2
9	Kt–B3	

Now that Black has already developed his Kt on Q2 the White Knight is much more actively posted on B3 than on Q2; nor need White worry about the eventual protection of his QBP.

9	...	P–B4

Black commits a scarcely noticeable and yet important inaccuracy in the opening. If he wanted to play P–B4 then it would have been better to have done it the move before and then to have developed his Kt on QB3. The Kt would be much more actively placed there and it could eventually have helped in the pressure on White's QB4 by Kt–QR4 or Kt–QKt5. Had Black played in this way then it would have been better for White to have developed his QKt on Q2.

Once, however, Black has already played 8 . . . QKt–Q2, it would have been better for him to have given up the idea of playing 9 . . . P–B4 and to have continued with, for instance, 9 . . . Kt–K5 and P–KB4. After the text-move, at all events, Black is beset by some disagreeable opening problems.

10	Q–K2	QPxP

With this exchange Black only worsens his position, since now White obtains a preponderance in the centre and he can have at his disposal the continuous threat of P–Q 5. Better was still 10 . . . Kt–K5, although even then after 11 KR–Q1 Black would not be happily placed.

11	KtPxP	Q–B2
12	QR–Q1	QR–Q1?

But this is indeed a mistake after which White can seize the initiative and obtain a clear positional advantage. Black must here choose the lesser evil and go in for 12 . . . PxP; 13 PxP, though then too White would stand rather better.

13	P–Q 5!

Experience teaches us that White always gets an advantage in such positions when he can carry out the thrust P–Q 5 without

incurring a disadvantage elsewhere. This is in fact the case in
the present game. Black cannot now continue 13 . . . PxP; 14
PxP, KtxP; 15 KtxKt, BxKt; since after 16 BxPch, KxB; 17
RxB, Kt–B3; 18 R–Kt5! would allow White a most dangerous
attack.

| 13 . . . | P–QR3 |

Black is forced to leave his opponent with this strong central
pawn and has now been fixed in a bad position. With the
text-move he protects himself against the threat of 14 P–Q6,
and plans to close the position after 14 P–K4, with 14 . . . P–K4
and thus lighten his defensive task. But with the ensuing
exchange White opens up lines for his pieces and saddles his
opponent with a weakness on K3 against which the spearhead
of White's attack will soon be directed.

| 14 | PxP | PxP |
| 15 | Kt–KKt5 | Q–B3 |

White was actually threatening 16 KtxKP, since after 16 . . .
Q–B3 White has the defence 17 Kt–B4. Now the weakness on
K3 becomes fixed.

| 16 | P–B4 | P–R3 |
| 17 | Kt–B3 | Q–B2 |

Now we can sum up the results of the opening. White's
pieces are ideally developed, his adversary is saddled with a
marked weakness on K3, and in the square KKt6 he possesses
a fine outpost for his pieces in the enemy position. On the other
hand Black's pieces lack the requisite outposts in the centre and
he is without a suitable plan for active counterplay. His one
chance lies in the thrust P–K4 and the following part of the
game is centred round this problem.

| 18 | Kt–KR4 | B–Q3 |
| 19 | B–Kt1 | |

White, having attained an undoubted positional advantage,
now continues imprecisely and thus allows his opponent some
real counter-play by means of the thrust P–K4. This advance
cannot be executed at once since then 20 Kt–B5! affords White
a whole series of formidable threats. Hence Black must still
regroup his pieces, in the first place by R–K1 and Kt–B1, which

would, incidentally, also protect the KKt3 square. Taking this into consideration, White should have continued here with 19 B–Kt6!, preventing the regrouping already mentioned and rendering most of the Black pieces practically without a move.

19	. . .	KR–K1
20	Q–KB2	Kt–B1
21	Q–Kt3	

Black could not, during the last few moves, play P–K4 because of White's Kt–B5 but by now this advance has become a genuine threat. With the text-move White once again prevents P–K4 because of 22 Kt–B5 and he himself threatens 22 P–K4. Naturally, too, an immediate 21 P–K4, P–K4; 22 P–B5 would have been a good continuation for White but he hopes to achieve more by the text-move.

| 21 | . . . | Kt–R4 |

It is difficult to find anything better for Black since otherwise he has no means of dealing with the threat of 22 P–K4.

| 22 | Q–R3 | Kt–B3 |
| 23 | Kt–Kt6 | |

Very strong here too was 23 P–Kt4, inaugurating a direct attack on the King. But the text-move, with which White aims at the control of KKt6, is equally good.

| 23 | . . . | P–K4 |

At length Black has managed to carry out this advance and so free his position to some extent. Nor can he any longer delay doing this since, for instance, after 23 . . . Q–B2; 24 Kt–K5, Q–B2; 25 Kt–Kt4 would yield White a most formidable attack.

| 24 | Kt–Q5! | |

Although here White possesses other good continuations, for example, 24 KtxKt etc., the text-move constitutes the most effective way of furthering his attack. White now opens up both diagonals for his Bishops, thereby lending fresh force to the attack. Unfortunately, both players had got into some time trouble by now, and this circumstance had a really upsetting influence on the further course of the game.

24 ...	BxKt

After 24 ... KtxKt; 25 PxP would be even more unpleasant.

25 PxP!	BxKP

Naturally not 25 ... BxBP; when there would follow 26 PxKt!, BxR; 27 RxB, with a decisive attack.

Black (Spassky)

White (Keres) to play

26	KtxB?

Here the upsetting effect of time trouble becomes evident. During the game both players were convinced that White could not play here 26 BxB, RxB; 27 KtxR, since then Black would win a piece by 27 ... B–K3; 28 Q–Kt3, RxR; 29 RxR, Kt–R4. But both had overlooked that Black's combination contained a big hole. Instead of 28 Q–Kt3? White could of course play 28 B–B5! and thus, with the exchange to the good, obtain an easily won position.

After the mistaken text-move White loses the greater part of his advantage. A position with material equality arises, one in which White retains only a slight positional superiority on account of the attacking chances on the King-side.

26	...	B–K3
27	Q–Kt3	RxR
28	RxR	P–QKt4

Black, having emerged from the worst of his difficulties, suddenly finds himself unable to form any settled plan. Since at the moment White is threatening nothing, Black thinks he has time to undertake some activity on the Queen-side. But it would have been better to have utilized the time at his disposal to ease his position by further exchanges and to have played 28 . . . Kt(B3)–Q2. Naturally in this event too White would have retained some pressure, for example, after 29 B–K4, Ktx Kt; 30 BxKt, Q–K2; 31 B–QB6, R–B1; 32 R–Q6 etc., but at any rate Black would avoid the direct attack.

29   R–KB1   Kt(B3)–Q2?

A mistake in time trouble that loses off-hand. Black overlooks the ensuing Queen sacrifice and now loses a piece. Naturally, 29 . . . Kt(B1)–Q2 would also not do because of 30 KtxKt, QxQ; 31 KtxKtch, but after 29 . . . Kt(B1)–R2 or 29 . . .Kt(B3) –R2 no direct win for White can be found. He could for example play 30 R–B4 with a fine position and excellent attacking chances, but even so Black could still put up a stubborn resistance.

30   QxPch!   resigns.

After 30 . . . KxQ; 31 KtxKtdisch, K–Kt1; 32 Kt–B6ch, followed by 33 Kt–Q 5disch White wins a piece.

Game 66

SICILIAN DEFENCE

F.I.D.E. Interzonal Tournament at Gothenbourg, 1955

	P. Keres	O. Panno
1	P–K4	P–QB4
2	Kt–KB3	P–Q3
3	P–Q4	PxP
4	KtxP	Kt–KB3
5	Kt–QB3	P–QR3

The variation in the Sicilian Defence chosen by Black here was very popular at Gothenbourg and new methods of development were discovered, both for White and for Black. In the present game White employs a continuation that is nowadays very well-known but was practically new territory at Gothenbourg.

| 6 | B–Kt5 | P–K3 |
| 7 | P–B4 | |

This pawn advance instead of 7 Q–B3, as up to this time had been the usual continuation, caused Black many a headache at Gothenbourg. Amongst the various continuations tried here Panno selects the sharpest but in the sequel he risks changing his plan and hence gets into difficulties.

| 7 | . . . | Q–Kt3 |
| 8 | Q–Q2 | |

Practice teaches us that White can also very well continue here with 8 Kt–Kt3, since the endgame arising out of 8 . . . Q–K6ch; 9 Q–K2, QxQch; 10 BxQ, is very favourable for White. Hence nowadays Black plays 7 . . . P–R3 in this variation so as to play Q–Kt3 only after White has retreated his Bishop to R4. Then 9 Kt–Kt3 would be a double-edged pawn sacrifice because of 9 . . . Q–K6ch.

The text-move is naturally much sharper since after the acceptance of the pawn sacrifice the game becomes so complicated that it is very difficult to find the best continuation, even in home analysis.

| 8 | . . . | Kt–B3 |

Whilst one cannot exactly single out this move as a mistake it is, however, illogical and allows White a very agreeable position. Once Black has already played 7 . . . Q–Kt3 then he should carry on with 8 . . . QxP as well. In justification of Black's play it must, however, be said that no final valuation of the worth of the complications that occur in the variation that was employed here for the first time has been achieved even years afterwards. So the right decision would have been all the more difficult for Panno to make since he was presented with the problem without having been able to prepare for it beforehand.

| 9 | O–O–O | QxKt |

Black can be hardly blamed for making this exchange since, for example, after 9 . . . B–K2 there could follow 10 Kt–B3 with the troublesome threat of 11 P–K5. Once Black has refrained from capturing on QKt2 he always has to contend with opening difficulties.

10	QxQ	KtxQ
11	RxKt	Kt–Q2

There is scarcely anything better that one can recommend
against the highly unpleasant threat of 12 P–K5, which would
follow, for instance, after 11 ... B–Q2. After 11 ... P–R3 White
has at his disposal two good continuations:— 12 B–R4 and 12
BxKt, PxB; 13 B–K2 etc.

12	B–K2	P–R3
13	B–R4	P–KKt4

Black has no time for 13 ... B–K2, since after 14 BxB, KxB;
15 KR–Q1, he can no longer defend Q3. With the text-move
Black embarks on an interesting plan of campaign. He makes a
temporary pawn sacrifice, in return for which he obtains the
fine post of K4 for his pieces, thereby gaining some counterplay.
His plan has a good positional basis and would have had every
prospect of success if White did not possess such an advantage in
development.

14	PxP	Kt–K4!

Naturally not 14 ... B–K2 because of the reply 15 B–Kt3.
With the text-move Black indirectly protects the pawn, since
after 15 PxP, BxPch; 16 K–Kt1, B–K6 Black would obtain
excellent counterplay. White, however, makes use of the fact
that Black must lose yet another move in regaining his pawn to
initiate a dangerous action on the Queen's wing.

15	Kt–R4!

Black (Panno)

White (Keres) to play

This move, with which White succeeds in getting his Kt to QKt6, thereby practically cutting off his opponent's Queen's wing pieces from the ensuing play, really is the decisive move, basically speaking. Despite desperate efforts Black is not able to build up a satisfactory defence from now till the end of the game.

15 . . .	B–K2?

After this Black's position can be considered as virtually lost, since now he will be unable, right to the very end of the game, to free the pieces shut in on the Queen's wing. Although too the continuation 15 . . . P–Kt4; 16 Kt–Kt6, R–QKt1; 17 KtxB, RxKt; 18 P–R4, would not have been satisfactory for Black, still he must choose the lesser evil and try by 18 . . . Kt–B3 to organise some sort of resistance.

16	Kt–Kt6	R–QKt1
17	B–Kt3	PxP
18	KR–Q1	P–B3

This second protection of the Knight is necessary, since 18 . . . B–Q2 would cost him a piece after 19 BxKt, and further-more there is the very disagreeable threat of 19 BxKt, PxB; 20 R–B4, etc. Now at last Black intends to get his QB into play by 19 . . . B–Q2 but that is not so easy.

19   P–B4!

So that after 19 . . . B–Q2 he has the powerful reply of 20 P–B5!

19 . . .	O–O
20 R(Q4)–Q2	P–B4

Black can no longer make any useful move and therefore decides upon the text-move, so as to initiate some sort of counter-play. But with it he merely hastens the inevitable collapse. It is, however, clear that passive play will not alter the end-result, but merely lengthen the duration of the resistance.

21   P–B5!

This is even more effective than an immediate 21 PxP, PxP, followed by 22 P–B5, since after the text-move Black's QB remains shut in forever.

| 21 | . . . | P–B5 |
| 22 | PxP | BxP |

A rather more stubborn resistance was provided here by
22 . . . B–Q1; 23 B–B2, BxKt; 24 BxB, B–Q2, by which Black
would at least have freed his pieces on the Queen's wing. But
in that case too the White Bishops, in conjunction with the
extra pawn would have brought about a decision.

| 23 | RxB | PxB |
| 24 | PxP | R–B2 |

Here at least he should have played 24 . . . Kt–B2; 25
R(Q6)–Q2, P–K4, to which White would have replied 26
B–B4. After the text-move Black gets into a tragic-comic
stalemate position.

| 25 | K–Kt1! | |

It is not always the case that a strong attacking move has this
innocent appearance. Now, however, there is threatened both
26 R–Q8ch, and 26 R–QB1, winning a piece. Hence Black's
reply is forced.

25	. . .	R–B2
26	R–Q8ch	K–Kt2
27	R–QB1!	Kt–B3

This reminds one of chess-problems in which Black often
defends his pieces by placing them in a stalemate position. But
Black has nothing better if he wishes to avoid losing a piece
immediately by 27 . . . RxRch; 28 KxR.

| 28 | P–K5 | K–Kt3 |
| 29 | B–Q3ch | K–B2 |

After 29 . . . K–R4; 30 R–R8ch, K–Kt5; 31 R–R3, the Black
King is in a mating net.

| 30 | R–R8 | K–K2 |
| 31 | B–Kt6! | resigns. |

The final position is quite unique. Without incurring great
loss in material Black can only move his KKt and QR pawns,
and in addition there is threatened a mate on K1. This game
would certainly have given Grandmaster Nimzowitsch much
pleasure.

Game 67

SICILIAN DEFENCE

F.I.D.E. Interzonal Tournament at Gothenbourg, 1955

	P. Keres	M. Najdorf
1	P–K4	P–QB4
2	Kt–KB3	P–Q3
3	P–Q4	PxP
4	KtxP	Kt–KB3
5	Kt–QB3	P–QR3
6	B–Kt5	P–K3
7	P–B4	

The energetic thrust, which is certainly much more dangerous for Black then 7 Q–B3, was a very popular variation at Gothenbourg. One of the chief ways for Black to prevent White's projected 8 Q–B3 and 9 O–O–O here is the keen counter-attack 7 . . . Q–Kt3, which both Panno and Fuderer tried against me in this tournament (Nos. 66 and 68). In both cases I continued in gambit style with 8 Q–Q2.

Panno did not risk accepting the pawn sacrifice but continued 8 . . . Kt–B3, and then after 9 O–O–O, QxKt; 10 QxQ, KtxQ; 11 RxKt, had the worse ending (No. 66). Fuderer, on the other hand, bravely made the capture 8 . . . QxP; 9 R–QKt1, Q–R6; but then after 10 P–K5, did not choose the best defence 10 . . . PxP; 11 PxP, KKt–Q2 and instead continued 10 . . . KKt–Q2? Then, however, a second pawn sacrifice 11 P–B5! yielded White a decisive attack (No. 68).

Later, too, a whole series of games were played with this Gambit variation, with up-and-down results. Despite all the research that has been made, it is still not yet clear for which side this extremely complicated way of playing is favourable and hence its employment in many an important encounter can be anticipated.

In this game Najdorf makes use of another defensive possibility, which he had specially prepared in previous analysis for this occasion.

7	. . .	B–K2
8	Q –B3	P–R3
9	B–R4	P–KKt4!?

This was the innovation that the Argentine players had prepared against the text-variation. With it Black attempts, at the cost of a pawn, to obtain full control of the important K4 square. Owing, however, to Black's behindhand development the whole idea appears to be of doubtful worth.

10 PxP KKt–Q2

This retreat allows White to make a most promising Knight sacrifice which in practice sets Black insoluble defensive problems. Although later analysis was perhaps able to show that Black could somehow or other defend himself satisfactorily in the ensuing phase of the game, his task over the board with a limited amount of time at his disposal must be regarded as hopeless.

Better therefore seems 10 . . . PxP; 11 BxKtP, QKt–Q2, by which Black does at least ensure himself control of the K4 square, although that, in my opinion, provides insufficient compensation for the pawn.

11 KtxP!

In this same round the games Geller-Panno and Spassky-Pilnik were also played, so that there arose a small match between the Soviet and the Argentine players. The Argentine masters had apparently made joint preparation for the encounter, since the same position occurred on each board, and on each board too White now played this promising sacrifice. Black comes under the fire of a withering attack against which there is hardly a completely satisfactory defence.

| 11 | . . . | PxKt |
| 12 | Q–R5ch | K–B1 |

At first glance White now seems to have some difficulties in pursuing his attack successfully. The trouble is that Black is now threatening to place his Knight on a strong defensive post on K4, whence it will be able to beat back all White's attempts at attack. For instance, after 13 B–B4, Kt–K4; 14 O–Och, K–Kt2; 15 B–KKt3, QKt–B3! Black will have succeeded in establishing his Knight on the K4 outpost.

However, Black still has at his disposal a surprising continuation of the attack by which he is able to prevent his opponent from occupying this outpost.

13   B–Kt5!

The idea of this move, at first glance an astonishing one, becomes a little clearer when one takes into account the variation 13 ... Kt–K4; 24 B–Kt3. Now 15 BxKt is threatened and Black can no longer protect his outpost, since after 14 ... QKt–B3 or 14 ... QKt–Q2 the QKt would be simply captured by the Bishop, after which would follow 16 BxKt with a winning attack. This continuation was played in the Geller-Panno game. Black could find nothing better than 14 ... BxP and soon was in a totally lost position after 15 O–Och, K–K2; 16 BxKt, etc ...

Here it should be observed that after 13 ... Kt–K4 White must play 14 B–Kt3 immediately. Whereas if first 14 O–Och? K–Kt2 and then 15 B–Kt3, Black would still have the defence of 15 ... PxP!

13   ...   K–Kt2

This defence is naturally much stronger than Panno's 13 ... Kt–K4 and demands from White careful and resourceful play in the continuation of the attack. Of course neither 13 ... PxB; 14 O–Och, nor 13 ... Q–K1; 14 O–Och, K–Kt2; 15 PxPch, etc. will do for Black.

A defence for Black that well deserves consideration is here, however, 13 ... R–KR2, which was used by Fischer against Gligoric at Portoroz, 1958. Gligoric replied with 14 Q–Kt6, R–B2; 15 QxPch, K–Kt1; 16 Q–Kt6ch, R–Kt2; 17 QxPch, K–R1; 18 BxKt, KtxB; 19 O–O–O, whereupon Black successfully defended himself against all the threats by 19 ... Kt–K4!. The game soon ended in a draw.

Much more dangerous for Black, however, after 13 ... R–KR2 is the attack 14 O–Och, K–Kt1; 15 P–Kt6, R–Kt2. Now 16 QxP is not good for White because of 16 ... Kt–K4! but he can obtain a very dangerous attack by 16 R–B7! e.g. 16 ... BxB (after 16 ... B–Kt4; 17 BxKt, KtxB; 18 QR–KB1, Black's pieces are practically paralysed) 17 QxP, RxR; 18 PxR ch, KxP; 19 Q–R7ch, and, despite being two pieces down, White still has very good attacking prospects and a draw whenever he likes to take it. Closer investigation of this position would take us too far and does not in any case belong to the scope of the actual game played.

14 O–O   Kt–K4

In this position the defence 14 . . . Q–Kt1 also came into consideration for Black. White could then continue the attack with 15 P–Kt6!, e.g.:—15 . . . BxB; 16 QxB! (stronger than 16 R–B7ch, QxR; 17 PxQ, B–B3; 18 BxKt, KtxB; 19 R–KB1, which would, all the same, yield White a strong attack) 16 . . . Q–Q1; (after 16 . . . PxB; there follows 17 Q–K7ch, KxP; 18 R–B3, etc.) 17 R–B7ch, KxP; 18 R–K7! and Black can scarcely hope to defend successfully so vulnerable a King. As we see, after the Knight sacrifice a particularly complicated welter of variations have arisen and an exact analysis of these, even after the game, is not so easy. It would seem, however, that the general opinion about this position must favour White.

15 B–Kt3   Kt–Kt3

We see once again in this position the necessity for the move 13 B–Kt5! since Black can neither support his Kt on K4 by 15 . . . QKt–B3, or by 15 . . . QKt–Q2. An interesting possibility is presented to White by 15 . . . Q–Kt1, and that is 16 BxKtch, PxB; 17 B–K8!, QxB; 18 PxPch, winning.

With the text-move Black temporarily protects all the threatened points and himself threatens 16 . . . PxP, and this forces White to take swift action.

16 PxPch   RxP
17 R–B7ch!

Without this resource White's attack would be at a dead end.

17 . . .   KxR
18 QxR   PxB

For the moment Black is two pieces up, has repelled the first enemy wave of attack and now plans to escape with his King to the Queen's wing via K1. But White gets back a piece at once, after which he has two pawns for the sacrificed piece and still retains excellent attacking chances in view of the unfavourable position of the enemy pieces. So even with the best defence Black has scarcely any real prospects of saving the game.

The other defensive possibilities were not noticeable better.
After 18 . . . Q–R1 for example White wins with the pretty
19 R–B1ch, B–B3; 20 B–K8ch!, KxB; (or 20 . . . QxB; 21 Q–R7
ch, etc.) 21 QxKtch, K–K2; 22 RxB! etc. Equally the attempt
at saving Black from loss by 18 . . . B–B3 fails against 19 Q–R7ch,
K–B1; 20 QxKt, PxB; 21 R–B1 etc.

19   R–B1ch   K–K1

after 19 . . . B–B3 White wins at once by 20 Q–R7ch, K–B1; 21
QxKt.

20   QxKtch   K–Q2
21   R–B7   Kt–B3

Black (Najdorf)

White (Keres) to play

Here Black could have chosen a whole series of different
defensive possibilities, but not one would have turned out to be
sufficient to save the game. It is obvious that the two pawns for
the piece in conjunction with the favourable attacking prospects
and Black's undeveloped position constitute ample compensation even without exact analytical proof. If, for example,
Black had continued here with 21 . . . P–Kt5, then a fresh
piece sacrifice, 22 Kt–Q5!, would have followed and after
22 . . . PxKt; simply 23 PxP! with very strong threats.

It is rather more difficult to demonstrate a clear analysis of
the win after 21 . . . K–B3, but Black also is beset by permanent
difficulties after this. For instance, White could play 22 Q–R7,
B–Kt4; 23 P–K5, P–Q4; 24 Q–Q3, or else 22 . . . P–Kt5; 23

Kt–Q 5, PxKt; 24 PxPch, in both cases with an attack so fierce
that in practice Black would be left with no saving chances.

The text-move seems the most natural reply, but now comes
a fresh surprise.

22   Kt–Q 5!

This fresh piece sacrifice leaves the opponent in a plight
quite without resource. The immediate threat is simply 23
KtxB, followed by 24 B–R4 etc.

22   . . .   RxP

Acceptance of the sacrifice by 22 . . . PxKt would give White
decisive threats after 23 QxPch, K–K1; 24 Q–Kt6!, e.g.:—
24 . . . Q–Kt3ch; 25 B–B2, or 24 . . . B–K3; 25 R–B3disch,
(also simply 25 QxB is of course enough) 25 . . . K–Q2; 26 PxP!
and if 26 . . . BxP; then 27 Q–B5ch, B–K3; 28 R–Q 3ch, and
White wins.

23   P–R4

It is interesting to observe that up to now the game has gone
exactly as in the Spassky-Pilnik encounter. Here Spassky
played 23 P–R3, rekindling the threat of 24 KtxB, followed by
25 B–R4, but there is of course no noticeable difference between
the two pawn moves. Black is now faced by the same difficulties
that were present on the previous move.

23   . . .   Q–R1

After 23 . . . PxKt there would again follow 24 QxPch, K–K1;
25 Q–Kt6! etc.

24   KtxB

The simplest continuation, although 24 R–Kt7 would also
have won, e.g.:—24 . . . PxKt; 25 QxPch, K–K1; 26 Q–Kt6ch,
K–Q2; 27 Q–Kt4ch, K–K1; 28 R–Kt8ch, etc.

24   . . .   KtxKt
25   Q–Kt5   resigns.

In the Spassky-Pilnik game, where the KRP was still back on
R3, Black still continued with 25 . . . R–R8ch; 26 K–R2, Q–Q1;
27 QxPch, K–B2; but here too he had to strike his colours after
28 Q–B5ch, K–Kt1; 29 BxPch, K–R1; 30 BxKt, R–R4; 31
Q–Kt4.

This exceptionally exciting game, full of sacrifices, is of a type rarely seen in contests between grandmasters.

Game 68

SICILIAN DEFENCE

F.I.D.E. Interzonal Tournament at Gothenbourg, 1955

	P. Keres	A. Fuderer
1	P–K4	P–QB4
2	Kt–KB3	P–Q3
3	P–Q4	PxP
4	KtxP	Kt–KB3
5	Kt–QB3	P–QR3
6	B–Kt5	P–K3
7	P–B4	Q–Kt3

This game was played some rounds after the Keres-Panno encounter (No. 66). Since Fuderer here decides upon repeating the variation used by Panno and then too on the capture of the pawn on QKt7 it must certainly have been only after an exhaustive analytical preparation. The present game, however, shows yet once again that the consequences of the complications arising out of 8 . . . QxP are not so easily estimated, more particularly in such a brief space of time as was available for Fuderer to make the said preparation.

8	Q–Q2	QxP

The logical follow-up of his previous move. The text-move is, at all events, more to the purpose than Panno's 8 . . . Kt–B3. One must also bear in mind that Fuderer feels especially at home in complicated and incalculable positions, much more than in quiet positional play.

9	R–QKt1	

Another interesting possibility here is 9 Kt–Kt3 when Black would continue with either 9 . . . Kt–B3 or 9 . . . Q–R6. All the same, White need not look for other ways of attack until it has been proved convincingly that 9 R–QKt1 is inadequate.

9	. . .	Q–R6
10	P–K5	KKt–Q2?

At the time this game was played the whole variation, as has already been mentioned, was hardly analysed at all and hence both players had to solve a great part of the complicated problem immediately over the board. Nowadays everybody knows that this retreat is faulty and that it is first necessary to insert the exchange 10 ... PxP; 11. PxP. An exhaustive research into the complications arising from this naturally does not come within the scope of the present game. One can only observe that, even after the analysis and researches of a number of years it is not yet definitely fixed which side has the advantage.

One thing stands out clearly from the present game however: the immediate retreat of the Knight is not really playable for Black since it leaves him easy prey to the ensuing fierce King-side attack.

Black (Fuderer)

White (Keres) to play

11   P–B5!

With this surprising pawn sacrifice White opens up a number of lines of action for his piece, and obtains a decisive attack, in comparison with which the two pawns minus play hardly any role. It is very important for White, in addition to the opening up of the KB file, to weaken the K6 square, so that in the ensuing phase of the game Black always has to keep his eye on the various sacrificial possibilities at this point.

Perhaps with his last few moves Black was only reckoning with the possible regain of the pawn by 11 R–Kt3. Q–R4; 12 PxP, after which he would have obtained a good game by 12 ... Kt–B4.

| 11   ... | KtxP |

There is nothing better for Black, since he has to give added
protection to his K3 square. Thus, for example, after 11 . . .
QPxP, White can continue either with 12 KtxP, PxKt; 13
PxP, or also very strongly with 12 PxP! PxKt; 13 PxPch, KxP;
14 B–B4ch, with a fierce attack. With the text-move Black
seemingly disposes of every danger, but only seemingly.

| 12   PxP | PxP |
| 13   B–K2! | |

Although White has two pawns less, he can allow himself
this quiet further development of his forces. The point is that
Black, in the next phase of the game, will find it intensely
difficult to evolve an acceptable plan by which he at least may
get his King into safety, more or less. And Black must hurry up
his counter-play since after castling White already threatens a
direct assault on the King.

| 13   ... | QKt–B3 |
| 14   KtxKt | PxKt |

After the game 14 . . . KtxKt was recommended by a number
of commentators. But one cannot then see how, after 15 O–O,
Black could have improved his position. On the contrary, in
addition to other threats, he would have to reckon with 15
Q–B4. The text-move appears to be more logical, since with it
Black does at least retain the good defensive post for his Kt on
K4. But however Black plays, he can never overcome the
greatest drawback of his position, to wit, the insecure position of
his King and his insufficient development.

| 15   Kt–K4! | |

Now there is threatened 16 R–Kt3, followed by 17 KtxPch,
and this forces Black's reply.

| 15   ... | P–Q4 |
| 16   O–O | Q–R5 |

Black was forced to weaken the position of his Kt on K4
by 15 . . . P–Q4, and this affords White fresh opportunities of
continuing his attack by Q–Q4 or Q–B4. When we add to this
the further threat of 17 B–R5ch, then we come to the conviction
that Black no longer has a satisfactory defence against all this,

With the text-move Black protects himself against the first two threats, but now the third is decisive.

17 B–R5ch   K–Q2

Black no longer has a defence. After 17 . . . P–Kt3; 18 Kt–B6 ch is of course decisive, and after 17 . . . Kt–Kt3; 18 BxKtch, PxB; 19 Q–B2! one cannot see any defence to the threatened mate on KB7.

18 RxB!   resigns.

After 18 . . . RxR; 19 Kt–B5ch, wins.

Game 69

RUY LOPEZ, BERLIN DEFENCE

Second Game of the match in Hamburg, 1956.

P. Keres	W. Unzicker
1 P–K4	P–K4
2 Kt–KB3	Kt–QB3
3 B–Kt5	Kt–B3

If Unzicker wanted to surprise his opponent in his choice of an opening variation, then he fully succeeded in so doing. I expect from a specialist in the Ruy Lopez like Unzicker something very different from this line of play, quite forgotten already some fifty years back and one which is deemed, and rightly, to be not very favourable for Black. But perhaps my adversary had prepared an innovation here?

4 O–O	KtxP
5 P–Q4	B–K2
6 Q–K2	Kt–Q3
7 BxKt	KtPxB

Everything so far has gone according to known theory. It is also known that Black has a difficult position after 7 . . . QPxB; 8 PxP, Kt–B4; 9. R–Q1, B–Q2; 10 P–K6! PxP; 11. Kt–K5 ctc. and hence Black is forced to play his Knight to the dismal square QKt2.

8 PxP	Kt–Kt2
9 Kt–B3	O–O
10 Kt—Q4	

The usual continuation, the so-called Rio de Janeiro variation, is here 10 R–K1, preventing the thrust of P–Q4 for the
moment. From praxis we learn, however, that after the further
10 ... Kt–B4; 11 Kt–Q4, Kt–K3; 12 B–K3, KtxKt; 13 BxKt,
P–QB4; 14 B–K3, P–P–Q4; 15 PxP e.p., BxP; Black's two
Bishops in an open position are sufficient compensation for the
weaknesses on the King-side. Perhaps it was in this very variation that Unzicker had prepared an improvement.

The text-move has been seldom used in praxis, but in my
opinion this neglect is ill-deserved. White now attacks QB6 and
so prevents Black from playing P–Q4. In order to force through
this advance Black is practically compelled to give up his K
Bishop. With this, however, the thrust P–Q4 loses much of its
original force, since the Black pawn structure betrays many
weaknesses. The present game is a characteristic example of
the difficulties with which Black has to contend after the
text-move.

               10 . . .   B–B4

If now 10 . . . Kt–B4, then 11 R–Q1, Q–K1; 12 Kt–B5,
leaves Black very uneasy (12 . . . P–B3; 13 B–R6! etc.).

               11 R–Q1   BxKt

Here Black could try 11 . . . R–K1, since then the continuation 12 KtxP, Q–R5; 13 P–KKt3, Q–R6; 14 Kt–Q4, P–Q3
would not be especially good for White. But White would then
reply 12 Q–R5! and if then 12 . . . P–Kt3; 13 Q–B3, BxKt; 14
RxB, RxP; 15 B–B4, with a dangerous attack in return for
his pawn sacrifice.

               12 RxB   P–Q4

Here too 12 . . . R–K1; would be met by 13 Q–R5. Black has
now indeed been able to get in P–Q4 but at a seemingly high
price. He has weaknesses on the black squares, his Kt is still
badly placed on Kt2, there is no piece to protect the King and
in addition White is better developed.

But how can White take advantage of these drawbacks in the
opponent's position? 13 P–QKt4 seems to be a good method,
since it threatens P–Kt5 and then 13 . . . B–K3 would not do on
account of 14 Q–R6. Another possibility is the exchange 13
PxP e.p., by which White opens up the position and then hopes

to exploit the weakness of the hanging pawns. In the game
White chooses the second possibility.

13 PxP e.p.   PxP
14 P–QKt4!

A very good move that fixes Black's pawn weaknesses,
threatens an eventual P–Kt5 and for a long time keeps the
Black Knight out of the game. It is clear that Black has been
unable to solve the opening problem satisfactorily.

14 . . .   R–K1

This whole method of play is of considerable age, almost
fifty years, and was first used in the game Schlechter–Reti,
Vienna, 1914. In that game Reti defended himself with 14 . . .
Q–B3, but after 15 B–K3, B–B4; 16 QR–Q1, P–QR3; 17
P–Kt4! he soon fell into insurmountable difficulties. The move
Unzicker chooses is more logical, since with it Black does at
least control the K file. But it is insufficient for the rehabilitation
of the whole variation.

15 B–K3   B–K3
16 Q–B3

In reply to 16 Q–R5, Black has the defence 16 . . . Q–B3 and
if then 17 Kt–K4, Q–K4. The text-move is directed against
the advance of 16 . . . P–Q4.

16 . . .   Q–Q2?

After this Black gets into great difficulties since now White
has a free hand on the Kingside. Despite the seeming dangers
Black must bring himself to play here 16 . . . P–Q4. If then 17
P–Kt5, not 17 . . . PxP; which would give White a clear
advantage by either 18 KtxQP, or 18 KtxKtP, but the courage-
ous 17 . . . P–QB4! After the further moves 18 R(Q4)–Q1,
P–Q5; 19 QxKt, Q–R4, there has arisen a complicated position
in which in any case Black wins his piece back with good
prospects of equality.

It would therefore be perhaps better for White after 16 . . .
P–Q4 to refrain from the advance 17 P–Kt5, and proceed
positionally with 17 B–B4, Kt–Q3; 18 BxKt, QxB, when he
would retain some advantage on account of his control of the
black squares.

17   Kt–K4   B–B4?

Yet another inaccuracy which could indeed be classed as the
decisive mistake since now the Black King is submitted to the
concentrated attack of all White's pieces. Here it was essential
for Black to have played 17 . . . B–Q4. In reply White must not
make the Kt sacrifice of 18 Kt–B6ch, since after 18 . . . PxKt;
19 R–Kt4ch, K–B1, no continuation of the attack is to be seen.
But the simple continuation 18 P–B4!, BxKt; 19 RxB, ensures
White a clear positional advantage owing to the unfavourable
position of the enemy Knight, although Black could still obtain
some counter-play by 19 . . . P–QR4.

18   Kt–Kt3!

By means of this pawn sacrifice the last piece is diverted
from the defence of Black's King-side. In practice Black is
forced to accept the sacrifice, since after 18 . . . B–Kt3; 19
P–KR4! is very strong.

18   . . .   BxP
19   R–QB1   B–R5
20   Kt–R5

An inaccuracy which enables Black to put up a stubborn
resistance. Here White rejects the continuation 20 Kt–B5, so as
not to give Black the opportunity of defending himself by 20 . . .
R–K3. Whereas now in reply 21 Q–Kt4 would win offhand.
But here the natural attacking move 20 Kt–B5, was undoubtedly
the quickest way to win. After 20 . . . R–K3 there could follow
21 R–R4, when one cannot see how Black could successfully
defend himself against the many threats, such as 22 Q–R3, 22
Q–R5, or 22 B–Q4.

20   . . .   P–KB4!

An excellent defensive move with which Black deprives his
opponent of the important attacking square KKt4 and at the
same time protects his own KKt2. If White now tries 21 B–R6,
Black plays 21 . . . Q–K3! threatening mate on the back rank.
However, White still finds a way of livening up his attack.

21   R–KB4

Now he threatens not only 22 RxP, but also 22 B–Q4, which,
for instance, after 21 . . . R–KB2, would gain command of

KKt7 (22 ... R–B2; 23 BxP!). Also 21 ... Q–K3; 22 RxKBP, R–KB1 would not work since White then replies 23 KtxP!, KxKt; 24 Q–Kt4ch, winning the Queen.

21	. . .	R–K2
22	RxKBP	R–B2

And so Black hopes to force the exchange of Rooks, thereby warding off a direct attack, but soon there comes a bitter surprise.

Black (Unzicker)

White (Keres) to play

23 KtxP!

This piece sacrifice, which breaks up Black's King-side beyond redemption, is only rendered possible by the fact that Black's pieces are stranded inactively on the Queen's wing and cannot speed to the help of the King in time.

23 . . . RxKt

The best defence, 23 ... KxKt obviously fails against 24 B–R6ch or 24 Q–Kt4ch, and after the seemingly workmanlike defence 23 ... QR–KB1 White wins by the elegant 24 Kt–K6! For example:—24 ... RxR; 25 Q–Kt4ch, K–R1; 26 KtxR, or 24 ... QxKt; 25 Q–Kt4ch, Q–Kt3; (or 25 ... K–R1; 26 B–Q4ch, R–B3; 27 RxR! etc.) 26 R–KKt5 and White has a decisive advantage in material

24 B–R6 Q–K2

The Rook cannot of course move since after 24 ... R–B2; 25 R–Kt5ch wins. But the attempt to bring up fresh reserves to the aid of the King by 24 ... R–K1 fails, as White then plays 25 P–R4, with the threat of 26 BxR. With the text-move Black protects his KB1 and does indeed threaten to play 25 ... R–Kt3. Hence White must capture at once on KKt7.

	25	BxR	QxB

After 25 ... KxB; White wins by 26 Q–B3ch, K–Kt1; 27 R–B3, with the threats of either 28 R–Kt3ch, or 28 R–K1. Obviously the Black King, bereft of all help, cannot make a long stand against the attack of the enemy heavy pieces.

	26	P–R4	P–KR3

Losing offhand, but there was no longer any adequate defence against the threat of 27 R–KKt5. Rather more obstinate was indeed 26 ... R–KB1, but then too White wins easily, continuing with either 27 R–K1, or with 27 RxRch, QxR; 28 Q–Kt4ch, K–R1; 29 Q–Q4ch, Q–Kt2; (or 29 ... K–Kt1; 30 R–B3, etc.) 30 QxP etc.

	27	R–QB4!	resigns.

Game 70

CARO-KANN DEFENCE

Alekhine Memorial Tournament in Moscow, 1956.

	P. Keres	H. Golombek
1	P–K4	P–QB3

In the last decade Master Golombek has scarcely answered the move 1 P–K4 with any other reply than the Caro Kann Defence. Naturally, this circumstance has its good sides since Golombek knows all the inner mysteries of this defence really well. But, on the other hand, preparation for the game is made noticeably easier for the opponent when he is practically hundred per cent sure beforehand what his adversary is going to play.

Still, when one takes into account the solid character of the Caro Kann Defence, then one can hardly anticipate any especial surprises and hence Master Golombek has obtained thoroughly satisfactory results with his system.

2	P–Q4	P–Q4
3	Kt–QB3	PxP
4	KtxP	B–B4

One of the most solid systems in the Caro Kann Defence, which, it should be observed, was employed also by Botvinnik in his last world championship matches. Praxis has shown that now White cannot obtain any noticeable advantage, although he usually retains the somewhat freer position.

| 5 | Kt–Kt3 | B–Kt3 |
| 6 | B–QB4 | |

A recommendation of the ex-world champion, Dr. Euwe. It cannot be claimed that this continuation is stronger for White than the usual (up to now) 6 P–KR4, P–KR3; 7 Kt–B3 etc. but nevertheless it has its advantages. The most important of these, in my opinion, is the fact that the possibilities arising thereafter have not been sufficiently tried in practice and therefore both players are already forced to think for themselves from the very first moves. But thereby Master Golombek is bereft of one of his trump cards, that is to say, his superior knowledge of the inner mysteries of this opening. Even the reverse is true, since this advantage now swings over to his adversary who has been able to prepare the variations arising after 6 B–QB4 quietly and calmly at home.

| 6 | . . . | P–K3 |

6 . . . Kt–Q2 has been recommended by many commentators here, so as to meet 7 KKt–K2, with 7 . . . P–K4. In my opinion, however, the whole plan is fundamentally false, since the opening up of the position can only favour White with his better development. And indeed after 8 O–O Black is faced by the problem as to what he should do with his centre pawns.

| 7 | KKt–K2 | |

The commencement of an interesting idea. In the ensuing phase of the game White wants to set in motion an attack against the enemy King's position by P–KB4-5, and for this reason avoids developing his Knight on KB3, so as not to get in the way of the pawn advance. In addition White threatens when the occasion arises to play his Knight to B4 followed by

P–KR4, which would leave Black's Bishop on Kt3 in somewhat
of a dilemma. Hence Black must play the opening with the
utmost accuracy in order to avoid getting into difficulties.

7   . . .   Kt–B3

After this natural developing move White is able to carry
out his plan unhindered. Hence, after the game, Golombek
held that 7 . . . B–Q3 would have been more exact, so that,
after 8 O–O, Q–B2; 9 P–B4, Black can protect his KB4 once
more with 9 . . . Kt–K2. White would therefore have to alter
his plan after 7 . . . B–Q3 and could, for example, continue
with 8 P–KR4, P–KR3; 9 Kt–B4, with a very promising game.

8   O–O   B–Q3
9   P–B4!

Now White's intentions are clear. He wants to open up the
KB file by P–B5 and activate his pieces for the attack against
the enemy King position. Thus for example after 9 . . . O–O; 10
P–B5, PxP; 11 KtxP, Black would get into real difficulties
owing to numerous threats. Hence Golombek essays radical
measures against these threats, but without marked success.

9   . . .   Q–B2

After 9 . . . Kt–K5 White can still continue 10 P–B5!, for
example: 10 . . . BxKt; 11 KtxB, KtxKt; 12 PxB!, KtxR; 13
PxPch, and if 13 . . . KxP; then, in addition to the simple
QxKtch, 14 Q–Kt4, R–K1; 15 B–KR6! is also a very strong
attacking continuation. With the text-move Black hopes he has
prevented 10 P–B5, since after a double exchange on KB5
White's KRP would be hanging. But a painful surprise lies in
wait for him.

10   P–B5!

White still carries out the advance according to plan! The
pawn sacrifice offered by the text-move is very interesting and,
if accepted, assures White excellent attacking prospects. Black
has, however, little choice, since a refusal of the sacrifice
would also give White a lasting initiative. It would seem that
Black has not handled the opening very successfully.

10   . . .   PxP
11   KtxP   BxPch

In a later game against Fichtl in the Chess Olympiad at Munich, 1958, Golombek did not risk taking the pawn and continued here with 11 ... BxKt; 12 RxB, QKt–Q2. But it is hardly likely that this continuation can be completely satisfactory for Black. White, with his two Bishops and excellent development has undoubtedly the better prospects.

21   K–R1   O–O?

A mistake due to the fact that Black has not bestowed sufficient attention to the ensuing encirclement of his Bishop. Black's best defence here undoubtedly consisted in 12 ... BxKt; 13 RxB, getting rid of White's strong Knight, and then 13 ... B–Q3. Although it would not then be easy for White to obtain a concrete advantage, he would still retain strong positional pressure in return for the pawn sacrifice. It is true that an immediate 14 Kt–B4 would lead to nothing because of 14 ... Q–K2! but 14 B–KKt5, QKt–Q2; 15 Kt–B4 is a good continuation since Black cannot well play 15 ... O–O–O; on account of 16 BxP etc.

Black (Golombek)

White (Keres) to play

13   P–KKt3!

This cuts off the retreat of the Bishop and Black must now lose material. The ensuing combination is indeed not difficult to find, but all the same it requires exact calculation.

13   . . .   BxKt

White's task would be rather more complicated after 13 ... Kt–Kt5; though with this move Black would run the risk of

losing a whole piece. There could follow, for example, 14
R–B4, BxKt; (or 14 . . . B–R4; 15 Q–B1 etc.) 15 RxB, BxP; 16
Q–Kt1, and Black loses material after 16 . . . Kt–B7ch; 17
K–Kt2, Kt–K5; 18 Q–K3. Not sufficient too is 13 . . . Q–Q2,
when White obtains a clear advantage by 14 Q–Q 3, Kt–Kt5;
15 Q–K4! However Black plays, loss of material is inevitable.

> 14   RxB   BxP
> 15   RxKt!

The simplest method of rendering his advantage crystal-
clear. But also possible was 15 Q–Kt1, since after the Queen
move neither 15 . . . B–R5; 16 B–KR6, nor 15 . . . Kt–K5;
16 Q–K3, are particularly enticing for Black.

> 15   . . .   Q–K2!

Golombek defends himself most resourcefully in a difficult
position. After 15 . . . PxR; 16 Q–Kt1, Black's position would
be hopeless on account of his broken King-side. Now, on the
other hand, after 16 KtxB, QxR, Black would stand comparatively well. White therefore decides to pursue his chief aim—the
breaking up of the enemy pawn position on the King's wing.

> 16   Q–B1!   Q–K5ch

After 16 . . . QxR; 17 QxQ, PxQ; 18 KtxB, White would
have attained his aim. But if Black tries 16 . . . Kt–Q2 then
there comes 17 RxP(B7), Q–R5ch; 18 K–Kt2, Q–R7ch; 19
K–B3, and White retains his extra piece. Also possible is the
original 17 R–R6.

> 17   Q–B3

17 K–Kt1, Q–R5; 18 Q–B3 etc. would lead to the same
position.

> 17   . . .   Q–R5ch
> 18   K–Kt2   Q–R7ch
> 19   K–B1

With this Black's "attack" is at an end and White's advantage
in material must prove decisive. It is interesting to observe that
White's King is safe from the attack of the enemy pieces even
without the usual pawn protection.

19	. . .	Q–R6ch
20	Q–Kt2	QxQch
21	KxQ	PxR
22	KtxB	

Now one can reckon up the successful outcome of the combination begun on the 13th move. Black has, it is true, a Rook and two pawns for the two enemy Bishops, materially speaking, sufficient compensation. But Black's pawns on the King's wing are broken and weak, and it is this circumstance that weighs the balance in White's favour. Black, despite the ensuing desperate resistance, is no longer able to save his position.

22	. . .	Kt–Q2
23	B–KR6	KR–K1
24	K–B3	K–R1

White was threatening a decisive attack on the KKt file. Thus for example 24 . . . Kt–B1 would meet with the strong reply 25 Kt–R5!, R–K2; 26 KtxPch, K–R1; 27 R–R1, with mating threats.

| 25 | Kt–R5 | R–KKt1 |

Black has nothing better against the threat of 26 B–Kt7ch, followed by 27 R–KKt1. But now White wins the exchange and this leaves him a piece up.

26	BxP	R–Kt3
27	BxR	PxB
28	Kt–Kt3	

Now Black cannot even try to cut off the return route of the Bishop by 28 . . . P–KKt4, since then 29 R–K1 wins. Further resistance with a piece less is naturally hopeless.

28	. . .	R–K1
29	B–B4	K–Kt2
30	Kt–K4	P–KKt4
31	Kt–Q6	R–K3
32	B–Kt3	P–Kt3
33	R–K1	RxR
34	BxR	K–Kt3
35	Kt–B8	P–B4
36	PxP	KtxP

37	KtxRP	P–B4
38	B–B2	Kt–Q2
39	B–Q4	K–R4
40	Kt–B8	Kt–B1
41	Kt–K7	P–B5
42	Kt–B5	Kt–Kt3
43	Kt–Kt7ch	K–R3
44	K–Kt4	Kt–B1
45	Kt–B5ch	resigns.

Game 71

SICILIAN DEFENCE

Alekhine Memorial Tournament in Moscow, 1956

	P. Keres	M. Botvinnik
1	P–K4	P–QB4
2	Kt–KB3	Kt–QB3

The former world champion Botvinnik is one of the few grandmasters who have not allowed themselves to be carried away by the fashionable variation 2 . . . P–Q 3 followed by an eventual P–K3 and once again he employs the old classical set-up.

3	P–Q4	PxP
4	KtxP	Kt–B3
5	Kt–QB3	P–Q 3
6	B–KKt5	P–K3
7	Q–Q2	P–KR3

This is one of the ex-world champion's pet variations in the Sicilian Defence. Black is here forced, after the exchange 8 BxKt, to recapture with the pawn, since, as is well-known, 8 . . . QxB loses a pawn without sufficient compensation because of 9 Kt(Q4)–Kt5. There arises in this variation a sharp type of play exacting methodical pursuit of the main objectives and in this line Botvinnik has obtained many a fine practical success. However, the most recent games played with this variation have tended to show that Black's solid defensive position together with his two Bishops still bears too passive a character and provided he plays with sufficient energy White should attain the more promising position.

Certain doubts too about the suitability of this complicated system of defence arise from the circumstance that this game was played in the last round when Botvinnik needed only half a point to make sure of first prize. Apparently the ex-world champion was convinced that the best way to make sure of a draw is to play a fighting game rather than to adopt quiet tactics aiming at simplification.

8	BxKt	PxB
9	O-O-O	P-R3
10	P-B4	P-KR4

Botvinnik usually, in previous games starting with this variation, chose the continuation 10 ... B-Q2, so as to complete the development of his Queen's wing as soon as possible. The text-move is, however, necessary sooner or later, in order to avert the positional threat of B-K2-R5, since on R5 the Bishop would exert disagreeable pressure on Black's position. Thus, for example, White, in the game Bondarevsky-Botvinnik, XIX U.S.S.R. Championship 1951, after 10 ... B-Q2; 11, B-K2, Q-Kt3; 12 B-R5, KtxKt; 13 QxKt, QxQ; 14 RxQ, R-KKt1; 15 P-KKt3, obtained strong positional pressure despite the exchange of Queens.

11	K-Kt1	B-Q2
12	B-K2	Q-Kt3
13	Kt-Kt3!	

In the game Keres-Petrosian, Amsterdam 1956, White allowed here the simplification 13 KR-B1, QxKt; 14 QxQ, KtxQ; 15 RxKt, B-B3, after which it is very difficult for White to assault the enemy position with any degree of success. With the text-move White prevents this possibility, which, in view of the constricted position of his opponent, is absolutely logical.

| 13 | ... | O-O-O |
| 14 | KR-B1 | Kt-R4 |

Black seeks to relieve his task by further exchanges and to deprive his opponent of the possibility of obtaining a concrete

advantage eventually by a direct attack on the King. Nevertheless the text-move is somewhat premature and forms the basis of
difficulties later on for Black. Here he must play the quiet
14 . . . K–Kt1, when White would continue with 15 R–B3,
with also a threat on Black's KRP.

15   R–B3

Lasting pressure also comes from the simple exchange
15 KtxKt, QxKt; 16 R–B3, so that, after 16 . . . K–Kt1, White
can continue 17 Q–Q4, B–K2; 18 P–QKt4, Q–B2; 19 Kt–Q5!,
PxKt; 20 R–B3, B–B3; 21 PxP. The text-move is however
equally good.

15	. . .	KtxKt
16	RPxKt	K–Kt1
17	Kt–R4!	

By permitting the exchange on QKt3, White has ensured
his Knight the QR4 square and now threatens a dangerous
attack on the King.

17   . . .   Q–R2

Here of course the Queen is out of play but it is not easy to
recommend anything better for Black. The exchange 17 . . .
BxKt would give Black the advantage of two Bishops and
afford White the opportunity of instituting troublesome
pressure on the white squares by R–QKt3. After 17 . . . Q–B2,
however, there could follow 18 Q–Q4, B–K2; 19 R–B3, B–B3;
20 Kt–Kt6, with the unpleasant threat of 21 Kt–Q 5.

18   P–B5!   B–K2

This normal defensive move loses a pawn in surprising
fashion, but Black's position was already difficult. The exchange
18 . . . PxP; 19 PxP, B–B3; would it is true yield Black good
piece-play, but his pawn position would be hopelessly shattered
and White could retain the clearly better position by for
example either 20 R–R3, or 20 R–Kt3. Now, in return for his
pawn Black does at least arrive at some reasonable piece-play.

19   PxP   PxP

Black (Botvinnik)

White (Keres) to play

20 RxP!

This sacrifice seems at first glance very obvious since clearly
Black cannot now reply 20 . . . BxR because of 21 QxPch,
followed by 22 Kt–Kt6ch, winning the Queen. All the same its
refusal requires exact calculation.

20   . . .   R–R2

Naturally not 20 . . . BxKt because of 21 RxP, but here chief
notice must be taken of the counter-attack 20 . . . P–Kt4, with
the idea of meeting 21 R–B7, with B–K1. White could then
obtain a fine attacking position by the exchange sacrifice 22
RxB, QxR; 23 Kt–B5, but even stronger would be 22 R–Kt7!,
PxKt; 23 Q–Kt4ch, K–R1; 24 P–K5! when Black would have
no adequate defence.

With the text-move Black simply surrenders a pawn and
hopes to gain counter-play in the ensuing phase of the game
through his two Bishops. The active position of White's
pieces, in conjunction with the unfavourable situation of
Black's Queen, make these prospects a little illusory.

21 R–Kt6!   P–Kt4

Black cannot leave his Queen for ever in this stalemate
position, but now new attacking possibilities open up for White
on the Queen-side.

22   Kt–B3   Q–B4
23   Kt–R2!

Once this Knight has attained Q3 via Kt4 with win of a tempo White's advantage is definitively assured.

23	. . .	K–R2
24	Kt–Kt4	R–KB1
25	B–B3	P–R5
26	P–R3	B–B1

An attempt to pursue the White Rook by 26 . . . B–K1; 27 RxP, B–Q2 would be in vain since White could simply reply 28 R–Kt6, B–K1; 29 Kt–Q3, followed by 30 R–R6 etc. Black must wait to see how White intends to strengthen his position.

27	Kt–Q3	Q–B2

After 27 . . . Q–Q4; 28 Q–K1 could be unpleasant.

28	Kt–B4	R–B3

Naturally not 28 . . . B–B3? 29 RxB! followed by 30 Q–Q4ch etc. After the text-move Black hopes for 29 RxR, BxR; 30 QxP, QxQ; 31 RxQ, B–K4; 32 R–Q8, BxKt; 33 RxB, when he can put up an obstinate resistance in the endgame with Bishops of opposite colour. White, however, is not content with such a small advantage.

29	B–Kt4!	RxR

After 29 . . . R(R2)–B2 another pawn would be won by 30 KtxP, BxKt; 31 BxB, ensuring White, in addition, a really good attack.

30	KtxR	B–Kt2

Black no longer has a defence against the threat of 31 KtxB followed by 32 QxQP. In time trouble Black apparently overlooks that the pawn on K4 is indirectly protected, and now he loses yet another pawn, whereupon all resistance is naturally hopeless.

31	BxP	B–Q1
32	B–Q5	BxB
33	QxB	R–B2
34	P–K5	resigns.

4

TOURNAMENTS AND EVENTS IN THE
YEARS 1957–1958

NINETEEN FIFTY-SEVEN was once again a year rich in various events for me. At the beginning of the year I took part in the XXIVth U.S.S.R. Championship at Moscow. My start was only moderate. After a draw with Mikenas there followed a loss to Spassky, then a difficult draw with Chasin and only in the fourth round did I manage to win a good positional victory over Furman. In my game against Boleslavsky in the fifth round I introduced an innovation in a well-known variation of the Sicilian Defence and, since my opponent did not find the right defence, I obtained a quick win. There ensued a series of draws and when, after ten rounds, I cast a glance at the tournament table, it did not present at all an agreeable aspect to me. In the lead with $7\frac{1}{2}$ points was Tolush, then in tip-top form, whereas I, with my $5\frac{1}{2}$ points was far down in the middle of the tournament table.

In the next couple of rounds I managed to improve my position to a marked degree, since I won both games and had got as far as a share of third place. But after the 15th round I was in fact at the head of the table, half a point ahead of my nearest rivals. Then, however, I lost a weakly played game against Tal, and this meeting was decisive as regards the first prize. Before the last round I was in fourth place, half a point behind the three leaders. Although in the last round I won a very riskily played game against Antoshin, this was not sufficient for first place, since Tal won against Tolush and so ensured coming first alone. I shared second and third prizes with Bronstein, half a point behind the winner. In this tournament, too, I gave up too many half points against those who figured at the bottom of the table, which prevented my attaining a higher place. On the whole, however, I could be pleased with my play.

Shortly after the Championship I went in company with Grandmaster Kotov on a long journey to South America. My participation in the annual tournament at Mar del Plata proved to be successful. My form seemed really good and the games followed one after another without any especial strain, despite the hot climate. At the end of the tournament I had an exciting duel with grandmaster Najdorf as we had the same score by the time the last round commenced. I won comparatively quickly in this last round whereas Najdorf fought out a dramatic struggle with Panno. Najdorf obtained a clearly won position and in addition Panno was in great time trouble. But then Najdorf continued so carelessly that he not only lost all his advantage but even in the end had to submit to a defeat. Thus I won first prize with the good score of 15 out of 17, without losing a game. We went on to Chile where we took part in a small tournament at Santiago. I won first prize, conceding only two draws. Two games from this tour are given in the present collection, from the Mar del Plata Tournament, against Eliskases (No. 72) and Lombardy (No. 73) the last-named game possessing some theoretical value.

Scarcely had I returned home than I had to leave for Lenigrad to take part in the match against Yugoslavia. Then I went on with the Soviet team to Vienna to play in the first European Team Championship. In both events I played quiet, calm chess without any particular pretensions and obtained in both tournaments taken together two wins and eight draws. In the autumn our Hungarian chess friends came to Tallinn to play a friendly match. I had an unhappy result in that I lost both games to grandmaster Barcza.

At the turn of the year, after a long interval, I once again took part in the Hastings Christmas Congress. This time I was in especially good form and won one game after another. From the first eight games I acquired 7½ points. Although I lost in the last round to Gligoric I still finished up in first place alone. Amongst the games I played in this tournament my brevity against Clarke (No. 74) merits attention, as it has a certain theoretical value.

In the summer there came the annual match with Yugoslavia, in which I was due to play four games against Gligoric. In one game I achieved a pretty win (No. 75), in another I succumbed to a strong King-side attack, whilst the other two ended in draws.

I also played in the U.S.S.R. Team Championship at Wilno in which, to everybody's surprise, Estonia occupied an excellent fourth place. Towards the end of the year the F.I.D.E. Olympiad took place at Munich. This time I was playing on board three for the U.S.S.R. and I obtained the best result on that board with 7 wins 5 draws and no losses.

Game 72

FRENCH DEFENCE

International Tournament at Mar del Plata, 1957.

	P. Keres	E. Eliskases
1	P–K4	P–K3
2	P–Q4	P–Q4
3	Kt–QB3	

The text-move usually leads to sharper variations than the other possibility 3 Kt–Q2. Since Eliskases belongs in his style to the school of quiet positional players, I made up my mind from the very start to strive after complications as much as possible and the text-move affords good opportunities for these.

3	. . .	B–Kt5
4	P–K5	P–QB4
5	P–QR3	BxKtch
6	PxB	Kt–K2

The most customary reply, by which Black already declares his willingness to go in for possibly great complications stemming out of 7 Q–Kt4. Hence the more cautious prefer 6 . . . Q–B2 here, which could lead to the game continuation by transposition, but which would allow Black, after 7 Q–Kt4 to defend his KKt2 square simply by 7 . . . P–B4.

7	Kt–B3	QKt–B3

Many experts hold that the sally 7 . . . Q–R4 is more energetic here, but this is disputable, more particularly when this move is bound up with the blockading idea of Q–R5. Thus for example after 7 . . . Q–R4; 8 Q–Q2, Q–R5 White can continue with 9 PxP, whereupon the game assumes quite another character and the blockade of R5 becomes illusory. In general, the question of one or other methods of play depends on the taste of each individual player and so it is very difficult to make an objective judgment.

8   P–QR4   Q–B2

Here the sally 8 . . . Q–R4 is deemed better, so as to continue after 9 B–Q2 or 9 Q–Q2 with 9 . . . B–Q2 and according to circumstances P–B5 followed by O–O–O. The text-move is bound up with another idea, preparing a counter-attack on White's centre by P–B3, for which purpose the Queen undoubtedly stands better on B2. It would seem that here too preference is given according to each player's taste since it is difficult, objectively speaking, to favour one system rather than the other.

9   Q–Q2

White would like to play the Bishop to R3 but an immediate 9 B–R3 would allow simplification by 9 . . . PxP; 10 PxP, Q–R4ch; 11 Q–Q2, QxQch; 12 KxQ, Kt–B4 etc., by which White would only attain a somewhat better ending. In order to prevent this possibility White makes this move which at first sight seems a little strange. As a preparation for his idea, however, White could have played better 9 B–K2 followed by O–O, thereby posing his opponent some tricky problems.

9   . . .   P–QKt3

Black plays illogically. Once he has chosen his system with the move Q–B2 he should logically continue with 9 . . . P–B3! which indeed was recommended by Grandmaster Bondarevsky. As the game Smyslov–Bondarevsky, Parnu 1947, showed Black, after the further 10 KPxP, KtPxP; 12 B–K2, P–B5; 12 Q–R6, Kt–Kt3; 13 Kt–R4, T–KKt1; 14 B–R5, Q–Kt2 obtains a thoroughly satisfactory position.

10   B–Q3

The question as to whether here White can better develop his Bishop on Q3 or K2, constitutes a really important problem.

Usually 10 B–K2 is played so as not to present the opponent with a tempo after the move P–B5 which would be necessary in any case. However White regards the move 10 B–Q 3 in order in the present position since after 10 . . . P–B5; 11 B–K2, P–B3 the opening of the diagonal QR3–KB8 can be utilised for the promising pawn sacrifice 12 B–R3! PxKP; 13 PxKP, KtxP; 15 Kt–Q4!

| 10 | . . . | B–Q2 |
| 11 | O–O | P–B5 |

It is difficult to find anything better for Black. If for example 11 . . . Kt–R4, then the answer 12 Q–Kt5 is very troublesome. Should Black attempt to prevent this Queen sally by 11 . . . P–KR3 then there could follow 12 Q–B4. In the game Belavienetz–Botvinnik, XIth U.S.S.R. Championship 1939, after 12 . . . P–B5; 13 B–K2, O–O; 14 B–R3, White obtained a clear advantage.

Through his inconsequent handling of the opening Black has already got into marked difficulties from which it is not so easy to find a way out.

| 12 | B–K2 | Kt–B4 |

If now 12 . . . P–B3; then naturally White would not exchange on B6, but could offer a highly promising pawn sacrifice with 13 B–R3! The position after 13 . . . PxP; 14 PxP, KtxP; 15 Kt–Q4! would certainly provide little joy for Black. It can be confidently asserted that White has emerged from the opening with a clear positional advantage.

| 13 | B–R3 | P–KR4 |
| 14 | KR–K1 | P–B3 |

Now, once White can adequately protect the K5 point this move has no force. On the other hand Black must try something, since for example after 14 . . . O–O–O; 15 P–Kt3 White would be gradually preparing to play P–KR3 and P–KKt4, and can also interpose the moves 15 Kt–Kt5, B–K1 with success.

15	B–KB1	O–O–O
16	P–Kt3	K–Kt2
17	B–R3	QR–K1

By now Black must reckon with the threat of 18 BxKt, PxB; 19 B–Q6, Q–B1; 20 PxP, PxP; 21 Kt–R4, by which his pawn position on the King's wing would be torn to pieces. After the text-move White tranquilly increases his pressure along the K file, and that by doubling his Rooks there.

18   R–K2   KR1

Black possesses no possibility of active counter-play and has to pursue a waiting policy. To 18 . . . P–R5; White can simply reply 19 B–KKt4, if he does not want to go in for the possible win of a pawn by 19 BxKt, followed by 20 PxP and 21 KtxP. The continuation 18 . . . Kt–R4 also constitutes no threat since after 19 QR–K1, BxP; White wins back the pawn with advantage by 20 PxP and 21 RxP

19   QR–K1   Q–B1

White was threatening to win a pawn by 20 BxKt, PxB; 21 P–K6, B–B1; 22 Kt–R4. If Black tries to relieve his position by exchanges with 19 . . . PxP, then there can follow more or less as in the game 20 BxKt, PxB; 21 PxP, B–K3; 22 Kt–Kt5 etc. In addition, too, 20 KtxP, KtxKt; 21 RxKt, Kt–Q 3; 22 P–B3, or 22 BxKt, is very strong.

20   BxKt

White cannot strengthen his position to any degree now, and hence the attack initiated by this exchange is fully justified.

20   . . .   PxB
21   Kt–R4

Very strong too would have been 21 PxP, PxP; 22 Kt–R4, but White believes there is no need to hurry with this exchange.

21   . . .   PxP

Black has nothing better, since after 21 . . . R–R3 there follows 22 PxP, RxP; 23 Q–Kt5, and furthermore there is threatened Kt–R4–Kt6–B4, or also simply 22 PxP; 21 . . . P–KKt4 could be considered but then White plays simply 22 Kt–B3, when Black would have as an additional burden the weakness on KKt5. After the further 22 . . . P–B5 the exchange sacrifice 23 KPxP, RxR; 25 RxR, B–Kt5; 25 KtxP, BxR; 26 QxB, etc. would win very easily.

22 PxP!

Black can indeed close the K file, but now White's pressure is transferred to the Black QP and this is much more difficult to defend. First of all White gets his Kt to the strong post on KB4, from which point it is an effective aid in the attack on Q5.

22	...	B–K3
23	Kt–Kt6	R–R3
24	Kt–B4	Q–Q2
25	R–Q1	R–Q1
26	B–Q6	

These moves are easy to understand and, at least on the part of Black, practically forced. With the text-move it seems all up with the pawn on Q4, but Eliskases still contrives to find a clever defence.

26 ...   B–B2!

A fine trap. If White now at once pockets the pawn with 27 KtxQP, then there comes the surprising reply 27 ... KtxP! and the endgame after 28 KtxPch, (Or 28 Kt–B7ch, QxKt!; 29 BxQ, RxQ, followed by Kt–B6ch, etc.) 28 ... PxKt; 29 BxKt, QxQ; 30 R(K2)xQ, RxR; 31 RxR, affords Black good drawing chances on account of the Bishops of opposite colour.

But White need not hurry to make the capture on Q5. With his next move he first secures the strong post of his Kt on B4 and then quietly prepares to capture on Q5.

Black (Eliskases)

White (Keres) to play

27   P–R4!   RxB

A desperate decision. But Black is by now convinced that he cannot in any other way successfully defend his QP against the threat of 28 Q–K3 followed by Q–B3. By the sacrifice in the text Black obtains a pawn in return for the exchange, but this does not prove sufficient to save the game. White with his strong Knight and control of the K file retains a positional advantage possesses a positional advantage sufficient for the win.

	28	PxR	QxP
	29	Q–K3	Q–R6.

But not 29 . . . R–K1 on account of 30 RxP. The counter-attack on the Queen's wing initiated by the text-move is about as hopeless as the other attempts to defend the position, but in fact by 29 . . . P–Kt3 the relatively toughest resistance could have been made.

	30	Q–B3	P–Kt3

Now 30 . . . Q–Q3 is too late because of the simple 31 KtxRP.

	31	KtxQP	K–Kt2
	32	R–K7ch	

This move is indeed forcing, but nevertheless the more modest 32 R(K2)–Q2 or 32 K–Kt2 would have ended the game more quickly owing to the threat of 33 Kt–Kt4. In the ensuing endgame Black, though the exchange down, can put up a stubborn resistance.

	32	. . .	KtxR
	33	KtxKtdisch	K–R3
	34	RxR	QxKt
	35	R–Q1	Q–K3

The ending after the exchange of Queens 35 . . . Q–K5; 36 QxQ, PxQ; 37 R–Q4 is naturally hopeless. The text-move is directed against the threat of 36 Q–B6.

| | 36 | P–R5! | |

With this attacking lines are opened up against the Black King, and this brings about a speedy decision.

36 . . .   B–K1

Black cannot well take the pawn. After 36 . . . KxP; 37
Q–Kt7 wins and after 36 . . . PxP White strengthens the attack
decisively by 37 Q–B4, since Black cannot defend himself on the
black squares. The text-move in no way alters the position.

37 PxP   B–B3

This counter-attack along the long diagonal is Black's only
hope of a counter-chance.

38 R–R1ch   KxP
39 Q–B4!   Q–K5

A little better was 39 . . . Q–Q4, to which White would reply
40 Q–Kt8ch, and after 40 . . . B–Kt2; could choose between
41 QxPch, K–B2; 42 Q–R5ch, with an easily won ending, and
41 . . . P–B3!. In the last case Black cannot capture by 41. . .
QxP because of 42 Q–Q 3ch because of 42 Q–Q 3ch followed
by R–Kt1ch and mate to follow.

After the text-move Black is mated.

40 Q–Kt8ch   B–Kt2
41 Q–Q6ch   resigns.

After 41 . . . Q–B3 or 41 . . . B–B3 he is mated in a few moves
starting with 42 R–Kt1ch.

Game 73

Q.P. NIMZOWITSCH DEFENCE

Interzonal Tournament at Mar del Plata, 1957.

	W. Lombardy	P. Keres
1	P–Q4	Kt–KB3
2	P–QB4	P–K3
3	Kt–QB3	B–Kt5
4	P–K3	

Custom and fashion play nowadays just as important a
rôle in the openings repertoire as before. Whereas round about
twenty years ago the continuation 4 Q–B2 was almost always
chosen in the Nimzowitsch Defence, this move has nowadays

practically disappeared from tournament praxis. Instead the
move 4 P–K3 has taken its place and driven practically every
other variation into the background. However, after another
twenty odd years it may well be that we shall meet with the
move 4 P–K3 just as seldom as nowadays we do 4 Q–B2 or
4 Kt–B3.

4	. . .	P–QKt3
5	Kt–K2	B–R3

This move, introduced into tournament praxis by Bronstein
(in his match with Botvinnik in 1951) contains a number of
interesting tournament problems and one of the most complicated of these is used in the present game.

6   P–QR3

Lately, the continuation 6 Kt–Kt3, has also been employed,
so as to get to P–K4 as quickly as possible. If then Black were to
reply 6. . . P–B4, then there follows 7 P–Q 5, PxP; 8 PxP, BxB; 9
KxB! followed by P–B3 and P–K4 with excellent play for White
as the game Geller-Matanovic, match U.S.S.R–Yugoslavia,
1958, demonstrates. Grandmaster Reshevsky has also enjoyed
some fine victories with this system.

6   . . .   B–K2

Many hold that this retreat is dubious and recommend
instead 6. . . BxKtch; 7 KtxB, P–Q4. Praxis shows that, with it,
Black also obtains excellent results, but the text-move is more
ambitious and leads to more interesting positions.

7	Kt–B4	P–Q4
8	PxP	BxB
9	PxP	

This pie.e sacrifice has, in recent years, been deemed
insufficient for White, even though White gets two pawns and
really good attacking prospects in return for his piece. Instead,
the continuation 9 KxB, PxP; 10 P–KKt4 has become popular
and this, for example, yielded White a quick win in the second
match game between Botvinnik and Smyslov, 1954.

I can hardly believe that this seemingly risky way of play is
so strong that Black must abandon the whole variation on its

account. At all events, after the text-move there arises an
interesting position rich in chances for both sides, and one
about which theory has certainly not said the last word as yet.

9	. . .	B–R3
10	PxPch	KxP
11	P–K4	

The attempt at attack by 11 Q–Kt3ch, K–K1; 12 Kt–K6, is
known to be insufficient on account of 12 . . . Q–Q2!, although
with it White does obtain a third pawn for his piece. The
text-move is a recommendation of Grandmaster Bondarevsky's
and is certainly more dangerous for Black, since Black's King's
position is still most insecure and the mobile White pawn
centre can eventually become highly dangerous. Black must
therefore initiate an immediate attack against the enemy
centre, before White has found time to complete his development.

| 11 | . . . | P–B4! |
| 12 | B–K3 | |

White conducts the attack with considerable cunning. If
now Black heedlessly captures the pawn with 12 . . . PxP, then
he has to undergo a fierce attack after 13 Q–Kt3ch, K–K1; 14
O–O–O, on account of the open centre.

Another enticing possibility here was 12 P–Q5, but the Black's
task would be even lighter. He could, for example, play 12 . . .
QKt–Q2; 13 Kt–K6, (after 13 P–Q6, B–KB1; Black threatens
Kt–K4) 13 . . . Q–QKt1; 14 P–B4, R–K1, so as to give back
the piece after 15 P–K5, with 15 . . . KtxKP. The somewhat
insecure position of White's King in this variation would not
allow him to utilise the full force of his centre pawns.

Bad of course would be 12 P–K5, when by 12 . . . QxP! Black
would win back his piece with an overwhelming position.

| 12 | . . . | Kt–B3 |
| 13 | Q–Kt3ch | |

An interesting continuation by which White relieves his
centre Q pawn of attack. Black is now forced to continue with
13 . . . P–B5, since after 13 . . . K–K1; 14 Q–R4, White, owing
to the threat of 15 P–Q5, would win his piece back. White

has, however, no choice, since after 13 P–Q5, Kt–K4 Black would
soon attain a winning position.

13   . . .   P–B5
14   Q–Q1

Now White once again threatens 15 P–K5, after which the
Knight has no good square of retreat. White could here of
course have won a tempo by 14 . . . Q–R4, but this move also
has its drawbacks, since the Queen is not particularly well
placed on R4. After 14 . . . Q–QB1; 15 P–K5, the Black Knight
has the good square KKt5 at its disposal and it seems unlikely
that White could develop a successful attack from this line.

14   . . .   B–Q3!

Black rightly decides to give back the piece in return for two
pawns. In so doing he nullifies the enemy attempts at attack and
with his two Bishops he attains an excellent position that solves
the problems of the opening in a completely satisfactory manner.
An attempt to retain the piece would have left Black in an
unsatisfactory position, for example: 14 . . . R–KB1; 15 P–K5,
Kt–K1; 16 Q–B3, with several nasty threats.

15   P–K5

White must seize the opportunity while he can since Black
was threatening 15 . . . BxKt followed by the capture of the QP.

15   . . .   KtxKP
16   PxKt   BxKP
17   Kt(B4)–Q5

After the return of the piece Black has obtained the initiative
and already White must occupy himself with the task of
equalising the position. However, the exchanges resulting from
the text-move can only favour Black since the latter would very
much like to get down to an endgame where, with his two
Bishops and the Queen-side pawn majority, he would possess
excellent winning prospects. Hence White should try to retain
as many pieces as possible and to engineer complications in the
middle-game.

17 Q–R4 would be of little value in this respect since Black
answers simply 17 . . . Q–B1; 18 O–O, B–Kt2, when the White

Queen would be badly placed on R4. But more promising was
17 Q–B3. Black would then reply 17 . . . Q–QB1 and would
still have the better game, but White would obtain better
chances than in the game.

	17 . . .	R–K1
	18 KtxKt	

After 18 Q–B3, there would now follow simply 18 . . . K–Kt1.
After the text-move Black could at once transpose into the
endgame by 18 . . . QxQch; 19 RxQ , BxKt, but he prefers to
wait for a more favourable moment.

	18 . . .	QxKt
	19 O–O!	B–Kt2

Naturally Black is not going to take the pawn as this would
lead, after 19 . . . BxKt; 20 PxB, QxP?; 21 Q–Q7ch, followed by
22 B–Q4, even to a won position for White.

	20 Q–Kt4	Q–K3

Black discerns that, despite the strong diagonal for the Bishop
on QKt2–KR8, he possesses no real attacking prospects and
hence returns to his old plan. Now White is practically forced
to exchange Queens, since after 21 Q–R5ch, K–Kt1 Black does
eventually attain a King-side attack by proceeding with Q–QB3
and R–K3.

The ensuing endgame is strategically won for Black, since
the two Bishops and the Queen-side pawn majority must result
in a decisive advantage for him sooner or later. But first of all
he has, in practice, a number of problems to solve.

	21 QxQch	RxQ
	22 QR–Q1	B–QB3
	23 B–Q4	B–B2

Naturally, Black does not want to exchange off one of his
two strong Bishops. But now all preparations have been made
on the Queen's wing and the pawn storm can commence.

	24 P–B3	

A good move with which White ensures for his Kt a supporting point on K4. Instead 24 P–B4 would have only appeared to

be more active and in actual fact would have merely increased the scope of the black Bishop.

$$24 \quad \ldots \qquad P\text{–}QKt4$$
$$25 \quad KR\text{–}K1 \qquad RxRch$$

Exchange of a pair of Rooks is very welcome for Black, since it lessens enemy counter-chances and adds to the strength of the pawn advance.

$$26 \quad RxR \qquad P\text{–}QR4$$
$$27 \quad Kt\text{–}K4!$$

The Knight is excellently posted here and in the ensuing phase of the game poses Black some very difficult problems. Naturally, White must not play here 27 BxP, because of 27 . . . B–Kt3ch, whilst after 27B–K5, B–Q1; 28 Kt–K4 Black can play 28 . . . BxKt; 29 RxB, R–B1, followed by 30 . . . P–Kt5.

$$27 \quad \ldots \qquad P\text{–}R3$$
$$28 \quad B\text{–}B2$$

White now intends to continue with 29 B–Kt3, which would force the exchange of Bishops and at the same time sets his adversary a small trap. For if now 28 . . . B–K4?, then 29 Kt–Kt5ch, K–B3; 30 Kt–R7ch! etc.

This waiting move with the Bishop is rendered possible by the fact that Black is not yet threatening 28 . . . P–Kt5 because of 29 PxP, PxP; 30 B–B5, etc. since this would be very troublesome on account of the threats of 31 BxP, and 31 Kt–Q6ch. On the other hand White cannot utilise this small pause to bring his King nearer to the centre, since after 28 K–B2, Black can indeed continue with 28 . . . P–Kt5! and if then 29 PxP,PxP; 30 B–B5, R–R7! with considerable advantage to Black.

$$28 \quad \ldots \qquad R\text{–}K1$$
$$29 \quad B\text{–}Q4$$

Despite acute time-trouble White here refrains from transposing to a Rook endgame with 29 B–Kt3, BxB; 30 PxB, BxKt; 31 PxB, since this would have given Black a clear advantage after 31 . . . P–Kt5!

$$29 \quad \ldots \qquad P\text{–}Kt5$$

Simpler than a preparatory 29 . . . R–Q1, which would, however, after 30 B–B3, (or 30 B–B5, R–Q4 etc.) 30 . . . R–QKt1 followed by 31 . . . P–Kt5 have also assured Black of the upper hand.

30	PxP	PxP
31	B–B5	BxKt!

Now that the pawns are sufficiently advanced it is time to exchange off one of the Bishops. The text-move constitutes the simplest way to win, although too 31 . . . P–Kt3 was quite possible.

32	PxB

The endgame after 32 RxB, RxR; 33 PxR, can be won by Black in two different ways. Firstly, he can play 33 . . . P–Kt6!; 34 B–Q4, K–K3; 35 K–B2, B–K4; 36 K–K3, P–B6! with an immediate win, and secondly he can also win by 33 . . . B–K4; 34 BxP, BxP; 35 B–B5!, P–B6; 36 B–Q4, B–R8; 37 B–K3, K–K3, 38 K–B2, K–K4; 39 K–B3, B–Kt7; when the QBP will cost White his Bishop.

32	. . .	B–K4

Black, convinced that the endgame is easily won, taking into consideration too the time trouble of his opponent, becomes a little careless, and thus makes the win much more difficult. The pawn exchange allowed by the text-moves is all the more welcome for White in that it relieves him of the burden of his QKtP. The logical continuation here was 32 . . . P–Kt6! and this, because of the threat of 33 . . . B–K4, would have won quickly, for example: 33 B–Q4, B–R4; 34 R–K2, R–Q1; 35 B–K5, R–Q2; followed by 36 . . . K–K3, with an easy win.

Black (Keres)

White (Lombardy) to play

33 R–QB1?

White loses his way in great time-trouble and now succumbs without a fight. Much better chances of defence were afforded by 33 BxP, BxP, since then Black would be faced by great difficulties in exploiting his advantage. Even so, Black's strong passed pawn would eventually have brought about a decision in his favour as the following possibilities show.

(1) 34 R–K2, B–Q5ch; 35 K–B1, R–QKt1 and the Black Rook breaks into White's position with decisive effect.

(2) 34 K–B2, B–Q5ch; 35 K–B3, R–QKt1; and if now 36 R–Q1, then 36 ... B–K4 with similar consequences to those of the first variation.

(3) 34 K–B1, K–B3!; 35 R–K2, (White has no useful move) 35 ... B–K4 and with the attack on KR7 Black gains the necessary tempo for playing 36 ... R–QK1.

33 ...   P–B6!

White's idea lay in 33 ... BxP?; 34 RxP, R–QB1; 35 RxP! etc. The advance of the BP is immediately decisive. After 34 P–QKt3, in addition to 34 ... R–QKt1, Black can also play simply 34 ... R–QB1; 35 BxP, P–B7 etc.

34 PxP   BxP
35 R–B1ch

Otherwise he loses the KP at once.

35 ...   K–K3
36 R–Kt1   R–QKt1!

Simpler than 36 ... R–QB1, which would have allied White to put up some resistance still by 37 BxP, R–QKt1; 38 BxB, RxRch. White must now allow the further advance of the QKtP, since after 37 R–Kt3, K–K4 would win for Black.

37 K–B2   P–Kt6
38 K–K2   P–Kt7
39 K–Q3   B–K4
40 P–Kt3   R–Q1ch

Here the game was adjourned and White sealed his move.

41 K–K3

In his adjournment analysis White now ascertained that

Black could win a piece by force as follows: 41 ... R–QB1!
42 B–Q4, R–B8; 43 RxP, R–K8ch. If then 44 K–Q3, R–Q8ch;
or if 45 K–Q2, simply 44 ... BxB; 45 R–Kt4, B–B7 etc.

Hence White resigns.

Game 74

RUY LOPEZ, STEINITZ DEFENCE DEFERRED

International Tournament at Hastings, 1957–58

	P. Keres	P. H. Clarke
1	P–K4	P–K4
2	Kt–KB3	Kt–QB3
3	B–Kt5	P–QR3
4	B–R4	P–Q3

This form of the Steinitz Defence gives Black a secure position
with rather greater possibilities of activity than the same
defence without the move 3 ... P–QR3.

5	P–B3	B–Q2
6	P–Q4	P–KKt3
7	B–KKt5	

The usual continuation here is 7 O–O, B–Kt2; 8 PxP, PxP,
but praxis shows that then White finds it very difficult to break
through his opponent's strong defensive position. With the
text-move White aims at taking the game from the usual
theoretical paths, but he can scarcely reckon on obtaining
better results than with the normal move 7 O–O.

7	...	P–B3

The simplest counter is undoubtedly 7 ... B–K2, whereupon
White can continue 8 BxB, QxB; 9 O–O, Kt–B3; 10 QKt–Q2,
in the hope of being able to exploit later on the small weakness
created on the King's wing by P–KKt3. After the text-move an
interesting position arises with chances for both sides.

8	B–K3	B–Kt2?

Surprisingly enough, this normal developing move would
seem to be a mistake after which Black is in difficulties. Here he
should have played 8 ... Kt–R3 at once, when I intended

continuing with 9 PxP. After 9 . . . BPxP; 10 B–KKt5, followed
by 11 B–B6, would be very troublesome for Black and if 9 . . .
QPxP, then White plays simply 10 O–O, followed eventually
by P–QB4 and Kt–B3.

9   P–KR4!

This energetic thrust casts a clear light on the inadequacies
of Black's position. If Black tries to stop the further advance of
this pawn by 9 . . . P–KR4, then, after 10 PxP, he is faced by an
unpleasant alternative. After 10 . . . BPxP; 11 Kt–Kt5, White
obtains absolute control of the KKt5 square, whilst after 10 . . .
QPxP; 11 P–B4, followed by 12 Kt–B3, White exerts great
pressure on the centre.

Hence Black decides to allow White's P–R5, but this yields
White other advantages.

| 9   . . . | Kt–R3 |
| 10 P–R5 | Kt–KKt5 |

Black has to reckon with the disagreeable threat of 11 Kt–R4,
which, for example, would be possible after 10 . . . Kt–R4.

| 11 B–B1 | Kt–R4 |
| 12 Kt–R4! | |

This strong move threatens in the first place 13 QxKt, and in
addition 13 P–B3, Kt–R3; 14 RPxP, etc. The ensuing positional
struggle is waged around the KB5 point. If White succeeds in
forcing his opponent to play P–KKt4 and then can occupy the
KB5 square with his Kt, he can expect to attain a marked
positional advantage.

| 12 . . . | P–QKt4 |

With this he retains, at any rate, his white-squared Bishop as
a protection of KB4. Hence there came into consideration for
White on the previous move to make an immediate exchange on
Q7 and only after this to continue with Kt–R4.

| 13 B–B2 | P–KB4? |

Black should have acknowledged that he was defeated in the
struggle for his KB4 square and continued with 13 . . . P–Kt4;
14 Kt–B5, BxKt; 15 PxB, Kt–R3, although the resulting position
would hardly cause him much joy. With the text-move Clarke

aims at bringing about complications, but should in fact merely lose a pawn without any compensation whatsoever.

14 KPxP

White sees that he gets the advantage with this capture and therefore does not look for any better way of play. Much stronger, however, was 14 P–B3! which, after 14 . . . Kt–KB3 (or 14 . . . Kt–R3; 15 RPxP), 15 P–R6, B–KB1; 16 KPxP, would have led to the win of a pawn and furthermore have still retained a clear positional advantage. After the text-move, on the other hand, Black gets concrete counter-play.

14 . . .   PxRP!
15 PxP   BxKP

After 15 . . . PxP; 16 Kt–Q2, White enjoys an ideal post for his Knight on K4.

16 Kt–B3   O–O

If Black had hoped to protect his pawn on KR4 by combinational means then this hope soon proves false and the Black King speedily succumbs to a concentrated attack by the White pieces. Comparatively better was 16 . . . Q–K2, although even then White's advantage after 17 Q–K2, or 17 KtxB, would be beyond doubt.

Black (Clarke)

White (Keres) to play

17 RxP!   Kt–KB3

A simple recognition by Black that he has lost a pawn, after having satisfied himself that an attempt to recover the lost material would have a tragic end. Thus for example 17 . . .

Q–KI? is simply met by 18 R–Kt5ch, and the combination
17 . . . BxPch, planning to meet 18 KtxB, with 18 . . . Q–KIch,
would, after 18 K–BI!, B–KB3 (or 18 . . . B–Kt2; 19 Q–Q 5ch,
K–RI; 20 RxPch! etc.) 19 Kt–Kt5! yield White a fierce attack.

18	R–R3	Q–K2
19	K–BI	K–RI?

Black wants to vacate the square KKtI for his Rook as a
precaution against the threat of 20 B–R6, but his King is badly
placed on RI and allows White to increase his advantage
decisively. It is, however, difficult to recommend any satisfactory continuation for Black. He could perhaps still try
19 . . . R–B2.

20   Kt–R4!

It is interesting to observe that in fact White wins this game
with the move Kt–KR4. For the first time, on the 12th move,
when it ensures White a positional advantage and now for the
second when it wins a decisive amount of material. There is
now threatened not only 21 Kt–Kt6ch, but also 21 P–KB4,
winning a piece. Black cannot meet both threats.

20   . . .   R–KKtI

Black is still hoping for 21 Kt–Kt6ch, RxKt; 22 PxR, BxR,
etc. but now White puts his other threat into execution.

21   P–KB4!

This practically finishes the game, since now Black loses a
piece. Ensuing attempts by Black to arrive at some sort of
attack are naturally unsuccessful and afford White no noticeable difficulties.

21	. . .	Kt–Kt5
22	PxB	PxP
23	Q–K2	

He could of course also have played 23 Kt–Kt6ch, RxKt;
24 PxR, but White is content with his win of a piece and avoids
further useless complications.

23	. . .	QR–KBI
24	Kt–Q2	Kt–R3

Now it is true that the KBP falls but with it the position is simplified and Black's attacking possibilities become even more remote.

25	Kt(Q2)–B3	KtxP
26	KtxKt	BxKt
27	BxB	RxB
28	Q–K4	Q–B2
29	P–KKt4!	R–B3
30	K–Kt2	Kt–B5
31	B–Kt5	resigns.

After 31 ... RxB; 32 KtxR, R–B7ch; 33 K–Kt1, the checks are at an end, and after other Rook moves 32 QR–R1 is decisive.

Game 75

RUY LOPEZ, MORPHY DEFENCE

Match U.S.S.R.–Yugoslavia at Zagreb, 1958

	P. Keres	S. Gligoric
1	P–K4	P–K4
2	Kt–KB3	Kt–QB3
3	B–Kt5	P–QR3
4	B–R4	Kt–B3
5	O–O	B–K2
6	Kt–B3	

This old continuation has been practically forgotten in modern master tournaments, but nevertheless provides good opportunities for obtaining interesting and exciting positions. Praxis shows that it is not so easy for Black to defend himself as is usually supposed. Anyway, in recent years I have obtained very good results with it.

6	...	P–QKt4

The quiet continuation 6 ... P–Q3 is held by many to be better here. This leads after 7 BxKtch, PxB; 8 P–Q4, Kt–Q2; 9 PxP; 10 Kt–QR4 to a position which is hard to judge. Black must try to find compensation for his pawn weaknesses on the Queen's wing in the two Bishops.

7	B–Kt3	P–Q3
8	Kt–Q5	

White must make this move at once, since Black is threatening to exchange off the strong Bishop by 8 . . . Kt–QR4.

8   . . .   B–Kt2!

A move recommended by Panno that constitutes one of the best replies to White's system of development. It is known that after 8 . . . Kt–QR4 White has very good prospects by 9 KtxB, QxKt; 10 P–Q4, and, too, the sharp continuation 8 . . . KtxP; 9 P–Q4, (according to Euwe 9 KtxB, QxKt; 10 P–Q4, is also very strong) 9 . . . B–Kt2 is not so clear in its consequences as is generally believed.

In the game Keres-Barcza, Tallinn 1957, Black had success with 8 . . . O–O; 9 P–B3, KtxP; 10 P–Q4, B–Kt2; but this was rather due to inexact play on White's part. Later it was shown that white could have obtained a strong attack by 11 Q–Q3, Kt–B3; 12 Kt–Kt5!

9   KtxKtch

There is nothing better since after 9 R–K1, Black carries out his threat of 9 . . . Kt–QR4, and if then 10 KtxB, QxKt; 11 P–Q4, Black plays 11 . . . KtxB; 12 RPxKt, KtxP, and one cannot see what White has got for his pawn. But if White plays 9 P–B3, then there can follow 9 . . . KtxP; 10 P–Q4, Kt–R4, and once again White has no worthwhile compensation for his pawn. The exchange by the text-move simplifies the position, however, and permits Black to solve his opening problem satisfactorily.

9   . . .   BxKt
10   B–Q5

With this pin White obtains nothing more than a further simplification of the position, and hence here 10 P–B3, merited more consideration.

10   . . .   Q–B1

After 10 . . . Kt–R4; 11 BxB, KtxB; 12 P–Q4, White still has rather the better position.

11   R–K1

There seems no cause for this move at the moment and hence more normal appears 11 P–B3, O–O; 12 P–Q4, as occurred in the game Sanguinetti-Panno, Mar del Plata 1958.

11	. . .	O–O
12	P–B3	Kt–K2

Black carelessly allows his opponent the opportunity of
retaining his King's Bishop and this piece proves superior to
its colleague on QKt7 in the ensuing play. In a game played
between the same opponents in a later round Gligoric continued
more exactly here with 12 . . . Kt–R4 and soon completely
equalised the position by 13 BxB, QxB; 14 P–Q4, P–B4.

13	B–Kt3!	P–B4
14	P–Q4	Q–B2
15	P–QR4!	

With this move White commences an action on the Queen's
wing, the point of which in actual fact is directed against the
enemy King's position. Black does not observe the threatened
danger in time and after a scarcely noticeable inexactitude he
suddenly finds himself in a difficult position.

15	. . .	B–B3
16	RPxP	RPxP
17	RxR	RxR?

Surprisingly enough, this natural move turns out to be the
decisive mistake, since the text-move leaves Black's KB2
unprotected and allows White to institute a very dangerous
attack on the King's wing. Correct here was 17 . . . BxR,
whereupon White can continue 18 P–R3, so as to make the
eventual manoeuvre Kt–R2–Kt4. In this case White would have
stood rather better but at all events Black would not be
threatened by any direct danger.

18 B–Kt5!

Gligoric had apparently underestimated the strength of this
sally. The trouble is that Black must not now play 18 . . . BxB,
since after 19 KtxB, he can no longer adequately protect the
KB2 square. For example: 19 . . . P–B5; 20 Q–R5, PxB; 21
QxBPch, K–R1; 22 Kt–K6, and Black loses his Queen. Hence
he must allow the exchange on his KB3, thereby decisively
weakening his King's wing and allowing White to institute a
dangerous attack there.

18	. . .	P–B5

With this he does at least close the dangerous Bishop diagonal.

19   BxB   PxB

After 19 . . . PxB; White can either win a pawn simply by
20 BxB, QxB; 21 P–Q 5, followed by 22 QxP, or else combina-
tionally by 20 PxP! PxB; 21 PxQP, etc., in both cases with
marked advantage.

20   B–B2   Kt–Kt3

Thus the strong move 21 Kt–R4 is prevented temporarily at
any rate. But White at once drives the Knight away from Kt3.

21   P–R4!   K–R1

Eventual counter-play on the KKt file forms Black's only
counter-chance. Otherwise the White attack would develop
and grow by itself on the King's wing.

22   P–KKt3   R–KKt1
23   K–R2   Q–Q2

Black is preparing to play B–Kt2–B1, but White gets in his
attack a move earlier. With the following move White opens
up a path for his Queen and plans an eventual Kt–B1–K3.

24   Kt–Q2   B–Kt2

Black (Gligoric)

White (Keres) to play

An attempt to obtain counter-play by 24 . . . P–Q4, would
only lead to a further opening up of the game, without noticeably relieving Black's position. White could then continue,
with 25 Q–B3, Q–K3; 26 KPxP, BxP; 27 B–K4, with a clear

advantage in position. The following variation serves as an example: 27 . . . BxB; 28 KtxB, PxP; 29 Kt–Kt5!, Q–Kt3; (the combinational counter-thrust 29 . . . KtxP, so as to meet 30 PxKt, with 30 . . . Q–Q3ch, followed by 31 . . . PxB, gives White a clear advantage after 30 Q–B4!, Q–B3; 31 KtxPch, K–B2; 32 QxKt, etc.) 30 Kt–K6! (30 R–K6! also came into consideration) 30 . . . PxKt; 31 QxPch, R–Kt2; 32 P–R5, and White wins his piece back together with a lasting initiative.

Perhaps this variation offered Black somewhat better chances in practice, since after the text-move he has no counter-play whatsoever and can only passively wait to see how White proposes to strengthen his attack. Passive defence in such positions is, however, usually hopeless.

25 Q–B3

With this attack on the KBP White frustrates all Black's attempts at counter-play.

25 . . . Q–K3

25 . . . K–Kt2 fails against 26 P–R5, Kt–K2; 27 P–R6ch, whilst if 25 . . . Q–K2; 26 Kt–B1, followed by 27 Kt–K3 is decisive. The fact that White has to spend a tempo (26 P–Q5) in dealing with the text-move is of no real importance.

26 P–Q5 Q–K2
27 R–QR1!

Since Black has been able to concentrate a sufficient number of pieces round his King White can have little hope of deciding the game through a direct King attack. Hence he initiates an action with the text-move on the other wing, thereby practically forcing the ensuing Rook exchange. But through this Black loses one of the most important pieces defending his King, and the absence of this piece makes itself felt later on.

27 . . . R–R1
28 RxRch BxR
29 P–Kt3!

Forcing an exchange on Kt3 and thereby opening up a way for attack on the pawn on QKt5, which now must fall, sooner or later. White's position is by now strategically won.

29	. . .	PxP
30	KtxP	K–Kt2
31	P–R5	Kt–B1
32	B–Q3	Q–Q2
33	Q–K2	

A good continuation here was of course also 33 P–R6ch, KxP; 34 QxPch, Kt–Kt3; 35 B–K2, with the threat of 36 P–Kt4. Black would therefore have to play 35 . . . Q–K2 and after 36 QxQ, KtxQ; 37 BxP, the ending is easily won for White. But the text-move is even stronger, since with it White also wins a pawn and still keeps the Queens on the board.

33	. . .	P–B4

A desperate attempt at counter-play, but Black no longer has a defence. Thus, for example, 33 . . . Q–B1 would not save the pawn, since after 34 BxP, QxP; 35 Q–Kt4ch, White would get a mating attack: 35 . . . K–R1; 36 P–R6, Kt–Kt3; 37 Q–Q7!, or 35 . . . K–R3; 36 Q–Kt8, QxKt; 37 QxKtch, etc.

Naturally hopeless also is the attempt to save the game by 35 . . . Kt–Kt3; 36 PxKt, QxKt; 37 PxPch, KxP; 38 Q–K6ch, K–Kt2; 39 Q–K7ch, etc.

34	BxP	Q–B1
35	P–QB4	

Now White has a pawn more together with the better position and the issue of the game is no longer in any doubt.

35	. . .	P–R3

After 35 . . . PxP; 36 QxP, P–B4; 37 Q–R4! is most unpleasant for Black.

36	Kt–Q2	Kt–R2
37	PxP	Kt–B3

More exact was 37 . . . QxKBP, which would have led to the game continuation after 38 Kt–K4, Kt–B3; 39 KtxP. After the text-move White could keep a second pawn with any danger by 38 P–Kt4, but, in view of some time trouble, he does not want to alter his plan, once made.

38	Kt–K4	QxKBP
39	KtxP	Kt–Kt5ch

After 39 ... QxRPch; 40 QxQ, KtxQ; 41 B–B6 is of course decisive.

40	K–Kt1	QxP
41	P–B3	

This was White's sealed move. Sufficient for a win were also the moves 41 Q–B3, or 41 Kt–K8ch, followed by 42 P–B3, but the text-move ends the game just as quickly.

41	...	Kt–B3
42	Q–K3!	resigns.

Black is practically paralysed. After 42 ... Q–Kt3; there follows 43 QxP, and the continuation 42 ... Q–Kt4; 43 QxQch, PxQ; 44 B–B6! loses the Bishop, since Black cannot capture on B3.

5

THE CANDIDATES' TOURNAMENTS, 1959–1962

Translator's Note

THE games that follow, together with their notes, were handed to me by Keres after the publication of the Estonian original collection of his games and they do not appear in either the Russian or German versions. As he did not add an introduction I give my own here.

1959 started off on a not particularly good note since Keres came as low as equal 7th and 8th with Averbach at the 26th U.S.S.R. Championship at Tiflis. Still, he was ahead of a number of great players, notably Korchnoi, Geller and Bronstein.

There followed a better result at the very strong international tournament held at Zurich to commemorate the 150th anniversary of the founding of the Zurich Chess Club. He had an excellent equal 3rd and 4th together with Bobby Fischer, scoring 10½ out of 15 and coming a point below the winner, Tal. We give his game against Gligoric from this event (No. 76).

Then there came the most important event of the year, the Candidates' Tournament in Yugoslavia. As I was the controller of this event I was able to study the play at close hand. It was a fascinating and exciting struggle between two great players, Tal and Keres. Keres, to quote his own words "played well, but Tal played better". So Tal won the right to challenge Botvinnik for the world title; but Keres was an excellent second and had the distinction of defeating Tal in their individual match by 3–1. From the last phase of the tournament, that at Belgrade, we give his magnificent win over Tal (No. 77).

Over the turn of the year 1959–60 Keres took part in a short international tournament at Stockholm. First place in this was shared between the Soviet grandmaster Kotov and the Swedish master Martin Johannson with 7 points. Keres was next with

6½ and was robbed of first prize by losing to the Swede, Skold. A double round match in May between Estonia and Finland ended in honours even, Keres losing one and winning one against Ojanen. In a match tournament in July and August at Hamburg between the U.S.S.R. and West Germany he scored 5½ out of 7 without losing a game and at the Leipzig Olympiad he obtained the best result on Board Three with a score of 10½ out of 13.

In 1961 he started off with an indifferent result in a match between the U.S.S.R. and Yugoslavia at Belgrade where, on Board Two, he scored only 50%, 2½ out of 5. But, at the Zurich International Tournament he played beautiful chess, coming first with 9 points out of 11, beating, amongst others, Petrosian.

The final of the European Team Championship was played in Oberhausen in West Germany in June. Here he scored 6 out of 8 on third board without losing a game. From this event we give his game against Hort (No. 78).

The year ended with a very strong tournament at Bled in Yugoslavia where he tied for fifth place with Gligoric and Petrosian with 12½ points out of 19, below Tal and Fischer.

Once again, at the beginning of 1962, he had an indifferent result in a Soviet Championship. In the 29th U.S.S.R. Championship at Baku he came equal 8th to 11th with 11 points out of 20, together with Cholmov, Gipslis and Smyslov.

Then came the great Candidates' Tournament at Curacao in which he missed winning the event by the narrowest margin. A loss to Benko in the penultimate round (after he had beaten him thrice in previous rounds!) cost him first place and he came equal second with Geller with 17 points half a point behind Petrosian. This was the fourth time Keres had come second in a Candidates' Tournament. We give a win against Tal from this event (No. 79).

A match was played at Moscow between Keres and Geller to determine who should be classed second and thus have the right to take part in the next Candidates'. It was a very evenly contested affair. When the 8th and last game was reached the score was 3½–3½. Keres had to win the last game since, in the event of a draw, Geller would gain the right to play in the

Candidates' as he had the superior Sonneborn-Berger score at Curacao. However, Keres won the match with a beautiful game that concludes this book (No. 80).

Game 76
RUY LOPEZ, MORPHY DEFENCE

International Tournament at Zurich, 1959

	P. Keres	S. Gligoric
1	P–K4	P–K4
2	Kt–KB3	Kt–QB3
3	B–Kt5	P–QR3
4	B–R4	Kt–B3
5	O–O	B–K2
6	R–K1	P–QKt4
7	B–Kt3	O–O
8	P–B3	P–Q3
9	P–KR3	B–Kt2

I have played a whole series of Ruy Lopezes against Gligoric and in so doing we have both tried out various methods of development. Usually Gligoric has employed the popular Tschigorin system 9 . . . Kt–QR4; 10 B–B2, P–B4, followed by Q–B2. In the present game he intends to experiment with a new system.

10	P–Q4	Kt–QR4

This sequence of moves chosen by Black was at one time combined by Flohr with an interesting pawn sacrifice, viz. 10 . . . PxP; 11 PxP, P–Q4; 12 P–K5, Kt–K5; 13 Kt–B3, Kt–R4; 14 B–B2, P–KB4; 15 PxP e.p., BxP; etc. Practical experience of this variation, however, has shown that the ensuing Black initiative is not quite worth the extra pawn for the opponent.

11	B–B2	Kt–B5

This move is the start of the new system Gligoric has prepared. Of course, Black could have transposed here to the usual paths of the Tschigorin Defence by 11 . . . P–B4.

12	P–QKt3	Kt–Kt3
13	QKt–Q2	

Naturally White cannot win a pawn by 13 PxP, PxP; 14 QxQ, QRxQ; 15 KtxP, because of 15 . . . KtxP etc. After the text-move, however, K4 must be protected.

13 . . .   QKt–Q2

After five moves this Knight has now retreated to a square which it could have reached at once from the original position. This loss of time gives one justified qualms about the system chosen by Gligoric. It is, however, in no way easy to exploit such a loss of time in a closed position so as to obtain a concrete advantage. In the ensuing phase of the game, in fact, White is unable to bring out fully into the open the dark side of Black's schemes.

14 B–Kt2   P–B4
15 Kt–B1

Both sides have completed the development of their forces and now it is a question of forming a promising plan for the coming middle-game. The text-move is by itself of course not bad, but this is only on the condition that, in the ensuing phase of the game, White pursues a concrete line of departure. Another very good idea here is that recommended by Vukovic: 15 P–QR4, followed eventually by B–Q 3 and Q–K2, so as to force the QKt pawn to clarify its position and eventually win the important QB4 square for his pieces.

15 . . .   R–K1
16 P–QR4

But with this, however, two good plans are confused, and nothing good can arise therefrom. If White wanted to play P–QR4, then he should have played it on the move before as already mentioned. But after he has played 15 Kt–B1 it is necessary to make use of another plan. This consists of 16 PxKP, PxP; 17 P–B4!

White could then have utilised the circumstance of Black's Knight standing badly to occupy the vacated square and posted his Knight on Q4.

This would have ensured him a small but clear positional advantage.

16   . . .   B–KB1
17   Kt–Kt3

Here still 17 PxKP, PxKP; 18 Q–K2, was worthy of consideration. After the text-move White must give up all hope of
occupying the Q4 square.

17   . . .   Q–B2
18   Q–Q3

This move is tactically inaccurate and allows his opponent
to carry out a freeing thrust. Better was 18 Q–Q2, or if White
wants to concentrate on attacking the QKt pawn, then perhaps
18 B–Q3.

18   . . .   P–B5?

Black (Gligoric)

White (Keres) to play

Under the influence of the seeming threat of a twofold
capture on QKt4 Black allows himself to be put off his stroke
and with the text-move he releases the tension in the centre,
which, however, practical experience has shown as only favour-
ing the first player. From now on Black has to contend once
more with difficulties and he is never free from these right till
the end of the game.

The simplest way for Black of demonstrating the harmlessness
of the enemy threat is the logical 18 . . . P–Kt3. White cannot
then in any way play for the win of a pawn, e.g.: 19 RPxP,
RPxP; 20 QxP, BPxP; or 19 PxBP, KtxBP; or finally 19
PxKP, P–B5! with an eventual QPxP, in every case with a
satisfactory game for Black.

However, the opponent's heedless Queen move can most

energetically be exploited by Black with 18 . . . P–Q4! On
account of the threatened fork on K4 White then seems to have
nothing better than 19 PxQP, when 19 . . . KPxP follows. In
this position White's most reasonable line is 20 RPxP, RPxP;
21 QxKtP, BxP; 22 Q–Q3, without thereby retaining any real
prospects of a positional advantage.

19	KtPxP	PxBP
20	Q–Q2	P–Kt3?

Another weak move which merely increases Black's
difficulties. Here too he should have seized the opportunity of
freeing his position by 20 . . . P–Q4. Though it must be said that
this advance would not have the same force as if it had been
made a couple of moves earlier, since after 21 KPxP, White
obtains rather the better game, e.g.: 21 . . . KtxP; 22 B–R3,
BxB; 23 RxB, Kt–B5; 24 B–K4, or 21 . . . BxP; 22 KtxP,
KtxKt; 23 PxKt, RxP; 24 RxR, QxR; 25 R–K1, etc.

21	B–R3!	QR–Q1

Now 21 . . . P–Q4 would be bad because of 22 BxB, when the
weakness of Black's King-side would become evident. Once
Black has missed his chance of making the freeing move he
must confine himself to a difficult and passive defence.

22	QR–Kt1	B–B1
23	Q–K3	B–KKt2
24	PxP!	

With this, all possible eventual complications by means of
the advance P–Q4 are thwarted, and White obtains overwhelming pressure on the position. The Bishop on R3, in
conjunction with the open Q file and the weakness on QB5 now
bring to bear a pressure on the enemy position that can hardly
be withstood.

24	. . .	PxP
25	KR–Q1	B–B1

Black can no longer tolerate the strong Bishop on QR3, but
now the weaknesses on the King's wing make themselves felt.

Another attempt to relieve the position by 25 . . . Kt–B1 would soon seal the fate of the pawn on QB5 after 26 RxR, RxR; 27 Kt–B1.

26   BxB   RxB

After 26 . . . KtxB; 27 RxR, RxR, White has the deadly 28 Q–Kt5.

27   Q–Kt5!

This strong move almost paralyses his opponent's pieces and furthermore threatens to initiate a direct attack against the King by 28 Kt–B5. In order to obtain a little space Black must get in P–B3 in the ensuing phase of the game.

27   . . .   Kt–K1

Black scarcely has time to prepare for Kt–KKt1 by 27 . . . K–R1, since then White would put an awkward question mark to the pawn on QB4 by 28 R–Kt4. Perhaps it was Black's best practical counter-chance to surrender the QBP in the next few moves without a struggle, so as to obtain some little compensation in the freeing of his pieces. But one does not gladly make such concessions.

28   Q–K7

Naturally not 28 KtxP, because of 28 . . . P–B3; but now he threatens to make this capture. Black once again gives the pawn indirect protection.

28   . . .   Kt–Kt2
29   Kt–B1

Again 29 KtxP fails against 29 . . . QR–K1.

With the text-move this Knight starts on its journey to K3, from where it not only threatens the QBP and the important central square Q5, but can also be used eventually for an attack against the enemy King-side via KKt4.

29   . . .   Kt–K3

Black must not only concern himself with the threatened King-side attack but he must also bear in mind his weakness on QB5. Naturally, he would have much preferred to have driven away the White Queen from its dominating position by

29 ... KR–K1; but this would have resulted in the loss of the hapless pawn after 30 Q–Kt4, followed by 31 Kt–K3. However, instead, Black's method of play now brings him under the fire of a mating attack.

30	Kt–K3	Kt–B5
31	K–B1	

Something must be done against the threat of 31 ... Kt–K7ch. Now Black's best chance lay in giving up the QBP by 31 ... KR–K1; 32 Q–Kt4, with the hope of fishing in troubled waters thereafter.

31	...	P–B3?

This fresh weakening of the King's position leads inevitably to the loss of the game. There now follows a pretty final attack.

32	Kt–Kt4!	Kt–Q6

He has no saving resource. An attempt to do so by 32 ... QR–K1 would be refuted by 33 KtxPch!, and this move is also playable after 32 ... K–R1. However, White was threatening to win the exchange by 33 Kt–R6ch.

33	RxKt!

Much more decisive than 33 Kt–R6ch, K–R1; 34 Kt–B7ch, RxKt; 35 QxR, when Black could still put up a resistance by 35 ... R–B1; 36 Q–K7, Q–B4; 37 QxQ, Kt(Q2)xQ.

33	...	PxR
34	B–Kt3ch	K–R1
35	KtxBP!	

The mating square is KR7 and in order to attain this the square KKt5 must be made available by this second sacrifice.

35	...	RxKt
36	Kt–Kt5	

Now the manoeuvre has been accomplished; Black has either to surrender his Queen or allow himself to be mated.

36	...	RxPch
37	K–Kt1!	

Naturally, 37 KxR would also have won, but the text-move is more according to plan.

37	. . .	R–B8ch
38	K–R2	resigns.

Game 77

Q.G.D. TARRASCH DEFENCE

Candidates' Tournament, Belgrade, 1959

	M. Tal	P. Keres
1	Kt–KB3	P–Q4
2	P–Q4	P–QB4

This game was played in the last tour, five rounds before the end of the tournament. At that moment Tal was leading by a margin of 2½ points over me. I had therefore to play for a win at all costs in order to retain even theoretical chances of gaining first place.

3	P–B4	P–K3
4	BPxP	KPxP
5	P–KKt3	

Known as the Schlechter-Rubinstein system, this is regarded nowadays as the best method of meeting the Tarrasch Defence.

5	. . .	Kt–QB3
6	B–Kt2	Kt–B3
7	O–O	B–K2
8	Kt–B3	O–O
9	B–Kt5	B–K3
10	PxP	

Many theoreticians hold that a strengthening of the central pressure by 10 R–B1 gives White a more enduring initiative here; but this immediate exchange on B5 also has its advantages.

10	. . .	BxP
11	Kt–QR4	

A new line, instead of the customary 11 R–B1. With the text-move White plans to initiate the well-known pressure on the QB5 square after 11 . . . B–K2 by 12 B–K3. Thus he would attain a position that would ensure him a lasting initiative without any possible danger of losing. Hence Black chooses a different, perhaps riskier, continuation so as to lead the game away from the usual paths.

11	. . .	B–Kt3
12	KtxB	PxKt
13	Kt–Q4	

An essay at appreciating the position that has now arisen might seem at first glance to make it appear much more favourable for White than it really is. He enjoys the advantage of two Bishops, controls the important Q4 square, whilst his opponent's pawn position reveals marked weaknesses on the Queen-side. But if one tries to suggest a plan by which White can increase his supposed advantage then one is pulled up sharp by unexpected difficulties. It becomes apparent that Black's position too contains various advantages that should not be underestimated. In the first place he has a good development, then he has a pawn in the centre, thereby fully controlling the important central square K5 and finally his Rooks may well become most active along the many open files. I am therefore far from convinced that White is in possession here of any advantage worth mentioning.

After the game Tal was much criticised for making the text-move, and in order to prevent the threat of 13 . . . P–Q5 the immediate retreat of the Bishop by 13 B–K3 was recommended. It is, however, unlikely that this would constitute any real strengthening of White's position. Black could then continue for example with 13 . . . R–R3 followed eventually by Q–Q2, but also both 13 . . . B–B4 and 13 . . . R–K1 deserve consideration. In my opinion, the reason why White gets into difficulties in the end lies chiefly in the fact that he underestimates the resources at Black's command.

| 13 | . . . | P–R3 |
| 14 | B–B4 | |

Now, after 14 B–K3, the sally 14 . . . Kt–KKt5, followed by 15 . . . Q–B3, would be very troublesome.

| 14 | . . . | Q–Q2 |

Black (Keres)

White (Tal) to play

15   P–QR3?

White overestimates his position and apparently imagines he can quietly increase his pressure in the centre by Q–Q 3, KR–Q1, QR–B1, etc. The text-move has as its purpose the protection of the QRP from attack by the Rook and prevention of an eventual Kt–QKt5 by Black. In fact, White's position is not overwhelming to the extent that he can completely ignore Black's counter-play. Something must of necessity be undertaken against the positional threat of 15 . . . B–R6, since after the exchange of the white-squared Bishops Black would in no way stand worse. I believe that White should decide to play here 15 KtxB, PxKt; 16 Q–Kt3, which would retain some chances of an advantage for him.

> 15   . . .   B–R6!
> 16   Q–Q 3   KR–K1
> 17   KR–K1

By now the KP stands in need of protection.

> 17   . . .   BxB
> 18   KxB   R–K5!

Black's pieces now take up very active positions and White is gradually pushed back on the defensive. Since the exchange on QB6 hardly comes into consideration, White must relinquish the important Q 4 square to his opponent and this means that the field of activity of his Bishop becomes still more limited.

| 19 | Kt–B3 | QR–K1 |
| 20 | B–Q2 | P–Q5! |

Now there is threatened, amongst other things, 21 ... Q–K3, by which the pressure on White's K2 would be strengthened to a disagreeable extent. White therefore decides to eliminate the strong pawn on Q4, but eventually has the disadvantage owing to his weaknesses on the white squares. It would therefore have been perhaps more logical to attack the enemy pawn weaknesses on the Queen-side at once by 21 Q–Kt5.

| 21 | P–K3 | Q–Q4 |
| 22 | PxP | |

Practically forced, since Black was threatening to win a pawn by 22 ... PxP. After the text-move the pretty 22 ... Kt–K4 leads to nothing because of the cool reply 23 Q–B3!, but Black can gain the advantage in the end by quite normal moves.

22	...	RxP
23	RxRch	KtxR
24	Q–K2	Kt–Q3
25	B–K3	R–Q6

Black's pieces now control the whole board. Especially burdensome for White is the pin on the Knight on KB3 and the weakness on the white squares. Naturally now 26 BxP would be suicide on account of 26 ... Kt–B5, but even with other continuations White would hardly be in a position to avoid material loss. One can now see how quickly the situation has changed after the inaccuracy on White's fifteenth move.

26	K–Kt1	Kt–B5
27	Kt–K1	R–Kt6
28	R–B1	

White must now surrender material. It goes without saying that 28 B–B1 fails against 28 ... Kt–Q5, whilst 28 R–Q1, Q–K5 would merely drive the Black Queen to a better square. With the text-move White hopes to relieve his position a little after 28 ... KtxKtP; 29 R–Kt1, but Black has a stronger continuation.

28   . . .   KtxB!
29   PxKt   Q–K4

Now White must give up the pawn under much less propi-
tious circumstances since 30 Kt–Q 3 would be utterly fatal on
account of 30 . . . Q–K5. One might think that White's
position is due to break up in a few moves, but Tal's resourcefulness in procuring counter-chances in this wretched position
must be admired.

30   Kt–Kt2   RxKtP
31   Q–Q3   Q–K3

Black has obtained a clearly won position, but, under the
influence of approaching time-trouble, he noticeably falters,
and allows his opponent some counter-chances. Here he needed
only to have fixed the White Knight by 31 . . . P–KKt4! after
which there would exist no further technical problems in the
way of the win.

32   Kt–B4   R–Kt6

Perhaps 32 . . . Q–R7 was also possible, but Black quite
rightly avoids unnecessary complications when in time-
trouble. After 32 . . . Q–R7; 33 Q–K4, RxP; 34 R–B1, White's
pieces would be very actively placed, and this circumstance
could hardly be outweighed by the gain of the unimportant
pawn on KR2.

33   R–B3

Objectively better was probably 33 KtxQ, RxQ; 34 Kt–Q4,
so as to try and save the ensuing Rook ending. Black could then
reach a promising Rook ending by 34 . . . RxRP; 35 KtxKt,
PxKt; 36 RxP, R–Kt6, or perhaps even better continue 34 . . .
Kt–K4, after which White must be wrecked by his numerous
weaknesses. With Queens on the board White has to conduct a
much more difficult defence owing to his vulnerable King's
position.

33   . . .   RxR
34   QxR   Q–K5
35   Q–Kt3   P–QKt4!

The exchange of the QKt pawn for the King pawn is an
excellent bargain, since the result is a further weakening of the

position of White's King. White has no choice, since 36 . . .
Kt–K4 is a strong threat.

36	QxP	QxPch
37	K–B1	Q–B6ch
38	K–Kt1	Q–K6ch
39	K–B1	P–Kt4

Black has repeated his moves in time-trouble so as to reach
the desired 40th move. But now he must vary in order to
avoid three-fold repetition of position. The text-move cannot
be termed bad but 39 . . . Kt–Q 5! won more quickly. Then
40 QxP loses a piece on account of 40 . . . P–Kt4, and the
ending after 40 Q–Q 3, QxQch; 41 KtxQ, P–QKt4, is naturally
completely lost for White.

40	Kt–K2	Kt–K4!

Black finds the right decisive plan. Good also was of course
simple protection by 40 . . . Q–K2, but the final attack inaugurated by the text-move is more effective. The only surprising feature is that White is able more or less to defend his
position despite its apparently hazardous nature.

This was Black's sealed move on adjournment. White has
but little choice in reply, in view of the mating threat.

41	Q–B8ch

There is obviously no point in checking on either QR8 or
QKt8, and 42 Q–Kt2 would lead, after 42 . . . Q–Q7, or
perhaps even better 42 . . . P–Kt5, to a position that could
also have arisen later in the game.

42	. . .	K–Kt2
43	Q–KB5	Q–Q7!

Threatening to win the Knight by 44 . . . Q–K8ch. Once
again White has little choice.

44	Kt–Q4!

The only move. Immediate loss results after 44 Q–B3,
Q–Q8ch followed by Kt–K8ch, or 44 Q–K4, Q–Q8ch; 45 K–Kt2,
Q–B7ch followed by 46 . . . Q–B8ch. And also retreat with the
Knight by 44 Kt–Kt1 leads to a loss after 44 . . . Q–Q8ch;
45 K–Kt2, Q–B7ch, e.g. 46 K–B1, Q–Kt8ch followed by 47 . . .

Kt–B5ch, or 46 K–B3, Q–B7ch; 47 K–Kt4, P–R4ch; 48
KxKtP, P–B3ch; etc.

44 . . .   Q–K8ch

The Queen ending after 44 . . . Q–Q8ch; 45 K–Kt2, Kt–K8
ch; 46 K–B2, QxKtch; 47 KxKt, offers Black winning chances,
but these are nebulous on account of the strong passed pawn
on the QR file.

45 K–Kt2   Q–K6!

This is the best position attainable by Black from the
adjourned position. Despite the reduced amount of material
Black still retains a dangerous attack which leads by force to
the win of material. White must play very exactly to avoid
immediate collapse.

46 Q–Q5!

Again the only move. It is clear that protection of the Knight
by 46 Q–Kt4, or 46 Q–Q7, will not do on account of 46 . . .
Q–B7ch, and for this reason only Knight moves remain to be
considered. They lead, however, to inevitable loss, as the following lines show.

I: 46 Kt–Kt3, (or 46 Kt–B2, Q–K7ch followed by 47 . . .
QxKt) 46 . . . Q–K7ch; 47 K–R3, Kt–B5ch! followed by mate
or win of the Queen.

II: 46 Kt–B3, Q–K7ch; 47 K–R3, Kt–B7ch; 48 K–Kt2,
Kt–Q8disch!; 49 K–R3, Q–B8ch; winning the Queen.

III: 46 Kt–B6, Q–Q7ch; 47 K–R3, (or 47 K–Kt1, Q–B8ch;
48 Q–B1, Q–B4ch!, etc.) 47 . . . Kt–B7ch; 48 K–Kt2, Kt–Kt5
disch; 49 K–R3, P–R4; followed by mate on R7.

IV: 46 Kt–Kt5, Q–K7ch; 47 K–Kt1, (47 K–R1, Kt–K8!)
47 . . . Kt–K4 and Black wins.

46 . . .   Q–B7ch

Seemingly very strong here was 46 . . . Q–Q7ch; so as to
attain a decision after 47 K–R3, by 47 . . . Kt–B7ch; 48 K–Kt2,
Kt–Q8disch; 49 K–B3, or R3, P–Kt5ch! White then plays,
however, 47 K–B3! and one may search closely without
demonstrating a concrete win. The position is rich in interesting
possibilities.

47 K–R3   Q–B8ch
48 K–Kt4   Kt–B7ch!

Black (Keres)

White (Tal) to play

With this Black avoids a diabolical trap that would have
been easy to overlook even in adjournment analysis. Apparently Black can win easily here by 48 ... P–R4ch; 49 KxKtP (or
49 KxRP, Q–R6ch); 49 ... Q–B3ch; 50 KxP, Kt–K4; since
what can White do against the threatened mate on KR3?
The astonishing reply 51 Q–R6, however, transforms the
position into a win for White!

There is also no forced win to be seen after 48 ... Q–Q8ch;
49 K–B5! and hence Black must content himself with a small
gain in material.

$$49 \quad K–B5 \qquad Q–Q6ch$$

Equally, nothing better can be found here. After 49 ...
Q–Kt8ch; 50 K–K5, nothing concrete comes from either
50 ... Kt–Kt5ch; 51 K–Q6, Q–Kt1ch; 52 K–B5, or 50 ...
Kt–Q6ch; 51 K–Q6, Q–Kt1ch; 52 K–B6, and after 49 ...
Kt–Q8 dis ch, White saves the game by 50 Q–B3! An attempt
to win by 49 ... Q–R3, also leads to nothing clear after 50
Kt–B6.

$$50 \quad K–K5 \qquad Kt–Kt5ch$$
$$51 \quad K–Q6 \qquad QxRPch$$

At long last this source of danger is destroyed and Black can
devote his energies to the technical problem. Even though he
now soon wins yet another pawn, the win of the game is still
quite far off.

52	K-B7	Q-K2ch
53	K-B8	Kt-K6

It was this position that I had set as my aim in my adjournment analysis. Sooner or later White must yield up another
pawn and thus is left with a lost ending that nevertheless still
demands good technical handling on Black's part.

In addition an immediate 53 . . . Q-K1ch; 54 K-Kt7,
KtxP, was possible here, but Black did not wish to place his
Knight too far away from the centre of action.

54   Q-Kt5

Naturally not 54 Kt-B5ch, KtxKt; 55 QxKt, because of
55 . . . Q-K3ch.

54	. . .	Q-K5
55	Q-Kt2	K-Kt3
56	Q-Kt6ch	P-B3

Simpler technically was 56 . . . K-R4; 57 Q-KB6, K-Kt5!
etc. The text-move constitutes a weakening of the King's
position that affords White fresh defensive possibilities.

57	Kt-K6	Kt-B5
58	Q-R6	Kt-K4

Threatening 59 . . . Q-B3ch. A desperate attempt at attack
by 59 Kt-B8ch, K-B2; 60 Q-K6ch, would now lead to nothing
after 60 . . . KxKt; 61 QxPch, Kt-B2.

59   Kt-B7

Now White must lose further material and so a second
crisis approaches in the game.

60   Q-Q6

Naturally 60 Q-K6 fails against 60 . . . Q-KB4, and the
thrust 60 P-R4, would, after 60 . . . Q-B4ch! lose the pawn
under much more unfavourable circumstances, e.g. 61 K-Kt8
(or 61 K-Kt7, Q-B6ch, followed by 62 . . . QxP); 61 . . . Kt-Q2
ch; 62 K-R7, Q-B7ch.

The counter-attack initiated by the text-move is White's
only chance.

60	. . .	QxP
61	Kt-Q5	Q-KB7

Simplest was an immediate 61 ... QxP, as was to occur later in the game.

62   K–Kt7

If 62 Q–K6, then 62 ... Q–B4ch; 63 K–Kt7, Q–B1, and Black has adequately protected himself against all possible attacks. With the text-move White prepares for 62 Q–K6, and therefore Black decides to liquidate the position.

62   ...   QxP!

63   QxPch   K–R4

64   Q–K6!

White makes life as difficult as possible for his opponent. Now he threatens 65 Kt–B6ch, K–R5; 66 Kt–K4, followed by the capture of the RP.

64   ...   Kt–Kt5

65   Kt–K7

If first 65 Q–B7ch, K–R5; and then 66 Kt–K7, Black has the very good reply of 66 ... Q–Kt7ch, followed by 67 ... Q–K5.

65   ...   Q–B6ch

66   K–B8

After 66 K–B7, there would come 66 ... Q–B3.

66   ...   K–R5

67   Kt–B5ch   K–R6

68   K–Q8

Naturally not 68 KtxP, because of 68 ... Q–B1ch.

68   ...   P–R4

69   Q–KKt6   Kt–K4

70   Q–K6   Kt–Kt5

71   Q–KKt6   Kt–K4

This game was played in Round 24. Little wonder then that Black once again got into time trouble and, in order to gain time on the clock, had to repeat moves.

72   Q–K6   Q–Q6ch

73   Kt–Q4 dis ch

After a King move Black wins by 73 ... Q–Q2ch! with

exchange of Queens, followed by P–Kt5. No better too is 73 Kt–Q6 dis ch, Kt–Kt5ch, etc.

	73 . . .	Kt–Kt5
	74 Q–Q5	Kt–B7!

The simplest way to win. There is no longer any defence against the pawn advance.

75	K–K8	P–R5
76	Q–K5	Q–K5
77	Q–B6	Q–B5
78	Kt–B5	Kt–K5
79	Q–K6	Q–Kt5!

resigns.

The threat of 80 . . . Kt–Kt6 forces exchange of Queens at the very least. This game was a terrific struggle.

Game 78

RUY LOPEZ, STEINITZ DEFENCE DEFERRED

European Team Championship at Oberhausen, 1961

	J. Hort	P. Keres
1	P–K4	P–K4
2	Kt–KB3	Kt–QB3
3	B–Kt5	P–QR3
4	B–R4	P–Q3
5	P–Q4	

Certainly more promising for White in this position are the continuations 5 P–B3, or 5 BxKtch, PxB6 P–Q4, if he does not intend to play a gambit with the text-move.

5	. . .	P–QKt4
6	B–Kt3	KtxP
7	KtxKt	PxKt
8	B–Q5	

It is interesting to observe that this tame continuation is employed time and time again, despite the fact that with it White can only hope for equality. Given that White wishes to handle the opening in modest style and is merely aiming at an eventual draw, then here 8 P–QB3 is much more to the point.

After 8 . . . PxP, if he does not want to make a pawn sacrifice, he can make sure of a draw by repetition of moves with 9 Q–Q5, B–K3; 10 Q–B6ch, B–Q2; 11 Q–Q5, B–K3 etc.

8	. . .	R–Kt1
9	B–B6ch	B–Q2
10	BxBch	QxB
11	QxP	Kt–B3
12	O–O	B–K2
13	Kt–B3	O–O
14	P–QR4	

This position has already occurred many times in tournament-praxis and it has been demonstrated that Black has an excellent game. Usually the development of the QB is proceeded with here, but White must avoid some snags in so doing. Thus for example after 15 B–Kt5, P–Kt5 he would be forced to make the ignominious retreat 15 Kt–Q1, since 15 Kt–Q5? would lead to the loss of a piece after 15 . . . KtxKt 16 QxKt, R–Kt4. After 14 B–Q2, Black obtained an uncomfortably strong pressure in the game Stoltz-Alekhine, Bled 1931, by 14 . . . KR–K1 15 Q–Q3, P–Kt5 16 Kt–K2, Q–B3.

The attempt in the text-move to instil fresh life in the variation is not crowned with success.

14	. . .	KR–K1
15	Q–Q3	

A preceding exchange on QKt4 would be of no help to White since the open QR file can easily fall into Black's hands. In addition, the object of attack on QR6 would disappear.

15	. . .	P–Kt5
16	Kt–Q5	P–QR4
17	P–QKt3	

An inaccuracy that weakens the long diagonal and soon allows Black to seize the initiative. Much better was the natural development of a piece by 17 B–B4, although then 17 . . . KtxKt 18 QxKt, B–B3 might perhaps have a rather disturbing effect. Into consideration came also 17 KtxBch, QxKt 18 R–K1.

17	. . .	KtxKt
18	PxKt	B–B3
19	R–Kt1	P–B4!

Here this move is very good since after 20 PxP e.p., QxP, White's weakness on QB2 turns out to be much more of a handicap than his opponent's on Q3. Also worthy of consideration was 19 . . . P–B3, so as to force the opening of the QB file.

20	B–B4	B–K4
21	B–K3	

White conducts the middle-game with a certain lack of logic. It is clear that his Bishop will play an unimportant role in the ensuing phase of the game, and therefore 21 BxB was in order here. True, Black would also stand a little better then after 21 . . . RxB 22 KR–K1, QR–K1 on account of his control of the K file, but any particular danger for White would not exist.

21	. . .	QR–B1!

Threatening 22 . . . P–B5 23 PxP, QxP etc. In order to prevent this White must allow the enemy Queen to get to KB4.

22	Q–B4	Q–B4
23	Q–Kt5?	

White, having got into some difficulties, now loses his head. The desperate counter-attack begun with the text-move is hopeless and should lead speedily to a catastrophe. 23 QR–Q1 should have been tried, so as to consolidate the position by an eventual R–Q3.

23	. . .	QxP
24	QxRP	P–B4!

This move is enormously strong, since White has no satisfactory defence against the threat of 25 . . . P–KB5. Thus the game is already decided from the strategical point of view, but in practice there are still some interesting developments.

25	P–B3	B–Kt7!?

Here Black has a considerable choice of favourable continuations and eventually decides upon complications that are not by any means clear. He could have won a pawn with a good

position by 25 . . . BxPch 26 KxB, RxB, or he could have
forced White to allow him an all-important passed pawn in
the centre by 25 . . . P–B5 26 B–B2, B–Q 5 27 BxB, PxB. But
simplest was 25 . . . Q–Q6! followed by 26 . . . QxQP, when
Black would have pocketed a pawn with a good position,
without conceding the slightest counter-chance to his opponent.

26   Q–R6!

Very well played. Hort had got into an absolutely lost
position after playing the first part of the game indifferently.
From now on, however, he takes beautiful advantage of his
counter-chances and in consequence the game follows a very
interesting course.

26   . . .   QxP
27   B–B2   P–QB5

So as to meet 28 QxQP, with 28 . . . P–B6. Had Black
devoted more attention to the complications that now ensue,
then he would scarcely have opened up a path for the enemy
Bishop with the text-move. Good was 27 . . . Q–B7 followed
eventually by P–Kt6.

28   Q–Kt7!

Now White even threatens to win after 28 . . . P–B6? 29
B–Q4. White has suddenly obtained counter-play, and, affected
by shortage of time, Black does not find immediately the right
method of strengthening his position. The simplest way of
doing this was probably by 28 . . . Q–R6!, threatening 29 . . .
P–Kt6 followed by 30 . . . B–B3. If then 29 KR–Q1, simply
29 . . . QxRP can follow.

28   . . .   R–Kt1
29   Q–R7   R–R1?

Black falls victim to a hallucination. He believes that 29 . . .
Q–B7! fails on account of 30 RxB, QxR 31 B–Q4, but overlooks the winning parry of 31 . . . R–Kt2!

30   Q–Kt7   KR–Kt1

It was still not too late to get back into the variation mentioned
above by 30 . . . QR–Kt1. Now, however, White obtains
counter-play.

31	Q–Q7	Q–B7
32	QxQP	P–Kt6
33	Q–K6ch	K–R1
34	P–Q6	B–B3

In his strong passed QP White has suddenly obtained a dangerous counter that requires the most careful attention. Black cannot well play 34 . . . B–R6 or 34 . . . P–B6, since in both cases 35 B–Q4 would leave White's Bishop in a most active position and create dangerous threats on the KKt7 square. With both sides in time trouble Black now embarks on an interesting combination that renders the game highly complicated.

35   KR–B1

White had set his hopes on this move. Is Black now really forced to surrender one of his proud passed pawns and in consequence condemned to content himself with an extremely problematical end-game advantage?

35   . . .   QxRch!

A shocking surprise in time pressure. One must pay great and due credit to Hort for the fact that, despite the unexpectedness of this sacrifice, he does not lose his head in the ensuing phase of the game and defends himself in the best fashion possible.

36	RxQ	P–Kt7
37	R–Kt1	P–B6
38	Q–K2!	

The only move. After 38 QxP, RxP, White would no longer have an adequate defence against the threat of 39 . . . R–R8.

| 38 | . . . | RxP |
| 39 | P–Q7 | P–R3? |

Under great time pressure Black misses the best continuation. The threat of 40 Q–K8ch should have been parried by 39 . . . R–Kt1!, after which White would have had no good defence against the threat of 40 . . . R–R8. Better than the text-move was also an immediate 39 . . R(R6)–R1, so as to give his King a safety valve thereafter and only then to continue R(R1)–R8.

| 40 | Q–K8ch | K–R2 |

The time pressure over, White now had to seal his move. On account of the threats of 41 ... P–B7 and 41 ... R–R8, his alternatives are limited to two continuations, viz. 41 QxR, or 41 P–Q8 = Q. In practice it is not at all easy to find the right defence, especially when one considers that both players had fought out a tough and tense battle for five hours.

Black (Keres)

White (Hort) to play

41   P–Q8 = Q?

Surprisingly enough, this natural looking move, which not only attacks the Rook on QR4 but also threatens eventually at least perpetual check by 42 Q–Kt8ch, is the decisive mistake. Hort defended himself well and resourcefully when in time trouble, and now, when he once again has sufficient time for thought, he commits a fatal error after long reflection.

He could have retained excellent chances of saving the game here by the correct continuation 41 QxR!. After this move 41 ... R–R8 would not suffice on account of 42 R–KB1!, P–B7; 43 QxP!, when the White pawn on Q7 would save the day. He would, therefore, have to play 41 ... P–B7, and then practically forced is 42 QxP, BxQ 43 R–KB1. Now the only way for Black to retain winning chances lies in 43 ... R–R1! 44 B–Kt6, R–R8 45 P–Q8 = Q, RxRch 46, KxR, P–B8 = Qch. Then, after 47 K–B2, Black can, for example, embark on an attack with 47 ... B–B6! and this would probably gain him a pawn with good practical winning chances.

Be this as it may, one thing is clear. White must seize the

chance of playing 41 QxR!. With the text-move he probably
reckons only with 41 . . . P–B7, which would have led to perpetual check after 42 Q–Kt8ch. But something quite different
occurs.

| 41 | . . . | RxQ! |
| 42 | QxR(R4) | R–Q7! |

The position that has now arisen is very odd and perhaps the
most curious that I have ever had in the whole course of my
long chess-praxis. Black has only two pawns for the Queen, but
these pawns are so strong that nothing can be done against the
threat of 43 . . . P–B7.

43   RxP

In his adjournment analysis Hort could find nothing better
than this immediate return of the Rook. In actual fact, an
attempt to save the game by 43 Q–Kt5 would not work on
account of 43 . . . P–B7, though Black's task would have been
more difficult in this case. Naturally 44 QxPch would now lose
at once because of 44 . . . P–Kt3, but after 44 Q–B1! matters
are not so simple.

Since now the straightforward continuation 44 . . . PxR = Q
45 QxQ, R–Q3 would not be good enough on account of 46
B–K3!, R–R3 47 K–B2, P–Kt3 48 Q–B2, B–Kt2 49 B–B1,
R–Kt4 50 Q–Kt1, etc., Black must be more exact in dealing
with the problem. The following analysis should serve to show
that it is indeed possible to force a win.

After 44 Q–B1, Black continues best with 44 . . . R–Q4!,
threatening in some variations 45 . . . R–R4, for example after
45 P–Kt4. Then three main defensive possibilities come into
consideration for White, as follows:—

I: 45 B–K3, PxR = Q 46 QxQ, R–R4 47 K–B2, K–Kt1!
48 Q–B2, R–R8 49 Q–B8ch, K–B2 and White cannot obtain
perpetual check.

II: 45 P–Kt3, PxR = Q 46 QxQ, P–Kt3! 47 K–Kt2, B–Kt2
and one cannot see how White can prevent the threatened
transference of the Rook to QR8.

III: 45 P–Kt4 (or 45 R–K1, B–B6 etc.) 45 . . . R–R4!
46 RxP, BxR 47 B–K3, R–R8 48 QxR, BxQ 49 B–B1, PxP
50 PxP, B–B3 followed by 51 . . . B–Kt4 and Black wins.

The immediate capture on QKt7 lightens Black's task quite noticeably, since he now gains an important tempo for the execution of his winning plan.

| 43 | . . . | PxR |
| 44 | Q–Kt3 | R–Q1 ! |

Now Black threatens 45 . . . R–QR1 against which nothing can be done.

| 45 | Q–B2 | R–QKt1 |
| 46 | Q–Kt1 | |

After 46 QxPch, Black wins by 46 . . . K–R1 47 Q–Kt1, R–QR1 followed by 48 . . . R–R8.

| 46 | . . . | P–Kt3 |

There is no defence against the threat of 47 . . . R–QR1. White is lacking in just one tempo so as to get his King away from the back rank.

47	P–Kt4	R–QR1
48	K–Kt2	R–R8
49	Q–B2	P–Kt8=Q
50	Q–B7ch	B–Kt2
51	B–Q4	Q–B8ch
52	K–Kt3	P–B5ch

White could have spared himself this last portion of the game.

| 53 | KxP | Q–B8ch |
| | resigns | |

This game is not flawless, but contains so many original and interesting moments that its inclusion in this collection is well justified.

Game 79

RUY LOPEZ, MORPHY DEFENCE

Candidates' Tournament for the World Championship at Curacao, 1962

	M. Tal	P. Keres
1	P–K4	P–K4
2	Kt–KB3	Kt–QB3
3	B–Kt5	P–QR3
4	B–R4	Kt–B3

5	O–O	B–K2
6	R–K1	P–QKt4
7	B–Kt3	O–O
8	P–B3	P–Q3
9	P–KR3	Kt–QR4
10	B–B2	P–B4
11	P–Q4	

This position has occurred thousands of times in various tournaments and there is hardly a continuation here that has not been exhaustively analysed and proved in practice. Usually Black continues with 11 ... Q–B2, and then, after 12 QKt–Q2, he has a rich choice of different methods of development at his disposal. In the present game Black tries a new type of defence in which the idea is to dispense with the protecting Q–B2 move.

	11 ...	Kt–Q2
12	QKt–Q2	

I tried this system for Black in three games at Curacao, counting a transposition even in four, and obtained the excellent result of three points with it. This tends to show that it is not so easy for White to find a promising line against it.

The text-move is undoubtedly the normal method of development, and certainly more promising than the colourless line 12 PxBP, PxP 13 QKt–Q2, which Fischer tried against me. Probably Fischer himself did not entertain so high an opinion of the strength of this continuation, even though he won the game in question, since in a later game he abandoned 12 PxB, and closed the centre with 12 P–Q5.

| | 12 ... | BPxP |

After an immediate 12 ... Kt–QB3 there comes into consideration 13 P–Q5, or also 13 PxBP, followed by 14 Kt–B1.

13	PxP	Kt–QB3
14	P–R3	

In an earlier game of the same tournament Tal continued here against me 14 Kt–Kt3, but after 14 ... P–QR4 15 B–K3, P–R5 he was unable to obtain any advantage. The thrust 14 P–Q5, as recommended by a number of commentators, should

be equally innocuous for Black and allow him adequate
counter-play after 14 ... Kt–Kt5 15 B–Kt1, P–QR4.

14 ...   PxP

With this pawn exchange Black accepts the handicap of a
weakness on his Q 3 so as to obtain good play with his pieces
in compensation. Another move that also came into consideration was 14 ... B–B3, so as to meet 15 P–Q5 with 15 ... Kt–K2.

15 Kt–Kt3   Kt(Q2)–K4
16 Kt(B3)xP   B–B3

Now Black exerts marked pressure along the diagonal
KR1–QR8 and has approximately equalised the chances. The
good play with the pieces fully compensates for the pawn
weakness on Q 3.

17 B–Q2?

Tal tries for the biggest possible complications in every
position and simply cannot leave any chance untouched of
bringing them about. The combination initiated by the text-
move is indeed very complicated, but it eventually turns to
Black's advantage. It would therefore have been more advisable,
by 17 KtxKt, KtxKt 18 R–Kt1, to have relieved the pressure on
his QKt2 and thus prepared for the development of his QB.

17 ...   KtxKt
18 KtxKt   Kt–Q6!

With this Black falls in with the designs of his opponent, in
the belief that the ensuing complications are good for him. The
game now becomes very interesting.

19 Kt–B6

This move cannot really be classed as a mistake since it
belongs to the plan White has formulated. Continuations such
as 19 B–R5, QxB 20 QxKt, P–Kt3 or 19 BxKt, BxKt 20
R–Kt1, Q–B3, painfully striving after equality are naturally not
calculated to substantiate the correctness of White's 17th move.

19 ...   KtxBP!

The key-move to Black's counter-play. After 19 ... Q–Kt3
20 BxKt, QxKt 21 R–QB1, White would in fact stand rather
better.

Black (Keres)

White (Tal) to play

20   Q–B3?

It is a great pity that Tal did not choose the main variation here, 20 Q–R5!, which would have led to well-nigh unfathomable complications. Then the continuation as in the game 20 . . . KtxPch 21 K–R2, B–K4ch would not be good because of 22 QxB!, PxQ 23 KtxQ, RxKt, 24 B–R5, etc. In this line it would appear that 21 . . . Q–B2 is also not sufficient because of 22 P–K5!, P–Kt3 23 Q–B3 and Black must lose material.

In reply to 20 Q–R5, Black had intended playing 20 . . . Q–Kt3. Then White could continue the attack with 21 P–K5! It would be taking us too far here to attempt to analyse out all the possible developments thereafter. As an example let us adduce the following variations: 21 . . . Kt–K5dis ch 22 K–R2 (not however 22 B–K3, QxKt etc.) 22 . . . P–Kt3 23 PxB! (much more interesting than 23 Q–K2, QxKt 24 BxKt, BxPch 25 K–R1, P–Q4, when Black should be able to gain equality) 23 . . . PxQ 24 BxKt, and though White has only two minor pieces for the Queen, his counter-chances are not to be underestimated. This variation serves as a refutation of those critics who wished to characterise Tal's previous moves as complete oversights.

Later analyses have shown, however, that Black has a better defence. In the first place, in the variation 20 Q–R5, Q–Kt3 21 P–K5, Kt–K5dis ch 22 K–R2, instead of 22 . . . P–Kt3 he can play more simply 22 . . . BxPch! 23 KtxB, Kt–B3!. It is true that White can then retain some attack by 24 Q–R4, PxKt 25 B–B3 (or 25 B–Kt5, P–R3!), but this, after 25 ... R–K1! followed by 26 ... B–Kt2 should merely afford White prospects of equality.

Still more forcing, however, is the continuation 20 ... KtxPch 21 K–R2, P–Kt3! Now naturally 22 QxKt, B–K4ch! followed by 23 ... Q–B2, or 22 Q–Q 5, Q–Q2 followed by 23 ... B–Kt2 are hopeless for White, as is the end-game after 22 KtxQ PxQ etc. Therefore, 22 Q–B3 must be played, but then 22 ... B–K4ch! leads to the game-continuation with the unimportant difference that the KKtP is on Black's KKt3.

> 20   ...   KtxPch!

Avoiding the alternative 20 ... Q–Kt3 when White can obtain a dangerous attack by the sacrificial combination 21 P–K5, Kt–Kt5 dis ch 22 B–K3, KtxB 23 PxB, KtxB dis ch 24 K–R1, KtxKR 25 RxKt.

> 21   K–R2

Other moves too yield no better result. After 21 PxKt, or 21 QxKt, there follows 21 ... Q–Kt3ch, and after 21 K–R1, Q–Kt3 22 P–K5, there comes the devastating reply 22 ... B–Kt5! Whilst if White plays 21 K–B1, then 21 ... Q–Kt3 22 K–B1, B–Kt5 23 B–K3, BxQ24 BxQ, BxKt is enough to ensure Black's advantage. It must be admitted that the text-move gives Black his easiest task.

> 21   ...   B–K4ch!

The simplest way of foiling the enemy attempt at attack.

> 22   KtxB

After 22 K–R1, Black can play either 22 ... Q–R5 23 PxKt, B–Kt6! 24 Kt–K7ch, K–R1 25 KtxB, QRxKt or 22 ... Q–B2, in both cases with a winning game.

> 22   ...   PxKt
> 23   KR–Q1

White has no time to capture the Knight as his Bishop on Q2 is attacked. After 23 B–Kt4, there would follow 23 ... Kt–Kt4.

> 23   ...   Kt–B5!

Making Black's advantage manifest, since 24 BxKt is not to be feared on account of 24 . . . Q–R5ch. Now, with two pawns to the good, Black naturally has a won game.

24	P–KKt3	Kt–K3
25	B–B3	

After 25 B–Kt4, Black has the resource of 25 . . . Kt–Q5.

25	. . .	Q–Kt4
26	R–Q6	

An oversight in a lost position, but there was no longer anything that he could do. After 26 R–Q5, Q–R3ch followed by 27 . . . Kt–Kt4, Black would have a fierce attack on White's weakened King-side.

26	. . .	Q–R3ch
27	K–Kt1	

Or 27 K–Kt2, Kt–B5ch 28 PxKt, QxR with the same result as in the game.

27	. . :	Kt–Q5

Winning the exchange, after which further resistance is hopeless. Tal makes some more moves in the hope that his opponent might perhaps commit an inaccuracy under time-pressure.

28	RxQ	KtxQch
29	K–B2	PxR
30	KxKt	R–K1
31	R–R1	K–Kt2
32	B–Kt3	B–Kt2
33	B–Q2	P–B4
34	RxP	QR–Q1
35	R–Kt6	BxPch
36	K–K2	B–B6ch
37	K–K1	P–B5!

Thwarting White's last chance of activating his QB by B–R6ch.

38	B–B3	PxP
39	RxRP	R–Q5
40	R–R7ch	K–R3
41	R–KB7	

And White resigned without waiting for his opponent's reply. A game full of interesting moments.

Game 80
QUEEN'S GAMBIT DECLINED
SEMI-TARRASCH DEFENCE

Eighth Match-game, Moscow, 1962

	P. Keres	E. Geller
1	P–Q 4	Kt–KB3
2	P–QB4	P–K3

This was the last game of the match, which at the moment was equal, $3\frac{1}{2}$–$3\frac{1}{2}$. In the event of a drawn match Geller would have assured himself of the second place in the Candidates' Tournament as he had the better percentage according to the Berger System. Hence his choice of opening—usually Geller plays the Indian Defence with 2 . . . P–KKt3.

3	Kt–KB3	P–Q 4
4	Kt–B3	P–B4
5	BPxP	KtxP
6	P–K3	Kt–QB3
7	B–B4	

The variation in the text has been frequently played in recent years and usually White continues here with 7 B–Q 3. Which of the two Bishop moves is objectively the stronger remains undecided—I wanted to choose a less usual continuation so as to avoid prepared variations.

7	. . .	KtxKt

I cannot reconcile myself to this exchange and rather recommend here 7 . . . PxP 8 PxP, B–K2 9 O–O, O–O. After the text-move White has untrammelled control of the centre, and this means he has a clear-cut advantage.

8	PxKt	B–K2
9	O–O	O–O
10	P–K4	

But this advance is perhaps a little premature. Better would

be first 10 Q–K2, P–QKt3; 11 R–Q1, and only after 11 . . .
Q–B2 12 P–K4, when the QB can find an eventual development
along the diagonal QB1–KR6.

| 10   . . . | P–QKt3 |
| 11   B–Kt2 | |

It now becomes apparent that White must make preparatory
moves for his Q–K2, since otherwise his QP is en prise. Very
good too was 11 B–B4, but still the development of the Bishop
on QKt2 was much to my taste as this Bishop can often prove
very effective along the long diagonal.

| 11   . . . | B–Kt2 |
| 12   Q–K2 | Kt–R4 |

It can now be seen that Black is beset by a number of minor
difficulties. The thrust 13 P–Q 5, is always in the air and would,
for example, lead to an overwhelming position for White
after 12 . . . R–B1 13 P–Q 5!, PxP; 14 BxP, followed by an
eventual P–QB4. The text-move parries this threat, but now
the Knight remains out of play on the edge of the board. White
has emerged from the opening with the better prospects.

| 13   B–Q 3 | R–B1 |
| 14   QR–Q1 | |

Which of the two Rooks one must move is always a difficult
choice. Here White leaves his K Rook on its place so as to
make use of it on the K file after an eventual P–Q 5.

| 14   . . . | PxP |

Black must undertake something against the threat of 15
QPxP, and this exchange is the simplest way of dealing with it.
However, a marked drawback is connected with the manoeuvre:
suddenly White's QB comes to life. Black must be very much
on the qui vive not to fall victim to an overwhelming attack
after an eventual P–Q 5.

Therefore the question arises whether perhaps here 14 . . .
Q–B2 might not have been more to the point. White intended
to continue then 15 P–Q 5, retaining thereby some advantage.
In particular, the two minor pieces on Black's Queen-side
would then play a seemingly miserable role.

| 15   PxP | B–Kt5? |

Black wants to free his position by an eventual exchange on QB6, but the text-move leaves his King's position entirely without protection and thus facilitates the introduction of a dangerous attack on White's part. Hence 15 ... B–KB3 should have been tried, so as to relieve his position to some extent at least by the exchange of Bishops on the black squares after the thrust P–Q 5.

16   P–Q 5!

This advance is very strong and creates fresh advantages for White. Black must exchange pawns, since after 16 ... Q–K2 17 Kt–Q 4 would be terrifically strong, whilst 16 ... B–B6 would result in the loss of the exchange after 17 B–R3, R–K1 18 B–Kt5. However, after the exchange on Q 5 both White Bishops become extremely powerful.

| 16 | . . . | PxP |
| 17 | PxP | Q–K2 |

Apparently the best reply and one which anyway made me rack my brains the most during the game. Weaker is 17 ... R–K1, since after 18 Kt–K5, Black, on account of the threat of 19 BxPch, has no time to take advantage of the pin on the Knight. Very bad is naturally 17 ... BxP because of 18 Q–K5, P–B3 19 Q–R5 etc., and after 17 ... B–B6 18 B–B5, R–B5 19 Kt–K5 is very strong.

18   Kt–K5   P–B3

Black must continue actively since otherwise he would simply find himself lost positionally. For example, after 18 ... B–Q 3 White could inaugurate a winning attack by 19 Q–R5, P–Kt3 20 Kt–Kt4!. The consequences of the text-move are however equally unhappy for Black. One gains the impression that, after 16 P–Q 5!, Black's position is very difficult to defend.

19   Q–R5!

The sacrifice 19 BxPch, KxB 20 Q–R5ch, K–Kt1 21 Kt–Kt6, results in nothing concrete after 21 ... Q–Q2. But the attack started by the text-move must be decisive.

19	. . .	P–Kt3
20	KtxP	PxKt
21	BxKtP	Q–Kt2

Black (Geller)

White (Keres) to play

Black's defence is exceedingly difficult. White has already two pawns for the sacrificed piece and in addition practically all his pieces stand ready to attack the weakened enemy King. Even on general grounds it seems that Black can scarcely hope to emerge from his hopeless position safe and sound.

The text-move leads quite clearly to a loss, but it is difficult to find a satisfactory defence for Black. The chief possibility lies in 21 ... B–R3, when White can proceed with his attack in two promising ways.

Firstly there comes into consideration 22 B–B5, with the strong threat of 23 B–K6ch. If Black then plays 22 ... BxR, White, in addition to the mating attack by 23 B–K6ch, can also play simply 23 BxR, RxB 24 Q–Kt4ch, K–B2 25 QxR, and Black can hardly save this position.

The other continuation, 22 P–Q6, is perhaps still more forcing. Black cannot naturally then play 22 ... BxP because of 23 KR–K1, followed by 24 RxB. After 22 ... Q–KKt2, however, 23 P–Q7, R–B4 24 B–B5, or 23 ... QR–Q1 24 R–Q4, is sufficient to render further resistance useless.

Instead of 21 ... B–R3 Black could also try 21 ... R–QB2, so as to play the Rook over to the King-side to defend the King. But this attempt is insufficient. White can, for example, play in reply 22 P–Q6!, BxQP 23 KR–K1, and after the further 23 ... Q–Q1 (or 23 ... B–K4 24 RxB!, PxR 25 BxP, etc.) 24 R–Q4, Black's resistance cannot last long.

22 R–Q3   B–Q3

After 22 ... B–R3 23 R–KKt3, BxR White wins at once by 24 B–R7ch, K–R1 25 B–B5 dis ch, etc.

23 P–B4!   Q–R1

Just as hopeless as any other move. There is no adequate defence against the threat of 24 R–KKt3.

24 Q–Kt4   B–B4ch
25 K–R1   R–QB2

Or 25 ... Q–Kt2 26 R–KKt3, etc. The text-move leads to mate.

26 B–R7db ch!   K–B2
27 Q–K6ch   K–Kt2
28 R–Kt3ch

And Black resigns as mate follows next move.

LIST OF EVENTS

Below are listed the events in which Keres took part during the period covered by this volume (1952–1962). The reader will find the year, the place, the result, number of games played, how many won, how many lost and how many drawn and the number of points obtained (in that order across the page).

Tournaments

1952 Budapest	I	17	10	2	5	12½
1952 Helsinki	X	12	3	2	7	6½
1952 Moscow	X–XI	19	5	5	9	9½
1953 Tartu	I	19	17	0	2	18
1953 Zurich	II–IV	28	8	4	16	16
1954 Amsterdam	I	14	13	0	1	13½
1955 Hastings	I–II	9	6	1	2	7
1955 Moscow	VII–VIII	19	7	4	8	11
1955 Parnu	I	10	9	0	1	9½
1955 Gothenbourg	II	20	9	2	9	13½
1956 Amsterdam	II	18	3	1	14	10
1956 Moscow	I	12	7	0	5	9½
1956 Moscow	VII–VIII	15	4	2	9	8½
1957 Moscow	II–III	21	8	2	11	13½
1957 Mar del Plata	I	17	13	0	4	15
1957 Santiago	I	7	5	0	2	6
1957 Vienna		5	1	0	4	3
1958 Hastings	I	9	7	1	1	7½
1958 Munich	I	12	7	0	5	9½
1959 Tiflis	VII–VIII	19	5	3	11	10½
1959 Zurich	III–IV	15	7	1	7	10½
1959 Bled-Belgrade	II	28	6	15	7	18½
1960 Stockholm	III	9	6	1	2	7
1960 Leipzig	I	13	8	0	5	10½
1961 Zurich	I	11	7	0	4	9
1961 Oberhausen		8	4	0	4	6
1961 Bled	III–V	19	7	1	11	12½
1962 Baku	VIII–XI	20	4	2	14	11
1962 Curacao	II–III	27	9	2	16	17
		452	214	42	194	

Matches

1956 W. Unzicker		8	4	0	4	6
1962 E. Geller		8	2	1	5	4½
		16	6	1	9	

Other Events

1954 Estonia–Latvia (Tal)	2	1	0	1	1½
1954 U.S.S.R.–Argentine (Bolbochan)	4	1	1	2	2
1954 U.S.S.R.–France (Tartakower)	2	2	0	0	2
1954 U.S.S.R.–U.S.A. (Pavey, Kevitz)	4	3	1	0	3
1954 U.S.S.R.–England (Wade)	2	2	0	0	2
1954 U.S.S.R.–Sweden (Stoltz)	2	2	0	0	2
1955 U.S.S.R.–Hungary	7	3	0	4	5
1955 U.S.S.R.–U.S.A. (R. Byrne)	4	3	0	1	3½
1956 U.S.S.R.–Yugoslavia	7	2	1	4	4
1957 U.S.S.R.–Yugoslavia	5	1	0	4	3
1957 Estonia–Hungary (Barcza)	2	0	2	0	0
1958 U.S.S.R.–Yugoslavia (Gligoric)	4	1	1	2	2
1958 Wilnius Team Championship	7	1	0	6	4
1959 Estonia–Finland (Ojanen)	2	0	0	2	1
1959 Moscow Team Matches	8	5	0	3	6½
1959 Estonia–Latvia (Tal)	2	0	2	0	1
1960 Estonia–Finland (Ojanen)	2	1	1	0	1
1960 U.S.S.R.–West Germany	7	4	0	3	5½
1961 U.S.S.R.–Yugoslavia	5	1	1	3	2½
1962 U.S.S.R.–Holland (Bouwmeester)	2	0	0	2	1
	80	33	8	39	

OPENINGS INDEX

(The numbers are those of the games)

573

LIST OF OPPONENTS

(The numbers are those of the games)

RESHEVSKY on
The Fischer-Spassky Games

For the World Championship of Chess

by Samuel Reshevsky

International Grandmaster and United States Champion

Grandmaster Reshevsky, who has won the title of U.S. Chess Champion eight times, defeated Bobby Fischer in a match in 1960. He has covered this historic contest for the New York *Times* and a New York television network play by play, thoroughly annotating each move and analyzing each play. This indispensable book for all chess enthusiasts is the result of his expert coverage. Bobby Fischer has solidly defeated all other international champions on his way to this final challenge and Boris Spassky is one of the Russians who had held the World Chess Championship since 1948. This exciting book is the climactic conclusion of this Challenge of the Century. Illustrated. **$1.45**

NEW TRAPS IN THE CHESS OPENING

Al Horowitz

The famous Chess Editor of the New York *Times*, long-time publisher of *Chess Review*, and three-time U.S. Open Champion, has in this authoritative book assembled a collection of new and original (plus a few classic) chess traps—traps that have been brilliantly conceived and are decisive to the outcome of the game. Traps in the opening phases of a game are considered the most exciting and spectacular part of chess playing, and Mr. Horowitz, with diagrams and step-by-step analysis, clearly explains the techniques for setting each trap. The traps are grouped alphabetically according to 42 different modern opening gambits, ranging from "Alekhine's Defense" to the "Vienna Gambit." Each trap—175 in all—is shown in its entirety from first move to the mate or resignation or decisive loss of material. This is an indispensable book for all classes of players—from the very weak to the strongest—the wide range of modern "trappy" ideas, baits, themes and motifs described must be part of every good chess player's arsenal.

Cloth $4.50   **paper $1.45**